TAKING SIDES

Clashing Views on Controversio

Issues in American History, Volume II, Reconstrucion to the Present

TENTH EDITION

TAKING SIDES

Clashing Views on Controversial

Issues in American History, Volume II, Reconstruction to the Present

TENTH EDITION

Selected, Edited, and with Introductions by

Larry Madaras
Howard Community College

and

James M. SoRelle
Baylor University

McGraw-Hill/Dushkin
A Division of The McGraw-Hill Companies

To Maggie and Cindy

Photo Acknowledgment
Cover image: © 2003 by PhotoDisc, Inc.

Cover Art Acknowledgment
Charles Vitelli

Manufactured in the United States of America

Tenth Edition

123456789BAHBAH6543

Library of Congress Cataloging-in-Publication Data
Main entry under title:
Taking sides: clashing views on controversial issues in American history, volume ii, reconstruction to the present/selected, edited, and with introductions by Larry Madaras and James M. SoRelle.—
10th ed.
Includes bibliographical references and index.
1. United States—History—1865–. I. Madaras, Larry, *comp.* II. SoRelle, James M., *comp.*
973
0-07-285027-2
ISSN: 1091-8833

Printed on Recycled Paper

Preface

The success of the past nine editions of *Taking Sides: Clashing Views on Controversial Issues in American History* has encouraged us to remain faithful to its original objectives, methods, and format. Our aim has been to create an effective instrument to enhance classroom learning and to foster critical thinking. Historical facts presented in a vacuum are of little value to the educational process. For students, whose search for historical truth often concentrates on *when* something happened rather than on *why*, and on specific events rather than on the *significance* of those events, *Taking Sides* is designed to offer an interesting and valuable departure. The understanding that the reader arrives at based on the evidence that emerges from the clash of views encourages the reader to view history as an *interpretive* discipline, not one of rote memorization.

As in previous editions, the issues are arranged in chronological order and can be easily incorporated into any American history survey course. Each issue has an issue *introduction*, which sets the stage for the debate that follows in the pro and con selections and provides historical and methodological background to the problem that the issue examines. Each issue concludes with a *postscript*, which ties the readings together, briefly mentions alternative interpretations, and supplies detailed *suggestions for further reading* for the student who wishes to pursue the topics raised in the issue. Also, Internet site addresses (URLs), which should prove useful as starting points for further research, have been provided on the *On the Internet* page that accompanies each part opener. At the back of the book is a listing of all the *contributors to this volume* with a brief biographical sketch of each of the prominent figures whose views are debated here.

Changes to this edition   In this edition we have continued our efforts to maintain a balance between the traditional political, diplomatic, and cultural issues and the new social history, which depicts a society that benefited from the presence of African Americans, women, and workers of various racial and ethnic backgrounds. With this in mind, we present seven new issues: *Was It Wrong to Impeach Andrew Johnson?* (Issue 1); *Was the Ku Klux Klan of the 1920s an Extremist Movement?* (Issue 7); *Did Communism Threaten America's Internal Security After World War II?* (Issue 10); *Should President Truman Have Fired General MacArthur?* (Issue 11); *Was Dwight Eisenhower a Great President?* (Issue 12); *Did President Kennedy Effectively Manage the Cuban Missile Crisis?* (Issue 13); and *Is America Entering the Twenty-First Century in a Period of Decline?* (Issue 17). In all there are 14 new selections.

A word to the instructor   An *Instructor's Manual With Test Questions* (multiple-choice and essay) is available through the publisher for the instructor using *Taking Sides* in the classroom. A general guidebook, *Using Taking Sides in the*

Classroom, which discusses methods and techniques for integrating the pro-con approach into any classroom setting, is also available. An online version of *Using Taking Sides in the Classroom* and a correspondence service for *Taking Sides* adopters can be found at http://www.dushkin.com/usingts/.

Taking Sides: Clashing Views on Controversial Issues in American History is only one title in the Taking Sides series. If you are interested in seeing the table of contents for any of the other titles, please visit the Taking Sides Web site at http://www.dushkin.com/takingsides/.

Acknowledgments Many individuals have contributed to the successful completion of this edition. We appreciate the evaluations submitted to McGraw-Hill/Dushkin by those who have used *Taking Sides* in the classroom. We are particularly indebted to Maggie Cullen, Cindy SoRelle, Barry A. Crouch, Virginia Kirk, Joseph and Helen Mitchell, and Jean Soto, who shared their ideas for changes, pointed us toward potentially useful historical works, and provided significant editorial assistance. Megan Arnold performed indispensable typing duties connected with this project. Susan E. Myers and Elu Ciborowski in the library at Howard Community College provided essential help in acquiring books and articles on interlibrary loan. Finally, we are sincerely grateful for the commitment, encouragement, and patience provided over the years by David Dean, former list manager for the Taking Sides series; David Brackley, senior developmental editor; and the entire staff of McGraw-Hill/Dushkin. Indispensible to this project is Ted Knight, the current list manager.

Larry Madaras
Howard Community College

James M. SoRelle
Baylor University

Contents In Brief

PART 1   Reconstruction and the Industrial Revolution 1

Issue 1.   Was It Wrong to Impeach Andrew Johnson?   2
Issue 2.   Was John D. Rockefeller a "Robber Baron"?   24
Issue 3.   Did the Industrial Revolution Disrupt the American Family? 46
Issue 4.   Was City Government in Late-Nineteenth-Century America a "Conspicuous Failure"?   68

PART 2   The Response to Industrialism: Reform and War 91

Issue 5.   Did Yellow Journalism Cause the Spanish-American War?   92
Issue 6.   Did Racial Segregation Improve the Status of African Americans?   118
Issue 7.   Was the Ku Klux Klan of the 1920s an Extremist Movement? 142
Issue 8.   Did the Women's Movement Die in the 1920s?   168
Issue 9.   Was Information About the Attack on Pearl Harbor Deliberately Withheld From the American Commanders? 190

PART 3   The Cold War and Beyond   217

Issue 10.   Did Communism Threaten America's Internal Security After World War II?   218
Issue 11.   Should President Truman Have Fired General MacArthur? 244
Issue 12.   Was Dwight Eisenhower a Great President?   268
Issue 13.   Did President Kennedy Effectively Manage the Cuban Missile Crisis?   290
Issue 14.   Should America Remain a Nation of Immigrants?   306
Issue 15.   Did President Reagan Win the Cold War?   322
Issue 16.   Will History Consider William Jefferson Clinton a Reasonably Good Chief Executive?   346
Issue 17.   Is America Entering the Twenty-First Century in a Period of Decline?   374

Contents

Preface   i
Introduction: The Study of History   x

PART 1   RECONSTRUCTION AND THE INDUSTRIAL REVOLUTION   1

Issue 1.   Was It Wrong to Impeach Andrew Johnson?   2

YES: **Irving Brant**, from *Impeachment: Trials and Errors* (Alfred A. Knopf, 1972)   *4*

NO: **Harold M. Hyman**, from *A More Perfect Union: The Impact of the Civil War and Reconstruction on the Constitution* (Alfred A. Knopf, 1973)   *15*

Historian Irving Brant argues that President Andrew Johnson was the victim of partisan Republican politics and that the articles of impeachment passed by the House of Representatives violated the U.S. Constitution. Professor of history Harold M. Hyman contends that Congress's decision to impeach President Johnson was wholly justifiable on constitutional grounds in light of Johnson's repeated defiance of national law.

Issue 2.   Was John D. Rockefeller a "Robber Baron"?   24

YES: **Matthew Josephson**, from *The Robber Barons: The Great American Capitalists, 1861–1901* (Harcourt, Brace & World, 1962)   *26*

NO: **Ralph W. Hidy and Muriel E. Hidy**, from *History of Standard Oil Company (New Jersey), vol. 1: Pioneering in Big Business, 1882–1911* (Harper & Brothers, 1955)   *36*

Historian Matthew Josephson depicts John D. Rockefeller as an unconscionable manipulator who employed deception, bribery, and outright conspiracy to eliminate his competitors for control of the oil industry in the United States. Business historians Ralph W. Hidy and Muriel E. Hidy argue that Rockefeller and his associates were innovative representatives of corporate capitalism who brought stability to the often chaotic petroleum industry.

Issue 3.   Did the Industrial Revolution Disrupt the American Family?   46

YES: **Elaine Tyler May**, from "The Pressure to Provide: Class, Consumerism, and Divorce in Urban America, 1880–1920," *Journal of Social History* (Winter 1978)   *48*

NO: **Jacquelyn Dowd Hall, Robert Korstad, and James Leloudis**, from "Cotton Mill People: Work, Community, and Protest in the Textile South, 1880–1940," *The American Historical Review* (April 1986)   *57*

Elaine Tyler May, a professor of American studies and history, argues that the Industrial Revolution in the United States, with its improved technology, increasing income, and emerging consumerism, led to higher rates of divorce because family wage earners failed to meet rising expectations for material accumulation. History professors Jacquelyn Dowd Hall, Robert Korstad, and James Leloudis contend that the cotton mill villages of the New South, rather than destroying family work patterns, fostered a labor system that permitted parents and children to work together as a traditional family unit.

Issue 4.   Was City Government in Late-Nineteenth-Century America a "Conspicuous Failure"?   68

YES: **Ernest S. Griffith,** from *A History of American City Government: The Conspicuous Failure, 1870-1900* (National Civic League Press, 1974) *70*

NO: **Jon C. Teaford,** from *The Unheralded Triumph: City Government in America, 1860-1900* (Johns Hopkins University Press, 1984)   *79*

Professor of political science and political economy Ernest S. Griffith (1896–1981) argues that the city governments that were controlled by the political bosses represented a betrayal of the public trust. Professor of history Jon C. Teaford argues that municipal governments in the late nineteenth century achieved remarkable success in dealing with the challenges presented by rapid urbanization.

PART 2   THE RESPONSE TO INDUSTRIALISM: REFORM AND WAR   91

Issue 5.   Did Yellow Journalism Cause the Spanish-American War?   92

YES: **W. A. Swanberg,** from *Citizen Hearst: A Biography of William Randolph Hearst* (Charles Scribner's Sons, 1961)   *94*

NO: **David Nasaw,** from *The Chief: The Life of William Randolph Hearst* (Houghton Mifflin, 2000)   *108*

Journalist W. A. Swanberg argues that newspaper mogul William Randolph Hearst used the sensational and exploitative stories in his widely circulated *New York Journal* to stir up public opinion and to force President William McKinley to wage a war against Spain to free Cuba. Historian David Nasaw maintains that even if Hearst had not gone into publishing, the United States would have entered the war for political, economic, and security reasons.

Issue 6.   Did Racial Segregation Improve the Status of African Americans?   118

YES: **Howard N. Rabinowitz,** from "From Exclusion to Segregation: Southern Race Relations, 1865-1890," *The Journal of American History* (September 1976)   *120*

NO: **Leon F. Litwack,** from *Trouble in Mind: Black Southerners in the Age of Jim Crow* (Alfred A. Knopf, 1998)   *131*

Professor of history Howard N. Rabinowitz suggests that racial segregation represented an improvement in the lives of African Americans in that it
provided access to a variety of public services and accommodations from
which they otherwise would have been excluded in the late-nineteenth-
century South. Professor of American history Leon F. Litwack argues that
"the age of Jim Crow," wherein efforts by whites to deny African Americans
equal protection of the laws or the privileges and immunities guaranteed
other citizens seemingly knew no bounds, created a highly repressive
environment for blacks.

Issue 7.   Was the Ku Klux Klan of the 1920s an Extremist Movement?   142

YES: David H. Bennett, from *The Party of Fear: From Nativist Movements to the New Right in American History* (University of North Carolina Press, 1988)   *144*

NO: Stanley Coben, from *Rebellion Against Victorianism: The Impetus for Cultural Change in 1920s America* (Oxford University Press, 1991)   *154*

Professor of history David H. Bennett argues that the Ku Klux Klan of the
1920s was a traditional nativist organization supported mainly by fundamentalist Protestants who were opposed to the changing social and moral
values associated with the Catholic and Jewish immigrants. Professor of
history Stanley Coben asserts that local Klansmen were not a fringe group
of fundamentalists but solid, middle-class citizens who were concerned
about the decline in moral standards in their communities.

Issue 8.   Did the Women's Movement Die in the 1920s?   168

YES: William L. O'Neill, from *Everyone Was Brave: A History of Feminism in America* (Quadrangle Books, 1971)   *170*

NO: Anne Firor Scott, from *The Southern Lady: From Pedestal to Politics, 1830-1930* (University of Chicago Press, 1970)   *178*

Professor of history William L. O'Neill contends that the women's movement died following the success of the suffrage campaign because women
were not united in support of many of the other issues that affected them
and because the increasingly militant feminism of the Woman's Party alienated many supporters of women's rights. Anne Firor Scott, a professor
emeritus of history, maintains that the suffrage victory produced a heightened interest in further social and political reform, which inspired southern
women to pursue their goals throughout the 1920s.

Issue 9.   Was Information About the Attack on Pearl Harbor Deliberately Withheld From the American Commanders?   190

YES: Robert A. Theobald, from *The Final Secret of Pearl Harbor: The Washington Contribution to the Japanese Attack* (Devin-Adair, 1954)   *192*

NO: Roberta Wohlstetter, from *Pearl Harbor: Warning and Decision* (Stanford University Press, 1967)   *203*

Retired rear admiral Robert A. Theobald argues that President Franklin D. Roosevelt deliberately withheld information from the commanders at Pearl Harbor in order to encourage the Japanese to make a surprise attack on the weak U.S. Pacific Fleet. Historian Roberta Wohlstetter contends that even though naval intelligence broke the Japanese code, conflicting signals and the lack of a central agency coordinating U.S. intelligence information made it impossible to predict the Pearl Harbor attack.

PART 3 THE COLD WAR AND BEYOND 217

Issue 10. Did Communism Threaten America's Internal Security After World War II? 218

YES: **John Earl Haynes and Harvey Klehr,** from *Venona: Decoding Soviet Espionage in America* (Yale University Press, 1999) *220*

NO: **Richard M. Fried,** from *Nightmare in Red: The McCarthy Era in Perspective* (Oxford University Press, 1990) *231*

History professors John Earl Haynes and Harvey Klehr argue that army code-breakers during World War II's "Venona Project" uncovered a disturbing number of high-ranking U.S. government officials who seriously damaged American interests by passing sensitive information to the Soviet Union. Professor of history Richard M. Fried argues that the early 1950s were a "nightmare in red" during which American citizens had their First and Fifth Amendment rights suspended when a host of national and state investigating committees searched for Communists in government agencies, Hollywood, labor unions, foundations, universities, public schools, and even public libraries.

Issue 11. Should President Truman Have Fired General MacArthur? 244

YES: **John S. Spanier,** from "The Politics of the Korean War," in Phil Williams, Donald M. Goldstein, and Henry L. Andrews, Jr., eds., *Security in Korea: War, Stalemate, and Negotiation* (Westview Press, 1994) *246*

NO: **D. Clayton James with Anne Sharp Wells,** from *Refighting the Last War: Command and Crisis in Korea, 1950–1953* (Free Press, 1993) *256*

Professor of political science John S. Spanier argues that General Douglas MacArthur was fired because he publicly disagreed with the Truman administration's "Europe first" policy and its limited war strategy of containing communism in Korea. Biographer D. Clayton James and assistant editor Anne Sharp Wells argue that General MacArthur was relieved of duty because there was a lack of communication between the Joint Chiefs of Staff and the headstrong general, which led to a misperception over the appropriate strategy in fighting the Korean War.

Issue 12. Was Dwight Eisenhower a Great President? 268

YES: **Stephen E. Ambrose,** from *Eisenhower: The President, vol. 2* (Simon & Schuster, 1984) *270*

NO: **Arthur M. Schlesinger, Jr.,** from *The Cycles of American History* (Houghton Mifflin, 1986) *278*

Professor of history Stephen E. Ambrose (1936–2002) maintains that Dwight D. Eisenhower was a greater president than his predecessors and successors because he balanced the budget, stopped inflation, and kept the peace. Professor of the humanities Arthur M. Schlesinger, Jr., argues that Eisenhower failed as a president because he refused to tackle the moral and environmental issues at home and because he established a foreign policy that relied on covert CIA activities and threats of nuclear arms.

Issue 13.   Did President Kennedy Effectively Manage the Cuban Missile Crisis?   290

YES: **Theodore C. Sorensen,** from *The Kennedy Legacy* (Macmillan, 1969) *292*

NO: **Mark J. White,** from *The Cuban Missile Crisis* (Macmillan Press Ltd., 1996)   *297*

Theodore C. Sorensen, President John F. Kennedy's special assistant, argues that Kennedy effectively managed the Cuban Missile Crisis via a "carefully balanced and precisely measured combination of defense, diplomacy, and dialogue." Assistant professor of history Mark J. White castigates Kennedy "for the excessive belligerence of his Cuban policies before the missile crisis while praising him for his generally adroit management of the crisis."

Issue 14.   Should America Remain a Nation of Immigrants? 306

YES: **Reed Ueda,** from "The Permanently Unfinished Country," *The World & I* (October 1992)   *308*

NO: **Richard D. Lamm,** from "Truth, Like Roses, Often Comes With Thorns," *Vital Speeches of the Day* (December 1, 1994)   *314*

Professor of history Reed Ueda maintains that the sheer magnitude and diversity of immigrants continually reshapes the American character, making America a "permanently unfinished country." Former Colorado governor Richard D. Lamm argues that immigration should be severely curtailed. He contends that the most recent immigrants are members of the underclass who are culturally unassimilable and who take jobs away from the poorest citizens in an already overpopulated America.

Issue 15.   Did President Reagan Win the Cold War?   322

YES: **John Lewis Gaddis,** from *The United States and the End of the Cold War: Implications, Reconsiderations, Provocations* (Oxford University Press, 1992)   *324*

NO: **Daniel Deudney and G. John Ikenberry,** from "Who Won the Cold War?" *Foreign Policy* (Summer 1992)   *334*

Professor of history John Lewis Gaddis argues that President Ronald Reagan combined a policy of militancy and operational pragmatism to bring about the most significant improvement in Soviet-American relations since the end of World War II. Professors of political science Daniel Deudney and G. John Ikenberry contend that the cold war ended only when Soviet president Mikhail Gorbachev accepted Western liberal values and the need for global cooperation.

Issue 16.   Will History Consider William Jefferson Clinton a Reasonably Good Chief Executive?   346

YES: **Lars-Erik Nelson,** from "Clinton and His Enemies," *The New York Review of Books* (January 20, 2000)   *348*

NO: **James MacGregor Burns and Georgia J. Sorenson et al.,** from *Dead Center: Clinton-Gore Leadership and the Perils of Moderation* (Scribner, 1999)   *359*

Journalist Lars-Erik Nelson (1941–2000) argues that President Bill Clinton is a sadly flawed human being but was a reasonably good president whose administration was a time of peace and plenty for Americans. Political scientists James MacGregor Burns and Georgia J. Sorenson et al. argue that Clinton will not rank among the near-great presidents because he was a transactional broker who lacked the ideological commitment to tackle the big issues facing American society.

Issue 17.   Is America Entering the Twenty-First Century in a Period of Decline?   374

YES: **Paul Kennedy,** from "The Next American Century?" *World Policy Journal* (Spring 1999)   *376*

NO: **Gregg Easterbrook,** from "America the O.K.," *The New Republic* (January 4 & 11, 1999)   *384*

Professor of history Paul Kennedy argues that Europe and China have the potential to equal or exceed the United States in economic power in 25 years. Gregg Easterbrook, senior editor of *The New Republic,* maintains that in terms of health, wealth, and moral values, life in the United States has never been better for the vast majority of Americans.

Contributors   398
Index   404

Introduction

The Study of History

Larry Madaras

James M. SoRelle

In a pluralistic society such as ours, the study of history is bound to be a complex process. How an event is interpreted depends not only on the existing evidence but also on the perspective of the interpreter. Consequently, understanding history presupposes the evaluation of information, a task that often leads to conflicting conclusions. An understanding of history, then, requires the acceptance of the idea of historical relativism. Relativism means the redefinition of our past is always possible and desirable. History shifts, changes, and grows with new and different evidence and interpretations. As is the case with the law and even with medicine, beliefs that were unquestioned 100 or 200 years ago have been discredited or discarded since.

Relativism, then, encourages revisionism. There is a maxim that says, "The past must remain useful to the present." Historian Carl Becker argued that every generation should examine history for itself, thus ensuring constant scrutiny of our collective experience through new perspectives. History, consequently, does not remain static, in part because historians cannot avoid being influenced by the times in which they live. Almost all historians commit themselves to revising the views of other historians, by either disagreeing with earlier interpretations or creating new frameworks that pose different questions.

Schools of Thought

Three predominant schools of thought have emerged in American history since the first graduate seminars in history were given at the Johns Hopkins University in Baltimore, Maryland, in the 1870s. The *progressive* school dominated the professional field in the first half of the twentieth century. Influenced by the reform currents of Populism, progressivism, and the New Deal, these historians explored the social and economic forces that energized America. The progressive scholars tended to view the past in terms of conflicts between groups, and they sympathized with the underdog.

The post–World War II period witnessed the emergence of a new group of historians who viewed the conflict thesis as overly simplistic. Writing against the backdrop of the cold war, these *neoconservative* and *consensus* historians argued that Americans possess a shared set of values and that the areas of agreement within the nation's basic democratic and capitalistic framework are more important than the areas of disagreement.

In the 1960s, however, the civil rights movement, women's liberation, and the student rebellion (with its condemnation of the war in Vietnam) fragmented the consensus of values upon which historians of the 1950s centered their interpretations. This turmoil set the stage for the emergence of another group of scholars. *New Left* historians began to reinterpret the past once again. They emphasized the significance of conflict in American history, and they resurrected interest in those groups ignored by the consensus school. In addition, New Left historians critiqued the expansionist policies of the United States and emphasized the difficulties confronted by Native Americans, African Americans, women, and urban workers in gaining full citizenship status.

Progressive, consensus, and New Left history is still being written. The most recent generation of scholars, however, focuses upon social history. Their primary concern is to discover what the lives of "ordinary Americans" were really like. These new social historians employ previously overlooked court and church documents, house deeds and tax records, letters and diaries, photographs, and census data to reconstruct the everyday lives of average Americans. Some employ new methodologies, such as quantification (enhanced by advancing computer technology) and oral history, while others borrow from the disciplines of political science, economics, sociology, anthropology, and psychology for their historical investigations.

The proliferation of historical approaches, which are reflected in the issues debated in this book, has had mixed results. On the one hand, historians have become so specialized in their respective time periods and methodological styles that it is difficult to synthesize the recent scholarship into a comprehensive text for the general reader. On the other hand, historians now know more about new questions or ones that previously were considered to be germane only to scholars in other social sciences. Although there is little agreement about the answers to these questions, the methods employed and the issues explored make the "new history" a very exciting field to study.

The topics that follow represent a variety of perspectives and approaches. Each of these controversial issues can be studied for its individual importance to American history. Taken as a group, they interact with one another to illustrate larger historical themes. When grouped thematically, the issues reveal continuing motifs in the development of American history.

Economic Questions

Issue 2 explores the dynamics of the modern American economy through investigations of the nineteenth-century entrepreneurs. Were these industrial leaders robber barons, as portrayed by contemporary critics and many history texts? Or were they industrial statesmen and organizational geniuses? Matthew Josephson argues that John D. Rockefeller is a key example of a monopoly capitalist who utilized ruthless and violent methods in organizing the oil industry. More favorable and representative of the business historian approach is the interpretation of Ralph W. Hidy and Muriel E. Hidy. They conclude that Rockefeller was among the earliest organizational innovators and that he standardized production and procedures and created a large integrated Industrial Corporation.

The Outsiders: Laborers, Blacks, Women, Family, and Immigrants

In the wake of industrialization during the late 1800s, the rapid pace of change created new working conditions for the laboring class. How did laborers react to these changes? Did they lose their autonomy in the large corporations? Did they accept or reject the wage system? Were they pawns of the economic cycles of boom and bust, to be hired and fired at will?

In recent years, historians have shifted their focus to social issues. New questions have been asked and new frameworks have been developed. Issue 3 ponders whether or not the Industrial Revolution disrupted the American family. In her study of changing patterns of divorce between 1880 and 1920, Elaine Tyler May finds that higher consumer expectations, which resulted from the Industrial Revolution, disproportionately strained marital relations among the lower-middle and working classes because the husbands were unable to fulfill the economic demands of their wives. But in their study of cotton mill people in the Piedmont region of North and South Carolina, Jacquelyn Dowd Hall, Robert Korstad, and James Leloudis argue that rural families were able to use the mills to make a living and to keep their families and farms intact.

The Piedmont mills were composed of white workers only. By the 1890s rigid segregation laws and customs separated the white and black races in the South. Did segregation hurt or harm the black community? In Issue 6, Howard N. Rabinowitz advances a unique position. He argues that it was better for blacks to attend segregated schools, to ride segregated streetcars and trains, and to use segregated parks and restrooms rather than to be totally excluded from schools and other public facilities. Segregation, says Rabinowitz, was a halfway measure between total exclusion and full integration. But Leon F. Litwack disagrees with this interpretation. To the white Southerners, he argues, Negroes were segregated because they were considered inferior.

In the 1920s the Ku Klux Klan emerged as the leading anti-Catholic, anti-immigrant, antiforeign, pro-Americanism group in the nation. In Issue 7, David H. Bennett takes the traditional position that the Klan was a reactionary organization that was prone to violence and unwilling to accept the cultural and social changes of the decade. Stanley Coben, taking a more sympathetic view, sees the Klan less as a nativist group and more as a pressure group. Exhibiting real concerns about the changing moral standards in their communities, many Klan members entered politics and attempted to enforce the older, Victorian moral standards.

Issue 14 asks, Should America remain a nation of immigrants? In the first selection, Reed Ueda maintains that the sheer magnitude and diversity of U.S. immigrants has continually reshaped the American character and made America a "permanently unfinished country." In the second selection, Richard D. Lamm argues that immigration should be severely curtailed because the most recent immigrants are members of the underclass who are culturally unassimilable and who take jobs away from the poorest citizens of an already overpopulated America.

The United States and the World

As the United States developed a preeminent position in world affairs, the nation's politicians were forced to consider the proper relationship between their country and the rest of the world. To what extent, many asked, should the United States seek to expand its political, economic, and moral influence around the world?

This was a particularly intriguing question for a number of political, military, and intellectual leaders at the close of the nineteenth century, who pondered whether or not it was necessary to acquire an overseas empire to be considered one of the world's great powers. Many historians consider the Spanish-American war a turning point in American history. In Issue 5, W. A. Swanberg argues that newspaper mogul William Randolph Hearst used the sensational and exploitative stories in his widely circulated and nationally influential *New York Journal* to stir up public opinion and to push President William McKinley into a questionable war. Taking a broader view, David Nasaw asserts that even if Hearst had not gone into publishing newspapers, the United States would have entered the war for political, economic, and security reasons.

One of the most controversial historical issues concerns the events leading to America's entrance into World War II. In Issue 9, Robert A. Theobald contends that President Franklin D. Roosevelt deliberately withheld information from the Hawaiian army and naval commanders at Pearl Harbor in order to encourage the Japanese to make a surprise attack on the weak U.S. Pacific Fleet. Roberta Wohlstetter, however, maintains that even though naval intelligence broke the Japanese code, conflicting signals and the lack of a central agency coordinating U.S. intelligence information made it impossible to predict the Pearl Harbor attack.

After World War II, many Americans believed that the Russians not only threatened world peace but also could subvert America's own democratic form of government. How legitimate was the second great red scare? Did communist subversion threaten America's internal security? In Issue 10, John Earl Haynes and Harvey Klehr contend that recently released World War II intelligence intercepts prove that a sizable number of high-level governmental officials passed sensitive information to Russian intelligence. But Richard M. Fried argues that the 1950s became a "red nightmare" when state and national government agencies overreacted in their search for Communists in government agencies, schools, labor unions, and even Hollywood, violating citizens' rights of free speech and defense against self-incrimination under the First and Fifth Amendments.

The Korean War provided the first military test case of America's cold war policy of "containing" the expansion of communism. The conflict explored in Issue 11 also provided a classic case of civilian control over military officials. Should President Harry S. Truman have fired General Douglas MacArthur? John

S. Spanier argues that MacArthur was fired because he publicly disagreed with the Truman administration's Europe-first policy and its limited war strategy of containing communism in Korea. D. Clayton James, writing with Anne Sharp Wells, maintains that General MacArthur was relieved of duty because there was a lack of communication between the Joint Chiefs of Staff and the headstrong general as well as a misperception over the appropriate strategy for fighting the Korean War.

In fall 1962 Soviet premier Nikita Khrushchev felt that he could improve Russia's military position against the United States by supplying Cuba with launching pads for short-range and intermediate-range missiles aimed at the United States. Issue 13 presents contrasting views about the effectiveness with which President John F. Kennedy managed the Cuban Missile Crisis. In the first selection, Theodore C. Sorensen argues that the president resolved the crisis via a "carefully balanced and precisely measured combination of defense, diplomacy, and dialogue." In the second selection, Mark J. White gives a more critical assessment in which he castigates Kennedy "for the excessive belligerence of his Cuban policies before the missile crisis while praising him for his generally adroit management of the crisis."

Now that the cold war is over, historians must assess why it ended so suddenly and unexpectedly. Did President Ronald Reagan's military buildup in the 1980s force the Soviet Union into economic bankruptcy? In Issue 15, John Lewis Gaddis gives Reagan high marks for ending the cold war. By combining a policy of militancy and operational pragmatism, he argues, Reagan brought about the most significant improvement in Soviet-American relations since the end of World War II. According to Daniel Deudney and G. John Ikenberry, however, the cold war ended only when the Soviets saw the need for international cooperation to end the arms race, prevent a nuclear holocaust, and liberalize their economy.

Political and Social Successes and Failures

Issue 4 looks at the way urban government operated in the late nineteenth century. Ernest S. Griffith surveys the nature of municipal government in the last three decades of the nineteenth century and concludes that city politics was consumed by a "cancer of corruption" that predominated from 1880 to 1893. Jon C. Teaford, on the other hand, maintains that scholars like Griffith are too eager to condemn the activities of late-nineteenth-century municipal governments without recognizing their accomplishments. While admitting numerous shortcomings, Teaford argues that American city dwellers enjoyed a higher standard of public services than any other urban residents in the world.

With the passage of the Nineteenth Amendment in 1919, women gained the right to vote. How did this impact the political system? And how did it affect the women's movement in the 1920s with regard to other gender issues? In Issue 8, William L. O'Neill argues that in the 1920s the women's movement splintered and lost its force as women pursued more individualistic and personal goals and broke through Victorian constraints on social and sexual mores. But Anne Firor Scott concentrates on southern women and concludes that the 1920s witnessed significant efforts by women to seek reforms in areas of interest to members of their sex and to society as a whole.

The perspective gained by the passage of time often allows us to reevaluate the achievements and failures of a given individual. Such is the case with Dwight Eisenhower, president of the United States from 1953 to 1961. In Issue 12, Stephen E. Ambrose maintains that Eisenhower was a greater president than his predecessors and successors because he balanced the budget, stopped inflation, and kept the peace. Arthur M. Schlesinger, Jr., admits that Eisenhower was a moderate who consolidated and accepted the reforms of the New Deal in an era of conservatism. Nevertheless, Schlesinger refuses to accept the revisionist interpretation and considers Eisenhower a failed president in terms of both domestic and foreign policy.

One issue in this book that demonstrates that history can shed some light on contemporary political controversies is Issue 1 on whether or not President Andrew Johnson should have been impeached. Irving Brant takes the traditional view and argues that Johnson treated the 11 defeated Confederate states as legal entities who never left the Union, not as conquered provinces. Johnson favored a more lenient Reconstruction program than his Republican congressional opponents, and he vetoed their policies. Furthermore, Brant maintains, passage of the Tenure of Office Act wrongly nullified the president's constitutional right to fire cabinet members without the approval of Congress. Harold M. Hyman, in response, argues that Johnson deserved to be impeached because he obstructed the Reconstruction policies passed by the congressional Republican majority.

The last president of the twentieth century, William Jefferson Clinton, was the first president to be impeached since Johnson. Both presidents, however, were not convicted of their impeachment charges. Most historians consider Johnson a below-average president. Will history rank Clinton as a near-great, average, or below-average president? In the first selection of Issue 16, Lars-Erik Nelson argues that President Clinton is "a sadly flawed human being but a reasonably good President whose administration was, for Americans, a time of peace and plenty." In the second selection, James MacGregor Burns and Georgia J. Sorenson et al. argue that Clinton will not rank among the near-great presidents, because he is a transactional broker who lacks the ideological commitment to tackle the big issues facing American society.

The final issue in this reader looks to the future. Will the United States dominate the twenty-first century as it did the previous one? Or will America decline? Paul Kennedy argues that both Europe and China have the potential to equal or exceed the United States in economic power in 25 years. He also contends that a backlash might occur in countries that are faced with a population explosion, atmospheric pollution, and economies wrecked by the "creative gales of international capitalism." Gregg Easterbrook, in opposition, asserts that if you look at the population's health, wealth, education, and even moral values, life in the United States has never been better for the vast majority of Americans.

Conclusion

The process of historical study should rely more on thinking than on memorizing data. Once the basics of who, what, when, and where are determined, historical thinking shifts to a higher gear. Analysis, comparison and contrast, evaluation, and explanation take command. These skills not only increase our knowledge of the past but they also provide general tools for the comprehension of all the topics about which human beings think.

The diversity of a pluralistic society, however, creates some obstacles to comprehending the past. The spectrum of differing opinions on any particular subject eliminates the possibility of quick and easy answers. In the final analysis, conclusions are often built through a synthesis of several different interpretations, but even then they may be partial and tentative.

The study of history in a pluralistic society allows each citizen the opportunity to reach independent conclusions about the past. Since most, if not all, historical issues affect the present and future, understanding the past becomes necessary if society is to progress. Many of today's problems have a direct connection with the past. Additionally, other contemporary issues may lack obvious direct antecedents, but historical investigation can provide illuminating analogies. At first, it may appear confusing to read and to think about opposing historical views, but the survival of our democratic society depends on such critical thinking by acute and discerning minds.

On the Internet ...

Gilder Lehrman Institute of American History

The Gilder Lehrman Institute of American History offers an extensive collection of resources on American history. Search for information either by historical period or by topic.

```
http://www.gliah.uh.edu/index.cfm
```

The American President: Andrew Johnson

This site provides a wealth of biographical information on the 17th president of the United States, including his life before the presidency, his foreign and domestic affairs policies, and his family life, as well as supplemental resources.

```
http://www.americanpresident.org/KoTrain/Courses/
AJO/AJO_In_Brief.htm
```

John D. Rockefeller and the Standard Oil Company

This site, created by Swiss entrepreneur Francois Micheloud, provides a highly detailed history of the American oil industry, with John D. Rockefeller as a main focus. It includes the discovery of oil, the main players in the oil industry, the rise of the Standard Oil Company, the passing of the Sherman Antitrust Act, and the dismantling of Standard Oil, as well as both short and detailed chronologies of the company.

```
http://www.micheloud.com/FXM/SO/rock.htm
```

Industrial Revolution

This site provides an extensive list of links to pages on the Industrial Revolution grouped into categories, including Child Labor, Disparity of Wealth, Unions, and Urban Planning.

```
http://members.aol.com/TeacherNet/Industrial.html
```

PART 1

Reconstruction and the Industrial Revolution

*E*conomic expansion and the seemingly unlimited resources available in postbellum America offered great opportunity and created new political, social, and economic challenges. Political freedom and economic opportunity provided incentives for immigration to America. The need for cheap labor to run the machinery of the Industrial Revolution created an atmosphere for potential exploitation that was intensified by the concentration of wealth in the hands of a few capitalists. The labor movement took root, with some elements calling for an overthrow of the capitalist system, while others sought to establish political power within the existing system. Strains began to develop between immigrant and native-born workers as well as between workers and owners, husbands and wives, and parents and their children.

With the growth of industry, urban problems became more acute. Improvements in water and sewerage, street cleaning, housing, mass transit, and fire and crime prevention developed slowly because incredible population growth strained municipal services. Urban governments had limited powers, which often fell under the control of political bosses. Historians disagree as to whether or not attempts to remedy these problems through a brokered political system were successful.

- Was It Wrong to Impeach Andrew Johnson?

- Was John D. Rockefeller a "Robber Baron"?

- Did the Industrial Revolution Disrupt the American Family?

- Was City Government in Late-Nineteenth-Century America a "Conspicuous Failure"?

1

ISSUE 1

Was It Wrong to Impeach Andrew Johnson?

YES: Irving Brant, from *Impeachment: Trials and Errors* (Alfred A. Knopf, 1972)

NO: Harold M. Hyman, from *A More Perfect Union: The Impact of the Civil War and Reconstruction on the Constitution* (Alfred A. Knopf, 1973)

ISSUE SUMMARY

YES: Historian Irving Brant argues that President Andrew Johnson was the victim of partisan Republican politics and that the articles of impeachment passed by the House of Representatives constituted a bill of attainder in violation of the U.S. Constitution.

NO: Professor of history Harold M. Hyman contends that Congress's decision to impeach President Johnson was wholly justifiable on constitutional grounds in light of Johnson's repeated defiance of national law and his efforts to seize control of the army.

On December 19, 1998, the U.S. House of Representatives approved two articles of impeachment charging President Bill Clinton with committing "high crimes and misdemeanors" for allegedly thwarting an investigation of his personal relationship with White House intern Monica Lewinsky. As the case made its way to the Senate, media pundits and constitutional scholars across the nation provided the American people with a historical context for the first impeachment trial of an American president in 130 years. In doing so, they reminded their viewers and readers of the political drama played out in Washington, D.C., only three years after the end of the Civil War, when President Andrew Johnson escaped being removed from office by a single vote in the Senate.

Johnson, born into poverty in North Carolina in 1808, migrated to Tennessee at the age of 18 and, through a combination of ambition and hard work, made a name for himself in Democratic politics. As governor of the Volunteer State and the most prominent Southern politician to reject secession, Johnson attracted the attention of Abraham Lincoln, who offered him a spot as his vice presidential running mate on the Union Party ticket in 1864. In April 1965, shortly after their electoral success, Lincoln was assassinated. As a result, Johnson became president within days of the end of the Civil War and was confronted with the enormous responsibilities associated with restoring the states of the former Confederacy to the Union.

For radical Republicans, Andrew Johnson initially seemed a preferable architect of postwar Reconstruction than the martyred Lincoln. After all, Johnson had openly expressed his desire to punish members of the planter aristocracy by prohibiting them from political participation until they had obtained a pardon from Johnson himself. In fact, Johnson envisioned a new political order in the South that would empower poor whites at the expense of the traditional political elite—the planters.

The honeymoon between congressional Republicans and the new president, however, was short-lived. Johnson adopted a Reconstruction policy that was similar to the lenient program outlined by Lincoln prior to his death, and he celebrated the rapidity with which the former Confederate states were restored to the Union. Radical Republicans were shocked when Johnson accepted the new Southern governments—many of whose elected leaders had been waging war against the United States only a few months earlier—into the national fold. They were dismayed by the president's acquiescence to the discriminatory "Black Codes" adopted by each of these states in place of the defunct slave statutes and by his refusal to seek congressional advice on the Reconstruction process. Relations further deteriorated when Johnson vetoed the Civil Rights Act of 1866 and a bill to extend the life of the Freedmen's Bureau. With the aid of moderate Republicans, the radicals succeeded in overriding these presidential vetoes, but the die had been cast. Johnson continued to resist the implementation of the Military Reconstruction Acts passed by Congress a year earlier, and he attempted to remove Secretary of War Edwin Stanton from office in apparent violation of the Tenure of Office Act. For these offenses, in 1868 the House of Representatives adopted 11 articles of impeachment against Johnson.

Were these actions justified? Had Johnson overstepped the constitutional bounds of his office? Had he threatened the sanctity of the Constitution of the United States? Was he guilty of "high crimes and misdemeanors," as charged by his congressional critics? These questions are addressed in the following selections by Irving Brant and Harold M. Hyman.

Brant agrees that Johnson did a great deal to incur the wrath of congressional Republicans. However, he argues that these actions did not warrant impeachment proceedings. In fact, Brant asserts, the Tenure of Office Act was patently unconstitutional, and the articles of impeachment adopted by the House amounted to a bill of attainder, the legality of which is rejected by the Constitution of the United States.

Hyman supports the decision to impeach Johnson. He argues that Johnson obstructed numerous congressional measures and directly violated the Tenure of Office Act. In the wake of this defiant behavior, says Hyman, the Republicans were fully within their constitutional rights to impeach the president.

The Johnson Trial: Attainder by Impeachment

The impeachment trial of President Andrew Johnson presented a strange phenomenon that has gone unnoticed in histories. Besides rebutting the specific
charges against him, Johnson's counsel assailed the impeachment as a violation of the Constitution. By the nature of those charges, they contended, the
proceeding violated the clause forbidding Congress to pass bills of attainder.
Lawyer after lawyer hammered on that theme, but not once did a House Manager reply. The reason appears obvious: they regarded silence as a better strategy
than unconvincing denials.

What is a bill of attainder? The Supreme Court defined it in the very year
of the Johnson impeachment, when the Court struck down two laws passed
at the close of the Civil War that required lawyers and clergymen to take loyalty oaths as a precondition to practicing their profession. Said the Court in
Cummings v. *Missouri,* holding the oath for lawyers to be in violation of the
Constitution:

"A bill of attainder is a legislative act which inflicts punishment without
a judicial trial. If the punishment be less than death, the act is termed a bill of
pains and penalties. Within the meaning of the Constitution, bills of attainder
include bills of pains and penalties." . . .

President Andrew Johnson did many things that invited the wrath of a
Congress gripped by deep emotions after four years of civil war. Johnson, a
Tennessee senator who opposed the secession of his state and adhered to the
Union throughout the war, was given the vice presidential nomination in 1864
out of gratitude and party policy. The assassination of President Lincoln thrust
him into the Presidency on April 15, 1865, at the moment of transition from
war to peace, from preservation of the Union to the difficult and complex task
of restoring national government and national unity.

The immediate question was: Should the eleven Confederate states be regarded as still legally part of the Union, and treated as if they never had left it?
Or should they be regarded as conquered provinces, to be readmitted as states
under such conditions as Congress should prescribe and they should agree to?
President Johnson took the former view; Congress the latter. Each side invoked

From Irving Brant, *Impeachment: Trials and Errors* (Alfred A. Knopf, 1972). Copyright © 1972 by
Irving Brant. Reprinted by permission of Alfred A. Knopf, Inc. Notes omitted.

the name of Abraham Lincoln, but Lincoln's final policies put him much closer to the views of his successor than to those of the Radical Republican leadership in Congress.

On the crucial issue of "rebel suffrage" there were three successive post-war policies. In reorganizing Arkansas, Louisiana, Tennessee, and Virginia, Lincoln as commander in chief disfranchised only Confederate leaders. President Johnson, ruling alone in the April–December 1865 absence of Congress, extended the disfranchisement to Confederate generals and men owning property worth more than $20,000. His object was to let poor whites govern the South and to break up the big plantations. The Radical Republicans in Congress demanded full enfranchisement of the former slaves who, under the Johnson plan already in effect, were being held close to their former status.

In the Congress that convened in December 1865, Representative Thaddeus Stevens of Pennsylvania rose swiftly to leadership of the radicals by virtue of his personal drive and the intensity of his convictions. In the Senate Charles Sumner of Massachusetts, a veteran abolitionist, gained similar preeminence. In swift succession, over the President's veto, Congress passed a series of Reconstruction Acts largely designed to protect the black population. From the Radical Republicans also came the historic Thirteenth, Fourteenth, and Fifteenth Amendments, which, as far as infringement by state action is concerned, now form the bedrock of liberty and equality under the law for all American citizens and particularly safeguard Negro rights. To enforce the Reconstruction laws, the states of the late confederacy were divided into military districts ruled by Union troops.

Trouble mounted between Johnson and Congress. In the Cabinet, Secretary of War Edwin Stanton vigorously opposed the President's Reconstruction policies. Word spread that Stanton was to be asked to resign. Congress quickly passed "an Act regulating the tenure of certain offices," which became law (again over Presidential veto) on March 2, 1867. By its terms the President could not remove any head of department without the prior consent of the Senate.

This law was patently unconstitutional. The President's power to remove such officers without consent of the Senate was debated at length in 1789 and thoroughly established by a declaratory act of Congress, not conferring that authority but worded to recognize its existence as an exclusive constitutional power....

Andrew Johnson thus had constitutional warrant for disregarding the Tenure of Office Act, but nearly a year went by with Secretary Stanton still in office. On January 30, 1868, an event occurred that revealed the Stevens faction's hair-trigger attitude toward impeachment and its sweeping concept of the power to impeach. Congressman Schofield of Pennsylvania took the floor in the House and read a short editorial from the Washington *Evening Express* of the previous day. The paper asserted that at a large social gathering one of the justices of the Supreme Court "declared in the most positive terms" that all the Reconstruction acts "were unconstitutional, and that the court would be sure to pronounce them so." Warned that such remarks were indiscreet, "he at once repeated his views in a more positive manner." The Baltimore *Gazette* named the speaker: Associate Justice Stephen J. Field, whom President Lincoln had appointed to office.

Schofield moved that the Judiciary Committee make an inquiry "and report whether the facts constituted such a misdemeanor in office as to require the House to present to the Senate articles of impeachment against the said justice of the Supreme Court." The motion was instantly approved, leaving no doubt that the Radical Republican majority regarded Justice Field's remarks as impeachable. Besides being an invasion of freedom of speech, the House action clearly meant that anything its members regarded as a "misdemeanor in office" was a constitutional ground of impeachment, even though it had not the faintest taint of criminality. Field's remark was an indiscretion, but no reasonable person could call it an impeachable misdemeanor. If the Constitution means what it says, both on impeachment and on attainder, nothing could more plainly stamp such an impeachment as a bill of attainder in disguise.

In three weeks, the impeachment move against Justice Field dropped out of sight and out of mind. For on February 21 President Johnson removed Secretary Stanton from office for undercutting Presidential policies. Three days later the House of Representatives, by a majority of 126 to 47, voted articles of impeachment against the President.

Eleven articles were presented, but ten related to the Stanton episode. Primarily, the House charged as a high crime and misdemeanor that on February 21 the President did unlawfully "issue an order in writing for the removal of Edwin M. Stanton from the office of Secretary for the Department of War... which order was unlawfully issued with intent then and there to violate the act entitled 'An act regulating the tenure of certain civil offices,' passed March 2, 1867."

In the only unrelated article, the House charged that Andrew Johnson did, on August 18, 1866, "deliver with a loud voice certain intemperate, inflammatory, and scandalous harangues, and did therein utter loud threats and bitter menaces as well against Congress as the laws of the United States duly enacted thereby." These were the impeachable words of the President, cited by the House Managers:

"We have witnessed in one Department of the Government every endeavor, as it were, to prevent the restoration of peace, harmony and union... we have seen Congress pretend to be for the Union when every step they took was to perpetuate dissolution, and make disruption permanent. We have seen every step that has been taken, instead of bringing about reconciliation and harmony, has been legislation that took the character of penalties, retaliation and revenge."

The citing of such sharp but orderly political remarks as a ground of impeachment stamped the movement for what it was—a determination to oust President Johnson because of hostility to his policies, not for any impeachable misconduct.

Notable among the seven House Managers were General Benjamin F. Butler of Massachusetts, a famous orator who was embroiled in controversy throughout his life; John A. Bingham of Ohio, leading drafter and congressional expositor of the Fourteenth Amendment; George S. Boutwell of

Massachusetts, later Secretary of the Treasury under President Grant; and Thaddeus Stevens. They were armed with a brief on impeachment precedents furnished by Representative William Lawrence of Ohio.

President Johnson's quintet of legal defenders included some of the outstanding lawyers of the United States. Henry Stanbury resigned as Attorney General to head the group, but illness disabled him except for the opening and closing addresses to the Senate. Benjamin R. Curtis had been appointed to the Supreme Court in 1851 at the age of forty-one, but had resigned six years later in protest against the Dred Scott decision, from which he and one other justice dissented. William M. Evarts, a recognized leader of the American bar for several decades, was also a diplomat without office: President Lincoln had sent him twice to England to dissuade the British government from aiding the Confederate navy. W. S. Groesbeck and Thomas A. R. Nelson completed the team.

The trial commenced in mid-March, three weeks after the impeachment, with General Butler opening for the Managers. He began adroitly by showing familiarity with and at the same time misrepresenting the famous trial of Warren Hastings in England:

"May it not have been that the trial then in progress [in 1787] was the determining cause why the framers of the Constitution left the description of offenses because of which the conduct of an officer might be inquired of to be defined by the laws and usages of Parliament as found in the precedents of the mother country, with which our fathers were as familiar as we are with our own?"

This question by its implications carried multiple distortions, both of the Hastings case itself and of the deductions to be drawn from it—distortions magnified by Hastings's acquittal. The seven-year Hastings trial was indeed cited by George Mason, but only as a reason for extending the grounds of impeachment beyond treason and bribery. Instead of supporting Butler's implication that the case carried impeachment beyond criminal misfeasance in office, the accusatory articles against Hastings piled crime on crime.

More subtle and even more misleading was Butler's equation of "high crimes and misdemeanors" with "the usages of Parliament as found in the precedents of the mother country." Those precedents included prosecutions forced on Parliament by omnipotent kings, prosecutions initiated by Parliaments snatching omnipotence away from the monarchs, and prosecutions that were mere outbursts of unreasoning passion. They reflected the violations more than the inclusions of the common law.

Later in the Johnson trial defense counsel Evarts exposed this perversion of history by showing that in the Hastings trial itself, British precedents on impeachment were repudiated. Lord Loughborough, said Evarts, sought "to demonstrate that the ordinary rules of proceedings in criminal cases did not apply to parliamentary impeachments, which could not be shackled by the forms observed in the Courts below" (that is, below the House of Lords). Evarts quoted the words by which Lord Thurlow overthrew this contention:

"My lords, with respect to the laws and usage of Parliament, I utterly disclaim all knowledge of such laws. It has no existence. True it is, in times of despotism and popular fury, when to impeach an individual was to crush him by the strong hand of power, of tumult, or of violence, the laws and usage of Parliament were quoted in order to justify the most iniquitous or atrocious acts. But in these days of light and constitutional government, I trust that no man will be tried except by the laws of the land, a system admirably calculated to protect innocence and to punish crime."

Thus whenever a representative or senator in Congress cites British precedent to justify going beyond the Constitution, he invokes "despotism and popular fury... the strong hand of power, of tumult, or of violence." Was that what the framers intended when they limited the grounds of impeachment to "high crimes and misdemeanors"?

General Butler, of course, ignored Lord Thurlow's denunciation of historic British practices that destroyed them as valid precedents. Instead, he sought to buttress his position by extended examples, contained in the brief submitted by Representative Lawrence, which he placed at this point in the record of the trial.

Lawrence cited case after case, from Hallam and other legal historians, of great lords done to death by impeachment—and then undermined his cause by placing them in Hallam's context of history, which supported Thurlow. First employed by Edward III in 1376, the impeachment process was set to one side by Tudor kings who found bills of attainder more convenient. The House of Stuart brought impeachment back. Between 1620 and 1688, it was employed forty times by Stuart kings or by a Parliament in rebellion against those kings. Attainder and impeachment as described by Hallam (as well as by historian Thomas Erskine May) were used interchangeably to destroy political offenders, and almost by the same process. Impeachment permitted a defense before the House of Lords; attainder had no standards.

It is impossible that the framers of our Constitution, knowing this history, would have prohibited bills of attainder and yet allowed the same forbidden results, actuated by the same passion, to be put into effect by a power of impeachment modeled by silent implication on British precedent. The debate in the Constitutional Convention, the wording of the impeachment clauses, the wholehearted devotion of the framers to liberty and justice, combine to forbid such a thought. In portentous contrast, the spirit of attainder ran through the trial of President Andrew Johnson. With truth, candor and impassioned rhetoric, Senator Sumner revealed the political motive for the prosecution:

"Andrew Johnson is the impersonation of the tyrannical Slave Power. In him it lives again... and he gathers about him... partisans of slavery North and South. ... With the President at their head, they are now entrenched in the Executive Mansion. Not to dislodge them is to leave the country a prey to one of the most hateful tyrannies of history."

It was in this manner that the entire prosecution of President Johnson was conducted—in the spirit and actuality of a bill of attainder, with Johnson's counsel calling it by that name. It was brought in the form of impeachment solely because the Constitution prohibits bills of attainder. The House Managers thinly cloaked this purpose in their interpretations of the impeachment power.

General Butler put heavy reliance on Madison's remark in supporting the exclusive constitutional power of a President to remove his appointees from office, that if he made "wanton removal of meritorious officers," he would be subject to impeachment. Butler omitted the qualifying statement that the motive for such an action "must be that he may fill the place with an unworthy creature of his own." The Manager saw clear proof in this that the Senate had power to convict President Johnson for removing Secretary Stanton, regardless of the validity or invalidity of the Tenure of Office Act.

Such an argument revealed at one stroke the twin errors of Madison's statement and of the deduction Butler drew from it. In August 1867, without removing Stanton as Secretary of War, President Johnson nominated General Ulysses S. Grant to that position. The Senate, as was expected, defeated confirmation. The stage was set for Grant to seek the post by court action, thus testing the constitutionality of the Tenure of Office Act. However, the General refused to make the challenge. The Secretaryship of War was then offered to General William T. Sherman, who declined; political war was a bit too hellish. The President then removed Stanton and nominated Lieutenant General Lorenzo Thomas. None of these three men could be termed an "unworthy creature." Manager Bingham disclaimed criticism of Thomas; the crime was removal of Stanton. Thus by Madison's own terms, the President's removal of "meritorious" Secretary Stanton offered no constitutional ground of impeachment. Butler's misuse of Madison's words for such a purpose revealed the fallacy in Madison's argument, which he had thought up on the moment to score a point in polemics. General Butler summed up the Managers' position by quoting and concurring in these words of Representative Lawrence:

"We define therefore an impeachable high crime or misdemeanor to be one in its nature or consequences subversive of some fundamental or essential principle of government or highly prejudicial to the public interest, and this may consist of a violation of the Constitution, of law, of an official oath, or of duty, by an act committed or omitted, or, without violating a positive law, by the abuse of discretionary powers from improper motives, or for any improper purpose."

In other words, an impeachable misdemeanor was any action which the Senate regarded as improper, and which in its opinion proceeded from an improper motive. Butler turned to England for support:

"It is but common learning that in the English precedents the words 'high crimes and misdemeanors' are universally used; but any malversation in office highly prejudicial to the public interest, or subversive of some fundamental principle of government by which the safety of a people may be in danger, is a high crime against the nation, as the term is used in parliamentary law."

This obsolete British definition (done to death by Lord Thurlow) was the same as saying that President Johnson's 1866 speech criticizing Congress, and his transfer of the War Department from Edwin M. Stanton to Lorenzo Thomas, were impeachable either as "highly prejudicial to the nation" or as dangerous to the safety of its people. The Butler-Lawrence interpretation of "high crimes and misdemeanors" can be boiled down to the single word "maladministration," which the framers refused to put in the Constitution as a ground of impeachment. House Manager Bingham heightened this perversion of the framers' intentions by saying that in determining such grounds, the Senate was "a law unto itself"—a remark that gave the trial the precise quality of a bill of attainder.

Counsel for President Johnson referred to the 1789 debate in Congress on the President's power to remove officers, proving conclusively from Madison's speech (and acts of Congress based on it) that this power was recognized to lie in the President alone, unalterable by legislative action. General Butler conceded that if Johnson, instead of sending "his defiant message to the Senate," had said he was acting to test the constitutionality of the Tenure of Office Act, the House of Representatives might not have impeached him. So, said defense counsel Benjamin Curtis, the ground of impeachment was "not the removal of Mr. Stanton but the manner in which the President communicated the fact of that removal to the Senate after it was made."

Logically, this exchange of remarks, combined with the invalidity of the Tenure of Office Act, demolished the only charge against President Johnson that could fall within the definition of a "high misdemeanor." Curtis then proceeded to his main argument (which was a bit too broad, as it excluded all violations of state laws):

"My first position is, that when the Constitution speaks of 'treason, bribery, and other high crimes and misdemeanors,' it refers to, and includes, only high criminal offenses against the United States, made so by some law of the United States existing when the acts complained of were done, and I say that this is plainly to be inferred from each and every provision of the Constitution on the subject of impeachment."

He quoted the various clauses referring to "offenses," "conviction," "crimes," etc., in connection with impeachment, and said that the argument on this point was "vastly strengthened" by the Constitution's direct prohibition of bills of attainder and *ex post facto* laws. Curtis said:

"What is a bill of attainder? It is a case before the Parliament where the Parliament make the law for the facts they find. Each legislator (for it is in their legislative capacity they act, not in a judicial one) is, to use the phrase of the honorable Managers [Bingham], 'a law unto himself'; and according to his discretion, his views of what is politic or proper under the circumstances, he frames a law to meet the case and enacts it or votes in its enactment."

Still dwelling on Bingham's maladroit remark, Curtis went on:

"According to the doctrine now advanced bills of attainder are not prohibited by this Constitution; they are only slightly modified. It is only necessary for the House of Representatives by a majority to vote an impeachment and send up certain articles and have two thirds of this body vote in favor of conviction, and there is an attainder; and it is done by the same process and depends on identically the same principles as a bill of attainder in the English Parliament. The individual wills of the legislators, instead of the conscientious discharge of the duty of the judges, settle the result.

"I submit, then, Senators, that this view of the honorable Managers of the duties and powers of this body cannot be maintained."

In conclusion, Curtis turned to the article impeaching the President for slander of Congress in a speech. This, he said, was not only an attempt to set up an *ex post facto* law where none existed "prior to the act to punish the act"; it was a case where Congress was expressly prohibited, by the First Amendment, from making any law whatever, even to punish subsequent speech.

What was this law on freedom of speech designed to be? Was it to be, "as the honorable Managers seem to think it should be, the sense of propriety of each Senator appealed to"? That was "the same freedom of speech, Senators, in consequence of which thousands of men went to the scaffold under the Tudors and the Stuarts. . . . Is that the freedom of speech intended to be secured by our Constitution?"

This trial, Curtis predicted, would live in history as the most conspicuous American example either of justice or of injustice. It would (to paraphrase Edmund Burke) either exemplify that justice which is the standing policy of all civilized states, or it would produce "that injustice which is sure to be discovered, and which makes even the wise man mad, and which, in the fixed and immutable order of God's providence, is certain to return to plague its inventors."

The House Managers continued to provide defense with openings to call the impeachment a bill of attainder. Later in the trial, defense counsel Groesbeck put some of these remarks together. Without naming the Managers, he said that one of them (it was Butler) had stated that in sitting as a court of impeachment, the Senate "knew no law, either statute or common, and consulted no precedents save those of parliamentary bodies." Another (it was Bingham) had claimed that the Senate "was a law unto itself; in a word, that its jurisdiction was without bounds; that it may impeach for any cause, and there is no appeal from its judgment." A third (John A. Logan) said much the same as Bingham. And it was argued by Butler that when the words "high crimes and misdemeanors" were used, "they are without signification and intended merely to give solemnity to the charge." Under these interpretations "everything this tribunal may deem impeachable becomes so at once." Said Groesbeck, pursuing the issue of attainder:

"To sustain this extraordinary view of the character of this tribunal we have been referred to English precedents, and especially to early English precedents, when, according to my recollection, impeachment and attainder and bills of pains and penalties labored together in the work of murder and confiscation."

The Constitution, Groesbeck declared, placed limitations on the executive and judicial departments, and he had supposed the legislative was also limited. But according to the argument made in this trial, it was otherwise. The Senate "has in its service and at its command an institution [impeachment] that is above all law and acknowledges no restraint; an institution worse than a court martial, in that it has a broader and more dangerous jurisdiction."

The question of attainder was sharpened by a vitriolic attack on Johnson by Thaddeus Stevens, who asserted that the Senate had rendered final judgment against Johnson even before the House impeached him. It did so, he declared, in a resolution adopted on February 21 (three days before the House acted) declaring that the President had no power to remove Stanton. By that vote, Stevens maintained, the senators were committed to find him guilty. Exclaimed the fiery Radical Republican leader:

"And now this offspring of assassination turns upon the Senate... and bids them defiance. How can he escape the just vengeance of the law? Wretched man, standing at bay, surrounded by a cordon of living men, each with the ax of an executioner uplifted for his just punishment!"

Defense counsel Evarts seized on this as one more proof that the Managers were seeking to pass a bill of attainder. If, said he, judgment was rendered in that vote of February 21, "then you are here standing about the scaffold of execution." If so, of what service was the constitutional prohibition of bills of attainder? He asked, as had a fellow counsel:

"What is a bill of attainder; what is a bill of pains and penalties?... It is a proceeding by the legislature as a legislature to enact crime, sentence, punishment all in one.... [If you follow the Stevens rule] you are enacting a bill of pains and penalties upon the simple form that a majority of the House and two thirds of the Senate must concur, and the Constitution and the wisdom of our ancestors all pass for naught."

To emphasize the element of attainder, Evarts quoted the admission of House Manager Buchanan in the case of Judge Peck that to convict the judge of impeachable official misbehavior, "we are bound to prove that the respondent has violated the Constitution or some known law of the land." He endorsed the argument of his colleague Curtis, "upon the strict constitutional necessity, under the clause prohibiting *ex post facto* laws, and under the clause prohibiting bills of attainder," that articles of impeachment be confined to "what is crime against the Constitution and crime against the law."

Here was the clearest statement that to go beyond crimes against the laws and Constitution and give sanction to general ideas of misbehavior was to convert impeachment into both a bill of attainder and an *ex post facto* law. If the case of Warren Hastings was to be used as a guide, Evarts declared, the standard of impeachable misconduct must meet the specifications laid down by Edmund Burke as manager of the Hastings trial. He quoted Burke's opening address to the House of Lords:

"We know, as we are to be served by men, that the persons who serve us must be tried as men, and with a very large allowance indeed to human infirmity and human error. This, my lords, we knew, and we weighed before we came before you. But the crimes which we charge in these articles are not lapses, defects, errors of common human frailty, which, as we know, and feel, we can allow for. We charge this offender with no crimes that have not arisen from passions which it is criminal to harbor; with no offenses that have not their root in avarice, rapacity, pride, insolence, ferocity, treachery, cruelty, malignity of temper; in short, in nothing that does not argue a total extinction of all moral principle, that does not manifest an inveterate blackness, dyed ingrain with malice, vitiated, corrupted, gangrened to the very core."

Evarts could have carried his case further. For at the close of that seven years' trial the Lords, passing on Burke's catalog of heinous accusations, found Hastings not guilty. They found that his conduct consisted, not of crimes in office, but of errors of judgment in performance of his duties as governor general of India. For these he could not properly be impeached. Thus prosecution and defense, in combination, narrowed the grounds of impeachment permissible under British precedents. Both sides cast aside the Tudor-Stuart concept of impeachment. The British reform went further: Public opinion in and out of Parliament discarded the entire institution of impeachment. Except for one trivial case a few years later, no impeachment has taken place in Great Britain from 1786 to the present. But members of Congress claim that the framers, without saying so, embodied British concepts of impeachment in the Constitution, and cite as their only evidence the fact that the Constitution was written during the Hastings impeachment—which put an end to the British system.

Evarts's quotation from Burke brought to a climax the fundamental defense of President Johnson: that the articles of impeachment brought against him constituted a bill of attainder. The argument was answered by total silence. Not once was the word "attainder" spoken by any House Manager, nor did any touch on the concept of attainder. Any attempt at rebuttal would have brought the issue fully before the Senate, and the weakness of the Managers' denials would have given their arguments a hollow ring. Even the admission that grounds of argument on attainder existed might have given a new aspect to the trial, producing in some senatorial minds an unwillingness to cast a vote for an unconstitutional conviction. Indeed, the one-sided discussion had that tendency, reducing the case against Johnson to two narrowly technical points —denial by the Managers that when the President removed Secretary Stanton, he intended to test the constitutionality of the Tenure of Office Act, and the question of criminal libel in Johnson's criticism of Congress.

The defense met the first of these arguments by putting General William Tecumseh Sherman on the stand. He testified that when the post of Secretary of War was being offered to him, the President said: "If we can bring the case to the courts it would not stand half an hour." Pursuing that line, defense counsel Nelson argued that the Tenure of Office Act was unconstitutional, but that in any case impeachment was unwarranted because "the President acted from laudable and honest motives, and is not, therefor[e] guilty of any crime or misdemeanor."

Manager Bingham brought the case against President Johnson to a close by defining freedom of speech in terms of the Sedition Act of 1798. This he linked with an 1806 set of Army regulations by Congress in which military officers and soldiers were made subject to court-martial for using "contemptuous or disrespectful words" against the President, Vice President, or Congress. If those two laws are constitutional, declared Bingham, seditious utterances "are indictable as misdemeanors, whether made by the President or anybody else, and especially in an official charged with the execution of the laws." Indeed, he continued, seditious utterances by an executive officer always were indictable at common law:

"But, say counsel, this is his guaranteed right under the Constitution. The freedom of speech, says the gentleman, is not to be restricted by a law of Congress. How is that answered by this act of 1806, which subjects every soldier in your Army and every officer in your Army to court-martial for using disrespectful words of the President or of the Congress or of his superior officers? The freedom of speech guarantied by the Constitution to all the people of the United States, is that freedom of speech which respects, first, the right of the nation itself, which respects the supremacy of the nation's laws, and which finally respects the rights of every citizen of the Republic."

Thus an unconstitutional Sedition Act (so pronounced by the Supreme Court more than a century after it expired), and a military regulation laid down to maintain discipline in the Army, were to measure the right of the President of the United States to criticize Congress. What this meant was that the First Amendment was worthless without the enforcing strength of the Supreme Court. On the constitutional level, impeachment trials throughout American history have been prosecuted on the legal plane occupied by the Sedition Act of 1798. In every instance where the drive for impeachment has been politically motivated—the prosecutions of Judge Pickering, Justice Chase, and President Johnson, and the abortive moves against Justices Field and Douglas—the same passions that produced the Sedition Act of 1798 have inflamed and degraded the driving forces in Congress.

The ordeal of President Andrew Johnson ended on May 16, 1868, when, after a two-month trial, the Senate voted on the eleven articles of impeachment. The vote was the same on each: guilty, 35; not guilty, 19—only one short of the needed two thirds. Before the balloting began, Senator Lyman Trumbull of Illinois presented a written opinion in which he said:

"In view of the consequences likely to flow from this day's proceedings, should they result in conviction on what my judgment tells me are insufficient charges and proofs, I tremble for the future of my country."

The ferocity of the prosecution and closeness of the verdict combined to establish the Johnson impeachment as a menacing portent of the future. The failure of this case to serve as a permanent warning against perversion of the Constitution is more ominous still. Nevertheless, if the cogent and powerful arguments of the defense influenced a single senator—and they probably converted several—they prevented the deepest tragedy in American political history.

How to Set the Law in Motion

The Tenure law [Tenure of Office Act] provided that persons appointed by the President and confirmed by the Senate should not be removed without Senate concurrence. The President could suspend an official if the Senate was not in session, but must report the suspension to the Senate on its reassembly and ask its consent. Republican congressmen differed on the question of whether the Tenure bill embraced Lincoln holdovers such as War Secretary [Edwin M.] Stanton in Johnson's cabinet. But enough sentiment obtained to lock Stanton in to comfort those in and out of the Army who feared the quality of a Johnson-appointed successor, a pleasure increased by provisions in the Army Appropriations Act requiring Congress's assent to transfer orders directed to the commanding general from the President.

In unhappy chronological conjunction, ambitions and events transformed efforts during March 1867 at stability into nervous near crisis. All through spring and summer, the President and Attorney General Henry Stanbery interpreted the Reconstruction statutes to hamstring commanding generals. A central issue was a general's authority to remove from office provisional state civil officials who failed to enforce state and local laws when blacks and Unionists were the victims of illegality and violence. In late April, Mississippi resorted to the Supreme Court for a permanent injunction directed against the President and the Army commander in that state, to forbid enforcement there of the allegedly unconstitutional Reconstruction statute. But even Johnson and his Attorney General acknowledged that Mississippi's request was unprecedented and outrageous; no court could enjoin a President. Congress had required the President to execute a law constitutionally enacted with respect to procedure, Stanbery told the court. The Mississippi petition, without legal or historical merit, received no support in the Court.

Almost simultaneously, Georgia sought injunctions against enforcement of the Reconstruction statute in the state, naming the Secretary of War and generals from Grant down. Georgia's counsel stressed Congress's alleged obliteration of the state. Responding for the defendants, Stanbery insisted that the Court's jurisdiction ended at political matters, and the Congress's decision concerning Georgia's status was political. Accepting Stanbery's argument on May 13, 1867, the Supreme Court dismissed both petitions.

By denying the Georgia and Mississippi petitions, the Court avoided for its own convenience direct confrontation with Congress concerning the Reconstruction law's constitutionality. The jurists' grounds were historical and jurisprudentially proper; plaintiffs' counsel had misfired.

Congress's Reconstruction authorizations to the Army appeared to have passed all foreseeable constitutional and political obstacles that the provisional southern states and the President could raise and the Supreme Court would entertain. Despite partisan contrary assertion, no judicial decision yet issued questioned directly the Reconstruction law or the Army's derivative policies in the South. In substantial confidence and good humor, therefore, on July 19 Congress passed over Johnson's veto another supplement to the Reconstruction law. Directly contradicting the Attorney General's hamstringing efforts, it authorized Army commanders to follow Grant's precedent instructions and to remove provisional state and local officials who failed equally to enforce their states' civil and criminal statues. Retrospectively, along with the McCardle case and the impeachment, this amendment forms the context in which Reconstruction's beginning ended and in which Reconstruction's end began.

Under Congress's authorization and Grant's orders most Reconstruction commanders became involved in numerous details of life and labor including criminal-law enforcement, professional licensing, municipal police, and debt collections, without which more decent political action, racially defined, was impossible, according to General [Daniel] Sickles in South Carolina. Sickles suspended execution of debt-collection judgments and debt-imprisonment sentences issuing from all courts, including national tribunals. He explained to Grant that under the 1789 Judiciary Act federal courts were required to employ the procedures of forum state courts. But it was precisely to reform state procedures that Congress had ordered the Army to Reconstruction duty. Therefore Sickles had suspended existing state laws and derivative judgments that in his view were unfair to citizens. But it was all fruitless if national courts, employing state procedures, substantively reinforced that state's unjust processes and results. Federal courts obeyed Congress's 1789 order to use state procedures. Should not national judges obey also Congress's 1867 laws that the southern states' constitutions, laws, and procedures become at least as decent as those of other states?

Though Grant and Stanton sustained Sickles and other generals, it was clear that Reconstruction matters had gone awry. Even [Supreme Court Chief Justice Salmon P.] Chase felt that however worthy the goals, Congress had given the Army too much latitude and had upset both power separation and national-state relationships. Whether Chase objected more to Sickles's intrusions into state and local commercial tax, debt, labor, and criminal matters, or into inferior national court procedures, is not known. But he believed fervently in the maintenance of state governments as the base of the federal union. Chase revered the national judiciary as the pacific links for Union, and he saw nothing amiss in the tradition that national judges use applicable state pleadings and procedures. The Army as servants for Congress and the national courts was one matter; the Army as master of federal court procedures was quite another.

Conservatives sniffed the shifting wind and discerned opportunity in the Army's intrusion into property and judicial matters. Lawyers and southern politicos picked up the theme that Reconstruction laws were unconstitutional not only as infringements on civil liberties but also as deprivations of property rights. "The [South's] only gleam of hope for the Constitution then was in the Supreme Court," recalled Alabama's conservative constitutionalist, Hilary Herbert.

But appropriate litigation in the sense of dramatic, politically compelling qualities did not come up every day. A Louisiana suit remained obscure in state courts even though it challenged the Army's power to set aside interest payments on a municipality's debt and despite plaintiff's argument that the suspension deprived good-faith bondholders of property in a manner the national Supreme Court had declared unconstitutional in the Gelpcke v. Dubuque decision.

Nationwide political attention turned instead to William McCardle's suit. He was a Vicksburg newspaper publisher whose editorials encouraged violent resistance to racial-equality provisions of the Reconstruction statutes. Arrested and awaiting a military commission trial, McCardle sought release by means of a habeas corpus writ from the United States Circuit Court. Its judge denied his petition and remanded him to Army jurisdiction.

Responding sensitively to growing civil-law concerns among lawyers, Jeremiah Black and David Dudley Field, McCardle's counsel, without abandoning the basic theme of the Reconstruction law's unconstitutionality, played down civil-military aspects. In order to get the case to the Supreme Court the appellants had to overcome the Vallandigham and Milligan precedents, which, taken together, suggested that no Supreme Court jurisdiction existed in appeals from military authority and that only wartime executive extensions of Army courts over civilians were unjustifiable. Instead McCardle's counsel seized on Congress's 1867 Habeas Corpus law and insisted that it gave adequate jurisdiction to the Supreme Court to protect McCardle.

Many elements made McCardle's case dramatic. Although the Attorney General had appeared very recently on behalf of the government and its officers in the Georgia and Mississippi injunction litigation, he refused to appear against McCardle. Grant obtained for the Army the services of Senators Lyman Trumbull and Matthew Carpenter. Only a week after denying itself competency to issue Georgia the requested injunction against the Reconstruction law, the Supreme Court accepted jurisdiction of McCardle's appeal. A decision was possible adverse to the congressional statutes now being militarily enforced. Further, events determined that judgment in McCardle's case must issue in the superheated politics of the nation's first impeachment, which in its unique way was also testing issues implicit in McCardle's case.

In short, McCardle kept the Supreme Court in the most exposed salient of Reconstruction politics. As Henry Dutton noted, McCardle's case involved the fates of the South's states and Negroes, of the President of the United States, and of the Army. Unique among the world's courts, the United States Supreme Court was to determine national policy, the destiny of races, and the quality and direction of a great society.

Aware of context and implications, the government's counsel chose to fight McCardle's appeal on his selected battlefield. Carpenter boasted confidently that in his brief he had "avoided all talk of the rights of conquest, a theme that is very unpalatable to that [Supreme] court . . . & placed [Congress's] right to pass the [Reconstruction] law upon entirely peace powers of the [national] government. This foundation is as solid as a rock, & if that Court decides the case upon judicial, not political, points, we have a sure thing."

Congress made a surer thing of it. Over somnambulistic Democratic resistance and a tepid presidential veto—the impeachment was under way, after all—on March 27 Congress repealed the provisions of the February 1867 law that provided it appellate jurisdiction in McCardle's case. In April the Court acquiesced and dropped consideration of McCardle's appeal.

But it dropped only that litigation. Accepting Congress's jurisdiction limitation, Chase stipulated carefully that "Counsel [for McCardle] seems to have supposed, if effect be given to the repealing act . . . that the whole appellate power of the court in cases in *habeas corpus* is denied. But this is an error." Instead McCardle meant only that quite constitutionally, Congress determined the Court's jurisdiction, which it elected now partially to excise.

While McCardle's appeal made its way to Washington, the President asserted his alleged right to independent control over the Army, i.e., to issue orders contrary to Congress's Reconstruction purposes. In August 1867, complying with the Tenure law, he suspended Stanton and named Grant ad interim successor. The President relieved from command Sickles and other generals who had actively enforced Congress's Reconstruction statutes. Wearing two hats as commanding general and temporary War Secretary, Grant saw to it that the Army kept in motion Congress's basic Reconstruction directives involving redistricting, voter registration, and new state constitutional conventions. In December when Congress reassembled, as the Tenure law required, the President reported Stanton's suspension to the Senate. It refused approval. The President refused in turn to readmit Stanton to the Cabinet. Grant turned the War Office keys back to Stanton, who occupied the Secretaryship in defiance of the President.

Unable to reverse Reconstruction through appeals to voters, to standpat and retrograde congressmen, or to courts, the President, defying a national law, reached out for control over one of Reconstruction's two essential instruments, the Army. Therefore, despite the clear political hazards and ambiguities involved in the unprecedented move, the Republican center decided for impeachment, a wholly constitutional procedure.

Johnson's obstructive replacements of Reconstruction generals and rejection of Stanton were last straws calling impeachment into action. . . . Laws on confiscation, test oaths, Freedmen's Bureau courts, Civil Rights, and Military Reconstruction had suffered Johnson's nonenforcements, malforming interpretations, or outright obstructions. Yet his piecemeal impediments had kept impeachment only a minority dream. Fall elections in 1867 and a worrisome business recession had disposed many Republicans against further political unsettlements and made impeachment the more unlikely despite the President's now-open appointments of conservative generals to commands in the South.

Nevertheless, in early 1868 Johnson managed to transform the Republicans' search for stability into an impeachment consensus.

It was easier to decide on the need for the act than to know confidently how to proceed or to anticipate the consequences of success. Since 1789 impeachments had been whistled up sporadically for Presidents, but never came to action. A very small number of lesser official fry had been impeached.

The Republican decision to impeach Johnson was hardly an expression of partisan contempt for the Presidency, as distinguished from the incumbent. M. L. Benedict, author of the best inquiry into the subject, concludes that the impeachment grew from Republicans' incapacity to be legislative despots or to conceive of Military Reconstruction without the Army's Commander-in-Chief commanding. In Benedict's judgment, "Historians should view the... impeachment for what it was, ... one of the great legal cases of history in which American politicians demonstrated the strength of the nation's ... institutions by attempting to... give a political officer a full and fair trial in a time of political crisis."

This moral victory would have been impossible had the Constitution's sparse impeachment clause failed to work. Impeachment became another instance in the Civil War and Reconstruction when politicians and legal scholars reviewed history in order for the first time actually to apply a dormant part of the Constitution.

Fortunately for congressmen a useful literature was available by early 1868 as a result of abortive efforts at impeachment in 1867. In this literature, attitudes about the law and politics of impeachment—and impeachment mixed characteristics of a trial at law and of a political contest—were sharply variant. A narrow view, insisted on throughout the trial by Democrats and conservative Republicans, was that English and American precedents applied which allowed impeachment of an official only if he had committed an indictable criminal act. The broad view, taken up by Republicans, insisted that English precedents were not wholly applicable. There the House of Lords could punish as well as try any offender, including officials. Here Congress could only remove officials. Therefore American precedents failed to sustain a need for indictable crime as a reason for removal.

History leans strongly toward the broad Republican position. "That an impeached official can be tried in a criminal court after his trial on impeachment does not imply [that] only those who can be tried in a criminal court can be impeached," Benedict concluded. "It means, rather, that where an officer *is* impeached for an indictable offense, the impeachment does not preclude a later indictment." The Constitution's framers and ratifiers had themselves carefully sidestepped their own double-jeopardy, jury-trial, and pardon provisions when dealing with impeachments, envisaging instead a special political process set to lawlike procedures.

Perhaps any strictly legalistic analyses would have assumed the Constitution's creators. As John Norton Pomeroy noted just before the Johnson impeachment got under way, the men of 1787 aimed actually to check unpredictable future power abuses at the highest political level, where discretion had to exist, else free government could not live. Therefore the framers wrote into the Constitution a brooding impeachment threat rather than a precise weapon.

Impeachment's adversary features gave the President's counsel ample scope to develop the narrow tradition that an indictable offense was necessary for conviction, that the Tenure law did not cover Stanton, that the President had equal right with Congress to determine if a law was unconstitutional, and that by violating the disputed law the President aimed at a court test. These lawyerlike arguments-in-the-alternative well suited the substantively political yet procedurally legal contours of the impeachment proceeding. Concerning Stanton's amenability to the Tenure law, Benedict's careful analysis convinces that by the final vote on its passage congressmen had "concluded [that] the bill protected Stanton after all," and that Johnson's retention of Stanton in the Cabinet "was . . . a virtual reappointment" acquiring tenured status. On the matter of the President testing a law he thinks is unconstitutional by violating it, no evidence exists that Johnson actually tried for a court test. Benedict properly raises the derivative query, what if after violation a court or the Congress finds the law constitutional? As a defense, the President's argument raised endless abysses for the survival potential of American government.

This evaluation of the President's scattergun points suggests a need to re-evaluate also the Republicans' omnibus accusations against him. They too were equivalents to a lawyer's arguments-in-the-alternative aimed to sweep as wide horizons as possible. In terms of Republican intraparty factionalism in the House the impeachment articles sought to accommodate conservative and centrist waverers whose goals were won with the President's mark-time response to impeachment, and who therefore felt little or no compulsion to proceed on the unmarked road to conviction.

Mixtures of politics and law featured also the Senate's maneuvers in committee and on the floor concerning rules of procedure for the impeachment trial. If the Senate proclaimed itself a court then the presiding officer stipulated in the Constitution, the Chief Justice of the United States, could "vote" as well as interpret points of evidence and law. But if the Senate retained its noncourt character, the Chief Justice could not claim a vote. Deciding that the Senate was not a court, senators determined also that they had the power to overturn Chase's rulings on disputed questions of law and evidence.

But senators' efforts not to be bound by Chase's unpredictable rulings on law collapsed in the trial's first days. As Chase administered oaths to senators to do impartial justice, Democrats insisted that Ben Wade should not sit, since he would succeed Johnson if the President were removed. Chase ruled that Wade should sit, since the Senate was a court and his status as president of the Senate was irrelevant. The Chief Justice implicitly resolved in his own favor the matter of his right to vote. It all meant that the trial would proceed far more slowly than Republicans wished. The conservatives won time for reaction to set in.

In constitutional terms, Edward S. Corwin concluded, "the impeachers had the better of the argument for all but the most urgent situations." And there was the heart of the matter. For conviction of Johnson involved the nation's most urgent situations, ranging from the unhappy prospects of Wade as President supporting agrarian monetary and tariff heresies, of continuing racial instability southward, of Negro suffrage issues in northern states, and of political corruption everywhere. Republican centrists impeached the President for refusing to execute their statutes. If the impeachment swerved his course, conviction became unnecessary.

While the trial was on Johnson made clear his intention to name a moderate general to be Secretary of War; forwarded to the Senate the Reconstruction constitutions of Arkansas and South Carolina, created by terms of Congress's Reconstruction laws which he said were unconstitutional, including ratification of the detested Fourteenth Amendment and provisions for blacks' voting; and ceased obstructing the progress of congressional Reconstruction in other provisional states by devious interpretations of the laws or other overt means. Politically, the seven recusant Republican senators who voted not to convict Johnson merely affirmed impeachment's victory. Little wonder that contrary to tradition, they did not suffer disastrously at the hands of their constituents or party. Little wonder also that history is redressing opinion concerning the senators who voted finally and unavailingly to convict. They were, Benedict concludes, "motivated by the same desire for impartial justice [or lack of it] that historians and partisans ascribed only to the recusants."

Between die-hard Democrats convinced of the need to acquit the President and Radical Republicans determined to convict him, senators in the center wrestled to come to decision on ambiguous technical points. Days, weeks, and months passed in complex skirmishes on the admissibility of evidence and on such technical legal points as estoppel and the President's independent power of removal. An over-all review sustains Benedict's judgment: "After the events leading to impeachment... it is difficult to understand how anyone could have accepted at face value the moderate and reasonable interpretation Johnson's lawyers put on his activities." But because evidential disproofs of the President's inner intentions were impossible to evoke, because Republican senators wished to retain existing constitutional configurations, and because all senators wished to prevent the "Mexicanization" of the Presidency, Johnson benefited. He received the one vote needed to secure nonconviction; in mid-May the impeachment ended.

A kind of quiet returned to the Potomac. The President, smarting from his one-vote escape and his inability to win the Democratic party's 1868 nomination for a whole term, contented himself with giving a "little lecture on constitutional law" to such captive visitors as youthful political reporter Henry Adams. But the scholarly pose failed to conceal the stubborn activist. Immediately after the Senate vote, Johnson considered sliding in the detested [William] Seward as War Secretary, but, fortunately dissuaded, named conservative General John Schofield. The Senate consented "inasmuch as... Stanton has relinquished his place." Mutual ill-humor aside, the President's belated acquiescence in the impeachment's verdict indicated that at last he had learned the lesson which Republican congressmen had been trying for two years to teach him. Now Reconstruction would proceed as Congress had prescribed.

A profound psychological release, the impeachment was another of the proofs accumulating since early 1861 concerning the Constitution's tough workability. In terms of early 1868, it allowed a procedurally pacific institutional readjustment between the nation's governing branches, badly skewed in favor of the White House by reason of the War, another item in the South's debits. It was an article of Republican faith that Reconstruction of the South also involved improved equilibrium between the nation's branches, which helps to explain Congress's devotion to increasing the federal courts' jurisdictions and powers.

Contemporaries saw impeachment's nonviolent course and constructive outcome as proof of Reconstruction's terminal phase. From 1866–68 Congress had embodied in legislation the War's "logical results," according to publicist Samuel Bowles. Insuring the protection of these results without the second civil war which reasonable men feared, the impeachment began a two-year-long wrapping-up of the War's residuals. By 1870 Ignatius Donnelly believed that "not a single issue of the many which agitated us in the past remains alive to-day—slavery—reconstruction—rebellion—impartial suffrage—have all perished." However coarse, his perception required a view of impeachment as a constitutional process accompanied by enormous political hazards that had rasped the nation's tight nerves. Pressures increased on politicians to close off Reconstruction. These pressures played essential roles in determining impeachment's hair-breadth outcome, the 1868 presidential elections, the Fourteenth and Fifteenth Amendments' ratifications and enforcements, and the nature of certain Supreme Court judgments.

POSTSCRIPT

Was It Wrong to Impeach Andrew Johnson?

Authority for the impeachment and potential removal from office of federal officials is established in Article 1, Sections 2 and 3 of the Constitution of the United States, which delegate sole power to impeach to the House of Representatives and the power to try all impeachments to the Senate. This power, however, has been invoked only 16 times in 200 years and only twice—in the cases of Andrew Johnson and Bill Clinton—against a president of the United States. The other cases involved a U.S. senator (William Blount, 1798), a Supreme Court justice (Samuel Chase, 1804), a Cabinet officer (William Belknap, 1876), and 11 federal judges. Less than half of the cases have resulted in conviction and removal from office.

In *Federalist,* No. 65, Alexander Hamilton noted that impeachment was an instrument to be used when individuals engaged in misconduct that abused the public trust. Recognizing the political nature of such offenses, he warned,

> The prosecution of them ... will seldom fail to agitate the passions of the whole community, and to divide it into parties more or less friendly or inimical to the accused. In many cases it will connect itself with the pre-existing factions, and will enlist all their animosities, partialities, influence, and interest on one side or on the other; and in such cases there will always be the greatest danger that the decision will be regulated more by the comparative strength of parties, than by the real demonstrations of innocence or guilt.

Such was undoubtedly true in the case of Andrew Johnson.

For historical studies of Johnson's impeachment, see Michael Les Benedict, *The Impeachment and Trial of Andrew Johnson* (W. W. Norton, 1973) and Hans L. Trefousse, *Impeachment of a President: Andrew Johnson, the Blacks, and Reconstruction* (University of Tennessee Press, 1975). Johnson's biographers also devote attention to the impeachment. See Albert Castel, *The Presidency of Andrew Johnson* (Regents Press of Kansas, 1979); James E. Sefton, *Andrew Johnson and the Uses of Constitutional Power* (Little, Brown, 1980); and Hans L. Trefousse, *Andrew Johnson: A Biography* (W. W. Norton, 1989).

For more general studies of impeachment, see William H. Rehnquist, *Grand Inquests: The Historic Impeachments of Justice Samuel Chase and President Andrew Johnson* (William Morrow, 1992) and Michael J. Gerhardt, *The Federal Impeachment Process: A Constitutional and Historical Analysis* (Princeton University Press, 1996).

ISSUE 2

Was John D. Rockefeller a "Robber Baron"?

YES: Matthew Josephson, from *The Robber Barons: The Great American Capitalists, 1861–1901* (Harcourt, Brace & World, 1962)

NO: Ralph W. Hidy and Muriel E. Hidy, from *History of Standard Oil Company (New Jersey), vol. 1: Pioneering in Big Business, 1882–1911* (Harper & Brothers, 1955)

ISSUE SUMMARY

YES: Historian Matthew Josephson depicts John D. Rockefeller as an unconscionable manipulator who employed deception, bribery, and outright conspiracy to restrain free trade in order to eliminate his competitors for control of the oil industry in the United States.

NO: Business historians Ralph W. Hidy and Muriel E. Hidy argue that although Rockefeller and his associates at Standard Oil occasionally used their power ruthlessly, they were innovative representatives of corporate capitalism who brought stability to the often chaotic petroleum industry and made a significant contribution to the rapid development of the national economy as a whole.

Between 1860 and 1914 the United States was transformed from a country of farms, small towns, and modest manufacturing concerns to a modern nation dominated by large cities and factories. During those years the population tripled, and the nation experienced astounding urban growth. A new proletariat emerged to provide the necessary labor for the country's developing factory system. Between the Civil War and World War I, the value of manufactured goods in the United States increased 12-fold, and the capital invested in industrial pursuits multiplied 22 times. In addition, the application of new machinery and scientific methods to agriculture produced abundant yields of wheat, corn, and other foodstuffs, despite the decline in the number of farmers.

Why did this industrial revolution occur in the United States during the last quarter of the nineteenth century? What factors contributed to the rapid pace of American industrialization? In answering these questions, historians often point to the first half of the 1800s and the significance of the "transportation revolution," which produced better roads, canals, and railroads to move people and goods more efficiently and cheaply from one point to another. Technological improvements such as the Bessemer process, refrigeration, electricity, and the telephone also made their mark in the nation's "machine age." Government cooperation with business, large-scale immigration from Europe and Asia, and the availability of foreign capital for industrial investments provided still other underpinnings for this industrial growth. Finally, American industrialization depended upon a number of individuals in the United States who were willing to organize and finance the nation's industrial base for the sake of anticipated profits. These, of course, were the entrepreneurs.

American public attitudes have reflected a schizophrenic quality with regard to the activities of the industrial leaders of the late nineteenth century. Were these entrepreneurs "robber barons" who employed any means necessary to enrich themselves at the expense of their competitors? Or were they "captains of industry" whose shrewd and innovative leadership brought order out of industrial chaos and generated great fortunes that enriched the public welfare through the workings of the various philanthropic agencies that these leaders established? Although the "robber baron" stereotype emerged as early as the 1870s, it probably gained its widest acceptance in the 1930s, when, in the midst of the Great Depression, many critics were proclaiming the apparent failure of American capitalism. Since the depression, however, some historians, including Allan Nevins, Alfred D. Chandler, Jr., and Maury Klein, have sought to revise the negative assessments offered by earlier generations of scholars. In the hands of these business historians, the late-nineteenth-century businessmen have become "industrial statesmen" who skillfully oversaw the process of raising the United States to a preeminent position among the nations of the world. The following selections reveal the divergence of scholarly opinion as it applies to one of the most notable of these American entrepreneurs—John D. Rockefeller, founder of the Standard Oil Company, who came to epitomize both the success and excess of corporate capitalism in the United States.

Matthew Josephson, whose 1934 attack on monopolistic capitalism became the model for the "robber baron" thesis for post-depression-era historians, characterizes Rockefeller as a parsimonious, deceptive, and conspiratorial businessman. Rockefeller's fortune, Josephson argues, was built upon a series of secret agreements that wrung concessions from America's leading railroad magnates and allowed Rockefeller to decimate his competitors through the establishment of the South Improvement Company and, subsequently, Standard Oil.

Ralph W. Hidy and Muriel E. Hidy, on the other hand, accentuate Rockefeller's positive accomplishments in their study of Standard Oil of New Jersey. Rockefeller could be ruthless in his business dealings, they admit, but he operated within the law and introduced innovations that stabilized the petroleum industry, produced a mass-marketing system, and spearheaded the nation's economic growth in the late nineteenth and early twentieth centuries.

The Robber Barons

John Rockefeller who grew up in Western New York and later near Cleveland, as one of a struggling family of five children, recalls with satisfaction the excellent practical training he had received and how quickly he put it to use. His childhood seemed to have been darkened by the misdeeds of his father, a wandering vendor of quack medicine who rarely supported his family, and was sometimes a fugitive from the law; yet the son invariably spoke of his parent's instructions with gratitude. He said:

> ... He himself trained me in practical ways. He was engaged in different enterprises; he used to tell me about these things ... and he taught me the principles and methods of business.... I knew what a cord of good solid beech and maple wood was. My father told me to select only solid wood ... and not to put any limbs in it or any punky wood. That was a good training for me.

But the elder Rockefeller went further than this in his sage instructions, according to John T. Flynn, who attributes to him the statement:

> I cheat my boys every chance I get, I want to make 'em sharp. I trade with the boys and skin 'em and I just beat 'em every time I can. I want to make 'em sharp.

If at times the young Rockefeller absorbed a certain shiftiness and trading sharpness from his restless father, it was also true that his father was absent so often and so long as to cast shame and poverty upon his home. Thus he must have been subject far more often to the stern supervision of his mother, whom he has recalled in several stories. His mother would punish him, as he related, with a birch switch to "uphold the standard of the family when it showed a tendency to deteriorate." Once when she found out that she was punishing him for a misdeed at school of which he was innocent, she said, "Never mind, we have started in on this whipping and it will do for the next time." The normal outcome of such disciplinary cruelty would be deception and stealthiness in the boy, as a defense.

But his mother, who reared her children with the rigid piety of an Evangelist, also started him in his first business enterprise. When he was seven years old she encouraged him to raise turkeys, and gave him for this purpose the family's surplus milk curds. There are legends of Rockefeller as a boy stalking a turkey with the most patient stealth in order to seize her eggs.

This harshly disciplined boy, quiet, shy, reserved, serious, received but a few years' poor schooling, and worked for neighboring farmers in all his spare time. (His whole youth suggests only abstinence, prudence and the growth of parsimony in his soul.) The pennies he earned he would save steadily in a blue bowl that stood on a chest in his room, and accumulated until there was a small heap of gold coins. He would work, by his own account, hoeing potatoes for a neighboring farmer from morning to night for 37 cents a day. At a time when he was still very young he had fifty dollars saved, which upon invitation he one day loaned to the farmer who employed him.

"And as I was saving those little sums," he relates, "I soon learned that I could get as much interest for $50 loaned at seven per cent—then the legal rate of interest—as I could earn by digging potatoes for ten days." Thereafter, he tells us, he resolved that (it was better "to let the money be my slave than to be the slave of money.")

In Cleveland whither the family removed in 1854, Rockefeller went to the Central High School and studied bookkeeping for a year. This delighted him. Most of the conquering types in the coming order were to be men trained early in life in the calculations of the bookkeeper, Cooke, Huntington, Gould, Henry Frick and especially Rockefeller of whom it was said afterward: "He had the soul of a bookkeeper."

In his first position as bookkeeper to a produce merchant at the Cleveland docks, when he was sixteen, he distinguished himself by his composed orderly habits. Very carefully he examined each item on each bill before he approved it for payment. (Out of a salary which began at $15 a month and advanced ultimately to $50 a month, he saved $800 in three years, the lion's share of his total earnings! This was fantastic parsimony.)

He spent little money for clothing, though he was always neat; he never went to the theater, had no amusements, and few friends. But he attended his Baptist Church in Cleveland as devoutly as he attended to his accounts. And to the cause of the church alone, to its parish fund and mission funds, he demonstrated his only generosity by gifts that were large for him then—first of ten cents, then later of twenty-five cents at a time.

In the young Rockefeller the traits which his mother had bred in him, of piety and the economic virtue—worship of the "lean goddess of Abstinence" —were of one cloth. The pale, bony, small-eyed young Baptist served the Lord and pursued his own business unremittingly. His composed manner, which had a certain languor, hid a feverish calculation, a sleepy strength, cruel, intense, terribly alert.

As a schoolboy John Rockefeller had once announced to a companion, as they walked by a rich man's ample house along their way: "When I grow up I want to be worth $100,000. And I'm going to be too." In almost the same words, Rockefeller in Cleveland, Cooke in Philadelphia, Carnegie in Pittsburgh, or a James Hill in the Northwestern frontier could be found voicing the same hope. And Rockefeller, the bookkeeper, "not slothful in business . . . serving the Lord," as John T. Flynn describes him, watched his chances closely, learned every detail of the produce business which engaged him, until finally in 1858 he made bold to open a business of his own in partnership with a young Englishman named Clark (who was destined to be left far behind). Rockefeller's grimly accumulated savings of $800, in addition to a loan from his father at the usurious rate of 10 per cent, yielded the capital which launched him, and he was soon "gathering gear" quietly. He knew the art of using loan credit to expand his operations. His first bank loan against warehouse receipts gave him a thrill of pleasure. He now bought grain and produce of all kinds in carload lots rather than in small consignments. (Prosperous, he said nothing,) but began to dress his part, wearing a high silk hat, frock coat and striped trousers like other merchants of the time. His head was handsome, his eyes small, birdlike; on his pale bony cheeks were the proverbial side-whiskers, reddish in color.

At night, in his room, he read the Bible, and retiring had the queer habit of talking to his pillow about his business adventures. In his autobiography he says that "these intimate conversations with myself had a great influence upon my life." He told himself "not to get puffed up with any foolish notions" and never to be deceived about actual conditions. ("Look out or you will lose your head—go steady.")

He was given to secrecy; he loathed all display. When he married, a few years afterward, he lost not a day from his business. His wife, Laura Spelman, proved an excellent mate. She encouraged his furtiveness, he relates, advising him always to be silent, to say as little as possible. His composure, his self-possession was excessive. Those Clevelanders to whom Miss Ida Tarbell addressed herself in her investigations of Rockefeller, told her that he was a hard man to best in a trade, that he rarely smiled, and almost never laughed, save when he struck a good bargain. Then he might clap his hands with delight, or he might even, if the occasion warranted, throw up his hat, kick his heels and hug his informer. One time he was so overjoyed at a favorable piece of news that he burst out: ("I'm bound to be rich! *Bound to be rich!*") . . .

The discovery of oil in the northwestern corner of Pennsylvania by [Edwin L.] Drake in 1859 was no isolated event, but part of the long overdue movement to exploit the subsoil of the country. When thousands rushed to scoop the silver and gold of Nevada, Colorado and Montana, the copper of Michigan, the iron ore of Pennsylvania and New York, technical knowledge at last interpreted the meaning of the greasy mineral substance which lay above ground near Titusville, Pennsylvania, and which had been used as a patent medicine ("Kier's Medicine") for twenty years. The rush and boom, out of which numerous speculators such as Andrew Carnegie had drawn quick profits and sold out—while so many others lost all they possessed—did not escape the attention of Rockefeller. The merchants of Cleveland, interested either in handling the new illuminating oil or investing in the industry itself, had sent the young Rockefeller to spy out the ground.

He had come probably in the spring of 1860 to the strange, blackened valleys of the Oil Regions where a forest of crude derricks, flimsy shacks and storehouses had been raised overnight. Here he had looked at the anarchy of the pioneer drillers or diggers of oil, the first frenzy of exploitation, with a deep disfavor that all conservative merchants of the time shared. There were continual fires, disasters and miracles; an oil well brought a fortune in a week, with the market price at twenty dollars a barrel; then as more wells came in the price fell to three and even two dollars a barrel before the next season! No one could tell at what price it was safe to buy oil, or oil acreage, and none knew how long the supply would last.

Returning to Cleveland, Rockefeller had counseled his merchant friends against investments in oil. At best the refining trade might be barely profitable if one could survive the mad dance of the market and if the supply of oil held out. Repugnance was strong in the infinitely cautious young merchant against the pioneering of the Oil Creek rabble. Two years were to pass before he approached the field again, while his accumulations increased with the fruitful wartime trade in provisions.

In 1862, when small refineries were rising everywhere, when more and more oil fields were being opened, the prospects of the new trade were immensely more favorable. A Clevelander named Samuel Andrews, owner of a small still, now came to the firm of Rockefeller & Clark with a proposal that they back him in setting up a sizable oil-refinery. The man Andrews was something of a technologist: he knew how to extract a high percentage of kerosene oil from the crude; he was one of the first to use the by-products developed in the refining process. Rockefeller and his partner, who appreciated the man's worth, invested $5,000 at the start with him. The affair flourished quickly, as demand widened for the new illuminant. Soon Rockefeller missed not a day from the refinery, where Andrews manufactured a kerosene better, purer than his competitors', and Rockefeller kept the books, conducted the purchasing of crude oil in his sharp fashion, and saved old iron, waste oils, made his own barrels, watched, spared, squirmed, for the smallest bargains.

In 1865, with uncanny judgment, Rockefeller chose between his produce business and the oil-refining trade. He sold his share in the house of Rockefeller & Clark, and purchased Clark's share in the oil-refinery, now called Rockefeller & Andrews. At this moment the values of all provisions were falling, while the oil trade was widening, spreading over all the world. Several great new wells had come in; supply was certain—10,000 barrels a day. Concentrating all his effort upon the new trade, he labored unremittingly to entrench himself in it, to be ready for all the hazards, which were great. He inaugurated ruthless economies; giving all his attention "to little details," he acquired a numerous clientele in the Western and Southern states; and opened an export selling agency in New York, headed by his brother William Rockefeller. "Low-voiced, soft-footed, humble, knowing every point in every man's business," Miss Tarbell relates, "he never tired until he got his wares at the lowest possible figures." "John always got the best of the bargain," the old men of Cleveland recall: "'savy fellow he was!" For all his fierce passion for money, he was utterly impassive in his bearing, save when some surprisingly good purchase of oil had been made at the creek. Then he could no longer restrain his shouts of joy. In the oil trade, John Rockefeller grew up in a hard school of struggle; he endured the merciless and unprincipled competition of rivals; and his own unpitying logic and coldly resolute methods were doubtless the consequence of the brutal free-for-all from which he emerged with certain crushing advantages.

While the producers of crude oil contended with each other in lawless fashion to drill the largest quantities, the refiners at different industrial centers who processed and reshipped the crude oil were also engaged in unresting trade conflicts, in which all measures were fair. And behind the rivalry of the producers and the refiners in different cities lay the secret struggles of the large railroad interests moving obscurely in the background. Drew's Erie, Vanderbilt's New York Central, Thomson and Scott's Pennsylvania, extending their lines to the Oil Regions, all hunted their fortune in the huge new traffic, pressing the interests of favored shipping and refining centers such as Cleveland or Pittsburgh or Buffalo to suit themselves. It would have been simplest possibly to have oil-refineries at the source of the crude material itself; but the purpose of the railroads forbade this; and there was no way of determining the outcome in this matter, as in any other phase of the organization of the country's new resources, whose manner of exploitation was determined only through pitched battles between the various gladiators, wherein the will of Providence was seen.

Rockefeller, who had no friends and no diversions, who was "all business," as John T. Flynn describes him, now gave himself to incessant planning, planning that would defeat chance itself. His company was but one of thirty oil-refiners located in Cleveland; in the Oil Regions, at Oil City and Titusville, there were numerous others, including the largest refineries of all, more favorably placed for shipping. But in 1867 Rockefeller invited into his firm as a partner, a business acquaintance of his, Henry M. Flagler, son-in-law of the rich whiskey distiller and salt-maker S. V. Harkness. Flagler, a bold and dashing fellow, was deeply attracted by the possibilities of the oil business. Thanks to Harkness, he brought $70,000 into the business, which at once opened a second refinery in Cleveland. Within a year or two the firm of Rockefeller, Flagler & Andrews was the biggest refinery in Cleveland, producing 1,500 barrels a day, having its own warehouses, its export agency in New York, its own wooden tank cars, its own staff of chemists or experts who labored to improve or economize the manufacturing processes. The company moved steadily to the front of the field, surpassing its rivals in quality, and outselling them by a small, though not certain or decisive, margin. How was this done?

In the struggle for business, Rockefeller's instinct for conspiracy is already marked. The partnership with Flagler brought an access of fresh capital and even more credit. Then in a further step of collusion, this of profound importance, Rockefeller and Flagler approached the railroad which carried so many carloads of their oil toward the seaboard, and whose tariff figured heavily in the ultimate cost. They demanded from it concessions in freight rates that would enable them to meet the advantages of other refining centers such as Pittsburgh, Philadelphia and New York. Their company was now large enough to force the hand of the railroad, in this case, a branch of Vanderbilt's New York Central system; and they were granted their demands: a secret reduction or "rebate" on all their shipments of oil. "Such was the railroad's method," Rockefeller himself afterward admitted. He relates:

> A public rate was made and collected by the railroad companies, but so far as my knowledge extends, was seldom retained in full; a portion of it was repaid to the shipper as a rebate. By this method the real rate of freight which

any shipper paid was not known by his competitors, nor by other railroads, the amount being a matter of bargain with the carrying companies.

Once having gained an advantage Rockefeller pressed forward relentlessly. The volume of his business increased rapidly. Thanks to the collaboration of the railroad, he had placed his rivals in other cities and in Cleveland itself under a handicap, whose weight he endeavored to increase.

(The railroads, as we see, possessed the strategic power, almost of life and death,) to encourage one industrial group or cause another to languish.) Their policy was based on the relative costs of handling small or large volume shipments. Thus as the Rockefeller company became the largest shipper of oil, its production rising in 1870 to 3,000 barrels a day, and offered to guarantee regular daily shipments of as much as sixty carloads, the railroads were impelled to accept further proposals for rebates. It was to their interest to do so in view of savings of several hundred thousand dollars a month in handling. On crude oil brought from the Oil Regions, Rockefeller paid perhaps 15 cents a barrel less than the open rate of 40 cents; on refined oil moving from Cleveland toward New York, he paid approximately 90 cents against the open rate of $1.30. These momentous agreements were maintained in utter secrecy, perhaps because of the persisting memory of their illegality, according to the common law ever since Queen Elizabeth's time, as a form of "conspiracy" in trade.

In January, 1870, Rockefeller, Flagler & Andrews were incorporated as a joint-stock company, a form increasingly popular, under the name of the Standard Oil Company of Ohio. At this time their worth was estimated at one million dollars; they employed over a thousand workers and were the largest refiners in the world. Despite deeply disturbed conditions in their trade during 1870, profits came to them in a mounting flood, while in the same year, it is noteworthy, four of their twenty-nine competitors in Cleveland gave up the ghost. The pious young man of thirty who feared only God, and thought of nothing but his business, gave not a sign of his greatly augmented wealth, which made him one of the leading personages of his city. His income was actually a fabulous one for the time. The Standard Oil Company from the beginning earned something like 100 per cent on its capital; and Rockefeller and his brother owned a full half-interest in it in 1870. But with an evangelistic fervor John Rockefeller was bent only upon further conquests, upon greater extensions of the power over industry which had come into the hands of the group he headed.

In the life of every conquering soul there is a "turning point," a moment when a deep understanding of the self coincides with an equally deep sense of one's immediate mission in the tangible world. For Rockefeller, brooding, secretive, uneasily scenting his fortune, this moment came but a few years after his entrance into the oil trade, and at the age of thirty. He had looked upon the disorganized conditions of the Pennsylvania oil fields, the only source then known, and found them not good: the guerilla fighting of drillers, or refining firms, of rival railroad lines, the mercurial changes in supply and market value —very alarming in 1870—offended his orderly and methodical spirit. But one could see that petroleum was to be the light of the world. From the source, from the chaotic oil fields where thousands of drillers toiled, the grimy stream of the precious commodity, petroleum, flowed along many diverse channels to narrow into the hands of several hundred refineries, then to issue once more in a continuous stream to consumers throughout the world. Owner with Flagler and Harkness of the largest refining company in the country, Rockefeller had a strongly entrenched position at the narrows of this stream. Now what if the Standard Oil Company should by further steps of organization possess itself wholly of the narrows? In this period of anarchic individual competition, the idea of such a movement of rationalization must have come to Rockefeller forcibly, as it had recently come to others.

Even as early as 1868 the first plan of industrial combination in the shape of the pool had been originated in the Michigan Salt Association. Desiring to correct chaotic market conditions, declaring that "in union there is strength," the salt-producers of Saginaw Bay had banded together to control the output and sale of nearly all the salt in their region, a large part of the vital national supply. Secret agreements had been executed for each year, allotting the sales and fixing the price at almost twice what it had been immediately prior to the appearance of the pool. And though the inevitable greed and self-seeking of the individual salt-producers had tended to weaken the pool, the new economic invention was launched in its infantile form. Rockefeller's partners, Flagler and Harkness, had themselves participated in the historic Michigan Salt Association.

This grand idea of industrial rationalization owed its swift, ruthless, methodical execution no doubt to the firmness of character we sense in Rockefeller, who had the temper of a great, unconscionable military captain, combining audacity with thoroughness and shrewd judgment. His plan seemed to take account of no one's feelings in the matter. Indeed there was something revolutionary in it; it seemed to fly in the fact of human liberties and deep-rooted custom and common law. The notorious "South Improvement Company," with its strange charter, ingeniously instrumenting the scheme of combination, was to be unraveled amid profound secrecy. By conspiring with the railroads (which also hungered for economic order), it would be terribly armed with the power of the freight rebate which garrotted all opposition systematically. This plan of combination, this unifying conception Rockefeller took as his ruling idea; he breathed life into it, clung to it grimly in the face of the most menacing attacks of legislatures, courts, rival captains, and, at moments, even of rebellious mobs. His view of men and events justified him, and despite many official and innocent denials, he is believed to have said once in confidence, as Flynn relates:

> I had our plan clearly in mind. It was right. I knew it as a matter of conscience. It was right between me and my God. If I had to do it tomorrow I would do it again in the same way—do it a hundred times.

The broad purpose was to control and direct the flow of crude petroleum into the hands of a narrowed group of refiners. The refiners would be supported by the combined railroad trunk lines which shipped the oil; while the producers' phase of the stream would be left unorganized—*but with power over their outlet to market* henceforth to be concentrated into the few hands of the refiners.

Saying nothing to others, bending over their maps of the industry, Rockefeller and Flagler first drew up a short list of the principal refining companies who were to be asked to combine with them. Then having banded together a sufficient number, they would persuade the railroads to give them special freight rates—on the ground of "evening" the traffic—guaranteeing equitable distribution of freight business; and this in turn would be a club to force other elements needed into union with them. They could control output, drive out competitors, and force all foreign countries throughout the world to buy their product from them at their own terms. They could finally dictate market prices on crude oil, stabilize the margin of profit at their own process, and do away at last with the dangerously speculative character of their business.

Their plans moved forward rapidly all through 1871. For a small sum of money the "conspirators" obtained the Pennsylvania charter of a defunct corporation, which had been authorized to engage in almost any kind of business under the sun. Those who were approached by the promoters, those whom they determined to use in their grand scheme, were compelled in a manner typical of all Rockefeller's projects to sign a written pledge of secrecy:

> I, —— ——, do solemnly promise upon my honor and faith as a gentleman that I will keep secret all transactions which I may have with the corporation known as the South Improvement Company; that should I fail to complete any bargains with the said company, all the preliminary conversations shall be kept strictly private; and finally that I will not disclose the price for which I dispose of any products or any other facts which may in any way bring to light the internal workings or organization of the company. All this I do freely promise.

At the same time, in confidential pourparlers with the officials of the Erie, the Pennsylvania and the New York Central Railroads, the men of the Standard Oil represented themselves as possessing secret control of the bulk of the refining interest. Thus they obtained conditions more advantageous than anything which had gone before; and this weapon in turn of course ensured the triumph of their pool.

The refiners to be combined under the aegis of the South Improvement Company were to have a rebate of from 40 to 50 per cent on the crude oil they ordered shipped to them and from 25 to 50 per cent on the refined oil they shipped out. The refiners in the Oil Regions were to pay *twice as much* by the new code (though nearer to New York) as the Standard Oil Company at Cleveland. But besides the rebate the members of the pool were to be given also a "drawback" consisting of part of the increased tariff rate which "outsiders" were forced to pay. Half of the freight payments of a rival refiner would in many cases be paid over to the Rockefeller group. Their competitors were simply to be decimated; and to make certain of this the railroads agreed—all being set down in writing, in minutest detail—"to make manifests or way-bills of all petroleum or its product transported over any portion of its lines... which manifests shall state the name of the consignee, the place of shipment and the place of destination," this information to be furnished faithfully to the officers of the South Improvement Company.

The railroad systems, supposedly public-spirited and impartial, were to open all their knowledge of rival private business to the pool, thus helping to concentrate all the oil trade into the few hands chosen. In return for so much assistance, they were to have their freight "evened," and were enabled at last to enter into a momentous peace pact with each other by which the oil traffic (over which they had quarreled bitterly) was to be fairly allotted among themselves.

By January, 1872, after the first decade of the oil business, John Rockefeller, with the aid of the railroad captains, was busily carrying out a most "elaborate national plan" of his own for the control of his industry—such planned control as the spokesman of the business system asserted ever afterward was impossible. The first pooling of 1872, beautiful as was its economic architecture and laudable its motive, had defects which were soon plainly noticeable. All the political institutions, the whole spirit of American law still favored the amiable, wasteful individualism of business, which in Rockefeller's mind had already become obsolete and must be supplanted by a centralized, one might say almost *collectivist*—certainly coöperative rather than competitive—form of operation. Moreover, these "revolutionists" took little account of the social dislocations their juggernaut would bring. Like the railroad baron, Vanderbilt, working better than they knew, their eyes fixed solely upon the immediate task rather than upon some millennium of the future, they desired simply, as they often said, to be "the biggest refiners in the world...."

To the principal oil firms in Cleveland Rockefeller went one by one, explaining the plan of the South Improvement Company patiently, pointing out how important it was to oppose the creek refiners and save the Cleveland oil trade. He would say:

"You see, this scheme is bound to work. There is no chance for anyone outside. But we are going to give everybody a chance to come in. You are to turn over your refinery to my appraisers, and I will give you Standard Oil Company stock or cash, as you prefer, for the value we put upon it. I advise you to take the stock. It will be for your good."

(Then if the men demurred, according to much of the testimony at the Senate Investigation of 1876, he would point out suavely that it was useless to resist; opposition would certainly be crushed. The offers of purchase usually made were for from a third to a half the actual cost of the property.)

Now a sort of terror swept silently over the oil trade. In a vague panic, competitors saw the Standard Oil officers come to them and say (as Rockefeller's own brother and rival, Frank, testified in 1876): "If you don't sell your property to us it will be valueless, because we have got the advantage with the railroads."

The railroad rates indeed were suddenly doubled to the outsiders, and those refiners who resisted the pool came and expostulated; then they became frightened and disposed of their property. One of the largest competitors in Cleveland, the firm of Alexander, Scofield & Co., held out for a time, protesting before the railroad officials at the monstrous unfairness of the deal. But these officials when consulted said mysteriously: "*Better sell—better get clear—* better sell out—no help for it." Another powerful refiner, Robert Hanna, uncle of the famous Mark Alonzo, found that the railroads would give him no relief, and also was glad to sell out at 40 or 50 cents on the dollar for his property value. To one of these refiners, Isaac L. Hewitt, who had been his employer in boyhood, Rockefeller himself spoke with intense emotion. He urged Hewitt to take stock. Hewitt related: "He told me that it would be sufficient to take care of my family for all time ... and asking for reasons, he made this expression, I remember: *'I have ways of making money that you know nothing of.'* "

All this transpired in secret. For "silence is golden," the rising king of oil believed. Though many were embittered by their loss, others joined gladly. The strongest capitalists in Cleveland, such as the wealthy Colonel Oliver H. Payne, were amazed at the swift progress Rockefeller had made, at the enormous profits he showed them in confidence to invite their coöperation. Payne, among others, as a man of wealth and influence, was taken into the board of directors and made treasurer of the Standard Oil Company. (The officers of the South Improvement Company itself were "dummies.") Within three months by an economic *coup d'état* the youthful Rockefeller had captured all of Cleveland's oil-refining trade, all twenty-five competitors surrendered to him and yielded him command of one-fifth of America's output of refined oil.

Tomorrow all the population of the Oil Regions, its dismayed refiners, drillers, and workers of oil, might rise against the South Improvement Company ring in a grotesque uproar. The secret, outwardly peaceful campaigns would assume here as elsewhere the character of violence and lawlessness which accompanied the whole program of the industrial revolution. But Rockefeller and his comrades had stolen a long march on their opponents; their tactics shaped themselves already as those of the giant industrialists of the future conquering the pigmies. Entrenched at the "narrows" of the mighty river of petroleum they could no more be dislodged than those other barons who had formerly planted their strong castles along the banks of the Rhine could be dislodged by unarmed peasants and burghers.

Pioneering in Big Business, 1882–1911

From Chaos to Combination

During the years from 1882 to 1911 the leaders of the Standard Oil group of companies, including the Standard Oil Company (New Jersey), carried out an extraordinary experiment in the management of a business. John D. Rockefeller and his associates successfully created and applied a system for operating a large, integrated industrial enterprise which was one of the earliest representatives of Big Business, to use the phrase popular in the United States. As executives of the large combination those men contributed greatly to the rapid development of the American petroleum industry and through it to the growth of the economy as a whole. Being innovators, however, they also made numerous mistakes and learned only slowly that large size and concentrated economic power in a democratic society required conduct conforming to new rules set by popular demand.

The early life of the Standard Oil Company (New Jersey), generally referred to as Jersey Standard, was marked by rapid growth from infancy to early parenthood. Organized as one of the units of the Standard Oil Trust in August, 1882, for its first ten years the corporation existed primarily as the owner of a refinery and other manufacturing establishments at Bayonne; late in the decade the company acquired a few wholesaling facilities in the same northern New Jersey area. As a consequence of a court decision in Ohio in 1892, Standard Oil executives reorganized their enterprise under twenty corporations of which Jersey Standard was one of the three largest; top managers vested this company with direct ownership of extensive additional manufacturing and marketing properties and also made it one of the holding companies within the group of sister corporations. The Jersey Company continued to perform operating functions after it had become the parent of the entire combination in 1899.

As the apex of a pyramid of companies dominating the American petroleum industry, Jersey Standard naturally became the symbol of the much-distrusted Standard Oil "monopoly" in the public mind. In 1911 the Supreme Court of the United States, affirming that general conviction, broke up the

From Ralph W. Hidy and Muriel E. Hidy, *History of Standard Oil Company (New Jersey), vol. 1: Pioneering in Big Business, 1882–1911* (Harper & Brothers, 1955). Copyright © 1955, 1983 by Business History Foundation, Inc. Reprinted by permission of HarperCollins Publishers, Inc. Notes omitted.

combination by divesting the Standard Oil Company (New Jersey) of thirty-three affiliates, thus bringing to a close one eventful and significant phase of the corporation's history....

The Standard Oil Team and Its Early Policies

As an early corporate product of the Standard Oil combination, Jersey Standard fell heir to the policies and practices of the men who created the alliance. In the course of working together before 1882, this group of executives had set precedents for the management of the Standard Oil family of firms which were to influence vitally the life of the new company.

The Men Who Made Standard Oil

The Standard Oil alliance in 1881 was the creation of a team of men. As one man paraphrased John D. Rockefeller's own statement, the "secret of the success of the Standard Oil Company was that there had come together a body of men who from beginning to end worked in single-minded co-operation, who all believed in each other and had perfect confidence in the integrity of each other, who reached all their decisions after fair consideration with magnanimity toward each other" in order to assure "absolute harmony."

As an instrument for carrying out the ideas of those men, the combination necessarily took its character from those who made it and managed it. When they chose to create a new corporation, such as Jersey Standard, it became part of the mechanism for pursuing their policies. Extremely significant, therefore, for understanding the history of the company is acquaintance with the individuals who created and directed both the Standard Oil family of companies and the Jersey Company itself. Scores of men made material contributions to the early development of the combination but only a relatively few ranked as outstanding.

John D. Rockefeller (1839–1937) was captain of the team. By all odds the largest holder of shares, he probably would have been chosen the head for that reason alone. Although not the only person to have the conviction in the 1870's that the petroleum industry should be stabilized, he first formulated the idea that the only satisfactory means was to organize a commonly owned unit on a national scale. Allan Nevins has characterized Rockefeller as careful, patient, cautious, methodical, quick to observe and to learn, grave, pious, aloof, secretive, reticent, inscrutable, and taciturn. Rockefeller considered work a duty, loved simplicity, believed in discipline, and possessed little social warmth except with his family and intimate friends. He had a mind of extraordinary force, great power of concentration, and almost infinite capacity for detail. Although he was willing to make decisions and to act forcefully, he possessed not only remarkable foresight, broad vision, and cool judgment, but also willingness to consider the ideas of others.

In the early 1870's Rockefeller began to delegate most details of management to subordinates and thereafter devoted himself primarily to formulation of broad policy. His greatest contribution, beyond the concept of the Standard

Oil combination itself, was the persuasion of strong men to join the alliance and to work together effectively in its management. The remarkable fact was that Rockefeller, while still in his thirties, impressed a group of men, almost all older than himself, with his qualities of leadership. His most arduous task later was to preside over meetings of strongly individualistic, positive executives, while they discussed and determined, usually unanimously, strategy and tactics for the combination as a whole.

During the 1860's and 1870's the closest and strongest associate of John D. Rockefeller was Henry M. Flagler (1830–1913). Of average height, slight build, erect figure, unobtrusive and dignified manner, Flagler was an ambitious, patient, and shrewd man of business. It is difficult to determine where the ideas of Rockefeller stop and those of Flagler begin. They were warm personal friends; they talked over their business before, during, and after office hours. Flagler liked to build new things and possessed a faculty for reducing complex problems to their simplest components. His constructive imagination was as broad and as vivid as Rockefeller's. It was caught by a desire to develop Florida, and into its hotels, railroads, and other enterprises he put some $50,000,000, and more of his energy than into Standard Oil, during the 1880's and later. Yet he left his mark on the combination. Having an aptitude for legal affairs, he was a master in drawing up clear, concise contracts. The incorporation of Ohio Standard appears to have been his brain child, and he helped in the later organization of the Trust. Flagler also participated in many negotiations leading to entry of other firms into the Standard Oil family. His special function was the handling of all affairs concerning transportation of both raw materials and finished products, and he drove hard bargains with railroad managers. Gifted with a keen sense of humor and a feeling of personal responsibilities to employees, he won the warm respect and loyal support of most subordinates. Not the least important of Flagler's executive positions was the presidency of Jersey Standard during eight of its first seventeen years. . . .

Although never an executive, one other man colored the history of Standard Oil as much as many of the men who created and managed the combination. Samuel C. T. Dodd (1836–1907), the general solicitor of the organization from 1881 to 1905, began his practice at Franklin, Pennsylvania, in 1859. Short and rotund, affable and learned, he soon became expert in the legal technicalities of the petroleum business. A Democrat in politics, he actively participated in the Pennsylvania constitutional convention of 1872. Though Dodd thought the material prosperity of the United States was attributable "in a great measure" to large combinations of capital, he was equally convinced that they should be regulated by clearly framed laws. Outspokenly opposed to "unjust" railroad rate discriminations, he accepted the invitation to become counsel for Standard Oil in the Oil Regions in 1879 only on the condition that his employers fully recognize his determination to fight the practice of rebating. When Dodd, a Presbyterian elder, abandoned private practice to become general solicitor for Standard Oil in New York, he humorously explained his decision to become the "least victim of the monopoly" by remarking: "Well, as the ministers say when they get a call to a higher salary, it seems to be the Lord's will." Thereafter Dodd quietly and honestly told top managers what they could and could not do under existing law as he interpreted it and occasionally, as extant correspondence shows, advocated a course of action on moral rather than legal grounds. He had a most difficult assignment in charting a course for a large business in a period when a new public policy toward trusts and combinations was emerging.

The executives advised by Dodd were men of varied abilities and complementary qualities. While several of them had specialized at one time or another in separate functions of the petroleum industry, a number of them had broad experience over a number of years. Some were inventors. Others brought special aptitudes in organization and marketing. Almost all had begun their careers in mercantile enterprises. Before joining the Standard Oil alliance, all had engaged in either regional or national co-operative efforts. By 1882 they had worked together for a number of years; while differing in backgrounds and philosophies, they had evolved policies which were, with some modifications, to guide the Standard Oil combination throughout its early history and to affect the petroleum industry for a longer span of years.

Policies, Practices, and Precedents

Policies and practices pursued by Standard Oil executives during the years prior to 1882 emerged in a variety of ways. Some policies were evidenced by votes of directors of components of the alliance and gradually won more general acceptance among its members. In other instances precedents and practices developed into policies over time; no formalized statement ever indicated the direction in which the leaders were traveling, but in a succession of separate steps they evolved a significant behavior pattern.

Many of the concepts and procedures adopted by executives of the alliance stemmed from their early experience as small businessmen. Probably at no other time during the nineteenth century was economic activity more freely competitive than in the period from 1840 to 1865. The customs and mores of the small individual enterpriser became the accepted pattern for almost all men. Naturally enough, therefore, Rockefeller and his associates learned in their youth to believe in freedom of entry into any occupation, in the sanctity of private property, in the obligation of the owner to manage his own operations, and in the right to keep his business affairs secret, a concept dating from time immemorial. As a corollary of that idea, in courts or legislative investigative chambers a businessman testified to the legal truth, and no more, a practice still honored by general observance in spite of critical charges of evasiveness and ambiguity. Since most markets were local, every businessman could observe his competitors with relative ease, and did. His habit was to use any competitive device not clearly prohibited by law. Bargaining in the market place was almost universal, whether for products or for such services as the transportation of freight. Posted prices were a point of departure for haggling, and price reductions were the most widely utilized of competitive techniques.

In response to the chaotic and depressed years of the 1870's, however, Standard Oil men drastically modified some of their socially inherited concepts about competition. They apparently desired at first to bring all gatherers of crude oil and refiners of light petroleum fractions into one commonly owned unit—to create a monopoly. Late in the decade they added lubricating oil specialists and trunk pipelines to their list of components to be unified. By means of common ownership in an association of specializing firms, Rockefeller and his associates created a great horizontal and vertical combination, which, on the eve of the birth of Jersey Standard, maintained overwhelming dominance in gathering, storing, and processing petroleum and its derivatives.

Either by design or through pressure of circumstances, the Standard Oil group of executives had not achieved monopoly in any function by 1881. Strong minority interests in many domestic marketing companies within the alliance, and limited coverage of the market by them, set definite limits to the influence of top managers in that field of operations. In almost all sales for export foreign merchants bought oil from companies in the Standard Oil family and carried on marketing in foreign lands. The combination owned few producing properties. United Pipe Lines men failed to keep pace with expansion in Bradford production, and competing gathering and storing facilities kept appearing. Tide-Water Pipe had thrown the first trunk pipeline over the mountains toward the sea and remained a belligerent competitor. Under the agreement with the producers in 1880 the price of crude oil was set on the oil exchanges, not by Standard Oil. In manufacturing, the area of initial intent for monopoly, the top managers of the alliance had stopped short of their goal. They had refused to pay the prices asked by owners of some plants. Others had sprung up in response to inducements offered by the Pennsylvania Railroad, and in 1882 the editor of *Mineral Resources* noted that the combination had "for some reason" not renewed leases on a number of refineries, several of which were doing "a good trade" and "assuming considerable importance." Thus, by that year some of the firms classified by H. H. Rogers in 1879 as being "in harmony" with Standard Oil had gone their independent ways.

Standard Oil executives employed a variety of tactics in carrying out the expansionist program during the 1870's. After the consolidation in Cleveland and the disastrous South Improvement episode, Rockefeller and his associates first won the confidence of competitors through comprehensive voluntary association. They then brought into the alliance the strongest men and firms in specific areas or functions, a policy pursued, with some exceptions, until 1911. Exchange of stock in the different companies by individuals and guarantee of equality in management provided the final assurance needed to convince such strong individualists as [Charles] Lockhart, [William G.] Warden, [Charles] Pratt, and [Henry H.] Rogers that combination was to their advantage. All then co-operated eagerly in trying to unify the remaining firms in refining by bringing them into The Central Association, by buying plants whenever feasible, and by leasing other works. If a seller personally chose not to enter the combination, he usually signed an agreement not to engage in the petroleum business for a period of years. In any case, evidence in extant records substantiates the point that Standard Oil men completely and carefully inventoried all properties and paid "good," though not high, prices for them, including compensation for patents, trade-marks, brands, good-will, and volume of business. In many instances prices for properties reflected the desire of Standard Oil officials to enlist the inventive capacities or administrative abilities of the owners in the service of the alliance. The preponderance of the evidence indicates that Rockefeller and his fellow executives preferred to buy out rather than fight out competitors.

At the same time, when Standard Oil men felt it necessary to apply pressure as a means of persuading a rival to lease or sell his plant, they showed no hesitancy in utilizing the usual sharp competitive practices prevailing in the oil industry during the 1870's. On one occasion or another they pre-empted all available staves and barrels, restricted as completely as possible the available tank cars to their own business, and indulged in local price cutting. They meticulously watched and checked on competitive shipments and sales, sometimes in co-operation with railroad men, and diligently negotiated advantageous freight rates on railways, even to the point of receiving rebates or drawbacks on rivals' shipments. All acts were kept secret as long as possible. The size and resources of the alliance gave it overwhelming power, which was sometimes used ruthlessly, though it is worthy of note that numerous oilmen successfully resisted the pressure.

Within the alliance itself executives also retained many of their competitive habits. Although price competition almost completely disappeared within the combination, men and firms raced with each other in reducing costs, devising new techniques, developing products, improving their quality, and showing profits. Top managers believed in competition but not in the undisciplined variety.

In building the alliance the leaders of Standard Oil adopted a long-range view with emphasis on planning, even before they had achieved an organization to carry such an approach into successful operation. They showed a profound faith in the permanence of the industry, a belief not generally held in years when the petroleum business was characterized by instability, rapid exhaustion of producing fields, and doubts about the appearance of new ones. They wanted to plan and to have reasonable assurance that they were taking no more than calculated risks in pushing toward their objectives. A necessary requirement of planning was centralized policy formulation.

That responsibility devolved not upon one man but on a group of executives. The evolution of Standard Oil's committee system, the hallmark of its administrative methods, started early in the seventies. The original bylaws of Ohio Standard provided for an Executive Committee. Its first membership of two, John D. Rockefeller and Flagler, was increased to three during the consecutive terms of Samuel Andrews and O. H. Payne. [John D.] Archbold replaced the latter in 1879. William Rockefeller, Pratt, Warden, and [Jabez] Bostwick had joined the three Cleveland members the previous year. At that time the Executive Committee absorbed the "Advisory Committee," which had been established as early as 1873 to act in the New York area. William Rockefeller and Bostwick, its first members, had been joined by Pratt and Warden soon after they entered the alliance. The enlarged Executive Committee of 1878 held many of its almost daily meetings at 140 Pearl Street, New York, and two years later made four a quorum because of the geographic split in membership between Cleveland and New York. Members of other committees started consultations before 1882. If the making of decisions as a synthesis of opinion of a group after discussion is a characteristic of modern business, as a recent commentator has implied, then Standard Oil was modern in the 1870's.

In order to have easily available the best data and advice for making decisions, the Rockefellers and their associates built up staffs in Cleveland, New York, and other points. For the use of executives they collected, evaluated, and digested information on crude oil supplies, costs of manufacture, and markets all over the world. The practice of watching and reporting on marketing by competitors everywhere in the United States, not merely locally, was already inaugurated, though not yet systematized. S. C. T. Dodd was engaged as legal navigator; Standard Oil officials desired to operate within the law. A beginning was made in standardizing accounting procedures.

As the emergence of the Executive Committee and the formation of staffs indicated, the creation of the combination permitted a division of labor or specialization within the organization. As Archbold expressed the development in 1888, the grouping of talents within the alliance permitted "various individuals to take up the different features of the business as a specialty and accomplish greater efficiency than can possibly be accomplished by an individual who attempts to cover all in a business."

In the matter of finance, as in other aspects of operations, Ohio Standard set precedents on reporting and central review. In 1877 the directors of that company resolved that all persons responsible for different aspects of the business should make quarterly reports in writing to the board. Two years later, its members unanimously agreed that annual financial statements should be presented. In 1875 the directors had voted that expenditures for new construction in manufacturing exceeding $2,500 should be undertaken only with written consent of seven members of the board, but that resolution was repealed five years later and the company's Executive Committee was given full charge of all matters relating to repairs and new construction.

Since the goal of the members of the alliance was to maximize profits in the long run, they adopted practices to that end. Emphasis was placed on reducing costs, improving and standardizing the quality of products, and striving for new methods of refining, including the engaging of specialists. Stories about John D. Rockefeller's penchant for eliminating waste and effecting economies have been told and retold. As president of the Acme Oil Company in the Oil Regions, Archbold achieved substantial savings through buying supplies in quantity and by making annual contracts regarding the repairing of boilers and barrels for all plants under his jurisdiction. When he purchased a lubricating oil patent in 1879, Archbold guaranteed the owner, Eli E. Hendrick, a salary of $10,000 per year for ten years in return for the devotion of his inventive talents to Acme. Duplicating pipelines were removed, inefficient plants dismantled, strategically located refineries enlarged, and auxiliary manufacturing units developed, all in the name of economy and reduction of costs. By consistently stressing that practice in every function Standard Oil men moved gradually but inevitably toward mass manufacturing and, more slowly, toward mass marketing.

Gathering information, consultation, planning, and experimentation did not always lead to quick action, but the leaders of Standard Oil early indicated flexibility in adopting new methods and thoroughness in carrying them out. Critics voiced the opinion in the late 1870's that Standard Oil, having invested so much in refineries in the Oil Regions, could not take advantage of the pipeline revolution to establish large manufacturing units at the coast. Almost as soon as others had demonstrated the feasibility of building long trunk pipelines the Standard Oil group took action in 1879. It already possessed a system of gathering lines through the United Pipe Lines. After its organization in 1881, the National Transit Company pushed trunk pipeline building vigorously. By the next year it owned 1,062 miles of trunk lines, only 48 of which had been bought from firms outside the alliance. Its policies... illustrate the fact that Standard Oil was not always the earliest to initiate an innovation, but, once launched on a policy, the combination pushed it with a vigor and fervor made possible by efficient organization and ample financial resources.

Standard Oil's financial policy itself was an important element in the successful life of the combination and its components. Not only were the risks spread by the breadth of the alliance's activities, but profits made in one company or phase of the business flowed into development of another when desired. Early in the history of Standard Oil units short-term loans were often obtained from commercial banks, and temporary aid had to be obtained when the properties of The Empire Transportation Company were purchased. A conservative ratio of dividends to net income, however, was soon to permit the accumulation of funds for self-financing.

Ohio Standard furnished an example for the companies in the alliance on the matter of insurance against fire. On the assumption that loss by fire was a normal expense of the petroleum industry and could be carried by a large unit, the directors of the Ohio Company agreed in January, 1877, to insure property in any one place only on the excess of its valuation above $100,000.

As directors of The Standard Oil Company (Ohio), executives of the alliance also set a precedent regarding the ownership of producing properties. In April, 1878, apparently as a result of a suit by H. L. Taylor & Company against John D. Rockefeller and others for breach of contract in a joint producing operation, the directors unanimously voted not to invest any more money in the purchase of crude oil lands. Six months later they resolved to discontinue all activity in producing petroleum and instructed the Executive Committee to dispose of its properties. This point of view had an influence upon the Standard Oil alliance for a decade.

Quite the contrary was the action adopted in regard to pipelines. By 1881 the Standard Oil group was definitely launched on a program for large-scale expansion of its pipeline facilities and soon exercised a greater measure of control over the function. The combination poured an increasing quantity of capital into building lines; the profits from them provided a cushion for all operations of the alliance. The speculatively minded can ask whether the development of the oil industry would have been more rapid or socially beneficial had parallel pipelines competed with each other during the formative years of the industry, and whether the development would have been as efficient, or more so, had the railroad systems controlled competing lines, as had seemed possible in the 1870's. The point remains that the top managers of Standard Oil determined to keep this function in their own hands to the extent possible. . . .

The roots of Standard Oil's policies went deep into the personalities and early experiences of Rockefeller and his associates. Though few of their practices had been satisfactorily systematized by 1881, precedents had been established for many later policies of Jersey Standard and other members of the combination.

By the end of 1881 the general public was hard put to make an accurate estimate of Standard Oil's behavior. Legislative investigations and several legal cases had already elicited an enormous amount of conflicting testimony as to the relations of the combination with both railroads and competitors. Rockefeller and his associates had heightened uncertainty and speculation about their activities by their secrecy in building the alliance and by their evasive, often ambiguous, consistently legally accurate testimony on the witness stand. The very newness, size, dominance, and efficiency of the combination, not to mention its absorption of small competitors in adversity and its avid search for the lowest possible railroad rates, all tended to arouse antagonism. In 1882 S. H. Stowell closed his comments on Standard Oil in *Mineral Resources* with an unbiased observer's puzzlement: "There seems to be little doubt that the company has done a great work, and that through its instrumentality oil refining has been reduced to a business, and transportation has been greatly simplified; but as to how much evil has been mixed with this good, it is not practicable to make a definite statement." It was certain that through combination managers of Standard Oil had brought a measure of order to a formerly confused industry, though they thought that the administration of the alliance itself needed further systematization.

POSTSCRIPT

Was John D. Rockefeller a "Robber Baron"?

Regardless of how American entrepreneurs are perceived, there is no doubt that they constituted a powerful elite and were responsible for defining the character of society in the Gilded Age. For many Americans, these businessmen represented the logical culmination of the country's attachment to laissez-faire economics and rugged individualism. In fact, it was not unusual at all for the nation's leading industrialists to be depicted as the real-life models for the "rags-to-riches" theme epitomized in the self-help novels of Horatio Alger. Closer examination of the lives of most of these entrepreneurs, however, reveals the mythical dimensions of this American ideal. Simply put, the typical business executive of the late nineteenth century did not rise up from humble circumstances, a product of the American rural tradition or the immigrant experience, as is frequently claimed. Rather, most of these big businessmen were of Anglo-Saxon origin and reared in a city by middle-class parents. According to one survey, over half the leaders had attended college at a time when even the pursuit of a high school education was considered unusual. In other words, instead of having to pull themselves up by their own bootstraps from the bottom of the social heap, these individuals usually started their climb to success at the middle of the ladder or higher.

Earl Latham and Peter d'A. Jones have assembled excellent collections of the major viewpoints on the "robber baron" thesis in their respective edited anthologies *John D. Rockefeller: Robber Baron or Industrial Statesman?* (D. C. Heath, 1949) and *The Robber Barons Revisited* (D. C. Heath, 1968). For a critique of Josephson's work, see Maury Klein, "A Robber Historian," *Forbes* (October 26, 1987). Studies focusing specifically upon Rockefeller include David Freeman Hawke, *John D.: The Founding Father of the Rockefellers* (Harper & Row, 1980) and Ron Chernow, *Titan: The Life of John D. Rockefeller, Sr.* (Random House, 1998). Biographical studies of other late-nineteenth-century businessmen include Harold Livesay, *Andrew Carnegie and the Rise of Big Business* (Little, Brown, 1975) and Maury Klein, *The Life and Legend of Jay Gould* (Johns Hopkins University Press, 1986).

The works of Alfred D. Chandler, Jr., are vital to the understanding of American industrialization. See *The Visible Hand: The Managerial Revolution in American Business* (Harvard University Press, 1977) and *Scale and Scope: The Dynamics of Industrial Capitalism* (Harvard University Press, 1990). Chandler's most important essays are collected in Thomas K. McCraw, ed., *The Essential Alfred Chandler: Essays Toward a Historical Theory of Big Business* (Harvard Business School Press, 1988).

ISSUE 3

Did the Industrial Revolution Disrupt the American Family?

YES: Elaine Tyler May, from "The Pressure to Provide: Class, Consumerism, and Divorce in Urban America, 1880–1920," *Journal of Social History* (Winter 1978)

NO: Jacquelyn Dowd Hall, Robert Korstad, and James Leloudis, from "Cotton Mill People: Work, Community, and Protest in the Textile South, 1880–1940," *The American Historical Review* (April 1986)

ISSUE SUMMARY

YES: Elaine Tyler May, a professor of American studies and history, argues that the Industrial Revolution in the United States, with its improved technology, increasing income, and emerging consumerism, led to higher rates of divorce because family wage earners failed to meet rising expectations for material accumulation.

NO: History professors Jacquelyn Dowd Hall, Robert Korstad, and James Leloudis contend that the cotton mill villages of the New South, rather than destroying family work patterns, fostered a labor system that permitted parents and children to work together as a traditional family unit.

The Industrial Revolution fueled the rise of the United States to a preeminent position among the nations of the world by 1914. It affected virtually every institution—political, economic, and social—in the country. Politically, municipal, state, and federal governments recognized the benefits of cooperating in a variety of ways with corporate America, so much so that the doctrine of laissez-faire existed more in theory than in actual practice. Economically, industrialization laid the foundation for monopolization; fueled occupational opportunities for residents, both native and foreign-born; placed in jeopardy the value of skilled artisans; and transformed the workplace for millions of Americans. Socially, the economic forces dominating the United States in the last quarter of the nineteenth century played a significant role in encouraging geographical mobility, subordinating rural values to those associated with large industrial cities, and generating tensions and conflicts along racial, ethnic, class, and gender lines.

As the factory came to replace the farm as the workplace for more and more Americans, the United States developed an identifiable proletariat—a mass of unskilled, often propertyless workers whose labor was controlled by someone other than themselves. Moreover, despite the optimistic promises of "rags-to-riches" advancement associated with the American Dream, these workers could anticipate that they would remain unskilled and propertyless for their entire lives. Within the factories, mills, and mines of industrial America, corporate managers dictated company policy regarding wages, hours, and other conditions of employment and tended to view themselves, not the laborers, as the producers. Wages may have been relatively higher but so, too, were prices, and a dollar a day was not enough for a man to feed, clothe, and house his family, to say nothing of providing medical attention. Consequently, many working-class, married women entered the labor force to help make ends meet, not because they found the prospect of wage earning to be liberating. In doing so, they were accused of stepping outside their proper sphere of domesticity and of violating the Victorian "cult of true womanhood." Their children also moved into the industrial workforce since little physical strength was required to carry out many of the tasks of the factory. Also, the owners could justify paying youngsters lower wages, which reduced production costs.

This scenario suggests that the processes of industrialization had the potential to alter the traditional structure of the American family wherein the husband and father was expected to provide the necessities of life. What happened to the family during the Industrial Revolution? How similar or different was it from the preindustrial family? Did industrialization have a sustaining or transformative impact on family life in the United States? These questions are addressed from different perspectives by the selections that follow.

Elaine Tyler May compares divorce records in California and New Jersey for the 1880s and 1920 and finds that the increased prosperity of the industrial era created money problems that affected marriages among the wealthy and the poor alike. In particular, assumptions of vastly improved material circumstances did not always match the realities of household income. As a result, arguments over money created a "pressure to provide" that led to the breakup of many families.

In contrast, Jacquelyn Dowd Hall, Robert Korstad, and James Leloudis emphasize factors that maintained family stability during the Industrial Revolution. Their study of the culture of cotton mill villages in the South after Reconstruction presents a portrait of a much smoother transition from farm to factory than is often associated with the Industrial Revolution. Specifically, they describe a work environment in the cotton mills that preserved rather than destroyed the traditional family labor system.

Elaine Tyler May  **YES**

The Pressure to Provide

In an era of massive production of consumer goods, what determines the normative standard of living, and what constitutes the necessities of life? These questions became increasingly difficult to answer during the decades surrounding the turn of the century, when profound economic changes ushered in corporate America. Scholars have documented a number of crucial developments, including standardized industrial technology, a mushrooming national bureaucracy, a shorter work week, and increased wages. Some observers hail these changes for providing security and material abundance to enhance the home and enrich private life. Others lament the loss of the craft tradition, and the intrinsic satisfactions that went with it. Still others claim that consumerism was a ploy to buy off workers and women, making them complacent while discouraging effective unionization and political action. But, as yet, no study has used empirical data to probe the impact of these developments on American families, or determined how they affected individuals on different levels of the class order. This article examines and compares the effects of heightened material aspirations upon wealthy, white-collar, and blue-collar Americans. While the rising standard of living may well have enhanced family life for some among the comfortable classes, it often wreaked havoc in the homes of those who could not afford the fruits of abundance. It is no accident that the emergence of the affluent society paralleled the skyrocketing of the American divorce rate.

One way to explore the way in which prosperity took its toll is to examine the casualties themselves. I have used hundreds of divorce cases filed during these years to uncover some of the economic problems that plagued American marriages. The samples include 500 litigations from Los Angeles in the 1880s, and another 500 from 1920. A comparative sample includes 250 divorces filed throughout New Jersey in 1920. The proceedings cover a developing west-coast city with little manufacturing, and an eastern industrial state with a large rural population. Within the samples are individuals from virtually every ethnic group and occupational category. By comparing the accusations mentioned in the 1880s and in 1920, we can determine the effects of economic change over time, during these crucial transitional years. The testimonies of the litigants in these cases reveal the limits of abundance, and suggest that no class or locale was immune to the ill effects of rising material aspirations.

From Elaine Tyler May, "The Pressure to Provide: Class, Consumerism, and Divorce in Urban America, 1880–1920," *Journal of Social History*, vol. 12, no. 2 (Winter 1978). Copyright © 1978 by *Journal of Social History*. Reprinted by permission of *Journal of Social History*; permission conveyed via Copyright Clearance Center. Notes omitted.

Obviously, financial problems did not erupt in American homes with the onset of the corporate economy. In fact, money conflicts appeared in divorce cases well before the 20th century. Yet the turn-of-the-century decades did witness a profound change. In the first place, the number of divorces increased dramatically. Secondly, issues surrounding money—who should make it, how much is adequate, and how it should be spent—became increasingly prevalent. The divorce samples from Los Angeles and New Jersey reflect this trend. Although the percentage of cases filed on the grounds of "neglect to provide" did not rise significantly between the two samples taken, these problems did become more complicated in the later decades. The Lynds found a similar development in Muncie, Indiana. In spite of the fairly constant rate of neglect complaints in divorce litigations from 1890 to the 1920s, "economic considerations figure possibly more drastically than formerly as factors in divorce."

At first glance, this appears rather perplexing. The nation was more prosperous in the later period than the earlier, and the standard of living was rising steadily for all classes. Moreover, women found greater opportunities to work, and both males and females experienced increasing wages and more free time off the job. During the same years, an unprecedented abundance of consumer goods became available on a mass level. Presumably, these developments would contribute to easing tensions between husbands and wives rather than creating them, while fostering a more pleasant, epressive, and comfortable existence. However, with the standard of living rising, and affluence filtering down to a greater proportion of the population, the "provider" was often expected to fulfill the increased demands sparked by widespread prosperity.

The evidence in the divorce proceedings suggests that this was not a major problem in the 1880s. Although financial conflicts appeared often, there was no controversy over what constituted the necessities of life. Either a husband supported his family, or he did not. Virtually all of the cases in the early sample that dealt with issues of neglect were clear-cut. If a man did not provide enough food, clothing, and shelter for his wife to live comfortably, she was entitled to a divorce. No husband questioned that; and no quarrels ensued over what his obligation entailed.

... Women who placed heavy demands upon their husbands were not merely selfish or lazy. Although these were the years of women's presumed "emancipation," females still faced limited options outside the home. Middle-class wives in particular may have felt restless as well as powerless. While their numbers in the work force increased, it was still considered undesirable for a married woman to work. If a wife did seek employment, she did not have access to the most lucrative, prestigious, and rewarding occupations. Most jobs available to women were routine and monotonous, with low pay and few chances for advancement.

What was left, then, to give these married females personal satisfaction? Even at home they may have felt a sense of uselessness. Childbearing and household responsibilities utilized less of a woman's creative energies as the birth rate declined and labor-saving devices proliferated. New avenues for self-expression had to be explored. The economy offered little in the way of jobs; yet it provided seemingly unlimited possibilities for consumerism. Indeed, female emancipation found its most immediate expression not in the work force, but in the realms of styles and leisure pursuits. These were purchasable, provided one had the means. If wives began spending to adorn their homes and themselves, it may have reflected their constraints elsewhere. It is no wonder that, for some women, this gave rise to an obsession with material goods and private indulgence. Thus, they turned the full force of their pent-up energies to these endeavors.

With limited financial resources of their own, women often looked to men to provide the means for their consumption desires. This pressure was one of many new challenges facing 20th-century males. While public notice focused on new female activities, parallel shifts that affected men went virtually unnoticed. Males continued to work, their clothing styles remained practically unaltered, and their public behavior did not change dramatically. Yet they were experiencing a subtle transformation in sex-role expectations that, while not as obvious as the new status of women, was no less profound.

For white-collar men, the most far-reaching changes came with the maturation of the corporate system. The engulfing bureaucracies stabilized many uncertainties of the earlier era, and offered at least a modicum of security. The 20th-century businessman was less likely to enter business on his own, with the full burden of success or failure resting on his shoulders. If one followed the rules, he would advance up the hierarchy in a steady, predictable manner, and reach a moderate level of success and prosperity. There may have been [a] few examples of men making a fortune overnight within the modern system; but, in fact, the Carnegies of the previous era served as little more than encouragement to fantasies. The top of the ladder was virtually closed then as well as later. However, successful men had been models of 19th-century striving. In spite of new rewards, the corporations took away some of the unique triumphs of individual enterprise.

With the mechanization of industry, increasing production, the declining work week, and a rising standard of living, the benefits were obvious. In terms of purely material considerations, the corporate economy offered abundance and leisure. The tragedy, however, was that the aspiration for affluence was more widespread than the luxurious life itself. Even if an individual entered the white-collar ranks, he still faced enormous pressures to advance and succeed. Supplying increased demands necessitated continual striving. This was difficult enough for relatively successful businessmen, but infinitely more so for employees with modest salaries, or for petty proprietors without the cushion of corporate security.

We know from national statistics that the white-collar level of society shifted away from self-employed businessmen to corporate bureaucrats and clerical workers. Our Los Angeles samples reflect a similar trend. These white-collar groups, possibly more than any other level in society, were striving for upward mobility, afraid of slipping down the socioeconomic ladder, and concerned with deriving the fruits of their labor in tangible material goods. Arno Mayer has suggested that, historically, the petite bourgeoisie was possibly the most insecure and status-conscious level in western nations. This group had its own unique aspirations and cultural forms geared toward emulating the more affluent groups above them. If this premise holds for 20th-century America, and I believe it does, then petty proprietors facing competition from large corporations, as well as rank and file white-collar workers, would be feeling these pressures most intensely.

Looking at the divorce samples from Los Angeles, we find that, by 1920, the low-white-collar level is overrepresented, compared to its proportion of the general population. In the later sample, the proportion of divorces granted to the wealthy classes declined dramatically as the more bureaucratic clerical and sales categories mushroomed. At the same time, the percentage of petty proprietors in the work force shrank; but these small businessmen remained heavily overrepresented in the divorce samples. Those who remained among the entrepreneurial ranks may well have felt new pressures. As large chains and department stores began drawing local patrons and customers away from independent enterprises, owners of small shops and businesses may have faced increasing insecurity. To add to these burdens, many of them had to purchase goods from larger firms, making them dependent upon a national marketing system. Undersold by large competitors who often controlled production and supply as well as distribution, and bound by wholesale merchandise prices, they may have tried to cut costs by turning to family labor. This was not always a satisfactory solution, especially if proprietors of small concerns had to cope with diminishing returns as well as increasing consumer demands. It is perhaps no wonder that this group had more than its share of divorce.

Unfortunately, relatively few of the divorce litigants articulated how financial and status considerations affected their marriages and their lives. As with virtually every complex issue that eroded these relationships, we must glean insights from a handful of cases where evidence is rich and detailed. In terms of material considerations, we are able to discern a pattern of discontent for each of the major socioeconomic levels represented.... [A]ffluence did not preclude the possibility of money squabbles. The leisured wife of a man with means might make a quasi-career out of purchasing goods and adorning herself and her abode. Even wealthy husbands may have reacted against frivolous or wasteful expenditures. But if a man's income was consistently a measure below his wife's aspirations for comfortable living, the tension could become chronic and destroy a marriage that otherwise might have survived.

In the divorce proceedings, conflicts over status and mobility stand out in bold relief, particularly among white-collar families on the west coast. It is here that we can best perceive the intensified pressures placed upon men to supply heightened material desires. Norman Shinner, for example, admitted that he deserted his wife after five years of marriage because of his "inability to support her in the manner she desired on my salary, and on this account we could not live together in an amiable manner." Rather than struggling to meet up to his wife's aspirations, Norman Shinner simply left.

Oscar Lishnog faced similar difficulties. He married Martha in Chicago in 1908, and had four children prior to their Los Angeles divorce. While the Lishnogs appeared to be a fairly comfortable suburban family, financial strain ultimately caused their union to collapse. Oscar was in the insurance and real estate business, working as an employee or salesman rather than executive or proprietor. His income was steady but modest. He spent some time living apart from his family while working in San Pedro; nevertheless, Oscar and Martha exchanged frequent loving, chatty, but slightly distant letters to each other. He sent her money, she tried to save, and they expressed affection for one another. Now and then Martha would tell Oscar to "mind the store and not waste time or money." Revealing her material aspirations, she wrote that many of her neighbors owned automobiles, for there was no street car line nearby. This suggests that their Los Angeles home was in a fairly new suburban development, removed from the downtown district and transportation network. Martha also reminded her husband that she was paying mortgage on the house, and the "kids want a hammock." She usually closed with affection, saying she was "waiting for him."

But in 1920, Martha filed for divorce on the grounds of willful neglect, saying that Oscar spent his $35 per week salary in "riotous living away from his family," squandering his money while depriving his wife and children. Claiming that she was not skilled in any vocation, Martha said she had to rely on the charity of friends. She asked for custody of the children. Oscar denied the charges, insisting that he earned only $21 per week and gave it all to his wife except a small amount for living expenses. He asked that the divorce be denied, and, assuming that they would remain living apart, requested joint custody of the children. Nevertheless, the court granted Martha the divorce, plus custody, $9 per week for the children, and $3 per month for her "personal recreation." This final item, though minimal in amount, suggests that courts were willing to designate some money for amusements and consumption within the category of necessities—which men were required to provide. Whatever other problems may be hidden from our view that contributed to this couple's woes, it is clear that money was a sore spot for a long time. Oscar's salary was hardly abundant, and he was finally unable to supply the demands of his wife and children to maintain their suburban lifestyle.

Perhaps one of the most telling of these cases was the Los Angeles divorce of Margaret and Donald Wilton. She was a devout midwestern Protestant whose marriage to her clerk husband lasted two years. At one point, she wrote to her estranged spouse, hoping to be reconciled. She recommended that he read some bible passages relating to the duties of husbands and wives, and promised to be a "good Christian wife." In a revealing passage at the end, she wrote, "I heard something about you that made my heart sing with joy; you have climbed another rung on the ladder of success. I am proud to know it, dear...." In spite of Donald's improved status, their marriage was beyond repair. After a rather bitter case, Margaret Wilton was granted a divorce.

Families such as the ones mentioned above may not have suffered severe deprivation. But, like other 20th-century couples, they faced a greater potential for disappointment when a modicum of luxury became the anticipated norm. As the standard of living continued to climb, the golden age of affluence seemed imminent, and it was anticipated with almost religious fervor. For much of the American population, increasing prosperity appeared as a signal from the Divine that the culmination of progress was at hand. One observer perceived, "To most people a millennium implies spiritual overtones. So does the standard of living." For a male provider, then, inability to keep up with this sanctified progress meant failure and damnation.

Although these pressures were particularly acute for the lower middle class, they were also severe for workers. Financial difficulties among working-class couples, however, were qualitatively different from those facing white-collar families. Laborers faced a double-edged problem. They may not have felt the same status anxieties as petty proprietors or rank and file bureaucrats, but it was often difficult for them to make ends meet. Blue-collar families lived with the uncertainties of a fluid labor market and usually lacked the cushion of corporate security. Weak or non-existent labor unions left them virtually un-protected. This is not to deny the fact that some of the abundance filtered down among the working classes. By 1900, their improved circumstances prompted Samuel Gompers, when asked if he thought the conditions of workers were worsening, to reply, "Oh, that is perfectly absurd." In our samples, we find that financial conflicts among blue-collar families actually decreased somewhat between 1880 and 1920. However, their percentage of the total number of lit-igants increased markedly. This may reflect a number of factors. It is possible that in the 1880s, the very price of a divorce precluded legal action for many blue-collar couples. When they did come to court, nearly one-third of them included money conflicts among their complaints. By 1920, more workers may have been able to afford a divorce, and the wives might have been less likely to complain of financial desperation. Yet status and spending concerns might well have helped erode these unions as well. To add to the problem of meeting basic needs, working-class families also shared new consumer desires with their more affluent peers. But for those with meager incomes, luxuries were out of the question, and the affluence they saw everywhere around them only served to heighten frustrations.

Working-class couples, then, faced compounded difficulties. Often the breadwinner's earnings were inadequate and his job insecure. Moreover, he was subject to the same sorts of demands for mass-produced goods as his white-collar contemporaries. One of the crucial features of the consumer-oriented economy was the way it transcended class boundaries. On one level, this con-tributed to a certain superficial "classless" quality. But, on another level, it served to homogenize tastes in a society where wealth remained unequally dis-tributed. Once self-esteem and validation came to rest upon supplying material goods, those on the bottom rungs would be considered less worthy....

Alberta Raschke was a blue-collar wife in Los Angeles with a five-year-old daughter. She filed for a divorce on the grounds of desertion and neglect, claiming that her husband forced her to rely on her parents' charity. The couple married in Indiana in 1913, and separated four years later. At some point, Alberta came to California and William remained in Chicago. In a letter, she accused him of refusing to support her, and claimed that she was in a "weakened condi-tion." "You have had ample time to *make a man of yourself* in all these six years, if you cared for your wife and baby, instead of driving a wagon for $12 a week. You would not take work offered you at $21 a week, so it is not because you could not find better. I stood for all the terrible abuse you gave me, and went without the very necessities of life to see if you would not come to your senses, but now I am tired of waiting and have decided to file suit for divorce... I am as ever Alberta."

Although Alberta Raschke probably had a valid complaint, the pressure put upon William to "make a man" of himself may have been unfair. It is not clear why he did not take the job allegedly offered to him for more pay, but perhaps he simply enjoyed what he was doing. The conflict between working at a job one liked and working for money may have ultimately led to this divorce. Although William Raschke apparently found the lower paying job more satisfying, as far as his wife was concerned the primary purpose of his work was to make money. Undoubtedly, it was not easy for this woman to live on $12 a week with a five-year-old child. However, the equation of manhood with the ability to provide placed a particularly heavy burden on a working-class husband.

In general, working-class wives were less obsessed with status considerations and more concerned with bread and butter issues. Most blue-collar divorces that included money difficulties revolved around basic needs, similar to the conflicts that surfaced in the 1880s proceedings. These problems erupted frequently in New Jersey, where the majority of divorces were among blue-collar couples. It is important to keep in mind that New Jersey only permitted divorces on the grounds of adultery and desertion—not financial neglect. Nevertheless, money was at the heart of many New Jersey litigations. In fact, a number of these couples struggled, quite literally, just to keep a roof over their heads.

A severe housing shortage in urban areas placed serious strains on several marriages. Providers with meager earnings often found themselves unable to provide a home. Numerous couples lived with parents or other relatives, or moved from one form of lodging to another. For these couples, the inability to acquire adequate housing was the fundamental issue that destroyed their marriages. The Shafers were one such family. "I want one thing," pleaded Anna Shafer to her husband. "Won't you please come back and make a home for me, I don't care if it is only two rooms, if you can afford to pay for two rooms." They had been married since 1910, when they ran away together to Hoboken, New Jersey. Anna claimed that William deserted her three years later. She said that her husband was "a drinking man who never made a home or provided for her and their child," although he worked for an insurance company. Anna was granted a divorce and restored to her maiden name. The same problems ended the marriage of Harris and Catherine Martin, two blue-collar workers in Newark. "I told him I would go anyplace with him as long as he could furnish me with a home," explained Catherine. "I didn't care where it was, even if it was only one room and I was alone." But after three months they separated, and Catherine was granted a divorce plus the return of her maiden name.

Lack of housing and insecure work also disrupted the marriage of a Jewish couple in New Jersey, Sarah and Morris Dubin, who married in 1910, and had one child that died. Morris was a tailor by trade, but was unable to practice his craft. Instead, he worked for the railroad, and as a cook in a sanitarium. It appears that this duo had a rather stormy marriage, with Morris deserting now and then and Sarah continually begging him to make a home for her. Whenever she asked, "Why won't you make me a home and support me?" he replied, "I won't and can't live in Newark with you." Newark was particularly plagued by the housing shortage at this time, which aggravated the situation for Morris, who was unable to find work that utilized his tailoring skills. But the court had little mercy. The interviewer concluded that Morris was "apparently one of those people who find it difficult to settle down and perform his obligations for any length of time." Sarah won her suit and the return of her maiden name.

Although a chronic shortage of basic needs eroded most of these blue-collar marriages, a number of working-class couples quarreled over consumer spending and status concerns as well. A few cases illustrate how squabbles might ensue over how money should be spent. Emma Totsworth was 19 when she married David Totsworth, a 22-year-old machinist, in Jersey City. Five years later she deserted. When asked about their difficulties, David said they argued "over different things, like going out and clothes, no clean clothes and all around jealousy. Simple meanness. She spent money on clothes that should have gone for eating." It appears that David Totsworth preferred to see his hard-earned income used for less frivolous items.

Charles and Ada Davis were plagued by similar problems. They were married in New Jersey in 1902 and had one child. After nine years, Ada deserted and went to New York. Apparently Charles, a railroad brakeman, never managed to provide for her in the style that she wanted. According to the interviewer, Ada became "dissatisfied with her surroundings and complained of the style of life her husband afforded her. She wouldn't speak or recognize her husband sometimes for days at a time. Finally she left, saying she wanted to live where she wanted to, and also wanted him to support her." Charles' brother stood up for the aggrieved husband, saying that he "always worked steadily and was a good provider for his home and did everything he could for his wife and family that a man could do under his circumstances." But apparently it was not enough. Charles testified that Ada "insisted upon telling me how much more the neighbors had than she had, and what the neighbor's husband did, and what they didn't do. I told her that if she would stop listening to outsiders and live for me and our little girl as she had done up to that time, everything could be very nice and we could get along." But Ada's dissatisfaction increased until she finally left, and Charles was granted a New Jersey divorce on the grounds of desertion.

These blue-collar couples were plagued by status anxieties. Both Emma Totsworth and Ada Davis had aspirations for material goods beyond the reach of their husbands' pay checks. Some wives not only held their spouses' incomes in disdain, they also looked down upon the work itself. Olivia Garside was a New Jersey housekeeper bent on feverish social climbing. After 26 years of marriage and three children, she finally left her husband Frederick, a machinist, who could not supply the lifestyle she craved. According to Frederick,

> My wife never considered me her equal. She told me this shortly after her marriage, and she was never satisfied with anything I might undertake to do and that I was not as neat appearing as a professional man. She would say my conversation wasn't as it should be and she felt I was socially beneath her. I have always turned over every cent I made to my wife outside of my travelling expenses. I have never been intoxicated in my life. I would very

often work overtime and on Sundays around the neighborhood to earn a few dollars more. My wife always complained I wasn't making enough money.

This husband took pride in his hard work, his efforts to support his wife, his sobriety and discipline. But to his wife, he lacked polish and grace—and the ample income to go with it. The court granted Frederick a divorce on the grounds of desertion.

The evidence in these cases suggests that mass consumption was not necessarily a positive outgrowth of the society's industrial development, even though it held the potential for increased financial security and a more comfortable lifestyle. Rather, these marital conflicts represent a failure or inability to come to terms with the changing economic order. For affluent couples, tensions emerged over how the family's resources should be spent. For those among the lower-white-collar ranks, status considerations clashed with limited incomes, creating enormous pressures upon the family breadwinner. For many working-class couples, mass consumption remained virtually out of reach, contributing to a greater sense of economic insecurity and heightened frustrations.

The testimonies of divorce litigants reflect the discrepancy between material desires and reality, for it was difficult to meet the soaring demands put before every consumer's eyes. Perhaps many Americans did indeed benefit from new opportunities created by the mature industrial system. But among those whose marriages fell apart during these years, and undoubtedly among thousands more whose thoughts and feelings are beyond the reach of scholars, there was a great deal of disappointment, disillusion, and despair that the good life they had hoped for could not be grasped.

Jacquelyn Dowd Hall, Robert Korstad, and James Leloudis

Cotton Mill People

Textile mills built the New South. Beginning in the 1880s, business and professional men tied their hopes for prosperity to the whirring of spindles and the beating of looms. Small-town boosterism supplied the rhetoric of the mill-building campaign, but the impoverishment of farmers was industrialization's driving force. The post–Civil War rise of sharecropping, tenantry, and the crop lien ensnared freedmen, then eroded yeoman society. Farmers of both races fought for survival by clinging to subsistence strategies and habits of sharing even as they planted cash crops and succumbed to tenantry. Meanwhile, merchants who had accumulated capital through the crop lien invested in cotton mills. As the industry took off in an era of intensifying segregation, blacks were relegated to the land, and white farmers turned to yet another strategy for coping with economic change. They had sold their cotton to the merchant; now they supplied him with the human commodity needed to run his mills. This homegrown industry was soon attracting outside capital and underselling northern competitors. By the end of the Great Depression, the Southeast replaced New England as the world's leading producer of cotton cloth, and the industrializing Piedmont replaced the rural Coastal Plain as pacesetter for the region.

Despite the lasting imprint of textile manufacturing on regional development and labor relations, we have no modern survey of the industry's evolution. Nor has the outpouring of research on working-class history been much concerned with factory workers in the New South. To be sure, recent studies have uncovered sporadic, and sometimes violent, contention over the shape of the industrial South. But those findings have done little to shake the prevailing wisdom: The South's mill villages supposedly bred a "social type" compounded of irrationality, individualism, and fatalism. Unable to unite in their own interests, textile workers remained "silent, incoherent, with no agency to express their needs."

We have reached different conclusions. Our research began with a collaborative oral history project aimed at discovering how working people made sense of their own experience. We did not view memory as a direct window on the past. But we did presume the moral and intellectual value of listening to those who lacked access to power and, thus, the means of affecting historical debate.

Adapted from Jacquelyn Dowd Hall, Robert Korstad, and James Leloudis, "Cotton Mill People: Work, Community, and Protest in the Textile South, 1880–1940," *The American Historical Review*, vol. 91, no. 2 (April 1986). Copyright © 1986 by Jacquelyn Dowd Hall, Robert Korstad, and James Leloudis. Reprinted by permission of the authors. Notes omitted.

Our effort was repaid in two major ways. Oral autobiographies dissolved static images, replacing them with portrayals of mill village culture drawn by the men and women who helped create it. Workers' narratives also steered us away from psychological interpretations and toward patterns of resistance, cultural creativity, and structural evolution. Later we turned to the trade press, particularly the *Southern Textile Bulletin.* Published by David Clark in Charlotte, North Carolina, the *Bulletin* spoke for factory owners at the cutting edge of industrial innovation. Finally, from the eloquent letters textile workers wrote to Franklin D. Roosevelt and the National Recovery Administration, we gained a view of the New Deal from below. Together, retrospective and contemporary evidence revealed the social logic that underlay daily practices and suggested an analysis that distinguished one epoch from another in a broad process of technological, managerial, and cultural change.

☙

Nothing better symbolized the new industrial order than the mill villages that dotted the Piedmont landscape. Individual families and small groups of local investors built and owned most of the early mills. Run by water wheels, factories flanked the streams that fell rapidly from the mountains toward the Coastal Plain. Of necessity, owners provided housing where none had been before. But the setting, scale, and structure of the mill village reflected rural expectations as well as practical considerations. Typically, a three-story brick mill, a company store, and a superintendent's house were clustered at one end of the village. Three- and four-room frame houses, owned by the company but built in a vernacular style familiar in the countryside, stood on lots that offered individual garden space, often supplemented by communal pastures and hog pens. A church, a company store, and a modest schoolhouse completed the scene. By 1910 steam power and electricity had freed the mills from their dependence on water power, and factories sprang up on the outskirts of towns along the route of the Southern Railway. Nevertheless, the urban mill village retained its original rural design. Company-owned villages survived in part because they fostered management control. Unincorporated "mill hills" that surrounded towns such as Charlotte and Burlington, North Carolina, and Greenville, South Carolina, enabled owners to avoid taxes and excluded workers from municipal government. But the mill village also reflected the workers' heritage and served their needs.

Like the design of the mill village, the family labor system helped smooth the path from field to factory. On farms women and children had always provided essential labor, and mill owners took advantage of these traditional roles. They promoted factory work as a refuge for impoverished women and children from the countryside, hired family units rather than individuals, and required the labor of at least one worker per room as a condition for residence in a mill-owned house. But this labor system also dovetailed with family strategies. The first to arrive in the mills were those least essential to farming and most vulnerable to the hazards of commercial agriculture: widows, female heads of households, single women, and itinerant laborers. By the turn of the century, families headed by men also lost their hold on the land. Turning to the mills, they sought not a "family wage" that would enable a man to support his dependents but an arena in which parents and children could work together as they had always done.

The deployment of family labor also helped maintain permeable boundaries between farm and mill. The people we interviewed moved with remarkable ease from farming to mill work and back again or split their family's time between the two. James Pharis's father raised tobacco in the Leaksville-Spray area of North Carolina until most of his six children were old enough to obtain mill jobs. The family moved to a mill village in the 1890s because the elder Pharis "felt that all we had to do when we come to town was to reach up and pull the money off of the trees." From the farm Pharis saved his most valuable possession: his team of horses. While the children worked in the mill, he raised vegetables on a plot of rented ground and used his team to do "hauling around for people." Betty Davidson's landowning parents came up with the novel solution of sharing a pair of looms. "My father would run the looms in the wintertime," Davidson remembered, "and go to and from work by horseback. And in the summertime, when he was farming, my mother run the looms, and she stayed in town because she couldn't ride the horse. Then, on the weekends, she would come home."

This ability to move from farming to factory work—or combine the two—postponed a sharp break with rural life. It also gave mill workers a firm sense of alternative identity and leverage against a boss's demands. Lee Workman recalled his father's steadfast independence. In 1918 the superintendent of a nearby cotton mill came to the Workmans' farm in search of workers to help him meet the demand for cloth during World War I. The elder Workman sold his mules and cow but, contrary to the superintendent's advice, held on to his land. Each spring he returned to shoe his neighbors' horses, repair their wagons and plows, and fashion the cradles they used to harvest grain. "He'd tell the superintendent, 'You can just get somebody else, because I'm going back to make cradles for my friends.' Then he'd come back in the wintertime and work in the mill." This type of freedom did not sit well with the mill superintendent, but the elder Workman had the upper hand. " 'Well,' he told them, 'if you don't want to do that, I'll move back to the country and take the family.' "

Although Lee Workman's father periodically retreated to the farm, his sons and daughters, along with thousands of others, eventually came to the mills to stay. There they confronted an authority more intrusive than anything country folk had experienced before. In Bynum, North Carolina, the mill owner supervised the Sunday School and kept tabs on residents' private lives. "If you stubbed your toe they'd fire you. They'd fire them here for not putting out the lights late at night. Old Mr. Bynum used to go around over the hill at nine o'clock and see who was up. And, if you were up, he'd knock on the door and tell you to cut the lights out and get into bed." Along with surveillance came entanglement with the company story. Mill hands all too familiar with the crop lien once again found themselves in endless debt. Don Faucette's father often talked about it. "Said if you worked at the mill they'd just take your wages and put it in the company store and you didn't get nothing. For years and years they didn't get no money, just working for the house they lived in and what they got at the company store. They just kept them in the hole all the time."

The mill village undeniably served management's interests, but it also nurtured a unique workers' culture. When Piedmont farmers left the land and took a cotton mill job, they did not abandon old habits and customs. Instead, they fashioned familiar ways of thinking and acting into a distinctively new way of life. This adaptation occurred at no single moment in time; rather, it evolved, shaped and reshaped by successive waves of migration off the farm as well as the movement of workers from mill to mill. Village life was based on family ties. Kinship networks facilitated migration to the mill and continued to play a powerful integrative role. Children of the first generation off the land married newcomers of the second and third, linking households into broad networks of obligation, responsibility, and concern. For many couples, marriage evolved out of friendships formed while growing up in the village. One married worker recalled, "We knowed each other from childhood. Just raised up together, you might say. All lived here on the hill, you see, that's how we met." As single workers arrived, they, too, were incorporated into the community. Mary Thompson explained that the boarding houses run by widowed women and older couples "were kind of family like. There ain't no place like home, but I guess that's the nearest place like home there is, a boarding house." Mill folk commonly used a family metaphor to describe village life. Hoyle McCorkle remembered the Highland Park mill village in Charlotte as a single household knit together by real and fictive kin: "It was kind of one big family; it was a 200–house family."

Mill hands also brought subsistence strategies from the countryside, modifying them to meet mill village conditions. Just as farmers had tried to bypass the furnishing merchant, mill workers struggled to avoid "living out of a tin can." Edna Hargett's father planted a large garden every spring but could not afford a mule to help till the land. He made do by putting a harness around himself and having his children "stand behind and guide the plow." Louise Jones's family also gardened and raised "homemade meat." Her parents "had a big garden and a corn patch and a few chickens around the yard. We'd have maybe six or eight hens, and we'd let the hens set on the eggs and hatch chickens and have frying-size chickens, raise our own fryers." Self-sufficiency, however, was difficult to achieve, especially when every family member was working a ten- to twelve-hour day for combined wages that barely made ends meet. Even with their gardens, few families could sustain a varied diet through the winter months. As a result, pellagra was a scourge in the mill villages. Life was lived close to the bone.

Under these conditions, necessity and habit fostered rural traditions of mutual aid. Although each family claimed a small plot of land, villagers shared what they grew and "live[d] in common." In late summer and early fall, they gathered for the familiar rituals of harvest and hog killing. Paul and Don Faucette remembered how it was done in Glencoe, North Carolina. "We'd kill our hogs this time, and a month later we'd kill yours. Well, you can give us some, and we can give you some. They'd have women get together down in the church basement. They'd have a quilting bee, and they'd go down and they'd all quilt. They'd have a good crop of cabbage, [and] they'd get together and all make kraut." Villagers helped one another, not with an expectation of immediate return but with the assurance of community support in meeting their individual needs. "They'd just visit around and work voluntarily. They all done it, and nobody owed nobody nothing."

Cooperation provided a buffer against misery and want at a time when state welfare services were limited and industrialists often refused to assume responsibility for job-related sickness and injury. It bound people together and reduced their dependence on the mill owners' charity. When someone fell ill, neighbors were quick to give the stricken family a "pounding." "They'd all get together and help. They'd cook food and carry it to them—all kinds of food—fruits, vegetables, canned goods." Villagers also aided sick neighbors by taking up a "love offering" in the mill. Edna Hargett organized such collections in the weave room at the Chadwick-Hoskins Mill in Charlotte. "When the neighbors got paid they'd come and pay us, and we'd take their money and give it to [the family of the weaver who was ill], and they'd be so proud of it, because they didn't have any wage coming in." To the people we interviewed, the village was "just one big community and one big family" whose members "all kind of hung together and survived."

Community solidarity did not come without a price. Neighborliness could shade into policing; it could repress as well as sustain. Divorced women and children born out of wedlock might be ostracized, and kinship ties could give mill supervisors an intelligence network that reached into every corner of the village. Alice Evitt of Charlotte remarked that "people then couldn't do like they do now. They was talked about. My daddy would never allow us to be with people that was talked about. This was the nicest mill hill I ever lived on. If anybody done anything wrong and you reported them, they had to move." A Bynum proverb summed up the double-edged quality of village life. "If you went along, they'd tend to their business and yours, too, if you let them, your neighbors would. Tend to your business and theirs, too. And the old saying here, you know, 'Bynum's red mud. If you stick to Bynum, it'll stick to you when it rains.' "

Given such tensions, we were struck by how little ambivalence surfaced in descriptions of mill village life. Recollections of factory work were something else again, but the village—red mud and all—was remembered with affection. The reasons are not hard to find. A commitment to family and friends represented a realistic appraisal of working people's prospects in the late nineteenth- and early twentieth-century South. Only after World War II, with the expansion of service industries, did the Piedmont offer alternatives to low-wage factory work to more than a lucky few. Until then, casting one's lot with others offered more promise and certainly more security than the slim hope of individual gain. To be sure, mill people understood the power of money; they struggled against dependency and claimed an economic competence as their due. Nevertheless, they had "their own ideas ... about what constitute[d] the 'good life.' " Communal values, embodied in everyday behavior, distance mill folk from the acquisitiveness that characterized middle-class life in New South towns. . . .

⋅◉⋅

The physical and social geography of the mill village ... was less a product of owners' designs than a compromise between capitalist organization and workers' needs. For a more clear-cut embodiment of the manufacturers' will, we must look to the factory. The ornate facades of nineteenth-century textile mills reflected their builders' ambitions and the orderly world they hoped to create. The mill that still stands at Glencoe is an excellent example. Situated only a few hundred yards from the clapboard houses that make up the village, the mill is a three-story structure complete with "stair tower, corbelled cornice, quoined stucco corners, and heavily stuccoed window labels." In contrast to the vernacular form of the village, the architecture of the factory, modeled on that of New England's urban mills, was highly self-conscious, formal, and refined.

At Glencoe, and in mills throughout the Piedmont, manufacturers endeavored to shape the southern yeomanry into a tractable industrial workforce. Workers' attitudes toward factory labor, like those toward village life, owed much to the cycles and traditions of the countryside. Owners, on the other hand, sought to substitute for cooperation and task orientation a labor system controlled from the top down and paced by the regular rhythms of the machine. Barring adverse market conditions, work in the mills varied little from day to day and season to season. Workers rose early in the morning, still tired from the day before, and readied themselves for more of the same. For ten, eleven, and twelve hours they walked, stretched, leaned, and pulled at their machines. Noise, heat, and humidity engulfed them. The lint that settled on their hair and skin marked them as mill workers to the outside world. The cotton dust that silently entered their lungs could also kill them.

Owners enforced this new pattern of labor with the assistance of a small coterie of supervisors. As a rule, manufacturers delegated responsibility for organizing work and disciplining the help to a superintendent and his overseers and second hands. A second hand in a pre–World War I mill recalled, "You had the cotton, the machinery, and the people, and you were supposed to get out the production. How you did it was pretty much up to you; it was production management was interested in and not how you got it." Under these circumstances, supervision was a highly personal affair; there were as many different approaches to its problems as there were second hands and overseers. As one observer explained, "There was nothing that could be identified as a general pattern of supervisory practice."

At times, discipline could be harsh, erratic, and arbitrary. This was particularly true before 1905, when most workers in southern mills were women and children. Even supervisors writing in the *Southern Textile Bulletin* admitted that "some overseers, second hands, and section men have a disposition to abuse the help. Whoop, holler, curse, and jerk the children around." James Pharis remembered that "you used to work for the supervisor because you were scared. I seen a time when I'd walk across the road to keep from meeting my supervisor. They was the hat-stomping kind. If you done anything, they'd throw their hat on the floor and stomp it and raise hell."

In the absence of either state regulation or trade unions, management's power seemed limitless, but there were, in fact, social and structural constraints. Although manufacturers relinquished day-to-day authority to underlings, they were ever-present figures, touring the mill, making decisions on wages and production quotas, and checking up on the help. These visits were, in part, attempts to maintain the appearance of paternalism and inspire hard work and company loyalty. At the same time, they divided power in the mill. Workers had direct access to the owner and sometimes saw him as a buffer between themselves and supervisors, a "force that could bring an arbitrary and unreasonable [overseer] back into line." Mack Duncan recalled that in the early years "most all the mill owners seemed like they had a little milk of human kindness about them, but some of the people they hired didn't. Some of the managers didn't have that. They were bad to exploit people." Under these circumstances, the commands of an overseer were always subject to review. Workers felt free to complain about unjust treatment, and owners, eager to keep up production, sometimes reversed their lieutenants' orders. Federal labor investigators reported in 1910 that "when an employee is dissatisfied about mill conditions he may obtain a hearing from the chief officer of the mill . . . and present his side of the case. Not infrequently when complaints are thus made, the overseer is overruled and the operative upheld." . . .

◦◎◦

[The] tradeoff between a relatively relaxed work pace on the one hand and long hours and low wages on the other was tenuous at best. Despite manufacturers' efforts to create a secure world in the mill and village, there were recurrent symptoms of unrest. During the 1880s and 1890s, southern mill hands turned first to the Knights of Labor and then to the National Union of Textile Workers (NUTW) to defend their "freedom and liberty." In 1900 an intense conflict led by the NUTW flared in Alamance County, center of textile manufacturing in North Carolina, when an overseer at the Haw River Mill fired a female weaver for leaving her loom unattended. The next day, September 28, union members "threw up" their machines, defending the woman's right to "go when she pleased and where she pleased." By mid-October, workers at other mills throughout the county had joined in a sympathy strike.

The mill owners, conveniently overstocked with surplus goods, posted armed guards around their factories, declared they would employ only non-union labor, and threatened to evict union members from company-owned houses. Undeterred, the workers resolved to stand together as "free men and free women"; five thousand strong, they brought production in Alamance mills virtually to a halt. But by the end of November evictions had overwhelmed the NUTW's relief fund, and the Alamance mill hands were forced to accept a settlement on management's terms.

The Haw River strike capped more than two decades of unrest. During those years, Populists and factory laborers challenged the power of planters, merchants, and industrialists. Between 1895 and 1902, southern Democrats turned to race baiting, fraud, and intimidation to destroy this interracial movement. The passage of state constitutional amendments disfranchising blacks and many poor whites, accompanied by a flurry of Jim Crow laws, restructured the political system, narrowing the terms of public discourse, discouraging lower-class political participation, and making it impossible for opposition movements to survive.

As prospects for collective protest diminished, Piedmont mill hands opted for a personal strategy as old as the industry itself—relocation. In Alamance County alone, more than three hundred workers left to find new jobs in south Carolina and Georgia. "Among them," reported the *Alamance Gleaner,* "are a great many excellent people who prefer to go elsewhere rather than surrender rights and privileges which they as citizens deem they should own and enjoy." In choosing to leave in search of better conditions, the Haw River workers set a pattern for decades to come. Until the end of World War I, quitting was textile workers' most effective alternative to public protest or acquiescence. One student of the southern textile industry declared that a mill hand's "ability to move at a moment's notice was his Magna Carta, Declaration of Independence, and Communist Manifesto."

This movement from job to job could be touched off by any number of factors—curtailed production, a promise of higher wages, or a simple desire to move on—but it could also be a response to a perceived abuse of authority. Josephine Glenn of Burlington explained. "A lot of people in textile mills come and go. They're more or less on a cycle. They're not like that as a whole, but a lot of them are. They're dissatisfied, you might say, restless. They just go somewhere and work awhile, and, if everything don't go just like they think it should, why, they walk out. Sometimes they'd be mad, and sometimes they'd just get on a bender and just not come back. Maybe something personal, or maybe something about the work, or just whatever they got mad about. They'd just [say], 'I've had it,' and that was it." Workers expected to be treated with respect; when it was lacking, they left. George Dyer of Charlotte offered this advice: "Sometimes some boss don't like you, gets it in for you. It's best then just to quit. Don't work under conditions like that. I didn't want to work under a man that don't respect me."

The decision to move was usually made by men, and it could be hard on women and children. Family ties could fray under the wear and tear of factory life. Although Edna Hargett also worked in the mills, she was evicted from her house every time her husband quit his job. "He was bad about getting mad and quitting. He was just hot-tempered and didn't like it when they wanted to take him off his job and put him on another job. When you work in the card room, you have to know how to run about every piece of machinery in there. He liked to be a slubber, and they wanted to put him on drawing or something else. Well, he didn't like to do that." Edna understood her husband's motives but finally left to settle down and rear their children on her own.

Divorce, however, was uncommon. Most families stayed together, and their moves from mill to mill were facilitated by kinship and cushioned by community. A study completed in the late 1920s revealed that 41 percent of mill families had moved less than three times in ten years. Most settled families were headed by middle-aged men and women who had "just kept the road hot" before and immediately after marriage and had then stayed in a village they liked. This relatively stable core of residents made movement possible by providing the contacts through which other workers learned of job opportunities. Established residents also mitigated the ill effects of transiency and preserved ways of life that made it easy for newcomers to feel at home. Women played central roles in this process, keeping up with the events in the village, coordinating informal acts of relief, and keeping the web of social relations intact.

In these ways, the Piedmont became what journalist Arthur W. Page described in 1907 as "one long mill village." Individual communities were woven together—through kinship, shared occupational experiences, and popular culture—into an elaborate regional fabric. According to Lacy Wright, who worked at Greensboro's White Oak Mill, "We had a pretty fair picture, generally speaking, of what you might say was a 200-mile radius of Greensboro. News traveled by word of mouth faster than any other way in those days, because that's the only way we had. In other words, if something would happen at White Oak this week, you could go over to Danville, Virginia, by the weekend and they'd done heard about it. It looked like it always worked out that there would be somebody or another that would carry that information all around." Rooted in a regional mill village culture, workers like Wright took the entire Piedmont as their frame of reference.

POSTSCRIPT

Did the Industrial Revolution Disrupt the American Family?

In his study of family life in Plymouth Colony, John Demos identifies six important functions performed by the family in preindustrial America. As the central social unit, says Demos, the family served as business, school, vocational institute, church, house of correction, and welfare institution. This pattern prevailed for the most part until the Industrial Revolution, when these traditional functions began to be delegated to institutions outside the household. For example, children received their formal education in public schools and private academies established for that purpose, rather than from their parents. Similarly, religious instruction occurred more often than not in a church building on Sunday morning, not in a home where family members gathered around a table for Bible readings. The explanation for this change is that work opportunities existed outside the home, and various family members were spending less and less time in the physical presence of one another because of the exigencies of the industrial workplace. See John Demos, *A Little Commonwealth: Family Life in Plymouth Colony* (Oxford University Press, 1970) and *Past, Present, and Personal: The Family and the Life Course in American History* (Oxford University Press, 1986).

May's work offers a variation of Demos's interpretation by focusing upon the destructive influence of industrialization on the family, but May is less concerned with the altered functions of the family than with the powerful influence of heightened expectations of the acquisition of material wealth. Hall, Korstad, and Leloudis, on the other hand, suggest that the changes produced in American families were not as drastic as some scholars believe. Their portrait of cotton mill workers reveals significant levels of continuity with the rural past and the family labor patterns that were not all that different from those described by Demos for seventeenth-century Plymouth.

The study of the history of families is an outgrowth of the "new social history" that began to emerge in the 1960s. Since that time, scholars have devoted considerable attention to such topics as changing household structure and the influence of economic forces on family units and individual family members. For a general summary of the scholarly attention given to the American family, see Estelle B. Freedman's essay "The History of the Family and the History of Sexuality," in Eric Foner, ed., *The New American History*, rev. and exp. ed. (Temple University Press, 1997). Carl Degler, *At Odds: Women and the Family in America* (Oxford University Press, 1980); Steven Mintz and Susan Kellogg, *Domestic Revolutions: A Social History of American Family Life* (Free Press,

1988); and Stephanie Coontz, *The Social Origins of Private Life: A History of American Families, 1600–1900* (Verso, 1988) present introductory surveys of American family history. May expands the coverage of some of the issues explored in her essay in *Great Expectations: Marriage and Divorce in Post-Victorian America* (University of Chicago Press, 1980). Additional works addressing southern families in the industrial era include Carol Bleser, ed., *In Joy and in Sorrow: Women, Family, and Marriage in the Victorian South* (Oxford University Press, 1991) and Peter Bardaglio, *Reconstructing the Household: Families, Sex and the Law in the Nineteenth-Century South* (University of North Carolina Press, 1995). Tamara Hareven, *Family Time and Industrial Time: The Relationship Between the Family and Work in a New England Industrial Community* (Cambridge University Press, 1982) and Michael Grossberg, *Governing the Hearth: Law and the Family in Nineteenth-Century America* (University of North Carolina Press, 1985) are important monographs of the industrial era. For studies of family life among African Americans and immigrants, see E. Franklin Frazier, *The Negro Family in the United States* (University of Chicago Press, 1939); Herbert G. Gutman, *The Black Family in Slavery and Freedom, 1750–1925* (Pantheon, 1976); Virginia Yans McLaughlin, *Family and Community: Italian Immigrants in Buffalo, 1880–1930* (Cornell University Press, 1977); and Judith Smith, *Family Connections: A History of Italian and Jewish Immigrant Lives in Providence, Rhode Island, 1900–1940* (State University of New York Press, 1985). Finally, for the past quarter century, cutting-edge scholarship on the American family has appeared in the issues of the *Journal of Family History.*

ISSUE 4

Was City Government in Late-Nineteenth-Century America a "Conspicuous Failure"?

YES: Ernest S. Griffith, from *A History of American City Government: The Conspicuous Failure, 1870–1900* (National Civic League Press, 1974)

NO: Jon C. Teaford, from *The Unheralded Triumph: City Government in America, 1860–1900* (Johns Hopkins University Press, 1984)

ISSUE SUMMARY

YES: Professor of political science and political economy Ernest S. Griffith (1896–1981) focuses upon illegal and unethical operations of the political machine and concludes that the governments controlled by the bosses represented a betrayal of the public trust.

NO: Professor of history Jon C. Teaford argues that scholars traditionally have overlooked the remarkable success that municipal governments in the late nineteenth century achieved in dealing with the challenges presented by rapid urbanization.

During the late nineteenth century, American farmers based their grievances on revolutionary changes that had occurred in the post–Civil War United States. Specifically, they saw themselves as victims of an industrial wave that had swept over the nation and submerged their rural, agricultural world in the undertow. Indeed, the values, attitudes, and interests of all Americans were affected dramatically by the rapid urbanization that accompanied industrial growth. The result was the creation of the modern city, with its coordinated network of economic development, which emphasized mass production and mass consumption.

In the years from 1860 to 1920, the number of urban residents in the United States increased much more rapidly than the national population as a whole. For example, the Census Bureau reported in 1920 that the United States housed 105,711,000 people, three times the number living in the country on the eve of the Civil War. Urban dwellers, however, increased ninefold during the same period. The number of "urban" places (incorporated towns with 2,500 or more residents, or unincorporated areas with at least 2,500 people per square mile) increased from 392 in 1860 to 2,722 in 1920. Cities with populations in excess of 100,000 increased from 9 in 1860 to 68 in 1920.

Reflecting many of the characteristics of "modern" America, these industrial cities produced a number of problems for the people who lived in them—problems associated with fire and police protection, sanitation, utilities, and a wide range of social services. These coincided with increased concerns over employment opportunities and demands for transportation and housing improvements. Typically, municipal government became the clearinghouse for such demands. What was the nature of city government in the late-nineteenth-century United States? How effectively were American cities governed? To what extent did municipal leaders listen to and redress the grievances of urban dwellers? In light of James Lord Bryce's blunt statement in 1888 that city government in the United States was a "conspicuous failure," it is worthwhile to explore scholarly assessments of Bryce's conclusion.

In the following selection, Ernest S. Griffith surveys the nature of municipal government in the last three decades of the nineteenth century and concludes that city politics was consumed by a "cancer of corruption" that predominated in the years from 1880 to 1893. He identifies numerous factors that contributed to this unethical environment, as well as the disreputable and illegal lengths gone to that perpetuated the power of the bosses but prevented city government from operating in the true interest of the people.

In the second selection, Jon C. Teaford contends that scholars like Griffith are too eager to condemn the activities of late-nineteenth-century municipal governments without recognizing their accomplishments. Teaford argues that, although there were numerous shortcomings, American city dwellers enjoyed a higher standard of public services than any other urban residents in the world. Also, in contrast to the portrait of boss dominance presented by Griffith and others, Teaford maintains that authority was widely distributed among various groups that peacefully coexisted with one another. For Teaford, nineteenth-century cities failed to develop a political image but succeeded to a remarkable degree in meeting the needs of those who were dependent upon them.

Ernest S. Griffith

 **YES**

The Cancer of Corruption

Introduction

Corruption may be defined as personal profit at the expense of the public—stealing and use of office for private gain, including the giving and taking of bribes outside of the law. More broadly defined, it is any antisocial conduct that uses government as an instrument. Its twilight zone is never the same from age to age, from community to community, or even from person to person. . . .

Historically, the motivations of the electorate, the uses to which tax money and campaign contributions were put, the pressures of reward and punishment to which candidates and officeholders were subjected, were never very far from the gray zone in which the line between the corrupt and the ethical —or even the legal—had somehow to be drawn. Votes were "coin of the realm" in a democracy; office holding or power-wielding was secured by votes. They might be freely and intelligently given; they might be the result of propaganda, friendship, or pressure; they might be purchased by money or otherwise; they might be manufactured out of election frauds. Those who were members of the government, visible or invisible, were ultimately dependent on the voters for their opportunity to serve, for their livelihood, for the chance to steal or betray. These conditions existed in the late nineteenth century; with differing emphases they still exist today.

What, then, determined whether a late-nineteenth-century city government was corrupt or ethical, or something in between? Ethically speaking, the nadir of American city government was probably reached in the years between 1880 and 1893. Why and how? There was obviously no one answer. The time has long since passed when municipal reformers, not to mention historians, believed there was a single answer. There was present a highly complex situation—a *Gestalt,* or pattern—never identical in any two places, but bearing a family resemblance in most respects. The path to better municipal governance was long and difficult because of this very complexity. The story of the 1890's and of the Progressive Era of the first twelve or fifteen years of the twentieth century was the story of a thousand battles on a thousand fronts—the unraveling of a refractory network of unsuitable charters and procedures, of a human nature that at times led to despair, of an economic order that put a premium

From Ernest S. Griffith, *A History of American City Government: The Conspicuous Failure, 1870–1900* (National Civic League Press, 1974). Copyright © 1974 by The National Municipal League. Reprinted by permission of University Press of America.

on greed, of a social order of class and ethnic divisions reflected often in incompatible value systems—all infinitely complicated by rapidity of growth and population mobility....

Patronage

... [H]ow are we to account for the corrupt machine in the first place, and for what came to be its endemic character in American cities for two or three decades? This is part of a broader analysis, and will be undertaken presently. As always, in the end the legacy of a corrupt and corrupting regime was a malaise of suspicion, discouragement, and blunted ideals in society as a whole.

In examining the fact of corruption, it was obvious that the city—any city, good or bad—provided livelihood for scores, hundreds, even thousands of people directly employed. They would fight if their livelihood were threatened. There were also large numbers dependent upon the city for contracts, privileges, and immunities. Not as sharply defined, and often overlapping one or both of these categories, were persons who served as organizers, brokers, or instruments of these other two groups, and whose livelihoods therefore also depended upon the city. They, too, would fight to attain, keep, or augment this livelihood, and probably the sense of power (and occasionally the constructive achievements) that their positions carried with them. They were the "machine," the "ring," the "boss," the professional politician, the political lawyer. This is to say, for many people (as regards the city) employment, power, and access to those with power were matters of economic life or death for themselves and their families—and, if these same people were wholly self-seeking, to them the end justified the means.

First, consider the municipal employees. "To the victors belong the spoils" —the party faction and machine rewarded their own and punished the others. In 1889 the mayor of Los Angeles appointed all of his six sons to the police force, but this helped to defeat him in the next election. In the smaller cities, and in the larger ones before skills seemed essential, a change of administration or party was the signal for wholesale dismissals and wholesale patronage. This fact created the strongest incentive for those currently employed to work for the retention in power of those influential in their employment; that they had so worked constituted a logical basis for their dismissal; given the success of the opposing candidates. That the city might suffer in both processes was unimportant to those whose livelihood was at stake in the outcome of the struggle. Those involved, in many instances, would not even respect the position of school teacher, and could usually find ways and means to subvert the civil service laws when they emerged, in intent if not in formal ritual. In Brooklyn, for example, during the Daniel Whitney administration of 1885, only favored candidates were informed of the dates of the examinations in time to apply. Examinations were then leniently graded, to put it mildly. One illiterate received a grade of 97.5 per cent on a written test. About 1890, each member of the Boston city council received a certain number of tickets corresponding to his quota of men employed by the city. No one was eligible without such a ticket, and existing employees were discharged to make room if necessary.

Sale of Privileges and Immunities

As regards the sale for cash of privileges and immunities, many politicians and officials did not stop with the twilight zone of liquor violations, gambling, and prostitution, but went on to exploit what would be regarded as crime in any language or society. Denver (incidentally, at least until the 1960's) was one of the worst. From the late 1880's until 1922, Lou Blonger, king of the city's underworld, held the police department in his grasp. For many of these years he had a direct line to the chief of police, and his orders were "law." Criminals were never molested if they operated outside the city limits, and often not within the limits, either. He contributed liberally to the campaign funds of both parties, those of the district attorneys being especially favored. Blonger was sent to jail in 1922 by Philip Van Cise, a district attorney who had refused his conditional campaign contribution of $25,000.

Yet, it was the insatiable appetite of men for liquor, sex, and the excitement and eternal hope of gambling that proved by all the odds the most refractory and the most corrupting day-to-day element....

The police of most cities, and the politicians and officials, took graft or campaign contributions from the liquor interests so that they would overlook violations of the law. Judging from extant material of the period, corruption by the liquor trade occurred more frequently than any other. Over and over again the question of enforcement of whatever laws existed was an issue at the polls. The fact was that, at this time, the trade did not want *any* regulation and resented all but the most nominal license fee, unless the license in effect granted a neighborhood semimonopoly, and increased profitability accordingly. It was prepared to fight and pay for its privileges. Council membership was literally jammed with saloon keepers, and Buffalo (1880) was not too exceptional in having a brewer as mayor. Apparently in one instance (in Nebraska), the liquor interests resorted to assassination of the clerk of the U.S. Federal Circuit Court in revenge for his part in the fight against them.

More clearly illegal, because here it was not a question of hours of sale but of its right to exist, was commercial gambling. State laws and even municipal ordinances were fairly usual in prohibiting it, but these laws were sustained neither by enforcement nor by public opinion. If the public opinion calling for enforcement was present, the requisite ethical standard was not there that would preclude the offering and accepting of the bribes that made the continuance of gambling possible—except for an occasional spasm of raids and reform.

Oklahoma City will serve as a case study. At one point gambling houses regularly paid one fine a month. Four-fifths of the businessmen refused to answer whether they would favor closing such joints; going on record either way would hurt their business. Citing District Attorney William T. Jerome's views of attempts to secure enforcement of this type of law, one writer commented: "The corrupt politician welcomes the puritan as an ally. He sees in laws that cannot and will not be permanently enforced a yearly revenue in money and in power."

The situation regarding commercialized vice was similar. Laws and ordinances forbidding brothels were on the statute books. Brothels existed in every large city and most of the smaller ones. Especially in the Western cities where men greatly outnumbered women, they appeared in large numbers, and the same might be said of the commercial centers and the seaport towns. A boss like Boies Penrose of Philadelphia patronized them. So, in fact, did a number of presumably otherwise respectable citizens. Many of this last group also drew rent from the brothels.

What this meant to the city government of a place like Seattle may be illustrated by an episode in 1892:

> The police department thought it had a vested property right in the collections from prostitutes and gamblers. The new mayor, Ronald, was waited on almost immediately by a group of high ranking police officers who asked him how much of a cut he wanted out of the monthly "pay off" for gambling and prostitution. "Not a cent! Moreover, there isn't going to be any collection or places that pay protection money," he said as he pounded the table. The committee patiently explained that it was "unofficial licensing," a very effective way to control crime. The mayor exploded again and one of the captains took out a revolver and dropped it on the table. "Somebody is going to get hurt—maybe." The mayor tried as hard as ever anyone could to clean up, but found it impossible. He was powerless because he had no real support. He resigned in less than a year.

For the depths of degradation into which the combination of lust and greed can sink a city government, one can only cite the example of Kansas City, where girls at the municipal farm were sold by the politicians (who of course pocketed the money) and sent to brothels in New Orleans....

Each city, as the pressures of urban living forced regulation, found itself under conflicting demands. The people as a whole probably wanted "nuisances" cleared up—unsanitary dwellings, cattle in the streets, sign encroachments, garbage left around, and a hundred other annoying matters—the counterpart in today's world of illegal parking. But to the particular person involved, there was an interest in leaving things as they were—an interest for which he was prepared to pay by a tip or a vote. Compulsory education laws ran up against parents who regarded them as a violation of their God-given right to employ their children as they wished. Political revenge might well await the enforcer —the truant officer, health officer, inspector of meat, dairies, or housing, or policeman. Political and often pecuniary rewards awaited those who would overlook matters of this type. There were other favors, tips on the location of a proposed public improvement or on the location of a road or a park relevant to real estate value. These were advantageous to the official and his friends to know and to control for their own personal profit. Real estate profit through advance notice or an actual share in the decision on a municipal improvement or purchase was one of the most lucrative perquisites of councilors or the "ring" members. A special instance of this was the desire of many members of Congress for seats on the low-status District of Columbia Committee so as to secure advance information as to what would be profitable real estate purchases in the District. In general, these examples came under the heading of "honest graft" in those days, as not necessarily costing the city treasury an undue amount. The term was invented by George W. Plunkett of Tammany as a rationalization.

Graft From Contracts and Franchises

Quite otherwise were the profits, direct and indirect, from lucrative city contracts. Probably in the majority of cities there was a tacit understanding that a favored contractor would "kick back" a substantial amount (10 per cent or more being quite usual) either to party campaign funds for which accounting was rare, as fees to a "political lawyer," with the ultimate distribution uncertain, or as out-and-out bribes to those with the power to make the decisions. There were always any number of devices to evade the intent of the law, even in situations where the law called for competitive bidding. Pittsburgh for years found that William Flinn, one of its two bosses, was always the lowest "responsible" bidder for contracts. In other instances, specifications were such that only the favored one could meet them. In New Orleans, around 1890, in spite of the protests of the property owners, almost all paving was with rosetta gravel (in which one man had a monopoly). In other cases, the lowest bid was accepted, but there would be advance assurance (private and arranged) that the inspectors would not insist that the contractor meet the specifications. Contractors in Portland (Oregon) in 1893 whose men voted "right" were laxly supervised. In still other instances, the bidders themselves formed rings, bid high, and arranged for distribution of the contracts among themselves. This practice seems to have been a particular bent among paving contractors. William Gabriel of Cleveland, high in Republican circles, will serve as an example. This was not incompatible with generous bribes to municipal officials or rings as well. Graft in contracts extended to the schools—to their construction and to the textbooks purchased. Things were probably not so flagrant in Cleveland, where campaign contributions and not bribes were the favored means of business.

Franchises and privileges for the railroads and the various utilities came to be special sources of demoralization, particularly for the councils that usually had the responsibility for granting them. Initially, a community welcomed the railroad and even subsidized its coming. With growing urbanization, it looked forward to waterworks, lighting (gas or electricity), street cars (horse or cable), and eventually electricity and the telephone. The earliest of the franchises were likely to be most liberal with respect to rate allowed, duration, and service rendered. The cities wanted the utilities and often urged their coming. Later, as the latter proved enormously profitable, the stakes grew high, and betrayal of the public interest probably took place in the majority of cases. Power to grant franchises greatly increased the desirability of membership on the council. Hazen Pingree, mayor of Detroit in the early 1890's wrote:

> My experiences in fighting monopolistic corporations as mayor of Detroit, and in endeavoring to save to the people some of their right as against their greed, have further convinced me that they, the corporations, are responsible for nearly all the thieving and boodling with which cities are made to suffer from their servants. They seek almost uniformly to secure what

they want by means of bribes, and in this way they corrupt our councils and commissions.

Providence, in the 1890's allowed only property owners to vote. They elected businessmen to the city council. This council then awarded Nelson Aldrich, the state boss, a perpetual franchise, which he sold out at an enormous profit. He went to the Senate through wholesale bribery of rural voters, with money contributed by the sugar magnates for whom as congressman he had arranged a protective tariff. The city of Pawtucket, which sought to block a franchise, was overridden by the rurally dominated state legislature.

It was Lincoln Steffens who later dramatized beyond any forgetting the unholy link between the protected underworld, the city governments, and the portion of the business community in search of contracts and franchises—a link found in city after city. The story of his exposures belongs to the Progressive Era. At the time, these betrayals of the public interest were either not known or, if known, were enjoyed and shared, shrugged off and rationalized, or endured in futile fury.

Two or three further examples of documented franchise bribery might be cited. In 1884, in New York City, the Broadway Surface Railroad paid $25,000 to each of eighteen alderman and received the franchise. The rival company had offered the *city* $1 million. Another corporation set aside $100,000 to buy the council. The street-car companies of Indianapolis contributed to both political parties. So it went in city after city.

Some other examples of business corruption might be cited. Governor John P. Altgeld of Illinois sent a message (1895) to the state legislature, calling attention to the fantastically low rents paid by newspapers for school lands. In a most complex arrangement involving shipping companies, boarding-house keepers, "crimps" (recruiters of seamen), and the city authorities, the San Francisco waterfront instituted a reign of near-peonage, in which seamen were grossly overcharged for their lodging and shore "amenities," prevented from organized resistance, and virtually terrorized and blackmailed into signing on the ships again. In the early 1870's, local speculators of Dubuque, including two former mayors, bought up city bonds for a small amount and held out for redemption at par. Favored banks (that is, those contributing through appropriate channels to the city treasurer, the party, or the boss) received city deposits without having to pay interest thereon, or, as in Pittsburgh, paying the interest to the politicians. Finally, the employer power structure threw its weight and its funds in support of almost any administration that would protect strikebreakers, break up "radical" gatherings, and otherwise preserve the "American system" against alien ideas—this, without reference to the extent of the known corruption of the administration.

Theft, Assessment Favoritism, "Kickbacks," "Rake-Offs"

As might be expected, there were a number of examples of actual theft, most frequently by a city treasurer. Judges would occasionally keep fines. A certain amount of this was to be expected in an age of ruthless money-making when business ethics condoned all kinds of sharp practices in the private sector. What was more discouraging was that many of these thieves remained unpunished, as the machine with its frequent control over the courts protected its own. City officials of Spokane even stole funds contributed for relief after its great fire (1889).

How widespread was political favoritism in tax assessment would be extraordinarily difficult to determine. The practice of underassessment across the board to avoid litigation was almost universal, and in some communities it had a statutory base. Certainly many corporations were favored, in part because they were deemed an asset to the community's economic life. What was more probable was the widespread fear that, if a person were to criticize the city administration, he would find his underassessment raised. This particular form of blackmail took place in blatant fashion at one time in Jersey City. It also occurred under Park Board administration in the Bronx in 1874. From time to time, there would be exposures in the local press of assessment anomalies, but the press was itself vulnerable to punitive retaliation of this type because of its frequent underassessment.

The practice of compensating certain employees by fees instead of fixed salaries lingered on, in spite of or often because of the large amounts of money involved. Such employees were usually expected, by virtue of their election or appointment, to "kick back" a substantial portion to the party organization. Such "kickbacks" from the receiver of taxes amounted in Philadelphia to $200,000 in one of the years after 1873—divided among the small number who constituted the gas-house ring. Other compensations by the fee system were abandoned in 1873, and the employees were put on salaries. Some nominations and appointments were sold, with the receipts going, it was hoped, to the party campaign funds, concerning the use of which there was rarely in these days any effective accounting. Political assessments of city employees probably ruled in the majority of the cities.

How much graft in fact found its way into the pockets of the city employees for their betrayal of trust or, for that matter, for services they should have rendered in any event, how much "rake-off" the ring or the boss took, will never be known. What was graft and what was "rake-off" shaded into a gray zone after a while. The amount must have been colossal in the cities—certainly enough, had it been dedicated to municipal administration, to have enhanced efficiency and service enormously, or to have cut the tax rate drastically. Utility rates would have tumbled and service improved. . . .

Extortion and Blackmail

Extortion and blackmail, if not standard practice, were frequent enough to call for comment. Once in a while, as in Fort Worth (1877), they were used in an intriguing and perhaps constructive fashion. It was proposed that the sale of intoxicants be forbidden at the theaters. The ordinance was tabled, with the notation that it would be passed unless one of the theater owners paid his taxes.

In Brooklyn during the Whitney administration, the head of the fire department blocked an electric franchise until he was given one-fifth of the company's stock and several other politicians had taken a cut.

The newspapers were particularly vulnerable to blackmail. A threat of loss of the city's advertising was a marvelous silencer. In Tacoma (1889), enough businessmen believed a particular gambling house was a community asset that the newspaper that had denounced its protected status as a result lost heavily in both advertising and circulation.

The gangs of Detroit seemed to be immune in the 1880's and able to bring about the promotion or dismissal of a policeman. Sailors, tugmen, longshoremen made up the bulk of their personnel. In the early 1880's in Indianapolis, citizens were arrested on trumped-up charges and fined by judges who at that time were paid by the fines.

Police and the Courts

... [D]ifficulties stemmed from the key role played by the police in the electoral process, the graft from the under-world, and the desire on the part of the allegedly more respectable for immunities. In Tacoma, the mayor reprimanded the chief of police for raiding a brothel in which a number of the city's influential men were found. All these factors meant that in city after city the police force was really regarded as an adjunct of the political party or machine. In some of the smaller cities, the patronage aspect was expressed in extreme form. For example, until 1891 each new mayor of Wilmington (Delaware) appointed a new set of policemen, usually of his own party.

Nor were the courts immune as adjuncts to corruption. The district attorney and the judges, especially the local ones, were usually elected, and by the same processes as the mayors and councils. The same network of political and corrupt immunities that pervaded the police and stemmed from the rings and other politicians was present in the courts. Four hazards to justice were thus in a sense vulnerable to pressure and purchase—the stages of arrest, prosecution, the verdicts (and delays) of the judge, and the possibilities of a packed or bribed jury. William Howard Taft commented at a later date as follows:

> [The] administration of criminal law is a disgrace to our civilization, and
> the prevalence of crime and fraud, which here is greatly in excess of that in
> European countries, is due largely to the failure of the law to bring criminals
> to justice.

Quite apart from overt corruption, there were numerous ways in which courts could reward the party faithful, such as by appointment as favored bondsmen, stenographers, or auctioneers.

It was not surprising that an exasperated and otherwise respectable public occasionally fought back by violent means. In Cincinnati (1884), so flagrant had been the court delays and acquittals that a mass meeting, held to protest the situation, evolved into a mob bent on direct action. They burned the courthouse and attempted to storm the jail. For days the mob ruled. Police and militia failed, and only federal troops finally restored order. There were over fifty deaths. In Dallas, in the early 1880's, the "respectable" element, despairing of action by the city government in closing some of the worst resorts, took to burning them. Acquittal of the murderers of the chief of police of New Orleans by a probably corrupted jury was followed by lynchings....

Summary Scenario

This in general was the scenario of most American cities about 1890: fitful reforms, usually not lasting; charters hopelessly tangled, with no agreement on remedies; civil service laws circumvented in the mad search for patronage opportunities; election frauds virtually normal; an underworld capitalizing on man's appetites and finding it easy to purchase allies in the police and the politician; countless opportunities for actual theft; business carrying over its disgraceful private ethics into subverting city government for its own ends, and city officials competing to obtain the opportunity to be lucratively subverted; citizens who might be expected to lead reforms generally indifferent, discouraged, frightened, and without the time necessary to give to the effort; a community with conflicting value systems into which the exploiter entered, albeit with an understanding and a sympathy denied to those from another class; ballots complicated; a nomination process seemingly built to invite control by the self-seeking; sinecures used to provide fulltime workers for the party machine; state governments ready to step in to aid in the corruption if local effort proved inadequate; confusion over the claims of party loyalty; a press often intimidated and frequently venal; countless opportunities to make decisions that would favor certain real estate over other locations; a burgeoning population rapidly urbanizing and dragging in its train innumerable problems of municipal services and aspirations.

For the unraveling of this tangled mess, the reformer and the career administrator had no acceptable philosophy.

NO

Jon C. Teaford

Trumpeted Failures and Unheralded Triumphs

In 1888 the British observer James Bryce proclaimed that "there is no denying that the government of cities is the one conspicuous failure of the United
States." With this pronouncement he summed up the feelings of a host of Americans. In New York City, residents along mansion-lined Fifth Avenue, parish-
ioners in the churches of then-sedate Brooklyn, even petty politicos at party
headquarters in Tammany Hall, all perceived serious flaws in the structure of
urban government. Some complained, for example, of the tyranny of upstate
Republican legislators, others attacked the domination of ward bosses, and still
others criticized the greed of public utility companies franchised by the municipality. Mugwump reformer Theodore Roosevelt decried government by Irish
political machine hacks, the moralist Reverend Charles Henry Parkhurst lam-
basted the reign of rum sellers, and that pariah of good-government advocates,
New York City ward boss George Washington Plunkitt, also found fault, attacking the evils of civil service. For each, the status quo in urban government was
defective. For each, the structure of municipal rule needed some revision. By
the close of the 1880s the litany of criticism was mounting, with one voice after
another adding a shrill comment on the misrule of the cities.

During the following two decades urban reformers repeated Bryce's words
with ritualistic regularity, and his observation proved one of the most-quoted
lines in the history of American government. Time and again latter-day Jeremi-
ahs damned American municipal rule of the late nineteenth century, denounc-
ing it as a national blight, a disgrace that by its example threatened the survival
of democracy throughout the world. In 1890 Andrew D. White, then-president
of Cornell University, wrote that "without the slightest exaggeration . . . the city
governments of the United States are the worst in Christendom—the most expensive, the most inefficient, and the most corrupt." Four years later the reform
journalist Edwin Godkin claimed that "the present condition of city governments in the United States is bringing democratic institutions into contempt
the world over, and imperiling some of the best things in our civilization." Such
preachers as the Reverend Washington Gladden denounced the American city
as the "smut of civilization," while his clerical colleague Reverend Parkhurst

said of the nation's municipalities: "Virtue is at the bottom and knavery on top. The rascals are out of jail and standing guard over men who aim to be honorable and law-abiding." And in 1904 journalist Lincoln Steffens stamped American urban rule with an indelible badge of opprobrium in the corruption-sated pages of his popular muckraking exposé *The Shame of the Cities*. Books, magazines, and newspapers all recited the catalog of municipal sins.

Likewise, many twentieth-century scholars passing judgment on the development of American city government have handed down a guilty verdict and sentenced American urban rule to a place of shame in the annals of the nation. In 1933 a leading student of municipal home rule claimed that "the conduct of municipal business has almost universally been inept and inefficient" and "at its worst it has been unspeakable, almost incredible." That same year the distinguished historian Arthur Schlesinger, Sr., in his seminal study *The Rise of the City*, described the development of municipal services during the last decades of the nineteenth century and found the achievements "distinctly creditable to a generation... confronted with the phenomenon of a great population everywhere clotting into towns." Yet later in his study he returned to the more traditional position, recounting tales of corruption and describing municipal rule during the last two decades of the century as "the worst city government the country had ever known." Writing in the 1950s, Bessie Louise Pierce, author of the finest biography to date of an American city, a multivolume history of Chicago, described that city's long list of municipal achievements but closed with a ritual admission of urban shortcomings, citing her approval of Bryce's condemnation. Similarly, that lifelong student of American municipal history, Ernest Griffith, subtitled his volume on late-nineteenth-century urban rule "the conspicuous failure," though he questioned whether municipal government was a greater failure than state government.

Historians such as Schlesinger and Griffith were born in the late nineteenth century, were raised during the Progressive era, and early imbibed the ideas of such critics as Bryce and White. Younger historians of the second half of the twentieth century were further removed from the scene of the supposed municipal debacle and could evaluate it more dispassionately. By the 1960s and 1970s, negative summations such as "unspeakable" and "incredible" were no longer common in accounts of nineteenth-century city government, and historians professing to the objectivity of the social sciences often refused to pronounce judgment on the quality of past rule. Yet recent general histories of urban America have continued both to describe the "deterioration" of city government during the Gilded Age and to focus on political bosses and good-government reformers who were forced to struggle with a decentralized, fragmented municipal structure supposedly unsuited to fast-growing metropolises of the 1880s and 1890s. Some chronicles of the American city have recognized the material advantages in public services during the late nineteenth century, but a number speak of the failure of the municipality to adapt to changing realities and of the shortcomings of an outmoded and ineffectual municipal framework. Sam Bass Warner, Jr., one of the leading new urban historians of the 1960s, has characterized the pattern of urban rule as one of "weak, corrupt, unimaginative municipal government." Almost one hundred years after

Bryce's original declaration, the story of American city government remains at best a tale of fragmentation and confusion and at worst one of weakness and corruption.

If modern scholars have not handed down such damning verdicts as the contemporary critics of the 1880s and 1890s, they have nevertheless issued evaluations critical of the American framework of urban rule. As yet, hindsight has not cast a golden glow over the municipal institutions of the late nineteenth century, and few historians or political scientists have written noble tributes to the achievements of American municipal government. Praise for the nation's municipal officials has been rare and grudging. Though many have recognized the elitist predilections of Bryce and his American informants, the influence of Bryce's words still persists, and the image of nineteenth-century city government remains tarnished. Historians have softened the harsh stereotype of the political boss, transforming him from a venal parasite into a necessary component of a makeshift, decentralized structure. Conversely, the boss's good-government foes have fallen somewhat from historical grace and are now typified as crusaders for the supremacy of an upper-middle-class business culture. But historians continue to aim their attention at these two elements of municipal rule, to the neglect of the formal, legal structure. They write more of the boss than of the mayor, more on the civic leagues than on the sober but significant city comptroller. Moreover they continue to stage the drama of bosses and reformers against a roughly sketched backdrop of municipal disarray. The white and black hats of the players may have shaded to gray, but the setting of the historian's pageant remains a ramshackle municipal structure.

Nevertheless, certain nagging realities stand in stark contrast to the traditional tableau of municipal rule. One need not look far to discover the monuments of nineteenth-century municipal achievement that still grace the nation's cities, surviving as concrete rebuttals to Bryce's words. In 1979 the architecture critic for the *New York Times* declared Central Park and the Brooklyn Bridge as "the two greatest works of architecture in New York...each...a magnificent object in its own right; each...the result of a brilliant synthesis of art and engineering after which the world was never quite the same." Each was also a product of municipal enterprise, the creation of a city government said to be the worst in Christendom. Moreover, can one visit San Francisco's Golden Gate Park or enter McKim, Mead, and White's palatial Boston Public Library and pronounce these landmarks evidence of weakness or failure? Indeed, can those city fathers be deemed "unimaginative" who hired the great landscape architect Frederick Law Olmsted to design the first public park systems in human history? And were the vast nineteenth-century water and drainage schemes that still serve the cities the handiwork of bumbling incompetents unable to cope with the demands of expanding industrial metropolises? The aqueducts of Rome were among the glories of ancient civilization; the grander water systems of nineteenth-century New York City are often overlooked by those preoccupied with the more lurid aspects of city rule.

A bright side of municipal endeavor did, then, exist. American city governments could claim grand achievements, and as Arthur Schlesinger, Sr., was willing to admit in 1933, urban leaders won some creditable victories in the struggle for improved services. Certainly there were manifold shortcomings: Crime and poverty persisted; fires raged and pavements buckled; garbage and street rubbish sometimes seemed insurmountable problems. Yet no government has ever claimed total success in coping with the problems of society; to some degree all have failed to service their populations adequately. If government ever actually succeeded, political scientists would have to retool and apply themselves to more intractable problems, and political philosophers would have to turn to less contemplative pursuits. Those with a negative propensity can always find ample evidence of "bad government," and late-nineteenth-century critics such as Bryce, White, and Godkin displayed that propensity. In their writings the good side of the municipal structure was as visible as the dark side of the moon.

Thus, observers of the late-nineteenth-century American municipality have usually focused microscopic attention on its failures while overlooking its achievements. Scoundrels have won much greater coverage than conscientious officials. Volumes have appeared, for example, on that champion among municipal thieves, New York City's political boss William M. Tweed, but not one book exists on the life and work of a perhaps more significant figure in nineteenth-century city government, Ellis Chesbrough the engineer who served both Boston and Chicago and who transformed the public works of the latter city. Only recently has an admirable group of studies begun to explore the work of such municipal technicians who were vital to the formulation and implementation of public policy. But prior to the 1970s accounts of dualistic conflicts between political bosses and good-government reformers predominated, obscuring the complexities of municipal rule and the diversity of elements actually vying for power and participating in city government. And such traditional accounts accepted as axiomatic the inadequacy of the formal municipal structure. Critics have trumpeted its failures, while its triumphs have gone unheralded.

If one recognizes some of the challenges that municipal leaders faced during the period 1870 to 1900, the magnitude of their achievements becomes clear. The leaders of the late nineteenth century inherited an urban scene of great tumult and stress and an urban population of increasing diversity and diversion.... The melting pot was coming to a boil, and yet throughout the 1870s, 1880s, and 1890s, waves of newcomers continued to enter the country, including more and more representatives of the alien cultures of southern and eastern Europe. To many in 1870, social and ethnic diversity seemed to endanger the very foundation of order and security in the nation, and municipal leaders faced the need to maintain a truce between Protestants and Catholics, old stock and new, the native business elite and immigrant workers.

The rush of migrants from both Europe and rural America combined with a high birth rate to produce another source of municipal problems, a soaring urban population.... During the last thirty years of the century, the nation's chief cities absorbed thousands of acres of new territory to accommodate this booming population, and once-compact cities sprawled outward from the urban core. This expansion sprawl produced demands for the extension of services and the construction of municipal facilities. The newly annexed peripheral wards needed sewer lines and water mains; they required fire and police protection; and residents of outlying districts expected the city to provide paved streets and lighting. Municipal governments could not simply maintain their services at existing levels; instead, they had to guarantee the extension of those services to thousands of new urban dwellers.

Improved and expanded municipal services, however, required funding, and revenue therefore posed another challenge for city rulers.... Inflation in the 1860s and economic depression in the 1870s exacerbated the financial problems of the city, leading to heightened cries for retrenchment. And throughout the 1880s and 1890s city governments faced the difficult problem of meeting rising expectations for services while at the same time satisfying demands for moderate taxes and fiscal conservatism. This was perhaps the toughest task confronting the late-nineteenth-century municipality.

During the last three decades of the century, American city government did, however, meet these challenges of diversity, growth, and financing with remarkable success. By century's close, American city dwellers enjoyed, on the average, as high a standard of public services as any urban residents in the world. Problems persisted, and there were ample grounds for complaint. But in America's cities, the supply of water was the most abundant, the street lights were the most brilliant, the parks the grandest, the libraries the largest, and the public transportation the fastest of any place in the world. American city fathers rapidly adapted to advances in technology, and New York City, Chicago, and Boston were usually in the forefront of efforts to apply new inventions and engineering breakthroughs to municipal problems. Moreover, America's cities achieved this level of modern service while remaining solvent and financially sound. No major American municipality defaulted on its debts payments during the 1890s, and by the end of the century all of the leading municipalities were able to sell their bonds at premium and pay record-low interest. Any wise financier would have testified that the bonds of those purported strongholds of inefficiency and speculation, the municipal corporations, were far safer investments than were the bonds of those quintessential products of American business ingenuity: the railroad corporations.

Not only did the city governments serve their residents without suffering financial collapse, but municipal leaders also achieved an uneasy balance of the conflicting forces within the city, accommodating each through a distribution of authority. Though commentators often claimed that the "better elements" of the urban populace had surrendered municipal administration to the hands of "low-bred" Irish saloonkeepers, such observations were misleading. Similarly incorrect is the claim that the business and professional elite abandoned city government during the late nineteenth century to decentralized lower-class ward leaders. The patrician, the plutocrat, the plebeian, and the professional bureaucrat all had their place in late-nineteenth-century municipal government; each staked an informal but definite claim to a particular domain within the municipal structure.

Upper-middle-class business figures presided over the executive branch and the independent park, library, and sinking-fund commissions. Throughout the last decades of the nineteenth century the mayor's office was generally in the hands of solid businessmen or professionals who were native-born Protestants. The leading executive officers were persons of citywide reputation and prestige, and during the period 1870 to 1900 their formal authority was increasing. Meanwhile, the legislative branch—the board of aldermen or city council —became the stronghold of small neighborhood retailers, often of immigrant background, who won their aldermanic seats because of their neighborhood reputation as good fellows willing to gain favors for their constituents. In some cities men of metropolitan standing virtually abandoned the city council, and in every major city this body was the chief forum for lower-middle-class and working-class ward politicians.

At the same time, an emerging body of trained experts was also securing a barony of power within city government. Even before the effective application of formal civil service laws, mayors and commissioners deferred to the judgment and expertise of professional engineers, landscape architects, educators, physicians, and fire chiefs, and a number of such figures served decade after decade in municipal posts, despite political upheavals in the executive and legislative branches. By the close of the century these professional civil servants were securing a place of permanent authority in city government. Their loyalty was not to downtown business interests nor to ward or ethnic particularism, but to their profession and their department. And they were gradually transforming those departments into strongholds of expertise.

The municipal professional, the downtown business leader, and the neighborhood shopkeeper and small-time politico each had differing concepts of city government and differing policy priorities. They thus represented potentially conflicting interests that could serve to divide the municipal polity and render it impotent. Yet, during the period 1870 to 1900, these elements remained in a state of peaceful, if contemptuous, coexistence. Hostilities broke out, especially if any element felt the boundaries of its domain were violated. But city governments could operate effectively if the truce between these elements was respected; in other words, if ward business remained the primary concern of ward alderman, citywide policy was in the hands of the business elite, and technical questions were decided by experts relatively undisturbed by party politics. This was the informal détente that was gradually developing amid the conflict and complaints.

Such extralegal participants as political parties and civic leagues also exerted their influence over municipal government, attempting to tip the uneasy balance of forces in their direction. The political party organization with its ward-based neighborhood bosses was one lever that the immigrants and less affluent could pull to affect the course of government. Civic organizations and reform leagues, in contrast, bolstered the so-called better element in government, the respected businessmen who usually dominated the leading executive offices and the independent commissions. Emerging professional groups such as engineering clubs and medical societies often lent their support to the rising ambitions and growing authority of the expert bureaucracy and permanent civil servants. And special-interest lobbyists like the fire insurance underwriters also urged professionalism in such municipal services as the fire department. Municipal government was no simple dualistic struggle between a citywide party boss with a diamond shirt stud and malodorous cigar and a good-government reformer with a Harvard degree and kid gloves. Various forces were pushing and pulling the municipal corporations, demanding a response to petitions and seeking a larger voice in the chambers of city government.

State legislatures provided the structural flexibility to respond to these demands. The state legislatures enjoyed the sovereign authority to bestow municipal powers and to determine the municipal structure, but when considering local measures, state lawmakers generally deferred to the judgment of the legislative delegation from the affected locality. If the local delegation favored a bill solely affecting its constituents, the legislature usually ratified the bill without opposition or debate. This rule of deference to the locality no longer applied, however, if the bill became a partisan issue, as it occasionally did. But in most cases authorization for new powers or for structural reforms depended on the city's representatives in the state legislature, and each session the state assemblies and senates rubber-stamped hundreds of local bills. Thus, indulgent legislators provided the vital elasticity that allowed urban governments to expand readily to meet new challenges and assume new responsibilities....

Even so, this process of perpetual adjustment resulted in a mechanism that succeeded in performing the job of city government. Municipal leaders adapted to the need for experts trained in the new technologies and hired such technicians. Moreover, downtown businessmen and ward politicos, the native-born and the immigrants, Protestants and Catholics, loosened the lid on the melting pot and reduced the boiling hostility of the midcentury to a simmer. The cities provided services; they backed off from the brink of bankruptcy; and the municipal structure guaranteed a voice to the various elements of society in both immigrant wards and elite downtown clubs.

Why, then, all the complaints? Why did so many critics of the 1880s and 1890s indulge in a rhetoric of failure, focusing on municipal shortcomings to the neglect of municipal successes? Why was municipal government so much abused? The answer lies in a fundamental irony: The late-nineteenth-century municipal structure accommodated everyone but satisfied no one. It was a system of compromise among parties discontented with compromise. It was a marriage of convenience, with the spouses providing a reasonably comfortable home for America's urban inhabitants. But it was not a happy home. The parties to the nuptials tolerated one another because they had to. Nevertheless, the businessman-mayors and plutocrat park commissioners disliked their dependence on ward politicians, whom they frequently regarded as petty grafters, and they frowned upon the power of the immigrant voters. Likewise, the emerging corps of civil servants was irked by interference from laypersons of both high and law status. And the plebeian party boss opposed efforts to extend the realm of the civil servants who had performed no partisan duties and thus merited no power. None liked their interdependence with persons they felt to be unworthy, incompetent, or hostile.

Enhancing this dissatisfaction was the cultural absolutism of the Victorian era. The late nineteenth century was an age when the business elite could refer to itself as the "best element" of society and take for granted its "God-given" superiority. It was an age when professional engineers, landscape architects, public health experts, librarians, educators, and fire fighters were first becoming aware of themselves as professionals, and with the zeal of converts they defended their newly exalted state of grace. It was also an age when most Protestants viewed Catholics as papal pawns and devotees of Italian idolatry, while most Catholics believed Protestants were little better than heathens and doomed to a quick trip to hell with no stops in purgatory. The late nineteenth century was not an age of cultural relativism but one of cultural absolutes, an age when people still definitely knew right from wrong, the correct from the erroneous. The American municipality, however, was a heterogeneous polyarchy, a network of accommodation and compromise in an era when accommodation and compromise smacked of unmanly dishonor and unprincipled pragmatism. Municipal government of the 1870s, 1880s, and 1890s rested on a system of broker politics, of bargaining and dealing. . . .

Late-nineteenth-century urban government was a failure not of structure but of image. The system proved reasonably successful in providing services, but there was no prevailing ideology to validate its operation. In fact, the beliefs of the various participants were at odds with the structure of rule that governed them. The respectable elements believed in sobriety and government by persons of character. But the system of accommodation permitted whiskey taps to flow on the Sabbath for the Irish and for Germans, just as it allowed men in shiny suits with questionable reputations to occupy seats on the city council and in the municipal party conventions. The ward-based party devotees accepted the notions of Jacksonian democracy and believed quite literally in the maxim To the victor belong the spoils. But by the 1890s they faced a growing corps of civil servants more devoted to their profession than to any party. Although new professional bureaucrats preached a gospel of expertise, they still had to compromise with party-worshiping hacks and the supposedly diabolical forces of politics. Likewise, special-interest lobbyists such as the fire insurance underwriters were forced to cajole or coerce political leaders whom they deemed ignorant and unworthy of public office. Each of these groups worked together, but only from necessity and not because they believed in such a compromise of honor. There was no ideology of heterogeneous polyarchy, no system of beliefs to bolster the existing government structure. Thus late-nineteenth-century city government survived without moral support, and to many urban dwellers it seemed a bargain with the devil.

Twentieth-century historians also had reasons for focusing on urban failure rather than urban success. Some chroniclers in the early decades accepted rhetoric as reality and simply repeated the condemnations of critics such as Bryce, White, and Godkin. By the midcentury greater skepticism prevailed, but so did serious ills. In fact, the urban crisis of the 1960s provided the impetus for a great upsurge of interest in the history of the city, inspiring a search for the historical roots of urban breakdown and collapse. Urban problems were the scholars' preoccupation. Not until the much-ballyhooed "back-to-the-city" movement of the 1970s did the city become less an object of pity or contempt and more a treasured relic. By the late 1970s a new rhetoric was developing, in which sidewalks and streets assumed a nostalgic significance formerly reserved to babbling brooks and bucolic pastures.

The 1980s, then, seem an appropriate time to reevaluate the much-maligned municipality of the late nineteenth century. Back-to-the-city euphoria, however, should not distort one's judgment of the past. Instead, it is time to understand the system of city government from 1870 to 1900 complete with blemishes and beauty marks. One should not quickly dismiss the formal mechanisms of municipal rule as inadequate and outdated, requiring the unifying grasp of party bosses. Nor should one mindlessly laud municipal rule as a triumph of urban democracy. A serious appreciation of the municipal structure is necessary.

POSTSCRIPT

Was City Government in Late-Nineteenth-Century America a "Conspicuous Failure"?

The opposing viewpoints expressed by Griffith and Teaford represent a long-standing scholarly debate about the consequences of boss politics in the United States. James Bryce, *The American Commonwealth*, 2 vols. (Macmillan, 1888); Moisei Ostrogorski, *Democracy and the Organization of Political Parties* (1902; Anchor Books, 1964); and Lincoln Steffens, *The Shame of the Cities* (McClure, Phillips, 1904), present a litany of misdeeds associated with those who controlled municipal government. Political bosses, these authors charge, were guilty of malfeasance in office and all forms of graft and corruption.

Efforts to rehabilitate the sullied reputations of the machine politicians can be dated to the comments of one of Boss Tweed's henchmen, George Washington Plunkitt, a New York City ward heeler whose turn-of-the-century observations included a subtle distinction between "honest" and "dishonest" graft. A more scholarly effort was presented by Robert K. Merton, a political scientist who identified numerous "latent functions" of the political machine. According to Merton, city bosses created effective political organizations that humanized the dispensation of assistance, offered valuable political privileges for businessmen, and created alternative routes of social mobility for citizens, many of them immigrants, who typically were excluded from conventional means of personal advancement.

There are several excellent urban history texts that devote space to the development of municipal government in the late nineteenth century. Among these are David R. Goldfield and Blaine A. Brownell, *Urban America: From Downtown to No Town* (Houghton Mifflin, 1979); Howard P. Chudacoff and Judith E. Smith, *The Evolution of American Urban Society*, 3rd ed. (Prentice Hall, 1981); and Charles N. Glaab and A. Theodore Brown, *A History of Urban America*, 3rd ed. (Macmillan, 1983). Various developments in the industrial period are discussed in Blake McKelvey, *The Urbanization of America, 1860–1915* (Rutgers University Press, 1963) and Raymond A. Mohl, *The New City: Urban America in the Industrial Age, 1860-1920* (Harlan Davidson, 1985). Boss politics is analyzed in William L. Riordon, *Plunkitt of Tammany Hall* (E. P. Dutton, 1963); Robert K. Merton, *Social Theory and Social Structure* (Free Press, 1957); and John M. Allswang, *Bosses, Machines, and Urban Voters: An American Symbiosis* (Kennikat Press, 1977). The most famous urban boss is analyzed in Alexander B. Callow, Jr., *The Tweed Ring* (Oxford University Press, 1966) and Leo Hershkowitz, *Tweed's New York: Another Look* (Anchor Press, 1977). Scott Greer, ed., *Ethnics, Machines, and the American Future* (Harvard University Press, 1981) and Bruce M. Stave and Sondra Astor Stave, eds., *Urban Bosses, Machines, and Progressive Reformers,* 2d ed. (D. C. Heath, 1984) are excellent collections of essays on urban political machinery. Significant contributions to urban historiography are Sam Bass Warner, Jr., *Streetcar Suburbs: The Process of Growth in Boston, 1870–1900* (Harvard University Press, 1962); Stephan Thernstrom, *Poverty and Progress: Social Mobility in the Nineteenth-Century City* (Harvard University Press, 1964); Gunther Barth, *City People: The Rise of Modern City Culture in Nineteenth-Century America* (Oxford University Press, 1980); and Martin V. Melosi, *Garbage in the Cities: Refuse, Reform, and the Environment, 1880–1980* (Texas A & M University Press, 1982).

On the Internet ...

The Spanish-American War

This site from the Hispanic Division of the Library of Congress details events leading up to and occurring during the Spanish-American War. Included are links to pages on many of the key players, with a particular emphasis on Cuban patriots.

http://lcweb.loc.gov/rr/hispanic/1898/trask.html

The Roaring 20's and the Great Depression

This is an extensive anthology of Web links to sites on the Roaring 20s and the Great Depression.

http://www.snowcrest.net/jmike/20sdep.html

Sallie Bingham Center for Women's History and Culture

The Sallie Bingham Center for Women's History and Culture is an integral part of Duke University's Special Collections Library, which houses a broad range of rare and unique primary source material. This page offers links to online collections, archives, and bibliographies on women's history.

http://odyssey.lib.duke.edu/women/

World War II Resources

This site links to primary source materials on the Web related to World War II, including original documents regarding all aspects of the war. From here you can see documents on Nazi-Soviet relations from the archives of the German Foreign Office, speeches of Franklin D. Roosevelt on foreign policy, and much more.

http://metalab.unc.edu/pha/

PART 2

The Response to Industrialism: Reform and War

*T*he maturing of the industrial system, a major economic depression, agrarian unrest, and labor violence all came to a head in 1898 with the Spanish-American war. The victory gave overseas territorial possessions to the United States and served notice to the world that the United States was a "great power." At the end of the nineteenth century, the African American population began fighting for civil rights, political power, and integration into society. Spokespeople for the blacks began to emerge, but their often unclear agendas frequently touched off controversy among both black people and white people.

The 1920s are often portrayed as a hedonistic interlude for everyone between the Progressive and New Deal reform eras. Organizations like the Ku Klux Klan revealed a number of tensions between the values of the nation's rural past and the new social and moral values of modern America. There is also controversy over whether the women's movement in those years lost momentum once the vote was achieved. The onset of a more activist federal government accelerated with the Great Depression. With more than one-quarter of the workforce unemployed, Franklin D. Roosevelt was elected on a promise to give Americans a "New Deal." World War II short-circuited these plans and led to the development of a cold war between the United States and the Soviet Union.

- Did Yellow Journalism Cause the Spanish-American War?

- Did Racial Segregation Improve the Status of African Americans?

- Was the Ku Klux Klan of the 1920s an Extremist Movement?

- Did the Women's Movement Die in the 1920s?

- Was Information About the Attack on Pearl Harbor Deliberately Withheld From the American Commanders?

ISSUE 5

Did Yellow Journalism Cause the Spanish-American War?

YES: W. A. Swanberg, from *Citizen Hearst: A Biography of William Randolph Hearst* (Charles Scribner's Sons, 1961)

NO: David Nasaw, from *The Chief: The Life of William Randolph Hearst* (Houghton Mifflin, 2000)

ISSUE SUMMARY

YES: Journalist W. A. Swanberg argues that newspaper mogul William Randolph Hearst used the sensational and exploitative stories in his widely circulated *New York Journal* to stir up public opinion and to force President William McKinley to wage a war against Spain to free Cuba.

NO: Historian David Nasaw maintains that even if Hearst had not gone into publishing, the United States would have entered the war for political, economic, and security reasons.

Although Spanish rule over Cuba dated from 1511, most American presidents from the 1840s through the 1890s assumed that Cuba's strategic location, 90 miles from Florida, made it inevitable that the island would eventually come under some form of American control. American politicians were convinced that Spain was a declining power with limited influence in the Americas. However, repeated attempts to buy the island from Spain failed. Meanwhile, Cuban insurgents unsuccessfully rebelled against the Spanish government from 1868 until 1878. In 1894, in the midst of a depression, the U.S. Congress imposed a tariff on Cuban sugar, which had been entering the United States duty-free. An economic depression also hit the island and encouraged another rebellion against Spanish rule. The Spanish government retaliated by imposing a policy of "reconcentration." Approximately 300,000 Cubans were rounded up into fortified towns and camps to separate the insurgents from their supporters. As the atrocities were played up by sensationalist American newspapers, a new Spanish government came to power in Madrid that modified "reconcentration" and promised Cuba some autonomy.

Three events in the first few months of 1898 sabotaged a peaceful resolution of the Cuban crisis. On February 9 the *New York Journal* published a stolen private letter from Enrique Dupuy de Lome, the Spanish minister in Washington, that cast doubt on the sincerity with which the Spanish government was pursuing a policy of autonomy for Cuba. Even worse, de Lome stated, "McKinley is weak and a bidder for the admiration of the crowd, besides being a would be politician who tries to leave a door open behind himself while keeping on good terms with the jingos of his party."

The second event stirred up public opinion even more than the de Lome letter. Early in January antireform, pro-Spanish loyalists rioted in Havana. In response, President William McKinley ordered the battleship U.S.S. *Maine* to Havana's harbor to protect the lives of American citizens. On February 15 the *Maine* blew up, killing 260 American service personnel. Two separate investigations were made. The Spanish government said that the explosion was caused by internal failures, while the U.S. panel reported that a mine destroyed the *Maine*.

The third factor that pushed McKinley in the direction of a confrontation with Spain were the reports—official and unofficial—that the president received from public officials. In June 1897 William J. Calhoun, a political friend of the president, reported that the principal cause of the war "can be found in the economic conditions that have prevailed there for many years past." Calhoun's picture of the countryside outside of the military posts was particularly gloomy. Events moved rapidly in spring 1898. There were failed attempts at negotiating an end to "reconcentration," establishing an armistice in the Spanish-Cuban war, and setting up a truly autonomous government with a Cuban relationship to Spain similar to that of Canada's to Great Britain.

Why did President McKinley intervene in Cuba? In his address to Congress on April 11, 1898, the president listed four reasons: (1) "To put an end to the barbarities, bloodshed, starvation, and miseries now existing there"; (2) "to afford our citizens in Cuba protection and indemnity for life and property"; (3) to avoid "very serious injury to the commerce, trade, and business of our people, and by the wanton destruction of property and devastation of the island"; and (4) "the present condition of affairs in Cuba is a constant menace to our peace ... where our traditional vessels are liable to seizure and are seized at our very door by war ships of a foreign nation, the expenditures of filibustering and the irritating questions and entanglements thus arising."

Implied in the president's message was the goal of independence for Cuba. Congress supported McKinley's request for intervention with a joint resolution that contained one exception: Senator Henry M. Teller of Colorado added an amendment that forbade the United States from annexing Cuba.

Historians continue to debate the reasons for the war. In the following selection, W. A. Swanberg argues that the war was started by propaganda created by the new yellow journalism of newspaper mogul William Randolph Hearst. In the second selection, David Nasaw contends that even if Hearst had not gone into publishing, political, economic and security reasons would have brought the United States into a war against Spain.

Citizen Hearst

The Cuban Joan of Arc

The Power of the Press

The two loudest warmongers in the United States, [William Randolph] Hearst and [Joseph] Pulitzer, were both six feet two inches tall, both millionaires who spent money royally while they espoused the causes of the masses. Both were singularly shy. The similarity ended there. Hearst was in a perfect health, placid and courteous. Pulitzer was blind, a nervous wreck who could fly into profane rages. Hearst was at his office daily, exercising personal control. Pulitzer was rarely at his proud, gold-domed skyscraper. He was only occasionally at his New York home on East Fifty-fifth Street, which was equipped with soundproof rooms to shield his quaking nerves. The rest of the time he was either at one of his four other mansions in Maine, New Jersey, Georgia and France, or aboard his palatial ocean-going yacht *Liberty,* keeping in touch with his editors by telegram or cable. Hearst believed in fighting Spain almost from the start of the Cuban trouble. Pulitzer, at first opposed to United States involvement, came around reluctantly for war, as he later candidly admitted, because it meant circulation.

It is safe to say that had not Pulitzer been locked in a bitter circulation struggle with Hearst, and had he not witnessed the added circulation Hearst's frenetic treatment of the Cuban news brought him, Pulitzer and his mighty *World* would have remained on the side of peace. Thus Hearst, in addition to his own potent newspapers, was responsible for dragging the morning and evening *World,* with the largest circulation in the nation, into the pro-war camp.

These two men addressed literally millions of Americans. In 1897, the circulation of Pulitzer's two papers was more than 800,000 daily. Hearst's morning and evening *Journal* were hardly 100,000 behind, and his San Francisco *Examiner* had 80,000. They had on their pro-war side the influential New York *Sun,* with about 150,000. Through the Associated Press and other news-service affiliations, the *Journal, World* and *Sun* dispatches were reprinted in many other important papers across the nation.

Against them they had the strongly anti-war *Herald* (100,000), the *Evening Post* (25,000), the conservative *Tribune* (75,000) and the high-priced *Times* (three cents, under 25,000 circulation). The remaining several New York papers were even smaller, had no funds for coverage of the Cuban rebellion, and exercised small weight.

The total circulation of New York's pro-war newspapers was about 1,560,000, against the anti-war total of 225,000.

However, all of these papers were of much more than local moment. The prestige of the large New York dailies on either side was a strong and determining influence on hundreds of fresh-water editors throughout the country who knew little of foreign affairs and traditionally had looked to the New York journals for guidance since the days of [Horace] Greeley, [James Gordon] Bennett and [Henry Jarvis] Raymond. Since the newspapers were the greatest mass medium then existing, their influence in shaping public opinion would be decisive. And since the New York newspapers in one way or another swayed most of the rest, it could be said that—given a situation where war or peace hung in almost equal balance—the clacking Underwoods and Remingtons in the grubby warrens around Printing House Square would decide whether it would be the olive branch or the sword.

No one could discount the national influence of the anti-war *Herald, Post, Tribune* and *Times.* Yet the plain fact was that their relatively quiet, sensible columns were dull newswise. They were like reasonable men speaking in normal tones. Naturally they were outshouted by the screams of the *Journal* and *World.* The majority of the public found it more exciting to read about the murder of Cuban babies and the rape of Cuban women by the Spaniards than to read conscientious accounts of complicated political problems and injustices on both sides. The hero-villain concept of the war was simple, easy to grasp and satisfying. In addition to having the loudest voices and the most money, Hearst and Pulitzer had the best writers and illustrators and had many more dispatch boats, jeweled swords and correspondents in Key West and Cuba than all the other papers combined. Hearst alone sent a total of at least thirty-five writers and artists to "cover the war" at various times. . . .

The Fate of the *Maine*

Hail Thee City Born Today!

. . . Like Caesar and Napoleon, Hearst enjoyed power. He derived pleasure from controlling masses of people, manipulating them to bring about events of national or international importance. Unlike Caesar and Napoleon, the bashful Hearst did his manipulating from behind the scenes with the aid of cylinder presses and tons of newsprint. By now, most other newspaper proprietors in New York regarded him with aversion as a man who would do anything for sensation, devoid of honesty or principle, a Polyphemus of propaganda who ate his enemies and kept his Cyclops eye on circulation. They misjudged the man by his methods. An incurable romantic, swayed by gusts of sentiment, Hearst was sincerely devoted to the Cuban cause and at the same time felt that American interests demanded the expulsion of Spain from the hemisphere. But he had no scruples against linking these defensible aims with a ruthless and vulgar drive for circulation, so that in the view of people of taste he had no unselfish impulses at all.

Considerations of taste in journalism did not disturb him. He had long since decided that the great majority of people, the masses, had no time or training for such a luxury as taste and could be reached and molded most effectively by the noise, sensation and repetition which he liked himself. Since these are the ingredients of modern mass advertising, Hearst deserves some dubious recognition as a pioneer.

His megalomania had grown. In San Francisco, his campaigns had been largely local, even his feud with the S.P. being inspired by local grievances. In New York he had started with local sensations—murders, public utility franchises, soup kitchens, bicycle carnivals. Now he was expanding his zone of operations into the nation and the world. His enemies were McKinley, Hanna, Weyler, Spain, France. The liberation of Miss Cisneros had been so successful that Hearst now had Karl Decker mapping an expedition to Devil's Island to free the wronged Captain Dreyfus and humiliate France as Spain had been humiliated.

In Spain, the American newspaper outcry, the continuation of the Cuban rebellion and the uprising in the Philippines caused the fall of the government and the formation of a new cabinet. Spain, with only some 18,000,000 people, grievously in debt, naturally feared the rich United States with its 75,000,000. In its anxiety to retain Cuba, its most treasured possession, it pocketed American insults and took steps to mollify the Yankees as well as the Cuban rebels. The new government under Práxedes Mateo Sagasta almost entirely accepted the United States position on Cuba. It promised the Cubans self-government under Spain. It dismissed General Weyler, who left Havana to the accompaniment of a valedictory in Hearst's *Journal* calling him "the monster of the century" who should be hanged for his "innumerable murders." It replaced him with General Ramón Blanco y Erenas, a kindly man not yet known as a murderer. It would be General Blanco's job to install the autonomous Cuban government and restore order.

But Hearst demanded independence for Cuba, not mere autonomy. He wrote a letter dated December 1, 1897, addressed to the unrecognized president of an unrecognized republic.

His Excellency Bartolomé Masso,

President of the Republic of Cuba:

Sir:—Will you kindly state through the New York *Journal,* acting for the people of the United States, the position of the Cuban Government on the offer of autonomy for the island by the Government of Spain?. . . .

—Yours truly, W. R. Hearst.

Although some would dispute Hearst's right to act for "the people of the United States," Señor Masso did not. Apparently the letter was smuggled through to Masso, who eventually replied from Camaguey in part:

> ... We hold ourselves an independent nation, unrecognized though we may be by the civilized world. Autonomy is not for one moment considered by us. We absolutely reject it.
>
> We have no faith left in Spain or her promises....

Along with Hearst, the insurgents with one voice rejected autonomy. Estrada Palma branded the conciliatory measures as ruses to defeat the rebellion by typical Spanish treachery. Rebel army leaders warned that all Cubans who cooperated with the new Spanish schemes would be considered "traitors to the republic," meaning that they would be shot on sight. The militarily feeble rebels could not have taken this intransigent stand had they not seen how American public opinion had already forced the Spaniards to back down. Counting on further American support to drive the Spaniards out entirely, they continued their pillaging of plantations and villages.

The *Journal* agreed that the Cubans "would be fools if they trust Spanish promises," and boasted that "Spain fears the *Journal* and Karl Decker." Not surprisingly, attempts were made to dynamite the *Journal*'s Havana office. But President McKinley, impressed by the conciliatory efforts of the Sagasta government, was disposed to give it every opportunity for success. When Spain agreed to permit American contributions of food and clothing to be distributed to destitute Cubans by the Red Cross, and the relief work got under way, the outlook for peace on the troubled island seemed improved at last....

In Cuba, Consul General Lee kept hearing rumors of an "anti-American plot" in Matanzas. Although this never materialized, he urged protection for American nationals and property in Cuba. It was on Lee's recommendation that the twenty-four-gun battleship *Maine* was moved first to Key West, then to Havana, as a "friendly act of courtesy" to Spain. Spain, not deceived by the polite words, readied its armored cruiser *Vizcaya* to pay a "friendly visit" to New York.

The *Maine*, commanded by solemn, bespectacled Captain Charles D. Sigsbee, passed under the guns of Morro Castle and anchored in Havana harbor on January 25, 1898. The Spanish commander sent a case of fine sherry to Sigsbee and his officers, who later went ashore to dine with General Lee and enjoy a bullfight.

Hearst had hardly been aware of the *Maine* when she was launched in San Francisco in 1890, but now she loomed large. "OUR FLAG IN HAVANA AT LAST," headlined the *Journal,* urging that American vessels occupy all Cuban ports and demand the withdrawal of the Spanish troops, i.e., to make war. Although Captain Sigsbee and his men were enjoying a quiet sojourn in Havana, the *Journal* saw so many war clouds there that it momentarily forgot its *bête noire,* the Spanish minister in Washington, Dupuy de Lome. De Lome, who for three years had conducted himself with dignity in the capital despite painful provocation, chose this moment to commit an error. He wrote a letter critical of President McKinley to a friend in Havana, José Canalejas. A rebel sympathizer, Gustavo Escoto, who worked in Canalejas' office, read the letter, saw its propaganda possibilities, and stole it, boarding the next boat for New York.

The letter brought joy to Estrada Palma and the Peanut Club. Palma was so grateful to the *Journal* for its efforts for Cuba that he translated the letter and took it in person to the *Journal* office, handing it in triumph to Sam Chamberlain. In commenting on McKinley's pacific message to Congress, De Lome wrote:

> The message has undeceived the insurgents, who expected something else, and has paralyzed the action of Congress, but I consider it bad.... Besides the natural and inevitable coarseness with which he [McKinley] repeats all that the press and public opinion of Spain have said of Weyler, it shows once more what McKinley is: weak and catering to the rabble and, besides, a low politician who desires to leave the door open to himself and to stand well with the jingoes of his party....

Although this was a private letter, stolen, and although the *Journal* had leveled far worse insults of its own about McKinley multiplied by some 800,000 circulation, it flew into a front-page rage at De Lome that lasted for five days. The letter was too provocative for the Peanut Club to give it exclusively to the *Journal*. It gave it to all the newspapers, handing the *Journal* a beat, however, in giving it exclusive right to publish a facsimile. The *Journal* used *all of its front page* to publicize the letter, headlining it "THE WORST INSULT TO THE UNITED STATES IN ITS HISTORY" and demanding the minister's instant dismissal. It dredged up a book which De Lome had published twenty-two years earlier, stressing critical remarks he had made about American women. It perpetrated an enormity in doggerel:

> Dupuy de Lome, Dupuy de Lome, what's this I hear of you?
> Have you been throwing mud again, is what they're saying true?
> Get out, I say, get out before I start to fight.
> Just pack your few possessions and take a boat for home.
> I would not like my boot to use but—oh—get out, De Lome.

It ran a huge Davenport cartoon showing an angry Uncle Sam thumbing away a quaking De Lome, with a one-word caption, "Git." "Now let us have action immediate and decisive," it said. "The flag of Cuba Libre ought to float over Morro Castle within a week." All this went out over the Associated Press.

In Washington, De Lome instantly cabled his resignation to Madrid. This took the sting out of the State Department's demand for his dismissal, for he was already packing. The Spanish government promptly disavowed his letter and apologized for it. In a few days, United States officials realized that what the *Journal* and a few other New York newspapers chose to construe as a gross affront was nothing more than a comic diplomatic blunder. In Cuba, the new autonomous government was beginning to function. The outlook was promising. The De Lome incident would have been forgotten had it not been followed almost immediately by an event of violence and tragedy that still poses one of history's impenetrable mysteries.

The *Maine* had now been in Havana for three weeks. Its usefulness there was questionable, since there were no anti-American demonstrations. Navy Secretary John D. Long had contemplated recalling it early in February, only to desist because of Consul General Lee's advice that it stay. On the sultry night of February 15, as the clear bugle notes of "Taps" pealed across the quiet harbor, Captain Sigsbee was in his cabin writing a letter in some embarrassment to his wife. He explained that in a uniform pocket he had discovered a letter to her from an old friend which he had forgotten for ten months. He had just sealed the envelope at 9:40 when the *Maine* blew up all around him.

Though shaken, Sigsbee was unhurt. The vessel's lights blacked out. Screams came from wounded and dying men. Fire broke out forward, causing small-caliber ammunition to start popping like firecrackers. Survivors jumped into the water as the ship began settling slowly into the mud. Dazed bluejackets put out a boat to pick up the swimmers. Other boats came from the Spanish cruiser *Alfonso XII* and an American vessel nearby. Spaniards and Americans joined gallantly in the dangerous rescue work as ammunition continued to explode. At his palace, Spain's General Blanco burst into tears at the news and sent officers to express regret and organize assistance. Of the *Maine*'s 350 officers and men, 260 died in the catastrophe. Sigsbee dispatched a telegram to "Secnav" in Washington, describing it and adding:

> Public opinion should be suspended until further report.... Many Spanish officers including representatives of General Blanco now with me to express sympathy.

Hearst had left the *Journal* earlier than usual that evening, probably to go to the theater. He returned to his apartment in the Worth House quite late without stopping at his office. He found his man Thompson waiting for him.

"There's a telephone from the office," Thompson said. "They say it's important news."

Hearst telephoned the *Journal*. "Hello," he said. "What is the important news?"

"The battleship *Maine* has been blown up in Havana Harbor," the editor replied.

"Good heavens, what have you done with the story?"

"We have put it on the first page, of course."

"Have you put anything else on the front page?"

"Only the other big news," said the editor.

"There is not any other big news," Hearst said. "Please spread the story all over the page. This means war."

There Is No Other News

Hearst's coverage of the *Maine* disaster still stands as the orgasmic acme of ruthless, truthless newspaper jingoism. As always, when he wanted anything he wanted it with passionate intensity. The *Maine* represented the fulfillment not of one want but two—war with Spain and more circulation to beat Pulitzer.

He fought for these ends with such abandonment of honesty and incitement of hatred that the stigma of it never quite left him even though he still had fifty-three years to live.

Intelligent Americans realized the preposterousness of the idea that Spain had blown up the *Maine*. Proud Spain had swallowed insult to avoid a war she knew she would lose. Her forbearance had borne fruit until the explosion in Havana caused journalistic insanity in New York. The disaster was the worst blow Spain could have suffered. The *Maine* might have been wrecked by an accidental explosion of her own magazines. If she was sunk by plotters, it was most reasonable to suspect those who stood to gain from the crime—the Cuban rebels, whose cause was flagging and would be lost unless the United States could be dragged into the struggle. There was one other possibility: that a group of Spaniards or Cuban loyalists, working off their hatred unknown to the Spanish government, were responsible.

Even the *Journal* admitted disbelief that Spain had officially ordered the explosion. But this was tucked away in small type and later disavowed. The big type, the headlines, the diagrams, the cartoons, the editorials, laid the blame inferentially or flatly on Spain. For a week afterward, the *Journal* devoted a daily average of eight and one-half pages to the *Maine* and war. In the face of Sigsbee's wise suggestion that "public opinion be suspended," the *Journal* lashed public opinion day after day.

Some idea of the *Journal's* enormities, though an inadequate one, is given by a day-by-day recapitulation of its headlines and stories.

February 16: "CRUISER MAINE BLOWN UP IN HAVANA HARBOR." This was simple truth, written before the propaganda machine got into motion. It was the last truthful front-page headline for almost two weeks.

February 17: "THE WARSHIP MAINE WAS SPLIT IN TWO BY AN ENEMY'S SECRET INFERNAL MACHINE." The cause, of course, was unknown. This issue had a seven-column drawing of the ship anchored over mines, and a diagram showing wires leading from the mines to a Spanish fortress on shore—a flight of fancy which many readers doubtless took as fact. The hatred of Spaniards for Americans was mentioned. The caption read, "If this [plot] can be proven, the brutal nature of the Spaniards will be shown in that they waited to spring the mine until after all men had retired for the night." The *Journal* said, "Captain Sigsbee Practically Declares that His Ship was Blown Up by a Mine or Torpedo." Sigsbee said no such thing. He later wrote, "A Spanish officer of high rank ... showed me a New York paper of February 17 in which was pictured the *Maine* anchored over a mine. On another page was a plan showing wires leading from the *Maine* to shore. The officer asked me what I thought of that. It was explained that we had no censorship in the United States. . . . Apparently the Spanish officer could not grasp the idea."

February 18: "THE WHOLE COUNTRY THRILLS WITH THE WAR FEVER." This came at a time when Spanish and Cuban military, civil and ecclesiastical leaders were giving the victims a solemn state funeral in Havana, with every mark of respect, dedicating the plots used at Colon Cemetery to the United States in perpetuity. On this day, for the first time, the combined circulation of the morning and evening *Journal* passed a million.

February 20 (over a drawing:) "HOW THE MAINE ACTUALLY LOOKS AS IT LIES, WRECKED BY SPANISH TREACHERY, IN HAVANA BAY."

February 21: "HAVANA POPULACE INSULTS THE MEMORY OF THE MAINE VICTIMS." This was over a story alleging that Spanish officers had been overheard to boast that any other American ship visiting Havana would "follow the *Maine.*"

February 23: "THE MAINE WAS DESTROYED BY TREACHERY."

Although the *Journal* knew all along who sank the ship, it offered $50,000 reward for the solution of the mystery. It also began a drive for a memorial to be erected to those lost in the explosion, Hearst donating the first $1000. It began as usual by soliciting famous men whose participation could be exploited, among them ex-President Cleveland. Cleveland won some measure of immortality by replying, "I decline to allow my sorrow for those who died on the *Maine* to be perverted to an advertising scheme for the New York *Journal.*" Other "big names" were less percipient, General Nelson Miles, Levi Morton, Chauncey Depew and O. H. P. Belmont being among the many who lent their prestige to the drive.

On February 18, at this most inopportune of times, the Spanish cruiser *Vizcaya* arrived in New York harbor from Cartagena on her "courtesy call." Her commander, Captain Antonio Eulate, shocked when informed of the *Maine* tragedy, ordered his colors half-masted and said he would take no part in any festivities planned in his honor. In view of the public hysteria, the police and naval authorities took strenuous measures to protect the *Vizcaya,* surrounding her with a cordon of patrol boats. The *World,* almost as frenetic in its Hispanophobia as the *Journal,* warned that the *Vizcaya* might have treacherous intentions, saying, "While lying off the Battery, her shells will explode on the Harlem River and in the suburbs of Brooklyn." However, the *Vizcaya* did not fire a shot.

The Spanish authorities, incensed by the *Journal*'s warmongering, retaliated. *Journal* men were forbidden to board the *Vizcaya.* More important, the *Journal* was denied further use of the cables from Havana. It took cognizance of this with an announcement headed, "SPANISH COURTESIES TO AN AMERICAN NEWSPAPER," and boxed on the front page with a flowing American flag. It read:

> The *Journal* takes great pride in announcing that on account of its too decided Americanism and its work for the patriots of Cuba this newspaper and its reporters have been forbidden entrance on board the Spanish warship *Vizcaya;* its dispatches are refused transmission over the Government cables from Havana.
>
> These Spanish acts, of course, do not prevent the *Journal* from getting all the news.... The *Journal* is flattered by these delicate attentions from Spain.... It expects to merit still more attention when the United States decides to end Spanish misrule and horrors in America.

The *Journal* also presented its readers with a newly-devised "Game of War With Spain," to be played by four persons with cards. Two contestants would portray the crew of the United States battleship *Texas,* doing their best to "sink" the other two, who manned the *Vizcaya.*

Hearst had rounded up a carefully-selected group of jingoistic legislators who were not averse to a free trip to Cuba. Senators Hernando Money of Mississippi, John W. Thurston of Nebraska and J. H. Gallinger of New Hampshire, and Representatives William Alden Smith of Michigan and Amos Cummings of New York, embarked from Fort Monroe on the Hearst yacht *Anita* as "*Journal* Commissioners" to make a survey of conditions on the island and to write reports for the *Journal,* their expenses being paid by Hearst. Representatives Smith and Cummings were members of the House Foreign Affairs and Naval Affairs committees respectively. The *Journal* meanwhile appealed to its readers to write their Congressmen, and said it had so far relayed 15,000 such letters demanding war.

The *Journal* raged at Senator Mark Hanna for deprecating the war talk. It referred to him frequently as "President Hanna," to indicate how completely McKinley was his puppet. The cowardly peace policy of the administration was dictated by a base desire for profits in Wall Street, which could be depressed by war. "President Hanna... announced that there will be no war," said the *Journal.* " ... This attitude is fairly representative of the eminently respectable porcine citizens who—for dollars in the money-grubbing sty, support 'conservative' newspapers and consider the starvation of... inoffensive men, women and children, and the murder of 250 [*sic*] American sailors ... of less importance than the fall of two points in a price of stock."

Anyone advocating peace was a traitor or a Wall Street profiteer, probably both. When Navy Secretary Long dared to say that "Spanish official responsibility for the *Maine* explosion might be considered eliminated," Long joined the *Journal*'s list of officials who had sold out the nation's honor to Wall Street. This was all part of a money-making coup engineered by Hanna, said the *Journal,* with Long as his pawn, for Hanna had advised his friends before the announcement to buy stocks which rose several points as a result of Long's words and netted them $20,000,000.

The treasonous President McKinley had already publicly stated his opinion that the *Maine* was wrecked by an accidental explosion of her own magazines. The perfidious Secretary of the Navy had defended Spain. In Havana at the time was sitting a United States naval board of inquiry, sending down divers to examine the *Maine*'s hull and taking testimony from survivors in an effort to determine the cause of the disaster. Spain had asked, and been promised, that no American newspaper correspondents would take part in the investigation. The *Journal,* with the *World* and *Sun* close behind, was whipping public fury to a point where all these official efforts were rendered useless, a trivial shadow play unheard behind the din of the headlines.

The Nearest Approach to Hell

In Cuba, Hearst's junketing group of Senators and Congressmen were finding plenty of destitution, which indeed was so bad that it could scarcely be exaggerated. The *Journal* praised them as "brave congressmen [who] faced death to get at the truth in Cuba." Each of the five legislators wrote articles for the *Journal* describing the suffering they saw. Mrs. Thurston, wife of the Senator from Nebraska, who had accompanied her husband, wrote an especially stirring appeal to *Journal* mothers:

> Oh! Mothers of the Northland, who tenderly clasp your little ones to your loving hearts! Think of the black despair that filled each [Cuban] mother's heart as she felt her life-blood ebb away, and knew that she had left her little ones to perish from the pain of starvation and disease.

While in the harbor of Matanzas, Mrs. Thurston suffered a heart attack and died aboard the Hearst yacht—a misfortune the *Journal* blamed on the destitution she had seen. The five *"Journal* Commissioners" returned to make speeches in Congress praising the *Journal*'s patriotic motives and declaring that newspaper reports of conditions in Cuba were not exaggerated. For weeks, while the naval court continued its investigation in Havana, American citizens were conducted into a theater world of Cuban horror, Spanish treachery and United States dishonor staged with primitive efficiency by Producer-Director Hearst and aped by the rabble-rousing Pulitzer (now sadly reduced to the role of imitator) and the respected *Sun.* Edwin Godkin vainly tried to stem the tide in his *Evening Post,* with its puny 25,000 circulation.

"... when one of [the yellow journals] offers a yacht voyage," Godkin wrote, "with free wine, rum and cigars, and a good bed, under the guise of philanthropy, or gets up a committee for Holy purposes, and promises to puff it, it can get almost any one it pleases to go on the yacht voyage and serve on the committee—senators, lawyers, divines, scholars, poets, presidents and what not.... Every one who knows anything about 'yellow journals' knows that everything they do and say is intended to promote sales.... No one—absolutely no one—supposes a yellow journal cares five cents about the Cubans, the *Maine* victims, or any one else. A yellow journal is probably the nearest approach to hell, existing in any Christian state."

Theodore Roosevelt, who had displeased the *Journal* as head of the New York police, was now Assistant Secretary of the Navy under Long and a jingo after Hearst's own heart. Roosevelt had decided instantly that the *Maine* was sunk by treacherous Spaniards. He privately referred with contempt to McKinley as having "no more backbone than a chocolate eclair." The *Journal,* always doubly glad when it could praise itself as it rapped its enemies, quoted Roosevelt in a front-page interview as saying: "It is cheering to find a newspaper of the great influence and circulation of the *Journal* tell [*sic*] the facts as they exist and ignore the suggestions of various kinds that emanate from sources that cannot be described as patriotic or loyal to the flag of this country."

Roosevelt immediately repudiated the statement, saying, "The alleged interview with me in today's New York *Journal* is an invention from beginning to end. It is difficult to understand the kind of infamy that resorts to such methods." Roosevelt later won a reputation for occasional denials of indiscreet things he had said, but perhaps in this instance it is safer to trust him than the *Journal.*

Long before the Navy report on the *Maine* was ready, the *Journal* anticipated it with sheer falsehood, saying, "the Court of Inquiry finds that Spanish government officials blew up the *Maine*," and that the warship "was purposely moved where a Spanish mine exploded by Spanish officers would destroy it." "The *Journal* can stake its reputation as a war prophet on this assertion: There will be a war with Spain as certain as the sun shines unless Spain abases herself in the dust and voluntarily consents to the freedom of Cuba." The Spaniards were universally painted as such cowardly, two-faced wretches that Madrid editors not surprisingly began railing at the "Yankee pigs," which in turn was faithfully reported by the *Journal* and its contemporaries.

Under these daily onslaughts, multiplied by many extra editions and news-service transmission from coast to coast, the nation was seething. The public was deceived, misled and tricked by its only source of information. McKinley, a kindly man of peace, could deal expertly with legislators but lacked the dynamism, the spark of leadership that grips and sways the public mind. The country was getting away from him. The Presidency of the United States was being preempted by batteries of cylinder presses.

On March 28, McKinley handed the report of the naval court to Congress. The court's opinion was that "the *Maine* was destroyed by the explosion of a submarine mine, which caused the partial explosion of two or more of the forward magazines." The court admitted its inability to fix the blame. A Spanish court of inquiry which had made a similar investigation, but which the Americans had denied an opportunity for close inspection, found for an accidental explosion within the ship. This report was ignored. The guilt for the disaster, if guilt there was, was a mystery then as it is today. No one ever collected the *Journal*'s $50,000 reward.

However, public sentiment was so inflamed that the United States court's opinion that the explosion came from outside and thus was not accidental was enough to lay the blame on Spain. The *Journal*, dissatisfied, declared that the truth was being hidden from the public, saying, "the suppressed testimony shows Spain is guilty of blowing up the *Maine*." Even the heavens demonstrated the inevitability of war. On the night of April 4, the moon was surrounded by two pale rings. "Many persons insisted," said the *Journal*, "that the contact of the two rings meant nothing short of war; the smaller ring standing for the pretension of Spain in the Island of Cuba and the larger circle for the United States and its immensely superior power."

This whimsy was lost in the prevailing theme of American dishonor. "Write to your Congressmen at once," the *Journal* urged its readers. " ... Give Congress a chance to know what the people think." The same issue featured a cartoon depicting Hanna, with his puppet McKinley stuck in his back pocket, poking a white feather into the star-studded hat of Uncle Sam, and suggested satirically that the stars on the flag be changed to dollar signs and the stripes to rows of dollar bills. It ran a front-page headline in three-inch type: "HANNA VS. HONOR." When some Ohio politicians charged that Hanna was elected to the Senate by fraud, the *Journal*'s cartoon showed him in prison stripes with the caption, "Here is Our 'President-Maker!' How Do You Like Him?" It warned that "Spain's powerful flotilla" was believed to be "stealing toward our shore." Blasting McKinley and his Wall Street bosses for waiting for Spain to strike the first blow, it demanded, in an issue dotted with American flags, "In the name of 266 [*sic*] American seamen, butchered in cold blood by the Spaniards, what is a 'blow' in the McKinley concept of war?" It ran an imaginative drawing showing Spanish soldiers bayoneting helpless Cubans, with the caption, "The wires bring news of the butchery of two hundred more reconcentrados.... Two hundred murders more or fewer is of little importance in Spain's record, and McKinley can hardly be expected to get excited about this."

The *Journal* pointed out how ridiculously easy it would be to crush Spain. It talked of organizing a regiment of giant athletes including Heavyweights Bob Fitzsimmons and James J. Corbett, Ballplayer Cap Anson, Hammer Thrower Jim Mitchell and Indian Footballer Red Water, all of whom agreed to join. "Think of a regiment composed of magnificent men of this ilk!" glowed the *Journal.* "They would overawe any Spanish regiment by their mere appearance. They would scorn Krag-Jorgensen and Mauser bullets."

According to the *Journal,* volunteers were itching to avenge the *Maine.* Frank James, ex-bandit brother of the legendary Jesse, offered to lead a company of cowboys. Six hundred Sioux Indians were ready and willing to scalp Spaniards in Cuba. The *World* improved on this, reporting the statement of "Buffalo Bill" Cody that 30,000 Indian fighters could clear the Spaniards out of Cuba in sixty days. The *Journal* came back with a report of riots in Havana that had "2,000 AMERICANS IN PERIL," presenting a four-column drawing showing exactly how the Navy would bombard Morro Castle and land men around Havana. *Journal* reporters were sent to interview the mothers of sailors who died in the *Maine* living in the New York area. All made pathetic appeals for vengeance.

"How would President McKinley have felt, I wonder," said one of them, "if he had a son on the *Maine* murdered as was my little boy? Would he then forget the crime and let it go unpunished while the body of his child was lying as food for the sharks in the Spanish harbor of Havana?" Another mother was quoted as saying in part, "I ask that mine and other mothers' sons be avenged.... I ask it for justice [*sic*] sake and the honor of the flag."

In Madrid, United States Minister Stewart Woodford was working efficiently for peace, although he was ostracized by Spanish society as De Lome previously had been in Washington. Being out of range of the *Journal,* which attacked his peace efforts as "twaddle," he felt that peace could be preserved. It would have been had not his efforts been junked by the administration. He found the Spanish government ready to go the limit to avoid war. "They cannot go further in open concessions to us," Woodford earlier had informed McKinley, "without being overthrown by their own people here in Spain.... They want peace if they can keep peace and save the dynasty. They prefer the chances of war, with the certain loss of Cuba, to the overthrow of the dynasty." On April 9, Woodford cabled that the Queen's government had gone still farther and had surrendered to all the important United States demands, even to the extent of offering to grant an immediate armistice there. Woodford was confident that this last concession meant peace, saying:

> I hope that nothing will now be done to humiliate Spain as I am satisfied that the present government is going, and is loyally ready to go, as fast and as far as it can. With your power of action sufficiently free, you will win the fight on your own lines.

Here was the key to an amicable settlement, if the United States wanted it. But McKinley knew that the majority of the American people, misled by their newspapers, wanted war. He knew that many legislators, influenced by their angry constituents, wanted war. And he knew that his administration and the Republican party would suffer unpopularity and loss of confidence if it made a stand for peace.

Mr. McKinley bowed to Mr. Hearst. He went over to the war party. Without taking any stand, he submitted the whole problem to Congress in a message given on April 11. He dramatized his own abandonment of peace by burying the all-important Spanish concessions in the last two paragraphs of his speech. Everybody knew that this meant war, but the *Journal* was impatient at the delay in making it official, as one of its headlines showed:

SUICIDE

LAMENTED

THE MAINE

AGED MRS. MARY WAYT ENHALED [*sic*] GAS THROUGH A TUBE.

GRIEVED OVER OUR DELAY

"The Government May Live in Dishonor," Said She,

"I Cannot."

Possibly the President was surprised at the peace sentiment still existing when the Senate on April 19 passed a war resolution by the narrow vote of 42 to 35. Only four more Senators on the peace side would have swung the balance, indicating that determined Presidential leadership might have foiled Hearst. But when the House concurred with the Senate in a 310–6 vote for war, it demonstrated that McKinley, had he won peace, would have won unpopularity along with it.

It was an unnecessary war. It was the newspapers' war. Above all, it was Hearst's war. It is safe to say that had not Hearst, with his magnificently tawdry flair for publicity and agitation, enlisted the women of America in a crusade they misunderstood, made a national heroine of the jail-breaking Miss Cisneros, made a national abomination of Dupuy de Lome, made the *Maine* a mistaken symbol of Spanish treachery, caused thousands of citizens to write their Congressmen, and dragged the powerful *World* along with him into journalistic ill-fame, the public would have kept its sanity, McKinley would have shown more spunk, at least four more Senators would have taken counsel with reason, and there would have been no war.

"The outbreak of the Spanish-American war found Mr. Hearst in a state of proud ecstasy," recalled James Creelman, who was working with Hearst daily. "He had won his campaign and the McKinley Administration had been forced into war." Willis Abbot wrote: "Hearst was accustomed to refer to the war, in company with his staff, as 'our war.'"

He rallied the United States with a headline in four-inch type:

"NOW TO AVENGE THE MAINE!"

David Nasaw    **NO**

"How Do You Like the *Journal's* War?"

There are no accounts of Hearst's life nor are there histories of the Spanish-American War that do not include some discussion of the role of the Yellow Press in general and Hearst in particular in fomenting war in Cuba. Still, it is safe to say from the vantage point of one hundred years that even had William Randolph Hearst never gone into publishing, the United States would nonetheless have declared war on Spain in April of 1898. That Hearst has received so large a measure of credit or blame for that "glorious war" is a tribute to his genius as a self-promoter. It was Hearst who proclaimed the war in Cuba to be the *New York Journal's* war and he who convinced the rest of the nation that without the Hearst press leading the way there would have been no war.

The first Cuban revolution against Spanish colonialism had begun in 1868, when Hearst was five years old, and was only subdued after ten years of fighting. In early 1895, the rebellion was reignited after the United States imposed a new American tariff on Cuban exports that led to massive unemployment on the sugar plantations and economic hardship throughout the island. By the fall, the Cuban revolutionaries had freed enough territory from Spanish rule to proclaim their own provisional government. "The reports indicate that Cuba is likely to gain her independence," the *San Francisco Examiner* editorialized in August of 1895, "but not before many battles have been fought, many lives have been lost, much property has been destroyed." Concluding that Spain was prepared to "fight a war to extermination" in Cuba, the *Examiner* called on the government in Washington to protect the innocent men, women, and children of Cuba from the fate that had recently befallen the Armenians at the hands of the Turks: "It may not be our duty to interfere in Turkey, but we certainly cannot permit the creation of another Armenia in this hemisphere... Cuba is our Armenia, and it is at our doors.... We are determined that no more butcheries and arsons shall be laid to our door. Cuba must not stand in the relation to us that Armenia does to England."

In early 1896, Spain responded to the growing insurrection in Cuba by sending 150,000 troops to the island commanded by General Valeriano Weyler (soon to be known in the American press as "Butcher" Weyler). Weyler tried to quell the rebellion by herding Cuban peasants into concentration camps to prevent them from supporting the rebel armies with food and new recruits. Hundreds of thousands of Cubans were forced from their land to die of starvation and disease behind barbed wire. The suffering was unimaginable. Pulitzer's *World,* Dana's *Sun,* and the *Journal,* which were fed a steady diet of stories from the Junta, the rebels' unofficial diplomatic and publicity arm, covered the events in Cuba as if they were happening next door.

That Spain had no moral or political right to maintain a colonial empire in the New World was not, for Hearst, a matter of debate. But this was not the primary reason why the Cuban conflict was given a prominent place on his front pages. What made Cuba such a compelling story was the fact that events on the island lent themselves to Hearst's favorite plot line. Here was raw material for tales of corruption more horrific than any yet told. The villains were lecherous and bloodthirsty Spanish officials and army officers; the victims, innocent Cuban women and children; the heroes, crusading *Journal* reporters and their publisher.

"Credible witnesses have testified," read an editorial from December 1896, "that all prisoners captured by Weyler's forces are killed on the spot; that even helpless inmates of a hospital have not been spared, and that Weyler's intention seems to be to murder all the pacificos in the country.... The American people will not tolerate in the Western Hemisphere the methods of the Turkish savages in Armenia, no matter what the cost of putting an end to them might be. Twenty Spains would prove no efficacious obstacle in the way of a righteous crusade like that. Let us not act hastily, but let us act."

In early 1897, Hearst offered Richard Harding Davis $3,000 a month plus expenses to serve as the *Journal's* special correspondent in Cuba. Artist Frederic Remington was sent along to illustrate Davis's articles. The two were transported to Cuba—with a full crew of assistants—in Hearst's new steam-driven 112-foot yacht, the *Vamoose,* which he had purchased in the early 1890s and kept moored in New York. Unfortunately the *Vamoose,* though a magnificent-looking yacht and reportedly the fastest ship in New York Harbor, was entirely unsuited for the mission. After three attempts at landing, the captain had to turn back. Davis was so frustrated at being marooned offshore that, as he wrote his mother, he lay on the deck and cried. The *Vamoose* returned to Key West, where Hearst wired his reporters an additional $1,000 to buy or lease another boat. Davis and Remington decided instead to take the regularly scheduled passenger steamer to Havana.

Hearst made the most of his stars' heroic entry onto the battle-scarred island. In mid-January, the *Journal* reported triumphantly that its representatives had caught up with the insurgent Cuban army. Davis was outraged. As he had written his mother a few days earlier, not only had he not found any army in the field, he had in his entire time in Cuba not "heard a shot fired or seen an insurgent.... I am just 'not in it' and I am torn between coming home and making your dear heart stop worrying and getting one story to justify me being here and that damn silly page of the Journal's.... All Hearst wants is my name and

I will give him that only if it will be signed to a different sort of a story from those they have been printing."

While Davis never did find any fighting, he was able to find enough material to write a few magnificent front-page stories on the devastation the war had visited on Cuba and its peoples. Frederic Remington was not so fortunate. Disgusted by the lack of action and his inability to find scenes worth illustrating, he telegrammed Hearst from Havana that he wished to return to New York. "Everything is quiet. There is no trouble here. There will be no war." Hearst, according to James Creelman, who wrote about the incident in his autobiography, answered Remington by return cable, "Please remain. You furnish the pictures, and I'll furnish the war."

Though many pages have been written about these telegrams, there is no record of them outside of Creelman's 1901 autobiography. Hearst himself, in a letter to the *London Times* in 1907, referred to the intimation that he was chiefly responsible for the Spanish war as a kind of "clotted nonsense" which "could only be generally circulated and generally believed in England."

Despite his disclaimers, Hearst might well have written the telegram to Remington, but if he did, the war he was referring to was the one already being fought between the Cuban revolutionaries and the Spanish army, not the one the Americans would later fight. There is no mention of or reference to American intervention in the telegrams; the groundswell that would lead to intervention after the sinking of the *Maine* had not yet begun. The war in question, the war Hearst may have claimed he would furnish, was the one between Cubans and Spaniards being waged in January of 1897, not the one that would be declared in Washington fifteen months later.

The question that is much more interesting than whether or not Hearst wrote the telegram is why its contents have been so universally misinterpreted. The answer is simple: Hearst, with his genius for self-promotion, so deftly inserted himself and his newspapers into the narrative of the Spanish-American War that historians and the general public have accepted the presumption that he furnished it.

❦

Though Hearst tried his best to keep Cuba on his front pages, events conspired against him. By April of 1897, Cuba was no longer front-page news. Hearst focused his attention instead on the threatened war between Greece and Turkey, dispatching to the front a full complement of star reporters led by Stephen Crane, Julian Ralph, two "female correspondents," and a full "contingent of Greek couriers, translators, and orderlies."

By the summer of 1897, peace having settled over Greece, Hearst and his editors were left without a viable front-page story cycle. They found it in August in Cuba where, as they reported in huge bold headlines and artfully engraved line drawings, Evangelina Cosio y Cisneros, the young and innocent daughter of a jailed insurgent, had been cast into an airless dungeon for daring to protect her chastity against the brutal advances of a lust-crazed Spanish colonel. Evangelina was the perfect heroine for Hearst's melodrama: a beautiful eighteen-year-old "Cuban Joan of Arc, with long black hair." As Creelman recalled in his autobiography—no doubt with some embellishment—Hearst, on hearing of Evangelina's plight, took command of the newsroom and barked out orders to the assembled editors and reporters:

> "Telegraph to our correspondent in Havana to wire every detail of this case. Get up a petition to the Queen Regent of Spain for this girl's pardon. Enlist the women of America. Have them sign the petition. Wake up our correspondents all over the country. Have distinguished women sign first. Cable the petitions and the names to the Queen Regent. Notify our minister in Madrid. We can make a national issue of this case.... That girl must be saved if we have to take her out of prison by force or send a steamer to meet the vessel that carries her away—but that would be piracy, wouldn't it?"

"Within an hour," continues Creelman's account, "messages were flashing to Cuba, and to every part of the United States. The petition to the Queen Regent was telegraphed to more than two hundred correspondents in various American cities and towns. Each correspondent was instructed to hire a carriage and employ whatever assistance he needed, get the signatures of prominent women of the place, and telegraph them to New York as quickly as possible."

Hearst himself telegraphed the most prominent women in the nation, including Mrs. McKinley in the White House: "Will you not add your name to that of distinguished American women like Mrs. Julia Ward Howe ... who are cabling petitions to Queen Regent of Spain for release of Evangelina Cisneros eighteen years old ... who is threatened with twenty years imprisonment? She is almost a child, sick, defenseless, and in prison. A word may save her. Answer at our expense. William Hearst."

Hundreds of responses followed—from Clara Barton, Mrs. Jefferson Davis, President McKinley's mother, and many more—each one of them reproduced on the pages of the *Journal*. While the *World*, citing the American consul general in Havana, screamed that the Cisneros story was more hoax than fact, and *Town Topics*, the weekly guide to gossip and politics in New York, echoing the opinion of the city's respectable classes, complained that the *Journal*'s coverage was both "senseless and pernicious," Hearst continued to trumpet the story, with the focus shifted from what had been done to Evangelina Cisneros to what the *Journal* was doing for her.

As it became apparent that Spain was not about to release Evangelina, Hearst ordered the reporter and adventurer Karl Decker to sail for Cuba and help Evangelina escape. Miraculously, with the help of some well-placed bribes, Decker succeeded in springing Cisneros from her dungeon and transporting her to New York City: "An American Newspaper Accomplishes at a Single Stroke What the Red Tape of Diplomacy Failed to Bring About in Many Months." In New York, Hearst dressed Evangelina like a princess in a long white gown, installed her in a suite at the Waldorf, and paraded her through the streets to a huge rally at Madison Square Garden, followed by a dinner at Delmonico's, a ball in the Waldorf's Red Room, and a trip to Washington, D.C., for a reception with President McKinley at the White House.

Hearst's rescue of Cisneros was significant not because, as his supporters and critics would later argue, it embarrassed the Spanish and pushed the United States toward involvement in the Caribbean, but because it strengthened his sense of entitlement and bolstered his confidence that because he was acting on behalf of the American people, he could make his own rules—subverting, if need be, common sense and international law.

⟡

The Evangelina Cisneros rescue was a sideshow. The real story was being played out in Cuba, where the insurgents continued their battle for independence, and in Spain, where the new Liberal party government found itself caught between the Cuban insurrectionists, who demanded complete independence, and the Conservative opposition, army officers, Spanish landholders in Cuba, and colonial officials, who threatened civil war should the Liberal government cede the island to the Cubans. With no compromise possible, the war continued. American businessmen watched hopelessly as the Cuban economy disintegrated, trade halted, and tens of millions of dollars in American investments were rendered virtually worthless.

On January 11, 1898, antigovernment riots broke out in Havana, incited this time not by the Cuban revolutionaries but by Spanish army officers who feared that the government in Madrid might give in to the revolutionaries. President McKinley ordered the battleship U.S.S. *Maine* to sail from Key West to protect American interests on the island.

Two weeks later, a representative of the Cuban Junta appeared at the *Journal* office with a stolen letter in which Dupuy de Lôme, the Spanish ambassador to the United States, referred to President McKinley as "weak, vacillating, and venal." The Cubans had offered the letter to the *Herald,* but when the *Herald* editors delayed publication pending authentication, the rebels withdrew it and marched to Hearst's office. The *Journal* published the letter next morning in an inflammatory English translation. The headline read, "Worst Insult to the United States in Its History."

Under ordinary circumstances, Hearst could have wrung headlines out of this story for weeks, but events were now moving so fast he did not have to. On the evening of February 15, 1898, the U.S.S. *Maine,* under circumstances which even today are not entirely clear, exploded in Havana Harbor, instantly killing more than 250 of the sailors, marines, and officers on board. This event, if we are to judge only from the size of the headlines, became at once the biggest newspaper story since the assassination of President Lincoln.

According to Hearst's account, he was awakened with news of the *Maine*'s sinking by his butler, George Thompson:

> "There's a telephone call from the office. They say it's important news."

> The office was called up.

> "Hello, what is the important news?"

"The battleship Maine *has been blown up in Havana Harbor."*

"Good heavens, what have you done with the story?"

"We have put it on the first page of course."

"Have you put anything else on the front page?"

"Only the other big news."

"There is not any other big news. Please spread the story all over the page. This means war."

While President McKinley convened a naval court of inquiry to determine the cause of the *Maine* explosion and newspapers across the country cautioned readers to await the gathering of evidence before jumping to conclusions, Pulitzer's *World* and Hearst's *Journal* determined, after only forty-eight hours, that the explosion had been detonated by a Spanish mine. "Destruction of the Warship *Maine* Was the Work of An Enemy," read the *Journal's* front-page headline on February 17, 1897. In the middle of the page was a drawing of the *Maine* in Havana Harbor with a mine placed directly underneath it. The caption read: "The Spaniards, it is believed, arranged to have the *Maine* anchored over one of the Harbor mines. Wires connected the mine with a powder magazine and it is thought the explosion was caused by sending an electric current through the wire."

"*Maine* is great thing. Arouse everybody. Stir up Madrid," Hearst telegrammed James Creelman in London. Having determined that the Spanish were responsible for the explosion, Hearst positioned the *Journal* in the center of the story as the hero who would avenge the murder of the American sailors. He offered a $50,000 reward for the solution to the mystery of the *Maine* explosion, began a drive for a *Maine* memorial and contributed the first $1,000, devised a new "War with Spain" card game, enlisted a delegation of senators and congressmen to travel to Cuba on a Hearst yacht as "*Journal* commissioners," and implored his readers to write their congressmen. The combined circulation of the morning and evening *Journals* reached one million and continued to grow.

Pulitzer and his editors tried but failed to keep up with Hearst's newspapers on this, the biggest story since the Civil War. The *World* did not have the funds—or the Hearst-owned yachts—to send dozens of correspondents and artists to report firsthand on Cuba, nor did it have the staff to put out six to eight pages of articles, editorials, cartoons, interviews, and illustrated features on the Cuban crisis each day. The *Journal's* coverage was bigger, more spectacular, more varied, and more imaginative than that of any other paper in the city. There were dozens of stories on the *Maine* explosion, on the funeral procession for the *Maine* victims, on the mounting horrors in "Butcher" Weyler's death camps, on the findings of the "*Journal* commissioners" to Cuba. While McKinley awaited the report from his naval court of inquiry on the cause of the *Maine* explosion, the Hearst papers attacked the president together with Mark Hanna, the "conservative" newspapers that refused to join the crusade, and "the eminently respectable porcine citizens" who resisted the call to battle. To graphically demonstrate to the public how easy it would be to win this war, the *Journal* contacted America's most famous oversized athletes, including heavyweight champions James J. Corbett and Bob Fitzsimmons, baseball star Cap Anson, and champion hammer-throwers and wrestlers, to ask if they would consider joining a regiment of athletes. "Think of a regiment composed of magnificent men of this ilk!" the *Journal* gloated on March 29, 1898. "They would overawe any Spanish regiment by their mere appearance."

"Whatever else happens, the *World* must go," declared *Town Topics* in early April. "It has been beaten on its own dunghill by the *Journal,* which has bigger type, bigger pictures, bigger war scares, and a bigger bluff. If Mr. Pulitzer had his eyesight he would not be content to play second fiddle to the *Journal* and allow Mr. Hearst to set the tone."

⋘◉⋙

When, less than two months after the *Maine* explosion, Congress passed a joint resolution demanding that Spain "relinquish its authority and government on the island of Cuba" and directing the president "to use the land and naval forces of the United States to carry these resolutions into effect," Hearst's *Journal* greeted the news, in headlines a full four inches high, "NOW TO AVENGE THE MAINE!" Five days later, on April 25, rockets were set off from the roof of the *Journal* building to celebrate the signing of the declaration of war and the *Journal* offered a prize of $1,000 to the reader who came up with the best ideas for conducting the war. A week later, Hearst, unable to contain his euphoria, asked on the very top of his front page, "How do you like the *Journal's* war?"

Though Hearst claimed that the war in Cuba was the *Journal's* war, it was not. President McKinley had not asked for a declaration of war, nor had Congress granted him one, to please William R. Hearst. The "yellows" had been clamoring for war for several years, with no discernible effect, their strident voices balanced by more conservative Republican voices like Whitelaw Reid's *Tribune* and E. L. Godkin's *Evening Post,* which urged restraint. Hearst was a cheerleader not a policy maker. McKinley had his own sources of information in Cuba; he did not need a Hearst or Pulitzer to tell him what was going on there nor did he place much trust in what they had to say. According to the historian Walter LaFeber, he did not even read the "yellows." As John Offner, the author of *An Unwanted War,* has concluded, sensational journalism had "only a marginal impact" on the decision to go to war with Spain: "Hearst played on American prejudices; he did not create them. Although he and other sensationalists supplied many false stories, they did not fabricate the major events that moved the United States.... Had there been no sensational press, only responsible editors, the American public nevertheless would have learned about the terrible conditions in Cuba [and] would have wanted Spain to leave."

What prompted McKinley, Congress, and most of the business community to support intervention in early 1898, after resisting for so many years, was the recognition that Spain had lost control of Cuba and would not be able to regain it. Politically, McKinley could not afford to allow the Democrats to blame him and his party for so much human suffering and bloodshed so close to home. Economically, he could not allow the millions of dollars invested on the island to lie fallow or, worse yet, be lost forever should the Cubans oust the Spanish.

POSTSCRIPT

Did Yellow Journalism Cause the Spanish-American War?

In his biography of the newspaper mogul, Swanberg argues that Hearst sent dozens of his first-rate reporters into Cuba to publicize the failure of the Spanish government to maintain control over the last vestiges of its empire in the Caribbean. The Spanish government contributed to the Hearst propaganda machine with its imprisonment of Evangelina Cosio y Cisneros, the letter of Spanish minister de Lome castigating President McKinley as "weak... catering to the rabble, and... [a] low politician," and, finally, what later proved to be the accidental blowing up of the battleship *Maine* in Havana harbor. There is little doubt that in major cities like San Francisco and New York the Hearst newspapers—with their sensational headlines, inflammatory stories, and artistic sketches—greatly impacted public opinion.

Marcus M. Wilkerson, *Public Opinion and the Spanish American War: A Study in War Propaganda* (Russell & Russell, 1932, 1967) and Joseph E. Wisan, *The Cuban Crisis as Reflected in the New York Press (1895-1898)* (Octagon Press, 1934, 1965) both support Swanberg's view that newspaper propaganda caused the Spanish-American War. Interestingly, the two books were written in the 1930s and reprinted in the 1960s, both periods of antiwar sentiments in the United States. Some journal articles discount the impact of pro-war newspapers on public opinion in midwestern states. See Mark M. Welter, "The 1895-98 Cuban Crisis in Minnesota Newspapers: Testing the 'Yellow Journalism' Theory," *Journalism Quarterly* (Winter 1970) and Harold J. Sylvester, "The Kansas Press and the Coming of the Spanish American War," *Historian* (vol. 31, 1969), pp. 251-267, which examines 18 newspapers and finds that only 2 are highly jingoistic.

The history of the American newspaper receives its fullest treatment in Frank Luther Mott, *American Journalism: A History, 1690-1960,* 3rd ed. (Macmillan, 1962). Though detailed, it contains an excellent chapter entitled "Yellow Journalism and the War With Spain." Briefer but useful is John Tebbel, *The Compact History of the American Newspaper* (Hawthorn Books, 1963). The correspondents' views of the war from the bottom up can be found in Joyce Milton, *The Yellow Kids: Foreign Correspondents in the Heyday of Yellow Journalism* (Harper & Row, 1989) and Charles H. Brown, *The Correspondent's War: Journalists in the Spanish-American War* (Charles Scribner's Sons, 1967).

Nasaw disagrees with Swanberg and others who argue that Hearst started the Spanish-American War. In a massive biography, and based on an examination of Hearst papers that were previously unavailable to researchers, Nasaw makes several telling points. First, Hearst sent veteran reporter Richard Harding

Davis and artist Frederick Remington to Cuba to write about the war. Supposedly, when Remington cabled Hearst that "everything is quiet," Hearst replied, "Please remain. You furnish the pictures and I'll furnish the war." According to Nasaw, the evidence for this exchange is very slim. The actual telegrams have never been found. The story originates in veteran reporter James Creelman's autobiography, *On the Great Highway: The Wanderings and Adventures of a Special Correspondent* (Lothrop, 1901). If Hearst said this, Nasaw argues, he was probably referring to the war between the Cuban rebels and the Spaniards. In 1907 Hearst himself referred to the notion that he was responsible for the Spanish-American War as "clotted nonsense."

Nasaw, like Ian Mugridge in *The View From Xanadu: William Randolph Hearst and United States Foreign Policy* (McGill-Queens University Press, 1995), argues that Swanberg and others have failed to demonstrate a causal link between propaganda, public opinion, and emotionalism and the decision for war made by President McKinley, his cabinet, and Congress. Such an interpretation assumes that McKinley was a passive individual with the "backbone of a chocolate éclair" (to quote then–assistant secretary of the navy Theodore Roosevelt) who could be easily swayed by Cuban rebels, big business, or Hearst himself to go to war. Recent biographers of McKinley see him as a man in charge of situations, a decision maker who reluctantly went to war when Spain refused to allow him to mediate the dispute between the Cuban rebels and the Spanish government. Why the breakdown in relations occurred is clear in hindsight. Spain wanted an armistice and was willing to grant Cuba autonomy. The United States wanted Cuba to become independent, a goal the Spanish government was not willing to concede. See, for example, John L. Offner, *An Unwanted War: The Diplomacy of the United States and Spain Over Cuba, 1895–1898* (University of North Carolina Press, 1992); H. Wayne Morgan, *America's Road to Empire: The War With Spain and Overseas Expansion* (John Wiley, 1965); and Lewis L. Gould, *The Spanish-American War and President McKinley* (University of Kansas Press, 1982). Both Morgan and Gould have also written full-scale biographies of McKinley.

Why the *Maine* was sunk is as controversial today as it was in 1898. In 1976 the Naval History Division of the Department of the Navy published Admiral Hyman D. Rickover's *How the Battleship Maine Was Destroyed*. Disputing the official naval verdicts in 1898 and 1911, Rickover concluded that a fire in a coal bunker had detonated munitions in an adjacent magazine. The February 1998 *National Geographic* uses computer technology to present both sides of the controversy. Joseph R. L. Sterne, in "Battleship Blowup Still a Mystery," *The Baltimore Sun* (February 15, 1998), summarizes the most recent scholarship.

Three books that detail the military as well as the social and diplomatic aspects of the war are Frank Friedel's pictorial *The Splendid Little War* (Little, Brown, 1958) and two other full-scale studies: David F. Trask, *The War With Spain in 1898* (Macmillan, 1981) and Ivan Musicant, *Empire by Default: The Spanish-American War and the Dawn of the American Century* (Henry Holt, 1998).

ISSUE 6

Did Racial Segregation Improve the Status of African Americans?

YES: Howard N. Rabinowitz, from "From Exclusion to Segregation: Southern Race Relations, 1865–1890," *The Journal of American History* (September 1976)

NO: Leon F. Litwack, from *Trouble in Mind: Black Southerners in the Age of Jim Crow* (Alfred A. Knopf, 1998)

ISSUE SUMMARY

YES: Professor of history Howard N. Rabinowitz suggests that racial segregation represented an improvement in the lives of African Americans in that it provided access to a variety of public services and accommodations from which they otherwise would have been excluded in the late-nineteenth-century South.

NO: Professor of American history Leon F. Litwack argues that "the age of Jim Crow," wherein efforts by whites to deny African Americans equal protection of the laws or the privileges and immunities guaranteed other citizens seemingly knew no bounds, created a highly repressive environment for blacks.

In the late nineteenth and early twentieth centuries, most black Americans' lives were characterized by increased inequality and powerlessness. Although the Thirteenth Amendment had fueled a partial social revolution by emancipating approximately 4 million southern slaves, the efforts of the Fourteenth and Fifteenth Amendments to provide all African Americans with the protections and privileges of full citizenship had been undermined by the U.S. Supreme Court.

By 1910, 75 percent of all African Americans resided in rural areas. Ninety percent lived in the South, where they suffered from abuses associated with the sharecropping and crop-lien systems, political disfranchisement, and antagonistic race relations, which often boiled over into acts of violence, including race riots and lynchings. Black southerners who moved north in the decades preceding World War I to escape the ravages of racism instead discovered a society in which the color line was drawn more rigidly to limit black opportunities.

Residential segregation led to the emergence of racial ghettos. Jim Crow also affected northern education, and competition for jobs produced frequent clashes between black and white workers. By the early twentieth century, then, most African Americans endured a second-class citizenship reinforced by segregation laws (both customary and legal) in the "age of Jim Crow."

The response by black Americans to the developing patterns of racial segregation in the late nineteenth century was often reflected in the philosophies of those recognized as "leaders of the race." Prior to 1895 the foremost spokesman for the nation's African American population was former slave and abolitionist Frederick Douglass, whose crusade for blacks emphasized the importance of civil rights, political power, and immediate integration. Historian August Meier has called Douglass "the greatest living symbol of the protest tradition during the 1880's and 1890's." At the time of Douglass's death in 1895, however, this tradition was largely replaced by the emergence of Booker T. Washington. Born into slavery in Virginia in 1856, Washington became the most prominent black spokesman in the United States as a result of a speech delivered in the year of Douglass's death at the Cotton States Exposition in Atlanta, Georgia. Known as the "Atlanta Compromise," this address, with its conciliatory tone, found favor among whites and gave Washington a reputation as a "responsible" spokesman for black America.

One of the earliest and most outspoken critics of Washington's program was his contemporary, W. E. B. Du Bois. In a famous essay in *The Souls of Black Folk* (1903), Du Bois leveled an assault upon Washington's apparent acceptance of segregation and attachment to industrial education. By submitting to disfranchisement and segregation, Du Bois charged, Washington had become an apologist for racial injustice in the United States. He also argued that Washington's national prominence had been bought at the expense of black interests throughout the nation.

In more reflective moments, Du Bois undoubtedly understood the immense difficulty of eradicating Jim Crow laws in a South where whites embraced the doctrine of white supremacy with great fervor. As a witness to the Atlanta race riot of 1906, he also knew the dangers of challenging the "white man's laws" too forcefully. Moreover, both Du Bois and Washington recognized that segregation, no matter how firmly entrenched, was not slavery and that certain benefits presented themselves to African Americans within this otherwise discriminatory caste system.

In the first of the selections that follow, Howard N. Rabinowitz asserts that racial segregation improved the circumstances of black southerners who had only recently been removed from chattel slavery by providing them access to education and public facilities, such as restaurants, theaters, parks, and transportation—areas from which blacks had been excluded prior to the war.

Leon F. Litwack, in the second selection, emphasizes the harshest realities confronting African Americans in a Jim Crow world. Subjected to insults, humiliations, and physical violence on a routine basis, black southerners living in the late nineteenth and early twentieth centuries, according to Litwack, faced "the most repressive period in the history of race relations in the South."

Howard N. Rabinowitz

 **YES**

From Exclusion to Segregation: Southern Race Relations, 1865–1890

S ince the appearance in 1955 of C. Vann Woodward's *The Strange Career of Jim Crow*, extensive research has been devoted to uncovering the origins of racial segregation in the South. Woodward challenges the traditional view that the restrictive Jim Crow codes were the product of the immediate post-Reconstruction period. Emphasizing the legal side of segregation, he argues that the separation of the races grew out of forces operating in the last decade of the nineteenth and the first years of the twentieth century. He has modified his original position, but the existence of a law enforcing segregation remains the key variable in evaluating the nature of race relations. Because of the alleged absence of these statutes, Woodward contends that "forgotten alternatives" existed in the period between redemption and the full-scale arrival of Jim Crow.

Although George Tindall had in part anticipated Woodward's arguments, it is the "Woodward thesis" over which historians have chosen sides. Charles E. Wynes, Frenise A. Logan, and Henry C. Dethloff and Robert P. Jones explicitly declare their support for Woodward (even though much of their evidence seems to point in the opposite direction); and the same is true of the more recent implicit endorsements by John Blassingame and Dale Somers. In his study of South Carolina blacks, however, Joel Williamson, unlike Woodward, emphasizes customs rather than laws and sees segregation so entrenched in the state by the end of Reconstruction that he refers to the early appearance of a "duo-chromatic order." Vernon Lane Wharton's account of Mississippi blacks reaches a similar conclusion, and it has been used to support the arguments of Woodward's critics. Richard C. Wade's work on slavery in antebellum southern cities, Roger A. Fischer's studies of antebellum and postbellum New Orleans, and Ira Berlin's treatment of antebellum free Negroes also question Woodward's conclusions.

The debate has been fruitful, shedding light on race relations in the postbellum South. But the emphasis on the alternatives of segregation or integration has obscured the obvious "forgotten alternative"—exclusion. The issue is not merely when segregation first appeared, but what it replaced. Before the Civil War, blacks were excluded from militia companies and schools, as well as most hospitals, asylums, and public accommodations. The first postwar governments

From Howard N. Rabinowitz, "From Exclusion to Segregation: Southern Race Relations, 1865–1890," *The Journal of American History*, vol. 63, no. 2 (September 1976). Copyright © 1976 by The Organization of American Historians. Reprinted by permission. Notes omitted.

during presidential reconstruction generally sought to continue the antebellum policy of exclusion. Nevertheless, by 1890—before the resort to widespread de jure segregation—de facto segregation had replaced exclusion as the norm in southern race relations. In the process the integration stage had been largely bypassed. This shift occurred because of the efforts of white Republicans who initiated it, blacks who supported and at times requested it, and Redeemers who accepted and expanded the new policy once they came to power.

The first postwar governments, composed of Confederate veterans and elected by white male suffrage, saw little need to alter the prewar pattern of exclusion of blacks from most sectors of southern life.

During the period from 1865 to 1867 southern whites sought to limit admission to poorhouses, orphanages, insane asylums, and institutions for the blind, deaf, and dumb to whites. The states that established systems of public education, such as Georgia, Arkansas, and Texas, opened the schools to whites only. The North Carolina public school system, which dated from antebellum years, was initially closed because of fears that it would be forced to admit blacks. Savannah officials made the same decision about their city's parks. Meanwhile, hotels, restaurants, and many theaters continued to exclude blacks.

Nevertheless, the policy of segregation rather than exclusion was already being forced upon the South. In Richmond and Nashville, for example, the United States Army and the Freedmen's Bureau made the local conservative governments provide poorhouse facilities to indigent blacks. In both cases blacks were placed in quarters separate from whites. The Nashville Board of Education, fearing that it would be forced to integrate its newly opened school system, voluntarily set up separate schools for blacks in 1867. A year earlier the new Nashville Street Railway, which previously had excluded blacks, began running a separate car for them. On the state level, Alabama conservatives admitted blacks for the first time on a segregated basis to the state insane asylum.

Further undermining the policy of exclusion were the practices in those facilities that had experienced the shift from exclusion to segregation during earlier years. The use of separate streetcars for blacks in New Orleans, for example, superseded exclusion during the antebellum and war years. Steamboats and railroads had for many years segregated those few blacks who traveled as paying passengers. This practice continued, and Texas, Mississippi, and Florida strengthened it through the passage of laws. Whatever exclusion there had been on boats and trains had not been forced; it had resulted from the absence of a large black clientele. Cemeteries suffered no such shortage. While most private cemeteries excluded all blacks except faithful servants, public cemeteries had by law or custom assigned blacks to special sections. This procedure continued after the war. Some places of amusement continued to exclude blacks; others retained their earlier pattern of segregated seating; still others as in Nashville opened their doors to freedmen for the first time, although on a segregated basis. Traveling circuses, especially popular with blacks, went so far in Montgomery as to establish separate entrances for the races. The Georgia Infirmary in Savannah and the Charity Hospital in New Orleans similarly continued as they had before the war to provide blacks with segregated medical care at city expense.

Most white southerners remained committed to exclusion as the best racial policy. They were thwarted by the imposition of congressional reconstruction in March 1867 and thereafter were forced by military and civilian authorities to grant new privileges and services to blacks. Nonetheless, the net effect of the Radical measures on race relations in the southern states was to institutionalize the shift from exclusion to segregation. . . .

The Republicans stood for more than segregation. They called for separate but equal treatment for blacks. During debates on congressional civil rights legislation, for example, Senator Joshua Hill of Georgia and Representative Alexander White of Alabama argued that separate provisions for blacks in public carriers, places of amusement, or hotels and restaurants was not a violation of civil rights if the accommodations were equal to those of whites. The Alabama Republican party in its 1874 platform declared that "the republican party does not desire mixed schools or accommodations for colored people, but they ask that in all these advantages they shall be equal. We want no social equality enforced by law." Tennessee's Republican governor signed a separate but equal accommodations measure in 1881, and a Georgia Republican legislature passed a similar bill in 1870. Alabama Republicans pushed for such a measure and congratulated those railroads that voluntarily provided separate but equal accommodations. The Republican legacy to the Redeemers therefore consisted of the seemingly mutually exclusive policies of segregation and equality. . . .

White opinion was not unified, but most Redeemers also adopted the rhetoric of the Republicans' separate but equal commitment. Despite the failure to honor this commitment, in several instances the Redeemers actually moved beyond their predecessors to provide segregated, if unequal, facilities in areas previously characterized by exclusion. Some whites distinguished between segregation and discrimination. Thus Tennessee law prohibited "discrimination" in any place of public amusement that charged a fee but nevertheless maintained that this provision did not outlaw "separate accommodations and seats for colored and white persons."

Additional public institutions opened their doors to blacks for the first time under the Redeemers. Among those states making initial provision for Negro blind, deaf, and dumb were Texas, Georgia, Alabama, Tennessee, and South Carolina; and in 1887, the same year that Tennessee provided a Negro department for the previously all-white and privately run Tennessee Industrial School. North Carolina opened its Colored Orphan Asylum.

Segregation may have also replaced exclusion in other areas of southern life after Reconstruction rather than integration. As early as 1872, Atlanta's Union Passenger Depot had a "Freedmen's Saloon," and at least by 1885 Nashville's Union Depot had "a colored passenger room." In 1885 Austin, Texas, was among the Texas cities required by city ordinance to have separate waiting rooms for both races. It is not known what facilities existed for blacks before the appearance of these Negro waiting rooms. The experiences of Montgomery, Alabama, and Raleigh, North Carolina, however, are instructive. The new Union Depot in Montgomery was described in 1877 as having "a ladies waiting room" and a "gents' waiting room"; the original plans for the Raleigh Union Depot in 1890 included a "ladies waiting room" and a "gentlemen's waiting room." Although there was no reference to a Negro waiting room, the use of the words "gents," "gentlemen," and "ladies" rather than "men" and "women" suggests the exclusion of blacks. The mention of three waiting rooms at the Montgomery Depot in 1885—one each for "ladies," "gentlemen," and "colored people"—and the revised plans for the Raleigh Depot that contained a separate waiting room for blacks suggest further evidence of the shift from exclusion to segregation.

Segregation persisted or replaced exclusion in theaters. For the most part blacks were confined to separate galleries. In Richmond, however, because of the 1875 Civil Rights Act blacks won access to a segregated portion of the once exclusively white dress circle. Most restaurants and hotels continued to exclude blacks, as did the better barrooms. Some bars catering to whites charged blacks outrageous prices or provided poor service; less subtle was the sign over the bar of a Nashville saloon in 1884—"No drinks sold to colored persons." In 1888 the Atlanta *Constitution* reported that of Atlanta's sixty-eight saloons, five served only blacks and only two catered to both blacks and whites. On those instances when blacks were admitted to primarily white restaurants, bars, and hotels, the races were carefully segregated. A restaurant in the rear of a Nashville saloon served "responsible and well behaved colored people" in its kitchen; the Planters Hotel in Augusta, Georgia, seated blacks at separate tables in the dining room; the St. Charles, the only Richmond hotel to accept a black delegate to the 1886 Knights of Labor convention, gave him second-class quarters and seated him at a table in the dining room farthest from the door and behind a screen; and in answer to the Civil Rights Act, Montgomery's Ruby Saloon set up "a small counter" apart from the main bar for black customers. Such examples probably marked only a transitory stage on the way to total segregation.

With the exception of New Orleans, athletic events in the South were rigidly segregated. Most cities had at least two black baseball teams. Militia companies similarly engaged in racially separated competition. Segregated places in parades and observances, usually in the rear, were provided for blacks as well.

Prostitution also suffered the effects of segregation. Even in New Orleans, houses of prostitution offering white and black women to a mixed clientele had become a rarity by 1880. White and black prostitutes resided on separate blocks in Atlanta. When two well dressed mulattoes sought admission to a brothel on Collins Street that served only whites, they were driven off by gunfire. If taken to court, the prostitutes would likely have found the spectators racially separated, and perhaps, like the procedure in Savannah's mayor's court in 1876, they would have sworn on a Bible set aside for their particular race.

The situation in parks was more complex. There were few formal parks and pleasure grounds in antebellum cities, and blacks were excluded from those that existed. Indeed, it was not until the mid-1870s, in most cases after Republicans had relinquished control of local governments, that the park movement began to affect southern urban life. Most of these new parks were privately owned, often by streetcar companies that used them to encourage traffic on their lines, but municipally owned parks became common by the 1880s.

Increasingly blacks were barred from many parks. Sometimes this can be surmised only from the language of the local press. In other cases speculation is unnecessary. Blacks taking the street railway to Atlanta's Ponce de Leon Springs in 1887 were informed "politely but forcibly" by policemen that they would not be admitted. Three years later blacks were excluded from the city's Inman Park. Already Atlanta blacks had begun to gravitate to the grounds and woods around Clark University, leading the Atlanta *Constitution* to call for construction of a park for them in that area. Then, too, in most southern cities blacks and whites continued to frequent separate picnic groves while the large all-white cemeteries served as parks for whites.

Nevertheless, the existence of separate parks for whites and blacks as a general phenomenon seems to have been the product of the post-1890 period. As of 1882, Nashville's Watkins Park was visited by "persons of all shades and sizes." As late as 1890, blacks and whites were invited to watch a Negro militia company drill in Atlanta's Piedmont Park, and on Independence Day, blacks were among the mostly white crowd that enjoyed the facilities at the city's Grant Park. Montgomery's Highland and Raleigh's Pullem Park were apparently open to blacks and whites as well.

In the absence of separate parks, segregation within the grounds became the norm. Although blacks enjoyed access to Atlanta's Ponce de Leon Springs until the late 1880s, the two races entertained themselves at separate dance halls and refreshment stands. Blacks attending the two free concerts given at Nashville's Glendale Park were barred from the new pavillion while those visiting Raleigh's Brookside Park could not use the swimming pool. When a new zoo opened in Atlanta's Grant Park, it contained eight cages occupying the center of the building and stretching from end to end. An aisle was railed off on each side of the row of cages: one was for blacks, the other for whites. "There is no communication between them," the Atlanta *Constitution* observed, "and two large double doors at each end of the building serve as entrance and exit to the aisles...."

Segregation also seems to have been the rule at expositions and fairs. Nashville Negroes had fairgrounds purchased by a black organization. Blacks could attend certain functions at the white fairgrounds but specifically which functions and when is not always clear. Negroes were barred, for example, from the interstate drill competition held in 1883. But again admittance of both races went hand in hand with segregation. There was a special gate provided for blacks in the exposition building at a Nashville fair in 1875; there was a "colored people's saloon" in addition to the main grandstand saloon at the 1871 Georgia State Fair in Macon; and at the Southern Exposition held in Montgomery in 1890 the two races ate in separate restaurants....

The situation in public conveyances is less discernible and there seems to have been a greater divergence in practice. As under the Republicans, steamboats remained the most segregated form of travel. Although Virginia did not pass a law requiring the racial separation of passengers on steamboats until 1900, the *City of Richmond* in service to Norfolk since 1880 had from its inception "a neat and comfortable dining room for colored passengers in the lower cabin." George Washington Cable discovered in 1887 that Louisiana Negroes had to confine themselves to a separate quarter of the boats called the "Freedman's bureau." And to Frederick Douglass it seemed ironic that the Negro had more freedom on steamboats as a slave since "he could ride anywhere, side by side with his white master.... [A]s a freeman, he was not allowed a cabin abaft the wheel."

Although there was greater integration in train travel, blacks were generally confined to the smoking and second-class cars. Occasionally they were provided with separate first class accommodations equal to those given to white passengers. During her trip through the United States in 1883, Iza Duffus Hardy was especially struck by the variety of methods used on trains to keep Negroes "in their place." On the train leaving Charleston, Negroes were in a separate second class car although they did pay a lower fare than whites. At Savannah on the Florida Express, the Negroes rode in the forward part of the smoking car nearest the engine. Somewhat farther south Hardy found a car labeled "For Coloured Passengers," that she discovered "was in every respect exactly like the car reserved for us 'white folk,' the same velvet seats, ice water tank; every comfort the same—and of course, the same fare." As opposed to this rare instance of a first-class car, the car assigned to Negroes in Charleston was described by her traveling companion, Lady Duffus Hardy, as "seedy looking." The association of Negroes with smoking cars was pronounced. While traveling on the Central Railroad in Georgia, Alexander Stephens and two other noted Georgians were ejected from a first-class Negro car because they had seen blacks in it and had assumed it was a second-class car where they could smoke.

The first class cars for Negroes on the Central Railroad reflected an effort by certain railroads and sympathetic whites to provide separate but equal accommodations for blacks able to afford first-class rates. Noting the noncompliance with the 1881 statute providing for separate but equal accommodations for the races on Tennessee's railroads, Nashville's *American* observed in 1885:

> The blacks are forced into the smoking cars where they are subjected not only to all the annoyance of smoke and dirt, but often to the additional hardship of association with the roughest and most quarrelsome class of whites.... Now these things *should not be.* They are bad for the black race and they are equally bad for the white race. The law which provides for separate cars and equal accommodations is right. It is only law which can be just to both of these classes of citizens, and at the same time prevent race conflicts, which would disturb the peace of the community.

As early as 1870, the Orange Railroad passenger trains in Virginia had a special car exclusively for Negroes where smoking was prohibited. A regular smoking car was to be used by both blacks and whites. The Houston and Texas Central agreed in 1883 to provide "separate, exclusive, equal accommodations for colored patrons." Two years later a Louisville and Nashville train running between Montgomery and Mobile had a first-class coach "specially provided for colored people." In the opinion of the Atlanta *Constitution,* it "was as good in every sense as the [white] car.... There was no smoking or disorder permitted."

In a case involving alleged discrimination on an Alabama railroad in 1887, the Interstate Commerce Commission held that different cars for the races could indeed be used provided that the accommodations were equal and that Negroes paying first-class fare received first-class facilities.

In only one area of southern life was the shift to segregation relatively incomplete by 1890. Most southern streetcar systems initially excluded blacks; separate cars for the races followed. Once blacks gained entrance to the white cars, documenting the existence of segregation becomes difficult. August Meier and Elliott Rudwick argue that segregation "declared after being instituted in many places prior to and just after the Civil War." There is evidence to support the contention that streetcars were the most integrated southern facility. Referring to the color line, the Nashville *American* observed in 1880 that "in Tennessee there is such a line, as every man, white and black, well knows, but on our street cars the races ride together without thought of it, or offensive exhibition, or attempt to isolate the colored passenger." Ten years later, when there was a rumor that the president of one of Richmond's street railways had been asked to provide separate cars for black passengers, the Richmond *Planet,* a Negro newspaper, expressed surprise and counseled against the plan since "we do not know of a city in the south in which discrimination is made on the street cars." In 1908 Ray Stannard Baker sadly concluded that "a few years ago the Negro came and went in the street cars in most cities and sat where he pleased, but gradually Jim Crow laws or local regulations were passed forcing him into certain seats at the back of the car."

Segregation, however, may have been more prevalent than these accounts indicate. In Richmond and Savannah segregated streetcars persisted at least until the mid-1870s. But segregation on horsecars could be inconvenient and expensive to maintain. Because the horses could pull only one rather small car at a time, the segregation of passengers required either the use of an entirely separate car and horse for blacks or limited them to a portion of the already crowded cars open to whites. This problem was remedied by the appearance on southern streets at the end of the 1880s of the dummy streetcar and the later electrification of the lines. The steam driven dummy derived its name from the attempt to disguise the engine as a passenger car in order to cut down on noise and to avoid frightening horses. Since it had two cars or else a single car larger than that pulled by horses, segregation of the races was easier.

Montgomery initiated dummy service in 1886 with the forward cars reserved for whites and the rear cars for blacks. Two years later the dummy also made possible the first clear indication of segregation in Atlanta. The dummy service, begun by the Metropolitan Street Railway Company in September 1888, included two cars plus the engine—one painted yellow for whites, the other red for blacks. Likewise, the first documented case of segregation in a Nashville streetcar after 1867 was contained in an 1888 report about a Negro minister's sermon. It simply noted that "in a sermon Sunday night, [the minister] attacked the management of the dummy line for insisting that he should move to another car or get off." During the following two years, however, the newspapers reported additional instances of blacks being told to go to separate cars.

The period of seeming flexibility came to an end with the passage of statutes enforcing segregation. Both blacks and the streetcar companies often objected to Jim Crow measures. But what were they protesting? Was it segregation or legal segregation that blacks were against? Did the streetcar owners object to any form of racial separation or simply to one that made them supply additional cars, usually an unprofitable venture. The fact that many Nashville blacks would have settled for separate cars in 1905 as long as there were black fare collectors suggests that the boycotts were not simply against segregation. The twentieth-century practice of dividing streetcars into black and white sections lends credence to the view that white owners objected less to the initiation of segregation than to the law requiring more cars. As the Richmond *Planet* noted, southern managers realized that "separate cars would not pay and what was worse there would be more trouble on account of it." Thanks to the cooperation of local officials the managers could handle the "trouble"; financial aspects were another matter.

Then, too, why would streetcars be immune from segregation, given its prevalence in most other areas of southern life? One answer would seem to rest less with the absence of white hostility than in the circumstances in which streetcars operated. The resistance of white managers might be a reason, but as important was the greater leverage blacks exercised over streetcar policy as compared, for example, to railroad policy. Clearly boycotts presented a more serious threat to local streetcar lines than they did to a railroad that drew passengers from many communities. In addition, boycotts could be better organized because of the existence of alternative means of transportation. Whether by using hacks, private carriages, or by simply walking, Negroes could go about their business without the streetcars.

This essay has been primarily concerned with the pervasiveness of segregation in the postbellum South as it came to replace exclusion as the dominant characteristic of race relations. It has been argued that both white Republicans and Redeemers came to embrace this new policy, though often for different reasons. But what helped to assure this shift was the attitude of the blacks themselves.

Blacks on occasion did challenge segregation. During Richmond's celebration of the passage of the Fifteenth Amendment, a Negro minister was accused by the Richmond *Dispatch* of saying that "the negroes must claim the right to sit with the whites in theatres, churches, and other public buildings, to ride with them on the cars, and to stay at the same hotels with them." Similarly after Tennessee passed its Jim Crow law in 1881, a minister from Nashville argued that "no man of color [should] ride in a car simply because it is set apart and *labeled* 'exclusively for negroes,' but rather let every individual choose of the regular coaches the one in which to ride." And six years later when Charles Dudley Warner asked a group of leading Nashville black businessmen "What do you want here in the way of civil rights that you have not?" the answer was, "we want to be treated like men, like anybody else regardless of color.... We want public conveyances open to us according to the fare we pay; we want the privilege to go to hotels and to theatres, operas and places of amusement....

[We] cannot go to the places assigned us in concerts and theatres without loss of self respect."

Negroes opposed segregation by deeds as well as by words. By 1870, Charleston, New Orleans, Richmond, Mobile, and Nashville were among the cities to experience challenges to exclusion or segregation on their streetcars. Suits were brought also against offending railroad companies. Challenges to segregation were most pronounced after passage of the 1875 Civil Rights Act. For the most part, blacks failed to break down the racial barriers in theaters, hotels, restaurants, public conveyances, and bars. More isolated and equally unsuccessful attempts occurred with decreasing frequency in subsequent years.

Despite this opposition to segregation, the majority of blacks, including their leaders, focused their attention elsewhere. The failure of a sustained attack on segregation perhaps resulted from the lack of support from white allies and the courts. There were other reasons as well. Five prominent Nashville blacks, for example, argued that Negroes would not use passage of the Civil Rights Act "to make themselves obnoxious" since they "had too much self respect to go where they were not wanted." Besides, they said, such actions would lead only to disturbances and "colored people wanted peace and as little agitation as possible." Bishop Henry M. Turner echoed this view in 1889, telling a reporter that "I don't find much trouble in traveling at [sic] the south on account of my color, for the simple reason that I am not in the habit of pushing myself where I am not wanted." A similar attitude might have governed the response of "several really respectable colored persons" in Charleston to the attempt of a Negro to buy a ticket for the orchestra or dress circle of the Academy of Music in 1870. Calling the move a cheap political trick, they "avowed their willingness to sit in the places provided for their own race when they visited the Academy."

Economic pressures also led blacks to accept segregation. Negroes who relied on a white clientele were especially reluctant to serve members of both races. Shortly after the passage of the Civil Rights Act two Negro barbers in Edgefield, across the river from Nashville, refused to serve black customers. The previous year a Negro delegation had been ejected when it demanded shaves at the shop of a black barber in Chattanooga. Asked if their money were not as good as a white man's, the barber, fearful of the loss of his white customers, answered, "Yes just as good, but there is not enough of it." Both whites and blacks understood the focus of economic power. In 1875 the Nashville *Union and American* listed twelve blacks who had been testing compliance to the Civil Rights Act. The fact that "most of them got their reward by losing their situations" helps explain why there were not more protestors.

Other blacks sought to work out an equitable arrangement within the confines of a segregated order. They accepted segregation because it was seen as an improvement over exclusion and because they believed, or at least hoped, that separate facilities could be equal. A rider in 1866 on the Nashville streetcar set apart for blacks did not complain about the segregation, but threatened a boycott unless the company protected black passengers from abusive whites who forced their way into the car and used obscene language in front of black women. A Norfolk, Virginia, Negro observing that the city was building a new opera house suggested that "colored theatregoers... petition the managers to give them a respectable place to sit, apart from those of a lewd character." To one Atlanta citizen, writing during a period of racial tension in his city, it seemed that whites and blacks should "travel each in their own distinct paths, steering clear of debatable ground, never forgetting to render one to the other that which equity and good conscience demands." And when the Negro principal of the Alabama State Normal School brought suit against the Western and Atlantic Railroad on the ground that despite his possession of a first-class ticket he was ejected from the first-class car and removed to the Negro car, he admitted the right of the company to classify passengers by race, but maintained it was the duty of the railroad to furnish equal facilities and conveniences for both races. This belief in the need to guarantee separate but equal treatment was expressed in a resolution offered in the Virginia senate by a Negro legislator in 1870. It provided that whites would be forbidden from traveling in portions of boats, trains, and streetcars reserved for blacks. In a letter to the Richmond *Dispatch,* the legislator attributed his action to the fact that there was little possibility of blacks being allowed to ride wherever they wanted and this would protect them, especially the women, from the intrusion of undesirable whites.

In other areas, acceptance of segregation did not necessarily mean passivity on the part of blacks. Again, the targets of protest were exclusion and unequal treatment rather than segregation. For example, blacks placed more emphasis on securing better schools and welfare institutions than on achieving integrated institutions. Blacks went even further. They called for black control of separate facilities through the use of black staff or black directors of public institutions, such as penitentiaries and institutions for the blind, deaf, and dumb. The increase in the number of black colleges, like Tuskegee and Morris Brown, founded and run by blacks was another manifestation of this desire for control over separate institutions.

When the white community persisted in its policy of exclusion, blacks responded by opening their own hospitals, orphanages, hotels, ice cream parlors, and skating rinks. Part of this response was an accommodation to white prejudice; but it was also related to the development of a group identity among blacks. Though it cannot be equated with the racism of whites, by moving in this direction blacks themselves contributed to the emergence of the separate black and white worlds that characterized southern life by 1890.

Although the sanction of law underwrote much of the system of parallel facilities, the separation of the races was accomplished largely without the aid of statutes for as long as both races accepted its existence. As early as 1866, an English traveler, William Dixon, noted that the Negro in Richmond, Virginia, regardless of his legal rights, knew "how far he may go, and where he must stop." He knew also that "[h]abits are not changed by paper law." In 1880 two of the Negro witnesses testifying before a congressional committee pointed to this difference between the power of law and the power of custom. When asked if there were any laws in Alabama applied solely to one race, James T. Rapier answered: "Custom is law in our country now, and was before the war." Asked again if there were any discriminatory provisions in the constitution or state statutes, he replied: "None that I know of; but what we complain of is the administration of the law—the custom of the country." James O'Hara of

North Carolina made a similar statement. "These are matters [segregation in public accommodations] that are and must be regulated purely by prejudice and feeling, and that the law cannot regulate...."

Though prejudice persisted during the quarter century after 1865, a profound change occurred in southern race relations. The policy of exclusion was largely discarded. Instead, by 1890 segregation had been extended to every major area of southern life. Doubts remained as to the possibility of keeping Negroes fully "in their place" without resort to laws. During the last decade of the nineteenth and the first decade of the twentieth century, these doubts resulted in the legalization of practices in effect since the end of the war. As Gilbert Stephenson pointed out for train travel: "The 'Jim Crow' laws ... coming later, did scarcely more than to legalize an existing and widespread custom." For whether under Radical Reconstruction, or Redemption, the best that blacks could hope for in southern racial policy was separate but equal access. In fact, they usually met with either exclusion or separate but unequal treatment. Integration was rarely permitted. When it did occur, it was only at the initiation of whites and was confined as a rule to the least desirable facilities—cheap bars, inferior restaurants, second-class and smoking cars on trains. Whites were there because they chose to be; blacks were there because they had no choice.

Leon F. Litwack

White Folks: Acts

On boarding the streetcar, the woman took the most convenient seat available. "What do you mean?" the conductor shouted at her. "Niggers don't sit with white folks down here. You must have come from 'way up yonder." The woman replied that she was a visitor and had no knowledge of the new law. "Well, no back talk now," the conductor loudly admonished her, playing very much to his audience; "that's what I'm here [for]—to tell niggers their places when they don't know them." The whites in the car laughed over her discomfort. "Not one of them thought that I was embarrassed, wounded, and outraged by the loud, brutal talk of the conductor and the sneering, contemptuous expressions on their own faces." Rather than move to the Jim Crow section she left the car, prompting one of the passengers to remark, "These niggers get more impudent every day; she doesn't want to sit where she belongs."

After walking downtown, the woman attempted to use an elevator in a public building, only to be told to heed the sign posted at the entrance. "I guess you can't read," the elevator operator told her, "but niggers don't ride in this elevator; we're white folks here, we are. Go to the back and you'll find an elevator for freight and niggers." The whites who then occupied the elevator appeared to enjoy her dismay.

The day's events in this Alabama city had left their mark on the woman. As a native Southerner, the daughter of a former slave, it had not been her first experience with the ways of white folks, only a different manifestation of the same phenomenon. "I have been humiliated and insulted often," she declared, "but I never get used to it; it is new each time, and stings and hurts more and more." Her children, she knew, would be better educated than her generation, and she expected the accumulation of insults and humiliations to add to their dislike of whites. "I dread to see my children grow. I know not their fate.... It does not matter how good or wise my children may be, they are colored. When I have said that, all is said. Everything is forgiven in the South but color."...

Racial segregation was hardly a new phenomenon. Before the Civil War, when slavery had fixed the status of most blacks, no need was felt for statutory measures segregating the races. The restrictive Black Codes, along with the few segregation laws passed by the first postwar governments, did not survive Reconstruction. What replaced them, however, was not racial integration but an informal code of exclusion and discrimination. Even the Radical legislatures in which blacks played a prominent role made no concerted effort to force integration on unwilling and resisting whites, especially in the public schools; constitutional or legislative provisions mandating integration were almost impossible to enforce. The determination of blacks to improve their position during and after Reconstruction revolved largely around efforts to secure accommodations that equaled those afforded whites. Custom, habit, and etiquette, then, defined the social relations between the races and enforced separation in many areas of southern life. Whatever the Negro's legal rights, an English traveler noted in Richmond in 1866, he knows "how far he may go, and where he must stop" and that "habits are not changed by paper laws."

But in the 1890s whites perceived in the behavior of "uppity" (and invariably younger) blacks a growing threat or indifference to the prevailing customs, habits, and etiquette. Over the next two decades, white Southerners would construct in response an imposing and extensive system of legal mechanisms designed to institutionalize the already familiar and customary subordination of black men and women. Between 1890 and 1915, state after state wrote the prevailing racial customs and habits into the statute books. Jim Crow came to the South in an expanded and more rigid form, partly in response to fears of a new generation of blacks unschooled in racial etiquette and to growing doubts that this generation could be trusted to stay in its place without legal force. If the old Negro knew his "place," the New Negro evidently did not. "The white people began to begrudge these niggers their running around and doing just as they chose," recalled Sam Gadsden, a black South Carolinian born in 1882. "That's all there is to segregation, that caused the whole thing. The white people couldn't master these niggers any more so they took up the task of intimidating them."

What made the laws increasingly urgent was the refusal of blacks to keep to their place. In the late nineteenth century, economic and social changes swept through the South, introducing new sites and sources of potential racial contact and conflict; at the same time, white women in increasing numbers moved into the public arena and workplace. Both races availed themselves of the expanding means of rail transportation, with middle-class blacks in particular asserting their independence and social position. Refusing to be confined to the second-class or "smoking" car, they purchased tickets in the first-class or "ladies" car, much to the consternation of whites who resented these "impudent" assertions of social equality. In response to white complaints, conductors expelled blacks from the first-class seats they had purchased, resulting in disruptive incidents and litigation.

Segregation, even more than disfranchisement, came to be linked to white fears of social equality. The railroad and the streetcar became early arenas of confrontation, precisely because in no other area of public life (except the polling place) did blacks and whites come together on such an equal footing. "In their homes and in ordinary employment," as one observer noted, "they meet as master and servant; but in the street cars they touch as free citizens, each paying for the right to ride, the white not in a place of command, the Negro without an obligation of servitude. Street car relationships are, therefore, symbolic of the new conditions." In daily travel, the proximity of the races was likely to be much closer, more intimate, more productive of evil, as a New Orleans newspaper suggested: "A man that would be horrified at the idea of his wife or daughter seated by the side of a burly negro in the parlor of a hotel or at a restaurant cannot see her occupying a crowded seat in a car next to a negro without the same feeling of disgust." An English visitor heard the Jim Crow car defended not only as a necessary means to keep the peace but "on the ground of the special aversion which . . . the negro male excites in the white woman."

In South Carolina, where legislation segregating public transportation had been previously defeated, the question took on a new urgency in the late 1890s. Explaining that urgency and why it no longer opposed such legislation, a Columbia newspaper referred to the "many" and "constant" complaints over racial intermingling on the railway trains.

> The seeming humiliation put upon respectable colored people is to be regretted, but they suffer from the conduct of those of their race who have not appreciated the privileges which they were accorded on the railroads of this state. The obtrusiveness and hardly-veiled insolence of many negroes constantly offends ladies traveling and this settles it.

Legislators and editors voiced support of segregation while lamenting the passage of the "old Negro." The linkage seemed obvious. The new laws, explained a state senator, were not needed to protect whites from "good old farm hands and respectable negroes" but from "that insolent class who desired to force themselves into first class coaches."

To resolve this growing problem, state after state, beginning in the 1880s, responded by designating cars for whites and blacks, in many instances making the "smoking" or second-class car the only car available to black passengers. The same assertiveness by blacks on the urban streetcars and trolleys including the refusal to sit in separate sections or to give up seats to whites, prompted municipalities to take similar action. In Jacksonville, Florida, for example, the city council enacted a separate streetcar ordinance after reports of disturbances on the cars and growing complaints from whites about "the attitude" of black passengers.

Some municipalities prescribed separate cars; most settled on partitions that separated the races on the same car, with blacks relegated to the rear seats. On boarding a streetcar in Atlanta, for example, the passenger would see over each door a sign reading

White People Will Seat From Front of Car Toward the Back and Colored People from Rear Toward Front

With some exceptions, that became the standard arrangement. In Birmingham, blacks sat in the front section, and attempts to reverse the order clashed with custom. "After all," one white resident noted, "it is not important which end of the car is given to the nigger. The main point is that he must sit where he is told."

Variations appeared in the way municipalities chose to define and enforce the restrictions. In the absence of clear demarcations within the car, it might be left to the discretion of the conductor. "Heh, you nigger, get back there," an Atlanta conductor shouted, and the black man, who had taken a seat too far forward, complied with the demand. But in most places, as in New Orleans, screens clearly defined where blacks could sit, and if whites filled their section, the screen could be moved farther to the rear. To listen to black passengers, the restrictions were often enforced arbitrarily, almost always to their discomfort and disadvantage. In responding to the complaint of a black woman, who objected to a white man smoking in a car assigned black passengers, the conductor placed the entire Jim Crow apparatus in its proper context: "The law was made to keep you in your place, not the white people."

The new railway stations in Birmingham, Atlanta, Charleston, and Jacksonville impressed visitors with their spaciousness and impressive architecture. Each station also had its separate entrances, waiting rooms, and ticket offices marked "For White Passengers" and "For Colored Passengers." The rod separating the white section from the black section, unlike the screens in streetcars, as one visitor noted, was neither provisional nor movable "but fixed as the foundations of the building." Throughout the South, segregation was extended to waiting rooms, most often confining blacks to smaller and cramped quarters. In one station, the waiting rooms were designated "White Men," "White Women," "Black Men," and "Black Women," but some of the local whites became alarmed at the limited scope of the term "Black" and authorities substituted "Colored."

Although blacks had previously experienced segregation in various forms, the thoroughness of Jim Crow made it strikingly different. What the white South did was to segregate the races by law and enforced custom in practically every conceivable situation in which whites and blacks might come into social contact: from public transportation to public parks, from the workplace to hospitals, asylums, and orphanages, from the homes for the aged, the blind, deaf, and dumb, to the prisons, from saloons to churches. Not only were the races to be kept apart in hospitals (including a special section for black infants requiring medical attention), but some denied admission to blacks altogether. Laws or custom also required that black and white nurses tend only the sick of their own race. By 1885, most states had already legally mandated separate schools. Where intermarriage and cohabitation had not been outlawed, states quickly moved to place such restrictions in law.

The signs "White Only" and "Colored" (or "Negroes") would henceforth punctuate the southern landscape, appearing over the entrances to parks, theaters, boardinghouses, waiting rooms, toilets, and water fountains. Movie houses were becoming increasingly popular, and Jim Crow demanded not only separate ticket windows and entrances but also separate seating, usually in the balcony—what came to be known as the "buzzard roost" or "nigger heaven." And blacks came to learn that in places where they were permitted to mix with whites—stores, post offices, and banks, for example—they would need to wait until all the whites had been served. Special rules also restricted blacks when shopping in white stores, forbidding women, for example, from trying on dresses, hats, and shoes before purchasing them.

The rapid industralization of the South introduced another set of problems, increasing racial tensions in places employing both races. Where whites and blacks worked in the same factories, the law would now mandate segregation wherever feasible. The code adopted in South Carolina, for example, prohibited textile factories from permitting black and white laborers to work together in the same room, or to use the same entrances, pay windows, exits, doorways, or stairways at the same time, or the same "lavatories, toilets, drinking water buckets, pails, cups, dippers or glasses" at any time. Under certain conditions, such as an emergency, the code permitted black firemen, floor scrubbers, and repairmen to associate with white laborers.

Separation of the races often meant the total exclusion of black men and women from certain facilities. The expansion of recreation in the late nineteenth century mandated exclusion of blacks from most amusement parks, roller skating rinks, bowling alleys, swimming pools, and tennis courts. It was not uncommon to find a sign at the entrance to a public park reading "Negroes and Dogs Not Allowed." Excluding blacks from parks deprived them not only of a recreational area but of free public entertainment. "Think of it," a black visitor to Atlanta informed a friend in New York, "Negroes not allowed in some of the parks here, to listen to [a] band which plays here on Sundays." Some communities admitted blacks to parks on certain days, designated a portion for their use, or made arrangements for separate parks.

With few exceptions, municipal libraries were reserved for the exclusive use of whites. Between 1900 and 1910, some public libraries extended limited service—that is, blacks were still denied access to the reading room or the privilege of browsing in the stacks, but they might in some instances borrow books for home use. Rather than make any such provisions in the main library, some cities chose to establish separate branches to serve black patrons. But for whites who feared educated blacks, barring them from libraries altogether made eminently good sense. "[T]he libraries in the Southern States are closed to the low down negro eyes . . . because he is not worthy of an education," a Florida white man wrote to a northern critic. "All the mean crimes, that are done are committed by some educated negro. . . ." In one community, the librarian had a ready answer to a question about why blacks could not be permitted to check out books: "[T]he southern people do not believe in 'social equality.' "

Although most business establishments welcomed back customers, there were exceptions and restrictions. Many laundries, for example, posted signs reading "We Wash For White People Only"; in Nashville, a laundry declared on the sides of its delivery wagons and on advertisements in streetcars "No Negro Washing Taken." Where custom had largely governed which if any restaurants blacks could patronize, laws in some states mandated separate accommodations, often a small room with a separate entrance, and many restaurants barred blacks altogether.

In the early twentieth century, the growing availability of automobiles to both races precipitated a variety of measures. While some communities limited the access of black motorists to the public streets, others placed restrictions on where they might park. In much of the South, racial etiquette dictated that black drivers should make no effort to overtake buggies and wagons driven by whites on unpaved roads. Not only could such behavior be construed as "impudence," but also the white passengers might be enveloped by a cloud of dust. "As a rule," Benjamin Mays recalled, "Negroes did not pass white people on either a dusty or a muddy road.... I have been with my father when he apologized for passing a white driver by saying, 'Excuse me, Boss, I'm in a hurry.' Did this mean that my father mentally accepted or emotionally approved this cringing behavior? I doubt it.... It was a technique of survival."

If the use of roads could be legislated, so could a town's sidewalks, where custom had always dictated that blacks step aside to provide ample room for whites. In Danville, Virginia, after hearing complaints about black children occupying the entire sidewalk on their way to and from school, a new police rule limited their use of those sidewalks when white children were coming or going in the other direction. Of course, whether by law or custom, blacks of any age were expected to step aside when white adults approached.

In the towns and cities, segregated residential patterns were now legally sanctioned, making it difficult for blacks of any class to move into a white block and accelerating the appearance or growth of a distinct district designated as "darktown" or "niggertown." Whether by custom or ordinance, the newer and most rapidly growing cities tended to be the most segregated; by the mid-1890s, for example, racially exclusive sections characterized Atlanta, Richmond, and Montgomery. In some of the older antebellum communities, where house slaves and free blacks had lived near their white employers, black housing tended to be more widely scattered. Some whites thought laws or ordinances restricting where blacks could live were unnecessary, that public sentiment would expeditiously settle the issue. "[T]here is no use to make a law that says one set of men can do this or do that," a resident of Greensboro, North Carolina, argued. "In this white man's town when an African proposed to 'move into' a white section, he was given to understand that it wouldn't do. And if he had moved in he would have moved out a great deal quicker—and a pile of ashes would have marked the house. That is what the White Man will do, law or no law, and that is understood." In a small community south of Clinton, Mississippi, as in Forsyth County, Georgia, public sentiment and night riders imposed their own version of exclusivity by driving out all the black residents.

The legislation of Jim Crow affected all classes and ages, and it tended to be thorough, far-reaching, even imaginative: from separate public school textbooks for black and white children and Jim Crow Bibles on which to swear in black witnesses in court, to separate telephone booths, separate windows in the banks for black and white depositors, and Jim Crow elevators in office buildings, one for whites and one for blacks and freight. New Orleans went so far as to adopt an ordinance segregating black and white prostitutes; Atlanta confined them to separate blocks, while a Nashville brothel settled for a plan by which black prostitutes were placed in the basement and white prostitutes on the ground and upper floors. In Atlanta, the art school that had used black models needed no law to dispense with their employment.

Even as the laws decreed that black babies would enter the world in separate facilities, so blacks would occupy separate places at the end of their lives. The ways in which Jim Crow made its mark on the ritual of death could assume bizarre dimensions. Will Mathis, a convicted white felon, appealed to a judge that he be hanged at a different hour than Orlando Lester, a black man, and from a different set of gallows. The same plea was made by a white Tennessean convicted of the brothel murder of his wife. After he objected to going to the gallows with three black men, the authorities agreed to hang them first. Custom, if not ordinances, dictated that blacks and whites be buried in separate cemeteries. "If a colored person was to be buried among the whites," one observer noted sarcastically in Alabama, "the latter would all rise from their graves in indignation. How they tolerate the 'niggers' in heaven is a mystery, unless the mansions there are provided with kitchens and stables." On the edge of Little Rock, Arkansas, in still another unique expression of white supremacy, a section of the cemetery once reserved for blacks was converted into an exclusively white cemetery. "There are a lot of colored folks buried there and white folks on top of them," a black resident observed. "They didn't move the colored because there wasn't nobody to pay for moving. They just buried the whites on top of them."

Enforcement of the Jim Crow laws could be as harsh and vigorous as the spirit and rhetoric that had demanded them. Had these laws not been adopted, an English visitor thought, "the South would have been a nation of saints, not of men. It is in the methods of its enforcement that they sometimes show themselves not only human but inhuman." The often savage beatings and expulsions on railroads and streetcars attested not only to white determination to enforce the law but also to black resistance to its implementation. Calling the Jim Crow car an "unmixed blessing," a Richmond newspaper noted that those "ill-advised" blacks who had protested it "only accentuated its need and its usefulness." Law and custom interacted to keep blacks in their place, and it would be the responsibility of blacks to learn how to adapt to these conditions as way of life. That required a knowledge not only of local customs and laws but also of the way these might differ from place to place. "Every town had its own mores, its own unwritten restrictions," a black educator recalled. "The trick was to find out from local [black] people what the 'rules' were."

Perhaps the most revealing aspects of Jim Crow were the exceptions made for black domestic workers. If a black servant, for example, accompanied a white child into a railroad coach or into a park reserved for whites, that was perfectly acceptable, since the association did not imply an equal relationship. "Everything was all right," a Georgia house servant revealed, "so long as I was in the white man's part of the street car or in the white man's coach as a servant—a slave—but as soon as I did not present myself as a menial, and the relationship of master and servant was abolished by my not having the white children with me, I would be forthwith assigned to the 'nigger' seats or the 'colored people's coach.'" The same exception applied to black servants overseeing white children in public parks that barred blacks. Some of the parks bore signs reading "No Negroes Allowed on These Grounds Except as Servants." A black teacher ventured into a restricted park in Charleston in the company of a white friend and fellow teacher and precipitated no objections. "Of course," she noted, "every one thought I was her maid."

Whether in the exceptions made for black employees or in the quality of the facilities afforded blacks, the position of superior and inferior had to be absolutely clear. "The black nurse with a white baby in her arms, the black valet looking after the comfort of a white invalid," an Episcopal minister in Napoleonville, Louisiana, explained, "have the label of their inferiority conspicuously upon them; they understand themselves, and everybody understand them, to be servants, enjoying certain privileges for the sake of the person served. Almost anything the Negro may do in the South, and anywhere he may go, provided the manner of his doing and his going is that of an inferior. Such is the premium put upon his inferiority; such his inducement to maintain it." On this basis, the poorest illiterate white could claim a standing in society denied to the wealthiest and most intelligent and educated black. . . .

❧❦❧

In Richland County, South Carolina, in the 1920s, a black story-teller reflected about the law and the courts and how they operated half a century after the abolition of slavery. "Dere ain' no use. De courts er dis land is not for niggers. . . . It seems to me when it come to trouble, de law an' a nigger is de white man's sport, an' justice is a stranger in them precincts, an' mercy is unknown." The Bible, he noted, asked people to pray for their enemy, and so he offered up this prayer: "Drap on you' knee, brothers, an' pray to God for all de crackers an' de judges an' de courts an' solicitors, sheriffs an' police in de land. . . ."

As the storyteller suggested, the perversion of justice had become a lasting legacy of the New South. The mechanisms of legal violence—that is, violence sanctioned by the day-to-day workings of the legal system—functioned after Reconstruction as a formidable instrument of social control. In the name of the law and justice, whites (including those sworn to uphold and enforce the law) made a mockery of law and justice. The legal system was only one mechanism in the arsenal of white power, but it proved to be a critical and formidable one. Unequal justice interacted with disfranchisement, segregation, economic exploitation, inferior schooling, and violence to remind blacks of all ages and classes of where power rested in this society. By 1907, a newspaper in Yazoo, Mississippi, could observe with satisfaction how the South had become to all intents and purposes a closed society. "With every official in Mississippi a white man, and every jury composed of whites; every judge upon the bench white, and all elections conducted by and only participated in by whites, there can be no possible danger of negro rule."

In communities across the South, blacks came to perceive the law and its enforcers as an outside and alien force, an intrusive and repressive agency against which appeals for fairness and impartiality, humane and just treatment, were all but useless. Even as the United States in the wake of World War I promoted the cause of international justice, blacks demanded some semblance of domestic justice. In the black press and at black meetings, the abuse of the law and the double standard of justice applied to the two races took increasing precedence over other issues. The remark made in a Georgia court that not half of the blacks sentenced would be convicted if properly represented resonated with blacks throughout the South. Addressing a biracial audience in Oklahoma City, a black editor confided to them how black people thought about the legal system:

> I think you ought to know how the black man talks and feels at times when he knows that you are nowhere about, and I want to tell you, if you were to creep up to-night to a place where there are 10,000 Negroes gathered, you would find no division on this one point. I know that they all would say, "WE HAVE NO CONFIDENCE IN WHITE POLICEMEN." Let there be one hundred or one hundred thousand, they would with one accord all say, "WE HAVE NO CONFIDENCE IN THE WHITE MAN'S COURT." I think you ought to know this, for it is with what men think that we have to deal. They would say in such a meeting that they know before they get into the court what the verdict will be. If their cause is the cause of a black man against a white man they will say that they know that a verdict would be rendered in favor of the white man.

This view of southern justice rested on an abundance of evidence, on tens of thousands of cases tried and not tried. The differences between the courtroom and the lynch mob were not always clear in the New South. Nor in the eyes of black men and women were there discernible differences between a speedy trial and mob justice, between lawless lynchers and lawless judges, sheriffs, constables, policemen, wardens, and prison guards. "The fact is," a black educator noted in 1915, "that lynching has gone on so long in many parts of our country that it is somewhat difficult to draw at this time a sharp line marking off distinctly the point where the lynching spirit stops and the spirit of legal procedure commences. You cannot tell what the most peaceable community will do at any moment under certain conditions."

The most repressive period in the history of race relations in the South also became the most violent. The race chauvinism, the often rabid Negrophobia, the intense feelings and emotions stirred up by the campaigns to disfranchise and segregate blacks expressed themselves simultaneously in an era of unprecedented racial violence. Rather than allay white fears, the campaigns to repress blacks heightened those fears. Rather than provide safe alternatives, the campaigns exacerbated race relations. Once dehumanized, black life was cheapened and made even more expendable. The effort to solidify the subordination of black men and women knew no limits.

POSTSCRIPT

Did Racial Segregation Improve the Status of African Americans?

There is little question that racial segregation created a separate and subordinate status for African Americans. Rabinowitz's selection is important in that it recognizes that patterns of Jim Crow represented a middle ground between total exclusion and full integration and that few blacks living in the United States at the turn of the century could have assumed that integration was a realistic possibility. Moreover, Rabinowitz, in this and other works (see especially *Race Relations in the Urban South, 1865–1890* [Oxford University Press, 1978]), challenges the interpretation of the origins of segregation developed by C. Vann Woodward in *The Strange Career of Jim Crow* (Oxford University Press, 1955). Writing in the wake of the explosive response by white segregationists to the U.S. Supreme Court's decision in *Brown v. Board of Education of Topeka* (1954), Woodward attempted to restore some sense of calm by declaring that segregation of the races was not an "immutable folkway" of the South. Looking back at the first 25 years following the Civil War, Woodward depicted a South in which no color line was rigidly drawn. In other words, Woodward, a native southerner, was challenging the notion that prevailed among most whites in the mid-twentieth-century South that segregation of the races had been in force ever since emancipation. While making a distinction between customary and *de jure* segregation, Woodward argued that the latter form did not appear in full until 1890.

Rabinowitz demonstrates that, in fact, numerous examples of legal segregation of the races could be found in the South during the Reconstruction period, especially in southern cities. Litwack, in *North of Slavery: The Negro in the Free States, 1790–1860* (University of Chicago Press, 1961), and Richard C. Wade, in *Slavery in the Cities: The South, 1820–1860* (Oxford University Press, 1964), also make a case for an earlier starting point for Jim Crow. Woodward answered some of his critics in "The Strange Career of a Historical Controversy," published in his *American Counterpoint: Slavery and Racism in the North-South Dialogue* (Little, Brown, 1971).

Discussions of race relations in the late-nineteenth- and early-twentieth-century United States invariably focus upon the ascendancy of Booker T. Washington, his apparent accommodation to existing patterns of racial segregation, and the conflicting traditions within black thought, which were epitomized by the clash between Washington and Du Bois. A thorough assessment of the protest and accommodationist views of black Americans is presented in August Meier, *Negro Thought in America, 1880–1915* (University of Michigan Press, 1963). For a study that coincides with the tone set in the selection by Litwack, see Rayford Logan, *The Betrayal of the Negro: From Rutherford*

B. Hayes to Woodrow Wilson (Macmillan, 1965). By far the best study of Booker T. Washington is Louis Harlan's 2-volume biography *Booker T. Washington: The Making of a Black Leader, 1856–1901* (Oxford University Press, 1972) and *Booker T. Washington: The Wizard of Tuskegee, 1901–1915* (Oxford University Press, 1983). In addition, Harlan has edited the 13-volume *Booker T. Washington Papers* (University of Illinois Press, 1972–1984). For assessments of two of Washington's harshest critics, see Stephen R. Fox, *The Guardian of Boston: William Monroe Trotter* (Atheneum, 1970) and David Levering Lewis, *W. E. B. Du Bois: Biography of a Race, 1868–1919* (Henry Holt, 1993) and *W. E. B. Du Bois: The Fight for Equality and the American Century, 1919–1963* (Henry Holt, 2000). John H. Bracey, Jr., August Meier, and Elliott Rudwick, in *Black Nationalism in America* (Bobbs-Merrill, 1970), provide an invaluable collection of documents pertaining to black nationalism. See also Edwin S. Redkey, *Black Exodus: Black Nationalist and Back-to-Africa Movements, 1890–1910* (Yale University Press, 1969) and Hollis R. Lynch, *Edward Wilmot Blyden: Pan-Negro Patriot, 1832–1912* (Oxford University Press, 1967). Diverse views of Marcus Garvey, who credited Booker T. Washington with inspiring him to seek a leadership role on behalf of African Americans, are found in Edmund David Cronon, *Black Moses: The Story of Marcus Garvey and the Universal Negro Improvement Association* (University of Wisconsin Press, 1955); Tony Martin, *Race First: The Ideological and Organizational Struggles of Marcus Garvey and the UNIA* (Greenwood Press, 1976); and Judith Stein, *The World of Marcus Garvey: Race and Class in Modern Society* (Louisiana State University Press, 1986). Some of Garvey's own writings are collected in Amy Jacques-Garvey, ed., *Philosophy and Opinions of Marcus Garvey* (1925; Atheneum, 1969).

ISSUE 7

Was the Ku Klux Klan of the 1920s an Extremist Movement?

YES: David H. Bennett, from *The Party of Fear: From Nativist Movements to the New Right in American History* (University of North Carolina Press, 1988)

NO: Stanley Coben, from *Rebellion Against Victorianism: The Impetus for Cultural Change in 1920s America* (Oxford University Press, 1991)

ISSUE SUMMARY

YES: Professor of history David H. Bennett argues that the Ku Klux Klan of the 1920s was a traditional nativist organization supported mainly by fundamentalist Protestants who were opposed to the changing social and moral values associated with the Catholic and Jewish immigrants.

NO: Professor of history Stanley Coben asserts that local Klansmen were not a fringe group of fundamentalists but solid, middle-class citizens who were concerned about the decline in moral standards in their communities.

There have been three Ku Klux Klans in American history: (1) the Reconstruction Klan, which arose in the South at the end of the Civil War and whose primary purpose was to prevent the newly emancipated blacks from voting and attaining social and economic equality with whites; (2) the 1920s Klan, which had national appeal and emerged out of disillusionment with the aftermath of U.S. intervention in World War I and the changing social and economic values that had transformed America as a result of the full-scale Industrial Revolution; and (3) the modern Klan, which arose after World War II in the rural areas of the Deep South and (like the Reconstruction Klan) came about to prevent blacks from attaining the political and legal rights guaranteed by the passage of the civil rights legislation in the 1950s and 1960s.

The Klan of the 1920s was founded in 1915 by William J. Simmons, a Methodist circuit preacher, and 15 of his followers. For five years the resurrected Klan consisted of only 4,000 or 5,000 members in scattered Klans throughout

Georgia and Alabama. On June 7, 1920, Simmons signed a contract with two clever salespersons, Edward Clarke and Elizabeth Tyler, who pioneered some of the most remarkable organizing and mass marketing techniques of the pro-business decade of the 1920s. The campaign was an immediate success. Between June 1920 and October 1921, 85,000 men joined the Klan. Total membership figures are difficult to ascertain, but somewhere between 3 and 5 million people joined the Klan. This means that one of every four Protestant males in America was a member of the Klan.

The 1920s Klan differed greatly from its predecessors and successors because it had wide-ranging influence in politics across the nation. The Klan was not merely a southern movement but a national movement that was strongest in the Midwest and Southwest. Politically, Klan members dominated state legislatures in Oklahoma, Texas, and Indiana, and city councils in such far-western places as El Paso, Texas; Denver, Colorado; Anaheim, California; and Tillamook, Oregon. The Klan of the 1920s was the most powerful right-wing movement of the decade.

While the 1920s Klan disliked blacks, it focused its attacks upon the Catholic and Jewish immigrants who had been coming to America since the 1890s. Klansmen particularly disliked Catholics, who constituted 36 percent of the nation's population in 1920. Catholics were accused of placing loyalty to the pope ahead of loyalty to the nation. If Catholics gained political control, the Klan asserted, separation of church and state would end, and freedoms of speech, press, and religious worship would also be abolished.

The Klan was also inspired by the xenophobic (fear of foreigners) atmosphere of the time. America's participation in World War I had ended in public disillusionment. The U.S. Senate reflected the country's dislike of all things foreign when it refused to ratify President Woodrow Wilson's Treaty of Versailles. Antiforeign feelings were also reflected in the passage of the 1921 and 1924 reform laws, which severely curtailed immigration from southern and eastern Europe and completely excluded Japanese and other oriental groups.

Most explanations for the fall of the 1920s Klan seem unsatisfactory. Greed may have been one cause. There was a lot of money involved—it has been estimated that as much as $75 million in Klan initiation fees and wardrobes ended up in the pockets of various Klan leaders—and everyone seemed to have their hand in the till. Moral hypocrisy also infiltrated the Klan. While many Klan members were afraid of the changing standards of morality and supported Klan politicians who preached law and order, the opposite was often the case. Third, the depression of the 1930s and World War II may have contributed to the Klan's fall by directing people's energies elsewhere.

Was the 1920s Ku Klux Klan an extremist organization? According to David H. Bennett in the following selection, the Klan was a traditional nativist organization supported mainly by fundamentalist Protestants who were opposed to the changing social and moral values of the 1920s associated with the Catholic and Jewish immigrants. In the second selection, Stanley Coben asserts that most Klansmen were ordinary white, middle-class Protestants who composed what he has described elsewhere as "the largest grassroots conservative . . . movement in American history."

Traditional Nativism's Last Stand

Restating the Themes of Nativism

The Ku Klux Klan under Hiram Wesley Evans and associates offered a program reminiscent of its nativist progenitors, the Know Nothings and the APA. Klan papers and magazines, books and articles by Klan leaders, laid out the appeal of the new nativism.

One spokesman, Reverend E. H. Laugher, in *The Kall of the Klan of Kentucky*. explained that "the KKK is not a lodge or a society or a political party." Rather, it is a mass movement, "a crusade of American people who are beginning to realize that they have neglected their public and religious duty to stand up for Americanism." This meant remembering that America was discovered by Norsemen, colonized by Puritans, that the United States was "purely Anglo-Saxon and Nordic." It was essential to "preserve our racial purity," he insisted, to avoid "mongrelization." It was imperative to maintain separation of church and state because "the forces of Protestantism" were protectors of the "doctrine of Americanism." The Roman Catholic church, appealing to the polyglot peoples who threatened the good and pure society, must be blocked in its drive to dominate and destroy the great nation.

In *The Fiery Cross, The Kourier, The American Standard, Dawn, The Imperial Night-Hawk,* and other publications, Klan ideologists assaulted Catholics, Jews, and aliens. "Jesus was a Protestant," the faithful were told, he had "split with the priests" because he had truth and right on his side. The Roman Catholic church, laboring under "the growth of Popish despotism," was irreligious and un-American. In fact, the "Papacy's campaign against liberalism and freedom" made it a proper "ally of Mussolini's fascism," just as the church had been on the side of other autocracies since medieval times. In America, the "spirit of Bunker Hill and Valley Forge," that longing for democracy and individualism which informed the Revolution and the words of the Founding Fathers, was at odds with a "hierarchical Church, which, like an octopus, has stretched its tentacles into the very vitals of the body politic of the nation." The church's effort to undermine the public schools, to "reach out for the children of Protestantism," to "hit anywhere with any weapon" in an unscrupulous campaign to impose its will, meant that every Catholic in public life, from school board

From David H. Bennett, *The Party of Fear: From Nativist Movements to the New Right in American History* (University of North Carolina Press, 1988). Copyright © 1988 by University of North Carolina Press. Reprinted by permission. Notes omitted.

member to national politician, must be watched carefully. "Do you know," a Klan editorialist asked, "that eight states have Roman Catholic administrations, 690 public schools teach from the Roman Catholic catechism, sixty-two percent of all elected and appointed offices in the United States are now held by Catholics, who also are a majority of the teachers in many major city school systems?"

The threat of the church was everywhere. The "Romanized press" tried to propagandize a gullible public. Catholics evaded taxes as a matter of course, refusing to share the burdens of government, preferring to subsidize sinister schemes hatched by their prelates. The church used Jesuits to engage in "occult mental manipulations" and tried to "subjugate the Negro race through spiritual domination." The pope favored child labor, and because "20,000 ordained priests in America are vassals to this Imperial Monarch in Rome," the same could be expected of church leaders in the United States. Indeed, Catholics were in no sense trustworthy Americans; during the Great War, "German sentiment was the fruit of carefully prepared and skillfully disseminated Roman propaganda." But it would be wrong to conclude that the Klan was anti-Catholic, leaders insisted, because its arguments were "wholly and solely concentrated on being one hundred per cent American." In fact, one writer suggested, the Klan is "no more aimed at Roman Catholics than it would be aimed at Buddhists, Confucianists or Mohammedans, or anybody else who owes allegiance to any foreign person and/or religion."

Like the nineteenth-century nativists, Klan initiates were asked to protect America from the diabolical plans of Jesuits and other leaders of this un-American presence. From colonial days, anti-Catholicism had been a dominant theme in the history of these movements, a way of displacing fears and angers on alien intruders. In the 1920s, with Irish Catholics maintaining positions of prominence in urban and national politics, continuing to gain greater influence in a growing economy, Klan spokesmen returned to the old themes. The assault on the church was repeated in almost every Klan speech, article, and editorial. This modern Ku Klux Klan dressed its members in garb borrowed from the Reconstruction vigilante organization, but its real roots were in traditional nativism, stretching back much further in the American experience.

But to its attack on Catholicism, the modern Klan added an anti-Semitic element. The APA, emerging during the new immigration, had touched on this theme; Klan writers developed the argument. "Jews are everywhere a separate and distinct people, living apart from the great Gentile masses," said the author of *Klansmen: Guardians of Liberty*. But these people are not "home builders or tillers of the soil." Evans had made a similar argument in a speech at Dallas in December 1922: "The Jew produces nothing anywhere on the face of the earth. He does not till the soil. He does not create or manufacture anything for common use. He adds nothing to the sum of human welfare." Yet not only were Jews unproductive, Klan theoreticians insisted, they were un-American. They were not interested in integration: "No, not the Jew... he is different." These people, who "defied the melting pot for one thousand years," believed in their own superiority, in "Jewry Uber Alles." They hatched secret plans to advance their interests to "cause wars and to subjugate America." Certain conspiratorial Jews must be "absolutely and eternally" opposed when they plotted their "crimes and wrongs." They were nothing more than money-grubbing and immoral vultures, "moral lepers who gloat over human tragedy, rejoice in the downfall of the guileless and inexperienced." The unethical practices of Jewish businessmen—often seen as winners in the economic competition of the boom years—and the radical schemes of Jewish Marxists were considered equally repugnant, dangers to America. But so, too, was the cultural depravity of strategically placed "Semites" in the media. "Jew Movies Urge Sex and Vice," the Klan headline shouted like an echo from Ford's *Dearborn Independent;* "Jewish corruption in jazz" was a result of "their monopoly over popular songs." In the big cities, "ninety five per cent of bootleggers are Jews."

It was the Roaring Twenties, and as mores changed, as traditional social arrangements were overturned, as skirts went up and speakeasies flourished, as the movies and radio made their mark with Tin Pan Alley songs popularized by so many show business celebrities, the Klan found a way of identifying these disturbing developments in an antialien context, of standing up for America by assailing yet another band of un-Americans.

Still, the Jews were only one part of a larger alien problem in America. Again, like the Know Nothings and the patriotic fraternalists of the 1890s, these nativists were concerned with the threat they saw posed by all non-Anglo-Saxon immigrants and their descendants. Imperial Wizard Evans spoke of "the vast horde of immigrants who have reached our shores," these "Italian anarchists, Irish Catholic malcontents, Russian Jews, Finns, Letts, Lithuanians of the lowest class." Even after the Immigration Act of 1924, which Evans characterized as a "new era dawning for America" and took full credit for security—"typifying the influence exerted by our organization"—he warned that undesirables "are still bootlegged into the nation," still try to "flaunt our immigration laws." This "polyglotism" was intolerable, for many of the most recent immigrants from southern and eastern Europe and from Asia still could not read and write English. They were unfamiliar with American history and tradition, "were unaware that America is fundamentally an Anglo-Saxon achievement." And because these alien peoples "congregate in our great centers, our cities are a menace to democracy," they are "modern Sodoms and Gomorrahs." Is "Petrograd in its ruin and desolation a picture of New York in the future"? There was only one possible response. "America for the Americans," Evans exhorted, for if "this state of affairs continues, the American race is doomed to cultural destruction." In words that might have been lifted from a Know Nothing broadside, he continued: "Illiteracy, disease, insanity, and mental deficiency are still pouring in among us."

The "foreigners" were responsible for a host of social problems. Evans lectured on "our alien crime-plague" and Klan papers reported on alien thugs, Italian mobsters and rum runners, even a "Newark alien hiding whiskey in U.S. flag." The aliens threatened female virtue: "Foreign women sell their bodies for gain." They threatened the safety of American womanhood: "Women Are Struck Down by Foreign Mob," screamed one headline, "Aliens Poison Hoosier Women," said another. Some aliens were radicals: "Russians Would Make America Red, Peril is a Very Real One." Others would destroy the nation through political sabotage: "Use the Ballot, the Italian Ambassador Recommends, to Advance the Interests of Italians' Native Land." And over all these perils loomed the threat of Irish Catholic party machine manipulators. Leaders of the church in America, most formidable of the foreign operatives, these "Irish Romanists in Tammany... lead the Jews, Poles, Italians, Germans, Czechs, Magyars"; it was a "vast army under command of the Irish Roman ward heelers." The only way to deal with the foreign devils, to safeguard our sacred institutions, was to re-Americanize the land. Evans announced: "Against us are all the forces of the mixed alliance composed of alienism, Romanism, hyphenism, Bolshevism and un-Americanism which aim to use this country as a dumping ground for the fermenting races of the Old World." But "we of the Klan are on the firing line ... like the soldiers of the American Expeditionary Force in France, we stand up for America and take pride and joy in the wounds we receive ... the Knights of the Ku Klux Klan have become the trustees under God for Protestant American nationalism."

The cause of the Klan, in the phrases of its spokesmen, could not have been more noble, more dangerous, or more urgent. But among those many American values that Klansmen were sworn to protect, one had particular urgency. This was the protection of "womanhood." In pursuing this goal, the Klan invoked memories of that long line of femininity's defenders who marched under the banners of nativism, back to the days of Maria Monk.

A Texas Klansman, author of *Religious and Patriotic Ideals of the Ku Klux Klan,* reminded initiates that they had sworn to "promote good works and thus protect the chastity of womanhood, the virtue of girlhood, the sanctity of the home." Spokesmen repeatedly used the term "chivalry" in describing the movement's principles. The role of women in the literature of the Klan was explicitly traditional. They were the moral arbiters of society, for "even in the midst of all the pressing duties of maternal care and home making, women have found time to keep the spiritual fire of the nation burning on the altar ... women have been the conscience keepers of the race." But the role was not so traditional that women would be repressed, for it was "Rome Which Opposes the Advancement of Womanhood," said the headline, the Jesuits who favor policies pushing women into "semi-oriental seclusion." The Klan would preserve and protect women so they might aid in the shaping of American destiny; "the fate of the nation is in the hands of women." As one Klan newswriter put it, they can be "not only help meets but help mates." After all, the "very mentioning of the word 'woman' always arrests the attention of every true man. Whatever else the human heart may forget in the rough experiences of life, it cannot forget its mother."

The call to protect these fragile, sensitive, vulnerable women led to violence. Local Klans were accused of floggings, tar and featherings, and beatings in several states in the South, Southwest, and lower Midwest. The victims of the masked night riders often were alleged adulterers and wife-beaters, men said not to be supporting their families, men who had deserted their women. But the enemies of "pure womanhood" included sinners of both sexes. "Fallen women" were the targets in some rural bastions. Young women accused of prostitution or adultery were stripped naked, tarred, left half-conscious with their hair shorn. The sexual frustrations of these bands of white-robed small-townsmen, envious of the freedom exercised by millions of more liberated urbanites in the jazz age, finding perverse pleasure in this part of their crusade for morality, reveling in the projection of their anger and the displacement of their resentments of these symbolic villains, recalled the nunnery craze of the early nineteenth century.

In fact, another generation of nativists meant another resurgence of convent tales. *Dawn* [a major Klan paper in Chicago] offered "Convent Cruelties: The True Story of Ex-Nun Helen Jackson," advertising offprints of this sadomasochistic piece for many months after initial publication. Other Klan journals featured, among several exposés, "Behind Convent Walls" and "Roman Priest Alienates Innocent Women's Love."

Women who knew their role and understood their place were offered membership in affiliate groups open to "patriotic ladies." Simmons's Kamelai had been disbanded, but Hiram Evans introduced the Women of the Ku Klux Klan, an organization which absorbed such local groups as Ladies of the Invisible Empire in Louisiana and the Order of American Women in Texas. This new national organization established its own Imperial Palace, a pillared mansion in Little Rock, Arkansas. It sent its own kleagles [officials in the Klan] into the field, calling on Klansmen to influence wives and sisters to join. By fall 1924, when the Ku Klux Klan said its membership numbered in the millions, the women's auxiliary claimed a following of two hundred thousand. The initiates were not, as one anti-Klan writer suggested, "nativist amazons." They were expected to perform customary housewifely chores; they prepared food for Klan outings, picnics, and klambakes. In fact, their order was little more than the instrument of one man's authority. James Comer, Evans's early ally and grand dragon of the Arkansas Klan, bankrolled the Women of the Ku Klux Klan and controlled its activities. He forced the resignation of its imperial commander to install Robbie Gill, an initiate friend who would soon be his wife, as new leader. It was Commander Gill who told the Second Imperial Klonvocation: "God gave Adam Woman to be his comrade and counselor... Eve's name meant life, society, company. Adam was lord and master." Like earlier nativists, Klansmen never questioned the assumption of male dominance. The American dream they sought to protect had no room for sexual equality. But the image of threatened womanhood was essential to their own search for masculine validation, even as it had been in the days of *The Awful Disclosures of Maria Monk.* That had been another age in which economic growth and status anxiety served as a setting for the resurgence of the antialien crusade.

The attacks on Catholics and foreigners and the vows to protect imperiled American women tied the Ku Klux Klan to a long history of similar movements. It was traditional nativism's last stand. Its emergence in the 1920s raised questions to which contemporary journalists and academics offered a variety of answers.

Reporter Robert L. Duffus, author of a series of anti-Klan articles in the *World's Work,* argued that many recruits came from "the back counties of the south and lower midwest," where men carry guns, women are objects of the deference but also of exploitation, and the disappointed seek causes outside themselves. Professor Frank Tannenbaum, writing in 1924, agreed in part, seeing Klansmen as seekers after "artificial thrills" as a way of dealing with the boredom of small-town life, people ready to use coercion in defense of social status, people "losing their grip" in a world of change. But Tannenbaum also looked to recent events as a source of this mood of restlessness. The Great War aroused human passions, he suggested, the "hope of a new and beatific world after the defeat of the German evil." The Klan offered an explanation of why the war brought no "dawning of Utopia." It was the Catholic, the radical, the foreigner who was in league with the devil.

Later, scholars would embrace some of these views. Though not sharing pro-Klan journalist Stanley Frost's rosy vision of Klansmen as a knighthood of admirable reformers, they agreed that the Klan represented a response to the war, a zeal to cleanse and reform American society. The rise of fundamentalist fervor in the 1920s, which provided an additional setting for the Klan, was seen as another reaction to the war. Anti-Catholicism was in the air in many parts of the nation in these years. As with fundamentalism, the Klan's crusade for conformity to old values and old social arrangements was seen as a "characteristic response to a common disillusion."

The Ku Klux Klan, like the Red Scare, was given new life by the souring of the international crusade. Almost all students of the Klan have made this point. But the reason why the Klan grew in the 1920s had more to do with social and economic strains in a society experiencing almost unprecedented growth.

Those who joined were not, as Duffus suggested, only losers in the boom years. Along with poor farmers, blue-collar workers, mechanics, and day laborers some bankers, lawyers, doctors, ministers, and prosperous businessmen were recruited in different regions. There were communities in which political careers and professional success depended on membership. But the Klan appealed more to those who were not members of any elite. Imperial Wizard and Emperor Evans observed: "We are a movement of the plain people, very weak in the matter of culture, intellectual support and trained leadership.... We demand a return of power into the hands of the everyday, not highly cultured, not overly intellectualized but entirely unspoiled and not de-Americanized average citizens of the old stock." The Klan everywhere appealed to those who believed that their older vision of America was at risk. In the struggle to preserve enduring American values, the movement offered a sense of common purpose in service of a cause greater than self. It offered an idealism that had a magnetic pull for many. Its shrewd managers, interested in money, power, and influence for themselves, knew how to package the movement. But the popularity of the Klan, once it began to spread across the land, did not depend on the Clarkes and Tylers or their successors as marketing specialists and salesmen. Like the earlier nativist fraternities, it was rooted in a longing for order, in misty memories of some stable and happy past, in fears of what new perils modernity might bring, in the search for community in an age of flux.

The movement provided community. Local Klans sponsored Sunday dinners and square dances, basketball tournaments and rodeos, carnivals and circuses, fireworks displays featuring "electric fiery crosses," social events of all kinds. It was comforting to be in the Klan, and it could be fun. Klansmen also took care of each other. Businessmen placed ads for Klan Klothes Kleaned or Krippled Kars Kured, expecting fraternal ties would result in new customers. Other activities offered bonding through unified action to clean up the community: boycotts of businesses run by "immoral men," committees to ferret out bootleggers and bars.

The communal ties seemed at one with religious conviction. The movement that defended Protestantism won the tacit endorsement of many clergymen, some who joined the order. Most nationally prominent church leaders stayed away from the Klan, and some Methodist, Presbyterian, and Episcopalian notables and publications even attacked it, but these assaults from influential cosmopolitans only served to underscore Evans's claims that his movement was the instrument of the mass of common people. The Klan made inroads in many Protestant communities, particularly among Southern Baptists and others influenced by fundamentalist concerns. A major part of the Protestant press remained silent on the issue, but many local church papers endorsed the goals of an organization that appealed for support in the name of old-time values and that old-time religion.

The Klan's growth was meteoric. In 1924, Stanley Frost reported that "some say it has six million members." Frost himself claimed only some 4.5 million in the movement. Robert Duffus put the number at 2.5 million in 1923. Other guesses ranged upward of 5 million. It was impossible to be certain; the Klan left only fragmentary local records and no national archives. But one modern scholar, using available data, estimated it had over 2 million recruits in 1924; another, in a careful review of conflicting claims, put it at over 2 million initiates across the years, with some 1.5 million at any one time. What is certain is that it had become a true mass movement, one of the major developments in the history of the 1920s, a great monument to the antialien impulse in America.

The Klan Across America

But it did not prosper equally in all sections of the country. In the Deep South, where the Klan was born, it exerted considerable influence in some states. Still, its membership never exceeded a quarter of a million....

The Klan lasted longer in Indiana, home of its most powerful, most successful organization in the United States. The man who was instrumental in recruiting a quarter of a million knights statewide—almost forty thousand in Indianapolis—was Grand Dragon David D. Stephenson. Only thirty years old in 1921, Stephenson had been one of the four key state leaders helping Evans oust Simmons before the first national meeting in Atlanta. Rewarded with the organizing rights for twenty-three states in the North, this charismatic figure, who liked to compare himself to Napoleon, already was a successful coal dealer when he joined the Invisible Empire. But in the Klan, he would make a fortune in recruitment fees and build a reputation as a mesmerizing orator, the super salesman of the national Klan.

In Indiana, his order sponsored parades and athletic contests, field days and picnics. It offered community and festivity, but always in the name of protecting Protestant America from its enemies. In "Middletown," the Lynds found it had become a working-class movement and "tales against the Catholics ran like wild fire" through Muncie. Local Klansmen vowed they would unmask only "when and not until the Catholics take the prison walls down from the convents and nunneries." Anti-Catholic, anti-Semitic, antiblack rhetoric filled Stephenson's colorful speeches: the Klan stood for temperance and patriotism, the aliens were threatening traditional American values. This appeal was so successful that store owners soon put TWK [Trade with a Klansman] in their windows; the secrecy of the order could be violated with little fear of retaliation in a state in which hundreds of thousands were flocking to join the most popular movement in memory. In fact, so many initiates paid their kleck-token to Stephenson that it was estimated he made between $2 and $5 million in eighteen months. The grand dragon acquired a ninety-eight-foot yacht, which he kept on Lake Huron, a fleet of automobiles, a palatial suburban home, and elaborate offices in downtown Indianapolis. There, the mayor opposed "Steven" and his order until a Klansman named Edward Jackson won the Republican primary for governor in 1923. Now the Klan took control of the county party machinery. Jackson's subsequent election gave Stephenson and his movement state power unmatched by any other Klan.

A high point was reached with the fabled Konklave at Kokomo, when "200,000 men and women filled with love of country"—in the words of the *Fiery Cross* (Indiana State Edition)—gathered for the Klan's greatest single meeting. Tens of thousands of cars brought members from across Indiana and Ohio. Stephenson, attired in a sequined purple robe and escorted by his team of personal bodyguards, finally mounted the rostrum. He explained that he was late for the meeting because "the President of the United States kept me counselling upon matters of state." He proceeded to deliver a quintessentially nativist exhortation, filled with pleas for America and plans for vigilant opposition to the aliens. Always a riveting stump speaker, Stephenson was most respected for his organizational skills. But his Bonapartist complex and rumors for numerous sexual indiscretions and alcoholic binges soon led to conflicts with state and national Klan leaders. Evans turned against him, and he resigned as state grand dragon in September 1923. But D. C. Stephenson was not through. He marshaled support for a special state meeting the following May, in which his followers elected him once against their grand dragon, thus rejecting the authority of national headquarters. Stephenson continued to flout the hierarchical authority of the national Klan, staying in power during the election year of 1924, a time which marked the KKK's most significant impact in American politics. But by 1925, the Indiana chief was caught up in the scandal that ended in his prison sentence, a sordid affair that fatally wounded not only the Indiana Klan but the national movement as well....

Although the Klan had suffered setbacks in Oklahoma, Texas, Colorado, Oregon, Illinois, and other states by early 1925, it still seemed a formidable national movement in the year after the election. Then came the Stephenson scandal in Indiana. The grand dragon was implicated in the death of a statehouse employee named Madge Oberholtzer. Although it was widely reported that he had known many attractive women in Indianapolis, D. C. Stephenson chose to lavish particular attention on Oberholtzer. She later testified that he compelled her to drink with him, finally forcing her at gunpoint to a train. In the private compartment he attacked and "sexually mutilated" her. Oberholtzer took a fatal overdose of drugs after this incident, but she lingered for weeks before her death; she had time to dictate the entire story to the prosecuting attorney, one of the new officials Stephenson could not control in Marion County. The revelations devastated the entire movement. The desperate grand dragon, on trial for murder, was abandoned by his former henchman, Governor Ed Jackson. Panicky Klan papers now assailed their leader. The *Indian Kourier* headline declared: "D. C. Stephenson Not a Klansman," and called him an "enemy of the order," reporting that he had been "repudiated by all true Knights of the Empire." Stephenson responded by revealing the contents of his "little black box," which contained records implicating many highly placed, Klan-backed officials as corrupters, providing evidence of their malfeasance of office. The movement did not recover in Indiana. While Stephenson languished in jail (he would not be released until 1956), the Klan found its political influence evaporating, its membership deserting by the thousands. Hypocrisy, greed, and dishonesty by the leadership was bad enough, but Stephenson's violation of the symbolic crusade for purity, chastity, womanhood, and temperance was too much. As the greatest of the state Klans dissolved, the national empire of the Ku Klux Klan began to crumble everywhere.

By late in the decade, the Klan was a shell of the powerful movement of 1923–24. Although thousands of hooded men marched in the last great parade down the boulevards of Washington in the summer of 1925, many more were abandoning the order. Al Smith's presidential candidacy in 1928 was the occasion for one final, convulsive anti-Catholic effort by the Invisible Empire, but Herbert Hoover's victory owed little to the Klan. In the 1930s, the shriveled movement receded from public view, and its remaining publicists turned away from Catholicism to communism when seeking the alien menace within. Hiram Wesley Evans, before he lost what had become the all but meaningless title of imperial wizard in 1939, even accepted the invitation of church leaders to attend the dedication of the Roman Catholic Cathedral, ironically built on the site of the old Imperial Headquarters in Atlanta. The old order was no more. By 1944, with the federal government pressing for the payment of back taxes on Klan profits from the prosperous 1920, remaining national officers officially disbanded the Ku Klux Klan.

Although small state and local organizations calling themselves Ku Klux Klan, using the terminology of the earlier movement, and dressing members in similar regalia would reemerge in the late 1940s to play occasional roles in antiblack and anti-civil rights violence up through the 1980s, the great Klan of the 1920s was long dead. It had faltered so quickly after the spectacular growth early in the decade for many reasons. It lacked a clear legislative agenda. It experienced heavy weather in the political struggles in several states, where adroit enemies could use its weaknesses to build support for their own interests. It was led, in many areas, by people who were the embodiment of precisely those qualities that Klan ideology asked initiates to oppose: heavy drinkers and swindlers, sexual exploiters and dishonest manipulators of the theme of patriotism. In the end, the movement that offered fraternity to men in tumultuous times, that provided a nativist response to the crisis of values troubling so many in the Roaring Twenties, could not endure the revelations of scandal, the lack of constancy, the confused policies of the leadership. Like its antialien progenitors, the Ku Klux Klan was a movement that symbolized a longing for order, a desire to displace anger and anxiety. With no programmatic reason for being, men would desert it if it ceased to fulfill its symbolic function. As major newspapers turned against it, as articulate figures in the ministry and education, as well as in public life, pointed to its hypocrisy and treated it with scathing contempt, the mass of members simply drifted away. As with the Red Scare, the patriotic activity of the 1890s, and the antialien excitement of the pre–Civil War years, nativism's last stand had a relatively short run.

The Guardians

The early twentieth-century assaults on Victorianism provoked a strong organized defense by fundamentalists, Prohibitionists, and various conservative and patriotic organizations. However, the huge nationwide Ku Klux Klan, with at least three million members, emerged as the most visible and powerful guardian of Victorianism during the 1920s.

Unlike the vigilante groups which had used the name Ku Klux Klan after the Civil War and during the mid-twentieth-century battles against integration, the Klan of the 1920s did not focus on protecting white supremacy in the South. At the height of the Klan's power in 1924, Southerners formed only 16 percent of its total membership. Over 40 percent of early twentieth-century Klan members lived in the three midwestern states of Indiana, Ohio, and Illinois. The Klan enrolled more members in Connecticut than in Mississippi, more in Oregon than in Louisiana, and more in New Jersey than in Alabama. Klan membership in Indianapolis was almost twice that in South Carolina and Mississippi combined.

Also, Klan members in the mid-1920s were not any more violent than other native, white, middle-class Protestant males. After the Klan organized nationally for maximum profit and political action in 1921, the organization expelled members and whole chapters charged with having taken part in vigilante activities. However, inconclusive newspaper and government investigations into the activities of a small minority of early Klansmen during 1921 gave the organization a violent image. The name Ku Klux Klan (adopted mainly because of the Klan's role in the immensely popular film, *The Birth of a Nation*), the Klan's secrecy, and the order's refusal to admit anyone except native white Protestant males contributed to this image, especially among blacks, Catholics, Jews, and champions of civil liberties.

The image of the Klan held by critics of the organization during the 1920s was affected too by the Klan's rhetoric. That rhetoric reflected still widely accepted Victorian ideas about a racial hierarchy and about the dangers to American society posed by Catholics, blacks, Jews, and Asians. These popular beliefs had assisted the passage of immigration-restriction acts and had helped to defeat the presidential bid of Al Smith. They already had led to nationwide segregation and to disenfranchisement of southern blacks. Therefore, almost nowhere that Klans-backed politicians won power did Klan racist rhetoric need to be transformed into legislation. Nowhere did Klansmen running for office need to advocate violence under any circumstance, even against blacks in the South.

The near absence of Klan violence against southern blacks was explained, in part, by a perceptive editorial in the Savannah, Georgia, *Tribune,* a black-owned newspaper which strongly supported Marcus Garvey's black nationalist Universal Negro Improvement Association and was outspoken about civil-rights violations. The *Tribune's* editorial (whose conclusions were corroborated by other evidence), published July 13, 1922, stated:

> The evidence is that in the South the Ku Klux are not bothering with the Negroes. The naked truth is that when a band of lynchers sets out to kill a Negro they do not take the trouble to mask. They do not think it necessary to join a secret society, pay initiation fees and buy regalia when Negroes are the quarry.

A Georgia mob did not find it necessary to don masks before lynching Leo Frank in 1915, the year that the early twentieth-century Klan met to organize outside Atlanta.

༺❦༻

The Klan's primary objectives consisted of guarding the major Victorian concepts and the interests these protected. The ideas of character, largely reserved for white Protestants, the home and family in which character was formed, and distinctly separate gender roles stood foremost among these concepts. A series of articles entitled "The Klansman's Criterion of Character," published weekly from March 1 to March 29, 1924, in the Klan's national newspaper *Searchlight,* illustrated what the Klan expected of its leaders as well as of its ordinary members.

Jesus provided the chief model for *Searchlight's* definition of character: "He never compromised when dealing with the leaders of the Jews. He would not lie in order to save his own life." Jesus "was the unflinching, accomplishing, achieving Christ, because he was the purposeful, steadfast, determined Christ." Furthermore, Jesus accomplished his great mission on earth without the advantages enjoyed by members of the privileged business elites and the intelligentsia: "He controlled no centers of influence; He commanded neither learning nor wealth."

Searchlight implied that Klan members had undertaken the task of guarding, in the United States, Jesus' accomplishments:

> The Klan is engaged in a holy crusade against that which is corrupting and destroying the best in American life. The Klan is devoted to the holy mission of developing that which is right and clean and beneficent in our country. The Klan is active in its ministry of helpfulness and service.... Such enthusiastic devotion to right principles and the holy cause must characterize true Klansmen, if they are to be like Him whom they have accepted as their "Criterion of Character.

The "Kloran" of the "Knights of the Ku Klux Klan," the order's ritual book used to conduct all meetings and initiations, declared on its cover the order's dedication to "Karacter, Honor, Duty."

Every recent study that has examined the characteristics of klan members —in urban and rural communities of California, Colorado, Georgia, Indiana, Ohio, Oregon, Tennessee, Texas, and Utah—has found that Klansmen constituted a cross section of the local native white Protestant male population, except for the very top and bottom socioeconomic levels of that population. Virtually every Klan candidate for state and local office appealed to this constituency—Klan and non-Klan—with promises to reduce or eliminate those results of character defects which threatened the home and family: violations of Prohibition especially, but also drug abuse, prostitution, gambling, political corruption, traffic violations, and Sunday blue-law offenses.

As local Klan chapters, or Klaverns, prepared to sweep almost every political office in rural Fremont County, Colorado, the county's Klan leaders invited a national Klan lecturer, "Colonel" McKeever, to help bring out the Klan vote. Speaking to an overflow audience in the Canon City armory (1920 population of 4,551), the county's largest community, McKeever proclaimed a typical Klan message.

> The Klan stands for law enforcement; money and politics must cease to play a role [particularly in Prohibition enforcement] in our courts. The Klan stands for the American home; there is no sanctuary like a mother's heart, no altar like a mother's knee. The Klan stands for good men in office.

The Klan attempted to combat all "forces of evil which attack the American home." Threatening the "purity of women," claimed an editorial in the *Fiery Cross,* Indiana's Klan newspaper, were businessmen who employed female secretaries: "Everyone knows of instances where businessmen insist on dating secretaries and imply that should they refuse, their jobs are in danger." ...

Klan membership held a strong attraction for large numbers of men who already belonged to secret white Protestant fraternal organizations.... The Klan offered a more blatant racism, anti-Catholicism, and anti-Semitism, as well as direct participation in politics to members of such societies as the Masons, Odd Fellows, and Knights of Pythias. Moreover, the basic objectives of these other orders resembled those of the Klan in respects more important than ritual and fraternity. The most recent and discerning historian of the Freemasons, Lynn Dumenil, summarized the fundamental Masonic aims: "Not only would America become homogeneous again, but the perpetuation of the values of native, Protestant Americans would be assured."

Kleagles received instructions to contact local ministers, fraternal lodge members, and potentially favorable newspaper editors upon entering a community. They were to ascertain the strongest needs of local white Protestants with the aid of these contacts and to begin enrolling members....

The most thorough statistical analyses of Klan membership during the 1920s have been written by Christopher Cocoltchos, Leonard Moore, and Robert Goldberg. A clear pattern emerges from Cocoltchos's information about Orange County, California, Moore's study of Indiana, and Goldberg's analysis of the Colorado Klan. Other recent books and articles support their conclusions.

These studies of members' characteristics found that Klansmen represented a near cross section of the white Protestant male population in their communities. Everywhere, the Klan fought to overcome the power of business and professional elites, except in some small towns. Outside those towns, few members of these elites joined the Klan, and those who did tended to be the younger members who evidently believed that their ambitions could be best furthered by the Klan.

In these communities as a whole, Catholics, blacks, Jews, and recent immigrants formed a very small part of the population. The few exceptions were the black population of Indianapolis, which almost equaled the proportion of blacks in the country; the German Catholic population of Anaheim, California, which led the anti-Klan elite there; and the Mexican-American Catholic population of Orange County, which was thoroughly segregated when the Klan was organized and which the Klan consequently ignored altogether. The percentages of those minorities in these communities were insignificant compared with the proportions of these same minorities in major cities like New York, Chicago, Cleveland, and St. Louis, where native white Protestants constituted a minority of the residents (in some cases, less than one-quarter).

Klansmen were concentrated in middle white-collar positions and among small businessmen. Those who were blue-collar workers were overwhelmingly in skilled positions. Members belonged to all major Protestant denominations, but the Klan included very few members of fundamentalist sects. They attended services in Northern Methodist and Disciples of Christ churches especially. Klansmen generally had lived in their communities longer than nonmembers, usually at least ten years before they joined the order, yet they tended to be younger. Well over three-quarters of them were married. They belonged to more civil and fraternal organizations, particularly to the Masons. They possessed greater wealth, more property, and registered to vote in 1924 in much larger proportions than did nonmembers in their communities. Klansmen in the mid-1920s decidedly were not a fringe group of vigilantes; they were solid middle-class citizens and individuals of high Victorian character.

Indiana served as the focal point of Klan power in America. The Indiana Klan enrolled more members and a much larger proportion of the state population than did the Klaverns of any other state. The state capital, Indianapolis, was referred to by a leading historian of the Klan as the "Center of Klandom."

Information about Klan members' characteristics in three Indiana communities, representative of the states' large and small cities and of its rural town, illustrates the Klan's composition in Indiana. The three communities are Indianapolis, a major industrial and commercial city whose population in 1920 was 314,000; Richmond, an industrial city with a population of 27,000 in 1920; and Crown Point, a commercial township of 4,312, which served the surrounding farming area.

Individuals in high white-collar occupations among Indianapolis's Klan members equalled almost exactly the proportion of men with that status in the city as a whole. However, the Indianapolis Klan contained none of the high executives of the city's largest corporations—such as Van Camp, one of the largest food canning companies in the nation; Eli Lilly, a major pharmaceutical manufacturer; and the Stutz and Dusenburg motor-car companies. Disciples of Christ, Lutheran, and United Brethren ranked highest among the church affiliations of Indianapolis's Klansmen.

About 75 percent of Richmond's Klan members occupied white-collar or skilled-worker positions compared to 64 percent of non-Klansmen in such positions. However, non-Klansmen filled the city's highest white-collar jobs in considerably larger proportions than did Klansmen. The greatest differences between the Protestant church affiliations of Richmond's Klan members and those of Richmond's citizens as a whole lay in the much higher proportion of Klansmen who belonged to Presbyterian, United Brethren, Disciples of Christ, and Episcopal congregations.

The occupational profile of Crown Point's Klan members resembled that of Indianapolis and Richmond Knights. Moore found that "Crown Point's wealthiest citizens did not appear to play any role in the Klan." Sixty-one percent of Crown Point's church-member Knights belonged to Methodist, Lutheran, Presbyterian, or Disciples of Christ congregations.

In each of these three Indiana communities, Kleagles and local Klan organizers used vocal and written criticism of American Catholics, blacks, Jews, and recent immigrants as part of their recruiting rhetoric. However, Moore concluded that the Indiana Klan "did not employ violence as a strategy, and only a tiny fraction of the hooded order's membership ever engaged in violent or threatening acts."

The characteristics of Orange County Klansmen differed little from those of the Indiana members. For fast growing Anaheim, the county seat, Cocoltchos derived statistical information for Klan, non-Klan, and active anti-Klan residents. The latter included those who had joined the club devoted to defeating the Klan politically and also those who had signed both of the petitions opposing the Anaheim Klan.

A much higher proportion of Anaheim Klansmen held professional and administrative jobs than did non-Klansmen, but twice as high a percentage of active anti-Klansmen—who included the city's established business, professional and farming elite—occupied such positions as Klan members. Klansmen worked in trade, service, and skilled positions in greater proportions than did either of the other groups.

Over half the Anaheim Klansmen with a specific church affiliation belonged to Disciples of Christ and Northern Methodist congregations. Catholic was the largest single church affiliation among those actively opposed to the Klan—over 25 percent.

Cocoltchos also collected statistics for Anaheim Klan leaders and the anti-Klan elite, which led activities in the city directed against the Klan. His data proved very informative for an understanding of the Klan's conflicts with the Anaheim business and professional elite.

The anti-Klan elite of three hundred individuals overlapped to a very large extent Anaheim's traditional elite. The median age of the elite in 1924 was fifty-four years compared to forty-two-and-a-half years for Klan leaders. The median years of prior residence in Anaheim was thirty-and-a-half years for the elite and fifteen years for Klan leaders in 1924. Ninety percent of elite members belonged to civic clubs, while 72 percent of Klan leaders did.

Forty-five percent of the elite occupied professional and administrative positions compared to 27 percent of the Klan leaders. Half of the latter worked in the retail and wholesale trades. The median wealth of Klan leaders amounted to $7,460 compared to $36,534 for members of the anti-Klan elite. Seventy-two percent of Klansmen had already run for or held public office in 1924 compared to 55 percent of the elite. The Klan leaders, despite their role as prosperous community activists, faced a near united front of Anaheim's wealthy, well-entrenched business, professional, and large farmer elite.

In the smaller city of Fullerton, California, Klansmen differed from the non-Klan population largely in their much larger proportion of members working in service and skilled jobs. Klan members owned more property and acknowledged much greater median wealth. A significantly higher proportion of them were married, belonged to civic clubs, and voted in 1924. Klansmen belonged predominantly to Disciples of Christ, Northern Methodist, Episcopalian, and Northern Baptist churches.

Half of the Ku Klux Klan's members in Colorado lived in the capital and largest city, Denver. A much higher percentage of Denver's Klansmen worked in both high and middle white-collar occupations than did members of the male population as a whole. However, Goldberg found that "Denver's elite clubs listed only a handful of Klansmen among their members," and none belonged to the most prestigious social clubs, such as the Denver Club, the Denver Country Club, and the University Club. Only one Klan member was listed in Denver's Social Register. A much lower proportion of Klansmen than male citizens of Denver worked in skilled, semi-skilled, and unskilled labor jobs. Goldberg was unable to collect information about individual church membership, but over 70 percent of Denver's Disciples of Christ churches, 33 percent of its Methodist churches, and 25 percent of its Baptist churches actively supported the Klan.

A Kleagle did not arrive in Canon City, Colorado (with a population of 4,551 in 1920) and surrounding rural Fremont County until 1923. Of the Klan's members between 1924 and 1928, 40 percent occupied high or middle white-collar positions. Only 1.5 percent worked at unskilled jobs. One-quarter of Canon City's Klansmen belonged to the Masons as well. Klan-member ministers guided the town's Methodist and Baptist churches and the fundamentalist Church of Christ congregation.

These statistics bear out Leonard Moore's conclusions about the meaning of the latest books and articles about the Klan:

> Together, these recent works make it nearly impossible to interpret the 1920's Klan as an aberrant fringe group.... In-depth analysis of state and community Klans from different regions of the country make it clear ... that the Klan was composed primarily of average citizens representing nearly all parts of America's white Protestant society....

Leonard Moore summarized what he called the Klan's "basic message":

> The average white Protestant was under attack: his values and traditions were being undermined; his vision of America's national purpose and social order appeared threatened; and his ability to shape the course of public affairs seemed to have been diminished.

Basing its political activity upon this message and the failure of state and local elites to address it satisfactorily, the Klan won a high degree of political power and influence in the states of Alabama, California, Colorado, Georgia, Indiana, Kansas, Louisiana, Oklahoma, Oregon, and Texas. It took political control of hundreds of American cities and towns, including Akron, Atlanta, Birmingham, Dallas, Denver, El Paso, Evansville, Gary, Indianapolis, Little Rock, Oklahoma City, Portland, Oregon, Terre Haute, and Youngstown.

However, the powerful business elite of Richmond, Indiana, thwarted the Klan's political efforts. Richmond's major employers were International Harvester and the Pennsylvania Railroad. The successful anti-Klan forces were led by members of the Rotary Club, limited to representatives of the city's industrial corporations, top executives of its other businesses, and its most successful retail merchants. The Rotary received aid from the Kiwanis Club, dominated by small businessmen and city officials.

Explaining the Klan's near-total triumph in Indiana, Moore concluded that the state and local elites "stood nearly alone as a white Protestant social group unwilling to support the Klan." That group, he declared, surpassed Indiana's Catholics, blacks, and Jews as the order's chief opponents. When Indiana's Klan chapters sought political power, Moore found "their most powerful rivals were . . . the Rotary Club and the Chamber of Commerce, not the powerless or nonexistent ethnic minorities." When the Klan swept the state election of 1924, "the real victims were not the state's Catholics but the Republican . . . political establishment, which, almost overnight, found itself removed from power."

In Indianapolis, businessmen organized in the Chamber of Commerce and the Indiana Taxpayers' Association formed an important component of the Old Guard Republican establishment. School issues symbolized the conflict between the Old Guard and the Klan. Voters, led by the Klan, approved a series of school bond issues, meant to renovate dilapidated schools and to alleviate overcrowding in the city's elementary and high schools. The Chamber of Commerce and the Taxpayers' Associations organized a Citizen's League to hide their own opposition to all spending for schools, except for a segregated high school to educate the city's black children. The school board refused to appropriate funds for any other construction. In the school-board election of 1925, the Klan elected all five of its candidates to replace the five Citizen's League incumbents. A school construction program started soon afterward. Aided by voter mobilization for the school-board election, the Klan won virtually every city political office in 1925.

In Lake County, where Crown Point served as county seat, Moore concluded: "Prohibition enforcement and public corruption had a . . . preponderant influence on Klan political victories." Exports of liquor by Chicago criminal organizations had left Lake County soaked in alcohol and full of corruption. In the November 1924 elections, every Lake County candidate endorsed by the Klan—including those in Crown Point—won election. . . .

◆

Starting in the mid-1920s, the Ku Klux Klan ebbed in numbers and in influence. The three chief reasons for this decline were the inability of the order to achieve its promises, the demoralization of members because of scandals involving Klan leaders and spokesmen (whom members expected to appear and act more honestly than their opponents), and counter-attacks by the ethnic and religious groups and business elites which held political control of the nation's major cities.

After an initial burst of enthusiasm for the Klan, when it gained control of city, county, and state governments, inexperienced Klan elected officials found their programs rendered ineffective by professional politicians. Therefore voters—including Klan members—who had supported the Klan were disappointed by the order's accomplishments.

For example, in Indiana, where the Klan elected its candidate for governor and won large majorities in both houses of the legislature in 1925, Klansmen enacted only one of their proposals into law. That measure, obliging all public schools to teach their students about the United States Constitution, obtained bipartisan support.

Other bills introduced by Klan legislators—such as legislation mandating daily Bible reading in Indiana's schools, forcing parochial schools to use the same textbooks as public schools, and compelling public schools to hire only public-school graduates as teachers—failed to pass. Legislators, especially in the state senate, and the Klan governor killed such measures rather than face the controversy that such blatant attacks on religious liberty would cause. The near certainty of adverse judicial decisions increased the reluctance of these politicians (particularly those who hoped to seek national office) to risk their careers.

Indiana Grand Dragon David C. Stephenson's crimes damaged the Klan most. Stephenson collected over a million dollars from Klansmen between 1922 and 1924. Most of this was used to support a most un-Klansmanlike life-style. He bought luxurious automobiles, an imposing suburban home, and a yacht on which he entertained numerous women. He also purchased a large liquor supply. Several times, his drinking binges brought him close to arrest by police.

In April 1925, Stephenson took one of his female companions, twenty-eight-year-old Madge Oberholtzer of Indianapolis, on an overnight train ride to Hammond, Indiana. During this trip, Stephenson repeatedly raped Oberholtzer. When they arrived in Hammond, she bought and swallowed a deadly poison. It took effect during the return trip to Indianapolis, but Stephenson refused to let the suffering woman see a physician until they reached Indianapolis. By then it was too late.

Before Oberholtzer died, she gave police a full statement. The State of Indiana charged Stephenson with causing her suicide because he had forced her to lose "that which she held dearer than life—her chastity." Stephenson was indicted and convicted of kidnapping, rape, and second-degree murder. He received a sentence of life imprisonment.

Stephenson confidently expected a pardon from Indiana's Governor Ed Jackson, a Klansman. When Jackson refused his request, Stephenson offered to testify about the corruption of Jackson and other state and local Klan officials. As a result, Mayor John Duvall of Indianapolis went to prison for violating the Corrupt Practices Act—so did the county sheriff, its congressman, the city purchasing agent, and a large number of less important Klan officeholders. Based on Stephenson's testimony, a grand jury indicted Governor Jackson for bribery, but he escaped prison because the statute of limitations on his offenses had expired. Soon after these revelations Klan membership in Indiana began shrinking. Fewer than seven thousand members remained by 1928.

Stephenson's trial, well publicized by newspapers and magazines, distressed Klansmen throughout America. Their outrage increased when they learned about the crimes of Dr. John Galen Locke, Colorado's Grand Dragon and Denver's Exalted Cyclops. In January 1925, Locke arranged the kidnapping of Klan member Keith Boehm, a high-school student. Taken to Locke's office and threatened with castration unless he married his pregnant girlfriend, Boehm agreed to the marriage. Locke explained to the Denver *Post* that "When I learned of what happened... I meant to see to it that young Boehm, as a Klansman, should do the manly thing." The district attorney brought kidnapping and conspiracy charges against Locke. Luckily for Locke, Klan opponent Judge Ben B. Lindsay of the juvenile court disqualified himself from the case. Locke's attorney engineered changes of venue until the case landed before a Klansman judge who found technical reasons to dismiss it.

Then federal Treasury officials charged Locke with failing to report any income or to pay income taxes despite the fees he earned as a physician and from Klan initiation fees and commissions on the sale of Klan robes. Locke went to prison until Colorado's governor, who had been chosen by the Grand Dragon, established a fund to pay Locke's back taxes. Other Klansmen paid Locke's fine. Mass defections from Colorado's Klan began. Imperial Wizard Hiram Evans requested Locke's resignation, and Locke immediately complied.

In Anaheim, the politically defeated Chamber of Commerce and Rotary Club collected sufficient signatures on petitions late in 1924 to force recently elected Klan city council members into a recall election. Minor scandals and a failure to appreciably diminish Prohibition violations already had cost the Klan some support. Anaheim's Klan leader, Reverend Mr. Meyers, sought to renew Klan members' enthusiasm by bringing Protestant evangelist E. E. Bulgin to the city in January 1925 to conduct revival meetings. Bulgin arrived on January 11, set up his tent, and began the services.

A group of Anaheim's ministers sent Bulgin and local newspapers a letter inquiring whether he had been brought to Anaheim "for the express purpose of assisting in the re-election of the members of the city council whose removal is being sought because of their Klan affiliations." Bulgin proclaimed his neutrality concerning the election. At the following evening's revival meeting, however, Bulgin told his assembled flock that "the way to vote right and never make a mistake is to find out what side the ex-saloonkeepers, the bootleggers and the harlots are on and get on the other side." Bulgin's nightly meetings attracted large and enthusiastic audiences.

Representatives of the Chamber of Commerce and of the Rotary and the Lion's clubs of Anaheim contacted the Knights of Columbus and the Catholic Truth Society in many parts of the West, asking for information about Bulgin. An Okmulgee, Oklahoma, attorney replied that Bulgin's real specialty was selling stock in fictitious or worthless mining companies. In return, he had taken deeds to some citizens' homes. Telegrams from Eastland, Texas, and Lewiston, Idaho, stated that Bulgin had been chased out of those cities after being charged with fraud in numerous lawsuits. Two of Anaheim's newspapers printed these replies.

On February 3, 1925, almost 77 percent of Anaheim's voters—a larger proportion than the record turnout less than six months before that had elected the Klan councilmen—went to the polls. Every Klan-endorsed council member was recalled by a substantial margin.

The Ku Klux Klan paid dearly for its obvious role in reinvigorating Victorian racism and religious bigotry. Kenneth Jackson pointed out that "Relatively few reports of Klan-related violence between 1915 and 1924 are contained in the files of United States Department of Justice." However, in September 1923, the *Literary Digest,* a Klan opponent, published an article entitled "The Klan as a Victim of Mob Violence." The Indiana state *Fiery Cross* complained in 1924 that "The list of the outrages against Klansmen is so long that it would take weeks to compile even an incomplete list."

In dozens of cities—such as Fort Worth; San Antonio; Terre Haute; and Portland, Maine—Klan headquarters and meeting places were bombed and burned. After numerous warnings, the shop believed to be the publication headquarters of the Chicago Klan's journal, *Dawn,* was gutted by a bomb. An editorial in the *Fiery Cross* asked plaintively: Why does not anyone "ever read about halls of the Knights of Columbus being destroyed mysteriously?"

Catholics and blacks had threatened the Klan with violence. The editor of the *Catholic World,* published by the Paulist Fathers, warned early in 1923 that because of the Klan, Catholics "may be driven to self-defense, even to the extent of bloodshed." The equally staid *Bulletin* of the National Catholic Welfare Council declared:

> In this struggle for the supremacy of law and order over lawlessness and despotism, no quarter should be given those self-appointed patriots who distort and disgrace our Americanism and whose weapons are darkness, the mask, violence, intimidation and mob rule.

The Harlem-based radical black nationalist African Black Brotherhood proclaimed in its journal that "The nation-wide mobilization under the Christian cross and the Stars and Stripes of cracker America is plainly an act of war...., war of the cracker element of the white race against the whole Negro race." The Chicago *Defender,* the most widely read black newspaper in the United States, urged its readers in a front-page editorial to prepare to fight "against sons who now try to win by signs and robes what their fathers lost by fire and sword."

When the Klan began organizing in and around the nation's largest cities, members of the order soon discovered that white Protestant authority no longer prevailed throughout the land. In these cities Catholics, blacks, Jews, and recent immigrants formed a majority of the population—sometimes a very large majority.

Soon after Kleagles ventured into New York City, Irish Catholic Mayor John F. Hylan told his police commissioner in 1922: "I desire you to treat this group of racial and religious haters as you would the Reds and bomb throwers. Drive them out of our city." Two New York City grand juries commenced investigations of the Klan, and the New York City Council quickly passed legislation forcing associations not incorporated in New York to file membership lists. Klan members in New York and suburban Westchester County during the 1920s totalled about 16,000, less than Klan membership in Akron or Youngstown, Ohio.

Chicago's large Klan chapter did nothing to help enforce Prohibition laws. However, the West Suburban Ministers and Citizens Association organized to help enforce those laws in and around Chicago. Soon afterward, the association's leader, a minister, was found shot to death a block from Al Capone's headquarters in suburban Cicero. This warning ended private attempts to fight Prohibition offenses in Chicago.

The Chicago City Council appointed a five-man committee in December 1922 to investigate the Klan and then report back to the council. The five members were identified as Ald. Robert J. Mulcahy, Irish; Ald. Louis B. Henderson, black; Ald. U. S. Schwartz, Jewish; Ald. S. S. Walkowiak, Polish; and Ald. Oscar H. Olsen, Norwegian. Largely as a result of the committee's unanimous report, the city council resolved by a vote of fifty-six to two to rid Chicago's municipal payroll of Klansmen. The Illinois legislature also received the report and consequently passed a bill prohibiting the wearing of masks in public. The measure cleared the Illinois House of Representatives by a vote of 100 to 2, and the Illinois State Senate by 26 to 1. Illinois's Klansmen were thus forced to hold most of their parades, picnics, and other gatherings in Indiana and Ohio.

Boston's Mayor James Michael Curley barred Klan meetings in Boston, and the city council approved his order. He gave speeches before burning crosses and in an emotion-choked voice always proclaimed: "There it burns, the cross of hatred upon which Our Lord, Jesus Christ, was crucified—the cross of human avarice, and not the cross of love and charity...." Homes and stores of suspected Klansmen in Boston were bombarded with bricks and stones.

On the outskirts of major cities, where the Klan sometimes dared to march or meet, the Knights received even worse treatment. Ten thousand Klansmen gathered near Carnegie, just outside Pittsburgh, on August 25, 1923, to witness an initiation featuring an address by Imperial Wizard Hiram Evans. When they tried to march back to the heavily Catholic, immigrant, and black town, however, a mob stood in their path. The Klansmen continued marching through a hail of rocks and bottles. Then a volley of shots rang out. One Klansman lay dead, a dozen others fell seriously wounded, and about a hundred more suffered minor injuries. The other Klan members turned and ran.

Commenting on the Carnegie massacre, the Washington *Star* declared that "Parades of the Klan, with its masked and hooded members, tend to create disorder and rioting." An editorial in the Washington *Post* stated that the paper agreed with the *New York Times* that "The Klan is merely reaping as it has sown."

Other Klan meetings were broken up by lethal shotgun blasts. In New York's suburban county of Queens, police ended a Memorial Day parade of 4,000 Klansmen by waving waiting cars through the whole parade line.

Hiram Evans summarized the Klan's plight when he stated in March 1926 that "The Nordic American today is a stranger in large parts of the land his fathers gave him. Moreover, he is a most unwelcome stranger, and one most spat upon."

Evans described accurately the result of the Klan's defense as Victorianism's essence. The most important social trends and the great social reform movements of the nineteenth and twentieth centuries had indeed left Klansmen strangers in most of the land their ancestors had settled.

POSTSCRIPT

Was the Ku Klux Klan of the 1920s an Extremist Movement?

Bennett places the 1920s Ku Klux Klan within the nativist tradition of American right-wing political movements. He argues that Klan ideology reasserted its hostility toward the Catholic and Jewish immigrants from southern and eastern Europe who had poured into America since the 1890s. He points out that Irish Catholics were associated with the saloons and the political bosses who controlled the machines in the large cities. In Bennett's view, the Klan was made up of Protestant fundamentalists who wished to reassert the traditional values of an earlier America.

Coben argues that many Klansmen were attracted to the Klan because they were legitimately concerned with the breakdown of traditional standards of morality and the increases in alcohol consumption and crime that they believed were occurring in their communities. Coben also argues that Klansmen were more often middle-class businessmen, small shopkeepers, and skilled workers who were fighting the well-to-do businessmen, the large farmers, and their allied Catholic, Jewish, and black ethnic groups for political control.

Recent scholarship on the 1920s Klan has focused on its grass-roots participation in local and state politics. Klansmen are viewed less as extremists and more as political pressure groups whose aims were to gain control of various local and state government offices. The best overview of this perspective is Shawn Lay, ed., *The Invisible Empire in the West: Toward a New Historical Appraisal of the Ku Klux Klan of the 1920s* (University of Illinois Press, 1992).

Indiana was at the heart of the second Klan and is the focus of much recent research. A good starting point is William E. Wilson's "That Long Hot Summer in Indiana," *American Heritage* (August 1965). M. William Lutholtz gives a well-researched but old-fashioned interpretative journalistic study of Indiana's amoral, opportunistic grand dragon in *Grand Dragon: D. C. Stephenson and the Ku Klux Klan in Indiana, 1921–1928* (University of North Carolina Press, 1991), while Leonard J. Moore, in *Citizen Klansmen: The Ku Klux Klan in Indiana, 1921–1928* (University of North Carolina Press, 1991), sees the Indiana group as concerned, middle-class citizens who challenged the local elites to clean up the political and immoral corruption in the state in order to reinforce traditional family values. Nancy MacLean, in *Behind the Mask of Chivalry: The Making of the Second Ku Klux Klan* (Oxford University Press, 1994), argues that the second Klan's lower middle class subverted traditional Republican values into a "reactionary populism" that bore a "family resemblance" to the movement Adolf Hitler rode to power in the 1930s.

ISSUE 8

Did the Women's Movement Die in the 1920s?

YES: William L. O'Neill, from *Everyone Was Brave: A History of Feminism in America* (Quadrangle Books, 1971)

NO: Anne Firor Scott, from *The Southern Lady: From Pedestal to Politics, 1830–1930* (University of Chicago Press, 1970)

ISSUE SUMMARY

YES: Professor of history William L. O'Neill contends that the women's movement died following the success of the suffrage campaign because women were not united in support of many of the other issues that affected them and because the increasingly militant feminism of the Woman's Party alienated many supporters of women's rights.

NO: Anne Firor Scott, a professor emeritus of history, maintains that the suffrage victory produced a heightened interest in further social and political reform, which inspired southern women to pursue their goals throughout the 1920s.

On March 31, 1776, Abigail Adams wrote to her husband, John, "I long to hear that you have declared an independency—and by the way in the new Code of Laws which I suppose it will be necessary for you to make I desire you would Remember the Ladies, and be more generous and favourable to them than your ancestors." Apparently, John Adams, like so many husbands before and since, forgot his wife's supplication. Consequently, following the American Revolution, women benefited very little from the democratic forces that swept through the United States. Their failure to enjoy the same progress as men in terms of political democracy produced a status characterized by historian Gerda Lerner as "relative deprivation." This sense of deprivation helped to fuel the women's movement during the "age of reform" and culminated in the Women's Rights Convention of 1848 in Seneca Falls, New York.

The tone of the Seneca Falls meeting was set by Elizabeth Cady Stanton's presentation of the Declaration of Sentiments and Resolutions, which called for the elimination of the separate status of the two sexes by proclaiming that "all men and women are created equal." All of the resolutions passed unanimously except the one demanding women's suffrage. This proposal was finally adopted, but not without a floor fight. The right to vote, it appeared, was too radical.

Following the Civil War, suffragists hoped that the issue of women's political disfranchisement would be resolved satisfactorily in conjunction with efforts to extend voting rights to African Americans. The architects of the Fourteenth and Fifteenth Amendments, however, feared that proposals to enfranchise former slaves and women at the same time would jeopardize the primary goal of black political empowerment. Stanton argued that this decision made women relatively more powerless than before and renewed her call for women's suffrage. After 1890 the National American Woman Suffrage Association (NAWSA) began to view women's suffrage as a primary goal for the reform of American society. Benefiting from the organizational skills of Carrie Chapman Catt, who formulated her "Winning Plan" to gain the right to vote, American women won their campaign with the passage and ratification of the Nineteenth Amendment.

For many participants, the suffrage victory signaled the last step to full equality. For others, it marked another beginning. Was the struggle over? Had the final victory been won? Certainly there was no evidence that voting rights brought full equality for American women after 1920. On the other hand, there is some doubt about whether or not women in the 1920s developed the collective self-consciousness that had been displayed in the suffrage campaign and that would be required to achieve further gains in their status. What *did* happen to the women's movement in the 1920s? The selections that follow suggest the absence of a consensus on this question.

In the first selection, William L. O'Neill argues that, following the enactment of the Nineteenth Amendment, American women possessed no other reform initiatives to which they were committed so strongly as the right to vote. Without a unifying goal, the women's movement splintered along regional, racial, and class lines, and many women's organizations abandoned their interest in activism and operated primarily as social clubs. Furthermore, contends O'Neill, organizations like the League of Women Voters reflected much of the conservatism of the period, while the Woman's Party, under the leadership of Alice Paul, failed to temper its demands for an equal rights amendment with a willingness to engage in the art of political compromise.

In the second selection, Anne Firor Scott concentrates on southern women and concludes that the 1920s witnessed significant efforts by women to secure reforms in areas of interest to members of their sex and to society as a whole. By addressing issues such as child labor, minimum wage and maximum hour legislation, race relations, and political democracy, women contributed significantly to the success of progressivism in the South in the 1920s. Scott maintains that these efforts demonstrated the growing powers of the "new woman" of the postsuffrage era and revealed the desire of many women to increase their opportunities beyond the purely domestic sphere.

William L. O'Neill

The Post-Suffrage Era

The decline of social feminism after World War I was demoralizing to all concerned. Women reformers could, however, console themselves with the knowledge that their frustrations resulted from a nationwide swing to the right rather than any special defects peculiar to themselves. Ardent feminists were denied this comfort. The women's rights movement expired in the twenties from ailments that had gone untreated in its glory days. Chief among them was the feminists' inability to see that equal suffrage was almost the only issue holding the disparate elements of the woman movement together. Once it was resolved, voters who happened to be female were released from the politically meaningless category of "woman." This allowed their basic allegiances to come into play. As a popular journalist pointed out, "the woman 'bloc' does not tend to become more and more solidified, but tends to become more and more disintegrated. Women at the polling places in Vermont turn out to be different from women at the polling places in Iowa; and the differences of locality and of class turn out to overshadow the difference of sex." It quickly became evident that, except on matters like Prohibition and the sex lives of political figures, there was no women's vote. It also soon became clear that the anti-suffragists had more accurately foreseen the ballot's limitation than the suffragists. In 1920 it was still possible to argue, as Emily Greene Balch did, that if women voters were often ignorant and inexperienced, "they are also largely free from bad old political habits and traditions, and free to strike out a new political method, not dominated by party, in which social and moral values shall outweigh all others." At the first postwar convention of the International Woman Suffrage Alliance, Carrie Chapman Catt, while admitting that in many countries woman suffrage had come almost by accident as a consequence of the war, still believed "that had the vote been granted to women some twenty-five years ago when justice and logic and public opinion demanded... there would have been no World War."

The mood did not last long. By 1922 H. L. Mencken could say:

> Years ago I predicted that these suffragettes, tried out by victory, would turn out to be idiots. They are now hard at work proving it. Half of them devote themselves to advocating reforms, chiefly of a sexual character, so utterly preposterous that even male politicians and newspaper editors laugh

at them; the other half succumb absurdly to the blandishments of the old-time male politicians, and so enroll themselves in the great political parties. A woman who joins one of these parties simply becomes an imitation man, which is to say, a donkey. Thereafter she is nothing but an obscure cog in an ancient and creaking machine, the sole intelligible purpose of which is to maintain a horde of scoundrels in public office.

Unjust? Of course. Yet soon many suffragists admitted that fighting for the vote had been more rewarding than getting it. Mrs. Catt had expected this. Even before women voted in their first national election, she reminded them that they had no obligation to the major parties, for if either had "lived up to the high ideals of our Nation and courageously taken the stand for right and justice as against time-serving, vote-winning policies of delay, women would have been enfranchised long ago." It was partially for this reason that she founded the League of Women Voters [LWV], and the experience of 1920 confirmed her judgment. "Suffrage women last autumn numerously confessed that they found real politics 'pale and insipid' when it came time to use their first vote. It seemed sordid and commonplace to be striving merely to elect men whose platforms were so strangely confused they could not find a direct issue. They felt a vacancy where for years there had been purpose consecrated to an immortal principle." A few years later Mrs. Catt noted again that suffragists "are disappointed first of all because they miss the exaltation, the thrill of expectancy, the vision which stimulated them in the suffrage campaign. They find none of these appeals to their aspiration in the party of their choice."

It was one thing for the indomitable Mrs. Catt, whom no political party had anything of value to offer, to take this line; it was quite another for the typical suffragist who had been led to expect something more from the franchise than political tokens (such as the National Committee seats assigned women by both parties). Anne Martin, who several times ran for the Senate from Nevada, was annoyed in 1919 when the National Conference of Republican Women seemed more interested in the clichés of professional politicians than in her own efforts to organize a specifically feminine program. Having given up on the Republicans, she was even more discouraged when in 1924 the La Follette managers picked a Socialist candidate to run on the third-party ticket, even though she had outpolled him in a previous election. She saw the 1924 election as a debacle for women. Only one was elected to Congress, and she was not among the emancipated candidates supported by the Woman's party [WP]. Ignoring the women endorsed by the La Follette party, Miss Martin concluded that all the parties had shown themselves equally bigoted, and that by urging women to work within the established system "Mrs. Carrie Chapman Catt sounded the doom of feminism for many years to come." This was hardly fair to Mrs. Catt, who held no brief for the existing parties but saw no alternative to them, nor was it reasonable of Miss Martin to expect Mrs. Catt to organize another Woman's party when the drawbacks of that policy had, from a social feminist point of view, been so clearly demonstrated by the existing one.

Even so, women with more patience and less personal ambition than Anne Martin found the results of big-party politics disappointing. The first chairman of the Republican Women's Committee of Illinois observed that reform-minded women who joined the regular parties were simply swallowed up. Her experience demonstrated that while the parties were willing to give women symbolic appointments, they were carefully shut out of the decision-making process. This was not so much because they were women as because they were amateurs who did not share the regulars' passion for office. The professionals reasoned correctly that "once in the organization we could be controlled. Our nuisance value was gone. Not only that, our power for good was gone." It was a mistake, she concluded, to think women could reform the party from within.

Emily Newell Blair, who served as vice-chairman of the Democratic National Committee from 1921 to 1928, was less disillusioned but hardly more sanguine. She agreed that women had little influence on the parties, that they had been awarded few high offices, and that in general their services had not been adequately compensated. She thought there was a good reason for this. "Members of the party take responsibility and women have been backward about taking it. Their habit is to sit back and then complain because it is not offered them." Mrs. Blair understood the deeper problems enfranchisement had revealed. When women first gained the vote, she noted, male politicians had feared the consequences and treated women with respect and caution. But soon it became clear not only that women would not hang together, but that they would not even support for public office the best female candidates. Since there was no bloc vote, there was no reason for men to cater to it. All of which, she felt, resulted from the fundamental failure of suffragists to think deeply enough about what would happen when the vote was won. Anna Howard Shaw knew the suffragists had let their followers down in this respect. Once victory was assured, she told Mrs. Blair, "I am sorry for you young women who have to carry on the work in the next ten years, for suffrage was a symbol, and now you have lost your symbol. There is nothing for the women to rally round."

Before long it became evident that the League of Women Voters, though it did good work, was no substitute for the NAWSA [National American Women Suffrage Association]. It labored on too many fronts; the nature of its activities precluded either the exhilarating victories or heart-wrenching defeats that made life among the suffragists so exciting; and its determined neutrality denied it the passionate loyalties reserved for partisan organizations. Most of all, perhaps, the LWV lost a great many fights, and this did not commend it to younger women who came of age during the years when suffrage was a winning cause. Of course, politics as such diminished in interest during the 1920's, and many women who might otherwise have concerned themselves with public affairs were drawn off into the cultural, social, and recreational pursuits that made the New Era exciting. Marguerite Wells, while attempting to show that women profited from the vote, was forced to admit that "the net effect of suffrage on many clubs has been that they are less, rather than more, prone to 'take action' on political questions." And Rose Schneiderman, although she was careful to point out that she was no more disappointed in women's suffrage than she had been in men's suffrage, admitted that "the women's vote hasn't been of any sensible value in the measures which the Women's Trade Union League want. We started twelve years ago to fight for a forty-eight-hour week. We are still fighting for it, and I can't see that it is a bit easier now, that we make any more impression on the Legislature than we did before we could vote." So much for Florence Kelley's contention that politicians were unresponsive to the needs of working women because they could not vote. The rejoinder that woman suffrage was no worse in practice than man suffrage, although often used, was of course beside the point: a large part of the original justification for it had been that women would vote more sanely than men. If women were going to be no different as voters, there was little purpose to the long struggle except as a matter of simple justice, and mere justice was not why social feminists had invested so much in the cause....

By 1936 it was possible for John Gordon Ross to sum up the results of woman suffrage in terms that require little modification today. In their sixteen years as voters women had overthrown no bosses, and few women in politics had established independent power bases. Women bureaucrats were no better than men—though less corruptible. The vote had not made women mannish, as had been feared, "rather their new responsibilities have brought out only the undesirable traits that women have always had," that is, fussiness, primness, bossiness, and the tendency to make unnecessary enemies. They did not trust each other as candidates. They had not come up with any useful new political ideas. As voters they tended to be excessively moralistic and intolerant. Only about half as many women as men registered to vote, and when they went to the polls they voted as their husbands did. "After a fair trial of sixteen years, it seems just to appraise women's suffrage as one of those reforms which, like the secret ballot, the corrupt-practices acts, the popular election of senators, and the direct primary, promised almost everything and accomplished almost nothing."

Except for a slightly mean-spirited satisfaction in the deflation of suffragist pretensions, this still seems a fair appraisal. The percentage of women who register to vote is much higher now than in 1936, but otherwise the situation is little changed. Ross did, however, admit to one area in which women excelled politically—lobbying. But, he pointed out, they had been successful lobbyists long before they got the vote, and their prowess in this area did not in any way weaken his argument. Quite so, yet it did raise again the possibility that anti-suffragists had been right in thinking that the vote would diminish women's actual influence over politics. Emily Newell Blair later remarked that so long as the woman vote was an unknown quantity, professional politicians were obliged to respect it. Moreover, women in the pre-suffrage years spoke with virtually a single voice as they were never able to do again. Although some women of note opposed equal suffrage, almost none of them was publicly against the purposes of social feminism. In the Progressive era, before women were divided by partisan political affiliations, before the German scare and Russian scare unleashed an hysterical patriotism, before ex-suffragists fell out over their differing conceptions of equal rights, an apparent unanimity prevailed that lent great weight to the woman movement's expressions of opinion. Organized women did not understand the sources of their unity very well. They explained it by references to the bonds of motherhood and other more occult characteristics which supposedly bound them together, but it was no less real for being so misconstrued. As they did not understand the peculiar circumstances responsible for their unity, they could hardly preserve it in the postwar, postsuffrage, and post-Progressive world.

This is not to say, of course, that the woman movement could have been saved if only suffragists had adopted a sounder strategy in their voteless years, or if they had given up entirely on votes for women. The latter was not a real option. Too many years, too many tears had gone into the movement for anyone to arrest it on the eve of victory. Even if suffragists had appreciated that the vote would do organized women more harm than good, they would still have wanted it. Nor could they control the historical processes that were going to make class differences and ideological disagreements more important to women after 1917. But while recognizing that chance and circumstance sharply limited their field of maneuver, it is still clear that suffragists' neglect of certain alternatives was fatal to their larger purposes. They oversold the vote, which meant that both they and the generation that followed them were inevitably disillusioned with public affairs in general. They made too many compromises, from ignobly deserting their embattled sisters in the Woman's party to accepting American participation in a war they disliked. Practical politics made these choices essential, but expediency tarnished the moral quality that was the movement's most precious asset in the postsuffrage era. They failed to think seriously about what was to come after the federal amendment was passed. And, perhaps worst of all, in overconcentrating on politics they neglected other areas—economic, social, domestic—that more profoundly governed women's lives.

It might have been expected that the decline of feminism after 1920 would have been especially hard on the militant suffragists. They had wanted the vote more desperately than most women, and had risked more and suffered more to gain it. Militants lived a richly colored emotional life. Like children, zealots, and romantics, they were either way up or way down, but whether high or low they were always intense, doctrinaire, and assertive. Once their initial euphoria had passed, the members of the Woman's party, more so than other suffragists, found victory hardly less demoralizing than defeat. Previous setbacks had, after all, only been provisional; victory was final. Suffragists had sustained innumerable reverses with their morale intact. But the struggle had gone on for too long, had become, in fact, a way of life. Victory too long delayed loses its savor, and campaigns if endlessly prolonged become self-sustaining and self-justifying. Three generations of women had fought for the vote, and in doing so had become dependent on the cause to give their lives meaning. The vote was no compensation for the effort that had gone into winning it, no substitute for the emotions it displaced. The suffrage army was quickly demobilized. The thought patterns and modes of behavior it had required were not so easily converted to a peaceful, postsuffrage economy.

The NAWSA had anticipated some such denouement by founding in advance the League of Women Voters, a new bottle into which it hoped to pour the old feminist wine. But the prosaic LWV offered nothing to militants who, like discharged commandos, could see no way of using their special skills in the postwar world. Even before most women had a chance to cast their first vote, ultra-feminists were expressing their discontent and searching for ways to maintain the old faith. Mrs. Oliver Hazard Perry Belmont, an immensely rich and determined widow who had become the Woman's party's principal means of support, returned from Europe in July 1920 urging women to boycott the coming elections. "Husband your new power," she instructed them, adding that "suffragists did not fight for your emancipation for seventy years to have you now become servants to men's parties." Her vague admonitions became less opaque a few days later when she announced that the times demanded a new party to save women from the corruptions of big-party politics. Mrs. Belmont's lack of enthusiasm for the party system was widely shared. The League of Women Voters was, of course, scrupulously nonpartisan, in keeping with organized women's traditional aversion to regular politics, but many women were not. Charlotte Perkins Gilman endorsed Mrs. Belmont's position with some fervor:

> The power women will be able to exercise lies with their not joining in the party system of men. The party system of politics is a trick of men to conceal the real issues. Women should work for the measures they want outside of party politics. It is because the old political parties realize that women's influence will be negligible on the inside that they are so eager to get women to join with them.

On February 18, 1921, the old Woman's party was disbanded and a new one created in its stead. Florence Kelley was there and took its number in a slashing report for the *Survey*. She found the new Woman's party's position on the race issue singularly ignoble. The leadership declared that since Southern Negro women were discriminated against equally with Negro men, the principle of equal rights was not imperiled and the party not obliged to intervene. "An inglorious ideal of equality this! Acquiescence in the disfranchisement of millions of women, provided only that the men of their race also are deprived of their constitutional rights." The party's interpretation of equal rights in the industrial field was just as bad. It was inclined to regard protective legislation for working women as discriminatory, an attitude Mrs. Kelley believed to be both unjust and ill-informed. "How cruel, therefore, is the pretension of certain organizations of professional and business women to decide for the wage-earners, without consulting them, what statutory safeguards they are henceforth to do without." From the day of its birth, then, the battle lines between the new Woman's party and the social feminists for whom Mrs. Kelley spoke were clearly drawn. Although other social reformers were not so quick to react as Mrs. Kelley, she correctly gauged the dedication of the WP to equal rights thus construed, and prophetically warned Newton Baker that the struggle would go on "until an amendment of this general nature is adopted, or the leaders of the Woman's Party all die of old age."...

The Woman's party did earn much of the invective directed against it. Haughty and uncooperative under the best of circumstances, the party became truculent in the face of adversity. Mrs. Belmont and some other leaders were extraordinarily tactless. The party's manifesto began, "Women today, although enfranchised, are still in every way subordinate to men"—a statement which was not so much false as belittling of all that had been done for and by women in the recent past. The WP insisted that all grievances listed in the Seneca Falls declaration of 1848, save only votelessness, still obtained. This sweeping untruth irritated veteran suffragists who by the turn of the century had come to feel, as Susan B. Anthony put it, that "while women still suffer countless minor disadvantages, the fundamental rights have largely been secured except the suffrage." Equally offensive was the WP's claim to be the original suffragists' only heir. "Other women's organizations work for many things and for women incidentally; the Woman's Party works to acquire for women equal rights and opportunities, and this, in sum and substance, is the feminist movement."

The Woman's party sometimes appeared to have virtually a monopoly on the kind of woman condemned by the *American Mercury* as "a rabid feminist, one of the type that sees all history as a struggle between Woman, the beautiful builder, and Man, the eternal brute and wastrel." It continually obscured the merits of its program by flippancies which could only offend the serious. *Equal Rights* concluded one editorial on the probable judicial reaction to its amendment by observing that however "the courts may interpret the amendment, we can rest serene in our reliance on the righteousness of the principle of Equal Right for men and women and not worry as to the details of how it will work out. The establishing of a righteous principle will certainly bring only good results." But, of course, the "details of how it will work out" were precisely what the controversy over the amendment was all about.

Extreme feminists, while superb agitators, were hopelessly bad politicians with no feel for the bargaining and compromises that make the democratic machine go. Agitation had played its part in the suffrage struggle, but it was accompanied by a careful attention to the political arts. The Woman's party was, in this sense, completely unbalanced. Even when it did attempt to play politics, its approach was absurdly unrealistic. By 1924 it had given up its old strategy of attempting to hold the party in power responsible, but it was drifting toward a new and equally implausible theory—that a sufficient number of congresswomen would guarantee passage of the equal-rights amendment. For a time the party planned to support all women candidates, regardless of their position on the amendment, and urged women to vote exclusively for members of their own sex. Eventually the WP decided to support only those women candidates who endorsed the amendment. Five did so, all of them La Follette or minority candidates. All of them, despite the WP's help, were beaten. As usual, the party had gotten much, largely hostile, publicity, but the effort was so great and failure so complete that it never tried this tactic again.

... [T]he WP illustrates another familiar aspect of American social history: that radicals often more correctly analyze a given situation than their adversaries, but that the very traits responsible for their insight prevent them from exploiting it successfully. The militants were quick to understand that the vote had not materially improved the condition of women. They realized that many discriminatory laws and customs remained, and that to overcome them would require the same crusading energies that had gone into the suffrage campaign. In the end, this knowledge did them little good because the passions that led them to demand a feminist revival kept them from effecting it. Their theatrical demonstrations and doctrinaire rigor antagonized most other women, leaving the Woman's party in a position of solitary grandeur. Perhaps it didn't matter really. The feminist tide was ebbing so fast in the 1920's that it probably could not have been reversed under the best of circumstances. All the same, militancy insured the defeat of those hopes it meant to advance....

For all its symbolic triumphs, the WP had little to show at the decade's end for the nearly $800,000 it had spent since 1921. Wisconsin was still the only state with an equal-rights proviso in its constitution—the effects of which had been minimal. The party had been involved in preparing more than five hundred individual pieces of legislation across the country, but most of them were never made into law. It had alienated itself from the mainstream of organized womanhood and was soon to be confronted with an economic collapse that made its concentration on equal rights seem parochial if not downright cranky, and that was to dry up the supply of romantic youth which had given the organization its special force. From this point on the WP grew smaller, older, and poorer while the current of events moved ever more strongly against it.

Women With the Vote

Women have been saying for years that the world, and they themselves, would be changed if they were granted the right to vote. When Tennessee ratified the Nineteenth Amendment, the old dream became reality. Would the predicted consequences follow?

For more than two decades increasing numbers of southern women had become deeply engaged in efforts to build a system of public schools, to clean up prisons and abolish the convict lease system, to restrict the use of child labor, to improve the working conditions and reduce the hours of work of women and of factory workers generally, and to diminish racial discrimination in the South. Progress in all these areas had been slow, and the World War diverted the energies of many reformers. Now the war was over, women had the ballot, and the time had come when it was possible to believe, as one young North Carolina woman put it, that "the advent of women into political life would mean the loosening of a great moral force which will modify and soften the relentlessly selfish economic forces of trade and industry.... the ideals of democracy and of social and human welfare will undoubtedly receive a great impetus."

Whatever the future was destined to reveal about the long-run consequences of adding women to the electorate, at the outset there was a burst of energy, a new drive for accomplishment. Among those who had long supported the idea of suffrage there was no lack of confidence that women would live up to their new opportunity. In Baton Rouge the daughter of a former governor edited a weekly paper entitled *Woman's Enterprise* with the goal of proving to the world that women "are as fully alive to the demands of the times as are the sterner sex." The newspaper encouraged women to register and vote, urged them to run for office, and issued constant reminders to officeholders that women now intended to be heard on all important issues. Women, the *Enterprise* thought, far from voting as their menfolk directed, were on the way to becoming the politically influential members of their families. "Place one energetic woman on a commission and a general house cleaning will result such as Baton Rouge has never enjoyed," the editors confidently asserted; "inefficiency in every department will disappear."

In addition to politics the *Enterprise* carried a steady stream of articles on working women's problems, education for women, and the "new concept of

From Anne Firor Scott, *The Southern Lady: From Pedestal to Politics, 1830–1930* (University of Chicago Press, 1970). Copyright © 1970 by Anne Firor Scott. Reprinted by permission of University of Chicago Press. Notes omitted.

marriage." It also directed a good deal of attention to the accomplishments of young women enrolled at the Louisiana State University.

For those who had taken it seriously the suffrage movement had been an excellent school in political methods. In the first flush of post-suffrage enthusiasm, the old hands undertook to try to teach the ways and means of political action to as many of the newly enfranchised as they could persuade to be interested. Even before the Nineteenth Amendment was ratified, state suffrage organizations transformed themselves into leagues of women voters, to educate women and work for "needed legislation." Charles Merriam, a well-known political scientist, was persuaded to offer an intensive training course for women leaders at the University of Chicago. "Citizenship schools" blossomed over the landscape, offering everything from the most serious reading in political theory to the simplest instruction in ballot marking. Meanwhile women established legislative councils in a concerted effort to attain the laws they felt were needed. The Alabama council, for example, was made up of sixteen organizations ranging from the Woman's Trade Union League to the Methodist Home Missionary Council. In Texas the Joint Legislative Council published a carefully compiled record of the work of congressmen, state legislators, and judges.

The central political concern had to do with the problems of children. In nearly every state women were active in the effort to secure better child labor laws. The case of Virginia is instructive. In 1921 women's groups urged the legislature to establish a Children's Code Commission, and when the legislature took their suggestion, they persuaded the governor to appoint five of their number to the commission. When the commission, in turn, brought in twenty-four recommendations for new laws, ranging from a statewide juvenile court system to compulsory education, the women went to work to secure legislative approval of the recommendations. Eighteen of the twenty-four were adopted.

Also in 1921 a combination of women's groups in Georgia secured the passage of a children's code, a child-placement bill, and a training school bill. In 1923 Georgia women tried, but failed, to persuade the state legislature to ratify the federal child labor amendment. In Arkansas, by contrast, a woman member of the legislature, working in conjunction with the members of the women's clubs, was given credit for that state's ratifying the amendment. The wife of the man who led the floor fight against ratification was reported to be unable to conceal her delight that he had failed. In other states when women failed to secure ratification of the child labor amendment they turned their attention to strengthening state labor laws, an effort in which they were more successful.

In 1921 southern women, along with women from over the nation, brought pressure upon the Congress to pass the Sheppard-Towner Act for maternal and infant health. Nineteen of 26 southern senators voted for the bill. In the House, 91 of the 279 votes in support of the bill came from the South and only 9 of 39 votes against it. This law, which pioneered federal-state cooperation in welfare, was the first concrete national achievement of newly enfranchised women. Since the law provided for federal-state cooperative financing, it was necessary for the women to follow up their congressional efforts with work to secure the matching appropriations from state legislatures. This campaign elicited a great deal of enthusiasm among women in every southern state. It was in those states particularly, where the machinery of public health was not well developed, that the favorable effects of the Act were most visible.

Next to children the subjects of most general interest to politically minded women had to do with the working conditions and wages of women workers. In Arkansas, for example, as early as 1919 the suffrage organization began to work for minimum wages and maximum hours in cotton mills. In Georgia women joined the Federation of Labor in an effort to secure a limit on hours of work for women. The hearing on this last measure brought out "every cotton mill man in Georgia," and while a woman's eloquent testimony persuaded the committee to report the bill, the millowners had enough influence to prevent its being brought to a vote. As a result of what they had learned about the conditions in which many factory women worked, clubwomen and the League of Women Voters developed a deepening concern for the problems of industrial labor generally. This concern often brought them into conflict with husbands and friends. The businessman's cherished "cheap labor" might be seen by his wife as an exploited human being, especially when the worker was a woman or a child. For years southern ladies had been praised for their superior sensitivity to human and personal problems, and now that their "sphere" was enlarging, such sensitivity took them in directions not always welcome to their husbands.

This particular drama of wives against husbands was played out, among other places, in North Carolina. Textile manufacturing was a major economic interest in that state, and working conditions in many mills were far from ideal. Wages were low, and it was common to find numbers of young children at work. Soon after the passage of the Nineteenth Amendment, North Carolina women began to develop an aggressive interest in these matters. It occurred to them to ask the state government to invite the Woman's Bureau of the United States Department of Labor to investigate working conditions in North Carolina mills. This suggestion aroused a strong opposition among millmen and their business colleagues. The governor was polite to the women but adamant: North Carolina had no need for the federal government to tell it how to run its affairs. Textile journals and newspapers accused the offending women of being unwomanly, of mixing in things about which they knew nothing, and of being the dupes of northern manufacturers bent on spoiling the competitive advantage which child labor and cheap female labor gave the South. The YWCA, one of the groups supporting the idea of a survey, was warned that it would soon find itself without funds. The state president of the League of Women Voters was summoned before a self-constituted panel of millmen and lectured severely. She was told that her husband's sales of mill machinery would diminish as long as she and the league continued their unseemly interest in working conditions in the mills.

The progressive movement came fully into being in the South in the 1920s, especially in relation to state government. Southern women contributed significantly to the political effort which led to the adoption of a wide range of social legislation in those years. In public, women continued to defer to men, but in their private correspondence they described their own efforts as more practical than those of men.

As time went by a small number of very respectable southern women became deeply involved in what could only be called, in the southern context, the radical aspect of the labor movement. Lucy Randolph Mason, whose name testified to her Virginia lineage, began by working with the YWCA in Richmond and became, as she said, more and more concerned about the lack of social control in the development of southern industry. In her YWCA work she became acutely aware of industrial problems, for the young women in the Y, during the twenties, were preoccupied with the study of the facts of industrial life. They worked out a legislative program which included the abatement of poverty, abolition of child labor, a living wage in every industry, the eight-hour day, and protection of workers from the hardships of continued unemployment. At Randolph-Macon members of the Y studied the problems of coal miners, and at Westhampton those of unemployment. College girls across the South formed a committee for student industrial cooperation, seeking, as they put it, to Christianize the social order.

In January 1923 the National Consumers League sponsored a conference on industrial legislation for the Mississippi Valley states. The session on hours of work for women was chaired by a New Orleans woman, and the one on minimum wages by a Kentucky woman. In the same year the chairman of the Women in Industry Committee of the Mississippi League of Women Voters urged members of local leagues to inform themselves about the working conditions of the 15,000 working women in Mississippi "in restaurants and shops, in bakeries and laundries and fisheries," about their inadequate wages, and their need for safety and sanitary protection. All this was to be in preparation for the next session of the Mississippi legislature.

Middle-class southern women set up two schools for factory girls. One, sponsored by the YWCA at Lake Junaluska in North Carolina, offered what its founders called a brief social-religious education. Although the organizers of this school realized that political action to improve their wages and working conditions could not be accomplished by the working women alone, they felt that these summer conferences might stimulate girls to begin to study and think about their own problems. The other experiment was the Southern Summer School for Women Workers in Industry, founded at Burnsville, North Carolina, in 1927. An outgrowth of the famous Bryn Mawr workers summer school, it offered training to factory girls many of whom, when the upsurge of unionization occurred in the 1930s, would become labor organizers.

By 1931 the Southern Council on Women and Children in Industry, made up of women, had been formed to work for shorter hours and to try to bring an end to night work in the textile industry. Lucy Mason worked for this group too, before she went on to her major effort in the 1930s as an organizer for the CIO [Congress of Industrial Organizations].

It is curious in view of the deep conservatism of the majority of southern women, many of whom never registered to vote, that those who did choose to live an active life were often found on the progressive side of the political spectrum. Part of the explanation is that the person who was bold enough to assume a role unusual for women was also likely to be radical on social questions generally. As the president of the Tennessee League of Women Voters remarked:

> Some good souls are pleased to call our ideas socialistic. They are indeed uncomfortable often for some folk. Some timid souls of both sexes are only half converted to the new order... [yet] every clear thinking, right feeling and high minded man and woman should consecrate his best talents to the gradual reorganization of society, national and international.

One evidence of the advanced thinking of many of the southern women who were most active in public life was the important part they played in what came to be called the interracial movement. Beginning in 1919, at a time when many Negroes were leaving the South and many others were coming home from the war with a new view of life, the interracial movement of the twenties was built on the foundation laid in the previous decades....

In 1920 at a meeting of southern churchwomen in Memphis four Negro women came on invitation to speak of the needs of southern Negroes. One of them, Charlotte Hawkins Brown, head of a school for Negroes in North Carolina, told the gathering that she had been forcibly removed from a Pullman car on her way to the meeting. In the emotional stir of the moment the ninety-odd white churchwomen constituted themselves the Woman's Department of Will Alexander's Commission [on Interracial Cooperation]. The first head of this group was Mrs. Luke Johnson of Griffin, Georgia, under whose leadership interracial committees were organized in every southern state. Mrs. Johnson thought race was "one of the livest issues of the day and... a real test of Christianity and of citizenship."

In Texas the women's interracial organization was put together by an energetic widow, businesswoman, and former suffrage worker, Jessie Daniel Ames. By 1924 women there were working to improve Negro housing, schools, libraries, to secure Negro farm agents to work with Negro farmers, for better health care, a school for delinquent girls, adequate railroad accommodations, and for textbooks dealing with the economic and racial development of the Negro people. They proposed an anti-lynching law which would have made every member of a mob liable to murder charges. The group also attempted to investigate particular problems of intimidation, and organized a speakers' bureau to take the discussion of race issues to the state. In North Carolina Mrs. Bertha Newell, superintendent of the Bureau of Christian Social Relations of the Women's Missionary Council of the Methodist Church, and Clara Cox, a Friend from High Point, carried on the same kind of effort. In 1926 Mrs. Newell began working to secure better job opportunities for educated Negro girls.

Women tried to deal with racial conflict and black problems in many ways. When the National League of Women Voters decided in 1924 to establish a committee on Negro problems with membership from every state that had more than 15 percent Negro population, women in eight southern states accepted appointment. Many of these same women served on local interracial committees, of which there were finally about eight hundred in the South. In Tennessee white women organized a special citizenship school for Negro women. Some individuals offered personal support to their Negro fellow citizens. Mary Cooke

Branch Munford of Richmond made a room of her house permanently available to Negroes for public meetings, and a busy doctor's wife in Alabama waged a one-woman campaign for better Negro education. When the Richmond city council considered a segregation statute in 1929, it was Lucy Randolph Mason who, almost single-handedly, persuaded the council to defeat it. In April 1924 the Mississippi Federation of Women's Clubs set up a committee on the condition of the colored people, and the president of the Colored Women's Federation was invited to tell the white convention about the problems of Negro domestic workers.

The most dramatic aspect of women's interracial work was the crusade against lynching, which began in the early twenties. A group of Georgia women sent a message to the *New York World:*

> We are convinced that if there is any one crime more dangerous than others, it is that crime which strikes at the roots of and undermines constituted authority, breaks all laws and restraints of civilization, substitutes mob violence and masked irresponsibility from established justice and deprives society of a sense of protection against barbarism.

By 1930 under the leadership of Jessie Daniel Ames, who by that time had left Texas for Atlanta, the Association of Southern Women for the Prevention of Lynching took shape. At its peak this organization enrolled 40,000 small-town and rural churchwomen in an effort to bring to an end this most spectacularly disgraceful form of race conflict.

In the meantime southern white women inaugurated an increasing number of interracial meetings, in which there was fairly open discussion of the problems Negroes faced. Though Negro women leaders, for the most part, took care to eschew any demand for social equality, they did hammer away on such things as discrimination in the administration of justice, housing, Jim Crow cars, inferior education, and the need for the ballot. It seems likely that these efforts, ineffectual as they seemed in the face of the magnitude of the problem, nevertheless represented the opening wedge which would ultimately bring an end to the monolithic position of southerners on the issue of white supremacy. From slavery through Reconstruction and into the twentieth century, relationships between white and black women were quite unlike those common between white and black men, sharing as they did many concerns about children and home life across the color line. The fact that women were very active in the interracial movement is not surprising.

In the twenties white women were speaking of their sympathy for Negro women who were, like themselves, mothers and homemakers. One point they made over and over was the need to protect the chastity of Negro women from the aggression of white men. Just as one antebellum woman had candidly remarked that she did not know whether her grandmother's sympathy for abolition stemmed from sympathy for slaves or for white women, so it might be wondered whether part of the concern for the chastity of Negro women was a reflection of the white women's distaste for the half-hidden miscegenation which existed in every southern community.

◄◦►

The interest of women in humanitarian causes had deep roots in traditional feminine philanthropy. However, the twenties also witnessed the beginning of some newer interests. As they studied the mechanics of government in order to vote, women began to develop a concern for efficient organization. One of the tools for educating new voters to their responsibilities was the study of state and local government. As women went about looking at the way such governments actually operated they began to wonder whether they could be made more efficient. As early as 1922 women's groups in Virginia were working for improved election laws, and in the following year they undertook to learn about the executive budget. In 1924 the Virginia League of Women Voters concentrated upon tax administration, a subject which the controlling Democratic machine was not anxious to discuss. The same group successfully supported a bill to create a uniform fiscal year but failed in an effort to secure civil service, a conservation department, and reform of the county government and the state educational machinery.

Such interests were not confined to Virginia. Women in Georgia and Tennessee became convinced that outmoded constitutions were the source of much inefficiency; and in both states campaigns for constitutional revisions were launched and eventually succeeded. Kentucky women in 1927 began to work for home rule for cities, improvements in local charters, and the adoption of city manager government.

Women were interested not only in the structure of government; they wanted to make it more democratic. Their own long exclusion had made them sensitive to citizen participation. It was newly enfranchised women who invented the now commonplace idea of getting out the vote. In some places their efforts led to spectacular increases. In Alabama, for example, 54.4 percent of the qualified voters voted in 1924 following a get-out-the-vote effort, compared to less than 30 percent in 1920. One county, where women had been particularly active, turned out 84.1 percent of its qualified voters. Florida in the same year reported a 65.9 percent increase over 1920 in the number of voters going to the polls.

The poll tax was a subject of twofold concern. Women's groups opposed the tax on principle, but as long as it remained in force, they set out to collect it in order to increase the number of qualified voters. In 1925 Louisiana women collected $30,000 to this end. The work of North Carolina women for the Australian ballot, which finally succeeded in 1929, was another example of an effort to improve democratic procedures.

Close to home, yet a long way from women's traditional concerns, were two other political issues that developed strength in southern women's groups in the twenties: government ownership of Muscle Shoals and the regulation of utility rates. Interest in both these questions resulted from studies of the cost of living. The movement that would lead to the Tennessee Valley Authority gained the enthusiastic support of women in Alabama and Tennessee. On these as on other questions politically active women took a pragmatic view without reference to traditional free enterprise arguments.

... Many southern women showed an interest in running for elective office; and, though numerous obstacles lay between almost any woman and nomination, by 1930 only Louisiana had yet to have women in the state legislature. During the twenties women served as secretaries of state in Kentucky, Texas, and Louisiana, as clerks or deputy clerks of the Supreme Court in Georgia and Oklahoma, as commissioners of public welfare in North Carolina and Oklahoma, as commissioner of state lands in Arkansas, railroad commissioner in Florida, and superintendent of public instruction in Texas.

One woman who made her way to the center of power was Mrs. Nellie Nugent Somerville of Greenville, Mississippi, who had been an active politician long before the Nineteenth Amendment. At the first election after it was legal to do so, in 1923, she ran for the state legislature, in a campaign that was a model of thorough organization, and was elected. She had been observing party organization long enough to understand it rather well, and she hoped the newly enfranchised women would be similarly observant. She advised them to be certain they had a hand in choosing county committees and reminded them: "It now becomes the duty of women voters to take lively interests in the details of political machinery. When any meeting or election is ordered by your political party be sure you take part in it." ...

Another politically minded woman who reached a position of genuine power in the party was Sue Shelton White of Tennessee, an independent court reporter, secretary to members of the Tennessee Supreme Court, and from 1920 to 1926 secretary to Senator Kenneth McKellar. In 1915 she drafted the first mother's pension law to be presented to the Tennessee legislature, which finally passed in 1920. She went from her job in Senator McKellar's office to practice law in Jackson, Tennessee, and was sufficiently effective in Democratic politics to be invited to work for the Democratic National Committee. With Nellie Davis (Tayloe) Ross she helped lay the groundwork for the extensive women's program of the party during the early Franklin D. Roosevelt years. ...

An increasing number of southern women undertook simple party work of the doorbell-ringing and envelope-stuffing variety—a trend that still continues. And whether they helped make policy or not, women voters believed they were affecting the outcome of elections. Women claimed to have defeated James E. Ferguson and elected William P. Hobby governor of Texas in 1920. In Mississippi Henry L. Whitfield, former president of Mississippi State College for Women, was elected governor in 1923, largely through the efforts of alumnae of the college. South Carolina women thought they had a large hand in the defeat of Cole Blease. One South Carolina woman who worked through the whole campaign remarked innocently, "We made no partisan stand, we merely got out the vote." Tennessee Democrats, perhaps looking for a scapegoat, blamed women for the Republican victory in Tennessee in the 1920 election. The women themselves claimed credit for the return of Cordell Hull to Congress three years later.

In North Carolina in 1921 the federated women persuaded a reluctant governor to appoint their former president, Kate Burr Johnson, commissioner of charities and welfare. The legislature showed an equal reluctance to confirm the appointment, but, as Mrs. Johnson recalled it, "They were scared to death of what women with the vote might do, and one legislator was heard to remark, 'Well, we might as well put her in; she's pretty and won't give us any trouble.'" The forecast was inaccurate, since Mrs. Johnson, with the organized women behind her, became a prime mover in the struggle to secure a survey of working conditions in North Carolina mills, and by so doing soon stood high on the legislature's list of troublemakers....

Many of the women... who had been trained during the two or three decades before suffrage, and who had been acutely aware of the disadvantage of being barred from the polls, were eager to move into a more active and effective political role in 1920. Their general goals had been worked out in the preceding decades. Their underlying motivation was complex, but at least two main drives were clear: first, the drive to assert themselves as individual human beings with minds and capacities that could be used; and, second, the drive to improve the world in which they lived. The balance of these motives varied from person to person. Some, like Lucy Mason, were primarily interested in social reform:

> When I was fourteen, a missionary's sermon made me want to be a missionary myself. Later I recognized that religion can be put to work right in one's own community. It was this belief that took me into the Equal Suffrage League, and later the League of Women Voters, both of which were interested in labor and social legislation.

Others thoroughly enjoyed the game of politics and the feeling of power that occasionally accompanied it. Nearly all felt that significant reforms would be more easily achieved with women's help.

The Nineteenth Amendment changed a good many things, but it only partially modified southern culture. A number of difficulties remained in the way of women's full participation in public life. One major obstacle, in addition to the demands of home and family, was widespread male opposition, typified, perhaps, by the Texan who burned his wife's poll tax receipt to prevent her from voting. Equally important was the unwillingness of many women to assume and carry through large responsibilities. Often they had a vague desire to "do something" but needed leadership to find out what to do and how to do it, and there were never enough leaders to tap all the potential resources. A good example, no doubt an extreme one, was a Virginia town of which it was reported that when a certain Miss Terry was at home the town was alive with women's political activities but when she went to Europe all was quiet.

Around the handful of leaders there gathered a slowly growing number of supporters and workers, and when this support was effectively channeled, specific goals were achieved. In almost every instance—as in child labor reform, for example—groups of men were working to the same ends, and frequently there was cooperation. Women's efforts were crucial in the areas of race relations and factory regulation. Through it all, the outward aspect of the southern lady continued to be maintained as the necessary precondition for securing a hearing.

For some women, this was a perfectly compatible outward role, so long as their freedom of action was not seriously limited. Others impatiently called for an end to pedestals, but even they found it effective to operate within the ladylike tradition. The other side of the coin was that women were accused of not being proper southern ladies by those who objected to the substantive goals for which they were working, and who hoped thus to discredit the goals themselves. . . .

When all this is said, however, the fact remains that the post-suffrage burst of political and social effort created a milieu in which the emerging new woman could try her powers. Along with expanding opportunities for work, education, and associated activity, the franchise added another dimension to women's lives, and another option for women who wanted more than purely domestic experience.

POSTSCRIPT

Did the Women's Movement Die in the 1920s?

Most students today associate the Equal Rights Amendment (ERA) with the women's liberation movement of the 1960s and 1970s, but the history of this amendment dates back to the 1920s. Proposed for the first time in 1923, the amendment stated, "Men and women shall have equal rights throughout the United States and every place subject to its jurisdiction." This notion of full equality met significant opposition when it was proposed—as it has in recent years—including challenges from women's organizations. Groups such as the League of Women Voters complained that the Equal Rights Amendment, if ratified, would roll back protective legislation in the areas of minimum wage and maximum hour laws and would jeopardize penalties for rape and sexual offenses against women. Hence, many of the fruits of the Progressive Era would be lost. For Alice Paul, leader of the National Women's Party that supported the amendment, the protective legislation enacted in the past represented a conspiracy to deny women full equality by singling them out for special treatment. These laws, Paul argued, set women apart as a separate and unequal class. The ideological struggle suggested by these divergent positions continued into the 1930s and reflected the serious divisions that surfaced in the women's movement following the suffrage victory.

The status of women in the decade after suffrage receives general treatment in William H. Chafe, *The American Woman: Her Changing Social, Economic, and Political Roles, 1920–1970* (Oxford University Press, 1972); June Sochen, *Herstory: A Woman's View of American History* (Alfred, 1974); Mary P. Ryan, *Womanhood in America: From Colonial Times to the Present* (New Viewpoints, 1975); Sheila M. Rothman, *Woman's Proper Place: A History of Changing Ideals and Practices, 1870 to the Present* (Basic Books, 1978); Lois Scharf and Joan Jensen, eds., *Decades of Discontent: The Women's Movement, 1910–1940* (Greenwood Press, 1983); and Nancy Woloch, *Women and the American Experience* (Alfred A. Knopf, 1984). Discussions of feminism in the 1920s are presented in J. Stanley Lemons, *The Woman Citizen: Social Feminism in the 1920s* (University of Illinois Press, 1973); Lois Banner, *Women in Modern America: A Brief History* (Harcourt Brace Jovanovich, 1974); Susan D. Baker, *The Origins of the Equal Rights Amendment: Feminism Between the Wars* (Greenwood Press, 1981); Dorothy Brown, *Setting a Course: American Women in the 1920s* (Twayne, 1987); and Robyn Muncy, *Creating a Female Dominion in American Reform, 1890–1935* (Oxford University Press, 1991). Felice D. Gordon, *After Winning: The Legacy of the New Jersey Suffragists, 1920–1947* (Rutgers University Press, 1986) and Kristi Anderson, *After Suffrage: Women in Partisan and Electoral Politics Before the New Deal* (University of Chicago Press, 1996) focus specifically on the continuing struggle for political empowerment following the ratification of the Nineteenth Amendment. Christine Lunardini, in *From Equal Suffrage to Equal Rights: Alice Paul and the National Woman's Party, 1910-1928* (New York University Press, 1986), examines one of the controversial advocates for an equal rights amendment in the 1920s. Nancy F. Cott, in *The Grounding of Feminism* (Yale University Press, 1987), argues that the diversity within the women's movement created important paradoxes. For example, although feminists in the 1920s desired equality with men, unity among themselves, and gender consciousness, they also focused upon their differences from men, the diversity of women, and the elimination of gender roles. David M. Kennedy, in *Birth Control in America: The Career of Margaret Sanger* (Yale University Press, 1970), examines an important issue that attracted the interest of many women's groups in the 1920s, while Jacqueline Dowd Hall, in *Revolt Against Chivalry: Jessie Daniel Ames and the Women's Campaign Against Lynching* (Columbia University Press, 1979), explores the role of women in the area of race relations. A valuable historiographical essay is Estelle B. Freedman, "The New Woman: Changing Views of Women in the 1920s," *Journal of American History* (September 1974).

ISSUE 9

Was Information About the Attack on Pearl Harbor Deliberately Withheld From the American Commanders?

YES: Robert A. Theobald, from *The Final Secret of Pearl Harbor: The Washington Contribution to the Japanese Attack* (Devin-Adair, 1954)

NO: Roberta Wohlstetter, from *Pearl Harbor: Warning and Decision* (Stanford University Press, 1967)

ISSUE SUMMARY

YES: Retired rear admiral Robert A. Theobald argues that President Franklin D. Roosevelt deliberately withheld information from the commanders at Pearl Harbor in order to encourage the Japanese to make a surprise attack on the weak U.S. Pacific Fleet.

NO: Historian Roberta Wohlstetter contends that even though naval intelligence broke the Japanese code, conflicting signals and the lack of a central agency coordinating U.S. intelligence information made it impossible to predict the Pearl Harbor attack.

In 1899 and 1900 Secretary of State John Hay enunciated two notes, known as the Open Door policy. The first pronouncement attempted to provide equal access to commercial rights in China for all nations. The second note called on all countries to respect China's "territorial and administrative" integrity. For the next 40 years the open door was restated by every president from Theodore Roosevelt to Franklin Roosevelt for two reasons: (1) to prevent China from being taken over by Japan, and (2) to preserve the balance of power in the world. The Open Door policy appeared to work during World War I and the 1920s.

The Nine-Power Treaty of 1922 restated the Open Door principles, and its signatories agreed to assist China in forming a stable government. Japan supported the agreements because the world economy was reasonably stable. But the worldwide depression had a major effect on the foreign policies of all nations. Japan decided that she wanted to extend her influence politically as well as economically in Asia. On the night of September 18, 1931, an explosion, probably staged by Japanese militarists, damaged the Japanese-controlled South Manchurian Railroad. Japanese troops not only overran Chinese troops stationed in South Manchuria but within five months established the puppet state of Manchukuo. When the League of Nations condemned Japan's actions, the Japanese gave their two-year's notice and withdrew from the league. A turn for the worse came for the Chinese on July 7, 1937, when a shooting incident at the Marco Polo Bridge between Chinese and Japanese troops led to a full-scale war on China's mainland. President Franklin Roosevelt took a strong verbal stand in a speech he delivered on October 5, 1937, demanding that nations stirring up "international anarchy" should be quarantined.

Roosevelt aided the Chinese with nonembargoed, nonmilitary goods when he found a loophole in the neutrality laws. Japan's goal to establish a "new order in East Asia" was furthered by the outbreak of World War II in Europe in the fall of 1939 and the ease with which the German army overran and defeated France the following spring. In September 1940 Japanese forces occupied northern French Indochina (later known as Vietnam). Although Roosevelt was unable to stop Japan's military expansionism, he did jar them with economic sanctions. When the Japanese occupied southern Indochina on July 25, 1941, Roosevelt again jolted the Japanese government by issuing an order freezing all Japanese assets in the United States, which created major problems. Japan had only 12 to 18 months of oil in reserves for military use. A military statement had developed in the war with China in part because the United States was funneling economic and military aid to her ally. Consequently, Japan sought an accommodation with the United States in the fall of 1941. Japan tried to negotiate two plans that would have resulted in a partial withdrawal from Indochina and the establishment of a coalition government in China proper that would be partially controlled by the Japanese and would take place once the war stopped. In return, America would resume trade with Japan prior to the July 26 freezing of Japanese assets.

Because American cryptologists had broken the Japanese diplomatic code for a second time in the summer of 1941, American policymakers knew that these were Japan's final proposals. Secretary of State Cordell Hull sent the Japanese a note on November 26 that restated America's Open Door policy and asked "the government of Japan [to] withdraw all military naval, air, and police forces from China and from Indochina." When Japan rejected the proposal both sides realized this meant war. Where or when was the question. Japan's surprise December 7 attack on Pearl Harbor provided the answer.

In the following selection, Robert A. Theobald argues that President Roosevelt deliberately withheld information from the Hawaiian army and naval commanders at Pearl Harbor in order to encourage the Japanese to make a surprise attack on the weak Pacific Fleet. In the second selection, Roberta Wohlstetter maintains that even though naval intelligence broke the Japanese code, conflicting signals made it impossible to predict the Pearl Harbor attack.

The Final Secret of Pearl Harbor

Having been present at Pearl Harbor on December 7, 1941, and having appeared with Admiral Husband E. Kimmel when that officer testified before the Roberts Commission,[1] the author has ever since sought a full understanding of the background that made that day possible. For many years, he gathered and pieced together the available evidence which appeared to shed light upon the Washington happenings concerned with that attack. These studies produced very definite conclusions regarding the manner in which our country's strategy had been shaped to entice the Japanese to attack Pearl Harbor, and the efforts that have since been made to keep these facts from the knowledge of the American People.

For over three years, the thirty-nine-volume set which comprises the Record of Proceedings of all the Pearl Harbor Investigations has been available to the author. Serious study of these volumes has caused many revisions of errors in detail, but it has served to divest the writer's mind of all doubt regarding the soundness of his basic conclusions.

It is firmly believed that those in Washington who knew the facts, decided from the first that considerations of patriotism and loyalty to their wartime Commander-in-Chief required that a veil of secrecy should be drawn about the President's handling of the situation which culminated in the Pearl Harbor attack.

While there was great justification for this secrecy during the continuance of the war, the reasons for it no longer exist. The war is finished. President Roosevelt and his administration are now history. Dictates of patriotism requiring secrecy regarding a line of national conduct in order to preserve it for possible future repetition do not apply in this case because, in this atomic age, facilitating an enemy's surprise attack, as a method of initiating a war, is unthinkable. Our Pearl Harbor losses would preclude that course of action in the future without consideration of the increased destructiveness of present and future weapons. Finally, loyalty to their late President in the matter of Pearl Harbor would be better served today, if his friends would discard their policy of secrecy in favor of full publicity.

Another consideration which today strongly favors a complete understanding of the whole Pearl Harbor story, is the thought of justice to the professional reputations of the Hawaiian Commanders, Admiral Kimmel and General Short—a justice which is long overdue.

Throughout the war, maintenance of the national morale at the highest possible level demanded complete public confidence in the President and his principal military advisers. During that time, the public could not be given cause to assign a tithe of blame for the Pearl Harbor attack to Washington. And so, dating from the report of the Roberts Commission, most of the responsibility for Pearl Harbor has been placed upon the two Hawaiian Commanders. This carefully executed plan which diverted all suspicion from Washington contributed its full measure to the successful conduct of the war.

The time has come when full publicity should be given to the Washington contribution to the Pearl Harbor attack, in order that the judgment of the American people may assign to Admiral Kimmel and General Short no more than their just and proper share of the responsibility for that tragic day.

Manifestly, many readers will be reluctant to agree with the main conclusions which have been reached in this study. In recognition of this fact, the normal sequence of deductive reasoning is discarded in favor of the order used in a legal presentation. The case is stated at the outset, and the evidence is then marshalled and discussed. The reader is thus enabled to weigh each fact, as it is presented, against the conclusions, which have been firmly implanted in the mind of the author by the summation of these facts.

The sole purpose of the subject matter contained herein is a searching for the truth, and it is hoped that the absence of any ulterior motive is apparent throughout. Comments of a critical character concerning the official actions of officers frequently intersperse the pages which follow. No criticism of the officer is intended. Those officers were obeying orders, under circumstances which were professionally most trying to them. Such comments are necessary to a full understanding of the discussion of the moment, however, but there is no intention to impugn the motives of any individual. Patriotism and loyalty were the wellsprings of those motives....

Main Deduction: President Roosevelt Circumvents American Pacifism

In the spring of 1940, Denmark, Norway, Holland, Belgium and France were conquered by Germany, and throughout the remainder of that year Great Britain's situation was so desperate that many expected her collapse early in the ensuing year. Fortunately, however, the Axis powers turned East in 1941 to conquer Greece and to attack Russia.

There is every reason to believe that when France was overcome President Roosevelt became convinced the United States must fight beside Great Britain, while the latter was still an active belligerent, or later sustain the fight alone, as the last democratic stronghold in a Nazi world. Never, however, had the country been less prepared for war, both psychologically and physically. Isolationism was a dominant philosophy throughout the land, and the armed forces were weak and consequently unready.

The United States not only had to become an active participant in democracy's fight as quickly as possible, but a people, completely united in support of the war effort, had to be brought into the arena. But, how could the country be made to fight? Only a cataclysmic happening could move Congress to enact a declaration of war; and that action would not guarantee that the nation's response would be the completely united support which victory has always demanded. This was the President's problem, and his solution was based upon the simple fact that, while it takes two to make a fight, either one may start it.

As the people of this country were so strongly opposed to war, one of the Axis powers must be forced to involve the United States, and in such a way as to arouse the American people to wholehearted belief in the necessity of fighting. This would require drastic action, and the decision was unquestionably a difficult one for the President to make.

In this connection, it should be remembered that Japan, Germany, and Italy signed the Tripartite Treaty on September 28, 1940, by which the three nations agreed to make common cause against any nation, not then a participant in the European war or the Sino-Japanese conflict, which attacked one of the signatories.

Thereafter, the fact that war with Japan meant war with Germany and Italy played an important part in President Roosevelt's diplomatic strategy. Throughout the approach to war and during the fighting, the primary U.S. objective was the defeat of Germany.

To implement the solution of his problem, the President: (1) instituted a successful campaign to correct the Nation's military unpreparedness; (2) offered Germany repeated provocations, by violations of neutrality and diplomatic usage; (3) applied ever-increasing diplomatic-economic pressure upon Japan, which reached its sustained climax on July 25, 1941, when the United States, Great Britain, and the Netherlands stopped their trade with Japan and subjected her to almost complete economic encirclement; (4) made mutual commitments with the British Prime Minister at Newfoundland in August, 1941, which promised mutual support in the event that the United States, Great Britain, or a third country not then at war were attacked by Japan in the Pacific; (5) terminated the Washington conference with the note of November 26, 1941, which gave Japan no choice but surrender or war; (6) retained a weak Pacific Fleet in Hawaiian waters, despite contrary naval advice, where it served only one diplomatic purpose, an invitation to a Japanese surprise attack; (7) furthered that surprise by causing the Hawaiian Commanders to be denied invaluable information from decoded Japanese dispatches [or "Magic"] concerning the rapid approach of the war and the strong probability that the attack would be directed at Pearl Harbor.

This denial of information was a vital feature of enticing a Japanese surprise attack upon Pearl Harbor. If Admiral Kimmel and General Short had been given the knowledge possessed by the Washington authorities, the Hawaiian Commands would have been alerted against an overseas attack. The Pacific Fleet would have kept the sea during the first days of December, 1941, until the issue of peace or war had been decided. With the highly effective Japanese espionage in Hawaii, this would have caused Tokyo to cancel the surprise attack.

The problem which faced Lincoln during March of 1861 was identical in principle—to unite the sentiment of the North behind the policy of compelling the seceded Southern states by force of arms to return to the Union. For a month after his inauguration, he made no move, and then South Carolina's insistent demands for the surrender of Fort Sumter gave him the answer to his problem. He refused to surrender the fort, and dispatched a fleet to reprovision it. South Carolina then fired the first shots of the Civil War. Pearl Harbor was President Roosevelt's Fort Sumter.

Diplomatically, President Roosevelt's strategy of forcing Japan to war by unremitting and ever-increasing diplomatic-economic pressure, and by simultaneously holding our Fleet in Hawaii as an invitation to a surprise attack, was a complete success. Militarily, our ship and personnel losses mark December 7, 1941 as the day of tragic defeat. One is forced to conclude that the anxiety to have Japan, beyond all possibility of dispute, commit the first act of war, caused the President and his civilian advisers to disregard the military advice which would somewhat have cushioned the blow. The President, before the event, probably envisaged a *Panay* incident[2] of somewhat larger proportions. Despite the fact that the attack laid the foundation for complete victory, a terrific price was paid, as the following account of the ship, plane, and personnel losses discloses.

The Pearl Harbor Losses: Facts and Figures

The Japanese clearly intended that their entire surprise attack should be delivered against military objectives. The first waves of the attack were delivered against the airfields on the Island of Oahu—Army, Navy, and Marine Corps—to reduce the air-borne opposition as much as possible. The main attacks began 15 minutes after these preliminary attacks, and were primarily directed against the capital ships in Pearl Harbor. Damage inflicted upon smaller vessels was clearly the incidental consequence of the main operation. Very few planes dropped their bombs upon the city of Honolulu. Three planes did so in the late phases of the attack, but their last-minute changes of course indicated that this was done because those particular pilots did not care to encounter the severe anti-aircraft fire that was then bursting over their main target area.

In December, 1941, the capital ships of the Pacific Fleet numbered twelve: 9 Battleships; 3 Carriers. Of these, eight Battleships but none of the Carriers were present in Pearl Harbor at the time of the Japanese attack: the Battleship *Colorado* was in the Bremerton Navy Yard; the Carrier *Enterprise* was in a Task Force returning from Wake; the *Lexington* was in a Task Force ferrying planes to Midway; the *Saratoga* was on the West Coast, having just completed a Navy Yard overhaul.

The results of the Japanese air attacks upon the U.S. Pacific Fleet in Pearl Harbor on December 7, 1941, were as follows:

Battleships:

Arizona: total loss, as her forward magazines blew up;

Oklahoma: total loss, capsized and sank in harbor—later raised solely to clear harbor of the obstruction and resunk off Oahu;

California, West Virginia: sank in upright position at their berths with quarterdecks awash—much later raised, repaired, and returned to active war service;

Nevada: beached while standing out of the harbor, to prevent sinking in deep water after extensive bomb damage—repaired and returned to active war service;

Pennsylvania, Maryland, and Tennessee: all received damage but of a less severe character.

Smaller Ships:

Cruisers: *Helena, Honolulu,* and *Raleigh* were all damaged, but were repaired and returned to active war service;

Destroyers: Two damaged beyond repair; two others damaged but repaired and returned to active war service;

Auxiliary Vessels: 1 Seaplane Tender, 1 Repair Ship, both severely damaged but repaired and returned to active war service;

Target Ship: *Utah,* former battleship, sank at her berth.

The Japanese attacks upon the various Oahu airfields resulted in the following U.S. plane losses: Navy 80; Army 97.

U.S. military personnel casualties were: Navy, including Marine Corps, 3077 officers and enlisted men killed, 876 wounded; Army, including the Army Air Corps, 226 officers and enlisted men killed, 396 wounded. Total: 4575.

The Japanese losses were 48 planes shot down and three midget submarines destroyed. These vessels displaced 45 tons and were of little, if any, military value.

The Final Summation

Review of the American Moves
Which Led to the Japanese Attack

Our Main Deduction is that President Roosevelt forced Japan to war by unrelenting diplomatic-economic pressure, and enticed that country to initiate hostilities with a surprise attack by holding the Pacific Fleet in Hawaiian waters as an invitation to that attack.

The evidence shows how surely the President moved toward war after June, 1940. His conversation with Admiral Richardson in October, 1940, indicated his conviction that it would be impossible without a stunning incident to obtain a declaration of war from Congress.

Despite the conditions of undeclared war which existed in the Atlantic during the latter half of 1941, it had long been clear that Germany did not intend to contribute to the creation of a state of formal war between her and the United States. The Tripartite Treaty of September, 1940, however, supplied the President with the answer. Under that treaty, war with Japan meant war with Germany and Italy.

The highlights of the ever-increasing pressure upon Japan were:

1. the extension of financial and military aid to China in concert with Great Britain and the Netherlands, which began early in 1941;
2. the stoppage of Philippine exports to Japan by Executive Order on May 29, 1941;
3. the freezing of Japanese assets and the interdiction of all trade with Japan by the United States, Great Britain, and the Netherlands on July 25, 1941;
4. President Roosevelt's very frank statements of policy to Ambassador Nomura in their conference of August 17, 1941;
5. the termination of the Washington conference by the American note of November 26, 1941, which brought the war to the United States as the President so clearly intended it would.

That the Pearl Harbor attack was in accord with President Roosevelt's plans is attested by the following array of facts:

1. President Roosevelt and his military and naval advisers were well aware that Japan invariably started her wars with a surprise attack synchronized closely with her delivery of the Declaration of War;
2. In October, 1940, the President stated that, if war broke out in the Pacific, Japan would commit the overt act which would bring the United States into the war;
3. The Pacific Fleet, against contrary naval advice, was retained in Hawaii by order of the President for the alleged reason that the Fleet, so located, would exert a restrictive effect upon Japanese aggressions in the Far East;
4. The Fleet in Hawaii was neither powerful enough nor in the necessary strategic position to influence Japan's diplomatic decisions, which could only be accomplished by the stationing of an adequate naval force in Far Eastern waters;
5. Before that Fleet could operate at any distance from Pearl Harbor, its train (tankers, supply and repair vessels) would have had to be tremendously increased in strength—facts that would not escape the notice of the experienced Japanese spies in Hawaii;
6. President Roosevelt gave unmistakable evidence, in March, 1941, that he was not greatly concerned with the Pacific Fleet's effects upon Japanese diplomatic decisions, when he authorized the weakening of that Fleet, already inferior to that of Japan, by the detachment of 3 battleships, 1 aircraft carrier, 4 light cruisers, and 18 destroyers for duty in the Atlantic—a movement which would immediately be detected by Japanese espionage in Hawaii and Panama Canal Zone;

7. The successful crippling of the Pacific Fleet was the only surprise operation which promised the Japanese Navy sufficiently large results to justify the risk of heavy losses from land-based air attacks if the surprise failed;

8. Such an operation against the Fleet in Hawaii was attended with far greater chances of success, especially from the surprise standpoint, and far less risk of heavy losses than a similar attack against that Fleet based in U.S. West Coast ports;

9. The retention of the Fleet in Hawaii, especially after its reduction in strength in March, 1941, could serve only one possible purpose, an invitation to a surprise Japanese attack;

10. The denial to the Hawaiian Commanders of all knowledge of Magic was vital to the plan for enticing Japan to deliver a surprise attack upon the Fleet in Pearl Harbor, because, as late as Saturday, December 6, Admiral Kimmel could have caused that attack to be cancelled by taking his Fleet to sea and disappearing beyond land-based human ken.

Review of the Situation Known to Washington Before the Attack

From the beginning of the Washington conference in November, 1941, President Roosevelt and his advisers had repeated evidence that this was Japan's last and supreme effort to break the economic encirclement by peaceful means.

Throughout the negotiations, the Japanese secret dispatches stressed a "deadline date," after which "things were automatically going to happen."

Automatic events which were to follow the breakdown of such vital negotiations could only be acts of war, clear evidence that Japan intended to deliver a surprise attack to initiate the hostilities.

The fact that surprise was essential to the Japanese plans was repeatedly emphasized, on and after November 28, by the Tokyo dispatches and by telephone instructions to the two Ambassadors, cautioning them to keep alive the appearance of continuing negotiation.

Everyone familiar with Japanese military history knew that her first acts of war against China in 1894 and Russia in 1904 had been surprise attacks against the main fleets of those countries.

The only American Naval Force in the Pacific that was worth the risk of such an operation was the Fleet in Hawaiian waters.

The President and his military naval advisers well knew, on October 9, from the Tokyo dispatch to Honolulu of September 24, that Japan intended to plan a surprise air attack on the American Fleet in Pearl Harbor, and had daily evidence from the late decodes of certain Tokyo-Honolulu dispatches during the period, December 3–6 inclusive, that the planned attack was soon to occur.

On November 26, the recipients of Magic all had positive information from the Tokyo dispatch to Hong Kong of November 14 that Japan intended war with the United States and Great Britain if the Washington negotiations should fail.

The Tokyo dispatch to the Washington Embassy of November 28 definitely stated that the Japanese Government considered that the American note of the 26th had terminated all possibility of further negotiations.

The Tokyo-Berlin messages dated November 30 instructed the Japanese Ambassador to inform Hitler and von Ribbentrop that war between Japan and the Anglo-Saxon nations would come sooner than anyone expected.

The Japanese code-destruction messages of December 1 and 2 meant that war was extremely close at hand.

With the distribution of the Pilot Message at 3:00 P.M. on Saturday, December 6, the picture was complete for President Roosevelt and the other recipients of Magic, both in Washington and Manila. It said that the answer to the American note was about to arrive in the Embassy, that it was very lengthy, and that its delivery to the U.S. Government was to be especially timed. That timed delivery could only have meant that the answer was a Declaration of War, synchronized with a surprise attack. No other deduction was tenable.

The Saturday receipt of this definite information strongly supported the existing estimates in the War and Navy Departments, that the Japanese surprise attack would be delivered on a Sunday, and marked the morrow, Sunday, December 7, as the day. All this, beyond doubt, was known to President Roosevelt, General Marshall, and Admiral Stark at about 3:00 P.M. on that Saturday, Washington time, 21 hours before the next sunrise in Hawaii.

In obedience to the basic dictates of the Military Art, the information contained in the Pilot Message and the unmistakable implications thereof should have been transmitted to Admiral Kimmel and General Short at once. There was no military consideration that would warrant or tolerate an instant's delay in getting this word to those officers. There cannot be the slightest doubt that General Marshall and Admiral Stark would have had this done, if they had not been restrained from doing so by the orders of President Roosevelt. In the situation which then existed for them, no officer of even limited experience, if free to act, could possibly decide otherwise.

The fighting words in the selected passages of the 13-part message received on that same Saturday were merely additional evidence that this was a Declaration of War. The 14th part received early Sunday morning was further confirmation of that fact.

The 1:00 P.M. Washington delivery, ordered by the time-of-delivery dispatch, clearly indicated Pearl Harbor as the objective of the surprise attack, the final link in the long chain of evidence to that effect.

There Would Have Been No Pearl Harbor If Magic Had Not Been Denied to the Hawaiian Commanders

The recurrent fact of the true Pearl Harbor story has been the repeated withholding of information from Admiral Kimmel and General Short. If the War and Navy Departments had been free to follow the dictates of the Art of War, the following is the minimum of information and orders those officers would have received:

The Tokyo-Honolulu dispatches regarding the exact berthing of U.S. ships in Pearl Harbor and, in that connection, a reminder that Japan invariably started her wars with a surprise attack on the new enemy's Main Fleet; the dispatches concerning the Washington Conference and the deadline date after which things were automatically going to happen—evidence that this was Japan's last effort to solve U.S.-Japanese differences by peaceful means and the strong intimation of the surprise attack; the Tokyo-Hong Kong dispatch of November 14, which told of Japan's intentions to initiate war with the two Anglo-Saxon powers if the Washington negotiations failed; the Tokyo-Washington dispatch of November 28, which stated that the American note of November 26 had terminated those negotiations; the Pilot Message of December 6, which told that the Declaration of War was about to arrive in Washington, and that its delivery to the U.S. Government was to be especially timed, an essential feature for synchronizing the surprise attack with that delivery.

Not later than by November 28, the War and Navy Departments should have ordered the Hawaiian Commanders to place the Joint Army-Navy Coastal Frontier Defense Plans in effect, and to unify their Commands; the Navy Department should have ordered the mobilization of the Naval Establishment.

On November 28, the Chief of Naval Operations should have ordered Admiral Kimmel to recall the *Enterprise* from the Wake operation, and a few days later should have directed the cancellation of the contemplated sending of the *Lexington* to Midway.

... [N]ot one word of this information and none of the foregoing orders were sent to Hawaii.

General Marshall Looks Ahead, but Admiral Stark Lets the Cat Out of the Bag

Everything that happened in Washington on Saturday and Sunday, December 6 and 7, supports the belief that President Roosevelt had directed that no message be sent to the Hawaiian Commanders before noon on Sunday, Washington time.

General Marshall apparently appreciated that failure to act on the Declaration of War message and its timed delivery was going to be very difficult to explain on the witness stand when the future inevitable investigation into the incidents of those days took place. His avoidance of contact with the messages after the Pilot message until 11:25 on Sunday morning was unquestionably prompted by these thoughts. Otherwise, he would undoubtedly have been in his office by 8:00 A.M. on that fateful day.

Admiral Stark, on the other hand, did arrive in his office at 9:25 A.M. on Sunday, and at once accepted delivery of the full Declaration of War message. Against the advice of his assistants, he refused to inform Admiral Kimmel of its receipt. Forty minutes later, he knew that the 14-part message was to be delivered to the U.S. Government at 1:00 P.M., Washington time, which was 7:30 A.M., Hawaiian time, as was pointed out to him at once. Again, despite the urging of certain of his aides, he refused to send word to Admiral Kimmel.

Never before in recorded history had a field commander been denied information that his country would be at war in a matter of hours, and that everything pointed to a surprise attack upon his forces shortly after sunrise. No Naval Officer, on his own initiative, would ever make such a decision as Admiral Stark thus did.

That fact and Admiral Stark's decisions on that Sunday morning, even if they had not been supported by the wealth of earlier evidence, would reveal, beyond question, the basic truth of the Pearl Harbor story, namely that these Sunday messages and so many earlier ones, of vital import to Admiral Kimmel's exercise of his command, were not sent because Admiral Stark had orders from the President, which prohibited that action.

This deduction is fully supported by the Admiral's statement to the press in August, 1945, that all he did during the pre-Pearl Harbor days was done on order of higher authority, which can only mean President Roosevelt. The most arresting thing he did, during that time, was to withhold information from Admiral Kimmel.

President Roosevelt's Strategy Accomplishes Its Purpose

Thus, by holding a weak Pacific Fleet in Hawaii as an invitation to a surprise attack, and by denying the Commander of that Fleet the information which might cause him to render that attack impossible, President Roosevelt brought war to the United States on December 7, 1941. He took a fully aroused nation into the fight because none of its people suspected how the Japanese surprise attack fitted into their President's plans. Disastrous as it was from a naval standpoint, the Pearl Harbor attack proved to be the diplomatic prelude to the complete defeat of the Axis Powers.

As each reader will make up his own mind regarding the various questions raised by President Roosevelt's solution to his problem, nothing would be gained by an ethical analysis of that solution.

Notes

1. Admiral Kimmel had asked the author to act as his counsel before the Roberts Commission, but the Admiral was not allowed counsel. Nevertheless, although his status before the Commission was anomalous, the author did accompany the Admiral whenever the latter testified before that body, and late on the first day of that testimony was sworn as a witness. During the discussion connected with this swearing, the following exchange occurred:

    Justice Roberts: "So it is understood that you are not acting as counsel."
    Admiral Theobald: "No, sir."
    General McCoy: "The admiral is not on trial, of course."
    Justice Roberts: "No, this is not a trial of the admiral, in any sense."

    It has always been difficult to understand Justice Roberts' statement that Admiral Kimmel was not on trial. The Commission came into being to investigate the surprise attack upon the Fleet which he had commanded at the time, and it was generally recognized that the result of the inquiry would be the severe arraignments of Admiral Kimmel and General Short, which did constitute the principal findings of the Commission; findings which were given wide publicity at the earliest possible moment.

2. U.S.S. *Panay,* an American gunboat, sunk by Japanese bombing planes on the Yangtze River on December 12, 1937.

Surprise

If our intelligence system and all our other channels of information failed to produce an accurate image of Japanese intentions and capabilities, it was not for want of the relevant materials. Never before have we had so complete an intelligence picture of the enemy. And perhaps never again will we have such a magnificent collection of sources at our disposal.

Retrospect

To review these sources briefly, an American cryptanalyst, Col. William F. Friedman, had broken the top-priority Japanese diplomatic code, which enabled us to listen to a large proportion of the privileged communications between Tokyo and the major Japanese embassies throughout the world. Not only did we know in advance how the Japanese ambassadors in Washington were advised, and how much they were instructed to say, but we also were listening to top-secret messages on the Tokyo-Berlin and Tokyo-Rome circuits, which gave us information vital for conduct of the war in the Atlantic and Europe. In the Far East this source provided minute details on movements connected with the Japanese program of expansion into Southeast Asia.

Besides the strictly diplomatic codes, our cryptanalysts also had some success in reading codes used by Japanese agents in major American and foreign ports. Those who were on the distribution list for MAGIC had access to much of what these agents were reporting to Tokyo and what Tokyo was demanding of them in the Panama Canal Zone, in cities along the east and west coasts of the Americas from northern Canada as far south as Brazil, and in ports throughout the Far East, including the Philippines and the Hawaiian Islands. They could determine what installations, what troop and ship movements, and what alert and defense measures were of interest to Tokyo at these points on the globe, as well as approximately how much correct information her agents were sending her.

Our naval leaders also had at their disposal the results of radio traffic analysis. While before the war our naval radio experts could not read the content of any Japanese naval or military coded messages, they were able to deduce from a study of intercepted ship call signs the composition and location of the Japanese Fleet units. After a change in call signs, they might lose sight of some units, and units that went into port in home waters were also lost because the ships in port used frequencies that our radios were unable to intercept. Most of the time, however, our traffic analysts had the various Japanese Fleet units accurately pinpointed on our naval maps.

Extremely competent on-the-spot economic and political analysis was furnished by Ambassador Grew and his staff in Tokyo. Ambassador Grew was himself a most sensitive and accurate observer, as evidenced by his dispatches to the State Department. His observations were supported and supplemented with military detail by frequent reports from American naval attachés and observers in key Far Eastern ports. Navy Intelligence had men with radio equipment located along the coast of China, for example, who reported the convoy movements toward Indochina. There were also naval observers stationed in various high-tension areas in Thailand and Indochina who could fill in the local outlines of Japanese political intrigue and military planning. In Tokyo and other Japanese cities, it is true, Japanese censorship grew more and more rigid during 1941, until Ambassador Grew felt it necessary to disclaim any responsibility for noting or reporting overt military evidence of an imminent outbreak of war. This careful Japanese censorship naturally cut down visual confirmation of the decoded information but very probably never achieved the opaqueness of Russia's Iron Curtain.

During this period the data and interpretations of British intelligence were also available to American officers in Washington and the Far East, though the British and Americans tended to distrust each other's privileged information.

In addition to secret sources, there were some excellent public ones. Foreign correspondents for *The New York Times, The Herald Tribune,* and *The Washington Post* were stationed in Tokyo and Shanghai and in Canberra, Australia. Their reporting as well as their predictions on the Japanese political scene were on a very high level. Frequently their access to news was more rapid and their judgment of its significance as reliable as that of our Intelligence officers. This was certainly the case for 1940 and most of 1941. For the last few weeks before the Pearl Harbor strike, however, the public newspaper accounts were not very useful. It was necessary to have secret information in order to know what was happening. Both Tokyo and Washington exercised very tight control over leaks during this crucial period, and the newsmen accordingly had to limit their accounts to speculation and notices of diplomatic meetings with no exact indication of the content of the diplomatic exchanges.

The Japanese press was another important public source. During 1941 it proclaimed with increasing shrillness the Japanese government's determination to pursue its program of expansion into Southeast Asia and the desire of the military to clear the Far East of British and American colonial exploitation. This particular source was rife with explicit signals of aggressive intent.

Finally, an essential part of the intelligence picture for 1941 was both public and privileged information on American policy and activities in the Far East. During the year the pattern of action and interaction between the Japanese and American governments grew more and more complex. At the last, it became especially important for anyone charged with the responsibility of ordering an alert to know what moves the American government was going to make with respect to Japan, as well as to try to guess what Japan's next move would be, since Japan's next move would respond in part to ours. Unfortunately our military leaders, and especially our Intelligence officers, were sometimes as surprised as the Japanese at the moves of the White House and the State Department. They usually had more orderly anticipations about Japanese policy and conduct than they had about America's. On the other hand, it was also true that State Department and White House officials were handicapped in judging Japanese intentions and estimates of risk by an inadequate picture of our own military vulnerability.

All of the public and private sources of information mentioned were available to America's political and military leaders in 1941. It is only fair to remark, however, that no single person or agency ever had at any given moment all the signals existing in this vast information network. The signals lay scattered in a number of different agencies; some were decoded, some were not; some traveled through rapid channels of communication, some were blocked by technical or procedural delays; some never reached a center of decision. But it is legitimate to review again the general sort of picture that emerged during the first week of December from the signals readily at hand. Anyone close to President Roosevelt was likely to have before him the following significant fragments.

There was first of all a picture of gathering troop and ship movements down the China coast and into Indochina. The large dimensions of this movement to the south were established publicly and visually as well as by analysis of ship call signs. Two changes in Japanese naval call signs—one on November 1 and another on December 1—had also been evaluated by Naval Intelligence as extremely unusual and as signs of major preparations for some sort of Japanese offensive. The two changes had interfered with the speed of American radio traffic analysis. Thousands of interceptions after December 1 were necessary before the new call signs could be read. Partly for this reason American radio analysts disagreed about the locations of the Japanese carriers. One group held that all the carriers were near Japan because they had not been able to identify a carrier call sign since the middle of November. Another group believed that they had located one carrier division in the Marshalls. The probability seemed to be that the carriers, wherever they were, had gone into radio silence; and past experience led the analysts to believe that they were therefore in waters near the Japanese homeland, where they could communicate with each other on wavelengths that we could not intercept. However, our inability to locate the carriers exactly, combined with the two changes in call signs, was itself a danger signal.

Our best secret source, MAGIC, was confirming the aggressive intentions of the new military cabinet in Tokyo, which had replaced the last moderate cabinet on October 17. In particular, MAGIC provided details of some of the preparations for the move into Southeast Asia. Running counter to this were increased troop shipments to the Manchurian border in October. (The intelligence picture is never clear-cut.) But withdrawals had begun toward the end of that month. MAGIC also carried explicit instructions to the Japanese ambassadors in Washington to pursue diplomatic negotiations with the United States with increasing energy, but at the same time it announced a deadline for the favorable conclusion of the negotiations, first for November 25, later postponed until November 29. In case of diplomatic failure by that date, the Japanese ambassadors were told, Japanese patience would be exhausted, Japan was determined to pursue her Greater East Asia policy, and on November 29 "things" would automatically begin to happen.

On November 26 Secretary Hull rejected Japan's latest bid for American approval of her policies in China and Indochina. MAGIC had repeatedly characterized this Japanese overture as the "last," and it now revealed the ambassadors' reaction of consternation and despair over the American refusal and also their country's characterization of the American Ten Point Note as an "ultimatum."

On the basis of this collection of signals, Army and Navy Intelligence experts in Washington tentatively placed D-day *for the Japanese Southeastern campaign* during the week end of November 30, and when this failed to materialize, during the week end of December 7. They also compiled an accurate list of probable British and Dutch targets and included the Philippines and Guam as possible American targets.

Also available in this mass of information, but long forgotten, was a rumor reported by Ambassador Grew in January, 1941. It came from what was regarded as a not-very-reliable source, the Peruvian embassy, and stated that the Japanese were preparing a surprise air attack on Pearl Harbor. Curiously the date of the report is coincident roughly with what we now know to have been the date of inception of Yamamoto's plan; but the coincidence is fairly pure. The rumor was traced to a Japanese cook in the Embassy who had been reading a novel that began with an attack on Pearl Harbor. Consequently everyone concerned, including Ambassador Grew, labeled the rumor as quite fantastic and the plan as absurdly impossible. American judgment was consistent with Japanese judgment at this time, since Yamamoto's plan was in direct contradiction to Japanese naval tactical doctrine.

Perspective

On the basis of this rapid recapitulation of the highlights in the signal picture, it is apparent that our decisionmakers had at hand an impressive amount of information on the enemy. They did not have the complete list of targets, since none of the last-minute estimates included Pearl Harbor. They did not know the exact hour and date for opening the attack. They did not have an accurate knowledge of Japanese capabilities or of Japanese ability to accept very high risks. The crucial question then, we repeat, is, If we could enumerate accurately the British and Dutch targets and give credence to a Japanese attack against them either on November 30 or December 7, why were we not expecting a specific danger to *ourselves?* And by the word "expecting," we mean expecting in the sense of taking specific alert actions to meet the contingencies of attack by land, sea, or air.

There are several answers to this question.... First of all, it is much easier *after* the event to sort the relevant from the irrelevant signals. After the event, of course, a signal is always crystal clear; we can now see what disaster it was signaling, since the disaster has occurred. But before the event it is obscure and pregnant with conflicting meanings. It comes to the observer embedded in an atmosphere of "noise," i.e., in the company of all sorts of information that is useless and irrelevant for predicting the particular disaster. For example, in Washington, Pearl Harbor signals were competing with a vast number of signals from the European theater. These European signals announced danger more frequently and more specifically than any coming from the Far East. The Far Eastern signals were also arriving at a center of decision where they had to compete with the prevailing belief that an unprotected offensive force acts as a deterrent rather than a target. In Honolulu they were competing *not* with signals from the European theater, but rather with a large number of signals announcing Japanese intentions and preparations to attack Soviet Russia rather than to move southward; here they were also competing with expectations of local sabotage prepared by previous alert situations.

In short, we failed to anticipate Pearl Harbor not for want of the relevant materials, but because of a plethora of irrelevant ones. Much of the appearance of wanton neglect that emerged in various investigations of the disaster resulted from the unconscious suppression of vast congeries of signs pointing in every direction except Pearl Harbor. It was difficult later to recall these signs since they had led nowhere. Signals that are characterized today as absolutely unequivocal warnings of surprise air attack on Pearl Harbor become, on analysis in the context of December, 1941, not merely ambiguous but occasionally inconsistent with such an attack. To recall one of the most controversial and publicized examples, the winds code, both General Short and Admiral Kimmel testified that if they had had this information, they would have been prepared on the morning of December 7 for an air attack from without. The messages establishing the winds code are often described in the Pearl Harbor literature as Tokyo's declaration of war against America. If they indeed amounted to such a declaration, obviously the failure to inform Honolulu of this vital news would have been criminal negligence. On examination, however, the messages proved to be instructions for code communication after normal commercial channels had been cut. In one message the recipient was instructed on receipt of an execute to destroy all remaining codes in his possession. In another version the recipient was warned that the execute would be sent out "when relations are becoming dangerous" between Japan and three other countries. There was a different code term for each country: England, America, and the Soviet Union.

There is no evidence that an authentic execute of either message was ever intercepted by the United States before December 7. The message ordering code destruction was in any case superseded by a much more explicit code-destruction order from Tokyo that was intercepted on December 2 and translated on December 3. After December 2, the receipt of a winds-code execute for code destruction would therefore have added nothing new to our information, and code destruction in itself cannot be taken as an unambiguous substitute for a formal declaration of war. During the first week of December the United States ordered all American consulates in the Far East to destroy all American codes, yet no one has attempted to prove that this order was equivalent to an American declaration of war against Japan. As for the other winds-code message, provided an execute had been received warning that relations were dangerous between Japan and the United States, there would still have been no way on the basis of this signal alone to determine whether Tokyo was signaling Japanese intent to attack the United States or Japanese fear of an American surprise attack (in reprisal for Japanese aggressive moves against American allies in the Far East). It was only after the event that "dangerous relations" could be interpreted as "surprise air attack on Pearl Harbor."

There is a difference, then, between having a signal available somewhere in the heap of irrelevancies, and perceiving it as a warning; and there is also a difference between perceiving it as a warning, and acting or getting action on it. These distinctions, simple as they are, illuminate the obscurity shrouding this moment in history.

Many instances of these distinctions have been examined in the course of this study. We shall recall a few of the most dramatic now. To illustrate the difference between having and perceiving a signal, let us [look at] Colonel Fielder.... Though he was an untrained and inexperienced Intelligence officer, he headed Army Intelligence at Pearl Harbor at the time of the attack. He had been on the job for only four months, and he regarded as quite satisfactory his sources of information and his contacts with the Navy locally and with Army Intelligence in Washington. Evidently he was unaware that Army Intelligence in Washington was not allowed to send him any "action" or policy information, and he was therefore not especially concerned about trying to read beyond the obvious meaning of any given communication that came under his eyes. Colonel Bratton, head of Army Far Eastern Intelligence in Washington, however, had a somewhat more realistic view of the extent of Colonial Fielder's knowledge. At the end of November, Colonel Bratton had learned about the winds-code setup and was also apprised that the naval traffic analysis unit under Commander Rochefort in Honolulu was monitoring 24 hours a day for an execute. He was understandably worried about the lack of communication between this unit and Colonel Fielder's office, and by December 5 he finally felt that the matter was urgent enough to warrant sending a message directly to Colonel Fielder about the winds code. Now any information on the winds code, since it belonged to the highest classification of secret information, and since it was therefore automatically evaluated as "action" information, could not be sent through normal G-2 channels. Colonel Bratton had to figure out another way to get the information to Colonel Fielder. He sent this message: "Contact Commander Rochefort immediately thru Commandant Fourteenth Naval District regarding broadcasts from Tokyo reference weather." Signal Corps records establish that Colonel Fielder received this message. How did he react to it? He filed it. According to his testimony in 1945, it made no impression on him and he did not attempt to see Rochefort. He could not sense any urgency behind the lines because he was not expecting immediate trouble, and his expectations determined what he read. A warning signal was available to him, but he did not perceive it.

Colonel Fielder's lack of experience may make this example seem to be an exception. So let us recall the performance of Captain Wilkinson, the naval officer who headed the Office of Naval Intelligence in Washington in the fall of 1941 and who is unanimously acclaimed for a distinguished and brilliant career. His treatment of a now-famous Pearl Harbor signal does not sound much different in the telling. After the event, the signal in question was labeled "the bomb-plot message." It originated in Tokyo on September 24 and was sent to an agent in Honolulu. It requested the agent to divide Pearl Harbor into five areas and to make his future reports on ships in harbor with reference to those areas. Tokyo was especially interested in the locations of battleships, destroyers, and carriers, and also in any information on the mooring of more than one ship at a single dock.

This message was decoded and translated on October 9 and shortly thereafter distributed to Army, Navy, and State Department recipients of MAGIC. Commander Kramer, a naval expert on MAGIC, had marked the message with an asterisk, signifying that he thought it to be of particular interest. But what was its interest? Both he and Wilkinson agreed that it illustrated the "nicety" of Japanese intelligence, the incredible zeal and efficiency with which they collected detail. The division into areas was interpreted as a device for shortening the reports. Admiral Stark was similarly impressed with Japanese efficiency, and no one felt it necessary to forward the message to Admiral Kimmel. No one read into it a specific danger to ships anchored in Pearl Harbor. At the time, this was a reasonable estimate, since somewhat similar requests for information were going to Japanese agents in Panama, Vancouver, Portland, San Diego, San Francisco, and other places. It should be observed, however, that the estimate was reasonable only on the basis of a very rough check on the quantity of espionage messages passing between Tokyo and these American ports. No one in Far Eastern Intelligence had subjected the messages to any more refined analysis. An observer assigned to such a job would have been able to record an increase in the frequency and specificity of Tokyo's requests concerning Manila and Pearl Harbor in the last weeks before the outbreak of war, and he would have noted that Tokyo was not displaying the same interest in other American ports. These observations, while not significant in isolation, might have been useful in the general signal picture.

There is no need, however, to confine our examples to Intelligence personnel. Indeed, the crucial areas where the signals failed to communicate a warning were in the operational branches of the armed services. Let us take Admiral Kimmel and his reaction to the information that the Japanese were destroying most of their codes in major Far Eastern consulates and also in London and Washington. Since the Pearl Harbor attack, this information has frequently been characterized by military experts who were not stationed in Honolulu as an "unmistakable tip-off." As Admiral Ingersoll explained at the congressional hearings, with the lucidity characteristic of statements after the event:

> If you rupture diplomatic negotiations you do not necessarily have to burn your codes. The diplomats go home and they can pack up their codes with their dolls and take them home. Also, when you rupture diplomatic negotiations, you do not rupture consular relations. The consuls stay on.
>
>   Now, in this particular set of dispatches that did not mean a rupture of diplomatic negotiations, it meant war, and that information was sent out to the fleets as soon as we got it.... [1]

The phrase "it meant war" was, of course, pretty vague; war in Manila, Hong Kong, Singapore, and Batavia is not war 5000 miles away in Pearl Harbor. Before the event, for Admiral Kimmel, code burning in major Japanese consulates in the Far East may have "meant war," but it did not signal danger of an air attack on Pearl Harbor. In the first place, the information that he received was not the original MAGIC. He learned from Washington that Japanese consulates were burning "almost all" of their codes, not all of them, and Honolulu was not included on the list. He knew from a local source that the Japanese consulate in Honolulu was burning secret papers (not necessarily codes), and this back yard burning had happened three or four times during the year. In July, 1941, Kimmel had been informed that the Japanese consulates in lands neighboring Indochina had destroyed codes, and he interpreted the code burning in December as a similar attempt to protect codes in case the Americans or their British and Dutch allies tried to seize the consulates in reprisal for the southern advance. This also was a reasonable interpretation at the time, though not an especially keen one.

Indeed, at the time there was a good deal of evidence available to support all the wrong interpretations of last-minute signals, and the interpretations appeared wrong only *after* the event. There was, for example, a good deal of evidence to support the hypothesis that Japan would attack the Soviet Union from the east while the Russian Army was heavily engaged in the west. Admiral Turner, head of Navy War Plans in Washington, was an enthusiastic adherent of this view and argued the high probability of a Japanese attack on Russia up until the last week in November, when he had to concede that most of Japan's men and supplies were moving south. Richard Sorge, the expert Soviet spy who had direct access to the Japanese Cabinet, had correctly predicted the southern move as early as July, 1941, but even he was deeply alarmed during September and early October by the large number of troop movements to the Manchurian border. He feared that his July advice to the Soviet Union had been in error, and his alarm ultimately led to his capture on October 14. For at this time he increased his radio messages to Moscow to the point where it was possible for the Japanese police to pinpoint the source of the broadcasts.

It is important to emphasize here that most of the men that we have cited in our examples, such as Captain Wilkinson and Admirals Turner and Kimmel— these men and their colleagues who were involved in the Pearl Harbor disaster —were as efficient and loyal a group of men as one could find. Some of them were exceptionally able and dedicated. The fact of surprise at Pearl Harbor has never been persuasively explained by accusing the participants, individually or in groups, of conspiracy or negligence or stupidity. What these examples illustrate is rather the very human tendency to pay attention to the signals that support current expectations about enemy behavior. If no one is listening for signals of an attack against a highly improbable target, then it is very difficult for the signals to be heard.

For every signal that came into the information net in 1941 there were usually several plausible alternative explanations, and it is not surprising that our observers and analysts were inclined to select the explanations that fitted the popular hypotheses. They sometimes set down new contradictory evidence side by side with existing hypotheses, and they also sometimes held two contradictory beliefs at the same time. We have seen this happen in G-2 estimates for the fall of 1941. Apparently human beings have a stubborn attachment to old beliefs and an equally stubborn resistance to new material that will upset them.

Besides the tendency to select whatever was in accord with one's expectations, there were many other blocks to perception that prevented our analysts from making the correct interpretation. We have just mentioned the masses of conflicting evidence that supported alternative and equally reasonable hypotheses. This is the phenomenon of noise in which a signal is embedded. Even at its normal level, noise presents problems in distraction; but in addition to the natural clatter of useless information and competing signals, in 1941 a number of factors combined to raise the usual noise level. First of all, it had been raised, especially in Honolulu, by the background of previous alert situations and false alarms. Earlier alerts, as we have seen, had centered attention on local sabotage and on signals supporting the hypothesis of a probable Japanese attack on Russia. Second, in both Honolulu and Washington, individual reactions to danger had been numbed, or at least dulled, by the continuous international tension.

A third factor that served to increase the natural noise level was the positive effort made by the enemy to keep the relevant signals quiet. The Japanese security system was an important and successful block to perception. It was able to keep the strictest cloak of secrecy around the Pearl Harbor attack and to limit knowledge only to those closely associated with the details of military and naval planning. In the Japanese Cabinet only the Navy Minister and the Army Minister (who was also Prime Minister) knew of the plan before the task force left its final port of departure.

In addition to keeping certain signals quiet, the enemy tried to create noise, and sent false signals into our information system by carrying on elaborate "spoofs." False radio traffic made us believe that certain ships were maneuvering near the mainland of Japan. The Japanese also sent to individual commanders false war plans for Chinese targets, which were changed only at the last moment to bring them into line with the Southeastern movement.

A fifth barrier to accurate perception was the fact that the relevant signals were subject to change, often very sudden change. This was true even of the so-called static intelligence, which included data on capabilities and the composition of military forces. In the case of our 1941 estimates of the infeasibility of torpedo attacks in the shallow waters of Pearl Harbor, or the underestimation of the range and performance of the Japanese Zero, the changes happened too quickly to appear in an intelligence estimate.

Sixth, our own security system sometimes prevented the communication of signals. It confronted our officers with the problem of trying to keep information from the enemy without keeping it from each other, and, as in the case of MAGIC, they were not always successful. As we have seen, only a very few key individuals saw these secret messages, and they saw them only briefly. They had no opportunity or time to make a critical review of the material, and each one assumed that others who had seen it would arrive at identical interpretations. Exactly who those "others" were was not quite clear to any recipient. Admiral Stark, for example, thought Admiral Kimmel was reading all of MAGIC. Those who were not on the list of recipients, but who had learned somehow of the existence of the decodes, were sure that they contained military as well as diplomatic information and believed that the contents were much fuller and more precise than they actually were. The effect of carefully limiting the reading and discussion of MAGIC, which was certainly necessary to safeguard the secret of our knowledge of the code, was thus to reduce this group of signals to the point where they were scarcely heard.

To these barriers of noise and security we must add the fact that the necessarily precarious character of intelligence information and predictions was reflected in the wording of instructions to take action. The warning messages were somewhat vague and ambiguous. Enemy moves are often subject to reversal on short notice, and this was true for the Japanese. They had plans for canceling their attacks on American possessions in the Pacific up to 24 hours before the time set for attack. A full alert in the Hawaiian Islands, for example, was one condition that might have caused the Pearl Harbor task force to return to Japan on December 5 or 6. The fact that intelligence predictions must be based on moves that are almost always reversible makes understandable the reluctance of the intelligence analyst to make bold assertions. Even if he is willing to risk his reputation on a firm prediction of attack at a definite time and place, no commander will in turn lightly risk the penalties and costs of a full alert. In December, 1941, a full alert required shooting down any unidentified aircraft sighted over the Hawaiian Islands. Yet this might have been interpreted by Japan as the first overt act. At least that was one consideration that influenced General Short to order his lowest degree of alert. While the cautious phrasing in the messages to the theater is certainly understandable, it nevertheless constituted another block on the road to perception. The sentences in the final theater warnings—"A surprise aggressive move in any direction is a possibility" and "Japanese future action unpredictable but hostile action possible at any moment"—could scarcely have been expected to inform the theater commanders of any change in their strategic situation.

Last but not least we must also mention the blocks to perception and communication inherent in any large bureaucratic organization, and those that stemmed from intraservice and interservice rivalries. The most glaring example of rivalry in the Pearl Harbor case was that between Naval War Plans and Naval Intelligence. A general prejudice against intellectuals and specialists, not confined to the military but unfortunately widely held in America, also made it difficult for intelligence experts to be heard. McCollum, Bratton, Sadtler, and a few others who felt that the signal picture was ominous enough to warrant more urgent warnings had no power to influence decision. The Far Eastern code analysts, for example, were believed to be too immersed in the "Oriental point of view." Low budgets for American Intelligence departments reflected the low prestige of this activity, whereas in England, Germany, and Japan, 1941 budgets reached a height that was regarded by the American Congress as quite beyond reason.

◦◦◉◦◦

In view of all these limitations to perception and communication, is the fact of surprise at Pearl Harbor, then, really so surprising? Even with these limitations explicitly recognized, there remains the step between perception and action. Let us assume that the first hurdle has been crossed: An available signal has been perceived as an indication of imminent danger. Then how do we resolve the next questions: What specific danger is the signal trying to communicate, and what specific action or preparation should follow?

On November 27, General MacArthur had received a war warning very similar to the one received by General Short in Honolulu. MacArthur's response had been promptly translated into orders designed to protect his bombers from possible air attack from Formosan land bases. But the orders were carried out very slowly. By December 8, Philippine time, only half of the bombers ordered to the south had left the Manila area, and reconnaissance over Formosa had not been undertaken. There was no sense of urgency in preparing for a Japanese air attack, partly because our intelligence estimates had calculated that the Japanese aircraft did not have sufficient range to bomb Manila from Formosa.

The information that Pearl Harbor had been attacked arrived at Manila early in the morning of December 8, giving the Philippine forces some 9 or 10 hours to prepare for an attack. But did an air attack on Pearl Harbor necessarily mean that the Japanese would strike from the air at the Philippines? Did they have enough equipment to mount both air attacks successfully? Would they come from Formosa or from carriers? Intelligence had indicated that they would have to come from carriers, yet the carriers were evidently off Hawaii. MacArthur's headquarters also pointed out that there had been no formal declaration of war against Japan by the United States. Therefore approval could not be granted for a counterattack on Formosan bases. Furthermore there were technical disagreements among airmen as to whether a counterattack should be mounted without advance photographic reconnaissance. While Brereton was arranging permission to undertake photographic reconnaissance, there was further disagreement about what to do with the aircraft in the meantime. Should they be sent aloft or should they be dispersed to avoid destruction in case the Japanese reached the airfields? When the Japanese bombers arrived shortly after noon, they found all the American aircraft wingtip to wingtip on the ground. Even the signal of an actual attack on Pearl Harbor was not an unambiguous signal of an attack on the Philippines, and it did not make clear what response was best.

Note

1. *Hearings,* Part 9, p. 4226.

POSTSCRIPT

Was Information About the Attack on Pearl Harbor Deliberately Withheld From the American Commanders?

Theobald was an eyewitness to the Pearl Harbor attack. In his selection, he defends his former boss, Admiral Husband E. Kimmel of the U.S. Pacific Fleet, from responsibility for the fleet's lack of preparation prior to Japan's surprise attack. Theobald argues that President Roosevelt and his chief military aides deliberately withheld from Kimmel information that they had received from intelligence intercepts going to Japanese diplomats that the Japanese navy was going to attack Pearl Harbor on December 7. Why would Roosevelt do such a thing? Because, says Theobald, Roosevelt wanted to enter the war against Germany and Japan, but he could not mobilize a reluctant public for war unless the United States was attacked first. Disastrous as it was from a naval standpoint, says Theobald, "the Pearl Harbor attack proved to be the diplomatic prelude to the complete defeat of the Axis Powers."

Theobald wrote *The Final Secret of Pearl Harbor* in the 1950s at the height of the battle between the internationist historians, who defended Roosevelt's policies toward Germany and Japan, and the revisionists, who believed that Roosevelt unnecessarily and deliberately deceived the American public by enticing the Japanese to attack Pearl Harbor. Both groups held different assumptions about the nature of America's foreign policy before World War II. Internationalists believed that Germany and Japan constituted threats to world peace and the overall balance of power and that they had to be defeated with or without active U.S. participation in the war. Revisionist historians believed that Germany and Japan did not threaten America's security even if they controlled Europe and Asia. For the best defenses of President Roosevelt's foreign policies, see Robert Dallek, *Franklin Roosevelt and American Foreign Policy, 1932–1945* (Oxford University Press, 1979) and Waldo H. Heinrichs, *Threshold of War: Franklin D. Roosevelt and American Entry Into World War II* (Oxford University Press, 1988). Early revisionist studies of Roosevelt are summarized in Harry Elmer Barnes, ed., *Perpetual War for Perpetual Peace: A Critical Examination of the Foreign Policy of Franklin D. Roosevelt and Its Aftermath* (Caxton, 1953). Later criticisms include John T. Toland, *Infamy: Pearl Harbor and Its Aftermath* (Doubleday, 1982) and *Wind Over Sand: The Diplomacy of Franklin Roosevelt* (University of Georgia Press, 1988).

Theobald's account raises a number of questions. Did Roosevelt shift 3 battleships, 1 aircraft carrier, 4 light cruisers, and 18 destroyers for duty in the Atlantic in March 1941 to bolster lend-lease shipments to aid Great Britain in her struggle against Germany (a possibility that Theobald does not mention)?

Or was Roosevelt, who knew that their intelligence agents would be aware of the maneuvers, trying to entice the Japanese to attack Pearl Harbor? What about Theobald's charge that the commanders at Pearl Harbor were deliberately denied information about Japan's plans so that the Japanese Navy would be tempted to attack the fleet? If this is true, why wasn't Roosevelt tried as a war criminal (after his death)? Furthermore, if the president wanted to use the attack to get America into the war, why would he destroy most of his Pacific task force? Perhaps Gordon W. Prange is correct to reject revisionist historians in his massive, well-documented account *At Dawn We Slept: The Untold Story of Pearl Harbor* (McGraw-Hill, 1981). Prange faults the commanders at Pearl Harbor: Lieutenant General Walter C. Short, for example, was so obsessed with sabotage that ammunition was not available when the attack came. Short also failed to use radar and ignored Washington's orders to undertake reconnaissance.

Although most revisionists will disagree with her, Wohlstetter's analysis of the decision-making process provides an alternative to both the revisionist conspiratorial views of Roosevelt and his staunchest defenders. Wohlstetter makes several telling points. First, the intelligence community was organizationally divided between army and navy intelligence units in Washington, D.C., and Hawaii, so there was no systematic analysis of the decrypted diplomatic messages collectively known as MAGIC by the War Department's Signal Intelligence Service (SIS). Second, because of the abundance of information from public and private sources as well as from diplomatic intelligence intercepts, it was difficult to sort through the noise level and separate relevant materials from irrelevant materials. Third, the Japanese themselves provided misleading signals so that American observers would think the fleet was home—near the Marshall Islands. Fourth, even though President Roosevelt knew that war was coming with Japan, he thought the attack might be against Russia in Siberia, with its oil reserves, or in Southeast Asia against the British and Dutch possessions, especially Indonesia, with its important supply of rubber. Finally, Wohlstetter contends that even with an eight-hour warning, America's leaders in the Philippines were immobilized by bureaucratic indecisiveness and that Japanese planes destroyed most of the American aircraft at Clark Field because the planes were not moved to hidden areas.

The starting points for further study on Pearl Harbor are Hans Trefouse, *Pearl Harbor: The Continuing Controversy* (Krieger, 1982) and Akira Iriye, *Pearl Harbor and the Coming of the Pacific War: A Brief History With Documents and Essays* (St. Martin's Press, LLC, 1999). On Pearl Harbor itself see Gordon Prange, *Pearl Harbor: The Verdict of History* (McGraw-Hill, 1986). A trenchant analysis with a comprehensive bibliography of the whole period is Justus D. Doenecke and John E. Wiltz, *From Isolation to War: 1931–1941*, 2d ed. (Harlan Davidson, 1991). For a discussion of early interpretations, see Wayne S. Cole, "American Entry Into World War II: A Historiographical Appraisal," *Mississippi Valley Historical Review* (March 1957). For a more recent evaluation, see J. Gary Clifford, "Both Ends of the Telescope: New Perspectives on F.D.R. and American Entry Into World War II," *Diplomatic History* (Spring 1989).

On the Internet ...

Cold War Policies 1945–1991

This site presents U.S. government policies during the cold war, listed year by year from 1945 through 1991, as well as links to related sites.

http://ac.acusd.edu/history/20th/coldwar0.html

Cold War Hot Links

This page contains links to Web pages on the cold war that a variety of people have created. They run the entire spectrum of political thought and provide some interesting views on the cold war and the state of national security.

http://www.stmartin.edu/~dprice/cold.war.html

Great Warrior Leaders/Thinkers: Eisenhower, Dwight D.

Compiled by Janet L. Seymour, bibliographer at the Air University Library, Maxwell AFB, Alabama, this site lists Internet resources, books, documents, periodicals, and videos on Dwight D. Eisenhower.

http://www.au.af.mil/au/aul/bibs/great/eisen99.htm

American Immigration Resources on the Internet

This site contains many links to American immigration resources on the Internet. It includes a site on children's immigration issues, the Immigration and Naturalization Service home page, and a forum on immigration.

http://www.immigration-usa.com/resource.html

The New American Studies Web

The American Studies Web is one of the largest bibliographies of Web-based resources in the field of American studies. The editors have established a series of categories to help guide your search.

http://cfdev.georgetown.edu/cndls/asw/

PART 3

The Cold War and Beyond

*T*he postwar years were a period of both affluence and anxiety. By 1947 a cold war between the Western powers and the Russians was in full swing. By 1950 a hot war of "containment" was being fought in Korea.

From 1950 to 1974 most Americans were economically well-off. Presidents Harry S. Truman, Dwight D. Eisenhower, and John F. Kennedy managed an economy whose major problem was keeping inflation under control for a prosperous blue-collar labor force and an emerging baby boomer, white-collar class. In the 1960s and early 1970s, African Americans and women demanded that they be granted their civil, political, and economic rights as first-class citizens.

In the last quarter of the twentieth century, deindustrialization hurt blue-collar factory workers, but unprecedented prosperity bloomed for the managers of the high-tech economy. Controversy surrounds whether President Ronald Reagan's policies were responsible for the demise of the Soviet Union's empire. The reputations of Presidents Reagan and Bill Clinton are heavily dependent upon the future course of America's prosperity and power in the twenty-first century.

- Did Communism Threaten America's Internal Security After World War II?

- Should President Truman Have Fired General MacArthur?

- Was Dwight Eisenhower a Great President?

- Did President Kennedy Effectively Manage the Cuban Missile Crisis?

- Should America Remain a Nation of Immigrants?

- Did President Reagan Win the Cold War?

- Will History Consider William Jefferson Clinton a Reasonably Good Chief Executive?

- Is America Entering the Twenty-First Century in a Period of Decline?

ISSUE 10

Did Communism Threaten America's Internal Security After World War II?

YES: John Earl Haynes and Harvey Klehr, from *Venona: Decoding Soviet Espionage in America* (Yale University Press, 1999)

NO: Richard M. Fried, from *Nightmare in Red: The McCarthy Era in Perspective* (Oxford University Press, 1990)

ISSUE SUMMARY

YES: History professors John Earl Haynes and Harvey Klehr argue that army code-breakers during World War II's "Venona Project" uncovered a disturbing number of high-ranking U.S. government officials who seriously damaged American interests by passing sensitive information to the Soviet Union.

NO: Professor of history Richard M. Fried argues that the early 1950s were a "nightmare in red" during which American citizens had their First and Fifth Amendment rights suspended when a host of national and state investigating committees searched for Communists in government agencies, Hollywood, labor unions, foundations, universities, public schools, and even public libraries.

The 1917 triumph of the Bolshevik revolution in Russia and the ensuing spread of revolution to other parts of Eastern Europe and Germany led American radicals to believe that the revolution was near. It also led to a wave of anti-Bolshevik hysteria. In the fall of 1919 two groups of radicals—one native-born, the other foreign-born—formed the Communist and Communist Labor parties. Ultimately they would merge, yet between them they contained only 25,000 to 40,000 members.

The popular "front" policy, which lasted from 1935 to 1939, was the most successful venture undertaken by American Communists. The chief aim of the American Communists became not to increase party membership but to infiltrate progressive organizations. They achieved their greatest successes in the labor movement, which badly needed union organizers. As a consequence Communists controlled several major unions, such as the West Coast longshoremen and the electrical workers, and attained key offices in the powerful United

Autoworkers. Many American novelists, screenwriters, and actors also joined communist front organizations, such as the League of American Writers, and the Theatre Collective produced "proletarian" plays.

In the 1930s and 1940s the American Communist Party's primary success was its ability to establish a conspiratorial underground in Washington. The release of the Venona intercepts of American intelligence during World War II indicates that some 349 American citizens and residents had a covert relationship with Soviet intelligence agencies.

During the war the Federal Bureau of Investigation (FBI) and the Office of Strategic Services (OSS) conducted security clearances that permitted Communist supporters to work at high-level jobs if they met the qualifications. This changed in February 1947. In order to impress the Republicans that he wished to attack communism at home, President Harry S. Truman issued an executive order that inaugurated a comprehensive investigation of the loyalty of all government employees by the FBI and the Civil Service Commission.

Truman's loyalty program temporarily protected him from charges that he was "soft" on communism. His ability to ward off attacks against his soft containment policy against communism ran out in his second term. Alger Hiss, a high-level state department official, was convicted in 1949 of lying about his membership in the Ware Communist cell group. In September Truman announced to the American public that the Russians had successfully tested an atomic bomb. Shortly thereafter the Chinese Communists secured control over all of China when their nationalist opponents retreated to the island of Taiwan. Then on June 24, 1950, North Korea crossed the "containment" line at the 38th parallel and attacked South Korea.

The Republican response to these events was swift, critical, and partisan. Before his conviction, Hiss had been thoroughly investigated by the House Un-American Activities Committee. Had he led President Franklin D. Roosevelt and others to a sell-out of the Eastern European countries at the Yalta Conference in February 1945? Who lost China? Did liberal and leftist state department officials stationed in China give a pro-Communist slant to U.S. foreign policies in Asia?

Within this atmosphere Truman's attempt to forge a bipartisan policy to counter internal subversion of government agencies by Communists received a mortal blow when Senator Joseph A. McCarthy of Wisconsin publicly identified 205 cases of individuals who appeared to be either card-carrying members or loyal to the Communist Party.

How legitimate was the second great red scare? Did communism threaten America's internal security in the cold war era? In the following selections, John Earl Haynes and Harvey Klehr contend that a sizeable number of high-level U.S. government officials passed sensitive information to Russian intelligence, while Richard M. Fried argues that the 1950s became a "red nightmare" when state and national government agencies overreacted in their search for Communists, violating citizens' rights of free speech and a defense against self-incrimination under the First and Fifth Amendments.

Venona and the Cold War

The Venona Project began because Carter Clarke did not trust Joseph Stalin. Colonel Clarke was chief of the U.S. Army's Special Branch, part of the War Department's Military Intelligence Division, and in 1943 its officers heard vague rumors of secret German-Soviet peace negotiations. With the vivid example of the August 1939 Nazi-Soviet Pact in mind, Clarke feared that a separate peace between Moscow and Berlin would allow Nazi Germany to concentrate its formidable war machine against the United States and Great Britain. Clarke thought he had a way to find out whether such negotiations were under way.

Clarke's Special Branch supervised the Signal Intelligence Service, the Army's elite group of code-breakers and the predecessor of the National Security Agency. In February 1943 Clarke ordered the service to establish a small program to examine ciphered Soviet diplomatic cablegrams. Since the beginning of World War II in 1939, the federal government had collected copies of international cables leaving and entering the United States. If the cipher used in the Soviet cables could be broken, Clarke believed, the private exchanges between Soviet diplomats in the United States and their superiors in Moscow would show whether Stalin was seriously pursuing a separate peace.

The coded Soviet cables, however, proved to be far more difficult to read than Clarke had expected. American code-breakers discovered that the Soviet Union was using a complex two-part ciphering system involving a "one-time pad" code that in theory was unbreakable. The Venona code-breakers, however, combined acute intellectual analysis with painstaking examination of thousands of coded telegraphic cables to spot a Soviet procedural error that opened the cipher to attack. But by the time they had rendered the first messages into readable text in 1946, the war was over and Clarke's initial goal was moot. Nor did the messages show evidence of a Soviet quest for a separate peace. What they did demonstrate, however, stunned American officials. Messages thought to be between Soviet diplomats at the Soviet consulate in New York and the People's Commissariat of Foreign Affairs in Moscow turned out to be cables between professional intelligence field officers and Gen. Pavel Fitin, head of the foreign intelligence directorate of the KGB in Moscow. Espionage, not diplomacy, was the subject of these cables. One of the first cables rendered into coherent text was a 1944 message from KGB officers in New York showing that the Soviet Union had infiltrated America's most secret enterprise, the atomic bomb project.

By 1948 the accumulating evidence from other decoded Venona cables showed that the Soviets had recruited spies in virtually every major American government agency of military or diplomatic importance. American authorities learned that since 1942 the United States had been the target of a Soviet espionage onslaught involving dozens of professional Soviet intelligence officers and hundreds of Americans, many of whom were members of the American Communist party (CPUSA). The deciphered cables of the Venona Project identify 349 citizens, immigrants, and permanent residents of the United States who had had a covert relationship with Soviet intelligence agencies. Further, American cryptanalysts in the Venona Project deciphered only a fraction of the Soviet intelligence traffic, so it was only logical to conclude that many additional agents were discussed in the thousands of unread messages. Some were identified from other sources, such as defectors' testimony and the confessions of Soviet spies.

The deciphered Venona messages also showed that a disturbing number of high-ranking U.S. government officials consciously maintained a clandestine relationship with Soviet intelligence agencies and had passed extraordinarily sensitive information to the Soviet Union that had seriously damaged American interests. Harry White—the second most powerful official in the U.S. Treasury Department, one of the most influential officials in the government, and part of the American delegation at the founding of the United Nations—had advised the KGB about how American diplomatic strategy could be frustrated. A trusted personal assistant to President Franklin Roosevelt, Lauchlin Currie, warned the KGB that the FBI had started an investigation of one of the Soviets' key American agents, Gregory Silvermaster. This warning allowed Silvermaster, who headed a highly productive espionage ring, to escape detection and continue spying. Maurice Halperin, the head of a research section of the Office of Strategic Services (OSS), then America's chief intelligence arm, turned over hundreds of pages of secret American diplomatic cables to the KGB. William Perl, a brilliant young government aeronautical scientist, provided the Soviets with the results of the highly secret tests and design experiments for American jet engines and jet aircraft. His betrayal assisted the Soviet Union in quickly overcoming the American technological lead in the development of jets. In the Korean War, U.S. military leaders expected the Air Force to dominate the skies, on the assumption that the Soviet aircraft used by North Korea and Communist China would be no match for American aircraft. They were shocked when Soviet MiG-15 jet fighters not only flew rings around U.S. propeller-driven aircraft but were conspicuously superior to the first generation of American jets as well. Only the hurried deployment of America's newest jet fighter, the F-86 Saber, allowed the United States to match the technological capabilities of the MiG-15. The Air Force prevailed, owing more to the skill of American pilots than to the design of American aircraft.

And then there were the atomic spies. From within the Manhattan Project two physicists, Klaus Fuchs and Theodore Hall, and one technician, David

Greenglass, transmitted the complex formula for extracting bomb-grade uranium from ordinary uranium, the technical plans for production facilities, and the engineering principles for the "implosion" technique. The latter process made possible an atomic bomb using plutonium, a substance much easier to manufacture than bomb-grade uranium.

The betrayal of American atomic secrets to the Soviets allowed the Soviet Union to develop atomic weapons several years sooner and at a substantially lower cost than it otherwise would have. Joseph Stalin's knowledge that espionage assured the Soviet Union of quickly breaking the American atomic monopoly emboldened his diplomatic strategy in his early Cold War clashes with the United States. It is doubtful that Stalin, rarely a risk-taker, would have supplied the military wherewithal and authorized North Korea to invade South Korea in 1950 had the Soviet Union not exploded an atomic bomb in 1949. Otherwise Stalin might have feared that President Harry Truman would stanch any North Korean invasion by threatening to use atomic weapons. After all, as soon as the atomic bomb had been developed, Truman had not hesitated to use it twice to end the war with Japan. But in 1950, with Stalin in possession of the atomic bomb, Truman was deterred from using atomic weapons in Korea, even in the late summer when initially unprepared American forces were driven back into the tip of Korea and in danger of being pushed into the sea, and then again in the winter when Communist Chinese forces entered the war in massive numbers. The killing and maiming of hundreds of thousands of soldiers and civilians on both sides of the war in Korea might have been averted had the Soviets not been able to parry the American atomic threat.

Early Soviet possession of the atomic bomb had an important psychological consequence. When the Soviet Union exploded a nuclear device in 1949, ordinary Americans as well as the nation's leaders realized that a cruel despot, Joseph Stalin, had just gained the power to destroy cities at will. This perception colored the early Cold War with the hues of apocalypse. Though the Cold War never lost the potential of becoming a civilization-destroying conflict, Stalin's death in March 1953 noticeably relaxed Soviet-American tensions. With less successful espionage, the Soviet Union might not have developed the bomb until after Stalin's death, and the early Cold War might have proceeded on a far less frightening path.

Venona decryptions identified most of the Soviet spies uncovered by American counterintelligence between 1948 and the mid-1950s. The skill and perseverance of the Venona code-breakers led the U.S. Federal Bureau of Investigation (FBI) and British counterintelligence (MI5) to the atomic spy Klaus Fuchs. Venona documents unmistakably identified Julius Rosenberg as the head of a Soviet spy ring and David Greenglass, his brother-in-law, as a Soviet source at the secret atomic bomb facility at Los Alamos, New Mexico. Leads from decrypted telegrams exposed the senior British diplomat Donald Maclean as a major spy in the British embassy in Washington and precipitated his flight to the Soviet Union, along with his fellow diplomat and spy Guy Burgess. The arrest and prosecution of such spies as Judith Coplon, Robert Soblen, and Jack Soble was possible because American intelligence was able to read Soviet reports about their activities. The charges by the former Soviet spy Elizabeth Bentley that several dozen mid-level government officials, mostly secret Communists, had assisted Soviet intelligence were corroborated in Venona documents and assured American authorities of her veracity.

With the advent of the Cold War, however, the spies clearly identified in the Venona decryptions were the least of the problem. Coplon, Rosenberg, Greenglass, Fuchs, Soble, and Soblen were prosecuted, and the rest were eased out of the government or otherwise neutralized as threats to national security. But that still left a security nightmare. Of the 349 Americans the deciphered Venona cables revealed as having covert ties to Soviet intelligence agencies, less than half could be identified by their real names and nearly two hundred remained hidden behind cover names. American officials assumed that some of the latter surely were still working in sensitive positions. Had they been promoted and moved into policy-making jobs? Had Muse, the unidentified female agent in the OSS, succeeded in transferring to the State Department or the Central Intelligence Agency (CIA), the successor to the OSS? What of Source No. 19, who had been senior enough to meet privately with Churchill and Roosevelt at the Trident Conference? Was the unidentified KGB source Bibi working for one of America's foreign assistance agencies? Was Donald, the unidentified Navy captain who was a GRU (Soviet military intelligence) source, still in uniform, perhaps by this time holding the rank of admiral? And what of the two unidentified atomic spies Quantum and Pers? They had given Stalin the secrets of the uranium and plutonium bomb: were they now passing on the secrets of the even more destructive hydrogen bomb? And how about Dodger, Godmother, and Fakir? Deciphered Venona messages showed that all three had provided the KGB with information on American diplomats who specialized in Soviet matters. Fakir was himself being considered for an assignment representing the United States in Moscow. Which of the American foreign service officers who were also Soviet specialists were traitors? How could Americans successfully negotiate with the Soviet Union when the American negotiating team included someone working for the other side? Western Europe, clearly, would be the chief battleground of the Cold War. To lose there was to lose all: the task of rebuilding stable democracies in postwar Europe and forging the NATO military alliance was America's chief diplomatic challenge. Yet Venona showed that the KGB had Mole, the appropriate cover name of a Soviet source inside the Washington establishment who had passed on to Moscow high-level American diplomatic policy guidance on Europe. When American officials met to discuss sensitive matters dealing with France, Britain, Italy, or Germany, was Mole present and working to frustrate American goals? Stalin's espionage offensive had not only uncovered American secrets, it had also undermined the mutual trust that American officials had for each other.

The Truman administration had expected the end of World War II to allow the dismantling of the massive military machine created to defeat Nazi Germany and Imperial Japan. The government slashed military budgets, turned weapons factories over to civilian production, ended conscription, and returned millions of soldiers to civilian life. So, too, the wartime intelligence and security apparatus was demobilized. Anticipating only limited need for foreign intelligence and stating that he wanted no American Gestapo, President Truman abolished America's chief intelligence agency, the Office of Strategic Services. With the coming of peace, emergency wartime rules for security vetting of many government employees lapsed or were ignored.

In late 1945 and in 1946, the White House had reacted with a mixture of indifference and skepticism to FBI reports indicating significant Soviet espionage activity in the United States. Truman administration officials even whitewashed evidence pointing to the theft of American classified documents in the 1945 *Amerasia* case because they did not wish to put at risk the continuation of the wartime Soviet-American alliance and wanted to avoid the political embarrassment of a security scandal. By early 1947, however, this indifference ended. The accumulation of information from defectors such as Elizabeth Bentley and Igor Gouzenko, along with the Venona decryptions, made senior Truman administration officials realize that reports of Soviet spying constituted more than FBI paranoia. No government could operate successfully if it ignored the challenge to its integrity that Stalin's espionage offensive represented. In addition, the White House sensed that there was sufficient substance to the emerging picture of a massive Soviet espionage campaign, one assisted by American Communists, that the Truman administration was vulnerable to Republican charges of having ignored a serious threat to American security. President Truman reversed course and in March 1947 issued a sweeping executive order establishing a comprehensive security vetting program for U.S. government employees. He also created the Central Intelligence Agency, a stronger and larger version of the OSS, which he had abolished just two years earlier. In 1948 the Truman administration followed up these acts by indicting the leaders of the CPUSA under the sedition sections of the 1940 Smith Act. While the Venona Project and the decrypted messages themselves remained secret, the substance of the messages with the names of scores of Americans who had assisted Soviet espionage circulated among American military and civilian security officials. From the security officials the information went to senior executive-branch political appointees and members of Congress. They, in turn, passed it on to journalists and commentators, who conveyed the alarming news to the general public.

Americans' Understanding of Soviet and Communist Espionage

During the early Cold War, in the late 1940s and early 1950s, every few months newspaper headlines trumpeted the exposure of yet another network of Communists who had infiltrated an American laboratory, labor union, or government agency. Americans worried that a Communist fifth column, more loyal to the Soviet Union than to the United States, had moved into their institutions. By the mid-1950s, following the trials and convictions for espionage-related crimes of Alger Hiss, a senior diplomat, and Julius and Ethel Rosenberg for atomic spying, there was a widespread public consensus on three points: that Soviet espionage was serious, that American Communists assisted the Soviets, and that several senior government officials had betrayed the United States.

The deciphered Venona messages provide a solid factual basis for this consensus. But the government did not release the Venona decryptions to the public, and it successfully disguised the source of its information about Soviet espionage. This decision denied the public the incontestable evidence afforded by the messages of the Soviet Union's own spies. Since the information about Soviet espionage and American Communist participation derived largely from the testimony of defectors and a mass of circumstantial evidence, the public's belief in those reports rested on faith in the integrity of government security officials. These sources are inherently more ambiguous than the hard evidence of the Venona messages, and this ambiguity had unfortunate consequences for American politics and Americans' understanding of their own history.

The decision to keep Venona secret from the public, and to restrict knowledge of it even within the government, was made essentially by senior Army officers in consultation with the FBI and the CIA. Aside from the Venona code-breakers, only a limited number of military intelligence officers, FBI agents, and CIA officials knew of the project. The CIA in fact was not made an active partner in Venona until 1952 and did not receive copies of the deciphered messages until 1953. The evidence is not entirely clear, but it appears that Army Chief of Staff Omar Bradley, mindful of the White House's tendency to leak politically sensitive information, decided to deny President Truman direct knowledge of the Venona Project. The president was informed about the substance of the Venona messages as it came to him through FBI and Justice Department memorandums on espionage investigations and CIA reports on intelligence matters. He was not told that much of this information derived from reading Soviet cable traffic. This omission is important because Truman was mistrustful of J. Edgar Hoover, the head of the FBI, and suspected that the reports of Soviet espionage were exaggerated for political purposes. Had he been aware of Venona, and known that Soviet cables confirmed the testimony of Elizabeth Bentley and Whittaker Chambers, it is unlikely that his aides would have considered undertaking a campaign to discredit Bentley and indict Chambers for perjury, or would have allowed themselves to be taken in by the disinformation being spread by the American Communist party and Alger Hiss's partisans that Chambers had at one time been committed to an insane asylum.

There were sensible reasons... for the decision to keep Venona a highly compartmentalized secret within the government. In retrospect, however, the negative consequences of this policy are glaring. Had Venona been made public, it is unlikely there would have been a forty-year campaign to prove that the Rosenbergs were innocent. The Venona messages clearly display Julius Rosenberg's role as the leader of a productive ring of Soviet spies. Nor would there have been any basis for doubting his involvement in atomic espionage, because the deciphered messages document his recruitment of his brother-in-law, David Greenglass, as a spy. It is also unlikely, had the messages been made public or even circulated more widely within the government than they did, that Ethel Rosenberg would have been executed. The Venona messages do not throw her guilt in doubt; indeed, they confirm that she was a participant in her husband's espionage and in the recruitment of her brother for atomic espionage. But they suggest that she was essentially an accessory to her husband's activity, having knowledge of it and assisting him but not acting as a principal. Had they been introduced at the Rosenberg trial, the Venona messages would have confirmed Ethel's guilt but also reduced the importance of her role.

Further, the Venona messages, if made public, would have made Julius Rosenberg's execution less likely. When Julius Rosenberg faced trial, only two Soviet atomic spies were known: David Greenglass, whom Rosenberg had recruited and run as a source, and Klaus Fuchs. Fuchs, however, was in England, so Greenglass was the only Soviet atomic spy in the media spotlight in the United States. Greenglass's confession left Julius Rosenberg as the target of public outrage at atomic espionage. That prosecutors would ask for and get the death penalty under those circumstances is not surprising.

In addition to Fuchs and Greenglass, however, the Venona messages identify three other Soviet sources within the Manhattan Project. The messages show that Theodore Hall, a young physicist at Los Alamos, was a far more valuable source than Greenglass, a machinist. Hall withstood FBI interrogation, and the government had no direct evidence of his crimes except the Venona messages, which because of their secrecy could not be used in court; he therefore escaped prosecution. The real identities of the sources Fogel and Quantum are not known, but the information they turned over to the Soviets suggests that Quantum was a scientist of some standing and that Fogel was either a scientist or an engineer. Both were probably more valuable sources than David Greenglass. Had Venona been made public, Greenglass would have shared the stage with three other atomic spies and not just with Fuchs, and all three would have appeared to have done more damage to American security than he. With Greenglass's role diminished, that of his recruiter, Julius Rosenberg, would have been reduced as well. Rosenberg would assuredly have been convicted, but his penalty might well have been life in prison rather than execution.

There were broader consequences, as well, of the decision to keep Venona secret. The overlapping issues of Communists in government, Soviet espionage, and the loyalty of American Communists quickly became a partisan battleground. Led by Republican senator Joseph McCarthy of Wisconsin, some conservatives and partisan Republicans launched a comprehensive attack on the loyalties of the Roosevelt and Truman administrations. Some painted the entire New Deal as a disguised Communist plot and depicted Dean Acheson, Truman's secretary of state, and George C. Marshall, the Army chief of staff under Roosevelt and secretary of state and secretary of defense under Truman, as participants, in Senator McCarthy's words, in "a conspiracy on a scale so immense as to dwarf any previous such venture in the history of man. A conspiracy of infamy so black that, when it is finally exposed, its principals shall be forever deserving of the maledictions of all honest men." There is no basis in Venona for implicating Acheson or Marshall in a Communist conspiracy, but because the deciphered Venona messages were classified and unknown to the public, demagogues such as McCarthy had the opportunity to mix together accurate information about betrayal by men such as Harry White and Alger Hiss with falsehoods about Acheson and Marshall that served partisan political goals.

A number of liberals and radicals pointed to the excesses of McCarthy's charges as justification for rejecting the allegations altogether. Anticommunism further lost credibility in the late 1960s when critics of U.S. involvement in the Vietnam War blamed it for America's ill-fated participation. By the 1980s many commentators, and perhaps most academic historians, had concluded that Soviet espionage had been minor, that few American Communists had assisted the Soviets, and that no high officials had betrayed the United States. Many history texts depicted America in the late 1940s and 1950s as a "nightmare in red" during which Americans were "sweat-drenched in fear" of a figment of their own paranoid imaginations. As for American Communists, they were widely portrayed as having no connection with espionage. One influential book asserted emphatically, "There is no documentation in the public record of a direct connection between the American Communist Party and espionage during the entire postwar period."

Consequently, Communists were depicted as innocent victims of an irrational and oppressive American government. In this sinister but widely accepted portrait of America in the 1940s and 1950s, an idealistic New Dealer (Alger Hiss) was thrown into prison on the perjured testimony of a mentally sick anti-Communist fanatic (Whittaker Chambers), innocent progressives (the Rosenbergs) were sent to the electric chair on trumped-up charges of espionage laced with anti-Semitism, and dozens of blameless civil servants had their careers ruined by the smears of a professional anti-Communist (Elizabeth Bentley). According to this version of events, one government official (Harry White) was killed by a heart attack brought on by Bentley's lies, and another (Laurence Duggan, a senior diplomat) was driven to suicide by more of Chambers's malignant falsehoods. Similarly, in many textbooks President Truman's executive order denying government employment to those who posed security risks, and other laws aimed at espionage and Communist subversion, were and still are described not as having been motivated by a real concern for American security (since the existence of any serious espionage or subversion was denied) but instead as consciously antidemocratic attacks on basic freedoms. As one commentator wrote, "The statute books groaned under several seasons of legislation designed to outlaw dissent."

Despite its central role in the history of American counterintelligence, the Venona Project remained among the most tightly held government secrets. By the time the project shut down, it had decrypted nearly three thousand messages sent between the Soviet Union and its embassies and consulates around the world. Remarkably, although rumors and a few snippets of information about the project had become public in the 1980s, the actual texts and the enormous import of the messages remained secret until 1995. The U.S. government often has been successful in keeping secrets in the short term, but over a longer period secrets, particularly newsworthy ones, have proven to be very difficult for the government to keep. It is all the more amazing, then, how little got out about the Venona Project in the fifty-three years before it was made public.

Unfortunately, the success of government secrecy in this case has seriously distorted our understanding of post–World War II history. Hundreds of books and thousands of essays on McCarthyism, the federal loyalty security program, Soviet espionage, American communism, and the early Cold War have perpetuated many myths that have given Americans a warped view of the nation's history in the 1930s, 1940s, and 1950s. The information that these messages reveal substantially revises the basis for understanding the early history of the Cold War and of America's concern with Soviet espionage and Communist subversion.

In the late 1970s the FBI began releasing material from its hitherto secret files as a consequence of the passage of the Freedom of Information Act (FOIA). Although this act opened some files to public scrutiny, it has not as yet provided access to the full range of FBI investigative records. The enormous backlog of FOIA requests has led to lengthy delays in releasing documents; it is not uncommon to wait more than five years to receive material. Capricious and zealous enforcement of regulations exempting some material from release frequently has elicited useless documents consisting of occasional phrases interspersed with long sections of redacted (blacked-out) text. And, of course, even the unexpurgated FBI files show only what the FBI learned about Soviet espionage and are only part of the story. Even given these hindrances, however, each year more files are opened, and the growing body of FBI documentation has significantly enhanced the opportunity for a reconstruction of what actually happened.

The collapse of the Union of Soviet Socialist Republics in 1991 led to the opening of Soviet archives that had never been examined by independent scholars. The historically rich documentation first made available in Moscow's archives in 1992 has resulted in an outpouring of new historical writing, as these records allow a far more complete and accurate understanding of central events of the twentieth century. But many archives in Russia are open only in part, and some are still closed. In particular, the archives of the foreign intelligence operations of Soviet military intelligence and those of the foreign intelligence arm of the KGB are not open to researchers. Given the institutional continuity between the former Soviet intelligence agencies and their current Russian successors, the opening of these archives is not anticipated anytime soon. However, Soviet intelligence agencies had cooperated with other Soviet institutions, whose newly opened archives therefore hold some intelligence-related material and provide a back door into the still-closed intelligence archives.

But the most significant source of fresh insight into Soviet espionage in the United States comes from the decoded messages produced by the Venona Project. These documents, after all, constitute a portion of the materials that are still locked up in Russian intelligence archives. Not only do the Venona files supply information in their own right, but because of their inherent reliability they also provide a touchstone for judging the credibility of other sources, such as defectors' testimony and FBI investigative files.

Stalin's Espionage Assault on the United States

Through most of the twentieth century, governments of powerful nations have conducted intelligence operations of some sort during both peace and war. None, however, used espionage as an instrument of state policy as extensively as did the Soviet Union under Joseph Stalin. In the late 1920s and 1930s, Stalin directed most of the resources of Soviet intelligence at nearby targets in Europe and Asia. America was still distant from Stalin's immediate concerns, the threat to Soviet goals posed by Nazi Germany and Imperial Japan. This perception changed, however, after the United States entered the world war in December 1941. Stalin realized that once Germany and Japan were defeated, the world would be left with only three powers able to project their influence across the globe: the Soviet Union, Great Britain, and the United States. And of these, the strongest would be the United States. With that in mind, Stalin's intelligence agencies shifted their focus toward America.

The Soviet Union, Great Britain, and the United States formed a military alliance in early 1942 to defeat Nazi Germany and its allies. The Soviet Union quickly became a major recipient of American military (Lend-Lease) aid, second only to Great Britain; it eventually received more than nine billion dollars. As part of the aid arrangements, the United States invited the Soviets to greatly expand their diplomatic staffs and to establish special offices to facilitate aid arrangements. Thousands of Soviet military officers, engineers, and technicians entered the United States to review what aid was available and choose which machinery, weapons, vehicles (nearly 400,000 American trucks went to the Soviet Union), aircraft, and other matériel would most assist the Soviet war effort. Soviet personnel had to be trained to maintain the American equipment, manuals had to be translated into Russian, shipments to the Soviet Union had to be inspected to ensure that what was ordered had been delivered, properly loaded, and dispatched on the right ships. Entire Soviet naval crews arrived for training to take over American combat and cargo ships to be handed over to the Soviet Union.

Scores of Soviet intelligence officers of the KGB (the chief Soviet foreign intelligence and security agency), the GRU (the Soviet military intelligence agency), and the Naval GRU (the Soviet naval intelligence agency) were among the Soviet personnel arriving in America. These intelligence officers pursued two missions. One, security, was only indirectly connected with the United States. The internal security arm of the KGB employed several hundred thousand full-time personnel, assisted by several million part-time informants, to ensure the political loyalty of Soviet citizens. When the Soviets sent thousands of their citizens to the United States to assist with the Lend-Lease arrangement, they sent this internal security apparatus as well. A significant portion of the Venona messages deciphered by American code-breakers reported on this task. The messages show that every Soviet cargo ship that arrived at an American port to pick up Lend-Lease supplies had in its crew at least one, often two, and sometimes three informants who reported either to the KGB or to the Naval GRU. Their task was not to spy on Americans but to watch the Soviet merchant seamen for signs of political dissidence and potential defection. Some of the messages show Soviet security officers tracking down merchant seamen who had jumped ship, kidnapping them, and spiriting them back aboard Soviet ships in disregard of American law. Similarly, other messages discuss informants, recruited or planted by the KGB in every Soviet office in the United States, whose task was to report signs of ideological deviation or potential defection among Soviet personnel.

A second mission of these Soviet intelligence officers, however, was espionage against the United States.... The deciphered Venona cables do more than reveal the remarkable success that the Soviet Union had in recruiting spies and gaining access to many important U.S. government agencies and laboratories dealing with secret information. They expose beyond cavil the American Communist party as an auxiliary of the intelligence agencies of the Soviet Union. While not every Soviet spy was a Communist, most were. And while not every American Communist was a spy, hundreds were. The CPUSA itself worked closely with Soviet intelligence agencies to facilitate their espionage. Party leaders were not only aware of the liaison; they actively worked to assist the relationship.

Information from the Venona decryptions underlay the policies of U.S. government officials in their approach to the issue of domestic communism. The investigations and prosecutions of American Communists undertaken by the federal government in the late 1940s and early 1950s were premised on an assumption that the CPUSA had assisted Soviet espionage. This view contributed to the Truman administration's executive order in 1947, reinforced in the early 1950s under the Eisenhower administration, that U.S. government employees be subjected to loyalty and security investigations. The understanding also lay behind the 1948 decision by Truman's attorney general to prosecute the leaders of the CPUSA under the sedition sections of the Smith Act. It was an explicit assumption behind congressional investigations of domestic communism in the late 1940s and 1950s, and it permeated public attitudes toward domestic communism.

The Soviet Union's unrestrained espionage against the United States from 1942 to 1945 was of the type that a nation directs at an enemy state. By the late 1940s the evidence provided by Venona of the massive size and intense hostility of Soviet intelligence operations caused both American counterintelligence professionals and high-level policy-makers to conclude that Stalin had already launched a covert attack on the United States. In their minds, the Soviet espionage offensive indicated that the Cold War had begun not after World War II but many years earlier.

NO

Richard M. Fried

"Bitter Days": The Heyday of Anti-Communism

Even independent of [Joseph] McCarthy, the years 1950–1954 marked the climax of anti-communism in American life. The Korean stalemate generated both a bruising debate over containment and a sourness in national politics. Korea's sapping effect and a series of minor scandals heightened the Democratic Party's anemia. In addition, the 1950 congressional campaign, revealing McCarthyism's apparent sway over the voters and encouraging the GOP's right wing, signaled that anti-communism occupied the core of American political culture. "These," said liberal commentator Elmer Davis in January 1951, "are bitter days—full of envy, hatred, malice, and all uncharitableness."

Critics of these trends in American politics had scant power or spirit. Outside government, foes of anti-Communist excesses moved cautiously lest they be redbaited and rarely took effective countermeasures. Liberals seldom strayed from the safety of the anti-Communist consensus. Radicals met the hostility of the dominant political forces in Cold War America and fared poorly. In government, anti-communism ruled. Senate resistance to McCarthy was scattered and weak. In the House, HUAC [House Un-American Activities Committee] did much as it pleased. [President Harry S.] Truman upheld civil liberties with occasional eloquence, but he remained on the defensive, and his Justice Department often seemed locked in near-alliance with the Right in Congress. [Dwight D.] Eisenhower, when not appeasing the McCarthyites, appeared at times no more able to curb them than had Truman.

Even at his peak, McCarthy was not the sole anti-Communist paladin, though he cultivated that impression. As McCarthyism in its broader sense outlived the personal defeat of McCarthy himself, so, in its prime, it exceeded his reach. Its strength owed much to the wide acceptance, even by McCarthy's critics, of the era's anti-Communist premises. Along with McCarthy, they made the first half of the 1950s the acme of noisy anti-communism and of the ills to which it gave birth.

Soon after the 1950 campaign, skirmishing over the Communist issue renewed in earnest. In December Senator Pat McCarran joined the hunt for subversives by creating the Senate Internal Security Subcommittee (SISS). As chairman of that panel (and the parent Judiciary Committee), the crusty Nevada

Democrat packed it with such like-minded colleagues as Democrats James East-land and Willis Smith and Republicans Homer Ferguson and William Jenner. While McCarthy darted about unpredictably, McCarran moved glacially but steadily to his objective, crushing opposition.

McCarran's panel spotlighted themes that McCarthy had raised giving them a more sympathetic hearing than had the Tydings Committee. In Febru-ary 1951, federal agents swooped down on a barn in Lee, Massachusetts, seized the dead files of the Institute of Pacific Relations (IPR) and trucked them under guard to Washington. After sifting this haul, a SISS subcommittee opened an extended probe of the IPR, which led to a new inquest on "who lost China" and resulted in renewed loyalty and security proceedings, dismissals from the State Department and prosecution—all to McCarthy's greater, reflected glory.

The subcommittee acquired a reputation—more cultivated than deserved —for honoring due process. SISS was punctilious on some points: evidence was formally introduced (when an excerpt was read, the full text was put in the record); hearings were exhaustive (over 5,000 pages); witnesses were heard in executive session before they named names in public; their credentials and the relevance of their testimony were set forth; and some outward courtesies were extended.

The fairness was only skin-deep, however. Witnesses were badgered about obscure events from years back and about nuances of aging reports. Diplomat John Carter Vincent was even asked if he had plans to move to Sarasota, Florida. When he termed it a most "curious" question, counsel could only suggest that perhaps the Florida Chamber of Commerce had taken an interest. The sub-committee strove to ensnare witnesses in perjury. One China Hand called the sessions "generally Dostoyevskian attacks not only on a man's mind but also his memory." To have predicted Jiang's decline or Mao's rise was interpreted as both premeditating and helping to cause that outcome.

A product of the internationalist do-goodery of YMCA leaders in the 1920s, the IPR sought to promote peace and understanding in the Pacific. It had both national branches in countries interested in the Pacific and an international secretariat. Well funded by corporations and foundations in its palmier days, the IPR had more pedigree than power. McCarran's subcommittee insisted that IPR's publications pushed the Communist line on China. Louis Budenz testified that the Kremlin had assigned Owen Lattimore the job of giving the IPR journal, *Pacific Affairs*, a Party-line tilt. Budenz claimed that when he was in the Party, he received "official communications" describing Lattimore (and several China Hands) as Communists.

McCarran's panel spent a year grilling Lattimore, other IPR officials, and various China experts and diplomats as it tried to knit a fabric of conspiracy out of its evidence and presuppositions. McCarran claimed that, but for the machi-nations of the coterie that ran IPR, "China today would be free and a bulwark against the further advance of the Red hordes into the Far East." He charged that the IPR-USSR connection had led to infiltration of the government by persons aligned with the Soviets, of faculties by Red professors, and of textbooks by pro-Communist ideas. He called Lattimore "a conscious and articulate instrument of the Soviet conspiracy."

The hearings revealed naiveté about communism, showed that IPR principals had access to important officials during the war, and turned up levels of maneuvering that sullied IPR's reputation for scholarly detachment. Proven or accused Reds did associate with the IPR and may well have sought leverage through it. There were tendentious claims in IPR publications, as in one author's simplistic dichotomy of Mao's "democratic China" and Jiang's "feudal China." Lattimore was a more partisan editor of *Pacific Affairs* than he conceded. However, in political scientist Earl Latham's measured assessment, the hearings "show something less than subversive conspiracy in the making of foreign policy, and something more than quiet routine." Nor was it proven that IPR had much influence over policy. Perhaps the China Hands had been naive to think that a reoriented policy might prevent China's Communists from falling "by default" under Soviet control and thus might maintain American leverage. Yet those who argued that unblinking support of Jiang could have prevented China's "loss" were more naive still.

Unable to prove, in scholarly terms, its thesis of a successful pro-Communist conspiracy against China, SISS could still carry it politically. The loyalty-security program helped enforce it. New charges, however stale, motivated the State Department Loyalty-Security Board to reexamine old cases of suspected employees, even if they had been previously cleared. Moreover, nudged by the Right, Truman toughened the loyalty standard in April 1951, putting a heavier burden of proof on the accused. Thus under Hiram Bingham, a Republican conservative, the Loyalty Review Board ordered new inquiries in cases decided under the old standard....

The purge of the China Hands had long-term impact. American attitudes toward China remained frozen for two decades. Battered by McCarthyite attacks, the State Department's Far Eastern Division assumed a conservative bunkerlike mentality. Selected by President John F. Kennedy to shake the division up, Assistant Secretary of State Averell Harriman found it "a disaster area filled with human wreckage." Personnel who did not bear wounds from previous battles were chosen to handle Asian problems. Vincent's successor on the China desk was an impeccably conservative diplomat whose experience lay in Europe. JFK named an ambassador to South Vietnam whose prior work had been with NATO. In the 1950s, the field of Asian studies felt the blindfold of conformity as the momentum of U.S. foreign policy carried the country toward the vortex of Vietnam.

∞

The IPR Investigation was but one of many inquiries during the early 1950s that delved into Communist activities. The Eighty-first Congress spawned 24 probes of communism; the Eighty-second, 34; and the Eighty-third, 51. HUAC busily sought new triumphs. In 1953, 185 of the 221 Republican Congressmen asked to serve on it. But HUAC faced the problem all monopolies meet when competitors pour into the market. Besides McCarran and McCarthy, a Senate labor subcommittee probed Red influences in labor unions, two committees combed the U.N. Secretariat for Communists, and others dipped an oar in when the occasion arose.

In part HUAC met the competition with strenuous travel. Hearings often bore titles like "Communist Activities in the Chicago Area"—or Los Angeles, Detroit, or Hawaii. The Detroit hearings got a musician fired, a college student expelled, and UAW Local 600 taken over by the national union. In 1956 two Fisher Body employees were called before a HUAC hearing in St. Louis. When angry fellow workers chalked such slogans as "Russia has no Fifth amendment" on auto bodies and staged a work stoppage, the two men were suspended. The impact of junketing congressional probers was often felt in such local fallout rather than in federal punishments (though many witnesses were cited for contempt of Congress). That indeed was the point. A witness might use the Fifth Amendment to avoid perjury charges, but appearing before a committee of Congress left him open to local sanctions.

Lawmakers fretted over communism in the labor movement. The presence of left-wing unionists in a defense plant offered a frequent pretext for congressional excursions. HUAC addressed the issue often; McCarthy, occasionally; House and Senate labor subcommittees paid close heed. The liberal anti-Communist Hubert Humphrey held an inquiry designed both to meet the problem and to protect clean unions from scattershot redbaiting. Lest unions be handled too softly, in 1952 Pat McCarran, Herman Welker, and John Marshall Butler conceived the formidably labeled "Task Force Investigating Communist Domination of Certain Labor Organizations."

Attacks on radical union leadership from both within and without the labor movement proliferated in the early 1950s. During 1952 hearings in Chicago, HUAC jousted with negotiators for the Communist-led United Electrical Workers just as they mounted a strike against International Harvester. In 1953 McCarthy's subcommittee also bedeviled UE locals in New York and Massachusetts. Such hearings often led to firings and encouraged or counterpointed raids by rival unions. They hastened the decline of the left wing of the labor movement.

The UE was beset on all sides. When the anti-communist International United Electrical Workers Union (IUE), led by James Carey, was founded, Truman Administration officials intoned blessings. The Atomic Energy Commission pressured employers like General Electric to freeze out the UE; IUE literature warned that plants represented by the UE would lose defense contracts. The CIO lavishly funded Carey's war with the UE. Three days before a 1950 election to decide control of a Pittsburgh area local, the vocal anti-Communist Judge Michael Musmanno arrived at a plant gate to campaign for the IUE. Bedecked in naval uniform, he was convoyed by a detachment of National Guardsmen, bayonets fixed and flags unfurled. Many local Catholic clergy urged their flocks to vote for the IUE on the basis of anti-communism. Carey's union won a narrow victory.

These labor wars sometimes produced odd bedfellows. Carey criticized McCarthy, but the latter's 1953 Boston hearings helped the IUE keep control of key GE plants in the area. GE management declared before the hearings that it would fire workers who admitted they were Reds; it would suspend those who declined to testify and, if they did not subsequently answer the charges, would dismiss them. Thus besieged, the UE often settled labor disputes on a take-what-it-could basis.

Where left-wing unions maintained reputations for effective bargaining, anti-communism had limited effect. The UE's tactical surrender of its youthful militancy probably eroded its rank-and-file support more than did any redbaiting. Yet the Longshoremen's Union, despite Smith Act prosecutions against its leaders in Hawaii and the effort to deport Harry Bridges, kept control of West Coast docks. (Indeed, having come to tolerate Bridges by the 1950s, business leaders had lost enthusiasm for persecuting him.) Similarly, the Mine, Mill and Smelter Workers Union held onto some strongholds despite recurrent redbaiting. Weaker leftist unions like the United Public Workers or the Fur and Leather Workers succumbed to raiding and harassment.

In an era when mainline labor was cautious, organizing initiatives often did originate with more radical unions and so fell prey to anti-Communist attack. In 1953 a CIO retail workers' union, some of whose organizers were Communists, struck stores in Port Arthur, Texas. A commission of inquiry named by Governor Allen Shivers (then seeking reelection) found "clear and present danger" of Communist sway over Texas labor. Shivers claimed he had foiled a Communist-led union's "well-laid plans to spread its tentacles all along the Gulf Coast and eventually into *your* community." Other Southern organizing drives succumbed to redbaiting too.

By the 1950s, labor's assertiveness had waned; where it persisted, it met defeat; and new organizing drives were few. Internal dissent—indeed, debate —was virtually stilled. Its momentum sapped and its membership reduced by over a third, the CIO merged with the AFL in a 1955 "shotgun wedding." Having won a place within the American consensus, labor paid a dear price to keep it.

Conservatives feared Communist influence in the nation's schools as well as in its factories. The influence of the "Reducators" and of subversive ideas that ranged, in various investigators' minds, from outright communism to "progressive education" perennially intrigued legislators at the state and national levels.

The Communists' long-running control of the New York Teachers Union alarmed the Senate Internal Security Subcommittee. Previously, the 1940–41 Rapp-Coudert inquiry had led to the dismissal of a number of New York City teachers. In 1949 the Board of Education began a new purge. From 1950 to early 1953, twenty-four teachers were fired and thirty-four resigned under investigation. By one estimate, over three hundred New York City teachers lost their jobs in the 1950s. SISS thus served to reinforce local activities with its 1952–53 hearings in New York City. The refusal by Teachers Union leaders to testify about their affiliations established grounds for their dismissal under Section 903 of the city charter.

Ultimately, the probers failed in their aim to expose Marxist-Leninist propagandizing in Gotham's classrooms. Bella Dodd, a former Communist and Teachers Union leader, claimed that Communist teachers who knew Party dogma "cannot help but slant their teaching in that direction." A Queens College professor said he knew a score of students whom the Communists had "ruined" and turned into "misfits." Yet aside from a few parents' complaints and "one case where I think we could prove it," the city's school superintendent had no evidence of indoctrination. Though Communists had obviously acquired great leverage in the Teachers Union, SISS located its best case of university subversion in a book about *China*.

HUAC quizzed educators too, but its scrutiny of the movie industry earned higher returns when it resumed its inquiry into Hollywood in 1951. By then the Hollywood Ten* were in prison, the film industry's opposition to HUAC was shattered, and the blacklist was growing. Fear washed through the movie lots. The economic distress visited on Hollywood by the growth of television further frazzled nerves. Said one witness, the renewed assault was "like taking a pot shot at a wounded animal." When subpoenaed, actress Gale Sondergaard asked the Screen Actors Guild for help, its board rebuffed her, likening her criticism of HUAC to the Communist line. The Screen Directors Guild made its members take a loyalty oath.

Yet few secrets were left to ferret out: the identity of Hollywood's Communists had long ceased to be a mystery. Early in the 1951 hearings, Congressman Francis Walter even asked why it was "material . . . to have the names of people when we already know them?" For HUAC, getting new information had become secondary to conducting ceremonies of exposure and penitence. Would the witness "name names" or not?

Of 110 witnesses subpoenaed in 1951, 58 admitted having had Party involvements. Some cogently explained why they had since disowned communism. Budd Schulberg recalled that while he was writing *What Makes Sammy Run,* the Party told him to submit an outline, confer with its literary authorities, and heed its artistic canons. *The Daily Worker* received his book favorably, but after being updated on Party aesthetics, the reviewer wrote a second piece thrashing the novel. One screenwriter recalled how the Party line on a studio painters' strike shifted perplexingly in 1945: we "could walk through the picket lines in February, and not in June."

Witnesses seeking to steer between punishment and fingering co-workers faced tearing ethical choices. Naming known Reds or those previously named might stave off harm, but this ploy was tinged with moral bankruptcy. Some soured ex-Communists did resist giving names, not wanting, in actor Larry Parks's phrase, to "crawl through the mud to be an informer." Some named each other; some said little, ducking quickly behind the Fifth Amendment. Others told all. The 155 names that writer Martin Berkeley gave set a record. Others gabbed freely. Parrying with humor the oft-asked question—would he defend America against the Soviets?—actor Will Geer, already middle-aged, cheerfully agreed to fight in his way: growing vegetables and entertaining the wounded. The idea of people his vintage shouldering arms amused him; wars "would be negotiated immediately."

In this as in all inquiries, witnesses trod a path set with snares. The courts disallowed the Hollywood Ten's use of the First Amendment to avoid testifying,

---

* [The Hollywood Ten were members of the film industry who refused to testify before Congress in 1947 about communist infiltration of the industry.—Ed.]

so a witness's only protection was the Fifth Amendment guarantee against self-incrimination. Even this route crossed minefields. *Blau v. U.S.* (1950) ruled that one might plead the Fifth legitimately to the question of Party membership. However, the 1950 case of *Rogers v. U.S.* dictated caution: one had to invoke the Fifth at the outset, not in the middle, of a line of questions inching toward incrimination. Having testified that she herself held a Party office, the court ruled, Jane Rogers had waived her Fifth Amendment privilege and could not then refuse to testify about others.

HUAC tried to quick-march Fifth-takers into pitfalls. One gambit was a logical fork: if answering would incriminate him, a witness might use the Fifth; but if innocent, he could not honestly do so. Thus, the committee held, the witness was either guilty or lying—even though the courts did not accept this presumption of guilt. However, a new odious category, the "Fifth-Amendment Communist," was born. Such witnesses, whether teachers, actors, or others, rarely hung onto their jobs.

Legal precedent also demanded care in testifying about associations. One witness pled the Fifth in response to the question of whether he was a member of the American Automobile Association. HUAC members enjoyed asking if witnesses belonged to the Ku Klux Klan, hoping to nettle them into breaking a string of refusals to answer. On their part, witnesses devised novel defenses like the so-called "diminished Fifth." A witness resorting to the "slightly diminished Fifth" would deny present CP membership but refuse to open up his past or that of others; those using the "fully diminished Fifth," on the other hand, testified about their own pasts but no one else's. (The "augmented Fifth" was like the slightly diminished Fifth, but the witness also disclaimed any sympathy for communism.)

The question of whether to testify freely or take the Fifth convulsed the higher precincts of American arts and letters. Writer Lillian Hellman, subpoenaed in 1952, took the bold step of writing HUAC's chairman that she would take the Fifth only if asked to talk about others. She realized that by answering questions about herself, she waived her privilege and was subject to a contempt citation, but better that than to "bring bad trouble" to innocent people. She simply would not cut her conscience "to fit this year's fashions." When she testified, she did invoke the Fifth but scored a coup with her eloquent letter and managed to avoid a contempt citation. In 1956 the playwright Arthur Miller also refused to discuss other people but, unlike Hellman, did not take the Fifth. (His contempt citation was later overturned.)

Art came to mirror politics. Miller had previously written *The Crucible,* whose hero welcomed death rather than implicate others in the seventeenth-century Salem witch trials. Admirers stressed the play's relevance to modern witch-hunts. In contrast, Elia Kazan, who had named names, directed the smash movie *On the Waterfront,* whose hero (Marlon Brando), implored by a fighting priest (Karl Malden) to speak out, agreed to inform against criminals in a longshoremen's union. None of these works dealt with communism, but their pertinence to current political issues was not lost. Among the arbiters of American culture, these moral choices prompted heated debate, which still reverberated in the 1980s.

The issues were not only philosophical. The sanctions were real. Noncooperative witnesses were blacklisted, their careers in Hollywood shattered. Many drifted into other lines of work. Many became exiles, moving to Europe, Mexico, or New York. Some suffered writer's block. Some families endured steady FBI surveillance and such vexations as sharply increased life insurance premiums (for an assertedly dangerous occupation). Being blacklisted so dispirited several actors that their health was impaired, and premature death resulted. Comedian Philip Loeb, blacklisted and unemployable, his family destroyed, committed suicide in 1955.

Even though several hundred members of the entertainment industry forfeited their livelihoods after HUAC appearances, the studios, networks, producers, and the committee itself did not admit publicly that a blacklist existed. (Privately, some were candid. "Pal, you're dead," a soused producer told writer Millard Lampell. "They told me that I couldn't touch you with a barge pole.") In this shadow world, performers and writers wondered if their talents had indeed eroded. Had one's voice sharpened, one's humor dulled?

For blacklisting to work, HUAC's hammer needed an anvil. It was duly provided by other groups who willingly punished hostile or reluctant witnesses. American Legion publications spread the word about movies whose credits were fouled by subversion; Legionnaires (and other local true believers) could pressure theatre owners, if necessary, by trooping down to the Bijou to picket offending films. The mere threat of such forces soon choked off the supply of objectionable pictures at the source. Indeed, Hollywood, responding to broad hints from HUAC and to its own reading of the political climate, began making anti-Communist potboilers. These low-budget "B" pictures did poorly at the box office. They provided insurance, not profits.

Though entertainment industry moguls justified screening employees' politics by citing the threat from amateur censors, usually professional blacklisters made the system work. Blacklisting opened up business vistas on the Right. In 1950 American Business Consultants, founded by three ex-FBI agents, published *Red Channels,* a compendium listing 151 entertainers and their Communist-front links. *Counterattack,* an ABC publication started in 1947, periodically offered the same type of information. In 1953 an employee left ABC to establish Aware, Inc., which sold a similar service. Companies in show biz subscribed to these countersubversive finding aids and paid to have the names of those they might hire for a show or series checked against "the files." Aware charged five dollars to vet a name for the first time, two dollars for rechecks. It became habit for Hollywood, radio and TV networks, advertisers, and stage producers (though blacklisting had its weakest hold on Broadway) not to employ entertainers whose names cropped up in such files.

A few found ways to evade total proscription. Writers could sometimes submit work under pseudonyms. Studios asked some writers on the blacklist to doctor ailing scripts authored by others. The blacklisted writers received no screen credits and were paid a pittance, but at least they were working. Ostracized actors did not have this option. Said comedian Zero Mostel: "I am a man of a thousand faces, all of them blacklisted." A TV producer once called a talent agent to ask, "Who have you got like John Garfield?" He had Garfield himself, the agent exclaimed; but, of course, the blacklisted Garfield was taboo.

Unlike actors, blacklisted writers could also find work in television, which devoured new scripts ravenously. As in film, some used assumed names. Others worked through "fronts" (whence came the title of Woody Allen's 1976 movie). They wrote, but someone else put his name to the script (and might demand up to half of the income). Mistaken-identity plot twists worthy of a Restoration comedy resulted. One writer using a pseudonym wrote a script that he was asked, under a second pseudonym, to revise. Millard Lampell submitted a script under a phony name; the producers insisted that the script's writer appear for consultation; told that he was away and unavailable, they went for a quick fix: they asked Lampell to rewrite his own (unacknowledged) script.

The obverse of blacklisting was "clearance." Desperate actors or writers could seek absolution from a member of the anti-Communist industry. Often, not surprisingly, the person to see was one who had played a part in creating the blacklist. Roy Brewer, the chief of the International Alliance of Theatrical Stage Employees, had redbaited the leftist craft guilds, but helped rehabilitate blacklistees, as did several conservative newspaper columnists. The American Legion, which issued lists of Hollywood's undesirables, also certified innocence or repentance. A listee might get by with writing a letter to the Legion. Or he might be made to list suspect organizations he had joined and to tell why he joined, when he quit, who invited him in, and whom he had enticed. Thus the written route to clearance might also require naming names.

To regain grace, some sinners had to repent publicly, express robust patriotism in a speech or article, or confess to having been duped into supporting leftist causes. Typically, a blacklistee had to be willing to tell all to the FBI or to HUAC. Even liberal anti-Communists were "graylisted," and some had to write clearance letters. Humphrey Bogart had bought trouble by protesting the 1947 HUAC hearings against the Hollywood Ten. In his article, "I'm No Communist," he admitted he had been a "dope" in politics. Actor John Garfield, whose appearance before HUAC sent his career and life into a tailspin, was at the time of his death about to publish an article titled "I Was a Sucker for a Left Hook."

Like teachers and entertainers, charitable foundations also triggered the suspicion of congressional anti-Communists. These products of capitalism plowed back into society some of the vast wealth of their Robber Baron founders, but conservatives found their philanthropic tastes too radical. In 1952 a special House committee led by Georgia conservative Eugene Cox inquired into the policies of tax-exempt foundations. Did not "these creatures of the capitalist system," asked Cox, seek to "bring the system into disrepute" and to assume "a socialistic leaning"? . . .

⋅◈⋅

How deeply did anti-communism gouge the social and political terrain of the 1950s? With dissent defined as dangerous, the range of political debate obviously was crimped. The number of times that books were labeled dangerous, thoughts were scourged as harmful, and speakers and performers were rejected as outside the pale multiplied. Anti-Communist extremism and accompanying pressures toward conformity had impact in such areas as artistic expression, the labor movement, the cause of civil rights, and the status of minorities in American life.

For some denizens of the Right, threats of Communist influence materialized almost anywhere. For instance, Illinois American Legionnaires warned that the Girl Scouts were being spoonfed subversive doctrines. Jack Lait and Lee Mortimer's yellow-journalistic *U.S.A. Confidential* warned parents against the emerging threat of rock and roll. It bred dope use, interracialism, and sex orgies. "We know that many platter-spinners are hopheads. Many others are Reds, left-wingers, or hecklers of social convention." Not every absurdity owed life to the vigilantes, however. A jittery Hollywood studio cancelled a movie based on Longfellow's "Hiawatha" for fear it would be viewed as "Communist peace propaganda."

Books and ideas remained vulnerable. It is true that the militant Indiana woman who abhorred *Robin Hood*'s subversive rob-from-the-rich-and-give-to-the-poor message failed to get it banned from school libraries. Other locales were less lucky. A committee of women appointed by the school board of Sapulpa, Oklahoma, had more success. The board burned those books that it classified as dealing improperly with socialism or sex. A spokesman claimed that only five or six "volumes of no consequence" were destroyed. A librarian in Bartlesville, Oklahoma, was fired for subscribing to the *New Republic, Nation,* and *Negro Digest.* The use of UNESCO [United Nations Educational, Scientific, and Cultural Organization] materials in the Los Angeles schools became a hot issue in 1952. A new school board and superintendent were elected with a mandate to remove such books from school libraries.

Local sanctions against unpopular artists and speakers often were effective. In August 1950, a New Hampshire resort hotel banned a talk by Owen Lattimore after guests, apparently riled by protests of the Daughters of the American Revolution and others, remonstrated. Often local veterans—the American Legion and Catholic War Veterans—initiated pressures. The commander of an American Legion Post in Omaha protested a local production of a play whose author, Garson Kanin, was listed in *Red Channels.* A founder of *Red Channels* warned an American Legion anti-subversive seminar in Peoria, Illinois, that Arthur Miller's *Death of a Salesman,* soon to appear locally, was "a Communist-dominated play." Jaycees and Legionnaires failed to get the theatre to cancel the play, but the boycott they mounted sharply curbed the size of the audience.

Libraries often became focal points of cultural anxieties. Not every confrontation ended like those in Los Angeles or Sapulpa, but librarians felt they were under the gun. "I just put a book that is complained about away for a while," said one public librarian. Occasionally, books were burned. "Did you ever try to burn a book?" asked another librarian. "It's *very* difficult." One-third of a group of librarians sampled in the late 1950s reported having removed "controversial" items from their shelves. One-fifth said they habitually avoided buying such books.

Academics, too, were scared. Many college and university social scientists polled in 1955 confessed to reining in their political views and activities.

Twenty-seven percent had "wondered" whether a political opinion they had expressed might affect their job security or promotion; 40 percent had worried that a student might pass on "a warped version of what you have said and lead to false ideas about your political views." Twenty-two percent had at times "refrained from expressing an opinion or participating in some activity in order not to embarrass" their institution. Nine percent had "toned down" recent writing to avoid controversy. One teacher said he never expressed his own opinion in class. "I express the recognized and acknowledged point of view." Some instructors no longer assigned *The Communist Manifesto.*

About a hundred professors actually lost jobs, but an even greater number of frightened faculty trimmed their sails against the storm. Episodes far short of dismissal could also have a chilling effect. An economist at a Southern school addressed a business group, his talk, titled "Know Your Enemy," assessed Soviet resources and strengths. He was denounced to his president as a Communist. Another professor was assailed for advocating a lower tariff on oranges. "If I'd said potatoes, I wouldn't have been accused unless I had said it in Idaho." Some teachers got in mild trouble for such acts as assigning Robert and Helen Lynds' classic sociological study, *Middletown,* in class or listing the Kinsey reports on human sexuality as recommended reading. A professor once sent students to a public library to read works by Marx because his college's library had too few copies. Librarians logged the students' names.

The precise effect of all this professed anxiety was fuzzy. Many liberals claimed that Americans had been cowed into silence, that even honest anti-Communist dissent had been stilled, and that basic freedoms of thought, expression, and association had languished. The worriers trotted out appropriate comparisons: the witch trials in Salem, the Reign of Terror in France, the Alien and Sedition Acts, Know-Nothingism, and the Palmer raids. Justice William O. Douglas warned of "The Black Silence of Fear." Prominent foreigners like Bertrand Russell and Graham Greene decried the pall of fear they observed in America. On July 4, 1951, a *Madison Capital-Times* reporter asked passersby to sign a paper containing the Bill of Rights and parts of the Declaration of Independence. Out of 112, only one would do so. President Truman cited the episode to show McCarthyism's dire effects. McCarthy retorted that Truman owed an apology to the people of Wisconsin in view of that paper's Communist-line policies. Some McCarthy allies upheld the wisdom of refusing to sign any statement promiscuously offered.

McCarthy's defenders ridiculed the more outlandish laments for vanished liberties. A New York rabbi who blamed "McCarthyism" for the current spree of college "panty raids" offered a case in point. Conservative journalist Eugene Lyons was amused by an ACLU spokesman, his tonsils flaring in close-up on television, arguing "that in America no one any longer dares open his mouth." Such talk, said Lyons, led to "hysteria over hysteria." In their apologia for McCarthy, William F. Buckley and L. Brent Bozell snickered at such silliness. They found it odd that, in a time when left-of-center ideas were supposedly being crushed, liberals seemed to monopolize symposia sponsored by the major universities, even in McCarthy's home state, and that Archibald MacLeish and Bernard De Voto, two of those who condemned the enervating climate of fear, had still managed to garner two National Book Awards and a Pulitzer Prize. To Buckley and Bozell, the only conformity present was a proper one—a consensus that communism was evil and must be fought wholeheartedly.

But did such an argument miss the point? The successes enjoyed by prominent, secure liberals were one thing; far more numerous were the cases of those less visible and secure who lost entertainment and lecture bookings, chances to review books, teaching posts, even assembly-line jobs. The fight over the Communist menace had gone far beyond roistering debate or asserting the right of those who disagree with a set of views not to patronize them. People, a great number of whom had committed no crime, were made to suffer.

POSTSCRIPT

Did Communism Threaten America's Internal Security After World War II?

The "Venona Transcripts" represent only one set of sources depicting the Soviet spy apparatus in the United States. The Venona papers were not released to the public until 1995. Haynes and Klehr have also collaborated on two recent documentary collections based on the archives of the American Communist Party, which had been stored for decades in Moscow and were opened to foreign researchers in 1992. See *The Secret World of American Communism* (Yale University Press, 1995) and *The Soviet World of American Communism* (Yale University Press, 1998), both of which contain useful collections of translated Russian documents, which are virtually impossible to access. Haynes and Klehr's work also substantiates charges made by Allen Weinstein and his translator, former KGB agent Aleksandr Vassilieo, in *The Haunted Wood: Soviet Espionage in America* (Random House, 1999).

According to Fried, 24 teachers from New York City were fired and 34 resigned while under investigation between 1950 and early 1953. According to one estimate, over 300 teachers in the city lost their jobs because of their political beliefs. Similar dismissals took place in public universities and colleges across the country. Book burnings were rare, but many public libraries discarded pro-Communist books or put them in storage. In Bartlesville, Oklahoma, in 1950, librarian Ruth Brown was fired from her job after 30 years, ostensibly for circulating magazines like *The New Republic* and *The Nation,* which were deemed subversive. Actually, many agree that she was fired for supporting civil rights activism, a fact that the American Library Association left out when defending her. See Louise S. Robinson, *The Dismissal of Miss Ruth Brown: Civil Rights, Censorship, and the American Library* (University of Oklahoma Press, 2000).

Four books represent a good starting point for students: M. J. Heale, *American Anticommunism: Combating the Enemy Within, 1830–1970* (Johns Hopkins University Press, 1990) extends Americans' fears of subversion back to the Andrew Jackson years; Ellen Schrecker, *The Age of McCarthyism: A Brief History With Documents* (Bedford Books, 1994) blames both political parties for the excesses of the anti-Communist assault against radicals who were fighting against status quo race relations in the 1930s and 1940s; John Earl Haynes, *Red Scare or Red Menace? American Communism and Anticommunism in the Cold War Era* (Ivan R. Dee, 1996), which argues that anticommunism was a reasonable response to a real threat; and Richard Gid Powers, *Not Without Honor: The History of American Anticommunism* (Free Press, 1995), which portrays anticommunism as a mainstream political movement with many variations.

ISSUE 11

Should President Truman Have Fired General MacArthur?

YES: John S. Spanier, from "The Politics of the Korean War," in Phil Williams, Donald M. Goldstein, and Henry L. Andrews, Jr., eds., *Security in Korea: War, Stalemate, and Negotiation* (Westview Press, 1994)

NO: D. Clayton James with Anne Sharp Wells, from *Refighting the Last War: Command and Crisis in Korea, 1950–1953* (Free Press, 1993)

ISSUE SUMMARY

YES: Professor of political science John S. Spanier argues that General Douglas MacArthur was fired because he publicly disagreed with the Truman administration's "Europe first" policy and its limited war strategy of containing communism in Korea.

NO: Biographer D. Clayton James and assistant editor Anne Sharp Wells argue that General MacArthur was relieved of duty because there was a lack of communication between the Joint Chiefs of Staff and the headstrong general, which led to a misperception over the appropriate strategy in fighting the Korean War.

O n June 25, 1950, North Korea launched a full-scale attack against South Korea. President Harry S. Truman assumed that the Russians were behind the attack and that they wanted to extend communism into other parts of Asia. The United Nations Security Council unanimously passed a resolution condemning North Korea's well-planned, concerted, and full-scale invasion of South Korea and asked for a halt to the invasion and a withdrawal back to the 38th parallel.

The South Koreans, meanwhile, sent Truman a desperate appeal for help, and the president responded quickly. He bypassed Congress and did not ask for an official declaration of war. Instead he responded to the UN resolutions and ordered General Douglas MacArthur to use American naval and air forces to attack North Korean military targets south of the 38th parallel.

It soon became clear that South Korean ground troops could not withstand North Korea's well-coordinated attack. In response, Truman increased

America's military presence by ordering a naval blockade of North Korea and air attacks north of the 38th parallel. Sixteen nations sent troops, but South Korea and the United States contributed 90 percent of the ground troops, and the United States alone supplied 93 percent of the air forces and 85 percent of the naval forces. By September there were 210,000 American ground forces, and MacArthur was the UN commander.

At first the war went badly for the UN forces. The inexperienced South Korean and American troops were nearly pushed off the peninsula until they established a strong defensive perimeter near the southeastern tip of Korea. Then MacArthur launched an amphibious attack on Inchon, near the western end of the 38th parallel, which caught the North Koreans by surprise. Thousands surrendered and others fled across the 38th parallel chased by UN troops.

The attempt to unify the Korean peninsula under a pro-Western, anticommunist government was short-lived. MacArthur had assured Truman at their only face-to-face meeting in mid-October that the Chinese Communists would not enter the war. The general was mistaken. In late November contingents of "Chinese volunteers" entered North Korea and attacked the overextended UN forces. Instead of going home for Christmas as MacArthur had predicted, UN troops were soon pushed back into South Korea. Seoul, the capital of South Korea, was again captured by the Communists in January 1951. By the spring of 1951, however, UN troops had successfully pushed the Chinese Communists back across the 38th parallel.

As early as December 1950, the Truman administration had decided to shift its policy in Korea back to its original goal: contain communist expansion in Korea and restore the status quo prior to the North Korean attack of June 25. Since UN troops were in control of South Korea by the spring of 1951, Truman decided that the United Nations command would issue a statement that it was ready to arrange a cease-fire. No concessions were made to the Chinese, but it held out the possibility of negotiating broader issues in Asia.

The announcement proposing a truce was never made. When the Joint Chiefs of Staff informed MacArthur of the State Department's proposal, he undercut Truman by issuing his own directive to the Chinese, threatening to expand the war to the "coastal areas and intern bases" of China unless the enemy's commander-in-chief met with MacArthur to end the war and fulfill "the political objectives" of the UN forces in Korea.

Truman boiled over. He relieved MacArthur of all his duties in the Far East. Another two years and three months passed before the new president, Dwight D. Eisenhower, signed the truce accords ending the Korean War.

Should President Truman have fired General MacArthur? In the following selections, John S. Spanier provides a strong defense of Truman's limited war policy. He maintains that MacArthur was justifiably fired for his public disagreement with the Truman administration's policy of containing communism in Korea. D. Clayton James and Anne Sharp Wells argue that MacArthur was relieved because there was a lack of communication between the Joint Chiefs of Staff and the headstrong general and a misperception over the appropriate strategy for fighting the Korean War.

John S. Spanier  **YES**

The Politics of the Korean War

Introduction

Prior to June 25, 1950, Korea was outside the U.S. defense perimeter. On June 25, however, the defense of South Korea rose from low to highest priority as U.S. policy-makers considered the consequences of North Korea's aggression, aggression that they believed could not have occurred without Soviet instigation or support.

There were several reasons for this. First, South Korea, while not a U.S. ally, was an American protégé; Washington had helped the South Korean government with economic and military aid and had a responsibility toward the regime it had created.

Second, had the North Koreans gained control over the entire peninsula, they would, in the metaphor used by the Japanese, have "pointed the Korean dagger straight at Japan's heart." After Nationalist China's collapse in 1949, the United States needed Japan as an ally. It thus had to defend South Korea; otherwise, Japan might have chosen a neutral stance in the Cold War, which, with the attack on South Korea, had spread from Europe to Asia.

A third reason for the U.S. intervention was to preserve the recently established North Atlantic Treaty Organization (NATO). In the absence of a strong response in Korea, the United States commitment to Western Europe would have had no credibility.

Finally, the United States sought to achieve a broader milieu goal. President Truman recalled that, during the 1930s, the democracies, working through the League of Nations, had failed to react to the aggressions of Italy, Japan, and Germany. This failure had encouraged further aggression, destroyed the League, and eventually resulted in World War II. The United States wanted a post-war world free from aggression: the United Nations (UN) was still new and was widely perceived as a symbol of a more peaceful world. A failure to act in South Korea, therefore, would not only whet the appetite of the Soviet Union, but would also undermine the UN.

The resulting defense of South Korea was America's first experience with limited war. The interests at stake were compatible with the restoration of the status quo ante; the total defeat of North Korea, the unconditional surrender of

From John S. Spanier, "The Politics of the Korean War," in Phil Williams, Donald M. Goldstein, and Henry L. Andrews, Jr., eds., *Security in Korea: War, Stalemate, and Negotiation* (Westview Press, 1994). Copyright © 1994 by Westview Press, a member of the Perseus Books Group. Reprinted by permission of Westview Press, a member of Perseus Books Group, LLC. Notes omitted.

its armed forces, and the elimination of its government were not, as in World War II, a prerequisite for the achievement of American objectives. A limited war was the rational response to a less than total challenge. It would have made little sense for the United States to defend South Korea by attacking the Soviet Union because it believed Moscow to be the source of aggression. That would have been irrational; countries do not risk their existence for limited, although very important, interests.

This was particularly so in the nuclear era. It was no longer "a question of *whether* to fight a limited war, but of *how* to avoid fighting any other kind." Limited war would allow the United States to escape the all-or-nothing alternative —inaction or attacking the Soviet Union (later, as the U.S. and Soviet nuclear arsenals grew, referred to as suicide-or-surrender alternatives)—ensuring the walls of containment would not be breached and allowing the United States to pursue containment at an acceptable risk and cost without risking a war with the Soviet Union. . . .

The Drive to the Yalu

By definition, the key problem in a limited war is escalation. Escalation may, of course, be a perfectly acceptable, even desirable, course of action under certain circumstances as, for instance, in cease-fire negotiations. Attacking certain targets previously left as "privileged sanctuaries," for example, could provide the extra incentive needed for the adversary to be more conciliatory and end hostilities. However, it should be the political leaders who weigh the military and political risks and costs of escalation. Escalation should be a deliberate, conscious choice, not a quick response to a battlefield decision taken by the theater commander. To grant the theater commander the freedom to conduct the military campaign as he sees fit is to surrender this critical control.

The war, after the American-led forces crossed the thirty-eighth parallel, was a model of how *not* to fight a limited war. Beginning in late October, there were increasing reports of clashes between Chinese troops and South Korean and then American forces. In early November, MacArthur, in his flamboyant style, denounced the Chinese Communist intervention as one of the most flagrant violations of international law in history. Just as soon as he made this announcement, however, the Chinese Communist forces disengaged, arousing considerable speculation about the purpose of the Chinese intervention in Korea. Was it to protect the hydroelectric dams on the Yalu River? Was it to establish a deeper buffer zone, ranging from the narrow neck above Pyongyang, North Korea's capital, to the Yalu River frontier in order to keep U.S. troops at some distance and ensure they would not cross into China? Was it to drive American forces back to the thirty-eighth parallel, restoring the status quo ante? Or was it the total defeat of the coalition forces, unifying all of Korea in the process, the original North Korean objective?

No one really knew. The most likely aim seemed to be some sort of buffer. The initial intervention, followed by the breakoff, might have been intended to communicate to the American government not to approach the Chinese frontier with non-South Korean troops; or perhaps it was for all UN forces to stay south of a buffer area. In any event, the Chinese disengagement may have been intended to explore political solutions that would either preclude Chinese intervention altogether or limit it to northern-most Korea.

Even if it was only a ruse to gain time and build up Chinese forces for a drive to push the Americans into the sea, it is doubtful Chinese leaders were in full agreement about the desirability of a war with the world's most powerful country at a time when the Chinese hold on the mainland was not yet secure and the new regime faced mounting economic problems. Had diplomacy yielded an acceptable alternative that would have provided the new regime with security, a massive Chinese intervention with all its consequences might have been avoided.

Perhaps Truman's decision to pick his general and then let him determine how best to wage the war would have been workable with a general more in sympathy with administration objectives (like Matthew Ridgway, MacArthur's successor) or a less prestigious and politically powerful general, even if he were not particularly sympathetic to administration goals (like Mark Clark). Unfortunately, it proved impossible with MacArthur, the American viceroy in Tokyo.

Although MacArthur enthusiastically endorsed the President's decision in June and swore total loyalty, it was not long before the surface unity between Washington and Tokyo started to come apart. In late July, instead of sending one of his generals to gather information for the Joint Chiefs of Staff about the defensibility of Formosa, MacArthur decided personally to visit the island. At the end of his visit, MacArthur issued a statement warmly praising Chiang, who returned the compliment in a statement that referred not only to plans for the joint defense of Formosa, but talked of having laid the foundation for "Sino-American military cooperation." This suggestion of broader Nationalist-MacArthur (rather than U.S.) cooperation must have concerned the mainland regime, already upset by the second U.S. intervention in the Chinese civil war. MacArthur dismissed criticisms of his visit when he declared the purpose of his trip, which had been strictly military, had been "maliciously misrepresented to the public by those who invariably in the past have propagandized a policy of defeatism and appeasement in the Pacific."

Then, instead of leaving well enough alone, MacArthur sent a long message to the annual conference of the Veterans of Foreign Wars. He elaborated on the strategic significance of Formosa and declared that United States policy on Formosa came from defeatists and appeasers who did not "understand the Orient... (and) Oriental psychology," a specialty he had long claimed for himself. When the administration, the target of these verbal attacks, already irritated by MacArthur's visit to Formosa, learned of MacArthur's message, he was ordered to withdraw it—although by then it was too late to stop its widespread dissemination because it had been sent to press associations, newspapers, and magazines.

These were early indications that MacArthur was an uncontrollable force. His position, however, was strengthened when, on the day the Chinese forces broke off contact, the Republicans in the mid-term election increased their Senate representation by five to forty-seven and House representation by twenty-eight to 199 (with the Democrats holding 235 seats). Even more notable still was the defeat of several senior Democratic senators, like Scott Lucas, the majority leader, Millard Tydings, chairman of the Senate Armed Services Committee, and Francis Myers, the Democratic Whip (the first two were targets of Senator McCarthy). Reelected were Republican conservatives Robert Taft (now the party's leading presidential candidate for 1952), Eugene Milliken, Homer Capehart, and Alexander Wiley. Also elected on the Republican side were such pro-Nationalist and pro-McCarthy figures as Nixon and Dirksen.

The election was clearly overshadowed by McCarthy's tactics, McCarthy's charges and McCarthy's imitators. The upshot was to enhance McCarthy's influence in the Senate and the country and strengthen MacArthur's hand in the conduct of the Korean War as the Republicans stepped up their attacks of appeasement and "softness on Communism" on an administration that, by any objective standards, had repeatedly demonstrated its tough anti-Communist foreign policy. The political price for Truman to take on MacArthur had gone up. MacArthur must have felt virtually untouchable; he certainly acted as if he were.

His orders as he advanced into North Korea were quite specific: he was to destroy the Communist forces, provided that there were no signs of impending or actual Chinese or Soviet intervention; as a matter of policy, he was to use only South Korean troops near the Chinese and Soviet frontiers in order to eliminate any possibility of provocation. Secretary of Defense George Marshall sent him a directive stating he was to feel unhampered tactically and strategically in proceeding north of the parallel, words intended to apply to the crossing of the parallel, but which MacArthur interpreted to mean that he could wage the campaign as he saw fit.

Thus, in late October, MacArthur authorized the use of all ground forces in the drive toward the Yalu, despite the earlier orders against sending any but South Korean forces to the Chinese frontier. The Secretary of Defense and the Joint Chiefs, all junior officers when MacArthur was already a general, handled MacArthur with great solicitousness. The Secretary of State called their approach "timorous."

Perhaps MacArthur had sound reasons for issuing his authorization to proceed north, the JCS said; they "would like information of these reasons since the action contemplated was a matter of concern to them." MacArthur fired back that it was a matter of "military necessity" because of the inadequacies of the South Korean Army. The Army Chief of Staff, General Joseph L. (Lighting Joe) Collins, finding this explanation incredible, considered MacArthur's action a clear violation of his orders and was concerned MacArthur might fail to consult the JCS in a more serious situation.

A second clash between the JCS and MacArthur occurred on the 7th of November, the day after MacArthur had informed the world about the Chinese intervention, when he ordered a bombing attack on the Korean ends of the bridges across the Yalu. When his air component commander Far East Air Force Commander Lieutenant General George E. Stratemeyer checked this order with Washington, the Joint Chiefs were upset. They were concerned that some of the bombs might land on Chinese soil at the very moment when a UN meeting on the Chinese intervention was about to take place and the United States wanted support for a resolution calling on the Chinese to halt their aggression. Bombing along the Yalu would only intensify China's antagonism. While the President was willing to authorize the bombing if there were an immediate and serious threat to U.S. forces, MacArthur had sent no such message. His last message to the JCS on November 4 had been optimistic. He had doubted the Chinese intervention was a full-scale one; the message's tone was one of "don't worry." MacArthur was therefore reminded of previous orders that no bombing closer than five miles to the Chinese frontier was permitted.

MacArthur, furious, shot back a message that men and materiel were "pouring" across all bridges over the Yalu from Manchuria, not just jeopardizing, but threatening "the ultimate destruction" of UN forces. Every hour the bombing was postponed "will be paid for dearly in American and other United Nations blood." Stating he could not accept responsibility for the major calamity that would follow if he were not permitted to bomb the bridges, he demanded the chiefs bring this matter to the President's attention. Truman, seeking to avoid trouble if the issue became public, permitted the bombing to proceed, warning MacArthur again of the danger of escalating the conflict.

Thus, MacArthur, appealing over his military superiors' heads to the Commander in Chief himself, was allowed to do what he had initially intended to do through a fait accompli. He then followed this with a public message that the Chinese had not only grossly violated international law by their intervention, but that more Chinese forces were in reserve in the "privileged sanctuary" of Manchuria. He hinted that this privilege might not last. The chairman of the Joint Chiefs, General Omar Bradley, wrote afterwards that "this night we committed the worst possible error. . . . Right then—that night—the JCS should have taken the firmest control of the Korean War and dealt with MacArthur bluntly." The chiefs were concerned, however, that if they ordered him to a more defensible line across North Korea's "narrow waist," there would be "another burst of outrage, perhaps a tumultuous resignation and angry public charges of appeasement" just as the voters were showing up at the polls.

The climax in this tug of war between Washington and the general came over his decision to launch a "home by Christmas" offensive on November 24 with his forces on the left separated from those on the right (permitting the Chinese to drive through this center). In the weeks leading up to this, disaster might have been averted had MacArthur been ordered to take up defensive positions. The difficulty was that he would have claimed Washington was denying him victory and he might have had to be relieved. Consequently, everyone hesitated and wavered and lost the opportunity to ward off a catastrophe. General Ridgway thought the JCS held MacArthur in "almost superstitious awe" as a "larger than life military figure who had so often been right when everyone else had been wrong." Thus, they were afraid to challenge him and give him a flat order not to advance forward and split his thinly spread armies when Chinese intervention appeared probable and imminent. "Why don't the Joint Chiefs send orders to MacArthur and tell him what to do?" Ridgway asked one of the JCS members. "He wouldn't obey the orders. What can we do?" he was told in reply.

Recent evidence suggests the Chinese may have intended a full-scale intervention from the beginning. Nevertheless, it is clear that by not exploring alternatives to the advance to the Yalu and, above all, not restraining MacArthur in order to avoid domestic turmoil, the administration ensured an escalation that prolonged the war to 1953 and only postponed the inevitable clash with its head-strong theater commander.

MacArthur's Dismissal

When, on November 24, MacArthur launched his offensive and the Chinese launched theirs, the UN Command faced what the general called a "new war." MacArthur called for new guidelines. His recommendations were: a naval blockade of the Chinese coast; air bombardment of China's industrial complex, communication network, supply depots, and troop assembly points; the reinforcement of UN troops with Chinese Nationalist troops; and diversionary actions with a possible second front on the mainland facing Formosa.

There is also some evidence MacArthur recommended the use of atomic weapons, although he denied it publicly. These measures MacArthur assured the JCS, would not only win in Korea, but "severely cripple and largely neutralize China's capability to wage aggressive war, and thereby "save Asia from the engulfment otherwise facing it." While publicly claiming his prescription was a formula for victory in Korea, MacArthur had a broader objective, namely, to take advantage of Communist China's intervention to wage a preventive war. Ridgway, who took over the retreating army in Korea and was MacArthur's eventual successor, believed that MacArthur's concept of victory "was no less than the global defeat of communism."

MacArthur also made clear that, if his recommendations were rejected his command would have to be evacuated or be subjected to steady attrition. He could not defeat the Chinese forces unless the restraints imposed by Washington—which were "without precedent in history"—were lifted. Either Washington should let him conduct the war as he saw fit—and then he would win—or the United States should withdraw from Korea altogether.

This either-or position was very suspect in Washington. There was an underlying sense that MacArthur was deliberately exaggerating his predicament in order to compel the administration to accept his recommendations. Indeed, to Ridgway, MacArthur's suggestion of throwing in the towel without putting up any fight and his failure to go to Korea and use some of his famous rhetoric to rally his troops were disgraceful. Bradley wondered why an army with superior ground firepower and complete air superiority could not stem the Chinese advance, especially as Chinese logistical lines became longer and more vulnerable to air strikes.

Truman, in addition, felt MacArthur was trying to allay responsibility for the failure of his offensive by saying "he would have won the war except for the fact that we (in Washington) would not let him have his way... I should have relieved General MacArthur then and there." The reason Truman did not do this, he said, was he did not wish it to appear that MacArthur was being fired because the offensive had failed. "I have never believed in going back on people when luck is against them . . ."

The administration therefore did two things. It sent MacArthur a directive, addressed to all officials, that foreign and military policy statements were not to be released until cleared by the State or Defense Departments. It also sent General Collins to Korea. In December, while UN forces were still retreating, Collins reported back to the JCS that the situation was not as critical as MacArthur had pictured it and Korea could be held. MacArthur however, persisted in his demand that the limitations be lifted and his forces be reinforced or evacuated.

When Collins returned to Korea in January 1951, along with the Air Force Chief of Staff, General Hoyt S. Vandenberg, they discovered General Ridgway, who had been there less than a month, had revitalized the army. From that point, Washington:

> Looked beyond MacArthur to Ridgway for reliable military assessments and guidance. Although we continued to address JCS messages and directives to MacArthur, there was a feeling that MacArthur had been 'kicked upstairs' to chairman of the board and was, insofar as military operations were concerned, mainly a prima donna figurehead who had to be tolerated.

The Republicans, however, did not share the administration's assessment. The Republican right, true to its pre-war isolationism with its twin traditions of rejecting entangling alliances with European states and favoring unilateralism in Asia, opposed sending troops to Europe because that might provoke the Soviets whose manpower the United States could not match. It did so while supporting MacArthur's course of action, even though this would deepen the U.S. involvement in a war with Communist China, which also had vastly superior manpower resources.

The shock of Chinese intervention and the headlong U.S. retreat led the Truman Administration to reject MacArthur's military prescriptions. There were several reasons for this. First, the JCS doubted that air and naval power and the imposition of blockade could bring the conflict to an early conclusion. The successful implementation of MacArthur's strategy would require, contrary to the general's assessment, large reinforcements. Indeed, General Omar N. Bradley, the Chairman of the Joint Chiefs of Staff, thought the only way to gain a decisive result would be to fight an all-out war with China, which would be a lengthy affair and require a large commitment of U.S. forces.

A second concern was that MacArthur's recommendations might bring the Soviet Union into the conflict. The Soviet Union could no more afford to see Communist China defeated than China could tolerate the defeat of North Korea. Indeed, the Soviet Union, not Communist China, was America's principal and most powerful enemy. Therefore, the United States had to concentrate its focus and resources on Western Europe, which, as two world wars had amply demonstrated, was America's "first line of defense." The country could not afford to squander its huge, but nonetheless finite resources in what General Bradley described as "the wrong war, at the wrong place, at the wrong time, and with the wrong enemy." If there was a right war in the right place, it would have been with the Soviet Union, the primary enemy, fought in Europe, the area of primary security interest. However, the United States did not think it was ready for such a conflict in 1950 and 1951. Ever since the Soviet atomic explosion in 1949, Washington believed that, until the United States had built up its nuclear strength, in part to balance Soviet conventional superiority, it was imperative to avoid confrontation with Moscow.

Third, the European allies strongly opposed MacArthur for the same reasons as the administration: his prescription, if followed, would divert U.S. attention and power away from Europe and risk war with the Soviet Union. The allies were also dismayed by Washington's inability to control or discipline MacArthur. The result was a declining confidence in American political leadership and judgment. Moreover, the European members of NATO sought to counter the pressure exercised on the administration from the right. They were reluctant to condemn China and impose sanctions, in part because they felt MacArthur was not blameless in provoking China's intervention and in part because they feared a condemnation of China would strengthen those forces in the United States that wanted a war with China. The administration, caught in the middle, ultimately managed to obtain support in the UN for a resolution condemning Communist China, but at a price: no follow-up military action.

Thus, the unity of the Atlantic alliance was preserved. MacArthur and the Republicans threatened the cohesion of the alliance, one of the key reasons for the administration's defense of South Korea. Indeed, the United States could not simultaneously "go it alone" in Asia, as MacArthur and his supporters wanted, and pursue a policy of collective security in Europe.

After the Chinese intervention, the Administration took seriously the principles of crisis management, such as presidential control of military options, avoiding options likely to motivate the enemy to escalate, pauses in military operations, and coordinating military moves with political-diplomatic action. The administration also reverted to its initial objective of protecting only the security of South Korea. Without ever explicitly admitting it had made a mistake in crossing the thirty-eighth parallel, the administration recognized that the attempt to reunite Korea and eliminate Communist North Korea had led to a dangerous escalation. Ending the war could only be achieved by restoring the status quo ante on the Korean peninsula.

Further clashes with MacArthur were inevitable, as he was unwilling to reconcile himself to a war limited to Korea and the defense of only South Korea. As MacArthur saw the issue, the only way to prevent future Chinese Communist military expansion was by destroying its capability to wage war now. Negotiations to end the war on the basis of the status quo ante would leave China's war potential intact and, therefore, had to be prevented. The administration's assessment was very different. As UN forces approached the thirty-eighth parallel once more, after having imposed very heavy casualties upon the Chinese, the administration, unwilling to attempt forced reunification a second time, sought to explore the possibilities of ending hostilities on the basis of the prewar partition of the country. Washington believed that if made without threat or recrimination, such an offer might be well received in Beijing.

MacArthur was informed on March 20 that the President, after consultation with the allies, would announce his willingness to discuss suitable terms for concluding the war. On March 24, the general issued his own statement. Pointing out China's failure to conquer all of Korea despite its numerical superiority and the restrictions placed upon him, MacArthur suggested that the enemy "must by now be painfully aware that a decision of the United Nations to depart from its tolerant effort to contain the war to the area of Korea, through expansion of our military operations to his coastal areas and interior bases would doom Red China to the risk of imminent military collapse." He then offered to confer with the Chinese military commander about ending the fighting and achieving the UN objectives without being burdened by such "extraneous matters" as Formosa and China's seat in the UN.

By delivering this virtual ultimatum, asking Beijing to admit that it had lost the war or face an expansion of the conflict and total defeat, MacArthur sought to undercut the administration's effort to achieve a cease-fire and start negotiations to end the war. In a letter to the Republican Minority Leader in the House, Representative Joseph W. Martin, Jr., written on the 19th of March, but not released until April 5, the general elaborated that the restrictions imposed upon him were not in accord with "the conventional pattern of meeting force with maximum counter-force," which "we never failed to do in the past." He said Martin's view of allowing Chiang to open a second front on the Chinese mainland was "in conflict with neither logic nor tradition." The war in Asia must be met with "determination and not half-measures," for it was in Asia that the critical battle was being fought; if this battle was lost, Europe's fall would be inevitable.

The President was furious. MacArthur was continuing to challenge the principle of civilian authority. Not surprisingly, therefore, Truman fired MacArthur. It probably should have been done months earlier, but politically it was a risky and unpopular thing to do. MacArthur himself had finally left Truman with no option. Nevertheless, given the political situation in the United States, it took great courage for the President to fire the General. Indeed, the dismissal created a political furor.

Whether the dismissal of MacArthur encouraged the Chinese to begin cease-fire negotiations shortly afterwards is not known, but it had to reassure them that China itself would not be attacked and that U.S. aims no longer included the forceful unification of Korea. This was reaffirmed by the administration in the congressional hearings held after MacArthur returned triumphantly home. To the degree that there were internal differences in the Chinese leadership about the terms on which to settle the war, MacArthur's firing and administration statements may have strengthened those who—as in the U.S. government —were willing to settle on the basis of the pre-war division. The Soviets also appeared ready to explore the ending of hostilities; it was their UN representative who, responding to U.S. feelers, publicly declared (somewhat obliquely) in June that the Soviet people believed peace was possible.

It is also unknown to what extent the situation on the battlefield contributed to the Chinese and Soviet willingness to negotiate. Ridgway had not only rallied his demoralized and retreating army, but honed it into a deadly fighting force. He stopped repeated Chinese offensives in early 1951 by inflicting immense casualties on Chinese troops through the effective use of artillery and air power. Having suffered about a half million casualties in the eight months since the intervention and, with their May offensive broken, the Chinese were demoralized, unable to resist Ridgway's offensive, and placed on the defensive as their long logistical lines were exposed to constant air attacks and the supply situation became desperate.

Had the administration been willing to continue the offensive, the Chinese would have been in danger of being driven back, perhaps to North Korea's narrow neck. This might have encouraged China to conclude the war before their armies were ripped apart. Instead, when the Soviets and Chinese suggested that they were willing to talk about a cease-fire, the administration immediately agreed and halted the offensive. Pressured by public opinion to end the war and unsure that it could count on domestic support for such a tough bargaining strategy, the administration was unwilling to sacrifice more American lives in order to end the war at lines slightly north of where it had begun. The expectation was of a fairly rapid conclusion to the war. Thus, the cost of the Truman Administration's political weakness and inability to coordinate policy and strategy, so characteristic of the American belief that the two were divorced and that diplomacy would follow the use of force, was very high.

In the event, the negotiations dragged on until 1953. In stopping the offensive, the administration had inadvertently ensured the continuation of the war. The Chinese, reinforced, continued to resist, delaying a settlement while seeking to improve the terms for ending the war at little cost to themselves. During that time, 20,000 Americans were killed, more than in the first year of the war; among all UN forces, the figure of those who died in battle was about twice that of the earlier period.

The tragic irony was that the final terms President Eisenhower accepted were little different from those proposed by the UN early in the negotiations; but Eisenhower could accept terms that Truman could not. The Republican President, a moderate who had opposed Senator Taft for the nomination, was immune to charges by his party's right wing of appeasement and "coddling Communism" (not that it did not try, but finally, forced to fight, Eisenhower destroyed McCarthy). However, Harry Truman, a Democrat, despite his staunch record of anti-Communism in Europe and the containment of Soviet power, was vulnerable to such scurrilous charges even though the United States could have done little to prevent Chiang's regime from committing political suicide. Harry Truman, who had succeeded Franklin Roosevelt when he died, could have run for a second term in 1952. Instead, he chose not to run.

D. Clayton James with
Anne Sharp Wells

 **NO**

MacArthur's Dare Is Called

Differences in Strategy

The dismissal of General [Douglas] MacArthur in April 1951 is a watershed in the history of American strategic direction in the Korean conflict. For the ensuing two years and three months of hostilities and truce negotiations no major challenge would be offered to the Truman administration's manner of limiting the war except for a few Allied leaders who urged more compromises with the communists at Panmunjom than the American wished to make for the sake of a quicker end to the fighting. With the removal of MacArthur, moreover, the post-1945 trend of increasing input by the State Department of military policy was accelerated. By the bellicose nature of his criticism of the Truman administration's direction of the war, MacArthur had placed himself in the position of championing a military solution in Korea in the American tradition of preferring strategies of annihilation, instead of attrition. He left the scene as an uncompromising warrior, though, in actuality, his differences with Truman were not as simplistic as they appeared. During World War II, as in the Korean conflict, for instance, he had argued for a balanced global strategy that accorded high priorities to not only Europe but also Asia and the Pacific. In view of the sites where American boys have died in combat since 1945, perhaps that and other arguments of the fiery old general need not have been dismissed so lightly.

Contrary to popular accounts, the strategic aspect of the Truman–MacArthur controversy was not based on the President's advocacy of limited war and the general's alleged crusading for a global war against communism. MacArthur wanted to carry the war to Communist China in air and sea operations of restricted kinds, but he never proposed expanding the ground combat into Manchuria or North China. Both Washington and Tokyo authorities were acutely aware that the Korean struggle could have escalated into World War III if the Soviet Union had gone to war, but at no time did MacArthur wish to provoke the USSR into entering the Korean War. He predicted repeatedly that none of his actions would lead to Soviet belligerency, which, he maintained steadfastly, would be determined by Moscow's own strategic interests and its own timetable.

Yet there were significant strategic differences between Truman and MacArthur. The "first war," against North Korea, did not produce any major collisions between the general and Washington except on Formosa policy, which did not reach its zenith until the Communist Chinese were engaged in Korea. The strategic plans of MacArthur for a defensive line at the Naktong, for an amphibious stroke through Inchon and Seoul, and for a drive north of the 38th parallel all had the blessings of the President and the Joint Chiefs before they reached their operational stages. Even the Far East commander's plans for separate advances by the Eighth Army and the X Corps into North Korea and for an amphibious landing at Wonsan, though they raised eyebrows in Washington, did not draw remonstrances from his superiors, who viewed such decisions as within the purview of the theater chief. Sharp differences between MacArthur and Washington leaders only emerged after the euphoric days of October 1950 when it seemed the North Korean Army was beaten and the conflict was entering its mopping-up phase. Perhaps because of the widespread optimism that prevailed most of that month, neither Tokyo nor Washington officials were aware of a strategic chasm developing between them....

Perhaps it might not have been too late to avert war with Communist China if the Joint Chiefs [JCS] had focused less on MacArthur's impudence toward them and more on the strategic consequence at stake in the Far East commander's move, namely, the escalation of the war by Communist China rather than by the USSR. While MacArthur had largely discounted the possibility of the Soviet Union's entry into the war, he had not seemed greatly concerned about Communist China's possible belligerency. As he had cockily assured the President at Wake, his air power would decimate the Chinese Communist Forces if they tried to advance south of the Yalu. The aggressive move up to the border with American troops in the lead was imprudent adventurism on MacArthur's part, but, on the other hand, the Joint Chiefs' timidity toward him and their priority on his effrontery to them at such a critical strategic juncture left them fully as liable as he was for the decisive provocation of Peking....

While the Great Debate was heating up on Capitol Hill, the beginning of MacArthur's end occurred when [Army Chief of Staff General Joseph L.] Collins, his Army superior and the executive agent for the JCS in Far East matters, visited Tokyo and the Korean front on January 15–17, accompanied by Vandenberg, the Air Force chief. Their trip had been precipitated by a false dilemma MacArthur had posed to his superiors the previous week: As Truman saw it, the Tokyo commander declared the only alternatives were to "be driven off the peninsula, or at the very least suffer terrible losses." Collins reported that during their meeting at MacArthur's GHQ [general headquarters] in Tokyo, MacArthur again appealed for the four divisions. Upon visiting Ridgway [MacArthur's eventual successor] and his troops in Korea, however, Collins found a renovated force preparing to go on the offensive. He was able to return to Washington with the good news, backed by Vandenberg's findings also, that MacArthur was not only uninformed about the situation at the front but also deceitful in posing the false dilemma of evacuation or annihilation if they did not approve his proposals and troop requests. Ridgway's counsel, rather than MacArthur's, was thereafter increasingly sought by the Joint Chiefs and the President.

MacArthur had been found wanting in both strategy and stratagem. Far more crucial, the U.S. government had reaffirmed its foremost global priority to be the security of its Atlantic coalition. Similar to his plight during the Second World War, MacArthur again was arguing in futility for greater American strategic concern about Asia and the Pacific against a predominantly Europe-first leadership in Washington. Having spent over twenty-five years of his career in the Far East, MacArthur may have been biased in speaking out for a higher priority on American interests in that region. There is little question, however, that communist expansionism was mounting in East and Southeast Asia and that American leaders knew little about the susceptibilities of the peoples of those areas. To MacArthur, his struggle to get Washington's attention focused on the Pacific and Asia must have seemed as frustrating as the efforts by him and Fleet Admiral Ernest King to get more resources allocated to the war against Japan.

Despite the warmongering allegations leveled against him, MacArthur never proposed resorting to nuclear weapons while he was Far East chief. In December 1952, he did suggest in a private talk with Eisenhower and Dulles, the President-elect and the next secretary of state, that a line of radioactive waste materials be air-dropped along the northern border of North Korea, to be followed by conventional amphibious assaults on both coasts as well as atomic bombing of military targets in North Korea to destroy the sealed-off enemy forces. He saw this as "the great bargaining lever to induce the Soviet [Union] to agree upon honorable conditions toward international accord." It must be remembered, however, that he had been out of command for twenty months, and, besides, Eisenhower and Dulles scorned his counsel and never sought it again.

In truth, Presidents Truman and Eisenhower, not MacArthur, both considered the use or threat of nuclear force in the Korean War. On November 30, 1950, Truman remarked at a press conference that use of the atomic bomb was being given "active consideration," but Allied leaders, with British Prime Minister Clement R. Attlee in the forefront, exhibited such high states of anxiety over his comment that the President never openly discussed that option again. In January 1952, however, he confided in his diary that he was considering an ultimatum to Moscow to launch atomic raids against Soviet cities if the USSR did not compel the North Koreans and Red Chinese to permit progress in the Korean truce negotiations. "This means all out war," he wrote angrily but wisely reconsidered the next day. In the spring of 1953, President Eisenhower tried to intimidate the Chinese and North Koreans into signing an armistice on UN terms by threatening to use nuclear weapons, which by then included hydrogen bombs. MacArthur had nothing to do with these nuclear threats. Nevertheless, the canard of MacArthur as a warmonger who was eager to employ nuclear weapons in the Korean conflict has persisted in popular and scholarly writings over the years.

A Threat to Civil-Military Relations?

MacArthur's record of arrogant and near-insubordinate conduct during the previous decade on the world stage was well known to the leaders in Washington in 1950–1951. During World War II, President Roosevelt and General Marshall, the Army chief of staff, had been greatly annoyed when he attempted to get Prime Ministers Churchill and Curtin to press for more American resources to be allocated to the Southwest Pacific theater in 1942. MacArthur appeared to encourage anti-Roosevelt groups in American politics who tried in vain to stir up a draft of him for the Republican presidential nomination in 1944. As for defiance of his military superiors, MacArthur launched a number of amphibious operations prior to obtaining authorization from the Joint Chiefs. Admiral Morison observes that "the J.C.S. simply permitted MacArthur to do as he pleased, up to a point" in the war against Japan.

On several occasions during the early phase of the occupation of Japan, MacArthur defied Truman's instructions for him to come to Washington for consultations, the general pleading his inability to leave "the extraordinarily dangerous and inherently inflammable situation" in Japan. Truman was so irked that he quoted two of the general's declinations in his memoirs written nearly a decade afterward. In 1948, MacArthur again appeared willing to run against his commander in chief, but his right-wing supporters were unable to secure the Republican nomination for him. His dissatisfaction with Washington directives during the later phases of the occupation almost led to his replacement by a civilian high commissioner. His growing alienation from administration policies during the first eight months of the Korean fighting gave rise to speculation that he might head an anti-Truman ticket in the 1952 presidential race.

The administration officials who testified at the Senate hearings on MacArthur's relief clearly indicated that they viewed his attitude and conduct as insubordinate and a threat to the principle of civilian supremacy over the military. Secretary of Defense Marshall, probably the most admired of the witnesses representing the administration, was adamant about MacArthur's unparalleled effrontery toward his superiors:

> It is completely understandable and, in fact, at times commendable that a theater commander should become so wholly wrapped up in his own aims and responsibilities that some of the directives received by him from higher authorities are not those that he would have written for himself. There is nothing new about this sort of thing in our military history. What is new, and what had brought about the necessity for General MacArthur's removal, is the wholly unprecedented situation of a local theater commander publicly expressing his displeasure at and his disagreement with the foreign and military policies of the United States.
>
> It became apparent that General MacArthur had grown so far out of sympathy with the established policies of the United States that there was a grave doubt as to whether he could any longer be permitted to exercise the authority in making decisions that normal command functions would assign to a theater commander. In this situation, there was no other recourse but to relieve him.

The evidence accumulated in the Senate investigation of May and June 1951 demonstrates that virtually all of his transgressions fell under the category of disobedience of the President's "muzzling directives" of December 6, 1950. The general's responses, in turn, had revealed his deep opposition to administration policies. The press had widely publicized his blasts; indeed, many of his missives had gone to national news magazines and major newspapers by way of interviews with and correspondence to their publishers and senior editors or bureau chiefs. His false dilemma about evacuation or annihilation, which was rankling enough to his superiors since he seemed to pass responsibility to them, was a frequent theme in his flagrantly defiant public statements. McCarthyism had already left the national press in a feeding frenzy, so it was natural for reporters eager to exploit the popular hostility against Truman and [Dean] Acheson to give lavish attention to the antiadministration barbs of one of the nation's greatest heroic figures of World War II.

Most heinous to Commander in Chief Truman were the general's ultimatum to the head of the Chinese Communist Forces [CCF] on March 24 and his denunciation of administration policy read in the U.S. House of Representatives on April 5. The general had been told that Truman would soon announce a new diplomatic initiative to get a Korean truce before Ridgway's army advanced across the 38th parallel again. MacArthur arrogantly and deliberately wrecked this diplomatic overture by issuing his own public statement directed to the CCF leader, which scathingly criticized Red China's "complete inability to accomplish by force of arms the conquest of Korea," threatened "an expansion of our military operations to its coastal areas and interior bases [that] would doom Red China to the risk of imminent military collapse," and offered "at any time to confer in the field with the commander-in-chief of the enemy forces in the earnest effort to find any military means whereby realization of the political objectives of the United Nations in Korea ... might be accomplished without further bloodshed."

In sixteen or more instances in the previous four months the volatile Far East chief had made statements sharply chastising the administration for its errors or absence of policy in the Far East. MacArthur was bent now upon some dramatic gesture to salvage his waning stature. By late March, the UN commander became so paranoid that he believed that he had ruined a plot created by some in the United Nations, the State Department, and high places in Washington to change the status of Formosa and the Nationalists' seat in the UN.

Upon reading MacArthur's shocking statement of the 24th, the President firmly but secretly decided that day to dismiss him; only the procedure and the date had to be settled. Truman heatedly remarked to an assistant that the general's act was "not just a public disagreement over policy, but deliberate, premeditated sabotage of US and UN policy." Acheson described it as "defiance of the Chiefs of Staff, sabotage of an operation of which he had been informed, and insubordination of the grossest sort to his Commander in Chief." Astoundingly,however, the President, through the JCS, sent him a brief and mildly worded message on March 25 reminding him of the directives of December 6 and telling him to contact the Joint Chiefs for instructions if the Chinese commander asked for a truce.

The message from Washington on March 20 alerting him to the impending peace move also set off MacArthur's second climatic act of self-destruction in his endeavor to redirect American foreign and military policies to a greater focus on Asia's significance to the self-interests of the United States. That same day the general wrote Representative Joseph W. Martin, Jr., the House minority leader and a strong Asia-first and Nationalist China crusader. Martin had asked for comments on a speech by the congressman hitting Truman's weak support of Formosa, his limited-war strategy in Korea, and his plans to strengthen NATO. In his letter, MacArthur endorsed his friend Martin's views with enthusiasm but offered nothing new, even admitting that his positions "have been submitted to Washington in most complete detail" and generally "are well known." What made the general's comments different this time were their coincidence with the sensitive diplomatic maneuvering, Martin's dramatic reading of the letter on the floor of the House, and the front-page headlines MacArthur's words got. . . .

At the Senate hearings, MacArthur claimed the letter to Martin was "merely a routine communication." On the other hand, Truman penned in his diary on April 6: "MacArthur shoots another political bomb through Joe Martin. . . . This looks like the last straw. Rank insubordination. . . . I call in Gen. Marshall, Dean Acheson, Mr. Harriman and Gen. Bradley before Cabinet [meeting] to discuss situation." Acheson exclaimed that the Martin letter was "an open declaration of war on the Administration's policy." When Truman conferred with the above "Big Four," as he called them, he did not reveal that his mind had been made up for some time; instead, he encouraged a candid discussion of options and expressed his desire for a unanimous recommendation from them as well as the three service chiefs, Collins, Sherman, and Vandenberg.

Over the weekend Truman talked to key members of the Cabinet to solicit their opinions, while top State and Defense officials met in various groupings to discuss the issue. At the meeting of the President and the Big Four on Monday, April 9, the relief of General MacArthur was found to be the unanimous verdict of the President, the Big Four, and the service chiefs. . . .

MacArthur was the first to testify at the Senate hearings [in early May], and when he expounded on the harmonious relationship and identity of strategic views between him and his military superiors, he seems to have believed this sincerely, if naively. One by one, Marshall, Bradley, Collins, Sherman, and Vandenberg would later tell the senators that they were not in accord with MacArthur on matters of the direction of the war, relations with civilian officials, the value of the European allies, and the priority of the war in the global picture, among other differences. Not aware of how united and devastating against him his uniformed superiors would be, MacArthur set about describing a dichotomy in the leadership of the war from Washington, with Truman, Acheson, Harriman, and other ranking civilians of the administration, especially the State Department, which tended to have unprecedented input in military affairs by 1950–1951, being responsible for the policy vacuum, indecisiveness, and protracted, costly stalemate. On the other hand, he and the Pentagon leaders, along with most of the other senior American officers of the various services, wanted to fight in less limited fashion and gain a decisive triumph in order to deter future communist aggression.

MacArthur, thinking he spoke for his military colleagues, told the senators that Truman and his "politicians" favored "the concept of a continued and indefinite campaign in Korea ... that introduces into the military sphere a political control such as I have never known in my life or have ever studied." He argued that "when politics fails, and the military takes over, you must trust the military." Later he added: "There should be no non-professional interference in the handling of troops in a campaign. You have professionals to do that job and they should be permitted to do it." As for his recommendations for coping with the entry of the Red Chinese onto the battlefield, he maintained that "most" of them, "in fact, practically all, as far as I know—were in complete accord with the military recommendations of the Joint Chiefs of Staff, and all other commanders." Referring to a JCS list of sixteen courses of action that were under consideration on January 12, which included three of the four he had recommended on December 30, he claimed with some hyperbole, "The position of the Joint Chiefs of Staff and my own, so far as I know, were practically identical." He pictured his ties with the JCS as idealistic, indeed, unrealistic; "The relationships between the Joint Chiefs of Staff and myself have been admirable. All members are personal friends of mine. I hold them individually and collectively in the greatest esteem." It was a desperate endeavor to demonstrate that the basic friction lay between the civilian and the military leadership, not between him and the Pentagon, but it became a pathetic revelation of how out of touch he was with the Joint Chiefs. For want of conclusive proof as to his motivation, however, leeway must be allowed for MacArthur's wiliness, which had not altogether abandoned him: He may have been trying to exploit tensions between the State and Defense departments, with few uniformed leaders holding Acheson and his lieutenants in high regard.

Fortunately for MacArthur, Marshall and the Joint Chiefs, who had chafed over Acheson's obvious eagerness to see the proud MacArthur fall, felt an affinity with this senior professional in their field who had long commanded with distinction. They could not bring themselves to court-martial him. Further, Truman's terrible ratings in the polls—worse than Nixon's at the ebb of Watergate—and the firestorm that McCarthyism had produced for him and Acheson weakened him so politically that a court-martial of MacArthur would have been foolhardy in the extreme. During the first five days after MacArthur's relief, a White House staff count showed that Truman received almost thirteen thousand letters and telegrams on the issue, of which 67 percent opposed the President's action. By the end of the Senate hearings on the general's relief, much of the public, Congress, and the press had lost interest in the inquiry, though polls indicated that a majority of those who cared enough to give an opinion now were against MacArthur. The notion that he might have touched off World War III was on its way to becoming one of the more unfortunate myths about the general.

Insubordination, or defiance of authority, was the charge most frequently leveled against MacArthur at the time and later by high-ranking officials of the Truman administration, including those in uniform. Of course, there was no doubt of his insubordination in the minds of the two chief architects of his dismissal, Truman and Acheson. On numerous occasions during his days of testimony before the Senate committees, it will be recalled, MacArthur himself said that the nation's commander in chief was empowered to appoint and dismiss his uniformed leaders for whatever reason, which surely included rank insubordination. There was no serious question about Truman's authority to relieve MacArthur, but the President and the Joint Chiefs found such great difficulty in dismissing him because there was no genuine threat to the principle of civilian supremacy over the military in this case. MacArthur was not an "American Caesar" and held very conservative views of the Constitution, the necessity of civilian control, and the traditions and history of the American military. When the President finally decided to gird his loins and dismiss MacArthur, the action was swift and Ridgway replaced him smoothly and effectively in short order. All the President had to do was issue the order to bring about the change in command, and it was clear that his power as commander in chief was secure and unchallenged. The President and his Far East commander had differed over strategic priorities and the direction of the war, but their collision had not posed a serious menace to civilian dominance over the military in America.

Breakdowns in Command and Communication

A significant and often overlooked reason for the termination of MacArthur's command was a breakdown in communications between him and his superiors. During the Second World War, MacArthur and the Joint Chiefs of Staff sometimes differed in ways that indicated misconceptions more than strategic differences, but the two sides and their key lieutenants had personal ties between them that were lacking between the Tokyo and Washington leaders of 1950–1951. During the Korean War, the camps of Truman and MacArthur strongly influenced each man's perception of the other. This is not to say that on their own Truman and MacArthur would have become cordial friends. But their lieutenants undoubtedly were important in molding their judgments. Their only direct contact had been a few hours at Wake Island on October 15, 1950, of which a very small portion had been spent alone. Despite the fact that they had never met before and were never to talk again, they would go to their graves implacable enemies.

If the Truman-MacArthur personal relationship was limited to one brief encounter, the personal links between the Far East leader and the seven men who were the President's principal advisers on the Korean War—the Big Four and the service chiefs—were almost nil. Acheson never met him. Marshall visited him once during World War II while going to Eisenhower's headquarters numerous times. Bradley and Harriman had no personal ties with MacArthur at all prior to June of 1950, although each traveled to Tokyo to confer with him after the Korean hostilities commenced. None of the Big Four was an admirer of MacArthur's flamboyant leadership style, yet Marshall, who had been his military superior in World War II, had treated him with commendable fairness despite the Southwest Pacific commander's sometimes difficult ways. All of the Big Four were strongly committed to the security of West Europe, and all had considerable experience and friends there.

None of the service chiefs had any personal contacts with MacArthur of any importance prior to the outbreak of war in Korea, whereupon they made a number of trips to Tokyo to meet with him and his senior commanders and staff leaders. Collins was on the faculty of the United States Military Academy during MacArthur's last year as superintendent (1921–1922), and Vandenberg was a cadet for the three years (1919–1922) of his tenure. Neither of them, however, really got to know the aloof superintendent, though both knew much about him, especially his hero image from the battlefields of France and his efforts to bring reforms to the school despite faculty and alumni resistance. Collins and Vandenberg achieved their senior commands in the Second World War in the European theater; the former had seen combat first in the Solomons, which was not in MacArthur's theater. When he was on Admiral Chester W. Nimitz's staff during the war in the Pacific, Sherman conferred with MacArthur at three or more intertheater planning sessions. Sherman, who had the most significant pre-1950 personal contact with MacArthur, was his strongest supporter of the seven men on a number of his ideas and plans, notably the Inchon assault. On the other hand, Marshall, the oldest of the seven (like MacArthur, born in 1880), and the officer with seniority in the service, was the last of the group to be persuaded that MacArthur should be relieved of his commands.

Of these key advisers to the President, Acheson stands out for his vituperativeness toward the Tokyo commander. In a bitter exchange of press statements in the autumn of 1945 contradicting each other over estimated troop strength needed in occupied Japan, Acheson and MacArthur seemed to exhibit a deep and natural incompatibility. Acheson blamed MacArthur in part for trouble in getting his approval as under secretary of state passed by the Senate that fall. When he was secretary of state later, he visited Europe often but never Japan, and in 1949 he was behind the move to oust the general as head of the Allied occupation. Certainly as proud and arrogant as MacArthur, Acheson could be invidious. Writing nearly two decades after the dismissal, Acheson still harbored deep wrath: "As one looks back in calmness, it seems impossible to overestimate the damage that General MacArthur's willful insubordination and incredibly bad judgment did to the United States in the world and to the Truman Administration in the United States." Acheson was the abiding voice in Truman's ear from 1945 onward urging him to dump "the Big General," and it was he who primarily continued to stoke the long-cold coals even after most of his cohorts had let the fire die as far as public statements were concerned.

The sorry spectacle of MacArthur testifying at the Senate hearings about his harmonious relations with the Joint Chiefs not only exposed his ignorance of the situation but also pointed up how poorly the JCS had communicated their doubts and anxieties, as well as their anger, to the theater commander. It was an invitation to trouble to place him in the UN command in the first place because of both his prior record of defying authority and his long career of distinction and seniority in comparison to theirs. It should have been understood from the beginning of the Korean War that his past achievements gave him no claim to special privileges in obeying orders and directives, especially in such an unprecedented limited conflict that could quickly become a third world war. Time after time, especially after the Red Chinese intervention, the Joint Chiefs retreated from the policy guidance and new directives they should have given MacArthur and should have demanded his obedience. Instead, his intimidation of the Joint Chiefs led them to appease him.

On the other hand, MacArthur discovered that he could not awe or intimidate Truman. Indeed, at the end, the President dismissed him so abruptly and crudely that the general heard of it first from a commercial radio broadcast. Speaking as a professional, MacArthur later said, "No office boy, no charwoman, no servant of any sort would have been dismissed with such callous disregard for the ordinary decencies." For MacArthur, his erroneous image of Truman as a fox terrier yapping at his heels instead of a tough, decisive commander in chief was a costly failure in communication.

If the Joint Chiefs had been more responsible in keeping MacArthur on a short leash, perhaps the collision course between the President and the general might have been averted. The absurd spectacle of the Senate investigation into the general's relief, which bestowed upon Pyongyang, Peking, and Moscow an abundance of data on American strategy in the midst of war, surely could have been avoided. While MacArthur's career was terminated by the confrontation, Truman's also was cut short, the controversy mightily affecting his chances for reelection. Truman won over MacArthur, but it was a Pyrrhic victory politically.

MacArthur's relief was, in part, a legacy of World War II and the strategic priorities of that conflict. Roosevelt and his Joint Chiefs of Staff had early agreed to the British priority on the defeat of Germany because the Atlantic community of nations was vital to American national security and the threat by Japan was more distant. In the midst of another Asian war, MacArthur was sacrificed by a different President and his Defense and State advisers, who did not consider American strategic interests as menaced in East Asia as in Europe. It remains to be seen whether a century hence the Far East will loom as important to American self-interests as MacArthur predicted.

POSTSCRIPT

Should President Truman Have Fired General MacArthur?

In 1950 MacArthur's disagreements with Truman were twofold. First, he disliked the Truman administration's Europe-oriented policy of "containment" of Russian expansionism; second, he detested the defensive strategy that was implied in fighting a limited war under a containment policy.

MacArthur's sympathies lay with those who blamed the Truman administration for the "loss of China" to the Communists and hoped that the UN forces would push the Communists out of a reunified Korea. On his visit to Formosa on August 2, 1950, he embarrassed the Truman administration with his remarks that plans had been developed for the effective coordination of Chinese and American forces in case of an attack on the island. A few weeks later he was nearly fired after he sent a long message to the national commander of the Veterans of Foreign Wars, which stated, "Nothing could be more fallacious than the threadbare argument by those who advocate appeasement and defeatism in the Pacific that if we defend Formosa we alienate continental Asia."

Spanier contends that MacArthur stretched orders from the Defense Department and Joint Chiefs of Staff well beyond their original intent. Particularly upsetting to Truman was MacArthur's public statement telling Beijing to admit it lost the war or face expansion of the war into parts of China and risk total defeat. This pronouncement, says Spanier, "undercut the administration's effort to achieve a cease-fire and start negotiations to end the war." It also convinced the president that he had to fire the general. The Joint Chiefs of Staff agreed.

James is the author of a three-volume biography of MacArthur. The third volume—*Triumph and Disaster, 1945–1964* (Houghton Mifflin, 1985)—covers in greater detail MacArthur's role in post–World War II Asia. James admits that MacArthur was arrogant and at times difficult to deal with, but he asserts that the Joint Chiefs of Staff might have prevented MacArthur's firing if they had exerted more control over him.

Spanier agrees with James that the Joint Chiefs of Staff were timorous in dealing with MacArthur. This was likely because many of the Joint Chiefs were much younger than MacArthur, who was then 70 years old, and were afraid to challenge a "living legend." Furthermore, MacArthur had proven to a highly skeptical Joint Chiefs and Defense Department that his tactical abilities were still sharp, given the success of the surprise landing behind the lines of the enemy at Inchon.

Spanier and James agree that a more aggressive military policy might have ended the war two years earlier. Could UN field commander Matthew Ridgeway or MacArthur have forced the Chinese and North Koreans to accept a divided

Korea if they had pushed the Chinese to North Korea's narrow neck? Was the Truman administration too politically weak to do this? Was the administration's policy and strategy poorly coordinated? Could MacArthur have been persuaded to accept a compromise-negotiated settlement?

Students who wish to learn more should start with Richard Lowitt, ed., *The Truman-MacArthur Controversy* (Rand McNally, 1984). Walter Karp explores the aftermath of the controversy in "Truman vs. MacArthur," *American Heritage* (April/May 1984). There are three books that cover the controversy in detail and that are supportive of Truman's decision. Many consider the best to be John W. Spanier, *The Truman-MacArthur Controversy and the Korean War* (W. W. Norton, 1959, 1965). See also Trumball Higgins, *Korea and the Fall of MacArthur: A Precis in Limited War* (Oxford University Press, 1960) and Richard H. Rovere and Arthur Schlesinger, Jr., *The MacArthur Controversy and American Foreign Policy* (Transaction Books, 1992), which was originally published at the height of the controversy in 1951. Other defenses include *Memoirs by Harry S. Truman: Years of Trial and Hope, vol. 2* (Signet Paperback, 1956, 1965) and former secretary of state Dean Acheson's caustic *Present at the Creation* (W. W. Norton, 1969). One criticism of MacArthur's vision comes from retired brigadier general Roy K. Flint, former head of the history department at West Point, in "The Truman-MacArthur Conflict: Dilemma of Civil-Military Relationships in the Nuclear Age," in Richard H. Kohn, ed., *The United States Military Under the Constitution of the United States, 1789–1989* (New York University Press, 1991).

MacArthur's defense of his policies and anger over his firing can be found in his *Reminiscences* (McGraw-Hill, 1964) and in Charles A. Willoughby and John Chamberlain, *MacArthur: 1941–1951* (McGraw-Hill, 1954). Willoughby was an intelligence officer on MacArthur's staff.

For a good short history of the war, students should see Burton I. Kaufman, *The Korean War: Challenges in Crisis, Credibility and Command*, 2d ed. (McGraw-Hill, 1997). Kaufman has also edited *The Korean Conflict* (Greenwood Press, 1999), an excellent compendium of chronologies, biographical sketches, and bibliography. The starting point for all the recent research in Soviet archives pertaining to the Korean War are Rosemary Foot, "Making Known the Unknown War: Policy Analysis of the Korean Conflict Since the Early 1980's" and Robert J. McMahon, "The Cold War in Asia: The Elusive Synthesis." Both are essays from *Diplomatic History* that have been reprinted in Michael J. Hogan, ed., *America in the World: The Historiography of American Foreign Relations Since 1941* (Cambridge University Press, 1995).

ISSUE 12

Was Dwight Eisenhower a Great President?

YES: Stephen E. Ambrose, from *Eisenhower: The President, vol. 2* (Simon & Schuster, 1984)

NO: Arthur M. Schlesinger, Jr., from *The Cycles of American History* (Houghton Mifflin, 1986)

ISSUE SUMMARY

YES: Professor of history Stephen E. Ambrose (1936–2002) maintains that Dwight D. Eisenhower was a greater president than his predecessors and successors because he balanced the budget, stopped inflation, and kept the peace.

NO: Professor of the humanities Arthur M. Schlesinger, Jr., argues that Eisenhower failed as a president because he refused to tackle the moral and environmental issues at home and because he established a foreign policy that relied on covert CIA activities and threats of nuclear arms.

David Dwight Eisenhower (he reversed his name in high school) was the third of seven sons raised in a very modest household in Abilene, Kansas, in the 1890s. After graduating from high school, he worked for a year and then passed a competitive examination for an appointment to the U.S. Naval Academy. He was not accepted because he was considered too old.

Instead, he entered West Point in 1911, against the wishes of his pacifist parents. According to his major biographer, Stephen E. Ambrose, "Sports were his all-consuming passion." During his sophomore year a twisted knee ruined the potential All-American's football career. In 1915 a disconsolate Eisenhower graduated 61st in a class of 164.

At first his military career looked very unpromising. During World War I he took command of a tank training center and learned a good deal about armored warfare but gained no combat experience. In the early 1920s he spent most of his time coaching football teams on army posts and seemed disinterested in his profession.

Fortunately, he met General Fox Conner, a man who stimulated Eisenhower's thinking about military strategy. With Conner's assistance he went to the Command and General Staff School in Leavenworth, Kansas, and graduated first in his class. Conner convinced the young officer of two things that would greatly impact his future career: (1) The next war would be global, and (2) a certain General George C. Marshall would lead the American troops in this future worldwide conflict.

Why contemporary observers of Eisenhower's presidency underestimated his intellectual abilities to think and write clearly remains puzzling when one examines his early career. The young officer had developed a reputation as an excellent staff officer who was uncommonly good at preparing reports. In 1927 he wrote an excellent guidebook detailing the major battles of World War I. In the summer of 1941 Eisenhower's organizational skills gained public notoriety when he distinguished himself as the chief planner of the 3rd Army in the Louisiana maneuvers. Therefore, it was no accident that Army Chief of Staff George C. Marshall called Eisenhower to Washington a week after the Pearl Harbor attack and put him in the War Plans Division.

During World War II Eisenhower, as head of the Combined Chiefs of Staff, was forced to make numerous military decisions. He performed brilliantly. In November 1942 he directed the combined American and British invasion of North Africa. His organizational skills were stretched to the limit when he directed the largest landed invasion in history. More than 156,000 men hit the beaches of Normandy, France, on D-Day, June 6, 1944, to establish the long-awaited second front. Germany surrendered less than a year later.

Like his predecessors Washington, Jackson, and Grant, the emergence of General Eisenhower as a war hero made him presidential timber. Democratic leaders asked him to be Harry S. Truman's replacement in 1948. He turned them down because of his hostility to the New Deal. He served a short stint as the first NATO commander before he accepted the bid of the "establishment" Republican leaders to become their candidate in 1952. After a successful run in the primaries and a bruising floor fight at the Republican convention against the leading conservative candidate, Ohio senator Robert Taft, the general was nominated.

The main issues of the campaign were an unpopular war and corruption and communism in government. Candidate Eisenhower made a trip to Korea and promised to end the war. The public believed him, and he easily defeated his Democratic opponent, Illinois governor Adlai Stevenson.

In the following selections, Stephen E. Ambrose argues that Eisenhower ranks as one of America's greatest presidents because he balanced the budget, stopped inflation, and gave the nation eight years of peace and prosperity. Arthur M. Schlesinger, Jr., disagrees with this assessment. He emphasizes the negative side of Eisenhower's administration: his refusal to tackle the moral and environmental issues at home and his establishment of a foreign policy that relied upon covert CIA activities and that too often went to the brink with threats of nuclear war.

Stephen E. Ambrose

 **YES**

The Eisenhower Presidency:
An Assessment

Any attempt to assess Eisenhower's eight years as President inevitably reveals more about the person doing the assessing then it does about Eisenhower. Assessment requires passing a judgment on the decisions Eisenhower made on the issues of his time, and every issue was political and controversial. Further, all the major and most of the minor issues of the 1950s continued to divide the nation's political parties and people in the decades that followed. To declare, therefore, that Eisenhower was right or wrong on this or that issue tends to be little more than a declaration of the current politics and prejudices of the author. The temptation to judge, however, is well-nigh irresistible, and most of the authors who write about the 1950s give in to it.

Thus William Ewald, in *Eisenhower the President,* concludes "that many terrible things that could have happened, didn't. Dwight Eisenhower's presidency gave America eight good years—I believe the best in memory." There were no wars, no riots, no inflation—just peace and prosperity. Most white middle-class and middle-aged Republicans would heartily agree with Ewald. But a black American could point out that among the things that did not happen were progress in civil rights or school desegregation. People concerned about the Cold War and the nuclear arms race could point out that no progress was made in reducing tensions or achieving disarmament. People concerned about the Communist menace could point out that no Communist regimes were eliminated, and that in fact Communism expanded into Vietnam and Cuba. On these and every issue, in short, there are at least two legitimate points of view. What did not happen brought joy to one man, gloom to another.

One of the first serious attempts at assessment was by Murray Kempton in a famous article in *Esquire* magazine in September 1967. Kempton called the piece "The Underestimation of Dwight D. Eisenhower," and in it he admitted that Eisenhower was much shrewder and more in control of events than he, or other reporters, had ever imagined during the fifties. Eisenhower was "the great tortoise upon whose back the world sat for eight years," never recognizing "the cunning beneath the shell." Garry Wills took up the same theme in his 1970 book *Nixon Agonistes.* Such judgments were little more than confessions on the part of the reporters, and they shed little light on the Eisenhower Presidency.

Members of the academic community also confessed. Thus Arthur Schlesinger, Jr., who wrote speeches for Stevenson during the presidential campaigns of 1952 and 1956, was—at the time—critical of Eisenhower for failing to exercise vigorous executive leadership, as Schlesinger's heroes, Andrew Jackson, Franklin Roosevelt, and Harry Truman, had done. Later, after Watergate, Schlesinger wrote *The Imperial Presidency*. In that book, Schlesinger's major criticism of Eisenhower was that Eisenhower went too far in his use of executive powers, especially in his proclamation of the principle of executive privilege when he refused to turn over documents or personnel to McCarthy's investigating committee, and in his insistence on exclusive executive responsibility during foreign-policy crises.

To repeat, then: To say that Eisenhower was right about this or wrong about that is to do little more than announce one's own political position. A more fruitful approach is to examine his years in the White House in his own terms, to make an assessment on the basis of how well he did in achieving the tasks and goals he set for himself at the time he took office.

By that standard, there were many disappointments, domestic and foreign. Eisenhower had wanted to achieve unity within the Republican Party on the basis of bringing the Old Guard into the modern world and the mainstream of American politics. In addition, he wanted to develop within the Republican Party some young, dynamic, trustworthy, and popular leaders. He never achieved either goal, as evidenced by the 1964 Republican Convention, where the Old Guard took control of the party nominating a candidate and writing a platform that would have delighted Warren Harding, or even William McKinley. Franklin Roosevelt did a much better job of curbing the left wing of the Democratic Party than Eisenhower did of curbing the right wing of the Republican Party.

Eisenhower wanted to see Senator McCarthy eliminated from national public life, and he wanted it done without making America's record and image on civil-liberties issues worse than it already was. But because Eisenhower would not denounce McCarthy by name, or otherwise stand up to the senator from Wisconsin, McCarthy was able to do much damage to civil liberties, the Republican party, numerous individuals, the U.S. Army, and the Executive Branch before he finally destroyed himself. Eisenhower's only significant contribution to McCarthy's downfall was the purely negative act of denying him access to executive records and personnel. Eisenhower's cautious, hesitant approach—or nonapproach—to the McCarthy issue did the President's reputation no good, and much harm.

Eisenhower had wanted, in January of 1953, to provide a moral leadership that would both draw on and illuminate America's spiritual superiority to the Soviet Union, indeed to all the world. But on one of the great moral issues of the day, the struggle to eliminate racial segregation from American life, he provided almost no leadership at all. His failure to speak out, to indicate personal approval of *Brown v. Topeka,* did incalculable harm to the civil-rights crusade and to America's image.

Eisenhower had hoped to find a long-term solution for American agriculture that would get the government out of the farming business while strengthening the family farm. In this area, he and Secretary Benson suffered abject failure. The rich grew richer thanks to huge government payments for the Soil Bank, the government in 1961 was more closely and decisively involved in agriculture than it had been in 1953, and the number of family farms had dropped precipitously.

In 1953 Eisenhower had entertained wildly optimistic hopes for the peaceful uses of nuclear power. Electricity too cheap to meter, he believed, was just around the corner, as soon as nuclear power plants went into operation. New trans-ocean canals would be blasted open, artificial harbors created, enormous strides in medicine taken, the world's fertilizer problems solved, the energy for the industrialization of the Third World created. But as he left office in 1961, there had not been any such significant application of nuclear power to civilian purposes.

In foreign affairs. Eisenhower's greatest failure, in his own judgment, which he expressed on innumerable occasions, was the failure to achieve peace. When he left office, the tensions and dangers and costs of the Cold War were higher than they had ever been. In large part, this was no fault of his. He had tried to reach out to the Russians, with Atoms for Peace, Open Skies, and other proposals, only to be rebuffed by Khrushchev. But his own deeply rooted anti-Communism was certainly a contributing factor to the failure. Eisenhower refused to trust the Russians to even the slightest degree. He continued and expanded the economic, political, diplomatic, and covert-operations pressure on the Kremlin for his entire two terms. This was good policy for winning votes, and may even have been good for achieving limited victories in the Cold War, but it was damaging to the cause of world peace.

Allied with the failure to achieve peace was the failure to set a limit on the arms race (never mind actual disarmament, another of his goals). Better than any other world leader, Eisenhower spoke of the cost of the arms race, and its dangers, and its madness. But he could not even slow it down, much less stop it. The great tragedy here is opportunity lost. Eisenhower not only recognized better than anyone else the futility of an arms race; he was in a better position than anyone else to end it. His prestige, especially as a military man, was so overwhelming that he could have made a test ban with the Russians merely on his own assurance that the agreement was good for the United States. But until his last months in office, he accepted the risk of an expanding arms race over the risk of trusting the Russians.

When finally he was ready to make an attempt to control the arms race by accepting an unsupervised comprehensive test ban, the U-2 incident intervened. Fittingly the flight that Powers made was one Eisenhower instinctively wanted to call off, but one that his technologists insisted was necessary. In this case, as in the case of building more nuclear weapons, holding more tests, or building more rockets, he allowed the advice of his technical people to override his own common sense. That this could happen to Eisenhower illustrates vividly the tyranny of technology in the nuclear/missile age.

Another area of failure came in the Third World, which Eisenhower had hoped to line up with the Western democracies in the struggle against Russia. In large part, this failure was caused by Eisenhower's anti-Communism coupled with his penchant for seeing Communists wherever a social reform movement or a struggle for national liberation was under way. His overthrow of popularly elected governments in Iran and Guatemala, his hostility toward Nasser, his refusal to seek any form of accommodation with Castro, his extreme overreaction to events in the Congo, were one result. Another was a profound mistrust of the United States by millions of residents of the Third World. A third result of his oversimplifications was an overcommitment in Indochina, based on an obsession with falling dominoes.

In Central and Eastern Europe, Eisenhower had hoped to take the offensive against Communism. But his unrealistic and ineffective belligerency combined with his party's irresponsible advocacy of uprisings and liberation within a police state, produced the tragedy of Hungary in 1956, which will stand forever as a blot on Eisenhower's record. In his Administration, "roll back" never got started, as "stand pat" became the watchword. But the free world was not even able to stand pat, as Eisenhower accepted an armistice in Korea that left the Communists in control in the north, another in Vietnam that did the same, and the presence of Castro in Cuba.

These failures, taken together, make at first glance a damning indictment. According to Eisenhower's critics, they came about because of the greatest shortcoming of all, the failure to exert leadership. In contrast to FDR and Truman, Eisenhower seemed to be no leader at all, but only a chairman of the board, or even a figurehead, a Whig President in a time that demanded dramatic exercise of executive power. Eisenhower was sensitive about this charge, which he had heard so many times. When Henry Luce made it, in an August 1960 *Life* editorial, Eisenhower took time to provide Luce with a private explanation of his methods—"not to defend," Eisenhower insisted, "merely to explain."

He realized, he told Luce, that many people thought "I have been too easy a boss." What such people did not realize, he pointed out, was that except for his "skimpy majority" in his first two years, "I have had to deal with a Congress controlled by the opposition and whose partisan antagonism to the Executive Branch has often been blatantly displayed." To make any progress at all, he had to use methods "calculated to attract cooperation," and could not afford "to lash out at partisan charges and publicityseeking demagogues." In addition, the government of the United States had become "too big, too complex, and too pervasive in its influence for one individual to pretend to direct the details of its important and critical programming." Nothing could be accomplished without competent assistants; to command their loyalty, the President had to be willing to show patience, understanding, a readiness to delegate authority, and an acceptance of responsibility for honest errors.

Finally Eisenhower concluded, "In war and in peace I've had no respect for the desk-pounder, and have despised the loud and slick talker. If my own ideas and practices in this matter have sprung from weakness, I do not know. But they were and are deliberate or, rather, natural to me. They are not accidental."

Shortly after Eisenhower left office, his successor suffered an embarrassing defeat at the Bay of Pigs. In passing his own judgment on the event, Eisenhower concentrated his criticism on Kennedy's failure to consult with the NSC before deciding to act. He chided Kennedy for not gathering together in one room representatives of every point of view, so that he could hear both the pros and the cons. Since Eisenhower made such a major point of this failure to consult, it is only fair to apply the same standard to Eisenhower's own Administration. How well did he listen to every point of view before acting?

In some cases, fully. In other cases, hardly at all. In the various Far East crises that began with Korea in 1952 and continued through Dien Bien Phu, the Geneva Conference of 1954, and Formosa, he consulted with every appropriate department and agency, listened carefully to every point of view, and acted only after he was satisfied he had taken everything into consideration and was prepared for all possible consequences. But in other areas, he was surprisingly remiss. He did not give the anti-McCarthy people a full hearing, for example, and only once met with Negro leaders on civil-rights issues. Until 1958, he allowed himself to be isolated from the nuclear scientists opposed to testing. On national defense, he gave the proponents of more spending every opportunity to express their views, but except for one meeting with Senator Taft in 1953 he never listened to those who urged dramatic cuts. Advocates of more spending for domestic social programs or for tax cuts seldom got near Eisenhower. He kept the U-2 such a closely guarded secret that only insiders who were proponents of the program ever gave him advice on how to utilize the spy plane.

But on major questions involving the European allies, he consulted with the heads of government in Paris, Bonn, and London before acting (except at Suez; and the failure to consult there was no fault of his). His record, in short, was mixed, and hardly pure enough to justify his extreme indignation at Kennedy for Kennedy's failure to consult the NSC before acting at the Bay of Pigs.

How effective, if not dramatic, Eisenhower's leadership techniques were can be seen in a brief assessment of his accomplishments as President, an assessment once again based on his own goals and aspirations. First and foremost, he presided over eight years of prosperity, marred only by two minor recessions. By later standards, it was a decade of nearly full employment and no inflation.

Indeed by almost every standard—GNP, personal income and savings, home buying, auto purchases, capital investment, highway construction, and so forth—it was the best decade of the century. Surely Eisenhower's fiscal policies, his refusal to cut taxes or increase defense spending, his insistence on a balanced budget, played some role in creating this happy situation.

Under Eisenhower, the nation enjoyed domestic peace and tranquillity—at least as measured against the sixties. One of Eisenhower's major goals in 1953 was to lower the excesses of political rhetoric and partisanship. He managed to achieve that goal, in a negative way, by not dismantling the New Deal, as the Old Guard wanted to do. Under Eisenhower, the number of people covered by Social Security doubled as benefits went up. The New Deal's regulatory commissions stayed in place. Expenditures for public works were actually greater under Eisenhower than they had been under FDR or Truman. Nor were Eisenhower's public works of the boondoggle variety—the St. Lawrence Seaway and the Interstate Highway System made an enormous contribution to the economy. Eisenhower, in effect, put a Republican stamp of approval on twenty years of

Democratic legislation, by itself a major step toward bringing the two parties closer together. Eisenhower's positive contribution to domestic peace and tranquillity was to avoid partisanship himself. His close alliance with the southern Democrats, his refusal to ever denounce the Democratic Party as a whole (he attacked only the "spender" wing), his insistence on a bipartisan foreign policy, his careful cultivation of the Democratic leaders in Congress, all helped tone down the level of partisan excess. When Eisenhower came into the White House, his party was accusing the other party of "twenty years of treason." The Democrats in turn were charging that the Republicans were the party of Depression. When Eisenhower left office, such ridiculous charges were seldom heard.

In 1953, Eisenhower had also set as a major goal the restoration of dignity to the office of the President. He felt, strongly, that Truman had demeaned the office. Whether Truman was guilty of so doing depended on one's perception, of course, but few would argue against the claim that in his bearing, his actions, his private and social life, and his official duties as head of state, Eisenhower maintained his dignity. He looked, acted, and sounded like a President.

He was a good steward. He did not sell off the public lands, or open the National Wilderness Areas or National Parks to commercial or mineral exploitation. He retained and expanded TVA. He stopped nuclear testing in the atmosphere, the first world statesman to do so, because of the dangers of radiation to the people who had chosen him as their leader.

In the field of civil rights, he felt he had done as well as could be done. His greatest contribution (albeit one that he had grown increasingly unhappy about) was the appointment of Earl Warren as Chief Justice. In addition, he had completed the desegregation of the armed forces, and of the city of Washington, D.C., as well as all federal property. He had sponsored and signed the first civil-rights legislation since Reconstruction. When he had to, he acted decisively in Little Rock in 1957. These were all positive, if limited, gains. Eisenhower's boast was that they were made without riots, and without driving the white South to acts of total desperation. Progress in desegregation, especially in the schools, was painfully slow during the Eisenhower years, but he was convinced that anything faster would have produced a much greater and more violent white southern resistance.

In 1952, when he accepted the Republican nomination for the Presidency, Eisenhower called the party to join him in a "crusade." Its purpose was to clean the crooks and the Commies (really, the Democrats) out of Washington. Once those tasks had been accomplished, Eisenhower's critics found it difficult to discover what his crusade was aiming at. There was no stirring call to arms, no great moral cause, no idealistic pursuit of some overriding national goal. Eisenhower, seemingly, was quite content to preside over a fat, happy, satisfied nation that devoted itself to enjoying life, and especially the material benefits available in the greatest industrial power in the world. There was truth in the charge. Eisenhower's rebuttal also contained an elementary truth. The Declaration of Independence stated that one of man's inalienable rights was the pursuit of happiness. Eisenhower tried, with much success, to create a climate in the 1950s in which American citizens could fully exercise that right.

His greatest successes came in foreign policy and the related area of national defense spending. By making peace in Korea, and avoiding war thereafter for the next seven and one-half years, and by holding down, almost single-handedly, the pace of the arms race, he achieved his major accomplishments. No one knows how much money he saved the United States, as he rebuffed Symington and the Pentagon and the JCS and the AEC and the military-industrial complex. And no one knows how many lives he saved by ending the war in Korea and refusing to enter any others, despite a half-dozen and more virtually unanimous recommendations that he go to war. He made peace, and he kept the peace. Whether any other man could have led the country through that decade without going to war cannot be known. What we do know is that Eisenhower did it. Eisenhower boasted that "the United States never lost a soldier or a foot of ground in my administration. We kept the peace. People asked how it happened—by God, it didn't just happen, I'll tell you that."

Beyond keeping the peace, Eisenhower could claim that at the end of his eight years, the NATO alliance, that bedrock of American foreign policy, was stronger than ever. Relations with the Arab states, considering the American moral commitment to Israel, were as good as could be expected. Except for Cuba, the Latin-American republics remained friendly to the United States. In the Far East, relations with America's partners, South Korea, Japan, and Formosa, were excellent (they were still nonexistent with the Chinese). South Vietnam seemed well on the road to becoming a viable nation. Laos was admittedly in trouble, but it appeared to be the only immediate danger spot.

What Eisenhower had done best was managing crises. The crisis with Syngman Rhee in early 1953, and the simultaneous crisis with the Chinese Communists over the POW issue and the armistice; the crisis over Dien Bien Phu in 1954, and over Quemoy and Matsu in 1955; the Hungarian and Suez crises of 1956; the Sputnik and Little Rock crises of 1957; the Formosa Resolution crisis of 1958; the Berlin crisis of 1959; the U-2 crisis of 1960—Eisenhower managed each one without overreacting, without going to war, without increasing defense spending, without frightening people half out of their wits. He downplayed each one, insisted that a solution could be found, and then found one. It was a magnificent performance.

His place in history is, of course, a relative matter. He has to be judged against other Presidents, which means that no judgment can be fair, because he did not have the opportunities, nor face the dangers, that other Presidents did. We cannot know how great a leader he might have been, because he ruled in a time that required him, at least in his own view, to adopt a moderate course, to stay in the middle of the road, to avoid calling on his fellow citizens for some great national effort. He did not face the challenges that Washington did, or Lincoln, or Franklin Roosevelt. How he would have responded to setting precedents, rather than following them, or to a Civil War, or to a Depression, or to a world war, we cannot know. What we do know is that he guided his country safely and securely through a dangerous decade.

Shortly after Eisenhower left office, a national poll of American historians placed him nearly at the bottom of the list of Presidents. By the early 1980s, a new poll placed him ninth. His reputation is likely to continue to rise, perhaps even to the point that he will be ranked just below Washington, Jefferson, Jackson, Lincoln, Wilson, and Franklin Roosevelt.

In attempting to assess the Eisenhower Presidency, certain comparisons must be made. Since Andrew Jackson's time, only four men have served eight consecutive years or more in the White House—Grant, Wilson, Franklin D. Roosevelt, and Eisenhower. Of these four, only two—Grant and Eisenhower—were world figures before they became President. Of the four, only two—Eisenhower and Roosevelt—were more popular when they left office than when they entered. In contrast to his Democratic predecessors and successors, Eisenhower kept the peace; in contrast to his Republican successors, Eisenhower both balanced the budget and stopped inflation.

Eisenhower gave the nation eight years of peace and prosperity. No other President in the twentieth century could make that claim. No wonder that millions of Americans felt that the country was damned lucky to have him.

The Cycles of American History

Eisenhower

Eisenhower never sank so low as Hoover in the esteem of historians, but his comeback has been still more impressive. The fashion in the 1980s is to regard Hoover rather as Hoover himself regarded Prohibition—"a great social and economic experiment, noble in motive and far-reaching in purpose." He is seen as a deep social thinker but as a failed statesman. Eisenhower, on the other hand, has come with time to be seen as above all a successful statesman. The year after he left office, historians and political scientists in my fathers's poll of 1962 rated him twenty-second among American Presidents. In a poll taken by Steve Neal of the *Chicago Tribune* twenty years later, Eisenhower rose to ninth place. In Professor Robert K. Murray's poll the next year he finished eleventh. (Hoover meanwhile, despite revisionist ardor, dropped from nineteenth in 1962 to twenty-first in 1982 and 1983 polls.)

There are obvious reasons for Eisenhower's upward mobility. At the time the 1950s seemed an era of slumber and stagnation, the bland leading the bland. After intervening years of schism and hysteria, the Eisenhower age appears in nostalgic retrospect a blessed decade of peace and harmony Moreover, the successive faults of Eisenhower's successors—Kennedy's activism, Johnson's obsessions, Nixon's crookedness, Ford's mediocrity, Carter's blah, Reagan's ideology—have given his virtues new value. Historians should not overlook the capacity of Presidents to do more for the reputations of their predecessors than for their own. The final impetus was provided by the swing of the political cycle back to the private-interest mood of Eisenhower's own Presidency.

The opening of the papers in the Eisenhower Library in Abilene, Kansas, has speeded the revaluation by placing his character in striking new light. When he was President, most Americans cherished him as the national hero reigning benignly in the White House, a wise, warm, avuncular man who grinned a lot and kept the country calm and safe. His critics, whom he routed in two presidential elections, saw him as an old duffer who neglected his job, tripped up in his syntax, read Westerns, played golf and bridge with millionaires and let strong associates run the country in his name, a "captive hero." Both views assumed his kindness of heart and benevolence of spirit.

The Eisenhower papers powerfully suggest that the pose of guileless affability was a deliberate put-on and that behind the masquerade an astute leader moved purposefully to achieve his objectives. Far from being an openhearted lover of mankind, Eisenhower now appears a wily fellow, calculating, crafty and unerringly self-protective. Far from being a political innocent, he was a politician of the first water, brilliantly exploiting the popular illusion that he was above politics. Far from being an amiable bumbler, he feigned his incoherence to conceal his purposes. Far from being passive and uninterested, he had large and vigorous concerns about public policy.

The man who emerges, for example, from *The Eisenhower Diaries* is shrewd, confident and masterful. He is hard and cold in his judgement of his associates. Some entries reveal the famous Eisenhower temper. ("One thing that might help win this war is to get someone to shoot King," he wrote in 1942 about the imperious Chief of Naval Operations.) Others betray, while denying, his ambition. Occasional passages of ponderous philosophizing read as if they had been carefully indited for posterity.

We thought at the time that he lacked political experience. How wrong we were! Politics has few tougher training schools than the United States Army. Eisenhower, who began as a protégé of General MacArthur and then rose to eminence as a protégé of MacArthur's detested rival, General Marshall, was obviously endowed with consummate political talent. His later skill as President in distancing himself from his unpopular party infuriated Republican professionals but testified to his dazzling instinct for survival.

We must assume now that, however muddled he often appeared, Eisenhower knew perfectly what he was up to most of the time—not least when he encouraged his fellow citizens to think of him as (Good Old) Ike. Once, when the State Department pleaded with him to say nothing in a press conference about the then explosive question of Quemoy and Matsu, the besieged islands off the coast of China, he told James Hagerty, his press secretary, "Don't worry Jim, if that question comes up, I'll just confuse them." He confused us all. As Richard Nixon put it, Eisenhower was "a far more complex and devious man than most people realized, and in the best sense of those words."

Martin Van Buren, John Randolph of Roanoke once said, "rowed to his object with muffled oars." Phrased less elegantly, this is Fred I. Greenstein's thesis in his influential study of Eisenhower's administrative techniques. Greenstein ascribes six "political strategies" to Eisenhower—"hidden-hand" leadership; "instrumental"—i.e., manipulative—use of language; refusal to engage in personalities; taking action nevertheless on the basis of private personality analysis; selective delegation; and building public support. While the author concedes that these strategies were hardly exclusive to Eisenhower, the loving care with which they are described gives the impression of attributing uniquely to Eisenhower practices that are the stock in trade of political leaders. Thus: "Eisenhower ran organizations by deliberately making simultaneous use of both formal and informal organizations." What President does not?

I do not think that Greenstein fully considers the implications of a "hidden-hand Presidency." For in a democracy, politics must be in the end an educational process, resting above all on persuasion and consent. The Presidency, in Franklin D. Roosevelt's words, is "preeminently a place of moral leadership." The hidden-hand Presidency represents an abdication of the preeminent presidential role. The concept is even a little unjust to Eisenhower, who was not entirely averse to using the Presidency as a pulpit.

On the whole, however, as his political confidant Arthur Larson later wrote, "He simply did not believe that the President should exploit his influence as a dominant national figure to promote good causes that were not within his constitutional function as Chief Executive." In consequence, Larson regretfully continued, Eisenhower denied the country the "desperately needed ... educational guidance and moral inspiration that a President with a deep personal commitment to the promotion of human rights could supply." Larson was talking about civil rights. His point applies equally to civil liberties.

Racial justice and McCarthyism were the great moral issues of the Eisenhower years. Eisenhower evaded them both. This may be in part because of his severely constricted theory of the Presidency. But it was partly too because Eisenhower did not see them as compelling issues. He did not like to use law to enforce racial integration, and, while he disliked McCarthy's manners and methods, he basically agreed with his objectives. His failure, as his biographer Stephen E. Ambrose has said, "to speak out directly on McCarthy encouraged the witch-hunters, just as his failure to speak out directly on the *Brown v. Topeka* [school integration] decision encouraged the segregationists." It can be added that Eisenhower's failure to speak out directly on the Pentagon, at least before his Farewell Address, encouraged the advocates of the arms race.

Yet, whatever his defects as a public leader, we may stipulate that behind the scene Eisenhower showed more energy, interest, purpose, cunning and command than many of us understood in the 1950s; that he was the dominant figure in his administration whenever he wanted to be (and he wanted to be more often than it seemed at the time); and that the very talent for self-protection that led him to hide behind his reputation for muddle and to shove associates into the line of fire obscured his considerable capacity for decision and control....

It is on his handling of the problems of peace and war that Eisenhower's enhanced reputation rests. Robert A. Divine conveniently sums up the case for "a badly underrated President" in his *Eisenhower and the Cold War* (1981):

> For eight years he kept the United States at peace, adroitly avoiding military involvement in the crises of the 1950s. Six months after taking office, he brought the fighting in Korea to an end; in Indochina, he resisted intense pressure to avoid direct American military intervention; in Suez, he courageously aligned the United States against European imperialism while maintaining a staunch posture toward the Soviet Union. He earnestly sought a reduction in Cold War tensions.

Professor Divine draws a particular contrast with his predecessor, claiming that the demands of foreign policy outran Truman's ability and that the result was overreaction and tragedy for the nation and the world."

In fact, Eisenhower thought that Truman underreacted to the Soviet menace. "In the fiscal years, 1947, 1948, 1949, and 1950," Eisenhower wrote in his diary the day after his inauguration, "the defense fabric continued to shrink at an alarming extent—and this in spite of frequent... warnings that people like Jim Forrestal had been expressing time and time again." Forrestal had been Eisenhower's mentor regarding the "threat by the monolithic mass of communistic imperialism." When Forrestal killed himself in 1949, Eisenhower recalled their talks in 1945 about the Russians: "He insisted they hated us, which I had good reason to believe myself. I still do." In May 1953 Eisenhower complained to the legislative leaders that Truman "had let our armed forces dwindle after World War II and had thus invited the attack on Korea....

Eisenhower fully accepted the premises of the Cold War. He appointed the high priest of the Cold War as his Secretary of State. He allowed Dulles to appease Joe McCarthy, to purge the Foreign Service, to construct a network of military pacts around the globe and to preach interminably about godless communism and going to the brink and massive retaliation. Lord Salisbury, the quintessential British Tory and a leading figure in the Churchill cabinet, found Eisenhower in 1953 "violently Russophobe, greatly more so than Dulles," and believed him "personally responsible for the policy of useless pinpricks and harassing tactics the U.S. is following against Russia in Europe and the Far East."

Eisenhower's superiority to the other Cold War Presidents, revisionists argue, lay not in the premises of policy but in the "prudence" with which he conducted the struggle. It is true that, as a former general, Eisenhower was uniquely equipped among recent Presidents to override the national security establishment. Convinced that excessive government spending and deficits would wreck the economy, he kept the defense budget under control. He knew too much about war to send regular troops into combat lightly, especially on unpromising Third World terrain. Perhaps for this as well as for budgetary reasons —nuclear weapons cost less than large conventional forces—he contrived a military posture that made it almost impossible for the United States to fight anything short of nuclear war.

The doctrine of massive retaliation left the United States the choice, when confronted by local aggression in a distant land, of dropping the bomb or doing nothing. Eisenhower's critics feared he would drop the bomb. Most of the time his preference was for doing nothing—not always a bad attitude in foreign affairs. When the Democrats took over in 1961, they briskly increased conventional forces. Their theory was that enlarging the capability to fight limited wars would reduce the risk of nuclear war. The result was the creation of forces that enabled and emboldened us to Americanize the war in Vietnam. Had the Eisenhower all-or-nothing strategy survived, we might have escaped that unmitigated disaster. Or we might have had something far worse.

Eisenhower's budgetary concerns—"a bigger bang for a buck"—and his skepticism about the regular Army and Navy also had their disadvantages. They led him to rely exceptionally, and dangerously, on unconventional forms of coercive power: upon the covert operations of the Central Intelligence Agency, and upon nuclear weapons.

❧❦❧

Professor Divine in his apologia declines to write about CIA covert action "because the evidence on Eisenhower's role is not yet available." This is surprising from such a competent historian. *Eisenhower and the Cold War* was published five years after the many revealing volumes of the Church Committee inquiry had become available. Indeed, in the same year of *Eisenhower and the Cold War* two other books—*Ike's Spies* by Stephen E. Ambrose with R. H. Immerman and *The Declassified Eisenhower* by Blanche Wiesen Cook—submit an impressive amount of evidence about Eisenhower and the CIA. Moreover, the CIA is central to any work purporting to discuss Eisenhower and the Cold War.

Instead of sending regular forces into combat abroad, Eisenhower silently turned the CIA into the secret army of the executive branch. The CIA, as originally conceived in 1947, was supposed to concentrate on the collection and analysis of intelligence. Covert action began in 1948 under the Truman administration, and there was more of it than Truman later remembered (or knew about?). But it was mostly devoted to supporting friends—socialist and Christian trade unions, Italian Christian Democrats, anti-Stalinist intellectuals —rather than to subverting foes. As Kermit Roosevelt, the CIA operative in Iran, has written about his project of overthrowing the Mossadegh government, "We had, I felt sure, no chance to win approval from the outgoing administration of Truman and Acheson. The new Republicans, however, might be quite different."

Indeed they were. Where Truman had seen Mossadegh as an honest if trying nationalist, Eisenhower saw him as a tool of Moscow. Eisenhower, as Anthony Eden, the British Foreign Minister, reported to Churchill, "seemed obsessed by the fear of a Communist Iran." The new President promptly gave Kim Roosevelt the green light. In August 1953 the CIA overthrew Mossadegh and restored the Shah. (One result of this disruption of indigenous political evolution in Iran was to stir resentments that after festering a quarter century overthrew the Shah in 1979. By that time Washington would have been delighted if it could have had a Mossadegh rather than a Khomeini.)

His thorough and generally approved biographer Stephen E. Ambrose has noted Eisenhower's "penchant for seeing Communists wherever a social reform movement or a struggle for national liberation was under way." He saw Communists next in the reformist Arbenz government in Guatemala. The domino theory was already forming itself in Eisenhower's mind. "My God," he told his cabinet, "just think what it would mean to us if Mexico went Communist!" Exhilarated by success in Iran, the CIA overthrew the Arbenz regime in 1954.

Exhilarated once more, the CIA helped install supposedly pro-western governments in Egypt (1954) and Laos (1959), tried to overthrow the Indonesian government (1958) and organized the expedition of Cuban exiles against Castro (1960). In December 1955 Eisenhower specifically ordered the CIA to "develop underground resistance and facilitate covert and guerrilla preparations... to the extent practicable" in the Soviet Union, China, and their satellites; and to "counter any threat of a party or individuals directly or indirectly responsive to Communist control to achieve dominant power in a free-world country."

The CIA evidently construed the verb "counter" in drastic fashion. There are indications that CIA operatives in 1955 blew up the plane on which Chou En-Lai was scheduled to fly to the Afro-Asian conference in Bandung, Indonesia. There is no question about later CIA assassination attempts in the Eisenhower years against Castro and against the Congolese leader Patrice Lumumba. There is no evidence, however, that these operations were undertaken with Eisenhower's knowledge or approval. Given the strong evidence that the CIA so often acted on its own, one may well conclude that assassination was another of its private initiatives.

By 1956 the CIA was spending $800 million a year for covert action as against $82 million in 1952. That same year Eisenhower created a President's Board of Consultants on Foreign Intelligence Activities. Its members were private citizens of unimpeachable respectability (One was Joseph P. Kennedy, who remarked about the CIA after the Bay of Pigs, "I know that outfit, and I wouldn't pay them a hundred bucks a week.") The Board promptly commissioned Robert A. Lovett and David Bruce to take a look at the CIA's covert action boom.

Lovett had been Secretary of Defense and Undersecretary of State. Bruce had run the Office of Strategic Services in the European Theater of Operations and was a distinguished diplomat. Their report was stern and devastating. Those who made the 1948 decision to start a program of covert action, Lovett and Bruce said, "could not possibly have foreseen the ramifications of the operations which have resulted from it." CIA agents were making mischief around the planet, and "no one, other than those in the CIA immediately concerned with their day to day operation, has any detailed knowledge what is going on." Should not someone in authority, Lovett and Bruce asked, be continuously calculating "the long-range wisdom of activities which have entailed our virtual abandonment of the international 'golden rule,' and which, if successful to the degree claimed for them, are responsible in a great measure for stirring up the turmoil and raising the doubts about us that exist in many countries of the world today?" If we continue on this course, they concluded, "Where will we be tomorrow?"

Where indeed? The Board endorsed the report and warned Eisenhower in February 1957 that CIA covert action was "autonomous and free-wheeling" and that few projects received the formal approval of the 5412 Special Group, the National Security Council's review mechanism. In 1958 the Board asked Eisenhower to reconsider "programs which find us involved covertly in the internal affairs of practically every country to which we have access." Eisenhower paid no attention. In 1959 his own Special Assistant for National Security, Gordon Gray, told him that the 5412 Committee had little control over covert operations. The Committee began to meet more regularly, but the CIA continued to keep it in the dark—on assassination plots, for example. In its last written report to Eisenhower (January 1961) the Board declared that CIA covert action was not worth the risk, money and manpower it involved and had detracted "substantially" from the execution of the CIA'S "primary intelligence-gathering mission." The Board begged still one more time for "a total reassessment of our covert action policies."

Though this material was published in 1978, it was ignored both by Divine and by Ambrose. Eisenhower revisionism generally obscures Eisenhower's decisive personal role in converting the CIA from an intelligence agency into an instrument for American intervention around the world. This was a sea change from Truman's CIA. As Lovett told the Bay of Pigs board of inquiry in 1961, "I have never felt that the Congress of the United States ever intended to give the United States Intelligence Agency authority to conduct operations all over the earth."

Eisenhower did not bring this change about through inattention or inadvertence. The Second World War had persuaded him of the value of covert action, and CIA excesses during his Presidency did not shake his faith. He strongly opposed Senator Mike Mansfield's resolution calling for a joint congressional committee to oversee the CIA, telling one Republican congressman that "this kind of bill would be passed over my dead body." In his conference with President-elect Kennedy the day before the inauguration, Eisenhower observed of the CIA's anti-Castro expedition, "It was the policy of this government to help such forces to the utmost" and urgently recommended to Kennedy that "this effort be continued and accelerated."

Eisenhower's faith in covert action produced mindless international meddling that exacerbated the Cold War, angered American allies and in later years rebounded fiercely against American interests. Moreover, by nourishing and cherishing the CIA more than any President before Reagan had done, Eisenhower released a dangerous virus in American society and life.

⋅❀⋅

We are sensitive these days about the limitless horror of nuclear war. Revisionist historians condemn Truman for his allegedly unrepentant decision to drop the bomb in 1945. In fact, Truman behaved like a man much shaken by the decision. He had directed that the bomb be used "so that military objectives ... are the target and not women and children," and he was considerably disturbed when he learned that most of those killed at Hiroshima were civilians. . . .

Revisionist historians are similarly severe in condemning Kennedy for running the risk of nuclear war to get the Soviet missiles out of Cuba in 1962. They seem strangely unconcerned, however, that Eisenhower used the threat of nuclear war far more often than any other American President has done, before or since. Nuclear blackmail was indeed the almost inevitable consequence of the military posture dictated by "massive retaliation." It is said in his defense that Eisenhower used the threat in a context of American nuclear superiority that minimized the risk. But the same condition of nuclear superiority prevailed for, and must equally absolve, Truman and Kennedy.

Eisenhower began by invoking the nuclear threat to end the fighting in Korea. He let the Chinese know, he later told Lyndon Johnson, that "he would not feel constrained about crossing the Yalu, or using nuclear weapons." Probably the effectiveness of this threat has been exaggerated. The Chinese had compelling reasons of their own to get out of the war. The decisive shift in their position away from the forced repatriation of prisoners of war took place, as McGeorge Bundy has pointed out, after the death of Stalin in March 1953—and before Eisenhower sent his signals to Peking. In May 1953 General J. Lawton Collins, the Army Chief of Staff, declared himself "very skeptical about the value of using atomic weapons tactically in Korea." Eisenhower replied that "it might be cheaper, dollar-wise, to use atomic weapons in Korea than to continue to use conventional weapons." If the Chinese persisted, "it would be necessary to expand the war outside of Korea and . . . to use the atomic bomb." In December, Eisenhower said that, if the Chinese attacked again, "we should certainly respond by hitting them hard and wherever it would hurt most, including Peiping itself. This . . . would mean all-out war." A joint memorandum from the State Department and the Joint Chiefs of Staff called for the use of atomic weapons against military targets in Korea, Manchuria and China.

The next crisis came in 1954 in Vietnam. In March, according to Divine, Eisenhower was "briefly tempted" by the idea of American intervention, refusing, as he put it, to "exclude the possibility of a single [air] strike, if it were almost certain this would produce decisive results. . . . Of course, if we did, we'd have to deny it forever." As envisaged by General Twining of the Air Force and Admiral Radford, the strike would involve three atomic bombs. Opposition by Congress and by the British killed the idea. Whether this was Eisenhower's hope when he permitted Dulles to carry the air strike proposal to London remains obscure. It was at this time that he propounded what he called "the 'falling domino' principle . . . a beginning of a disintegration that would have the most profound influences," a disintegration that, he said, could lead to the loss of Indochina, then Burma, then Thailand, Malaya, Indonesia, then Japan, Formosa and the Philippines. This theory of the future entrapped Eisenhower's successors in the quicksands of Vietnam. The dominos did indeed fall in Indochina, as we all know now. But, with communist China invading communist Vietnam because communist Vietnam had invaded communist Cambodia, the dominos fell against each other, not against the United States.

Whatever Eisenhower's intentions regarding Vietnam, he definitely endorsed in May 1954 the recommendation by the Joint Chiefs to use atomic bombs in case of Chinese intervention if Congress and allies agreed. "The concept" in the event of a large-scale Vietminh attack, Dulles said in October, "envisions a fight with nuclear weapons rather than commitment of ground forces."

Eisenhower tried nuclear blackmail again during the Quemoy-Matsu crisis of 1955. In March of that year Dulles publicly threatened the use of atomic weapons. Eisenhower added the next day in his press conference, "I see no reason why they shouldn't be used just exactly as you would use a bullet or anything else." In the 1958 replay of the Quemoy-Matsu drama, Dulles said that American intervention would probably not be effective if limited to conventional weapons; "the risk of a more extensive use of nuclear weapons, and even of general war, would have to be accepted." "There [is] no use of having stuff,"

Dulles remarked over the phone to General Twining, "and never being able to use it."

"The beauty of Eisenhower's policy," Divine writes with regard to Quemoy and Matsu, "is that to this day no one can be sure whether or not... he would have used nuclear weapons." Nuclear blackmail may strike some as the beauty part, though we did not used to think so when Khrushchev tried it. In Eisenhower's case it was associated with an extraordinary effort to establish the legitimacy of nuclear war. One restraint on the use of the bomb was the opposition of American allies and of world opinion. This resistance Eisenhower was determined to overcome. As Dulles told the National Security Council on 31 March 1953, while "in the present state of world opinion we could not use an A-bomb, we should make every effort now to dissipate this feeling." The minutes of the meeting add: "The President and Secretary Dulles were in complete agreement that somehow or other the tabu which surrounds the use of atomic weapons would have to be destroyed." ...

In December 1954 Eisenhower ordered the Atomic Energy Commission to relinquish control of nuclear weapons to the Department of Defense. At the same time, he ordered Defense to deploy overseas a large share of the nuclear arsenal—36 percent of the hydrogen bombs, 42 percent of the atomic bombs—many on the periphery of the Soviet Union. The movement of American policy continued to disturb our British allies. . . .

Eisenhower's persevering effort was to abolish the "firebreak" between conventional and nuclear weapons. Fortunately for the world, this effort failed. By 1964 nearly everyone agreed with Lyndon Johnson when he said, "Make no mistake. There is not such thing as a conventional nuclear weapon."

In the first years in the White House Eisenhower regarded nuclear attack as a usable military option. He had no compunction about threatening such attack. He hoped to destroy the taboo preventing the use of nuclear weapons. But in fact he never used them. As Ambrose points out, "Five times in one year [1954] the experts advised the President to launch an atomic strike against China. Five times he said no." His campaign to legitimate the bomb was happily only a passing phase.

As the Soviet Union increased its nuclear arsenal, Eisenhower came to believe more and more strongly in the horror of nuclear war. The outlook was ever closer, he said in 1956, "to destruction of the enemy and suicide for ourselves." When both sides recognized that "destruction will be reciprocal and complete, possibly we will have sense enough to meet at the conference table with the understanding that the era of armaments has ended and the human race must conform its actions to this truth or die."

For all his early talk about the "same old whore," Eisenhower now sought better relations with the Soviet Union. As Sherman Adams, Eisenhower's chief of staff on domestic matters, later observed, "The hard and uncompromising line that the United States government took toward Soviet Russia and Red China between 1953 and the early months of 1959 was more a Dulles line than an

Eisenhower line." But Dulles retained his uses for Eisenhower, both in frightening the Russians and in enabling the President to reserve for himself the role of man of peace.

In his later mood, Eisenhower strove, less anxiously than Churchill and later Macmillan but a good deal more anxiously than Dulles, to meet the Russians at the conference table. In 1953 at the United Nations he set forth his Atoms for Peace plan, by which the nuclear powers would contribute fissionable materials to an International Atomic Energy Agency to promote peaceful uses of atomic energy. This well-intentioned but feckless proposal assumed that atoms for peace could be segregated from atoms for war—an assumption abundantly refuted in later years and the cause of dangerous nuclear proliferation in our own time. In 1955 at the Geneva summit he came up with a better idea, the creative Open Skies plan. A system of continuous reciprocal monitoring, Eisenhower argued, would reduce fears of surprise attack. The Russians turned Open Skies down as an American espionage scheme. Open Skies was a good idea; it deserves revival. In his second term, against the opposition of many in his own administration, Eisenhower fitfully pursued the project of a nuclear test ban.

He resented the mounting pressure from the Democrats and from the Pentagon to accelerate the American nuclear build-up. The Pentagon did not impress him. He knew all the tricks, having employed them himself. He used to say that he "knew too much about the military to be fooled." He refused to be panicked by perennial Pentagon alarms about how we were falling behind the Russians and dismissed the 'missile gap' of the late 1950s with richly justified skepticism.

Yet he weakly allowed the build-up to proceed. In 1959 he complained that the Pentagon, after agreeing a few years earlier that hitting seventy key targets would knock out the Soviet system, now insisted on hitting thousands of targets. The military, he said, were getting "themselves into an incredible position —of having enough to destroy every conceivable target all over the world, plus a threefold reserve." The radioactivity from atomic blasts at this level, he said, would destroy the United States too. The United States already had a stockpile of "five thousand or seven thousand weapons or whatnot." Why did the Atomic Energy Commission and the Department of Defense want more? "But then," writes Ambrose, "he reluctantly gave way to the AEC and DOD demands."

In 1960, when informed at a National Security Council meeting that the United States could produce almost 400 Minuteman missiles a year, Eisenhower with "obvious disgust" (according to his science adviser George Kistiakowsky) burst out, "Why don't we go completely crazy and plan on a force of 10,000?" The nuclear arsenal had now grown to a level that the Eisenhower of 1954 had considered "fantastic," "crazy" and "unconscionable." There were approximately 1000 nuclear warheads when Eisenhower entered the White House, 18,000 when he left.

For all his concern about nuclear war, for all his skepticism about the Pentagon, for all the unique advantage he enjoyed as General of the Armies in commanding confidence on defense issues, he never seized control of the military-industrial complex. "Being only one person," he lamely explained, he had not felt he could oppose the "combined opinion of all his associates." In the measured judgment of the Regius Professor of History at Oxford, the military historian Michael Howard, "The combination of his constant professions of devotion to disarmament and peace with his reluctance to take any of the harsh decisions required to achieve those professed objectives leaves an impression, if not of hypocrisy, then certainly of an ultimate lack of will which, again, denies him a place in the first rank of world statesmen."

Though Eisenhower carefully avoided war himself, he was surprisingly bellicose in his advice to his successors. He told Kennedy before the inauguration not only to go full speed ahead on the exile invasion of Cuba but, if necessary, "to intervene unilaterally" in Laos. So bent was Eisenhower on American intervention in Laos that Kennedy persuaded Macmillan to explain to him in detail the folly of such an adventure. When Vietnam became the issue in the mid-1960s, Eisenhower advised Lyndon Johnson to avoid gradualism, "go all out," declare war, seek victory, not negotiations, warn China and the Soviet Union, as Eisenhower himself had done over Korea, that the United States might feel compelled to use nuclear weapons to break the deadlock, and, if the Chinese actually came in, "to use at least tactical atomic weapons." The antiwar protest, Eisenhower declare, "verges on treason." When Johnson announced in 1968 that he was stopping most of the bombing of North Vietnam, Eisenhower, Ambrose writes, "was livid with anger, his remarks [to Ambrose] about Johnson's cutting and running unprintable." Eisenhower was more a hawk than a prince of peace.

"It would perhaps have been better for him, as in the last century for Wellington and Grant," Sir John Colville concludes, "if he had rested on his military laurels." Walter Lippmann remarked in 1964 that Eisenhower's was "one of the most falsely inflated reputations of my experience"—and he was speaking before the inflation was under way. In later years the Eisenhower boom has gathered momentum in cyclical response to a need and a time.

In due course the pendulum will doubtless swing back toward the view of Eisenhower presented in the illuminating early memoirs by men close to him—Sherman Adams's *Firsthand Report* (1961), Emmet Hughes's *The Ordeal of Power* (1963), Arthur Larson's *Eisenhower: The President Nobody Knew* (1968). In these works of direct observation, Eisenhower emerges as a man of intelligence, force and restraint who did not always understand and control what was going on, was buffeted by events and was capable of misjudgment and error. I lunched with Emmet Hughes in 1981. "Eisenhower was much more of a President than you liberals thought at the time," he said. "But Eisenhower revisionism has gone too far. Take Fred Greenstein of Princeton, for example. He is a nice fellow. But his thesis these days—Eisenhower the activist President—is a lot of bullshit."

Yet we were wrong to have underestimated Eisenhower's genius for self-presentation and self-preservation—the best evidence of which lies in his capacity to take in a generation of scholars.

POSTSCRIPT

Was Dwight Eisenhower a Great President?

Ambrose believes that Eisenhower's reputation will continue to rise to just a notch below Washington, Jefferson, Jackson, Lincoln, Wilson, and Roosevelt. Schlesinger thinks that the pendulum will push him back to the middle of the pack. Historians may quibble with Schlesinger's view that although Eisenhower has fooled the current generation of scholars, nobody will ever again view him as a kindly, grinning grandfather who read westerns and played golf with millionaires while his aides ran the country.

Most early assessments of Eisenhower were generally lukewarm or critical of his presidency. A good collection of these early appraisals appears in *Eisenhower as President* edited and introduced by Dean Albertson (Hill & Wang, 1963). Revisionist assessments were started in the late 1960s by journalists Murray Kempton and Garry Wills. The fullest portrait is Ambrose's two-volume *Eisenhower* (Simon & Schuster, 1983,1984), a portion of which is the first selection in this issue. Another assessment, Anthony James Joe's "Eisenhower Revisionism and American Politics," in Joann P. Krieg, ed., *Dwight Eisenhower: Soldier, President, Statesman* (Greenwood Press, 1987), is part of a symposium that was held at Hofstra University in March 1984.

The most carefully constructed revisionist analysis of Eisenhower is by Princeton University political scientist Fred I. Greenstein, *The Hidden-Hand Presidency: Eisenhower as Leader* (Basic Books, 1982). His arguments are summarized in "Eisenhower as an Activist President: A Look at New Evidence," *Political Science Quarterly* (Winter 1979–1980) and more recently in "Dwight D. Eisenhower: Leadership Theorist in the White House," in Fred I. Greenstein, ed., *Leadership in the Modern Presidency* (Howard University Press, 1988). The latter book is extremely useful because it contains detailed sketches of every U.S. president from Truman through Reagan.

Greenstein's thesis is fairly simple. Based upon a close examination of Eisenhower's diaries and most intimate personal papers, the author concludes that Eisenhower deliberately employed a convoluted speaking style at his press conferences and used his subordinates to carry out his policies. It remains to be seen whether or not Greenstein's analysis of Eisenhower's presidency will be substantiated by future historians. The postrevisionist critics, as Schlesinger predicted, have already begun to emerge. British historian Piers Brendon recalls how, as a boy of seven, he admired the leader of D-Day and savior of the Western world. Years later he became disillusioned with his hero, and he accused Eisenhower of chronic vacillation and moral obtuseness in *Ike: His Life and Times* (Harper & Row, 1986).

ISSUE 13

Did President Kennedy Effectively Manage the Cuban Missile Crisis?

YES: Theodore C. Sorensen, from *The Kennedy Legacy* (Macmillan, 1969)

NO: Mark J. White, from *The Cuban Missile Crisis* (Macmillan Press Ltd., 1996)

ISSUE SUMMARY

YES: Theodore C. Sorensen, President John F. Kennedy's special assistant, argues that Kennedy effectively managed the Cuban Missile Crisis via a "carefully balanced and precisely measured combination of defense, diplomacy, and dialogue."

NO: Assistant professor of history Mark J. White castigates Kennedy "for the excessive belligerence of his Cuban policies before the missile crisis while praising him for his generally adroit management of the crisis."

In 1959 the political situation in Cuba changed drastically when dictator Fulgencio Batista y Zaldívar was overthrown by a 34-year-old revolutionary named Fidel Castro, who led a guerilla band in the Sierra Maestra mountain range. Unlike his predecessors, Castro refused to be a lackey for American political and business interests. The left-wing dictator seized control of American oil refineries and ordered a number of diplomats at the U.S. Embassy in Havana to leave the country. President Dwight D. Eisenhower was furious. He imposed economic sanctions on the island and broke diplomatic ties shortly before he left office.

In April 1961 Eisenhower's successor, John F. Kennedy, supported an invasion at the Bay of Pigs in Cuba by a group of disaffected anti-Castro Cuban exiles to foster the overthrow of Castro. However, the invasion that took place in April 1961 was a disaster. Castro's army routed the invaders. Many were killed; others were taken prisoner.

The Kennedy administration secured Cuba's removal from the Organization of American States (OAS) in early 1962, imposed an economic embargo on the island, and carried out threatening military maneuvers in the Caribbean.

The isolation and possibility of a second invasion of Cuba probably influenced Soviet premier Nikita Khrushchev to take a more proactive stance to defend Cuba. In summer 1962 the Soviet premier sent troops and conventional weapons to the island. In September launching pads were being installed for medium- and intermediate-range nuclear ballistic missiles.

By September Kennedy was feeling the heat from Republicans such as New York senator Kenneth Keating, who charged that the Russians were bringing not only troops but nuclear weapons to the island. At first Kennedy was concerned with the political implications of the charges for the 1962 congressional races. On September 13 he assured the news reporters that the Cuban military buildup was primarily defensive in nature.

But the situation changed drastically on the morning of October 16 when National Security Council adviser McGeorge Bundy informed the president that pictures from U-2 flights over Cuba revealed that the Russians were building launching pads for 1,000-mile medium-range missiles as well as 2,200-mile intermediate-range ones. The president kept the news quiet. He ordered more U-2 flights to take pictures and had Bundy assemble a select group of advisers who became known as the Executive Committee of the National Security Council, or Ex-Comm. For six days and nights the committee met secretly and considered a wide range of options. By the end of the sixth day, the president favored a blockade, or what he called a "quarantine," of the island. On October 22 Kennedy revealed his plans for a quarantine over national television.

It took six days from the time Kennedy made his announcement for the participants to resolve the crisis. Mark J. White has succinctly summarized the resolution of the Cuban Missile Crisis in the introduction to his edited collection of documents entitled *The Kennedys and Cuba: The Declassified Documentary History* (Ivan R. Dee, 1999):

> During the second week of the crisis, from JFK's October 22 address to the achievement of a settlement six days later, Kennedy and Khrushchev initially fired off messages to each other, defending their own positions and assailing their adversary's. But a series of developments from October 26 to 28 suddenly brought the crisis to an end. Khrushchev's messages to JFK on October 26 and 27 proposed two different settlements: the first was an American pledge not to invade Cuba in return for withdrawal of Russian missiles from the island; the second called for an additional concession from Kennedy, the removal from the Soviet border of America's Jupiter missiles in Turkey. JFK managed to formulate a response to these offers that Khrushchev found acceptable: a public promise not to invade Cuba, and a private commitment to withdraw the Jupiters. The most dangerous episode of the entire cold war era ended, only twelve days after it had begun.

Did President Kennedy effectively manage the Cuban Missile Crisis? In the following selection, Theodore C. Sorensen argues that the president resolved the crisis via a "carefully balanced and precisely measured combination of defense, diplomacy, and dialogue." In the second selection, Mark J. White gives a more critical assessment.

Theodore C. Sorensen **YES**

Performance

The Berlin crisis of 1961, to be sure, had been a tough test of [John F.] Kennedy's mettle. Faced with a dangerous deadline which would have required him to abandon a commitment vital to our interests, confronted with a threatened squeeze too subtle for nuclear response but too serious to ignore, he found that he had inherited a "Berlin Contingency Plan" and a military capability in that area which gave him a choice of either nuclear holocaust or abject humiliation. He found as well that his allies and advisers were divided. Some said, in effect: Refuse to talk and fight if pressed. Others said, in effect: Refuse to fight and yield if pressed. Still others said, in effect: Refuse to fight or talk or yield, but think of something. Kennedy, making clear what we would and would not talk and fight about, shrewdly engaged [Soviet leader Nikita] Khrushchev in a long correspondence and other diplomatic exchanges on the issue, meanwhile building the deterrent power of our conventional forces (and mistakenly inspiring a national civil defense craze) and permitting the deadline to pass without notice.

Soviet long-range missiles in Cuba, however, represented a sudden, immediate and more dangerous and secretive change in the balance of power, in clear contradiction of all U.S. commitments and Soviet pledges. It was a move which required a response from the United States, not for reasons of prestige or image but for reasons of national security in the broadest sense. JFK's obligation as President in October 1962 was to find some way of effecting a removal of those nuclear weapons without either precipitating mankind's final war or trading away anyone's security. It was in a very real sense the world's first armed confrontation between two nuclear superpowers.

Ever since the successful resolution of that crisis, I have noted among many political and military figures a Cuban-missile-crisis syndrome, which calls for a repetition in some other conflict of "Jack Kennedy's tough stand of October 1962 when he told the Russians with their missiles either to pull out or look out!" Some observers even attributed Lyndon Johnson's decision to escalate in Vietnam to a conviction that America's military superiority could bring him a "victory" comparable to JFK's. That badly misread what actually happened. Kennedy himself took pains to point out to [West-German Chancellor Konrad] Adenauer and others that the Cuban outcome was not a "victory," that it was not achieved solely through military might, and that what success we had in this instance—with the Soviets at a geographic and world-opinion disadvantage—could not be counted on in instances, such as Berlin, which more directly affected Soviet security.

It is true that American military force—namely, a barrier of naval vessels around Cuba—before its effectiveness could be rendered less meaningful by the delivery of all missiles to the island, interposed itself against a potential Soviet force on its way to Cuba. It is true that our superiority in deliverable nuclear power, as well as our superiority in naval power, undoubtedly made the Soviets more cautious than they might otherwise have been about physically challenging our naval quarantine or retaliating with the blockade of West Berlin. It is also true that JFK's address sternly warned that any nuclear missile launched from Cuba against any nation in the Western Hemisphere would be regarded as a Soviet attack on the United States "requiring a full retaliatory response upon the Soviet Union." But these facts should not be taken out of context.

Kennedy in fact relied not on force and threats alone but on a carefully balanced and precisely measured combination of defense, diplomacy, and dialogue. He instituted the naval quarantine without waiting for diplomatic efforts, because once such efforts failed (and he was convinced they would fail), it would be too late to prevent completion of the missiles or get them out without more belligerent and dangerous measures. He chose the quarantine in preference to an air attack because it was a measured, limited step, it offered the Russians both room to maneuver and a peaceful way out, and it did not make armed conflict inevitable. He deliberately called it a "quarantine" rather than a "blockade," which is an act of war. He took no action that would risk civilian lives. He authorized no surprise attacks and no needless risk of American lives. He posed the issue as one between two powers restrained by mutual deterrence, instead of making the unpredictable [Fidel] Castro his opposite number.

Despite his anger at being deceived and his awareness that one misstep meant disaster, he remained cool at all times. He refused to issue any ultimatum, to close any doors, or to insist upon any deadlines, noting only that continued work on the missile sites would "justify" (not necessarily insure) further U.S. action. He made clear to the Soviets both in writing and through his brother that the United States was prepared to talk about peace and disarmament generally and about the presence of our missiles in Turkey specifically, once the Soviet provocation to peace had been withdrawn. He placed the dispute before the United Nations and corresponded with Khrushchev about it almost daily. He was careful to obtain sanction for the quarantine under international law, procuring unanimous authorization from the members of a recognized regional defense group, the Organization of American States (OAS), obtaining its members' multilateral participation, and invoking the self-defense provisions of the UN charter.

Even as Soviet ships and work on the missile sites proceeded, he avoided a confrontation that might force the Soviets to attack. Even after an American plane was shot down, he withheld retaliation in the hopes of an early settlement. On the final crucial Saturday night before the missiles were withdrawn, he adjourned our "Ex Comm" meeting as the hawks began to dominate the discussion and to urge an immediate air strike. He achieved a resolution that was in effect negotiated by mail, one that treated both powers as equals and restored the *status quo ante* instead of destroying Castro. Then he refused to crow or claim victory. He was at each step firm but generous to his adversaries and candid with his major allies, with the American public, and with the Congressional leaders, although he gave advance information to no one and sought advance approval from no one.

While oversimplified comparisons of drastically different situations are dangerous, it is interesting to take each of the above standards and apply it to this nation's role in Vietnam. My own view is that we might have avoided the disastrous escalation of that war had Presidents Kennedy and Johnson followed these same standards. I also think it highly possible that, had each of these standards not been followed in the Cuban missile crisis, this planet might now be in ashes. The medium-range missile sites under rapid construction in Cuba would all have been operational within a few days, according to the intelligence estimates, and some may already have been prepared to respond to any American attack by firing their deadly salvos upon the southeastern United States.

Some ask: What if Khrushchev had not backed down? Others say: Why did we settle for so little? The real question is: Where would we be if JFK had not pursued the above course and accepted Khrushchev's offer in a way that avoided the need for anyone to back down? It was indeed eyeball-to-eyeball, and fortunately both men blinked. Dean Acheson is right in crediting Kennedy with considerable good luck on this awesome occasion; but there was considerable good judgment as well as luck involved in the President's rejection of alternative recommendations, including the recommendation for bombing the missile sites which came from Acheson himself. (In short, among the ways in which JFK was lucky was in not taking Dean Acheson's advice!)

While some have since accused him of taking action to influence the Congressional elections, JFK at the time was convinced his course would hurt his party in the elections. It seemed clear on that fateful Saturday afternoon, October 20, when he made his decision for the quarantine, that an air strike would be a swifter and more popular means of removing the missiles before Election Day, and that a quarantine would encourage a prolonged UN debate and Republican charges of weakness in the face of peril. Yet he never contemplated changing that course for political reasons. Others have since accused him of overreacting for reasons of personal and national prestige to a move that did not really alter the strategic balance of power or pose an actual threat to our own security. But Kennedy recognized that appearances and reality often merge in world affairs; and if all Latin America had thought that the U.S. had passively permitted what was apparently a new threat to their existence, and if all our Western allies had thought that we would not respond to a sudden, secret deployment of missiles in our own hemisphere, then a whole wave of reactions contrary to our interests and security might well have followed.

Throughout this period the role of Robert Kennedy was unusually important. The President confided to me his concern that his Secretary of State in particular had been disappointingly irresolute during the few days preceding JFK's final formulation of the quarantine policy and too fatigued after guiding a brilliant execution of that policy during the following few days; that the Joint Chiefs of Staff had been dangerously inflexible in their insistence on an all-out military attack as the only course the Soviets would understand; and that sooner or later everyone involved would reflect what both Macmillan and McNamara termed the period of most intense strain they had ever experienced.

But brother Bob displayed not the "emotional dialectics" suggested by some but hardheaded and cool judgment. He was a leader without designation when our little "Executive Committee" group—Rusk, McNamara, Dillon, Bundy, Ball, Taylor, McCone, and a half-dozen others, including me—met with the President. He used his full powers of presence and persistence to extract specific suggestions and objections instead of generalities and to produce concrete progress instead of anxieties. He was instrumental in the early days in rejecting the proposal for surprise attack. He was instrumental in the final days in conveying to the Soviet Ambassador the position that finally prevailed. He helped shape, organize, and monitor the entire effort that remains a standard for all time.

Never before had the Soviets and the Americans peered so clearly at each other down the barrels of their nuclear cannons and contemplated the meaning of attack. The effect was to purge their minds, at least temporarily, of cold-war clichés. If nuclear war were suicidal, if nuclear blackmail were futile, if an accidental nuclear war would be disastrous, surely there had to be a more sensible way of competing against each other than building still more exorbitantly expensive nuclear weapons. The chief lesson learned from this first nuclear crisis was not how to conduct the next one—but how to avoid it.

Thus the air was cleared for John Kenedy's speech on June 10, 1963, at American University, the single most important foreign-policy speech in the entire Kennedy legacy. It summed up his views on peace, "a process, a way of solving problems ... the sum of many acts." It remained Americans that "enmities between nations, as between individuals, do not last forever." It offered friendship to the Russian people and admiration for their many achievements.

> And if we cannot now end our differences, at least we can help make the world safe for diversity. For in the final analysis our most basic common link is that we all inhabit this planet. We all breathe the same air. We all cherish our children's future. And we are all mortal.

That speech, Khrushchev indicated later, helped pave the way for the Nuclear Test Ban Treaty aimed at ending the radioactive poisoning of the atmosphere. Obtaining the Senate's consent to the ratification of that treaty was JFK's proudest moment, fulfilling one of his first priorities—but it was also the result of Kennedy at his educational best. The treaty was opposed by the chairman of the Senate Armed Service Committee, by the Senator who became the next Republican nominee for President, by three former Chiefs of Staff, and by other notables. Such a combination would normally have had enough to block the necessary two-thirds vote. Kennedy, fearing a repetition of Wilson's experience with the League of Nations, worked on his Joint Chiefs, on Minority Leader Everett Dirksen, on the Armed Services Preparedness Subcommittee, on the Joint Atomic Energy Committee, on every individual Senator he could, and on public opinion directly and indirectly. He was eminently successful.

Nor was he content with that one treaty. Like his brother Bob, he wanted his speeches remembered not for the words he used but for the action that resulted. In a period of a few months, he reached agreement with Moscow on a "hot line" for emergency communications, on banning weapons of mass destruction from outer space, on the first sale of surplus American wheat to the Soviet Union, on joint efforts regarding weather and communications space satellites, and on a cooperative program in nuclear studies. Earlier he had expanded cultural and scientific exchanges with the U.S.S.R., proposed mutual increases in consulates, removed at least one major trade restriction, offered a specific plan to implement the Soviet slogan of general and complete disarmament, conferred and corresponded with Soviet Chairman Khrushchev, and spoken directly to the Russian people via a front-page interview in *Izvestia*.

In his address to the United Nations two months before he was killed he urged still further steps, one of which—a treaty against the proliferation of nuclear weapons—became the subject for Bob Kennedy's first major speech as a United States Senator. The treaty was signed under Johnson's Administration and ratified under Nixon's.

John Kennedy did not do all this because he thought that all conflict or even danger had suddenly disappeared from Soviet–American relations. He recognized that two very different but very large and powerful nations, each necessarily concerned with events all over the world and each possessing a capacity to affect but not control those events, were bound to have conflicts of interest as well as ideology. Much as he understood and was fascinated by Khrushchev's rough ways, he sensed in him an air of recklessness which—combined with a national inferiority complex—could drag us all into war. But he also recognized that the two great powers had a common interest in devoting their resources to peaceful pursuits instead of stockpiling arms and that those common interests could maintain treaties more effectively than any international police force.

He did not share the view of some that the Americans and Soviets would ultimately form an alliance against the Chinese. But he did believe that both nations could cooperate in reducing the risks of detonating the entire planet. As a student of modern history, he regarded the greatest danger of all to be the danger of war by miscalculation—by a national mistakenly not expecting the other to respond, by a nation mistakenly going to war over an issue that could have been equitably settled, by a nation not accurately distinguishing the other's commitments or capability. In the modern age, the first such mistake could be the last.

Thus his prime objective since taking high office had been "to get the nuclear genie back into the bottle," as he put it in an early press conference. That is why his proudest moment was not the day Khrushchev took his missiles out of Cuba but the day the Test Ban Treaty was ratified. For that one limited step symbolized much more that was then developing—including a general recognition that the prospects for a Soviet–American nuclear war, which a few years earlier most people had thought to be ultimately inevitable, were largely diminished.

NO

Mark J. White

The Cuban Missile Crisis

From the end of October to December 1962, the last vestiges of the Cuban missile crisis dissolved. One thorny issue, created by Castro's refusal to permit UN officials on Cuban soil, was the provision of adequate inspection for the monitoring of the withdrawal of the missiles. That dilemma was resolved when Moscow agreed to discard the tarpaulins covering the weapons on the ships returning to the Soviet Union, thereby making it a simple matter for American U-2 planes to photograph the missiles on the departing vessels. The question of which Soviet weapons were to be regarded as offensive was another problem. Reversing the position he had taken in the ExComm [Executive Committee of the U.S. National Security Council] meeting on 28 October, Kennedy began to argue that the IL-28 bombers were offensive weapons and so had to be removed. When Khrushchev acceded to that demand and forced Castro to go along with it as well, JFK announced on 20 November that he would end the naval blockade. The Soviets withdrew all their IL-28s by 6 December. In this way, the settlement to the crisis over Cuba, forged by Kennedy and Khrushchev at the end of October, was implemented.

John and Robert Kennedy, Nikita Khrushchev, Adlai Stevenson, Kenneth Keating, and Dean Acheson had all played a role in making the Cuban missile crisis —or at least exacerbating it. It was Khrushchev who made the critical decision to install nuclear weapons in Cuba, but JFK's campaign to overthrow Castro (including, probably, Robert Kennedy's implementation of Operation Mongoose), helped to convince the Soviet leader that missiles were needed in Cuba to discourage an American attack. The president's policy of expanding America's nuclear arsenal and his decision to stress his country's strategic superiority in public also brought Khrushchev to the conclusion that he should emplace missiles on the Caribbean island. Keating, along with other Republicans, had in large measure caused Kennedy to promise the American public that he would take vigorous action to resist any Soviet missile deployment in Cuba, a pledge that made JFK feel compelled to confront Khrushchev in mid-October when he discovered that nuclear weapons were on the island. Even Stevenson had increased Cuban isolation and Castro's dependence on Khrushchev by laying the groundwork for the subsequent ejection of Cuba from the OAS [Organization of American States] during his trip to Latin America in the summer of 1961. Acheson, by insisting in the ExComm meetings that Kennedy order an air strike on the missile sites, made the crisis more dangerous than it would otherwise have been.

After the missile crisis, these six men travelled along divergent but in general equally hapless paths. A group of Kremlin rivals which included Leonid Brezhnev ousted Khrushchev from power in 1964, the same year that Keating lost his seat in the Senate to Robert Kennedy after a bitterly fought campaign. Assassins' bullets struck down John and Bobby Kennedy in 1963 and 1968. A heart attack on a London street in the summer of 1965 also cut short the life of Adlai Stevenson. Dean Acheson fared the best. Used by Presidents Johnson and Nixon as an *ad hoc* adviser, his reputation, tarnished in the early 1950s by the Korean War and McCarthy's attacks, continued its rehabilitation.

External and internal factors coalesced to bring about the Cuban missile crisis— and to determine the way it played out. External considerations were certainly important. Among the probable considerations prompting Khrushchev to put nuclear weapons in Cuba was the belief that this would help close the strategic gap with the United States, undercut the Chinese criticism that he was failing to support revolutionary clients, and provide him with a bargaining chip he could use to extract concessions from the West in Berlin. Kennedy's pre-missile crisis policies towards Cuba were propelled in part by the standard assumptions that generally underpinned American policy during the Cold War: monolithism, dominoes, and the lessons of the 1930s. Kennedy tried to overthrow Castro because he regarded him as Khrushchev's puppet and so felt his position as Cuban leader represented an unacceptable extension of Soviet power. He suspected that the Cuban Revolution, unless quashed quickly, might prove to be the first of a long sequence of leftist revolutions throughout Latin America. He believed that the failure of appeasement in the 1930s showed the necessity of an American commitment to counter the expansion of communist influence anywhere and especially in America's own backyard, as with Cuba.

The internal factors that were equally important in bringing about the missile crisis have usually received less attention from historians. Kennedy's relationship with the liberals in his administration, especially Stevenson, shaped his policies towards Cuba in important ways. If JFK had been more receptive to their arguments before the Bay of Pigs, he would have rejected the plan. If he had embraced their views after it, he would not have organised such a concerted campaign to overthrow Castro during the second half of 1961 and 1962. A Cuban policy grounded in the ideas of these liberals would have mitigated Khrushchev's fear of an imminent American attack on the island, and hence reduced the likelihood that he would have deployed missiles in order to protect Cuba. Furthermore, a decision by Kennedy to implement Stevenson's proposals during the first week of the October confrontation, offering Khrushchev a negotiated settlement at the same time that the blockade was announced, could have brought about a prompter and thus safer resolution to the crisis.

Kennedy's relationship with Republican opponents, particularly Senator Keating, also influenced his Cuban policies. Determined to refute their charges that he had responded weakly to the dangerous Soviet military build-up that was taking place in Cuba during the fall of 1962, Kennedy explained to the American public that the build-up was not a threat to the United States because it did not include offensive weapons. In this way, JFK acknowledged that the deployment of surface-to-surface nuclear missiles would represent an unacceptable challenge to American security, one requiring a swift and decisive response from his administration; and this in large measure was why he felt bound during the first week of the crisis to remove the missiles from Cuba with either a military strike, his initial preference, or a blockade, the alternative he came to prefer, rather than by means of the diplomatic strategy developed by Stevenson. The public commitments Keating and other Republicans had elicited in September 1962 also ensured that Kennedy would not react to the news in mid-October of missiles in Cuba by simply tolerating the deployment and explaining that decision to the American public (which he could possibly have done by saying the Soviets already had the ability to strike the American mainland with its ICBMs and by noting that the United States already had in Turkey what the Soviets had just acquired—nuclear weapons on the border of its adversary). Those September public pledges helped sustain JFK's determination to remove the missiles from Cuba during the second week of the crisis as well. His citation of them on numerous occasions indicated that they were always an important reference point for him.

Kennedy's campaign for the presidency in 1960 may have contributed to the coming of the missile crisis. To bolster his chances of reaching the White House, JFK pointed to the Eisenhower administration's failure to prevent Castro's rise to power, and promised to make amends by overthrowing the Cuban leader if elected. Kennedy, therefore, probably authorised the Bay of Pigs operation in part to make good on his election promise. Khrushchev's fear after the Bay of Pigs that Kennedy would try once again to remove Castro, but on the next occasion use American force directly to ensure success, was one of the key factors behind his decision to install missiles in Cuba. Hence, it can be argued that there was a nexus between the 1960 campaign and the missile crisis, with the former helping to bring about the Bay of Pigs of operation, which in turn helped convince Khrushchev of the need for missiles to protect Cuba, which obviously brought about the confrontation in October 1962.

Kennedy's conception of the relationship between public opinion and the foreign policy-making process also helped define his approach towards Castro. One of the lessons he drew from Britain's appeasement of Hitler in the late 1930s was that the public can exert an unhealthy influence over the pursuit of the national interest. In that case, the pressure applied by various interest groups had prevented British leaders from increasing military spending, a step made necessary by the threat of German aggression. In seeking to oust Castro, Kennedy was thus attracted to secret operations which could be used without triggering a public debate over the merits of that approach and objective. This explains why so many of JFK's Cuban policies, such as Mongoose, military contingency planning, and the assassination attempts he probably approved, were covert.

Domestic concerns were among the cluster of considerations that lay behind Khrushchev's decision to deploy missiles in Cuba. The Soviet leader probably felt that nuclear weapons in the Caribbean were helpful in part because they would allow him to make the argument to the rest of the Soviet leadership that this improvement to their strategic position meant that it was now safe to resume his suspended programme of cutting troop numbers in order to release resources for the civilian economy. Missiles in Cuba would also allow Khrushchev to use again the strategy of brinksmanship which the Kennedy administration's public assertion of American nuclear superiority had undermined in the fall of 1961. Fundamentally, brinksmanship was a device for accomplishing foreign policy objectives through rhetoric rather than the application of actual resources. In other words, it was part of Khrushchev's overall goal of concentrating more on domestic than defence needs.

Kennedy and Khrushchev were jointly responsible for the missile crisis. Khrushchev's decision to install medium and intermediate-range missiles in Cuba was an unnecessary risk. He could have enhanced Cuban security (and thereby undercut the Chinese charge that Moscow's support for leftist revolutions was inadequate) by deploying only troops and conventional weaponry on the island (and perhaps short-range, tactical nuclear weapons as well). Faced with the prospect of a direct clash with Soviet forces, Kennedy, in all likelihood, would have jettisoned any plan to attack Cuba. By accelerating the Soviet ICBM programme and by highlighting that policy in public, Khrushchev would have been able to placate the Soviet military, indulge his penchant for brinksmanship with credibility, repair the strategic nuclear balance that lay so conspicuously in America's favour, and to accomplish all that without moving the superpowers and Cuba to the brink of nuclear disaster.

Kennedy, however, was equally culpable. The sequence of events is important here. While it was obviously Khrushchev who made the decision to put missiles in Cuba, he did so only *after* Kennedy had ordered a CIA-organised invasion of the island, attempted to bring the Cuban economy to a standstill with a tight embargo on trade, arranged the diplomatic isolation of Cuba by working for its removal from the OAS, approved large-scale military manoeuvres in the Caribbean, and, although it is not clear whether Khrushchev knew of these, encouraged Operation Mongoose and contingency planning for an attack on Cuba, and probably approved various assassination attempts on Castro. That Kennedy showed no indication of even suspecting that these policies might appear threatening to Cuba's chief ally, the Soviet Union, was testimony to a remarkable myopia on his part. He likewise failed to perceive how the general increase in defence spending he carried out, his October 1961 decision to inform the public of America's nuclear superiority over the Soviets, and his tendency to emphasise this thereafter might have troubled Khrushchev. In the 1960 presidential campaign, JFK had predicted that the Cold War would reach its summit during the early 1960s. His policies towards Cuba and the Soviet Union helped make that a self-fulfilling prophecy.

Kennedy, moreover, may have missed opportunities to ameliorate relations with Moscow in early 1961, and with Havana both at that time and in August 1961 in the wake of the Che Guevara–Goodwin meeting. The offers made by Khrushchev and Castro could have been disingenuous, and even if they were not, they may have turned out to be problematic for JFK. For example, even though Khrushchev was interested in a Soviet–American rapprochement in early 1961, he may not have been willing to accept the status quo in Berlin as part of a *modus vivendi,* and this was plainly an essential requirement for the United States. None the less, Kennedy should have made a greater effort to explore these overtures. The Soviet and Cuban leaders were motivated to seek an improvement in relations with the United States out of self-interest, the former so that he could justify his defence cuts, and the latter to lessen the chances of a United States invasion and to help Cuba's ailing economy by, for example, encouraging Kennedy to restore Cuban–American trade to its pre-1959 levels. Precisely because Khrushchev and Castro were motivated by selfish rather than altruistic considerations, their attempts to open a dialogue with JFK were probably made in good faith. That their overtures were essentially at the private, diplomatic level also suggests that they were not public relations gimmicks. Despite all that, JFK did not respond to the offers from Moscow and Havana. Clearly, any improvement in the triangular Soviet–Cuban–American relationship that might have emerged from a decision by Kennedy to take advantage of these opportunities would have reduced the chances of Khrushchev offering and Castro accepting the deployment of missiles in Cuba.

Although Kennedy and Khrushchev shared the responsibility for causing the missile crisis, they also deserve the credit for defusing it. They managed to avoid a military clash on the seas. Khrushchev, with the letter he sent to JFK on 26 October, proved himself willing to be the first leader to offer the other concessions, and that message provided the basis for the final settlement. But Kennedy, ably assisted by his advisers, was able to dispel the confusion created by Khrushchev's two different offers on 26 and 27 October and to devise a shrewd and effective response to them.

Too often, portrayals of Kennedy's Cuban policies, as with assessments of his presidency in general, have been prone to oversimplification and exaggeration. JFK's record on Cuba was neither brilliant in the way that his supporters have insisted nor disastrous as his detractors have claimed: it was mixed. Kennedy's approach towards Castro before the missile crisis was utterly misguided. He tinkered with but never altered the assumptions on which American Cold War policies had been based. He exaggerated the threat posed by Castro to the United States. He implemented policies towards Cuba that were excessively hostile. He failed to take advantage of opportunities to improve relations with Havana and Moscow. He failed to listen to advisers who proposed creative alternatives to the policies he was carrying out.

During the first week of the missile crisis, Kennedy's performance was a mixture of the impressive and the disconcerting. If it had not been for the restraining hand of his advisers, especially Robert Kennedy, he may well have ordered a military strike on Cuba. Kennedy, in addition, should have paid far greater heed to Stevenson, whose policy proposals were on balance the most sensible and potentially efficacious of those devised by American officials during the early days of the crisis. On the other hand, the basic decision made by JFK during the first week—that a naval blockade should be implemented instead of the military attack recommended by the likes of Acheson—was sound. An air strike or invasion, given the likelihood that they would provoke the sort of forceful Soviet response that would make war virtually inevitable, were unacceptably dangerous alternatives.

During the second week of the crisis, Kennedy's overall performance was superb. He was perhaps excessively concerned with the presentation of the American case to the public, press, and international community; and, to be sure, his reluctance to promise not to invade Cuba, as Khrushchev requested, was the most disappointing feature of his thinking during the last days of the confrontation. None the less, as the crisis progressed, he became more flexible and conciliatory, more earnest in his efforts to avoid war. He resisted the temptation to react forcibly to seemingly intolerable Soviet provocations, like the shooting down of the U-2. At the height of the crisis on 27 October he turned to the removal of the Jupiters and the extension of the blockade to POL [petroleum, oil, and lubricants] as ways of avoiding the military options that some of his advisers wished to implement if Khrushchev rejected the Trollope ploy. In the end, Kennedy proved willing to make the concessions—the withdrawal of the Jupiters and the non-invasion pledge—needed to resolve the crisis. It is impossible to prove what JFK would have done had Khrushchev dismissed the Trollope initiative, demanded that the deal on the Jupiters be a public arrangement, and ignored any decision by JFK to add POL to the quarantine. At the end of that hypothetical lies a frightening area of uncertainty. Still, the weight of evidence, particularly Kennedy's comments during the 27 October ExComm meetings (though not the Cordier ploy), suggests that he would have accepted a public trade of the Jupiters before resorting to military action.

As with JFK, an evaluation of Khrushchev needs to be balanced. His decision in the spring of 1962 to install nuclear weapons in Cuba was probably not needed to fulfill his various foreign, domestic, and defence policy objectives. His belief that American intelligence would fail to detect the missiles in Cuba before the completion of the deployment was mistaken. Most importantly, Khrushchev should have realised that the Kennedy administration would not tolerate missiles in Cuba, that a confrontation over the issue was thus inevitable, and hence the decision to put nuclear weapons on the island was simply too dangerous a risk to take. Like JFK, however, Khrushchev's performance was far more impressive during the crisis itself. His decision to respect and not challenge the blockade on 24 October, the settlement he offered Kennedy two days later, and his willingness on 28 October to embrace the Trollope initiative were all crucial contributions to the resolution of the crisis.

Why were Kennedy and Khrushchev so much more effective in extricating themselves from the missile crisis than in preventing it? JFK's inability to challenge the assumptions behind American foreign policy during the Cold War and to think about the long-term consequences of his actions explain in part his anti-Castro policies and his unwillingness to respond positively to Khrushchev's initiatives. Khrushchev, with his de-Stalinisation drive, the military cutbacks he attempted, and his development of the concept of peaceful coexistence, showed signs of being capable of revising the premises behind the foreign policy he inherited. But his risk-taking proclivities and impulsiveness—in other words, his general lack of caution—meant that he was capable of committing an error as egregious as installing nuclear missiles in Cuba.

Despite these shortcomings, Kennedy and Khrushchev were quick on their feet, and that mental agility helped them on 27 and 28 October to stay probably two or three steps away from the point at which a military confrontation might have taken place. The other attribute that enabled them to reach a settlement was the genuine fear of nuclear war that they shared. This enlarged their willingness to offer concessions to end the crisis. Khrushchev, despite his use of brinksmanship, had expressed concern about the possibility of a nuclear exchange throughout his years as Soviet leader. For Kennedy, the crisis itself had a dramatic and educative effect on his thinking, creating in the midst of the confrontation the deep-seated fear of nuclear war that he did not previously appear to possess.

If it had not been for Kennedy's consistently hostile policies towards Cuba and the Soviet Union and for Khrushchev's miscalculations in the spring of 1962, there would have been no missile crisis. If, however, leaders with less ability than Kennedy and Khrushchev had been at the helm in October 1962, the outcome of that confrontation might not have been a peaceful settlement. For Kennedy and Khrushchev, then, the Cuban missile crisis represented both the summit and nadir of their foreign policies.

POSTSCRIPT

Did President Kennedy Effectively Manage the Cuban Missile Crisis?

Sorensen's selection expresses the views of a consummate insider, considering that Sorensen was President Kennedy's chief speechwriter and long-time adviser as well as a member of the Ex-Comm committee. He argues that Soviet missiles in Cuba threatened America's national security because they "represented a sudden, immediate and more dangerous and secretive change in the balance of power, in clear contradiction of all U.S. commitments and Soviet pledges." What Khrushchev did, essentially, was to threaten the status quo in the cold war by challenging America's military supremacy in the Western Hemisphere.

Sorensen portrays Kennedy as a moderate who rejected the hawks on the executive committee who wanted to deploy air strikes against Cuba. Instead, Kennedy chose to "blockade" Cuba (though he used the less-threatening military term *quarantine*) while engaging in official and unofficial negotiations.

Sorensen can be accused of being too upbeat about the aftermath of the crisis. It is true that Kennedy and Khrushchev agreed to install a hot line between Washington, D.C., and Moscow that would enable the major leaders to engage in instant communication should a similar crisis emerge. It is also true that Kennedy's June 10, 1963, speech at American University was more conciliatory than his more jingoistic inaugural address of 1961 and that it paved the way for the Nuclear Test Ban Agreement later that summer.

But the Cuban Missile Crisis also had its downside. The Russians were humiliated by the showdown, and Khrushchev was removed from power in 1964. For the next five years the Soviets expended large amounts of money modernizing their navy and taking the lead over the United States in ICBMs. In 1963, although Operation Mongoose was officially abolished, the Kennedy administration created a special group to try to assassinate Castro and to sabotage the Cuban economy whenever possible. Finally, then–secretary of defense Robert S. McNamara maintains that success in defusing the missiles in Cuba gave Kennedy and Johnson's staff the confidence that the administration could win the war in Vietnam by sending "advisers" to aid the South Vietnamese military in order to secure a victory against communism.

White asserts that Khrushchev probably placed intermediate-range missiles in Cuba to improve the Soviet strategic position in such a major way that he could then resume his suspended program of reducing troop numbers and concentrate on building up his domestic economy. Khrushchev could then resort to a policy of rhetorical brinkmanship and undercut the Kennedy administration's public policy of nuclear supremacy.

White also argues that Khrushchev overreached. Had the Russian premier enhanced Cuba with Russian troops, conventional weapons, and perhaps some tactical nuclear missiles, he could have protected Cuba from an invasion by the United States and at the same time cut Soviet military expenditures and rebuild its civilian economy. Would Kennedy have attacked Cuba under these conditions? White thinks not.

White also faults Kennedy for "missed opportunities" to ameliorate relations with Moscow in early 1961 and with Havana both at that time and in the summer of 1961, when Castro sent overtures of a possible settlement of economic and political differences in Cuban-American relations. Had Castro paid off the expropriated American oil companies and agreed not to engage in revolutionary activities in Latin America, the United States might have resumed trade with Cuba, and the missile crisis would never have taken place.

Unfortunately, Kennedy was a prisoner of the cold war assumptions of the post–World War II era. In the 1960 campaign, remembering the McCarthyite attacks on Harry S. Truman's containment policy, candidate Kennedy attacked Republicans Dwight D. Eisenhower and Richard M. Nixon for being soft on communism when they allowed Castro to take over Cuba. Even after the Bay of Pigs fiasco, how could a macho Kennedy administration negotiate with a communist regime 90 miles from the United States and not be politically vulnerable to attacks from the military, conservatives, and Republican right-wingers?

The literature on the Cuban Missile Crisis is enormous. The starting point is White's "The Cuban Imbroglio: From the Bay of Pigs to the Missile Crisis and Beyond," in his edited book *Kennedy: The New Frontier Revisited* (New York University Press, 1998). All the essays in this volume strive for an alternative to the Camelot and counter-Camelot interpretations of the Kennedy presidency. The same may be said of White's *Missiles in Cuba: Kennedy, Khrushchev, Castro and the 1962 Crisis* (Ivan R. Dee, 1997).

A superb collection of articles can be found in Robert A. Divine, ed., *The Cuban Missile Crisis* (Quadrangle Books, 1971), which contains older but still useful articles. Divine also reviews a number of books and collections of primary sources, secondary articles, and roundtable discussions in "Alive and Well: The Continuing Cuban Missile Crisis Controversy," *Diplomatic History* (Fall 1994). James Nathan has edited a collection of articles based on records opened by the American, former Soviet, and Cuban governments and collected by the independent National Security Archive. See the articles by Barton J. Bernstein, Richard Ned Lebow, Philip Brenner, and the editor himself in James A. Nathan, ed., *The Cuban Missile Crisis Revisited* (St. Martin's Press, 1992).

There are a number of primary sources that students can explore without visiting the archives. Mark J. White has edited *The Kennedys and Cuba: The Declassified History* (Ivan R. Dee, 1999). See also Laurence Chang and Peter Kornbluh, eds., *The Cuban Missile Crisis, 1962: A National Security Archive Documents Reader,* rev. ed. (New Press, 1998). Students are fortunate to have access to tape recordings of the Ex-Comm meetings. They have been transcribed along with some other meetings by Ernest R. May and Philip D. Zelikow and are reprinted in their edited book *The Kennedy Tapes: Inside the White House During the Cuban Missile Crisis* (Harvard University Press, 1997).

ISSUE 14

Should America Remain a Nation of Immigrants?

YES: Reed Ueda, from "The Permanently Unfinished Country," *The World & I* (October 1992)

NO: Richard D. Lamm, from "Truth, Like Roses, Often Comes With Thorns," *Vital Speeches of the Day* (December 1, 1994)

ISSUE SUMMARY

YES: Professor of history Reed Ueda maintains that the sheer magnitude and diversity of immigrants continually reshapes the American character, making America a "permanently unfinished country."

NO: Former Colorado governor Richard D. Lamm argues that immigration should be severely curtailed. He contends that the most recent immigrants are members of the underclass who are culturally unassimilable and who take jobs away from the poorest citizens in an already overpopulated America.

Historians of immigration tend to divide the forces that encouraged voluntary migrations from one country to another into push and pull factors. Historically, the major reason why people left their native countries was the breakdown of feudalism and the subsequent rise of a commercially oriented economy. Peasants were pushed off the feudal estates of which they had been a part for generations. In addition, religious and political persecution for dissenting groups and the lack of economic opportunities for many middle-class émigrés also contributed to the migrations from Europe to the New World.

America was attractive to settlers long before the American Revolution took place. While the United States may not have been completely devoid of feudal traditions, immigrants perceived the United States as a country with a fluid social structure where opportunities abounded for everyone. By the mid-nineteenth century, the Industrial Revolution had provided opportunities for jobs in a nation that had always experienced chronic labor shortages.

There were four major periods of migration to the United States: 1607–1830, 1830–1890, 1890–1925, and 1968 to the present. In the seventeenth and eighteenth centuries, the white settlers came primarily, though not entirely, from the British Isles. They were joined by millions of African slaves. Both groups lived in proximity to several hundred thousand Native Americans. In those years the cultural values of Americans were a combination of what history professor Gary Nash has referred to as "red, white, and black." In the 30 years before the Civil War, a second phase began when immigrants came from other countries in northern and western Europe as well as China. Two European groups dominated. Large numbers of Irish Catholics emigrated in the 1850s because of the potato famine. Religious and political factors were as instrumental as economic factors in pushing the Germans to America. Chinese immigrants were also encouraged to come during the middle and later decades of the nineteenth century in order to help build the western portion of America's first transcontinental railroad and to work in low-paying service industries like laundries and restaurants.

By 1890 a third period of immigration had begun. Attracted by the unskilled jobs provided by the Industrial Revolution and the cheap transportation costs of fast-traveling, steam-powered ocean vessels, immigrants poured in at a rate of close to 1 million a year from Italy, Greece, Russia, and other countries of southern and eastern Europe. This flood continued until the early 1920s, when fears of a foreign takeover led Congress to pass legislation restricting the number of immigrants into the United States to 150,000 per year.

For the next 40 years America was ethnically frozen. The restriction laws of the 1920s favored northern and western European groups and were biased against southern and eastern Europeans. The depression of the 1930s, World War II in the 1940s, and minimal changes in the immigration laws of the 1950s kept migrations to the United States at a minimum level.

In the 1960s the immigration laws were drastically revised. The civil rights acts of 1964 and 1965, which ended legal discrimination against African Americans, were also the impetus for immigration reform. The 1965 Immigration Act represented a turning point in U.S. history. But it had unintended consequences. In conjunction with the 1990 Immigration Act, discrimination against non-European nations was abolished and preferences were given to family-based migrants over refugees and those with special skills. Immigrants from Latin American and Asian countries have dominated the fourth wave of migration and have used the loophole in the legislation to bring into the country "immediate relatives," such as spouses, children, and parents of American citizens who are exempt from the numerical ceilings of the immigration laws.

Should America remain a nation of immigrants? In the following selection, Reed Ueda maintains that America is a permanently unfinished country as a result of immigration and that immigration continues to play a positive role in the nation's development. In the second selection, Richard D. Lamm makes a case for restricting current immigration to a total of 300,000 per year, a 75 percent reduction from the 1.2 million who have entered each year in the 1990s, because immigration has harmed America's participation in the global economy.

Reed Ueda

 **YES**

The Permanently Unfinished Country

$\mathbf{T}$ he twentieth century has been called the "American century" because of the rise of the United States to world leadership. It has also been the era when the country became a world immigrant nation. The historical role of the United States as the quintessential magnetic society built from immigration has expanded to accommodate greater ethnic diversity. By the 1990s, the flow of newcomers included people from every region and culture of the globe.

However, this "new diversity" is merely a child of old historic patterns. Unless this is grasped, we are likely to mistake this new diversity as a new threat or new utopia, when it is in reality an outgrowth of roots imbedded in our national past. Thus the question "How new is diversity?" should actually be, "How old is diversity?"

The historical record shows that ethnic diversity is as old as the United States. The first U.S. census in 1790 revealed that the majority of Americans then were not of English origin. California had a higher proportion of Asians in 1880 than it did in 1980. In 1900, the majority of inhabitants in the largest cities were immigrants or the children of immigrants. In 1910, more than 50 languages were spoken by immigrants in the United States. Government and census records of the past amply prove the longstanding reality of American diversity.

This phenomenal ethnic diversity is largely due to certain unique characteristics of American immigration. The first key feature is the sheer magnitude of immigration: By 1990, 57 million people had migrated to the United States, the largest international movement of population in history. More immigrants came to the United States than to all other major immigrant-receiving countries combined. From 1820 to 1930, 38 million people moved to the United States, while 24 million migrated to Canada, Argentina, Brazil, Australia, New Zealand, and South Africa combined. The United States attracted three-fifths of the population flocking to major immigration countries. From the mid-nineteenth century to the Great Depression, the United States received more than 30 million newcomers, while Argentina received 6.4 million, Canada 5.2 million, Brazil 4.4 million, and Australia 2.9 million.

The second defining feature of American immigration is that it encompasses the greatest variety of nationalities among all the modern international population movements. Fifteen percent of American immigrants came from Germany, 11 percent from Italy, 10 percent from Ireland, 9 percent from Austria-Hungary, 8 percent from Canada, and only 7 percent from England. More Latin American, Caribbean, and Asian immigrants have journeyed to America than to any other nation. By contrast, other English-speaking immigrant countries have drawn new settlers almost wholly from other English-speaking nations. Eighty percent of immigrants to Australia came from Great Britain, while in Canada 37 percent arrived from Great Britain and another 37 percent from the United States. Immigration into Latin America is limited chiefly to those of Iberian or Italian origin. In Argentina, 47 percent of the immigrants came from Italy and 32 percent from Spain; in Brazil, 34 percent came from Italy, 29 percent from Portugal, and 14 percent from Spain.

Every immigrant, from the Mexican farm laborer to the Polish steelworker, has been a bold adventurer on a voyage of discovery. Emma Lazarus was wrong in describing immigrants as "wretched refuse" in her poem "The New Colossus" that adorns the Statue of Liberty. In reality, the immigrants are brave, resourceful, and vigorous, with the immigrant resiliency to cope with tremendous social change and social loss.

The early immigrants made enormous sacrifices, and persevered to realize a new vision of man and society. They found that the novel American conditions of tolerance toward pluralism and variety made the forging of new identities and cultural ties inescapable. The immigrant American is a person who absorbs new ways from neighboring people who are different. The children of Japanese immigrants in Hawaii learn new games, new words, new values, new tastes in food, new dress and hairstyles, new friendships and relationships from their neighbors, who are Hawaiian, Filipino, German, Chinese, and Portuguese. Americans are not bound to tradition but are open to change and choices that come from outsiders. They learn from people unlike themselves about different foods, music, skills, arts and values. The American language is an immigrant language, a blending of many ethnic vocabularies.

A New Society

American immigrants have created a new society completely different from old societies like Sweden, Scotland, or Japan. These societies had taken strength from homogeneity. Solidarity came from all people being the same. American immigrants have built a society that substitutes a radical new self-definition for the nation. In the United States, the strength of the nation comes from the immense multiplicity of ethnic groups. Moreover, it hinges upon the existence of conditions that permit dissimilar groups to act and live together. The resultant mutual fusion and interdependency help integrate the nation. The large majority of nations in the world have little historical experience or political interest in operating as an immigrant-receiving nation. The German political leader Volker Ruhe expressed this viewpoint in 1991 by announcing "We [in Germany] are not an immigration country and we will not become one." But other societies—such as Japan, Norway, Scotland, Sweden, or Korea—also have no tradition of immigration and little interest in developing one.

By contrast, immigration has been the shaping force of the American nation and its role in world history. It has contributed an endless flux to American social history, making the nation, in the words of sociologist Nathan Glazer, "the permanently unfinished country." Immigration to America has adjusted the balance of human and material resources between nations, creating new international economic and cultural ties. Otto von Bismarck, the "Iron Chancellor" who unified Germany, called American immigration the "decisive fact" of the modern world.

Thus, at the heart of American history lies the cycle of national creation and recreation through immigration. The social foundation of the political nation has been a historical immigrant nation that has been ever-changing. Historically, three immigrant nations arose successively and fused into each other in the two centuries after the American Revolution, producing immense changes in social organization, cultural life, and nationality. The new republic built by Protestant colonials from the British Isles had to accommodate, by the Civil War, an immigrant nation of Irish Catholics and newcomers from Germany and Scandinavia. After the turn of the century, a new immigrant nation formed principally from migrations from southern and eastern Europe, with input also from east Asia, Mexico, and the Caribbean. In the late twentieth century, a multicultural immigrant nation coalesced out of the expansion of immigration onto a global stage. The United States, on the eve of the twenty-first century, is a cumulative fusion of these immigrant nations, a synthesis that has come to embody a "world" or international culture.

The contemporary multicultural focus on the differences and separate experiences of diverse groups often starts from a myopia toward the enormous magnitude of ethnic assimilation that is part of American history. When David Dinkins, the first black mayor of New York City, delivered his inaugural address, he paid homage to his city as a "beautiful mosaic." The discrete and static parts of the mosaic form an image employed to legitimize a model of ethnic relations that favors cultural preservationism. This image, however, only pictures one part of American social history, the unmelted elements found among all groups. The other part of the picture has been the chemistry of change in status, culture, and identity. This process has not been as far-reaching or uniform as the earlier image for ethnic relations, the melting pot, once described and predicted. But it would be unrealistic to ignore the dimensions of social mobility and acculturation experienced over the span of generations by every group since the arrival of immigrant ancestors.

It is a cliché to disparage the melting-pot model of ethnic relations as a path toward homogenization or even "Anglo-conformity." It is true that Anglo-Saxon nativists of the early twentieth century prescribed this method of dealing with ethnic pluralism. But, recently, this sterotypical view of the melting-pot culture has been resuscitated by journalists and advocates seeking to use it as a target for the movement to promote multicultural difference.

The melting pot as a social and cultural reality in history was never Anglo-conformist or homogeneous. It was the shared national culture, a fusion of elements taken from a multitude of group cultures. Assimilation has been a multidirectional process, undertaken with mutual concern among local groups.

Groups changed and merged like the images of a kaleidoscope, with astounding and unpredictable patterns of diversity that yet cohered into a unity. Moreover, many features of group life were left unmelted and unfused. Melting has been incomplete, not always linear, and it proceeded at a variety of paces for different groups. Northern European groups that were two or more generations removed from the Old World had the most attenuated sense of ethnic identity. Some examples of European groups that no longer stressed specific loyalties have been the Scotch-Irish, the Welsh, and the Dutch. Although they retained a stronger sense of special identity, the Norwegians, Danes, Swedes, and Germans have also grown distant from an ethnic identity based on the homeland. Americans descended from forebears who came from southern and eastern Europe, Asia, the Caribbean, and Latin America exhibited a stronger tendency to retain distinctive ethnic features.

One of the most sensitive signs of mutual assimilation or multidirectional fusion of American society has been intermarriage. The Japanese Americans and Jews who most stressed marriage within the ethnic group early in the twentieth century now marry out at the highest rates, about one out of two marrying spouses of other ethnic backgrounds. The dramatic story of the rise of intermarriage is recorded in the multiple ancestry table of the 1980 federal census.

Prejudice and discrimination based on ethnic identity have affected all groups at one time or other, but the immigrants found niches on the social pyramid that would provide a foothold for further ascent. The new immigrants —such as the Greeks, Jews, Italians, Slavs, Armenians, Chinese, Japanese, and Mexicans—faced severe exclusion from jobs, schools, and neighborhoods. Most workers advanced little and lived a life of transiency and grinding poverty. But equality of opportunity increased for their children and grandchildren, upon which they capitalized to chart a course of multigenerational advancement. The descendants of even the most impoverished and powerless immigrants have obtained better jobs, more education, and higher status than their immigrant forebears. In the media culture and political culture of mass parties they have achieved more representation and greater voice than their ancestors. Recent immigrants from Latin America, Asia, the Caribbean, and the Middle East appear to be starting their own multigenerational cycle of social mobility. Any verdict on America's identity as a land of opportunity must rest on the broader view of the promise of American life as directed to the children and grandchildren of immigrants.

The groups that were involuntarily incorporated into the nation through conquest and slavery, American Indians and African blacks, encountered greater difficulty in achieving social mobility. Treated as separate quasi-nations, Indians were quarantined in the reservation system; blacks had to struggle against slavery and its residual barriers. The elimination of poverty within the Indian and black populations remains a crucial challenge.

The immigrant's need to deal with outsiders who were different in order to survive made ethnic boundary crossing practical and opportunistic. An individual's opportunities increased according to the ability to diversify social contacts. To tap the full range of opportunity, it was necessary to overlook ethnic differences and loyalties. Ethnic group members were willing to ignore the religion or ancestry of the person with whom they developed instrumental and mutually beneficial social relations and economic ties. Immigrants could only gain political power and office by forming alliances with outsiders. No ethnic group constituted a secure majority except at the most localized level. In order to become a force, groups had to form coalitions that leapfrogged ethnic divisions. Ethnic groups in America lacked the size and power to isolate their members. Their members forged and dissolved linkages with people from other groups as made necessary by self-interest and permitted by the limits of discriminatory boundaries. The dynamic conditions of American society that detached people from families and groups of origin and reabsorbed them into new families and new communities created novel combinations of ethnic identity.

The kaleidoscopic complexity of American identity also reveals that the dynamics of social history have made ethnicity only a part of human identity. The nature of ethnic identity changed as it was outflanked and decentered by the forming of multiple identities and competing loyalties. Members of ethnic minorities forged overlapping bonds with other types of communities that increased as one generation succeeded the next. Even the youngest new Americans are shaped by the heterogeneous world of classmates and playmates.

In fact, many Americans have come not to identify with a particular ethnic group; their identity derives primarily from their occupation, consumer habits, generation, geographic location, and mass culture. In a special census survey in 1970, nearly half of the sample group of European origins chose not to identify with a specific ethnic heritage. If the sample had included Hawaiian persons of mixed ancestry, a similar pattern probably would have emerged. These populations represent a transnational group that has grown in size and importance, inclusive of the increasing numbers of people of mixed ethnic and racial parentage.

The conditions that promoted intergroup and intercultural fusion nevertheless retained the capacity to support the preservation of cultural heritages. American conditions have allowed the melted and the unmelted to coexist in equilibrium. The Jews, Koreans, Irish, and Armenians and others who were persecuted in their homelands saw melting-pot America as the land where they were at greatest liberty to maintain their way of life. This was the advantage of democracy that made the difficult journey worth it. Here, government left them alone to pursue their religion, build their neighborhood institutions, start their own schools. The tendency today is to see the historic United States as callously assimilationist. But let us not forget that immigrants throughout history voted with their feet that the United States was the most tolerant nation in the world. Today's sophisticates give in too readily to skepticism or cynicism about the historic nation as a haven of multicultural pluralism. The unsophisticated immigrants of 1910 found in America a place of refuge to protect their group life and culture. The Irish, Italians, Greeks, Japanese, Chinese, and Mexicans did not have activist government programs to protect their cultures, yet the historical record shows that their cultural identities were systematically and enduringly preserved. Irish parochial schools, Jewish religious schools, and German and Japanese language schools reached a flourishing pinnacle in the late nineteenth and early twentieth centuries, when public institutions did not give them support.

Americans have long seen their country as the land of opportunity and individual freedom. However, fears that the United States would disintegrate through the social disorders wrought by immigration have surfaced time and again. American authorities, such as the great economist Francis Walker and anthropologist Madison Grant, have sounded the alarm that immigration is a force corroding the nation.

Ultimately, their views gave way to the ascendant idea that immigration played a positive role in the nation's development. The intellectual turning points in this ideological change were marked by the work of historians Marcus Lee Hansen and Oscar Handlin. They viewed immigration as a source of the national ethos of liberty and individualism. Handlin's historical writings on immigration formed the intellectual and ethical capstone of the view of immigration as a liberating and nationalizing force. In his work, immigration was transfigured into a myth-history of the creation of modern identity. The immigrant American became the archetype of the individual freed from the shackles of prescribed roles by moving into an alien world to discover a new empowering identity. Immigration facilitated the fulfillment of the national and global destiny of the United States as the prototypical modern nation unified by the joint effort of dissimilar groups.

The vision of Hansen and Handlin can help refocus the public mind on the historic liberal conditions conducive to forging a national community. It is needed in our time to allay destructive anxiety over the new diversity. It also is needed to counteract the artificial division of society into separate ethnic classes under government social policies. The historically rooted forces that made American identity heterogeneous and transcendent of differences were ineluctable and are still vital. The mutual assimilation of immigrants, their need to establish interdependency with surrounding groups, and their vision of American democracy as the best haven for cultural pluralism probably ensure that voluntary and fluid identities will continue to make immigration a nationalizing experience.

Richard D. Lamm

 **NO**

Truth, Like Roses, Often Comes With Thorns

Delivered before the 1994 Harris Bank Family Conference, Chicago, Illinois, October, 15, 1994

I have never started a speech by citing Joseph Stalin, but I do so today. Joseph Stalin once said: "One man's death; that's a tragedy, a million men's death; that's a statistic." I have been intrigued with that quote in the health care context. In American health care, we have the rule of rescue where we will go to unfathomable expense to save an individual, but yet we have over 30 million people without basic health insurance. Hundreds of thousands of American women give birth without adequate prenatal care, and 40 percent of our city youths are not fully vaccinated . . . yet, we spend hundreds of millions of dollars on "long shot" medicine at the end of life.

Individualism is fine, and it is one of the things that has made America great. But when you come to social policies, quite often the focus on the individual is at conflict with what should be the ends of your social policy.

"The divergence between what is good for the individual and what is good for society is one of the key elements in the health care debate," observes one scholar.

This is true not only of the health care debate, but it is central to the debates about many other important national issues. Does the right of a homeless person, for instance, to loiter in a public library because it is his only form of shelter, supersede the right of the rest of society to use the library in safety and in comfort?

Does the right of a welfare mother to have additional children take precedence over the taxpayers' interest in her not having more kids?

It is a dilemma that we find when we try to formulate our immigration policies as well. Should we give greater weight to the interest of the individual immigrant, who simply wants to improve his or her life by settling in the U.S., than we do the interest society has in limiting immigration?

To govern is to choose. Yet, choosing does not come easy to Americans. Our whole cultural heritage is that we can do everything for everybody, not only in the health care area, but in virtually every other area. Walt Whitman called America "the bulging store house and the endless freight train." The idea of any limit is abhorrent.

Yet, we are borrowing over a billion dollars a day from our children and our grandchildren, and recklessly running up nation-threatening deficits. By not having the maturity to ask hard questions about our limited resources, we are not only doing many people injustice, but we are doing the future injustice. We are stealing from our children's heritage.

It is this kind of lack of forethought or consideration of consequences that has been the hallmark of our immigration policy for decades. Factoring in legal immigration, admission of refugees, political asylum seekers and illegal immigrants who settle permanently, the United States now admits between 1.2 million and 1.4 million people a year.

These are abstract numbers, so let me put them into context for you. I live in Denver, a city of approximately half a million people. In other words, our immigration policies are responsible for the equivalent of a new Denver every five months! And we will go on adding a new Denver every five months indefinitely, with no end in sight.

What's even more astounding is that nobody really seems to know why. It is perhaps the only important public policy that has no definable objective. We cannot even articulate a national interest here. Ask the people who make the immigration laws why we have large-scale immigration and your response is likely to be a platitude. "We're a nation of immigrants," or someone will recite Emma Lazarus' poem.

Thus, as far as anyone can discern, we are adding a new Denver every five months out of habit, or because a schoolgirl wrote a nice poem in 1883. We have an immigration policy that is doomed to fail because nobody knows what we're aiming for, because we have never even defined what a successful immigration policy might be. And, like so many of our other failures, it will be our children and grandchildren who will live with the consequences of our unwillingness to even think about what we're doing.

We have all heard the expression about the road to hell being paved with good intentions. In America, the road to overpopulation, social tensions, cultural conflict and economic instability is being paved with a well-meaning, but thoughtless, immigration policy.

When you see an immigrant on television, our whole heritage says we must be doing the right thing. But, I increasingly question whether we are. Of the 160 countries that belong to the United Nations, only three take any appreciable number of legal immigrants. The United States takes about one million a year, Canada takes about 150,000 per year, and Australia takes about 125,000. So, perhaps, 1.25 million people in a total pool of 3 billion people are lucky enough to come to one of the immigrant receiving countries. Yet, that pool increases about 90 million people a year, almost all of the increase in underdeveloped countries.

The maximum amount of "good" that the immigrant receiving countries can do to alleviate the pressures on those countries where people want to migrate is infinitesimally small—less than .05 percent.

The maximum amount of "good" that we can do from the standpoint of alleviating those pressures is ridiculously small. We may be able to save a few highly identified individuals that appear on the evening news. But, in terms of alleviating the pressures of world population, economic disruption, revolts, and revolutions, it is small. Most people will have to solve their problems within their country of origin. In an increasingly crowded world, we have to take great care not to engender unrealistic expectations.

What should be our immigration policy? I believe we should do what is right for America.

The United States accepted more than 9 million immigrants during the 1980s. In contrast to its European and Asian trading partners, the United States is the only major nation accepting large numbers of newcomers. Does the United States stand alone as the major immigration country because it knows something about immigrants that Europe and Japan do not? Or, has the United States resisted a revision of its immigration policies in a changing world?

We backed into this role as the major destination of immigrants without planning for the current wave of newcomers that are crowding our metropolitan areas and are posing massive problems for our health and educational institutions. Yet, today, many voices are heard arguing for more and more immigration and they come from the right and left. One commentator said it well:

> "The conservatives love their cheap labor; the liberals love their cheap cause."

Unfortunately, advocates of more immigration often confuse "pro-immigrant" and "pro-immigration." They believe that more must be done by government for the Hispanic and Asian immigrants currently arriving on our shores, and that doing more for the immigrants who are already here also means supporting further immigration. I am strongly "pro-immigrant" and favor assisting those already here to join our mainstream as soon as possible. I also believe that it is necessary to reduce the number of future immigrants if we are to adequately assist those already here.

Why do I, along with significant majority of the American people (according to recent polls), favor a reduction in levels of immigration? First, the presence of newcomers in such large numbers makes it impossible to deal with America's poor (whether native-born or immigrants) in compassionate and effective ways. The United States has a large, and growing, number of people —especially in the inner cities—with weak ties to the labor market, but strong links to welfare programs, crime, and drugs. Many immigrants also live in these cities. These immigrants gain a foothold in the labor market and then preserve the status quo because they do not complain about inferior wages or working conditions.

As long as eager immigrants are available, private employers are not going to make the difficult and costly adjustments needed to employ the American underclass. Instead, they continue to operate their sweatshops and complain about the unwillingness of Americans with welfare and other options to be enthusiastic seamstresses or hotel maids alongside the immigrants. If we are going to end "welfare as we now know it" we are going to have to end immigration "as we now know it."

The availability of immigrants keep private business from experimenting with effective ways to integrate the underclass into the work force. Yet, a tight labor market could provide a unique opportunity for private businesses to help lift people out of poverty and into the mainstream of American society. At a time when American minorities, Hispanic as well as African-American, suffer from double-digit unemployment, I believe it is immoral to continue accepting so many newcomers to compete with Americans for the jobs that are available. I believe a tight labor market is a great friend to the poor.

Hannah Arendt once observed that there is nothing more dangerous to a society than to have large numbers of human beings who are not economically vital. With or without immigration, changing technology and global economy are marginalizing large segments of people in our society.

We see evidence of it every day. The once self-sufficient blue collar worker who is now struggling to hang on, doing menial labor for menial wages. The proliferation of homeless, who have ceased even to have marginal value to our economy. These people already pose a monumental challenge to our society. Armies of people who have no personal stake in the current order, and a society that has no real use for such people, is a formula for disaster, as Arendt warned.

Not only are we failing to come to grips with this dangerous social pathology, but we are exacerbating it through our immigration policies. By tens of millions, we are importing immigrants to compete with our own economically marginal citizens.

The jobs that used to give the less educated in our country a stake in our society—the ability to contribute, to own a home, a college education for their children—those jobs are being lost to global competition. At a time when we should be engaging in a national effort to retrain such workers, to make them economically vital, we are doing something far different. We are forcing them to compete with a constantly growing pool of immigrant labor that further drives down wages and working conditions for those jobs that remain.

In the future, probably the not too distant future, we will pay the price for the short-term benefits of these immigration policies. We undermine the working class of this country at our own peril.

The second reason for reducing immigration is that the availability of such workers steers some of the economy in a losing direction. American products have to compete in international markets. The United States' competitive edge can be technological sophistication, quality and reliability, or price. Although large numbers of unskilled immigrants may help American businesses hold down wages and thus prices in order to remain competitive, a low-wage and low-price strategy simply cannot succeed in the global economy. Developing countries are becoming more adept at producing goods, such as garments and agricultural products, that are currently made in the United States by immigrant workers. Consequently, even wages which are low by United States standards are not low enough to compete with Malaysian seamstresses or Mexican farm workers.

Industries which rely on immigrant workers are often slow to innovate, and when developing countries ship similar products produced at even lower wages to the United States, these American businesses often turn protectionist. The result is familiar. The American industry which "needed" immigrant workers to survive and ensure, for example, that grapes do not cost $2.00 per pound soon complains that cheaper foreign grapes threaten the survival of the American grape industry and asks for restrictions on imports. This, in turn, drives up consumer prices.

The third reason for limiting immigration is to ease the adaptation of newcomers into American society and facilitate their acceptance by the resident population. Earlier immigration waves contributed to positive changes in American culture. Many of us here today are second and third generation Americans and we are justly proud of our heritage and the contributions our ancestors made to American society. However, the immigration wave at the turn of the twentieth century ended after 25 years, partly due to war and depression and also because of the 1920s restrictive legislation. As a result, immigration dropped from over one million annually in 1908–09 to under 100,000 in the 1930s. No such abrupt end to current immigration is in sight. The immigration laws of the 1920s were racist and are an embarrassing blot on the American conscience. Yet, by limiting the admission of newcomers, the new immigrants were encouraged to adapt to American society. And within two generations, they adapted with a vengeance—and in the process, improved society. Tsongas is now as American as Clinton. Valdez is as common as Smith.

Today, with immigration increasing year after year, it is difficult for new Americans to adapt to the United States as did previous immigrants. Rather, the old norms and languages are reinforced in ever-growing ethnic enclaves and we see a situation such as Miami where, according to the 1990 census, over half of the population of that city either do not speak English or speak it poorly.

Because of these dramatic shifts in demographic behavior, current and future immigrants—as well as the resident population—must adapt to a brand new social situation. Pressure was exerted on earlier waves of immigrants to "Americanize" and to conform to Anglo-Saxon norms. Instead, a new "melting pot" emerged within the population of European ancestry. What kind of cultural adaptation will be needed to insure that today's different ethnic groups assimilate into 21st century America? With a continuation of current levels of immigration, cultural separatism, where each group maintains its own identity at the expense of the greater whole, could easily emerge. I would argue strongly against such an eventuality.

The fourth reason to reduce immigration is to slow down rapid population growth. We are the world's fastest growing industrial nation. We add about three million people annually. If current demographic trends continue, with fertility once again above 2.0 and immigration levels surpassing one million annually, thanks to the 1990 legislation, our population could approach half a billion by 2050, or 145 million more people than today. Demographers Dennis Ahlburg and J.W. Vaupel foresee a population of 811 million by 2080—that's bigger than India today!

Several weeks ago, National Public Radio was airing a piece about politics in India. During the course of the report they aired a comment by a professor at an Indian university that ought to serve as a warning to those of us in America. The professor began his comments by saying:

"We are the world's largest democracy. But because India is so overpopulated, Indians have very few personal freedoms."

Personal liberty, the ability to "do our own thing" is very much dependent on the size of our population. The more people we have, the more rules and regulations we will require to govern what we do, when we do it, how we do it and where it can be done. When everyone is living cheek to jowl, it becomes impossible for you to do your own thing without it impinging on me.

As we grow not just in numbers, but in terms of people of different cultures living side by side, the tensions of overpopulation become even greater. A difficult situation is made all the more difficult because we begin to lose a consensus about how a crowded society should co-exist.

While population growth must eventually come to an end, when and at what point should that occur? Our infrastructure is already deteriorating; rapid population growth exacerbates this deterioration by increasing the burden on roads and water systems and creating demands for schools and other types of public investment. Americans are concerned about environmental issues, about air and water quality, and while population growth is not necessarily the major cause of environmental problems, more people are certainly an accomplice. Quality of life can improve more with reduced population growth.

I believe we must place our emphasis on helping those in need—where they are. In 1990, 58 percent of the $400 million that the United States committed to assisting refugees was spent to resettle 125,000 refugees in this country. By contrast, what we spent to help the 99 percent of world refugees we did not resettle, amounted to a paltry four cents a day per capita. Resettling the few, while neglecting the many, is at best stupid and at worst immoral.

In addition to what we spent resettling a handful of refugees, the federal government spent (according to the Center for Immigration Studies) in excess of $2 billion in 1990 to take care of the needs of recent immigrants. By all indications, those costs are rising rapidly. California reports that it cost $700 million last year to provide health care just to illegal aliens. That's not the cost for all immigrants in the state—that's just the health care bill for people who were in the country illegally to begin with!

From the point of view of the recently resettled refugee or immigrant, these have been resources well spent. For the countless millions barely surviving in the shanty towns of most of the third world, it was a gross misallocation of resources.

The underclass, the economic trajectory, cultural adaptation, and population growth are four reasons why I think that the United States should reevaluate its immigration policy. I am convinced that a continuation of current trends will produce problems that can be avoided.

I sincerely believe that legal immigration should be limited to no more than 300,000 people a year—a level that the majority of Americans feel comfortable with.

The sense that Americans want immigration of all kinds brought down to more manageable levels is growing more evident every day. In California, the national's most important political state and the national bellwether when it comes to political trends, this year's elections are being dominated by the immigration issue. In many respects, immigration has overshadowed the races for governor and senator in that state. Given California's political importance—it is unlikely that anyone can win the White House without winning California—any issue that so dominates the political agenda there is bound to become an issue in the 1996 presidential campaign.

We have an opportunity now for comprehensive immigration reform—and that is what is needed, a top to bottom overhaul of our immigration policies. During the last session of Congress, we saw the first encouraging moves in that direction. For the first time in nearly 30 years, legislation was introduced to reform a policy that most Americans agree does not serve the interests of our nation. Even more encouraging, these first attempts at serious immigration reform had bi-partisan support.

Limiting legal immigration and halting illegal immigration are often perceived as controversial issues. Quite the contrary. There is practically no other public policy matter on which there is greater political consensus among the American people. With a new congress... [and] with a clear message from the voters of California, ... we have an opportunity to make some real reforms....

Which brings me to the Federation for American Immigration Reform, or FAIR, a remarkable not-for-profit organization that I've been associated with now for almost fifteen years. It's made up of people from all across America, in all fifty states, governed by an all-volunteer Board of Directors from across the political spectrum. FAIR works more aggressively—and responsibly—than any other national organization to fight for the kinds of sensible changes I'm talking about here. With an annual budget of only about three million dollars, FAIR has taken on some of the entrenched interests on this issue, and, despite the rough and tumble nature of this debate, has emerged in the forefront of the national immigration dialogue today.

FAIR's program includes research and public education as well as comprehensive legislative solutions to control the costs of illegal immigration, end illegal immigration, set a national policy for legal immigration, and find ways to streamline and reduce the immigration flow down the line. But we can't do it all alone. We need your interest and support to achieve these monumental objectives....

One way or the other, our immigration dilemma will be resolved. As George Kennan has suggested, it will be resolved either by rational decisions at this end—or by the achievement of some sort of a balance of misery between this country and the vast pools of poverty that confront it. The choice is ours to make, and the longer we put it off, the more difficult it will be to make those rational decisions and the more certain it will be that that balance of misery will be achieved.

POSTSCRIPT

Should America Remain a Nation of Immigrants?

There are a number of similarities among the four waves of migration. The "push" factors of political oppression, religious persecution, and lack of economic opportunities have continued to attract immigrants to the United States. Contrary to legend, many mainstream Americans have never welcomed "the huddled masses." Politicians like Patrick Buchanan may deplore the large numbers of nonwhite Hispanics and Asians entering the United States, yet over 200 years ago Benjamin Franklin echoed similar sentiments about the "Palatine boors" from Germany who swarmed into Pennsylvania with little respect or knowledge of the English language and its customs.

The major differences among the four waves of migration center around America's evolving economy. Eighteenth-century colonial America's economy was primarily subsistence agriculture; between 1850 and 1925 America shifted to a market-oriented agricultural- and industrial-producing economy; since the 1950s America has shifted to a postindustrial, technetronic, consumption-based economic system. Meanwhile illegal immigrants from Mexico, who work at seasonal back-breaking jobs for agribusinesses, stream into the United States at a rate of 250,000 per year.

What effect will the recent immigration have on America's core culture? Since the newest phase only started in 1968, it is probably too soon to tell whether or not the "ethnic enclaves" of the Cubans in Miami and the Asian neighborhoods of New York City and Los Angeles will disperse, as occurred in earlier generations.

There is an enormous bibliography on the newest immigrants. A good starting point, which clearly explains the immigration laws and their impact on the development of American society, is Kenneth K. Lee, *Huddled Masses, Muddled Laws: Why Contemporary Immigration Policy Fails to Reflect Public Opinion* (Praeger, 1998). Another book that concisely summarizes both sides of the debate and contains a useful glossary of terms is Gerald Leinwand, *American Immigration: Should the Open Door Be Closed?* (Franklin Watts, 1995).

Because historians take a long-range view of immigration, they tend to weigh in on the pro side of the debate. See L. Edward Purcell, *Immigration: Social Issues in American History Series* (Oryx Press, 1995); Ueda's *Postwar America: A Social History* (Bedford Books, 1995); and David M. Reimers, *Still the Golden Door: The Third World War Comes to America,* 2d ed. (Columbia University Press, 1997) and *Unwelcome Strangers: American Identity and the Turn Against Immigration* (Columbia University Press, 1998).

ISSUE 15

Did President Reagan Win the Cold War?

YES: John Lewis Gaddis, from *The United States and the End of the Cold War: Implications, Reconsiderations, Provocations* (Oxford University Press, 1992)

NO: Daniel Deudney and G. John Ikenberry, from "Who Won the Cold War?" *Foreign Policy* (Summer 1992)

ISSUE SUMMARY

YES: Professor of history John Lewis Gaddis argues that President Ronald Reagan combined a policy of militancy and operational pragmatism to bring about the most significant improvement in Soviet-American relations since the end of World War II.

NO: Professors of political science Daniel Deudney and G. John Ikenberry contend that the cold war ended only when Soviet president Mikhail Gorbachev accepted Western liberal values and the need for global cooperation.

The term *cold war* was first coined by the American financial whiz and presidential adviser Bernard Baruch in 1947. Cold war refers to the extended but restricted conflict that existed between the United States and the Soviet Union from the end of World War II in 1945 until 1990. Looking back, it appears that the conflicting values and goals of a democratic/capitalist United States and a communist Soviet Union reinforced this state of affairs between the two countries. Basically, the cold war ended when the Soviet Union gave up its control over the Eastern European nations and ceased to be a unified country itself.

The Nazi invasion of Russia in June 1941 and the Japanese attack on America's Pacific outposts in December united the United States and the Soviet Union against the Axis powers during World War II. Nevertheless, complications ensued during the top-level allied discussions to coordinate war strategy. The first meeting between the big three—U.S. president Franklin Roosevelt, British prime minister Winston Churchill, and Soviet premier Joseph Stalin— took place in Teheran in 1943 followed by another at Yalta in February 1945. These high-level negotiations were held under the assumption that wartime harmony among Britain, the United States, and the Soviet Union would continue; that Stalin, Churchill, and Roosevelt would lead the postwar world as they had conducted the war; and that the details of the general policies and agreements would be resolved at a less pressing time.

But none of these premises were fulfilled. By the time the Potsdam Conference (to discuss possible action against Japan) took place in July 1945, Churchill had been defeated in a parliamentary election, Roosevelt had died, and President Harry S. Truman had been thrust, unprepared, into his place. Of the big three, only Stalin remained as a symbol of continuity. Details about the promises at Teheran and Yalta faded into the background. Power politics, nuclear weapons, and mutual fears and distrust replaced the reasonably harmonious working relationships of the three big powers during World War II.

By 1947 the Truman administration had adopted a conscious policy of containment toward the Russians. This meant maintaining the status quo in Europe through various U.S. assistance programs. The NATO alliance of 1949 completed the shift of U.S. policy away from its pre–World War II isolationist policy and toward a commitment to the defense of Western Europe.

In the 1960s the largest problem facing the two superpowers was controlling the spread of nuclear weapons. The first attempt at arms control took place in the 1950s. After Stalin died in 1953, the Eisenhower administration made an "open-skies" proposal. This was rejected by the Russians, who felt (correctly) that they were behind the Americans in the arms race. In the summer of 1962 Soviet premier Nikita Khrushchev attempted to redress the balance of power by secretly installing missiles in Cuba that could be employed to launch nuclear attacks against U.S. cities. This sparked the Cuban Missile Crisis, the high point of the cold war, which brought both nations to the brink of nuclear war before the Russians agreed to withdraw the missiles.

During the Leonid Brezhnev–Richard Nixon years, the policy of *détente* (relaxation of tensions) resulted in a series of summit meetings. Most important was the SALT I agreement, which outlawed national antiballistic missile defenses and placed a five-year moratorium on the building of new strategic ballistic missiles.

Soviet-American relations took a turn for the worse when the Soviets invaded Afghanistan in December 1979. In response, President Jimmy Carter postponed presenting SALT II to the Senate and imposed an American boycott of the 1980 Olympic Games, which were held in Moscow.

Détente remained dead during President Ronald Reagan's first administration. Reagan not only promoted a military budget of $1.5 trillion over a five-year period, he also was the first president since Truman to refuse to meet the Soviet leader. Major changes, however, took place during Reagan's second administration. In the following selections, John Lewis Gaddis argues that President Reagan combined a policy of militancy and operational pragmatism to bring about significant improvements in Soviet-American relations, while Daniel Deudney and G. John Ikenberry credit Soviet president Mikhail Gorbachev with ending the cold war because he accepted Western liberal values and the need for global cooperation.

The Unexpected Ronald Reagan

T he task of the historian is, very largely, one of explaining how we got from where we were to where we are today. To say that the Reagan administration's policy toward the Soviet Union is going to pose special challenges to historians is to understate the matter: rarely has there been a greater gap between the expectations held for an administration at the beginning of its term and the results it actually produced. The last thing one would have anticipated at the time Ronald Reagan took office in 1981 was that he would use his eight years in the White House to bring about the most significant improvement in Soviet-American relations since the end of World War II. I am not at all sure that President Reagan himself foresaw this result. And yet, that is precisely what happened, with—admittedly—a good deal of help from Mikhail Gorbachev.

The question of how this happened and to what extent it was the product of accident or of conscious design is going to preoccupy scholars for years to come. The observations that follow are a rough first attempt to grapple with that question. Because we lack access to the archives or even very much memoir material as yet, what I will have to say is of necessity preliminary, incomplete, and almost certainly in several places dead wrong. Those are the hazards of working with contemporary history, though; if historians are not willing to run these risks, political scientists and journalists surely will. That prospect in itself provides ample justification for plunging ahead.

The Hard-Liner

... President Reagan in March, 1983, made his most memorable pronouncement on the Soviet Union: condemning the tendency of his critics to hold both sides responsible for the nuclear arms race, he denounced the U.S.S.R. as an "evil empire" and as "the focus of evil in the modern world." Two weeks later, the President surprised even his closest associates by calling for a long-term research and development program to create defense against attacks by strategic missiles, with a view, ultimately, to "rendering these nuclear weapons impotent and obsolete." The Strategic Defense Initiative was the most fundamental challenge to existing orthodoxies on arms control since negotiations on that subject had begun with the Russians almost three decades earlier. Once again it called into question the President's seriousness in seeking an end to—or even a significant moderation of—the strategic arms race.

Anyone who listened to the "evil empire" speech or who considered the implications of "Star Wars" might well have concluded that Reagan saw the Soviet-American relationship as an elemental confrontation between virtue and wickedness that would allow neither negotiation nor conciliation in any form; his tone seemed more appropriate to a medieval crusade than to a revival of containment. Certainly there were those within his administration who held such views, and their influence, for a time, was considerable. But to see the President's policies solely in terms of his rhetoric, it is now clear, would have been quite wrong.

For President Reagan appears to have understood—or to have quickly learned—the dangers of basing foreign policy solely on ideology: he combined militancy with a surprising degree of operational pragmatism and a shrewd sense of timing. To the astonishment of his own hard-line supporters, what appeared to be an enthusiastic return to the Cold War in fact turned out to be a more solidly based approach to detente than anything the Nixon, Ford, or Carter administrations had been able to accomplish.

The Negotiator

There had always been a certain ambivalence in the Reagan administration's image of the Soviet Union. On the one hand, dire warnings about Moscow's growing military strength suggested an almost Spenglerian gloom [reflecting the theory of philosopher Oswald Spengler, which holds that all major cultures grow, mature, and decay in a natural cycle] about the future: time, it appeared, was on the Russians' side. But mixed with this pessimism was a strong sense of self-confidence, growing out of the ascendancy of conservatism within the United States and an increasing enthusiasm for capitalism overseas, that assumed the unworkability of Marxism as a form of political, social, and economic organization: "The West won't contain communism, it will transcend communism," the President predicted in May, 1981. "It won't bother to ... denounce it, it will dismiss it as some bizarre chapter in human history whose last pages are even now being written." By this logic, the Soviet Union had already reached the apex of its strength as a world power, and time in fact was on the side of the West.

Events proved the optimism to have been more justified than the pessimism, for over the next four years the Soviet Union would undergo one of the most rapid erosions both of internal self-confidence and external influence in modern history; that this happened just as Moscow's long and costly military buildup should have begun to pay political dividends made the situation all the more frustrating for the Russians. It may have been luck for President Reagan to have come into office at a peak in the fortunes of the Soviet Union and at a trough in those of the United States: things would almost certainly have improved regardless of who entered the White House in 1981. But it took more than luck to recognize what was happening, and to capitalize on it to the extent that the Reagan administration did.

Indications of Soviet decline took several forms. The occupation of Afghanistan had produced only a bloody Vietnam-like stalemate, with Soviet troops unable to suppress the rebellion, or to protect themselves and their clients, or to withdraw. In Poland a long history of economic mismanagement had produced, in the form of the Solidarity trade union, a rare phenomenon within the Soviet bloc: a true workers' movement. Soviet ineffectiveness became apparent in the Middle East in 1982 when the Russians were unable to provide any significant help to the Palestinian Liberation Organization during the Israeli invasion of Lebanon; even more embarrassing, Israeli pilots using American-built fighters shot down over eighty Soviet-supplied Syrian jets without a single loss of their own. Meanwhile, the Soviet domestic economy which [former Soviet premier Nikita] Khrushchev had once predicted would overtake that of the United States, had in fact stagnated during the early 1980s, Japan by some indices actually overtook the U.S.S.R. as the world's second largest producer of goods and services, and even China, a nation with four times the population of the Soviet Union, now became an agricultural exporter at a time when Moscow still required food imports from the West to feed its own people.

What all of this meant was that the Soviet Union's appeal as a model for Third World political and economic development—once formidable—had virtually disappeared, indeed as Moscow's military presence in those regions grew during the late 1970s, the Russians increasingly came to be seen, not as liberators, but as latter-day imperialists themselves. The Reagan administration moved swiftly to take advantage of this situation by funneling military assistance—sometimes openly sometimes covertly—to rebel groups (or "freedom fighters," as the President insisted on calling them) seeking to overthrow Soviet-backed regimes in Afghanistan, Angola, Ethiopia, Cambodia, and Nicaragua; in October, 1983, to huge domestic acclaim but with dubious legality Reagan even ordered the direct use of American military forces to overthrow an unpopular Marxist government on the tiny Caribbean island of Grenada. The Reagan Doctrine, as this strategy became known, sought to exploit vulnerabilities the Russians had created for themselves in the Third World: this latter-day effort to "roll back" Soviet influence would, in time, produce impressive results at minimum cost and risk to the United States.

Compounding the Soviet Union's external difficulties was a long vacuum in internal leadership occasioned by [President Leonid] Brezhnev's slow enfeeblement and eventual death in November, 1982; by the installation as his successor of an already-ill Yuri Andropov, who himself died in February 1984; and by the installation of his equally geriatric successor, Konstantin Chernenko. At a time when a group of strong Western leaders had emerged—including not just President Reagan but also Prime Minister Margaret Thatcher in Great Britain, President François Mitterrand in France, and Chancellor Helmut Kohl in West Germany—this apparent inability to entrust leadership to anyone other than party stalwarts on their deathbeds was a severe commentary on what the sclerotic Soviet system had become. "We could go no further without hitting the end," one Russian later recalled of Chernenko's brief reign. "Here was the General Secretary of the party who is also the Chairman of the Presidium of the Supreme Soviet, the embodiment of our country, the personification of the party and he could barely stand up."

There was no disagreement within the Reagan administration about the desirability under these circumstances, of pressing the Russians hard. Unlike several of their predecessors, the President and his advisers did not see containment as requiring the application of sticks and carrots in equal proportion; wielders of sticks definitely predominated among them. But there were important differences over what the purpose of wielding the sticks was to be.

Some advisers, like [Secretary of Defense Casper] Weinberger, [Assistant Secretary of Defense for International Security Policy Richard] Perle, and [chief Soviet specialist on the National Security Council Richard] Pipes, saw the situation as a historic opportunity to exhaust the Soviet system. Noting that the Soviet economy was already stretched to the limit, they advocated taking advantage of American technological superiority to engage the Russians in an arms race of indefinite duration and indeterminate cost. Others, including Nitze, the Joint Chiefs of Staff, career Foreign Service officer Jack Matlock, who succeeded Pipes as chief Soviet expert at the NSC, and—most important—[Secretary of State Alexander M.] Haig's replacement after June, 1982, the unflamboyant but steady George Shultz, endorsed the principle of "negotiation from strength": the purpose of accumulating military hardware was not to debilitate the other side, but to convince it to negotiate.

The key question, of course, was what President Reagan's position would be. Despite his rhetoric, he had been careful not to rule out talks with the Russians once the proper conditions had been met: even while complaining, in his first press conference, about the Soviet propensity to lie, cheat, and steal, he had also noted that "when we can, . . . we should start negotiations on the basis of trying to effect an actual reduction in the numbers of nuclear weapons. That would be real arms reduction." But most observers—and probably many of his own advisers—assumed that when the President endorsed negotiations leading toward the "reduction," as opposed to the "limitation," of strategic arms, or the "zero option" in the INF [intermediate-range nuclear forces] talks, or the Strategic Defense Initiative, he was really seeking to avoid negotiations by setting minimal demands above the maximum concessions the Russians could afford to make. He was looking for a way they believed, to gain credit for cooperativeness with both domestic and allied constituencies without actually having to give up anything.

That would turn out to be a gross misjudgment of President Reagan, who may have had cynical advisers but was not cynical himself. It would become apparent with the passage of time that when the Chief Executive talked about "reducing" strategic missiles he meant precisely that; the appeal of the "zero option" was that it really would get rid of intermediate-range nuclear forces; the Strategic Defense Initiative might in fact, just as the President had said, make nuclear weapons "impotent and obsolete." A simple and straightforward man, Reagan took the principle of "negotiation from strength" literally: once one had built strength, one negotiated.

The first indications that the President might be interested in something other than an indefinite arms race began to appear in the spring and summer of

1983. Widespread criticism of his "evil empire" speech apparently shook him: although his view of the Soviet system itself did not change, Reagan was careful, after that point, to use more restrained language in characterizing it. Clear evidence of the President's new moderation came with the Korean airliner incident of September, 1983. Despite his outrage, Reagan did not respond—as one might have expected him to—by reviving his "evil empire" rhetoric; instead he insisted that arms control negotiations would continue, and in a remarkably conciliatory television address early in 1984 he announced that the United States was "in its strongest position in years to establish a constructive and realistic working relationship with the Soviet Union." The President concluded this address by speculating on how a typical Soviet couple—Ivan and Anya—might find that they had much in common with a typical American couple—Jim and Sally: "They might even have decided that they were all going to get together for dinner some evening soon."

It was possible to construct self-serving motives for this startling shift in tone. With a presidential campaign under way the White House was sensitive to Democratic charges that Reagan was the only postwar president not to have met with a Soviet leader while in office. Certainly it was to the advantage of the United States in its relations with Western Europe to look as reasonable as possible in the face of Soviet intransigence. But events would show that the President's interest in an improved relationship was based on more than just electoral politics or the needs of the alliance: it was only the unfortunate tendency of Soviet leaders to die upon taking office that was depriving the American Chief Executive—himself a spry septuagenarian—of a partner with whom to negotiate.

By the end of September, 1984—and to the dismay of Democratic partisans who saw Republicans snatching the "peace" issue from them—a contrite Soviet Foreign Minister Andrei Gromyko had made the pilgrimage to Washington to re-establish contacts with the Reagan administration. Shortly after Reagan's landslide re-election over Walter Mondale in November, the United States and the Soviet Union announced that a new set of arms control negotiations would begin early the following year, linking together discussions on START [Strategic Arms Reduction Talks], INF, and weapons in space. And in December, a hitherto obscure member of the Soviet Politburo, Mikhail Gorbachev, announced while visiting Great Britain that the U.S.S.R. was prepared to seek "radical solutions" looking toward a ban on nuclear missiles altogether. Three months later, Konstantin Chernenko, the last in a series of feeble and unimaginative Soviet leaders, expired, and Gorbachev—a man who was in no way feeble and unimaginative—became the General Secretary of the Communist Party of the Soviet Union. Nothing would ever be quite the same again.

Reagan and Gorbachev

Several years after Gorbachev had come to power, George F. Kennan was asked in a television interview how so unconventional a Soviet leader could have risen to the top in a system that placed such a premium on conformity. Kennan's reply reflected the perplexity American experts on Soviet affairs have felt in seeking to account for the Gorbachev phenomenon: "I really cannot explain it." It seemed most improbable that a regime so lacking in the capacity for innovation, self-evaluation, or even minimally effective public relations should suddenly produce a leader who excelled in all of these qualities; even more remarkable was the fact that Gorbachev saw himself as a revolutionary—a breed not seen in Russia for decades—determined, as he put it, "to get out of the quagmire of conservatism, and to break the inertia of stagnation."

Whatever the circumstances that led to it, the accession of Gorbachev reversed almost overnight the pattern of the preceding four years: after March, 1985, it was the Soviet Union that seized the initiative in relations with the West. It did so in a way that was both reassuring and unnerving at the same time: by becoming so determinedly cooperative as to convince some supporters of containment in the United States and Western Europe—uneasy in the absence of the intransigence to which they had become accustomed—that the Russians were now seeking to defeat that strategy by depriving it, with sinister cleverness, of an object to be contained.

President Reagan, in contrast, welcomed the fresh breezes emanating from Moscow and moved quickly to establish a personal relationship with the new Soviet leader. Within four days of Gorbachev's taking power, the President was characterizing the Russians as "in a different frame of mind than they've been in the past.... [T]hey, I believe, are really going to try and, with us, negotiate a reduction in armaments." And within four months, the White House was announcing that Reagan would meet Gorbachev at Geneva in November for the first Soviet-American summit since 1979.

The Geneva summit, like so many before it, was long on symbolism and short on substance. The two leaders appeared to get along well with one another: they behaved, as one Reagan adviser later put it, "like a couple of fellows who had run into each other at the club and discovered that they had a lot in common." The President agreed to discuss deep cuts in strategic weapons and improved verification, but he made it clear that he was not prepared to forgo development of the Strategic Defense Initiative in order to get them. His reason —which Gorbachev may not have taken seriously until this point—had to do with his determination to retain SDI as a means ultimately of rendering nuclear weapons obsolete. The President's stubbornness on this point precluded progress, at least for the moment, on what was coming to be called the "grand compromise": Paul Nitze's idea of accepting limits on SDI in return for sweeping reductions in strategic missiles. But it did leave the way open for an alert Gorbachev, detecting the President's personal enthusiasm for nuclear abolition, to surprise the world in January, 1986, with his own plan for accomplishing that objective: a Soviet-American agreement to rid the world of nuclear weapons altogether by the year 2000.

It was easy to question Gorbachev's motives in making so radical a proposal in so public a manner with no advance warning. Certainly any discussion of even reducing—much less abolishing—nuclear arsenals would raise difficult questions for American allies, where an abhorrence of nuclear weapons continued to coexist uneasily alongside the conviction that only their presence could deter superior Soviet conventional forces. Nor was the Gorbachev proposal clear on how Russians and Americans could ever impose abolition, even if they themselves agreed to it, on other nuclear and non-nuclear powers. Still, the line between rhetoric and conviction is a thin one: the first Reagan-Gorbachev summit may not only have created a personal bond between the two leaders; it may also have sharpened a vague but growing sense in the minds of both men that, despite all the difficulties in constructing an alternative, an indefinite continuation of life under nuclear threat was not a tolerable condition for either of their countries, and that their own energies might very well be directed toward overcoming that situation.

That both Reagan and Gorbachev were thinking along these lines became clear at their second meeting, the most extraordinary Soviet-American summit of the postwar era, held on very short notice at Reykjavik, Iceland, in October, 1986. The months that preceded Reykjavik had seen little tangible progress toward arms control; there had also developed, in August, an unpleasant skirmish between intelligence agencies on both sides as the KGB, in apparent retaliation for the FBI's highly publicized arrest of a Soviet United Nations official in New York on espionage charges, set up, seized, and held *USNEWS* correspondent Nicholas Daniloff on trumped-up accusations for just under a month. It was a sobering reminder that the Soviet-American relationship existed at several different levels, and that cordiality in one did not rule out the possibility of confrontation in others. The Daniloff affair also brought opportunity though, for in the course of negotiations to settle it Gorbachev proposed a quick "preliminary" summit, to be held within two weeks, to try to break the stalemate in negotiations over intermediate-range nuclear forces in Europe, the aspect of arms control where progress at a more formal summit seemed likely. Reagan immediately agreed.

But when the President and his advisers arrived at Reykjavik, they found that Gorbachev had much more grandiose proposals in mind. These included not only an endorsement of 50 percent cuts in Soviet and American strategic weapons across the board, but also agreement not to demand the inclusion of British and French nuclear weapons in these calculations—a concession that removed a major stumbling block to START—and acceptance in principle of Reagan's 1981 "zero option" for intermediate-range nuclear forces, all in return for an American commitment not to undermine SALT I's ban on strategic defenses for the next ten years. Impressed by the scope of these concessions, the American side quickly put together a compromise that would have cut ballistic missiles to zero within a decade in return for the right, after that time, to deploy strategic defenses against the bomber and cruise missile forces that would be left. Gorbachev immediately countered by proposing the abolition of *all* nuclear weapons within ten years, thus moving his original deadline from the year 2000 to 1996. President Reagan is said to have replied: "*All* nuclear weapons? Well, Mikhail, that's exactly what I've been talking about all along.... That's always been my goal."

A series of events set in motion by a Soviet diplomat's arrest on a New York subway platform and by the reciprocal framing of an American journalist in Moscow had wound up with the two most powerful men in the world agreeing—for the moment, and to the astonishment of their aides—on the abolition of all nuclear weapons within ten years. But the moment did not last. Gorbachev went on to insist, as a condition for nuclear abolition, upon a ban on the laboratory testing of SDI, which Reagan immediately interpreted as an effort to kill strategic defense altogether. Because the ABM treaty does allow for some laboratory testing, the differences between the two positions were not all that great. But in the hothouse atmosphere of this cold-climate summit no one explored such details, and the meeting broke up in disarray, acrimony, and mutual disappointment.

It was probably just as well. The sweeping agreements contemplated at Reykjavik grew out of hasty improvisation and high-level posturing, not careful thought. They suffered from all the deficiencies of Gorbachev's unilateral proposal for nuclear abolition earlier in the year; they also revealed how susceptible the leaders of the United States and the Soviet Union had become to each other's amplitudinous rhetoric. It was as if Reagan and Gorbachev had been trying desperately to outbid the other in a gigantic but surrealistic auction, with the diaphanous prospect of a nuclear-free world somehow on the block. . . .

Negotiations on arms control continued in the year that followed Reykjavik, however, with both sides edging toward the long-awaited "grand compromise" that would defer SDI in return for progress toward a START agreement. Reagan and Gorbachev did sign an intermediate-range nuclear forces treaty in Washington in December, 1987, which for the first time provided that Russians and Americans would actually dismantle and destroy—literally before each other's eyes—an entire category of nuclear missiles. There followed a triumphal Reagan visit to Moscow in May, 1988, featuring the unusual sight of a Soviet general secretary and an American president strolling amiably through Red Square, greeting tourists and bouncing babies in front of Lenin's tomb, while their respective military aides—each carrying the codes needed to launch nuclear missiles at each other's territory—stood discreetly in the background. Gorbachev made an equally triumphal visit to New York in December, 1988, to address the United Nations General Assembly: there he announced a *unilateral* Soviet cut of some 500,000 ground troops, a major step toward moving arms control into the realm of conventional forces.

When, on the same day Gorbachev spoke in New York, a disastrous earthquake killed some 25,000 Soviet Armenians, the outpouring of aid from the United States and other Western countries was unprecedented since the days of Lend Lease. One had the eerie feeling, watching anguished television reports from the rubble that had been the cities of Leninakan and Stipak—the breakdown of emergency services, the coffins stacked like logs in city parks, the mass burials—that one had glimpsed, on a small scale, something of what a nuclear war might actually be like. The images suggested just how vulnerable both super-powers remained after almost a half-century of trying to minimize vulnerabilities. They thereby reinforced what had become almost a ritual incantation pronounced by both Reagan and Gorbachev at each of their now-frequent summits: "A nuclear war cannot be won and must never be fought."

But as the Reagan administration prepared to leave office the following month, in an elegiac mood very different from the grim militancy with which it had assumed its responsibilities eight years earlier, the actual prospect of a nuclear holocaust seemed more remote than at any point since the Soviet-American nuclear rivalry had begun. Accidents, to be sure, could always happen. Irrationality though blessedly rare since 1945, could never be ruled out. There was reason for optimism, though, in the fact that as George Bush entered the White House early in 1989, the point at issue no longer seemed to be "how to fight the Cold War" at all, but rather "is the Cold War over?"

Ronald Reagan and the End of the Cold War

The record of the Reagan years suggests the need to avoid the common error of trying to predict outcomes from attributes. There is no question that the President and his advisers came into office with an ideological view of the world that appeared to allow for no compromise with the Russians; but ideology has a way of evolving to accommodate reality especially in the hands of skillful political leadership. Indeed a good working definition of leadership might be just this —the ability to accommodate ideology to practical reality—and by that standard, Reagan's achievements in relations with the Soviet Union will certainly compare favorably with, and perhaps even surpass, those of Richard Nixon and Henry Kissinger.

Did President Reagan intend for things to come out this way? That question is, of course, more difficult to determine, given our lack of access to the archives. But a careful reading of the public record would, I think, show that the President was expressing hopes for an improvement in Soviet-American relations from the moment he entered the White House, and that he began shifting American policy in that direction as early as the first months of 1983, almost two years before Mikhail Gorbachev came to power. Gorbachev's extraordinary receptiveness to such initiatives—as distinct from the literally moribund responses of his predecessors—greatly accelerated the improvement in relations, but it would be a mistake to credit him solely with the responsibility for what happened: Ronald Reagan deserves a great deal of the credit as well.

Critics have raised the question, though, of whether President Reagan was responsible for, or even aware of, the direction administration policy was taking. This argument is, I think, both incorrect and unfair. Reagan's opponents have been quick enough to hold him personally responsible for the failures of his administration; they should be equally prepared to acknowledge his successes. And there are points, even with the limited sources now available, where we can see that the President himself had a decisive impact upon the course of events. They include, among others: the Strategic Defense Initiative, which may have had its problems as a missile shield but which certainly worked in unsettling the Russians; endorsement of the "zero option" in the INF talks and real reductions in START, the rapidity with which the President entered into, and thereby legitimized, serious negotiations with Gorbachev once he came into office; and, most remarkably of all, his eagerness to contemplate alternatives to the nuclear arms race in a way no previous president had been willing to do.

Now, it may be objected that these were simple, unsophisticated, and, as people are given to saying these days, imperfectly "nuanced" ideas. I would not argue with that proposition. But it is important to remember that while complexity, sophistication, and nuance may be prerequisites for intellectual leadership, they are not necessarily so for political leadership, and can at times actually get in the way. President Reagan generally meant precisely what he said: when he came out in favor of negotiations from strength, or for strategic arms reductions as opposed to limitations, or even for making nuclear weapons ultimately irrelevant and obsolete, he did not do so in the "killer amendment" spirit favored by geopolitical sophisticates on the right; the President may have been conservative but he was never devious. The lesson here ought to be to beware of excessive convolution and subtlety in strategy, for sometimes simple-mindedness wins out, especially if it occurs in high places.

Finally President Reagan also understood something that many geopolitical sophisticates on the left have not understood: that although toughness may or may not be a prerequisite for successful negotiations with the Russians—there are arguments for both propositions—it is absolutely essential if the American people are to lend their support, over time, to what has been negotiated. Others may have seen in the doctrine of "negotiation from strength" a way of avoiding negotiations altogether, but it now seems clear that the President saw in that approach the means of constructing a domestic political base without which agreements with the Russians would almost certainly have foundered, as indeed many of them did in the 1970s. For unless one can sustain domestic support—and one does not do that by appearing weak—then it is hardly likely that whatever one has arranged with any adversary will actually come to anything.

There is one last irony to all of this: it is that it fell to Ronald Reagan to preside over the belated but decisive success of the strategy of containment George F. Kennan had first proposed more than four decades earlier. For what were Gorbachev's reforms if not the long-delayed "mellowing" of Soviet society that Kennan had said would take place with the passage of time? The Stalinist system that had required outside adversaries to justify its own existence now seemed at last to have passed from the scene; Gorbachev appeared to have concluded that the Soviet Union could continue to be a great power in world affairs only through the introduction of something approximating a market economy, democratic political institutions, official accountability, and respect for the rule of law at home. And that, in turn, suggested an even more remarkable conclusion: that the very survival of the ideology Lenin had imposed on Russia in 1917 now required infiltration—perhaps even subversion—by precisely the ideology the great revolutionary had sworn to overthrow

I have some reason to suspect that Professor Kennan is not entirely comfortable with the suggestion that Ronald Reagan successfully completed the execution of the strategy he originated. But as Kennan the historian would be the first to acknowledge, history is full of ironies, and this one, surely, will not rank among the least of them.

**Daniel Deudney and
G. John Ikenberry**

 **NO**

Who Won the Cold War?

The end of the Cold War marks the most important historical divide in half a century. The magnitude of those developments has ushered in a wide-ranging debate over the reasons for its end—a debate that is likely to be as protracted, controversial, and politically significant as that over the Cold War's origins. The emerging debate over why the Cold War ended is of more than historical interest: At stake is the vindication and legitimation of an entire world view and foreign policy orientation.

In thinking about the Cold War's conclusion, it is vital to distinguish between the domestic origins of the crisis in Soviet communism and the external forces that influenced its timing and intensity, as well as the direction of the Soviet response. Undoubtedly, the ultimate cause of the Cold War's outcome lies in the failure of the Soviet system itself. At most, outside forces hastened and intensified the crisis. However, it was not inevitable that the Soviet Union would respond to this crisis as it did in the late 1980s—with domestic liberalization and foreign policy accommodation. After all, many Western experts expected that the USSR would respond to such a crisis with renewed repression at home and aggression abroad, as it had in the past.

At that fluid historic juncture, the complex matrix of pressures, opportunities, and attractions from the outside world influenced the direction of Soviet change, particularly in its foreign policy. The Soviets' field of vision was dominated by the West, the United States, and recent American foreign policy. Having spent more than 45 years attempting to influence the Soviet Union, Americans are now attempting to gauge the weight of their country's impact and, thus, the track record of U.S. policies.

In assessing the rest of the world's impact on Soviet change, a remarkably simplistic and self-serving conventional wisdom has emerged in the United States. This new conventional wisdom, the "Reagan victory school," holds that President Ronald Reagan's military and ideological assertiveness during the 1980s played the lead role in the collapse of Soviet communism and the "taming" of its foreign policy In that view the Reagan administration's ideological counter-offensive and military buildup delivered the knock-out punch to a system that was internally bankrupt and on the ropes. The Reagan Right's perspective is an ideologically pointed version of the more broadly held conventional wisdom on the end of the Cold War that emphasizes the success of the "peace-through-strength" strategy manifest in four decades of Western containment. After decades of waging a costly "twilight struggle," the West now celebrates the triumph of its military and ideological resolve.

The Reagan victory school and the broader peace-through-strength perspectives are, however, misleading and incomplete—both in their interpretation of events in the 1980s and in their understanding of deeper forces that led to the end of the Cold War. It is important to reconsider the emerging conventional wisdom before it truly becomes an article of faith on Cold War history and comes to distort the thinking of policymakers in America and elsewhere.

The collapse of the Cold War caught almost everyone, particularly hardliners, by surprise. Conservatives and most analysts in the U.S. national security establishment believed that the Soviet-U.S. struggle was a permanent feature of international relations. As former National Security Council adviser Zbigniew Brzezinski put it in 1986, "the American-Soviet contest is not some temporary aberration but a historical rivalry that will long endure." And to many hardliners, Soviet victory was far more likely than Soviet collapse. Many ringing predictions now echo as embarrassments.

The Cold War's end was a baby that arrived unexpectedly, but a long line of those claiming paternity has quickly formed. A parade of former Reagan administration officials and advocates has forthrightly asserted that Reagan's hardline policies were the decisive trigger for reorienting Soviet foreign policy and for the demise of communism. As former Pentagon officials like Caspar Weinberger and Richard Perle, columnist George Will, neoconservative thinker Irving Kristol, and other proponents of the Reagan victory school have argued, a combination of military and ideological pressures gave the Soviets little choice but to abandon expansionism abroad and repression at home. In that view, the Reagan military buildup foreclosed Soviet military options while pushing the Soviet economy to the breaking point. Reagan partisans stress that his dramatic "Star Wars" initiative put the Soviets on notice that the next phase of the arms race would be waged in areas where the West held a decisive technological edge.

Reagan and his administration's military initiatives, however, played a far different and more complicated role in inducing Soviet change than the Reagan victory school asserts. For every "hardening" there was a "softening": Reagan's rhetoric of the "Evil Empire" was matched by his vigorous anti-nuclearism; the military buildup in the West was matched by the resurgence of a large popular peace movement; and the Reagan Doctrine's toughening of containment was matched by major deviations from containment in East-West economic relations. Moreover, over the longer term, the strength marshaled in containment was matched by mutual weakness in the face of nuclear weapons, and efforts to engage the USSR were as important as efforts to contain it.

The Irony of Ronald Reagan

Perhaps the greatest anomaly of the Reagan victory school is the "Great Communicator" himself. The Reagan Right ignores that his anti-nuclearism was as strong as his anticommunism. Reagan's personal convictions on nuclear weapons were profoundly at odds with the beliefs of most in his administration. Staffed by officials who considered nuclear weapons a useful instrument of statecraft and who were openly disdainful of the moral critique of nuclear weapons articulated by the arms control community and the peace movement, the administration pursued the hardest line on nuclear policy and the Soviet Union in the postwar era. Then vice president George Bush's observation that nuclear weapons would be fired as a warning shot and Deputy Under Secretary of Defense T. K. Jones's widely quoted view that nuclear war was survivable captured the reigning ethos within the Reagan administration.

In contrast, there is abundant evidence that Reagan himself felt a deep antipathy for nuclear weapons and viewed their abolition to be a realistic and desirable goal. Reagan's call in his famous March 1983 "Star Wars" speech for a program to make nuclear weapons impotent and obsolete was viewed as cynical by many, but actually it expressed Reagan's heartfelt views, views that he came to act upon. As *Washington Post* reporter Lou Cannon's 1991 biography points out, Reagan was deeply disturbed by nuclear deterrence and attracted to abolitionist solutions. "I know I speak for people everywhere when I say our dream is to see the day when nuclear weapons will be banished from the face of the earth," Reagan said in November 1983. Whereas the Right saw anti-nuclearism as a threat to American military spending and the legitimacy of an important foreign policy tool, or as propaganda for domestic consumption, Reagan sincerely believed it. Reagan's anti-nuclearism was not just a personal sentiment. It surfaced at decisive junctures to affect Soviet perceptions of American policy. Sovietologist and strategic analyst Michael MccGwire has argued persuasively that Reagan's anti-nuclearism decisively influenced Soviet-U.S. relations during the early Gorbachev years.

Contrary to the conventional wisdom, the defense buildup did not produce Soviet capitulation. The initial Soviet response to the Reagan administration's buildup and belligerent rhetoric was to accelerate production of offensive weapons, both strategic and conventional. That impasse was broken not by Soviet capitulation but by an extraordinary convergence by Reagan and Mikhail Gorbachev on a vision of mutual nuclear vulnerability and disarmament. On the Soviet side, the dominance of the hardline response to the newly assertive America was thrown into question in early 1985 when Gorbachev became general secretary of the Communist party after the death of Konstantin Chernenko. Without a background in foreign affairs, Gorbachev was eager to assess American intentions directly and put his stamp on Soviet security policy. Reagan's strong antinuclear views expressed at the November 1985 Geneva summit were decisive in convincing Gorbachev that it was possible to work with the West in halting the nuclear arms race. The arms control diplomacy of the later Reagan years was successful because, as *Washington Post* journalist Don Oberdorfer has detailed in *The Turn: From the Cold War to a New Era* (1991), Secretary of State George Shultz picked up on Reagan's strong convictions and deftly side-stepped hard-line opposition to agreements. In fact, Schultz's success at linking presidential unease about nuclear weapons to Soviet overtures in the face of right-wing opposition provides a sharp contrast with John Foster Dulles's refusal to act on President Dwight Eisenhower's nuclear doubts and the opportunities presented by Nikita Khrushchev's détente overtures.

Reagan's commitment to anti-nuclearism and its potential for transforming the U.S-Soviet confrontation was more graphically demonstrated at the October 1986 Reykjavik summit when Reagan and Gorbachev came close to agreeing on a comprehensive program of global denuclearization that was far bolder than any seriously entertained by American strategists since the Baruch Plan of 1946. The sharp contrast between Reagan's and Gorbachev's shared skepticism toward nuclear weapons on the one hand, and the Washington security establishment's consensus on the other, was showcased in former secretary of defense James Schlesinger's scathing accusation that Reagan was engaged in "casual utopianism." But Reagan's anomalous anti-nuclearism provided the crucial signal to Gorbachev that bold initiatives would be reciprocated rather than exploited. Reagan's anti-nuclearism was more important than his administration's military buildup in catalyzing the end of the Cold War.

Neither anti-nuclearism nor its embrace by Reagan have received the credit they deserve for producing the Soviet-U.S. reconciliation. Reagan's accomplishment in this regard has been met with silence from all sides. Conservatives, not sharing Reagan's anti-nuclearism, have emphasized the role of traditional military strength. The popular peace movement, while holding deeply antinuclear views, was viscerally suspicious of Reagan. The establishment arms control community also found Reagan and his motives suspect, and his attack on deterrence conflicted with their desire to stabilize deterrence and establish their credentials as sober participants in security policy making. Reagan's radical anti-nuclearism should sustain his reputation as the ultimate Washington outsider.

The central role of Reagan's and Gorbachev's anti-nuclearism throws new light on the 1987 Treaty on Intermediate-range Nuclear Forces, the first genuine disarmament treaty of the nuclear era. The conventional wisdom emphasizes that this agreement was the fruit of a hard-line negotiating posture and the U.S. military buildup. Yet the superpowers' settlement on the "zero option" was not a vindication of the hard-line strategy. The zero option was originally fashioned by hardliners for propaganda purposes, and many backed off as its implementation became likely. The impasse the hard line created was transcended by the surprising Reagan-Gorbachev convergence against nuclear arms.

The Reagan victory school also overstates the overall impact of American and Western policy on the Soviet Union during the 1980s. The Reagan administration's posture was both evolving and inconsistent. Though loudly proclaiming its intention to go beyond the previous containment policies that were deemed too soft, the reality of Reagan's policies fell short. As Sovietologists Gail Lapidus and Alexander Dallin observed in a 1989 *Bulletin of the Atomic Scientists* article, the policies were "marked to the end by numerous zigzags and reversals, bureaucratic conflicts, and incoherence." Although rollback had long been a cherished goal of the Republican party's right wing, Reagan was unwilling and unable to implement it.

The hard-line tendencies of the Reagan administration were offset in two ways. First, and most important, Reagan's tough talk fueled a large peace movement in the United States and Western Europe in the 1980s, a movement that put significant political pressure upon Western governments to pursue far-reaching arms control proposals. That mobilization of Western opinion created a political climate in which the rhetoric and posture of the early Reagan administration was a significant political liability. By the 1984 U.S. presidential election, the administration had embraced arms control goals that it had previously ridiculed. Reagan's own anti-nuclearism matched that rising public concern, and Reagan emerged as the spokesman for comprehensive denuclearization. Paradoxically, Reagan administration policies substantially triggered the popular revolt against the nuclear hardline, and then Reagan came to pursue the popular agenda more successfully than any other postwar president.

Second, the Reagan administration's hard-line policies were also undercut by powerful Western interests that favored East-West economic ties. In the early months of Reagan's administration, the grain embargo imposed by President Jimmy Carter after the 1979 Soviet invasion of Afghanistan was lifted in order to keep the Republican party's promises to Midwestern farmers. Likewise, in 1981 the Reagan administration did little to challenge Soviet control of Eastern Europe after Moscow pressured Warsaw to suppress the independent Polish trade union Solidarity, in part because Poland might have defaulted on multibillion dollar loans made by Western banks. Also, despite strenuous opposition by the Reagan administration, the NATO allies pushed ahead with a natural gas pipeline linking the Soviet Union with Western Europe. That a project creating substantial economic interdependence could proceed during the worst period of Soviet-U.S. relations in the 1980s demonstrates the failure of the Reagan administration to present an unambiguous hard line toward the Soviet Union. More generally, NATO allies and the vocal European peace movement moderated and buffered hardline American tendencies.

In sum, the views of the Reagan victory school are flawed because they neglect powerful crosscurrents in the West during the 1980s. The conventional wisdom simplifies a complex story and ignores those aspects of Reagan administration policy inconsistent with the hardline rationale. Moreover, the Western "face" toward the Soviet Union did not consist exclusively of Reagan administration policies, but encompassed countervailing tendencies from the Western public, other governments, and economic interest groups.

Whether Reagan is seen as the consummate hardliner or the prophet of anti-nuclearism, one should not exaggerate the influence of his administration, or of other short-term forces. Within the Washington beltway, debates about postwar military and foreign policy would suggest that Western strategy fluctuated wildly, but in fact the basic thrust of Western policy toward the USSR remained remarkably consistent. Arguments from the New Right notwithstanding, Reagan's containment strategy was not that different from those of his predecessors. Indeed, the broader peace-through-strength perspective sees the Cold War's finale as the product of a long-term policy, applied over the decades.

In any case, although containment certainly played an important role in blocking Soviet expansionism, it cannot explain either the end of the Cold War or the direction of Soviet policy responses. The West's relationship with the Soviet Union was not limited to containment, but included important elements of mutual vulnerability and engagement. The Cold War's end was not simply a result of Western strength but of mutual weakness and intentional engagement as well.

Most dramatically, the mutual vulnerability created by nuclear weapons overshadowed containment. Nuclear weapons forced the United States and the Soviet Union to eschew war and the serious threat of war as tools of diplomacy and created imperatives for the cooperative regulation of nuclear capability. Both countries tried to fashion nuclear explosives into useful instruments of policy, but they came to the realization—as the joint Soviet-American statement issued from the 1985 Geneva summit put it—that "nuclear war cannot be won and must never be fought." Both countries slowly but surely came to view nuclear weapons as a common threat that must be regulated jointly. Not just containment, but also the overwhelming and common nuclear threat brought the Soviets to the negotiating table. In the shadow of nuclear destruction, common purpose defused traditional antagonisms.

A second error of the peace-through-strength perspective is the failure to recognize that the West offered an increasingly benign face to the communist world. Traditionally, the Soviets' Marxist-Leninist doctrine held that the capitalist West was inevitably hostile and aggressive, an expectation reinforced by the aggression of capitalist, fascist Germany. Since World War II, the Soviets' principal adversaries had been democratic capitalist states. Slowly but surely Soviet doctrine acknowledged that the West's behavior did not follow Leninist expectations, but was instead increasingly pacific and cooperative. The Soviet willingness to abandon the Brezhnev Doctrine in the late 1980s in favor of the "Sinatra Doctrine"—under which any East European country could sing, "I did it my way"—suggests a radical transformation in the prevailing Soviet perception of threat from the West. In 1990, the Soviet acceptance of the de facto absorption of communist East Germany into West Germany involved the same calculation with even higher stakes. In accepting the German reunification, despite that country's past aggression, Gorbachev acted on the assumption that the Western system was fundamentally pacific. As Russian foreign minister Andrei Kozyrev noted subsequently, that Western countries are pluralistic democracies "practically rules out the pursuance of an aggressive foreign policy." Thus the Cold War ended despite the assertiveness of Western hardliners, rather than because of it.

The War of Ideas

The second front of the Cold War, according to the Reagan victory school, was ideological. Reagan spearheaded a Western ideological offensive that dealt the USSR a death blow. For the Right, driving home the image of the Evil Empire was a decisive stroke rather than a rhetorical flourish. Ideological warfare was such a key front in the Cold War because the Soviet Union was, at its core, an ideological creation. According to the Reagan Right, the supreme vulnerability of the Soviet Union to ideological assault was greatly underappreciated by Western leaders and publics. In that view, the Cold War was won by the West's uncompromising assertion of the superiority of its values and its complete denial of the moral legitimacy of the Soviet system during the 1980s. Western military strength could prevent defeat, but only ideological breakthrough could bring victory.

Underlying that interpretation is a deeply ideological philosophy of politics and history. The Reagan Right tended to view politics as a war of ideas, an orientation that generated a particularly polemical type of politics. As writer Sidney Blumenthal has pointed out, many of the leading figures in the neoconservative movement since the 1960s came to conservatism after having begun their political careers as Marxists or socialists. That perspective sees the Soviet Union as primarily an ideological artifact, and therefore sees struggle with it in particularly ideological terms. The neoconservatives believe, like Lenin, that "ideas are more fatal than guns."

Convinced that Bolshevism was quintessentially an ideological phenomenon, activists of the New Right were contemptuous of Western efforts to accommodate Soviet needs, moderate Soviet aims, and integrate the USSR into the international system as a "normal" great power. In their view, the *realpolitik* strategy urged by George Kennan, Walter Lippmann, and Hans Morgenthau was based on a misunderstanding of the Soviet Union. It provided an incomplete roadmap for waging the Cold War, and guaranteed that it would never be won. A particular villain for the New Right was Secretary of State Henry Kissinger, whose program of détente implied, in their view, a "moral equivalence" between the West and the Soviet Union that amounted to unilateral ideological disarmament. Even more benighted were liberal attempts to engage and co-opt the Soviet Union in hopes that the two systems could ultimately reconcile. The New Right's view of politics was strikingly globalist in its assumption that the world had shrunk too much for two such different systems to survive, and that the contest was too tightly engaged for containment or Iron Curtains to work. As James Burnham, the ex-communist prophet of New Right anticommunism, insisted in the early postwar years, the smallness of our "one world" demanded a strategy of "rollback" for American survival.

The end of the Cold War indeed marked an ideological triumph for the West, but not of the sort fancied by the Reagan victory school. Ideology played a far different and more complicated role in inducing Soviet change than the Reagan school allows. As with the military sphere, the Reagan school presents an incomplete picture of Western ideological influence, ignoring the emergence of ideological common ground in stimulating Soviet change.

The ideological legitimacy of the Soviet system collapsed in the eyes of its own citizens not because of an assault by Western ex-leftists, but because of the appeal of Western affluence and permissiveness. The puritanical austerity of Bolshevism's "New Soviet Man" held far less appeal than the "bourgeois decadence" of the West. For the peoples of the USSR and Eastern Europe, it was not so much abstract liberal principles but rather the Western way of life—the material and cultural manifestations of the West's freedoms—that subverted the Soviet vision. Western popular culture—exemplified in rock and roll, television, film, and blue jeans—seduced the communist world far more effectively than ideological sermons by anticommunist activists. As journalist William Echikson noted in his 1990 book *Lighting the Night: Revolution in Eastern Europe*, "instead of listening to the liturgy of Marx and Lenin, generations of would-be socialists tuned into the Rolling Stones and the Beatles."

If Western popular culture and permissiveness helped subvert communist legitimacy, it is a development of profound irony. Domestically, the New Right battled precisely those cultural forms that had such global appeal. V. I. Lenin's most potent ideological foils were John Lennon and Paul McCartney, not Adam Smith and Thomas Jefferson. The Right fought a two-front war against communism abroad and hedonism and consumerism at home. Had it not lost the latter struggle, the West may not have won the former.

The Reagan victory school argues that ideological assertiveness precipitated the end of the Cold War. While it is true that right-wing American intellectuals were assertive toward the Soviet Union, other Western activists and intellectuals were building links with highly placed reformist intellectuals there. The Reagan victory school narrative ignores that Gorbachev's reform program was based upon "new thinking"—a body of ideas developed by globalist thinkers cooperating across the East-West divide. The key themes of new thinking—the common threat of nuclear destruction, the need for strong international institutions, and the importance of ecological sustainability—built upon the cosmopolitanism of the Marxist tradition and officially replaced the Communist party's class-conflict doctrine during the Gorbachev period.

It is widely recognized that a major source of Gorbachev's new thinking was his close aide and speechwriter, Georgi Shakhnazarov. A former president of the Soviet political science association, Shakhnazarov worked extensively with Western globalists, particularly the New York-based group known as the World Order Models Project. Goibachev's speeches and policy statements were replete with the language and ideas of globalism. The Cold War ended not with Soviet ideological capitulation to Reagan's anticommunism but rather with a Soviet embrace of globalist themes promoted by a network of liberal internationalists. Those intellectual influences were greatest with the state elite, who had greater access to the West and from whom the reforms originated.

Regardless of how one judges the impact of the ideological struggles during the Reagan years, it is implausible to focus solely on recent developments without accounting for longer-term shifts in underlying forces, particularly the widening gap between Western and Soviet economic performance. Over the long haul, the West's ideological appeal was based on the increasingly superior performance of the Western economic system. Although contrary to the expectation of Marx and Lenin, the robustness of capitalism in the West was increasingly acknowledged by Soviet analysts. Likewise, Soviet elites were increasingly troubled by their economy's comparative decline.

The Reagan victory school argues that the renewed emphasis on free-market principles championed by Reagan and then British prime minister Margaret Thatcher led to a global move toward market deregulation and privatization that the Soviets desired to follow. By rekindling the beacon of laissez-faire capitalism, Reagan illuminated the path of economic reform, thus vanquishing communism.

That view is misleading in two respects. First, it was West European social democracy rather than America's more free-wheeling capitalism that attracted Soviet reformers. Gorbachev wanted his reforms to emulate the Swedish model. His vision was not of laissez-faire capitalism but of a social democratic welfare state. Second, the Right's triumphalism in the economic sphere is ironic. The West's robust economies owe much of their relative stability and health to two generations of Keynesian intervention and government involvement that the Right opposed at every step. As with Western popular culture, the Right opposed tendencies in the West that proved vital in the West's victory.

There is almost universal agreement that the root cause of the Cold War's abrupt end was the grave domestic failure of Soviet communism. However, the Soviet response to this crisis—accommodation and liberalization rather than aggression and repression—was significantly influenced by outside pressures and opportunities, many from the West. As historians and analysts attempt to explain how recent U.S. foreign policy helped end the Cold War, a view giving most of the credit to Reagan-era assertiveness and Western strength has become the new conventional wisdom. Both the Reagan victory school and the peace-through-strength perspective on Western containment assign a central role in ending the Cold War to Western resolve and power. The lesson for American foreign policy being drawn from those events is that military strength and ideological warfare were the West's decisive assets in fighting the Cold War.

The new conventional wisdom, in both its variants, is seriously misleading. Operating over the last decade, Ronald Reagan's personal anti-nuclearism, rather than his administration's hardline, catalyzed the accommodations to end the Cold War. His administration's effort to go beyond containment and on the offensive was muddled, counter-balanced, and unsuccessful. Operating over the long term, containment helped thwart Soviet expansionism but cannot account for the Soviet domestic failure, the end of East-West struggle, or the direction of the USSR's reorientation. Contrary to the hard-line version, nuclear weapons were decisive in abandoning the conflict by creating common interests.

On the ideological front, the new conventional wisdom is also flawed. The conservatives' anticommunism was far less important in delegitimating the Soviet system than were that system's internal failures and the attraction of precisely the Western "permissive culture" abhorred by the Right. In addition, Gorbachev's attempts to reform communism in the late-1980s were less an ideological capitulation than a reflection of philosophical convergence on the globalist norms championed by liberal internationalists. And the West was more appealing not because of its laissez-faire purity, but because of the success of Keynesian and social welfare innovations whose use the Right resisted.

Behind the debate over who "won" the Cold War are competing images of the forces shaping recent history. Containment, strength, and confrontation— the trinity enshrined in conventional thinking on Western foreign policy's role in ending the Cold War—obscure the nature of these momentous changes. Engagement and interdependence, rather than containment, are the ruling trends of the age. Mutual vulnerability, not strength, drives security politics. Accommodation and integration, not confrontation, are the motors of change.

That such encouraging trends were established and deepened even as the Cold War raged demonstrates the considerable continuity underlying the West's support today for reform in the post-Soviet transition. Those trends also expose as one-sided and self-serving the New Right's attempt to take credit for the success of forces that, in truth, they opposed. In the end, Reagan partisans have been far more successful in claiming victory in the Cold War than they were in achieving it.

POSTSCRIPT

Did President Reagan Win the Cold War?

Now that the cold war is over, historians must assess why it ended so suddenly and unexpectedly. Did President Reagan's military buildup in the 1980s force the Russians into economic bankruptcy? Gaddis gives Reagan high marks for ending the cold war. By combining a policy of militancy and operational pragmatism, says Gaddis, Reagan brought about the most significant improvement in Soviet-American relations since the end of World War II. Deudney and Ikenberry disagree. In their view the cold war ended only when the Russians saw the need for international cooperation in order to end the arms race, prevent a nuclear holocaust, and liberalize their economy. It was Western global ideas and not the hard-line containment policy of the early Reagan administration that caused Gorbachev to abandon traditional Russian communism, according to Deudney and Ikenberry.

Gaddis has established himself as the leading diplomatic historian of the cold war period. His assessment of Reagan's relations with the Soviet Union is balanced and probably more generous than that of most contemporary analysts. It is also very useful because it so succinctly describes the unexpected shift from a hard-line policy to one of détente. Gaddis admits that not even Reagan could have foreseen the total collapse of communism and the Soviet empire. While he allows that Reagan was not a profound thinker, Gaddis credits him with the leadership skills to overcome any prior ideological biases toward the Soviet Union and to take advantage of Gorbachev's offer to end the arms race. While many of the president's hard-liners could not believe that the collapse of the Soviet Union was for real, Reagan was consistent in his view that the American arms buildup in the early 1980s was for the purpose of ending the arms race. Reagan, says Gaddis, accomplished this goal.

Deudney and Ikenberry give less credit to Reagan than to global influences in ending the cold war. In their view, Gorbachev softened his hard-line foreign policy and abandoned orthodox Marxist economic programs because he was influenced by Western European cosmopolitans who were concerned about the "common threat of nuclear destruction, the need for strong international institutions, and the importance of ecological sustainability." Deudney and Ikenberry agree that Reagan became more accommodating toward the Russians in 1983, but they maintain that the cold war's end "was not simply a result of Western strength but of mutual weakness and intentional engagement as well."

There is a considerable bibliography assessing the Reagan administration. Three *Washington Post* reporters have provided an early liberal and critical assessment of Reagan. Lou Cannon's *President Reagan: The Role of a Lifetime* (Simon & Schuster, 1991) is a perceptive account of a reporter who has closely followed Reagan since he was governor of California. Haynes Johnson's *Sleepwalking Through History: America in the Reagan Years* (W. W. Norton, 1991) is more critical than Cannon's biography, but it is a readable account of Reagan's presidency. Don Oberdorfer, a former Moscow correspondent for the *Washington Post,* has written *The Turn: From the Cold War to a New Era: The United States and the Soviet Union, 1983–1990* (Poseidon Press, 1991). Oberdorfer credits Secretary of State George Schultz with Reagan's turnaround from a hard-line to a détente approach to foreign policy. Historian Michael R. Beschloss and *Time* magazine foreign correspondent Strobe Talbott interviewed Gorbachev for *At the Highest Levels: The Inside Story of the End of the Cold War* (Little, Brown, 1993), which carries the story from 1987 through the Bush administration.

Early evaluations of Reagan by historians and political scientists are useful, although any works written before 1991 are likely to be dated in their prognostications because of the collapse of the Soviet Union. Historian Michael Schaller, in *Reckoning With Reagan: America and Its President in the 1980s* (Oxford University Press, 1992), argues that Reagan created an illusion of national strength at the very time it was declining. Political scientist Coral Bell analyzes the disparity between Reagan's declaratory and operational policies in *The Reagan Paradox: U.S. Foreign Policy in the 1980s* (Rutgers University Press, 1989). A number of symposiums on the Reagan presidency have been published. Two of the best are David E. Kyvig, ed., *Reagan and the World* (Greenwood Press, 1990) and Dilys M. Hill, Raymond A. Moore, and Phil Williams, eds., *The Reagan Presidency: An Incomplete Revolution?* (St. Martin's Press, 1990), which contains primarily discussions of domestic policy.

Not all scholars are critical of Reagan. Some of his academic and intellectual supporters include British professor David Mervin, in the admiring portrait *Ronald Reagan and the American Presidency* (Longman, 1990), and Patrick Glynn, in *Closing Pandora's Box: Arms Races, Arms Control, and the History of the Cold War* (Basic Books, 1992). A number of conservative magazines have published articles that argue that American foreign policy hard-liners won the cold war. Two of the most articulate essays written from this viewpoint are Arch Puddington, "The Anti–Cold War Brigade," *Commentary* (August 1990) and Owen Harries, "The Cold War and the Intellectuals," *Commentary* (October 1991).

Books on the end of the cold war will continue to proliferate. Michael J. Hogan has edited the earliest views of the major historians in *The End of the Cold War: Its Meaning and Implications* (Cambridge University Press, 1992). Michael Howard reviews five books on the end of the cold war in "Winning the Peace: How Both Kennan and Gorbachev Were Right," *Times Literary Supplement* (January 8, 1993).

ISSUE 16

Will History Consider William Jefferson Clinton a Reasonably Good Chief Executive?

YES: Lars-Erik Nelson, from "Clinton and His Enemies," *The New York Review of Books* (January 20, 2000)

NO: James MacGregor Burns and Georgia J. Sorenson et al., from *Dead Center: Clinton-Gore Leadership and the Perils of Moderation* (Scribner, 1999)

ISSUE SUMMARY

YES: Journalist Lars-Erik Nelson (1941–2000) argues that President Bill Clinton is a sadly flawed human being but was a reasonably good president whose administration was a time of peace and plenty for Americans.

NO: Political scientists James MacGregor Burns and Georgia J. Sorenson et al. argue that Clinton will not rank among the near-great presidents because he was a transactional broker who lacked the ideological commitment to tackle the big issues facing American society.

William Jefferson Clinton, born in Hope, Arkansas, on August 19, 1946, is the third-youngest president ever to hold the office. Similar to Abraham Lincoln, Clinton is considered a true embodiment of the "log cabin myth," which holds that anybody can become president. Both Lincoln and Clinton grew up in poor, dysfunctional southern families. Lincoln was born in Kentucky and was raised by a stepmother and a father whose unsuccessful ventures as a farmer caused the family to move four times before Lincoln was 21. Both had stepbrothers who were constantly in financial and legal trouble.

By the age of 16 Clinton knew he wanted to be a professional politician. After graduating from Georgetown University in 1968 with an international affairs degree, Clinton won a Rhodes scholarship and studied for two years at Oxford University. Like a number of his liberal and conservative counterparts of the 1960s, Clinton avoided the draft and earned a law degree from Yale University in 1973. His first experience in politics was as the Texas coordinator of George McGovern's presidential campaign in 1972. Ironically, Clinton served briefly as a staff attorney for the House Judiciary Committee, a year before the committee became preoccupied with investigating charges of impeachment against President Richard Nixon.

In the early 1970s Clinton returned to his home state and briefly taught law at the University of Arkansas. But, like Lincoln, politics was his real ambition. In 1974 he made a strong showing against an entrenched Republican incumbent in the House of Representatives but fared better in 1976 when he ran Jimmy Carter's presidential campaign in his home state and was elected state attorney general. In 1978, at age 32, Clinton became one of the youngest governors ever elected to the office.

In his first term Clinton tried to govern as a New Deal Democrat. He upgraded the state's highways but was forced to raise taxes on gasoline and auto licensing fees to pay the costs. Meanwhile, riots by 18,000 Cuban refugees at Fort Chaffee, Arkansas, which he was forced to quell in conjunction with a perception that the governor and his staff exhibited a streak of arrogance and overambitiousness, hurt his bid for reelection in 1980. Carter's failed presidency and the taxpayer revolt, which started in California and spread to the rest of the nation, left Clinton unemployed.

Clinton was down but not out. He ostensibly practiced law, but his real goal was to get reelected as governor. He began his campaign on television with an apology to the voters for raising highway taxes, blamed his mistakes on "youthful ignorance," and toured the state in an effort to listen to the concerns of his citizens. This strategy paid off. Clinton defeated his Republican opponent by a wide margin in 1982 and was reelected on four more occasions with little opposition through 1992.

Clinton thought about running for president in 1988 but decided to wait until 1992. He was only 45 but it was a propitious time. President George Bush was extremely popular in the winter of 1991 because he had led UN forces to victory over the Iraqis in Kuwait. Prominent Democrats considered it futile to run against a popular incumbent president. The challengers were a group of lesser Democrats whom Clinton was able to defeat in the primaries. On November 3, 1992, Clinton received only 43 percent of the popular vote, Bush 38 percent, and H. Ross Perot 19 percent, which was the second-highest percentage in American history for a third-party candidate. The margin of victory was much wider in the electoral college—Clinton's 370 votes to Bush's 168. Clinton won the election running as a centrist Democrat from Arkansas. He got Reagan Democrats in the northeast and midwestern states to come back to the fold.

Will history rank Bill Clinton as a near-great, average, or below average president? In the following selection, Lars-Erik Nelson takes Clinton's detractors head-on and challenges a number of conceptions that Americans hold about the presidency. In the second selection, James MacGregor Burns and Georgia J. Sorenson et al. argue that Clinton will not rank among the near-great presidents because he lacked the ideological commitment and overall vision to tackle the big issues facing American society.

Lars-Erik Nelson  **YES**

Clinton and His Enemies

Writing on the eve of the 1952 presidential election, the Cambridge political scientist D. W. Brogan described a peculiar trait in the American psyche, which he called "the illusion of American omnipotence." This, he elaborated, "is the illusion that any situation which distresses or endangers the United States can only exist because some Americans have been fools or knaves."[1]

Brogan was writing in the context of the debate over "Who lost China?," which was premised on the assumption that the convulsive Chinese Communist revolution, a forty-year struggle involving hundreds of millions of desperate people, could have been thwarted, or at least turned in a positive direction, by adroit diplomacy in Washington. The inanity of the China debate was instantly apparent (just as soon as Brogan put it into words), yet the illusion thrives. Even today, there are perfectly serious people who believe President Franklin D. Roosevelt was a knave for failing to stop the Nazi Holocaust or a fool for allowing the Red Army to occupy Eastern Europe at the end of World War II.

Brogan did not make the point, but the most obvious candidate for accusations of knavery is the president, especially now that whoever is in the White House is chief executive of the world's last superpower. In *Dead Center,* a survey of Bill Clinton's presidency, we see a modern extension of what Brogan described, the illusion of presidential omnipotence. In the current version, all that has gone wrong in America or the world at large—the slaughter in Kosovo, continuing inequality of wealth, the lack of national health insurance, even leaky roofs in our schools—can be blamed on Clinton. He is guilty, in the eyes of James MacGregor Burns and Georgia J. Sorenson, not because he is a knave or a fool, but, just as bad, because he is a centrist who shunned the radical changes and bold solutions that a more energetic and partisan leader could have achieved.

Burns and Sorenson, colleagues at the James MacGregor Burns Academy of Leadership at the University of Maryland, describe Clinton as a "transactional" president—one who makes deals—rather than a "transformational" one, who confronts political foes head-on and galvanizes the nation into taking fresh paths and shattering old habits. This is a fair assessment. Clinton has no large vision. As president, he has tried to reach across party lines. He has used opinion polls to assess and then act in accordance with the prevailing public sentiment, which will usually be more or less in the center. He has famously adopted a policy of "triangulation," trying to place himself at the apex of a triangle whose base angles are the preternaturally hostile congressional Republicans and Democrats. Though he is an eloquent speaker, he seldom directs his oratory against his enemies. Rather he lets them snarl themselves into incoherence.

The result is that Clinton has survived and prevailed over them. The Monica Lewinsky scandal guarantees that his presidency will be forever deemed a disappointment, not least to himself and his family. But by many measures his centrist strategy has worked. As Clinton enters his last year in the White House, the nation is not only at peace but it has no plausible foreign threats to its survival. Unemployment has remained low, and inflation has been held in check. Personal incomes are rising. Clinton's job approval rating hovers around 60 percent, even though his personal approval is about half that. Annual budget deficits, once projected to extend into infinity, have been eliminated. The national problem most debated at the moment appears to be nothing more immediate than shoring up the Social Security system so that it can pay its projected bills thirty years from now. Clinton has not only survived impeachment but outlasted his chief political opponents, former Senator Bob Dole of Kansas and former House Speaker Newt Gingrich of Georgia. Despite all the political shrieking against him that can be heard on radio and television, the country, under President Clinton, tootles along.

Burns and Sorenson, however, measure Clinton against a far stricter standard than mere peace and prosperity. They complain that he has failed to solve urgent national problems, and they attribute this failure to his centrism, which they regard as an inherently flawed ideology because it is incapable of effecting great, transformational change. Centrism would not have freed the slaves, or led America out of the Depression, or integrated the armed forces. Thus, in their eyes, Clinton is a failure. But the standard to which they hold him suffers from being based on the illusion of presidential omnipotence, and this illusion undermines their argument.

An example of the authors' complaint: Clinton prides himself on being the "Education President." And yet they write,

> A *New York Times* article reported "leaky school roofs, buckling auditorium floors, antiquated coal furnaces, and dangerously rotted window frames." This was not a depression town in the 1930s but booming New York City in November 1998. Teachers and parents could report thousands and thousands of such situations across the country. Education was still in crisis.

In their eyes, the Education President had failed to transform local public education. Yes, we may agree; but what they do not say is that the federal government has only a small role in public education, and Clinton's Republican opponents have been trying to reduce even that, by abolishing the Education Department. To fault a sitting president, even indirectly, for the rotting window frames in a New York City school verges on the bizarre.

As a second Clinton "failure," the authors cite "the grotesque income gap between the rich and the poor in America. Here again Clinton offered a host of proposals, some of which alleviated the direct symptoms of poverty." Yet income inequality remains. Why? "Clinton failed to exhibit the moral outrage that could have put inequality at the top of the nation's agenda." It is hard to believe that serious commentators would expect a moderate Democratic president, captive of the current campaign finance system, to agitate for class warfare against his own financial backers. But suppose he had: Would this or any other Congress have reenacted the steep progressive tax rates on income that were so triumphantly eliminated during the Reagan administration? Would the small business lobby have lessened its hostility to increases in the minimum wage? If Clinton had addressed income inequality in any meaningful way, he would have (a) failed to do much to change current income distribution and (b) been a one-term president.

On race, Clinton, in his open relations with African-Americans and his recruitment of them for his administration, has set an example that will be hard for successors to match. But even here he falls short of the Burns-Sorenson standard. "Historians of the future may see Clinton as a neoliberal, neo-civil-rights-radical, taking up Martin Luther King Jr.'s unfinished work toward an economic justice that transcends race," Burns and Sorenson concede.

> But while strong presidential leadership could potentially have created conditions and bridges across the racial divide, no such coalition—not even [Jesse] Jackson's Rainbow—had ever been sustained in the past. Such a coalition would take an act of transforming leadership on the order of the New Deal. It would take political capital, moral standing and the political will of Lincoln. Did Clinton have the will? The answer appeared to be no.

Clinton is not Lincoln.

Burns and Sorenson do not allow Clinton the excuse that he was presented with no opportunity to perform grand, Lincolnesque acts on race relations.

> Clinton had... misjudged Americans' relationship to their elected leaders. Again, as the sixties made plain, Americans would tolerate change—radical change—if leaders articulated values and visions consistently and succeeded in conveying a sense of urgency. Clinton did neither. His pursuit of racial justice was itself centrist.
>
>   In the end, Clinton was content to tinker, when he had a genuine opportunity to transform.

In the face of such ungenerous and unrealistic criticism, it is tempting to defend the Clinton presidency in spite of all its bungles, money-grubbing for contributions, foreign policy missteps, false starts, and changed directions. But we should not ignore some basic facts. Clinton, a moderate Democratic governor of Arkansas, was elected president in 1992 with 43 percent of the popular vote, hardly a mandate for sweeping personal leadership. As a governor of a small state, where politics were based more on personal relations than party divisions, he made appointments and dealt with the legislature without much concern for party affiliation. When he took office in Washington, he was supported by the smallest congressional majority of any president elected in this century (although some, most notably Richard Nixon, took office with one or both houses of Congress in the hands of the opposition). By nature and by circumstance, he was a centrist—a position that for him made political sense because, in his eyes, the Republican Party had moved so far to the right. There was a great political middle to be grabbed, and Clinton grabbed it.

◦◦◦

To the Republicans, however, Clinton was no centrist. He was a pot-smoking, draft-dodging, anti–Vietnam War liberal with a socialist wife who wanted to strip away your right to see your family doctor. It was Clinton's great, and as yet unexplored, misfortune that he was the first Democratic president to take office since the astonishing rise of the demagogic radio talk-show hosts and their counterparts on cable television. A caricatured view of Clinton as a dangerous, even subversive liberal was broadcast for three hours a day, every day, from coast to coast by Rush Limbaugh and echoed by his imitators across the country. They questioned his patriotism and his right to be commander in chief. They complained when Hillary Rodham Clinton replaced the White House chef, as if she had no right to fire Barbara Bush's cook. They made a major scandal of an incident in which Clinton supposedly delayed air traffic at Los Angeles International Airport while he got a haircut aboard Air Force One. He did get the haircut, but no other aircraft was delayed. Nevertheless, the LAX incident survives in memory as a Clinton scandal.

Clinton's heavy-handed replacement of seven employees of the White House travel office, career government officials who enjoyed no civil service protection in that particular job, was also transformed into a scandal out of all proportion to its seriousness. He was dogged by questions about his Whitewater real estate investments, which proved to be more or less innocent, and hounded by investigations in the press, in the Congress, and by freelance inquisitors backed in large part by the reclusive Michigan multimillionaire Richard Mellon Scaife.

Clinton certainly made mistakes. One of his earliest actions was an attempt to order the military to accept homosexuals. The policy was well-intentioned, but homosexuals have protested that its application has led to more harassment, not less. Clinton failed to understand how deeply the military establishment and its supporters throughout the country would resent any change, and it added to the caricature image of him as a traditional liberal pandering to the most outspoken left-wing special interests. Some of his early appointments were badly bungled, particularly that of Lani Guinier, a longtime friend whom he nominated to head the Justice Department's civil rights division without anticipating the predictably harsh reaction against her support for race-based proportional representation.

◆◦◆

To Burns and Sorenson, Clinton's biggest mistake was his health care plan, which tried to make use of existing insurance companies, doctors, hospitals, and health maintenance organizations rather than ignore these well-funded interest groups and start afresh. It was a relatively modest, well-intentioned initiative that was undermined by its complexity and the unnecessary secrecy with which it was drafted. The Health Insurance Association of America, which represents smaller insurance companies, ran TV commercials against it in which actors named "Harry" and "Louise" tried to frighten the public into believing that the government was about to take over and dictate their health care. Even *The New Republic,* which might have been expected to support a moderate Democratic president, ran a long, specious attack on the Clinton health plan's alleged failings.

Moderate though the plan was, it was too radical for the American political system. Clinton could be faulted for not trying, even after its defeat, to put forward a simpler and more modest plan so that at least some progress might have been made toward providing health care for the millions of people, mainly poor, who have no insurance whatever.

Yet Burns and Sorenson, who chide Clinton for the defeat and subsequent abandonment of his centrist proposal, argue that he should have pushed instead for a far more radical health reform, a Canadian-style "single-payer" system that would have taken all insurance companies out of the health care business and substituted for them a system of direct government payments to doctors. A single-payer plan has its virtues, but it would put an additional one seventh of the Gross National Product into the hands of government, and it would have gone down to defeat far faster and more decisively than the plan Clinton put forward. Nevertheless, Burns and Sorenson argue that only in this way can progress be made, by Hegelian clashes between extreme positions that might produce a new synthesis. It is an interesting theory, but it shows no awareness of political reality.

In his first two years in office, Clinton also pushed for a tax increase—promptly mischaracterized by his Republican opponents and a few Democrats as the biggest tax increase in history, even though it spared the middle class. One by one Republicans trooped to the House floor to warn the public that Clinton's 4.3-cent-a-gallon gasoline tax would cripple the economy and lead to widespread unemployment. They were wrong, but their charges that Clinton had raised everyone's taxes stuck in the public mind, nevertheless.

Clinton then antagonized congressional Democrats by pushing for approval of the North American Free Trade Agreement [NAFTA], promising that lowering the barriers to trade with Mexico would create hundreds of thousands of good new jobs. The labor unions and their congressional supporters were properly skeptical. NAFTA was approved, thousands of Americans lost their jobs as factories moved south across the border, and the hundreds of thousands of new jobs never materialized. NAFTA was not the disaster that labor feared— although it hit some workers so hard that their incomes have never recovered— but it was also not the panacea Clinton and his allies promised.

Third, he fought for approval of the Brady Bill, which put new restrictions on handgun sales and outlawed some types of semiautomatic rifles. This guaranteed him the hostility of one of the most powerful grass-roots lobbies in the country, the National Rifle Association, as well as enmity in even Democratic rural areas. Partly because of these three painful victories—the tax increase, NAFTA, and gun control—Clinton lost Democratic control of both House and Senate in the 1994 off-year congressional elections.

◆

From that point on, his presidency was under constant siege, a fact ignored by Burns and Sorenson, just as they ignore the relentless denunciations of Clinton and his wife by TV and radio commentators. This is an inexplicable omission. While trying to conduct the nation's business, the Clintons were investigated by two special prosecutors, Robert Fiske and Kenneth Starr, and a host of congressional committees. The Clintons were required to produce, under subpoena, documents going back decades. One inquisitor, Senator Alfonse D'Amato, subpoenaed the records of every telephone call from the White House to the 501 area code, i.e., Arkansas. Representative Dan Burton, an Indiana Republican, reenacted in his backyard the suicide of White House deputy counsel Vince Foster. A self-appointed gadfly, Larry Klayman of the group Judicial Watch, instituted a civil suit against the White House on behalf of Republicans whose FBI files had been stored there, and subjected White House officials to endless, rambling depositions. Utterly guiltless young men and women who had joined the Clinton administration in hopes of serving the country found themselves going into debt to pay lawyers' fees. So intense was the scrutiny that White House officials stopped taking notes in meetings or keeping records of their phone calls lest they be subpoenaed.

In addition to this, the Supreme Court ruled that a serving president could be subjected to a civil lawsuit while in office, which opened the way to the Paula Jones sexual harassment suit. This, in turn, led to the Lewinsky scandal. Four years after a special prosecutor was appointed to investigate him, Clinton finally committed a legal offense, falsely denying to Jones's lawyers that he had had sex with Lewinsky. By so doing he made himself fatally vulnerable to his enemies. The ensuing investigation and impeachment occupied the entire year of 1998 and the first month of 1999. So great was the congressional hostility to Clinton that at one point in 1997, when I asked then Speaker Gingrich seven times, in a semipublic forum, whether Clinton was the legitimately elected president of the United States, Gingrich, second in line to the presidency, seven times refused to say yes.

Dick Morris, Clinton's former pollster, records in *Vote.com* the burdens under which the Clinton White House labored:

> The sheer magnitude of the Clinton scandals is dizzying—Gennifer Flowers; the draft; pot smoking; the nanny tax; gays in the military; the $200 haircut; the travel-office firings; the Foster suicide; the Espy, Brown, Cisneros, and Babbitt investigations; Whitewater; the FBI files; the Rose Law Firm billing records; Chinese campaign contributions; advertising spending; Paula Jones; the China satellite waivers; the Web Hubbell job search; Chinese spies at Los Alamos.

It might be noted that in none of these controversies and scandals were the Clintons proved to have committed a crime, though at least one of them, the China-based fund-raising, stinks to high heaven.

·◈·

Under such unrelenting attack, it is remarkable that the Clinton White House was able to function at all. Robert Reich, who served as Clinton's first-term labor secretary, believes Clinton could and should have done more with his presidency. But in a critique written [in 1998] for *The Nation,* Reich noted that even Clinton's modest achievements have been overshadowed. "I fear," he writes, that "none will be remembered nearly as much as the viciousness of these years: the virulent spins and counterspins, the war rooms, the deadly battle over health care, the government shutdown and the stream of allegations over the White House travel office, Vince Foster's suicide, Whitewater, illegal fundraising and Gennifer, Paula, Kathy and Monica." Reich summed up Clinton's first-term plight this way: "A baby-boomer President who could charm snakes has tried to charm America and only infuriated the snakes." Clinton enraged the right with gun control, enraged organized labor with NAFTA, enraged liberals with welfare reform, and enraged Republicans by co-opting many of their issues.

And yet he wins consistently high job approval ratings. Morris explains part of this mystery in his book. Clinton, he says, was shrewdly—and with the help of Morris's polls—appealing to a younger generation, young families with children, whose concerns don't fit conventional political categories. Clinton's much-derided "small agenda" in fact meant a good deal to young parents. "He helped them get time off from work to bond with their newborn babies by passing the Family Leave Law," Morris writes.

> He made childhood immunization universal, inoculating children against disease and effectively inoculating their parents against Republican attacks on his administration.
>
> As their children came of preschool age, Clinton doubled the Head Start program so that it could accommodate all the children whose parents wanted it.... As their children grew older, X Generation parents worried more about issues like values, crime and violence. Clinton faced down the TV networks and made them implement a ratings system. Meanwhile, he got Congress to pass legislation requiring the installation of a V-chip in

each new television set.... To cut crime, Clinton got funds for 100,000 extra police and more money for drug counselors in schools.

When Clinton ensnared himself in a lurid scandal that had even grade schoolers asking about oral sex, many of the young parents blamed Republicans more for spreading their revelations into every household than they faulted Clinton for providing the ammunition. Clinton won their support, Morris says, by addressing, with careful political calculation, problems they actually faced at home. "He focused on topics like violence on television, teen smoking, national educational standards, school construction, and other areas that had never been part of the traditional congressional agenda."

Clinton's accomplishments may not seem like much in comparison to the Emancipation Proclamation or Dwight Eisenhower's support for the interstate highway system, the standards Burns and Sorenson use, but they improved the lives of a good many people in small but telling ways. Is that much of a legacy? We will not know for years to come.

In the eyes of Burns and Sorenson, Clinton fares no better on foreign policy. While Clinton vacillated on Bosnia, they write, 150,000 people were killed. They fault him for refusing to go it alone on Kosovo and for using air attacks rather than ground troops to repel Serbian forces. "The whole Kosovo episode once again illustrated the perils of moderation in foreign affairs, as in domestic," they write. Just how Clinton would have been able to use ground troops effectively in the face of vehement Pentagon and congressional opposition to taking losses Burns and Sorenson do not say.

William Hyland, a career national-security and intelligence expert who later served as editor of *Foreign Affairs,* is one of Clinton's more level-headed foreign-policy critics, and his survey of Clinton-era diplomacy, while stinging at times, is both more informed and more restrained than that of Burns and Sorenson. He faults the President chiefly for his inattention to foreign affairs until it is too late, creating a vacuum in which his subordinates "hijacked his foreign policy in the name of neo-Wilsonian internationalism, and for more than two years... engineered a series of failures and disasters."

In Hyland's view, Anthony Lake, Clinton's first National Security adviser, erred by putting too much stress on moral judgments as a driving force for American foreign policy, for example in Bosnia and China, while being unwilling, or unable, to devise policies to implement these judgments. He also accuses Secretary of State Madeleine Albright of being too willing to use force without an adequate sense of its dangers. Albright,who has seemed obsessed by the Munich agreement that sold out her native Czechoslovakia, has indeed been unusually bellicose. In a speech at Georgetown University in 1997, for example, she announced that America would never lift its economic sanctions against Iraq so long as Saddam Hussein was in power. It was a tough speech, but it gave Saddam no incentive to cooperate with United Nations arms inspections; Albright made it clear that even if he did, sanctions would continue. Similarly, Albright declared that Slobodan Milosevic understood no language other than force, which may have encouraged the Kosovo Liberation Army in the belief that America would support its stepped-up guerrilla war against Belgrade.

Hyland believes Clinton could have been more forceful in urging allies in 1993 to support the partition of Bosnia, according to the intricate plan worked out by former Secretary of State Cyrus Vance and former British Foreign Secretary David Owen. In addition, Clinton could have pressed harder for a policy of lifting the arms embargo on Bosnia's Muslims and carrying out air strikes against Bosnia's Serbs. The Bosnian Serbs, however, who controlled 70 percent of Bosnia, rejected the Vance-Owen plan, so it could only have been imposed—in all its complexity—at gunpoint. And the European allies, their peacekeeping troops on the ground outnumbered by the Serbs, wanted no US air strikes that might place their own troops at risk.

There is a whiff of the illusion of American omnipotence not only in Hyland's comments on the Balkans but also in the belief that more robust US diplomacy could have prevented the India-Pakistan nuclear arms race or averted the Asian economic collapse. But Hyland clearly recognizes the limits of US power when he dismisses the now current notion that more energetic American involvement could have created a free market and a functioning democracy in Russia.

The demoralization of Russia may be the most serious long-term development of the Clinton era, but here the administration's sins are more of style and tone than of substance. Certainly there was no need for US officials to act as cheerleaders and loan guarantors while so-called Russian reformers looted their country's wealth in the guise of privatization. Clinton's policymakers badly underestimated the depth of the corruption and criminality that pervades Russian society. But in dealing with Russia, Clinton had to work with the forces at hand. That meant backing Boris Yeltsin, with all his flaws, in preference to the resurgent Communist Party or the wacky fascism of Vladimir Zhirinovsky. As for another controversial part of Clinton's policy toward Russia, the expansion of the North Atlantic Treaty Organization to include Poland, Hungary, and the Czech Republic, Hyland seems dubious. While calling NATO expansion a significant achievement for the President, he also asserts that "building European security without, or against, Russia has not worked for four centuries."

⌖

Clinton has to his credit genuine achievements in mediating the Northern Ireland dispute and pushing the Israelis and Palestinians farther along toward a permanent peace settlement. None of Clinton's supposed foreign policy fiascoes has been as bone-headed as, say, the Reagan administration's disastrous deployment of Marines in Lebanon in 1983 or its attempt to court supposed moderates in Iran by selling them antiaircraft missiles. In the 1996 election, Republicans chose not to make much of an issue of Clinton's foreign policy except for an effort to revive Reagan's Strategic Defense Initiative, an expensive and probably unworkable scheme that has many doubters among Republicans as well as Democrats. It is also the case that although the administration's policy has been marked by false steps, misjudgments, and shifts in direction, no one has put forward a clear, generally accepted alternative to it. Hyland freely admits that, on the major issues—whether in China, the Balkans, or Russia—he has none himself. Burns and Sorenson fault Clinton for lacking a grand strategy in foreign affairs, but they also note that no one else has one either.[2]

Hillary Clinton defended the administration's overall record to Burns and Sorenson by making the rather modest claim that Clinton has proven that government can be made to work for ordinary people and that it is not, as Ronald Reagan portrayed it, an enemy:

> So whether it's [the] Family and Medical Leave [Act] or the Brady Bill or taking assault weapons off the streets or even, as he has done, trumpeting small measures like curfews or school uniforms—that can give people a sense that all is not lost, that they're not living in this sort of libertarian wilderness where it's every person for himself.

Mrs. Clinton did not mention here the administration's major experiments such as welfare reform and the repeal of restrictions on banking. Senator Daniel Patrick Moynihan warned in the course of the welfare debate that in ten years' time we will be seeing children sleeping on grates. As Michael Massing recently observed in these pages, welfare reform has so far been a mixed success; but beginning in the year 2000, "the program's time limits will begin to take hold, and when they do, the levels of homelessness and hunger could sharply rise."[3] This program, moreover, has not yet been confronted with an economic downturn.

As Republicans compete to succeed Clinton, their chief stated goal is not to repeal the legislative accomplishments of his administration but to "restore dignity to the office" —dignity they themselves did much to besmirch. No one proposes rolling back the 4.3-cent gasoline tax or legalizing assault weapons. With a few minor exceptions, Governor George W. Bush's foreign policy speech at the Reagan Library in California in November could have come out of Clinton's speechwriting shop. Senator John McCain of Arizona, Bush's leading rival for the Republican presidential nomination, is concentrating on campaign finance reform, deriding Clinton's money-raising techniques even while he, McCain, freely acknowledges that under the current system he raises large sums from the corporations he oversees as chairman of the Senate Commerce Committee.

Clinton is not a candidate for Mount Rushmore. Blighted by its scandals, both real, and fabricated, his administration has been at best a tepid success. He repaired the damage of the crippling deficits produced by Reaganomics. He may have altered the image of the Democratic Party as a collection of tax-and-spend liberals who are soft on crime. He advanced the cause of racial justice largely through personal example. His vow to staff an administration that "looks like America" seemed hokey when announced, but he has made it stick.

He has also set an example, in this vituperative age, of showing no malice. It is hard to remember a single harsh word that Clinton has uttered against his many enemies. He will have, as Burns and Sorenson emphasize, no grand achievements like freeing the slaves, conquering the Depression, rolling back communism, or any of the other major transformations that they ascribe, somewhat simplistically, to previous presidents. Ordinary people, if not historians, are likely to remember him as they see him now, a sadly flawed human being but a reasonably good President whose administration was, for Americans, a time of peace and plenty.

Notes

1. "The Illusion of American Omnipotence," *Harper's,* December 1952, p. 21.
2. For anyone who thinks that in the post–cold war era a single grand strategy is possible, I recommend a book, *World Conflicts,* from Scarecrow Press. It lists, in encyclopedic form, virtually every one of the world's continuing ethnic, religious, tribal, and cross-border conflicts. It is an essential guide to the real world of the twenty-first century and, as it summons up the regional hatreds on all continents, a devastating antidote to any lingering illusion about American omnipotence. Its author, Patrick Brogan, is the son of D. W. Brogan.
3. "The End of Welfare?," *The New York Review,* October 7, 1999, pp. 22–26.

James MacGregor Burns and Georgia J. Sorenson et al.

What Kind of Leadership?

At some point a two-term president begins to think more about his place in history and less about his standing in the polls and at the polls. His hope for eternal fame rises most acutely after his reelection, of course, but not only then. Presidents are now held responsible for leading their party to win in congressional elections; thus Clinton, and Hillary Rodham Clinton too, were blamed for the Republican takeover of Congress in 1994, then credited for some Democratic gains in 1998. A president is also expected to help his vice president succeed him, but in 2000 that will be Al Gore's responsibility.

During much of his life—and perhaps as early as seizing JFK's hand—Clinton aspired to be not only president but a "great" president. One of his most crushing reactions to the Monica S. Lewinsky revelations was that his behavior had relegated him to the standing of a run-of-the-mill president. He might even be downgraded to failure—a rating inexplicably accorded Jimmy Carter in one polling of presidential scholars.

What is greatness in the White House? For years scholars have been rating presidents without a clear and agreed-on set of criteria. In our view, the bottom-line answer is conviction and commitment, plus the courage and competence to act on beliefs and promises. The scholarly rating game shows some volatility over the years in the standings of presidents—Harry Truman improved the more we got to know some of his successors—but the continuing "greats" over the years are the committed leaders Washington, Lincoln, and Franklin Roosevelt, with Thomas Jefferson just behind.

Monuments are another form of rating, especially in Washington. There is a pecking order in those memorials. For a century or more Washington and Lincoln have had their monuments, joined by Jefferson a half century ago and by FDR in the past decade. Washington's is the most imposing, Lincoln's the most evocative, Jefferson's the most philosophical, and Roosevelt's the most revealing about himself and his First Lady. Then there is Mount Rushmore, with Washington, Jefferson, and Lincoln carved in mighty stone, along with Theodore Roosevelt. Mean-spirited people complained that TR got there only because he and the sculptor were friends, but admirers of this "near great" are satisfied that he made it on his own.

Could Clinton aspire to a monument in Washington? Of course every president now gets his home library, no matter how great or nongreat. But Clinton might want more. Could he even hope for Mount Rushmore? There appears to be an open spot next to TR. But Franklin Roosevelt idolators see two spots that could be reserved for FDR and—yes—Eleanor. Still, what if someday the South Dakotans might balance the present three easterners and one midwesterner with a famous southerner?

Of course all this is terribly elitist. Dozens of other presidents, along with hundreds of governors, congressmen, local politicos, judges, and even professors are memorialized in thousands of courthouses, libraries, parks, and schools across the country. The warp and woof of American leadership, they are portrayed holding swords, canes, bibles, scrolls, constitutions, the reins of horses. Not one, so far as we know, brandishes a balanced budget law.

The Price of Centrism

A contradiction lay at the heart of Clinton's leadership: if he truly aspired to presidential greatness, the strategy he had chosen ensured that he would never achieve it. Rather, long before his presidency he had resolved on a centrist path that called for the kind of transactional leadership that he would exercise in abundance, especially in foreign policy. As a master broker he raised the art of the deal to world-class levels. But he rejected the kind of transformational leadership that might have placed him among the historic "greats."

What form did their transformational leadership take? Washington consolidated a whole new constitutional system that he had helped create. Jefferson recognized that political parties were necessary to unify and democratize that system, and he, with James Madison, fashioned the first opposition party. Lincoln moved on from demanding union at any price to demanding emancipation at any price and established a moral leadership that would vitalize his country for more than a century. FDR's remarkable foresight in broadening the antigovernment Bill of Rights into an "economic bill of rights" provided a "people's charter" that helped Americans cope with the ravages of the Depression and inequality.

The huge successes of these and other presidents displayed their transformational leadership: creativity in fashioning new policies; the courage to press for reforms and other changes despite popular apathy and opposition; the conviction to stick to grand principles no matter how long their realization might take; the commitment to the people to fight for their welfare at any personal cost. What was required for "greatness," in short, was a lifelong struggle to help achieve real, intended, principled, and lasting change.

Clinton could claim that he was just as committed to centrism as those great leaders had been committed to liberalism or progressivism. But just what was Clinton's centrism? The confusion over the term was vividly dramatized when his and Rodham Clinton's health bill of 1993–94 came to be categorized as a radical departure from his centrism. In fact in most respects the health plan epitomized moderate "mainstream" thinking. Rejecting the Canadian plan, it sought to attain a liberal goal, universal health care, without alienating conservatives, such as highly paid doctors and insurance companies. It had no particular ideology; it was neither socialist nor laissez-faire.

Confusion on this score was understandable because there seemed to be several brands of centrism. To some it was a kind of shopping list including moderate, liberal, and indeed conservative policies, from which the White House could pick items almost at will to meet immediate political and legislative exigencies. For others it was a nice balancing act, choosing conservative stands such as the death penalty and matching it with a liberal position on, say, gun control, without much in the middle.

The White House itself seemed unable to clarify this new form of government, or how it fit into the broader political system. In the summer of 1995, in a speech at Georgetown University, Clinton lamented that politics had become more and more fractured, and "just like the rest of us, pluralized. It's exciting in some ways, but as we divide into more and more and more sharply defined organized groups around more and more and more stratified issues, as we communicate more and more with people in extreme rhetoric through mass mailings or sometimes semihysterical messages right before election on the telephone, or thirty-second ads designed far more to inflame than to inform, as we see politicians actually getting language lessons on how to turn their adversaries into aliens, it is difficult to draw the conclusion that our political system is producing the sort of discussion that will give us the kind of results we need." Clinton seemed less than certain that mere goodwill among elected officials could paint over deep cracks in the polity.

Again and again the President invoked symbols of common ground, national unity, middle-class values, political partnership. Again and again he fell into pieties, such as civility, good citizenship, "strong families and faith," provoking in the minds of some listeners the only response to such shibboleths: "Of course, and who's against them?"

At that point, the President occupied the middle of the middle ground—so tenaciously that the liberal press searched for a Rasputin and found him in Dick Morris, who had come back to advise Clinton in 1995 after having worked for such conservatives as Jesse Helms and Paula Hawkins. But Clinton did not really need an advisor or a speechwriter for the Georgetown address. He was speaking from his heart and mind about his present political lodging place. Still, even this speech, lengthy though it was, omitted vital questions.

What about the Republicans? Were they supposed to suspend their partisanship to join the President on some peaceful ground? Clinton did not seem to recognize that he was confronted by one of the most disciplined and doctrinaire parties in this century, or if he did, he still assumed he could make deals with it. But the Republicans had won in 1994 with a most forthright platform, the Contract with America. Why should they break their promises to the people in order to trade with the President? These Republicans could hardly forget that Clinton had defeated a GOP governor in Arkansas and later driven their own president out of the White House. Who was he to talk conciliation?

And what about the Democrats? The President did not once mention the words *Democrat* or *Democratic party* in his Georgetown speech, though he was still using the old party catchwords—justice, equality, compassion, the Jeffersonian pursuit of happiness. Two hundred years earlier Jefferson and Madison were busy founding the Democratic-Republican party that would pursue the ancient values of liberty, equality, and fraternity. Was the modern Democratic party to stand by impotent while Clinton dickered with Republicans on his newly rediscovered common ground?

"Centrism is fine when it is the result of competing interests," William Safire wrote in late 1997. "Thesis; antithesis; synthesis. But centrism is vapid when it is the suffocator of interests, seeking to please rather than trying to move. Clinton's approach, in most cases, has been to follow the primrose path of polling down the middle: his motto has become a firm 'there must be no compromise without compromise.' "

Clinton's major failure was his inability, during his centrist phases, to frame a coordinated policy program that would make of his centrism not just an electoral strategy but a vital center of change. He was not against a political strategy in principle—he would tell aides that he wanted a "strategy" for some undertaking, as though strategies could be ordered up like tractors from John Deere. He loved strategy so much, someone quipped, that he had several of them, often at the same time. Clinton still clung to his overarching values of fairness and justice, but furthering such values to the degree he wished called for a strategy of change. Would centrist politics produce the kind of transformation that Clinton had so often championed and still seemed to support?

Perhaps it would if Clinton pursued his brokering kind of leadership persistently and skillfully. But in his heart he was not content to be only a dealer—at times his lofty values summoned him to a higher, transforming level of leadership. Such leadership, however, called for steady commitment to values such as equality and justice, priorities among those values, capacity to mobilize support both in his party and in movements that could be linked with the party, tenacity in pursuing his long-run visions and goals. It was not enough to know Niccolò Machiavelli's famous distinction between the courageous lion and the wily fox. He also needed to remember another Machiavelli dictum, which he quoted to a group of *Washington Post* reporters: "It must be considered that there is nothing more difficult to carry out or more doubtful of success, nor dangerous to handle, than to initiate a new order of things." For reformers have enemies, Machiavelli explained, and only "lukewarm defenders."

Clinton had lost many of his liberal defenders within three years of his somewhere-left-of-center 1992 campaign for the presidency. But he had not won over his centrist supporters, who feared another lurch to the left. Close observers had been tracking Clinton's ambivalence. Bob Woodward noted how Clinton sought to placate conservative foes of the energy (BTU) tax, stating, "I've been fighting the wrong folks." Elizabeth Drew reported that the President's ambivalence was raising again the "character issue," which could be overcome only if Clinton could move forcefully ahead on his program. It was not the first time someone pronounced, "Clinton was in a race against himself."

"On the one hand, the President badly wants to look like a problem-solver who will work with anyone to overcome the barriers of party and ideology," E. J. Dionne Jr. wrote in mid-1995. But Clinton also understood that "the Republicans have been dominating the political debate, and to change that, Democrats need to take on the large questions, challenging the Republican view of government fundamentally, and with conviction."

But Clinton could not resort to venomous politics. He could not hate those who hated him—not even the House Republicans who were targeting his favorite programs for extinction. "The Republicans were unanimous in their hatred for me—and I welcome their hatred," Franklin Roosevelt cried out to a roaring Democratic crowd at the height of the 1936 election campaign, as he scorched "economic royalists" who occupied positions similar to those of the Gingrich Republicans sixty years later. Clinton could not speak in such tones. Facing an ideological party, he could not be ideological because he was a transactional broker who was not always persistent and skillful enough to make his dealing stick, and was a would-be transforming leader without the deep conviction necessary to that strategy. No wonder some Americans considered him neither a fox nor a lion, but a chameleon.

⚜

The clinching argument for centrism is simple: it works. While the ideologues are out there speechifying and pontificating, New Democrats are out there getting things done—not as fast as the "old" liberals would like, perhaps, but centrists get there step by step.

They have a point. The Clinton-Gore centrists can boast of hundreds of presidential and congressional acts leading to incremental progress. But the problem, as always, is not simply what the centrists have done. It is what they have done in comparison with the enormity of the problem and with the changes, some of them regressive, that others are fashioning. It is not only a battle of leaders but a battle of leaderships, economic and social and ideological as well as political.

"Government bureaucracies built a half or even a quarter century ago," Al From wrote in 1991, "are incapable of coping with the challenges of the 1990s—jobs lost to companies overseas, stagnant family incomes, a burgeoning underclass, homelessness, rampant drug abuse and crime and violence in our cities, crumbling roads and bridges, declining public schools, and a deterioration of moral and cultural values symbolized by the breakdown of the family. We need a new set of political innovations."

Eight years and trillions of dollars later, can we say that any of these fundamental problems have been solved? Some economic improvement, yes, but the problems still stare at us. Take education—a concern of Clinton and Rodham Clinton's from their earliest days in Arkansas and a key test of centrist strategy. "We have to be prepared to reform the systems we have made," Governor Bill Clinton told the Democratic Leadership Council in 1990. "As the governors' statement on national education goals says, we can't get there with the system we've got. That's why restructuring schools nationwide is so important."

Restructuring schools? Restructuring the educational *system*? In eight years we have seen a plethora of proposals and programs for federal loans, grants, testing (for teachers and students), school uniforms, aid to special education, recruiting volunteers to teach fourth-graders to read, the end of "social promotion" in schools, adding one hundred thousand new teachers in the primary grades—most of these worthy and helpful—but nothing that could be described as a transformation of our educational system. Centrism, with its incremental advances, cannot possibly achieve such a huge task. And education continues in crisis in the United States.

The centrists have an excuse—the intractability of the American political system. And one of the key arguments for centrism is that it is flexible enough to allow brokering within the interstices of the constitutional checks and balances. Still, it is the liberals, and the conservatives demanding systemic change, who have the main problem with all the veto traps and institutional blocks in the political system. But transformational leaders have learned that the system will respond if they work at it long enough and hard enough; and if this fails to work, they have ideas about rejuvenating the system. Centrists have hardly been forthcoming with ideas for "reconstruction": centrists don't do that sort of thing.

So, Clinton began his seventh year in office amid a political and institutional shambles. Indeed, as Alison Mitchell observed in the *New York Times,* when the 1997–98 Congress came to an end, "it stood identified less with any signature bill than with the paralysis of American politics near century's end." The lesson seemed clear; centrists can deal and bargain and transact from the center; they can gain incremental changes from the center; they cannot truly lead and transform from the center.

Thus, the cardinal question transcends Bill Clinton's or Al Gore's or Hillary Rodham Clinton's "greatness." It goes to core issues about the dynamics of progress, the role of conflict and consensus in democracy, the capacity of people to bring about far-reaching change, the requirements of leadership. It sharply poses the difference between the truly "vital center" that Arthur Schlesinger Jr. wrote about years ago and the mainstream, bipartisan, flaccid centrism of the 1990s.

The Myth of Presidential Virtue

While Clinton had been jibbing and yawing in his search for the political center, right, left, or middle, some close observers had been searching for a center in him, ethical, moral, or virtuous.

No words are more confused or abused than the language of good behavior. Dictionaries don't help; ours defines morality as ethics, ethics as morality, and virtue as both. But the distinctions are crucial. We define *virtue* as approved personal conduct, especially sexual; *ethical* as rectitude or right conduct, especially in nonprivate business or professional behavior; and *moral* as fidelity to the highest and broadest of national or community values, past and present, especially as proclaimed and continually reiterated in formal pronouncements such as presidential inaugural addresses over a long span of time.

The myth of the virtuous American president began early, with George Washington. The story of the cherry tree, although fabricated, symbolized the honesty and integrity that later ennobled the first president's leadership. Yet, he was succeeded, after the very proper John Adams, by his fellow Virginian Thomas Jefferson, who was shown many years later to have probably slept with his slave Sally Hemmings. This was not only unvirtuous but illegal as miscegenation under the laws of the day. But the myth survived and even flourished during the nineteenth century because the genteel press, though it might criticize a president's policies, would not conceive of investigating and exposing presidential peccadilloes, and even scholarly biographers rarely dug into sexual behavior.

Throughout the twentieth century, rumors drifted around about the extramarital sexual behavior—both before and during their presidencies—on the part of Harding, Franklin Roosevelt, Eisenhower, JFK, LBJ, and perhaps earlier of Woodrow Wilson. But the press was not yet so intrusive, or respectable biographers so bold, as to shatter the benign image of the virtuous president. Only years later did it become known, for example, that Harding had had sex with his young mistress in a White House "closet"; or that FDR had had a romance in his earlier Washington days with his wife's secretary or that the liaison was renewed in the White House during his final years; or that JFK had indulged in numerous trysts in the presidential mansion.

How long could the myth survive? Its destruction would require the combination of a reckless president, some bad luck, and rapacious journalists. This was the unintended feat of Bill Clinton. But when one strips away the exploitation of the "scandal" and considers the titillating specifics of the sexual behavior—the caressing, groping, undressing, and the rest—was there any difference between what literally went on in Harding's closet and in Bill and Monica's lovemaking? Only one differences so far as the myth was concerned—Harding's was never exposed in all its graphic detail by an independent prosecutor and sensationalized in the press.

Clinton was attacked not only for his sexual behavior, of course, but for lying about it. And few Americans would ever forget that indignant finger thrust out from the tube, as the President flatly denied the accusations against him. But the earlier transgressors had lied too—implicitly in the case of Jefferson, or with the covering-up by Harding and Kennedy, with the aid of a complicit press.

At issue is the president's right to privacy, including his right to protect it. Beginning with childhood, we all exercise that right, against intrusive parents, prying friends, interrogating employers. Whatever the law may say about the obstruction of justice, William Buckley Jr. wrote, "it is unrealistic to distinguish sharply between the offense of adultery and the offense of lying about it, inasmuch as the second offense goes hand in hand with the first. Anyone who commits adultery is expected to lie about it."

The right to privacy remains the issue. Perhaps presidents do not need it. Or perhaps they need it most of all.

⌁⟨⊙⟩⌁

The tragedy of Monicagate was intensely personal—the horrendous invasions of the privacy of Monica S. Lewinsky herself at the hands of an alleged friend

[Linda Tripp], the privacy of Bill Clinton and countless others at the hands of a rampaging prosecutor, and the intense distress for Hillary Rodham Clinton and daughter Chelsea. Everything revolved around the definition of virtue as sex. The tragedy quickly became political, as a media frenzy turned the ethical lesson of Monicagate upside down, grotesquely overemphasizing sex in the Oval Office and ignoring the nonsexual ethical implications. As a result the whole era rivals the Age of McCarthy in its confused and perverted priorities. It ignored the great lesson of American history that ethical concerns must trump private virtue in the public realms.

To free a president from public accountability for behavior in the private realm does not free him from ethical responsibilities in the public realm. Rather, it is to pinion him all the more tightly to his public obligations. It is to confront him with the ethical standards that Americans learn from their parents, teachers, ministers, scoutmasters, coaches, indeed, from the lofty heritage of Christian and Judaic teachings. The standards are old-fashioned but eternally new—rectitude, integrity, compassion, loyalty, responsibility, trustworthiness, civility, respect for all regardless of status, race, gender, or age.

Both the political and economic demands of transactional leadership require a set of more specific but still significant qualities for brokers and mediators—honesty, accountability, reciprocity, credibility, and prudence. How well would the presidents of this century meet both the broader and narrower tests? The answer is difficult because qualities such as rectitude and credibility are not easily definable and certainly not quantifiable. But we do know that presidents lie, dissemble, cover up, break promises, but that they also show compassion, treat people with respect, work hard for their intended goals. As academics we would grade presidents of this century ethically at around a "gentleman's C," with Richard Nixon lowering the collective grade and Jimmy Carter raising it.

How would Bill Clinton fare in this ethical lineup? Measured by the presidential leadership we have studied, we would place him in the middle of the middle, on the basis of Clinton's promises not met, trust not given him, public integrity questioned, along with his incremental progress and his compassion and respect for Americans not sharing in the promise of America. His standing rises a bit when combined with the "straight arrow" of Hillary Rodham Clinton. These evaluations, anecdotal and impressionistic, may well be modified when the Clinton-Gore leadership is evaluated in longer perspective, and with more factual information.

A pressing question that allows a more easily measurable answer, based on extensive historical data, is whether presidential ethics have declined over two centuries, and if so, whether the deterioration will continue. From the lofty ethical standards of Washington and most of the other founders, those standards declined during the nineteenth century as our political system became more democratized and more subject to bossism and corruption. This tendency was balanced by relatively strong parties that could enforce a measure of discipline on individual miscreants in order to protect their national image and popular vote appeal. As parties have declined in the twentieth century, this kind of collective control has yielded to highly personalistic politics that encourages candidates and officeholders to set their own ethical standards, if any, free of external influence. Bill Clinton—far more a manipulator of the national Democratic party than a disciplined agent of it—well exemplifies this trend.

Will the apparent overall decline in presidential ethics continue in the twenty-first century? Probably yes, for two reasons, political and intellectual.

Increasingly our political institutions and practices are forcing office seekers and -holders to resort to manipulation and deception. Our constitutional checks and balances have long compelled our political executives and legislators to be extraordinarily skillful in threading their way through the devices that thwart collective action. In the absence of strong parties that can unify and empower the rank and file in Congress and the state legislatures, factional leaders within the parties pursue their narrower ends by mobilizing money, interest groups, and legions of lobbyists. Policy—or the blocking of policy—falls into the hands of "transactional opportunists."

Nothing suggests any improvement in this situation; on the contrary, the problem will only worsen, and with it the tendency of politicians, including presidents, to take ethical shortcuts, fueled by money. The Constitution cannot be reformed to make for more responsible and accountable collective action, and the power of corporate money is bound to increase. The sheer incapacity of Congress to pass any effective control of campaign finance is a symptom of the malaise. Nor can presidents solve this problem; increasingly they are part of it.

Behind these political forces lies a pervasive intellectual doctrine—pragmatism. It is ludicrous how often this pretentious term—which today means only expedient, narrow, and short-run self-interest—is used in the press to defend mediocre political actors. "Don't worry folks, Senator Smith, who might talk like a visionary, is really down-to-earth, a practical man. He coaches Little League and makes bookcases in his basement. He will not be carried away by his ideals or principles. He's okay—a pragmatist." This kind of pragmatism has come to mean, ethically, "anything goes, if you can get away with it." The test is "what immediately works?"—with no consideration of broader, long-term aspects.

Fashioned by Harvardmen William James and Charles Sanders Peirce and others a century ago, pragmatism was a philosophical theory about truth and a refreshing reaction against the heavy Anglo-Hegelian European dogmas that dominated philosophical teaching in America. Pragmatism called for fresh thinking, intellectual innovation, new truths, practical experience. James described his kind of pragmatist: he "turns away from abstraction and insufficiency, from verbal solutions, from bad *a priori* reasons, from fixed principles, closed systems, and pretended absolutes and origins. He turns toward concreteness and adequacy, toward facts, toward action and toward power." James did not flinch from mentioning pragmatism's "cash-value."

So analytically based was this kind of pragmatism, so clearheaded in clarifying different kinds of thought and action, so relevant to American politics and markets, that the new doctrine established a dominant role in American thought in the twentieth century. But during that century the doctrine has been both trivialized and barbarized. Trivialized in its application to almost any business or political act needing a positive spin. Barbarized in its use as "practicality" to defend ethically dubious persons or acts. Thus the FDR White

House joked about some of the disreputable city bosses who trafficked with it; the Kennedy White House admitted it made use of rascals, but these were "our rascals"; the Bush White House compromised with some of the most egregious Christian-right extremists.

So today's "pragmatism" is not an ethical test of political leadership—it is merely winning votes in the next election. Almost anything legal—and much that borders on the illegal—is justified as the "practical" thing to do. But the pragmatists ignore broader and more long-run aspects of elections. How is the contest being waged? What broader stakes than winning are involved? How will defeat or victory impact the future? Winning elections obviously calls for practicality—but what about the role of vision and idealism?

Above all today's pragmatism is anti-ideology. But the pragmatists have made an ideology of pragmatism.

Pragmatism encourages compartmentalization—the separation of self-serving acts from their ethical implications. Bill Clinton is said to deal with his varied problems by putting them into separate boxes—a personal relations box, a budget box, an election box, a Southern Baptist box, a civil rights box. Perhaps this is understandable since, in a broader sphere, our government itself is compartmentalized, as the constitutional separation of powers distributes authority and accountability among House, Senate, White House, and judiciary, and subdivisions thereof, even apart from the division of powers between the national and state governments.

As the most dynamic and innovative branch, can the presidency regain the moral leadership that certain administrations have displayed in the past?

The Real Test: Moral Leadership

"Are you having fun?" *Rolling Stone* reporters asked Bill Clinton. It was around the end of his first year in the White House.

"You bet," he answered. "I like it very much. Not every hour of the day is fun. The country is going through a period of change."

"But are you having fun in this job?"

"I genuinely enjoy it."

Later in the interview one of the reporters told Clinton of a young man who had been disappointed by the President's performance and had asked the reporter to pass on his question: What was Clinton "willing to stand up for and die for"?

The President furiously turned on the reporter, his face reddening as his voice rose.

"But that's the press's fault too, damn it. I have fought more damn battles here for more things than any President in the last twenty years." Clinton raged on: he had not "gotten one damn bit of credit for it from the knee-jerk liberal press, and I am sick and tired of it and you can put that in the damn article." He got up there "every day, and I work till late at night on everything from national service to the budget to the crime bill and all this stuff and you guys take it and you say, 'Fine, go on to something else, what else can I hit him about?' " Clinton ranted on and on. He was amazingly self-revealing, a bit paranoid, and wildly off the mark.

The "knee-jerk liberal press." All Democratic presidents—FDR, JFK, LBJ, Carter—were criticized by liberals farther to the left, sometimes unfairly. It came with the job.

"I have fought and fought and fought and fought." What had he fought about? He had pursued a number of policies tenaciously—as he would in the next five years—but he was hardly the image of the Andy Jackson fighting president.

"I..." "I..." "I..." Clinton was remarkably narcissistic, even for a president. In happier moments Clinton boasted of his "White House team." This was a time when the White House troika of Bill, Al, and Hillary was especially influential.

"So if you convince them I don't have any convictions, that's fine, but it's a damn lie. It's a lie." He pointed to a couple of his policies, such as tax reform. Already the most common criticism of the President was his "lack of principle." And again, this was a standard charge against presidents—it too came with the territory.

"Do I care if I don't get credit? No." Of course Clinton did care immensely—that's what the shouting was about. "And you get no credit around here for fighting and bleeding..." But Clinton had not fought and bled—he had brokered and negotiated and compromised on a wide range of policies.

And clearly he was not a happy president, at least at this point. Political psychologist Stanley Renshon noted his "bitter sense of futility," which suggested the active-negative character types. This was a reference to the distinction that presidential scholar James David Barber had drawn between active-positive presidents (FDR, Truman, JFK, Carter), who were the most psychologically healthy, and the active-negatives, who dutifully carried out their presidential chores (Wilson, Hoover, LBJ, Nixon) but gained little happiness on the job. Had the cheery, sunny Bill Clinton who had started office as an active-positive, but then, frustrated by Congress and criticism, turned active-negative?

Perhaps it signified something simpler, and even more significant—Clinton's dissatisfaction with himself. Over and beyond his centrist strategy, his endless brokerage, his incremental steps, perhaps he still visualized himself ideally as a principled and visionary leader. Would he ever be in a position to display that kind of political leadership?

In the next five years he became a more seasoned president, more resilient and self-assured. In part this resulted from the sheer experience of governing, and his winning in 1996 the most glorious prize of American politics, a second presidential term. His job satisfaction also rose, ironically, after the Republican sweep of Congress in 1994, forcing him to define and defend his own policies.

Then Monicagate. Anyone who had seen Clinton reveal his vulnerabilities in the *Rolling Stone* interview, or in other incidents where he had lost his cool, could understand Clinton's excruciating mortification later in the titillating revelations. And now he had no one to blame—no "knee-jerk liberals" or hostile press—for his troubles, only his own reckless behavior.

At the beginning of his presidency Bill Clinton had preached and promised change—big change. His presidential leadership would be measured by the success of his economic and social reform. While he was vague on some details, his and Hillary Rodham Clinton's plans became clearer when they proposed a comprehensive new health program. Facing a Democratic Congress, still in his presidential honeymoon, the President reasonably expected that, like FDR and others, he would be granted support and leeway.

The reaction to the rejection of the health bill still remains a mystery. The rejection itself was understandable—the First Lady's plan, developed with Ira Magaziner, had significant flaws, including overelaborate details that evidently tried to anticipate the flood of executive and administrative orders that usually follow the presidential signing of a major bill. In the long history of reform, first efforts often fail; the measure is revived and the fight goes on. Not so with the health bill. The rejection by a centrist Congress triggered a vituperative reaction against the proposers in the White House, not the destroyers on the Hill. The proposal was not only a failure; it was an outrage.

The most important of the overreactors was the President himself. Of all politicians he should have recognized the enormity of the high-powered and heavily financed attack the pharmaceutical and other lobbies had launched in Congress. But the conservatives won a double victory—the killing of the bill and Clinton's return to the centrist, incremental strategy that he and his Democratic Leadership Council [DLC] colleagues had embraced in the late 1980s.

So gradualism was back in favor. And over the next few years Clinton offered scores and scores of policy bytes, most of them welcomed by the public as promising to address specific problems and deficiencies. Supported by his Vice President and First Lady, he was imaginative and indefatigable in pressing for these small but benevolent changes. But he was most firm, most willing to spend his political capital, not on controversial liberal policies but on such centrist, DLC-backed programs at NAFTA [North American Free Trade Agreement] and budget balancing.

The tragedy of the Clinton administration was its failure to tackle the big changes needed to overcome the most glaring deficiencies and inequalities in American society.

Consider education. Clinton had prided himself on being the Education Governor of Arkansas, but even with the indispensable help of Rodham Clinton and a number of initiatives, Arkansas was still near the bottom of state standings on education when he left Little Rock. Then he would be, above all, the Education President, on the premise that the states could not do the job without ample funding from Washington. Soon he was initiating a host of education policy bytes, most of them worthy. But no teacher or parent could enjoy the illusion in 1999 that public education as a whole had been dramatically improved.

A *New York Times* article reported "leaky school roofs, buckling auditorium floors, antiquated coal furnaces, and dangerously rotted window frames." This was not a depression town in the 1930s but booming New York City in

November 1998. Teachers and parents could report thousands and thousands of such situations across the country. Education was still in crisis.

Or remember an even more deep-seated problem—the grotesque income gap between the rich and the poor in America. Here again Clinton offered a host of proposals, some of which alleviated the direct symptoms of poverty. But income data told the real story. "Overall, from the late sixties to the midnineties," according to Douglas A. Hicks of the University of Richmond, "income inequality, measured by the standard indicator called the Gini coefficient, increased by over twenty percent for families, and by almost twenty percent for households." Seen another way—in terms of quintiles of the U.S. population—the top 20 percent of our income distribution now receives almost half of the total national income. This is a greater share than the middle 60 percent earns and thirteen times the share of the poorest 20 percent. Clinton failed to exhibit the moral outrage that could have put inequality at the top of the nation's agenda.

Or take the "environmental challenge," Al Gore's special bailiwick. Early administration initiatives were either junked in Congress, as with the proposed BTU energy tax, or drastically cut, as with the proposed boost of the gasoline tax. After 1994, Clinton's and Gore's main efforts were devoted to thwarting Republican attempts to reverse recent gains in environmental policy. That policy —really a cluster of policies—was so complicated by global, national, regional, and special interest (oil industry) politics as to defy easy generalization, but it can be noted that Clinton and Gore's second term neared its end with their old environmental comrades disenchanted by the administration's centrist and weak leadership in this area.

The great excuse of Clinton and Gore—as of all American leaders trying to fashion major change—was the intractability of a constitutional system that utterly fragmented policy. Yet previous presidents had confronted the two-hundred-year-old Constitution and managed somehow to bring off huge changes—Roosevelt's New Deal programs, JFK's economic policies, LBJ's civil rights achievements. Of course, they enjoyed Democratic Congresses, but consider Ronald Reagan's conservative programs. He faced mainly Democratic Congresses but he put through his right-wing policies. He had two big things going for him: conviction and consistency.

The blockage of Clinton-Gore policies in Congress might have tempted Gore to propose major changes in the constitutional and political system. After all, he was in charge of REGO, the exciting project of Reinventing Government. With his strong philosophical interests, his legal and religious education, and his hands-on experience in politics and journalism, he might have at least proposed some constitutional changes for consideration—most notably the abolition of the midterm congressional elections, which had regularly wreaked havoc on presidents no matter how well or poorly they were leading. But the Vice President limited himself to downsizing the huge federal bureaucracy and experimenting with some managerial improvements. Government was hardly reinvented.

So if it was Government Lite under Clinton and Gore, as critics contended, how could they judge the President's efforts, for all his tenacity and compassion, as anything more than Leadership Lite?

POSTSCRIPT

Will History Consider William Jefferson Clinton a Reasonably Good Chief Executive?

Burns and Sorenson et al. distinguish between *transformational* leaders who confront foes head-on and push the nation in new directions and *transactional* leaders who make deals with their foes in Congress in order to win incremental changes. Clinton, they charge, lacked an overall vision; consequently, when he did bargain with the enemy on proposals for tax reform, gun control, and international trade agreements with the North American Free Trade Agreement (NAFTA) he ended up losing control of Congress to the Republicans in 1994. As Robert Reich, Clinton's first-term labor secretary put it, "A baby-boom president who could charm snakes has tried to charm America and only infuriated the snakes."

Burns and Sorenson et al. also criticize Clinton for governing like a centrist Democrat instead of acting like a true liberal, such as Franklin D. Roosevelt. They ask, Why didn't Clinton take on the "economic royalists" and enact real programs of redistributing wealth in the form of a single-pay, government-controlled health plan or a welfare-reform program of living wage income subsidies for the poor? Many would agree that had Clinton pushed for these programs he would never have been elected in 1992, much less reelected in 1996. Burns discusses FDR's leadership further in his classic biography *The Lion and a Fox* (Harcourt Brace Jovanovich, 1956). Many say that Roosevelt had no overall vision for curing the ills of the depression in 1933. Furthermore, his New Deal was a hodgepodge of relief, recovery, and reform programs, which were invented on an almost daily basis in a desperate search to bring back prosperity. In at least two cases—the Social Security Act and the National Labor Relations Act—Roosevelt was a transactional leader who jumped on the bandwagon when it was certain these acts would pass in Congress.

In Nelson's view, Clinton had to govern as a centrist because Congress and the extremely conservative press, along with their right-wing demagogues on the radio, curbed any radical changes Clinton could make in areas of health and welfare reforms and real income redistributions of wealth and power. Nelson argues that Clinton's centrist position allowed him to be reelected because he initiated programs, according to his centrist guru Richard Morris, "on topics like violence on television, teen smoking, national education standards, school construction, and other areas that had never been part of the traditional congressional agenda."

Nelson maintains that in the area of foreign policy Clinton made incremental changes in mediating the Northern Ireland dispute and pushed the

Israelis and Palestinians along toward a permanent peace settlement. The critics argue that these agreements could easily fall apart. They also contend that Clinton was very slow in getting involved in Bosnia and Kosovo, and he was unable to disentangle himself from Somalia, a situation he inherited from the Bush administration. Yet the critics have not been able to formulate an alternative foreign policy. This may be due to the fact that there may be no grand strategy that fits all situations in the post–cold war world.

Both Burns/Sorenson et al. and Nelson play down the importance of Clinton's aberrant private life, especially his affair with Monica Lewinsky. Burns contends that Clinton should never have been impeached because only a president's public morality should be questioned, not his private behavior. While this distinction should probably be followed, nevertheless the impeachment hearings dwarfed public policy and dominated the media for almost a year. Would the country have been better off if Clinton had resigned, as would have quickly occurred in a government run by a parliamentary system?

The Clinton presidency has been under constant assessment, which will certainly continue. The starting point for his prepresidential career is David Maraniss, *First in His Class: A Biography of Bill Clinton* (Simon & Schuster, 1995). An interesting account is Stanley A. Renshon, *High Hopes: The Clinton Presidency and the Politics of Ambition* (Routledge, 1998). Political scientists analyze the first term of Clinton's presidency and two election victories in Stanley A. Renshon, ed., *The Clinton Presidency: Campaigning, Governing and the Psychology of Leadership* (Westview Press, 1995) and in Colin Campbell and Bert A. Rockman, eds., *The Clinton Legacy* (Chatham House, 2000). The British weigh in with Paul S. Herrnson and Dilys M. Hill, eds., *The Clinton Presidency: The First Term 1992–1996* (St. Martin's Press, 1997).

The insiders have also started to weigh in. An easy read, which became a best-seller, is George Stephanopoulos, *All Too Human: A Political Education* (Little, Brown, 1999), which should be compared with Dick Morris, *Behind the Oval Office* (Random House, 1997). Morris was Clinton's chief strategist behind his "comeback from the grave" in 1995 and 1996. Reporters also weigh in with varying degrees of success. The earliest accounts are Elizabeth Drew, *On the Edge* (Simon & Schuster, 1994) and Bob Woodward, *The Agenda* (Simon & Schuster, 1994) and *Shadow* (Simon & Schuster, 1999).

Finally, three important works deserve mention. Jacob Weisberg, former *New Republic* editor, asserts that Clinton altered the office of the presidency in "The Governor-President, Bill Clinton," *New York Times Magazine* (January 17, 1999); the focus of *Washington Post* media critic Howard Kurtz's *Spin Cycle: Inside the Clinton Propaganda Machine* (Free Press, 1998) is self-evident; and senior Clinton pollster and adviser Stanley B. Greenberg's *Middle Class Dreams: The New American Majority,* rev. ed. (Yale University Press, 1996) is a book of wide-ranging historical analysis, which President Clinton read and apparently absorbed.

ISSUE 17

Is America Entering the Twenty-First Century in a Period of Decline?

YES: Paul Kennedy, from "The Next American Century?" *World Policy Journal* (Spring 1999)

NO: Gregg Easterbrook, from "America the O.K.," *The New Republic* (January 4 & 11, 1999)

ISSUE SUMMARY

YES: Professor of history Paul Kennedy argues that Europe and China have the potential to equal or exceed the United States in economic power in 25 years.

NO: Gregg Easterbrook, senior editor of *The New Republic,* maintains that in terms of health, wealth, and moral values, life in the United States has never been better for the vast majority of Americans.

In 1941 *Time* magazine owner Henry Luce said that the twentieth century is the "American Century." Will the twenty-first century also be called America's century? Before attempting any predictions, a comparison of America in 1900 with America in the years 1950 and 2000 is in order.

The most visible changes in the United States over the past century have been in transportation and communication. In 1900 there were several transcontinental railroad systems connecting the east and west coasts. Mass transit inner-city transportation systems of trolleys, buses, and subways were also in place at the turn of the twentieth century. By the 1950s, however, cities were beginning to decline in population. People continued to work there, but the automobile carried the labor force to and from the suburban communities built alongside the federally funded interstate highway system. At the same time, trucks replaced trains as the main means for transporting goods to warehouses and factories, while airplanes were carrying passengers thousands of miles to conduct business and to enjoy vacations.

In addition to experiencing declining populations, cities have lost the consumer revolution to the mega–shopping malls. Even movie houses, live theatres, and art galleries have decentralized and relocated to the suburbs. Whether the personal home computer, the fax machine, e-mail, portable phones, the Internet, and satellite television systems have created a globalized community or an information-overload jungle remains to be seen.

By 1900 American capitalism had matured. The Industrial Revolution had created a system of oligopolies that dominated steel, oil, coal, meat packing, tobacco, and railroads because such industries needed large economies of scale to be competitive. Opposition to these "trusts" came from smaller competitors and middle-class consumers, who demanded that the national government either break them up into smaller units through antitrust laws or have state and federal agencies regulate their market practices. The first sign that government was to become a player came in 1902, when the Supreme Court declared a railroad monopoly formed by investment banker J. P. Morgan unconstitutional. A little less than a decade later, John D. Rockefeller's Standard Oil Company and the American Tobacco Company were broken up into smaller units.

There are some similarities between 1900 and 2000. Although the economy is much more decentralized today, monopolies in certain sectors of the economy are still prevalent. Wal-Mart and Home Depot, for example, have wiped out many smaller department and hardware stores. Also, Alan Greenspan, chairman of the Federal Reserve System, dominates monetary policy in the same way that Morgan's investment banking house controlled the money supply in the early twentieth century. Finally, there are many similarities between the dissolution of Rockefeller's Standard Oil Company in 1911 and the breakup of Bill Gates's Microsoft empire in 2000.

The 1950s represented the peak period of prosperity for the blue-collar worker. With the exception of the coal and textile industries, workers' wages were at an unusually high level. Strikes occurred periodically, but they were peacefully resolved. Although labor leader Samuel Gompers was dead, business unionism prevailed. Workers received higher hourly wages and better health, vacation, and retirement benefits, while the steel, automobile, and tobacco companies passed the increased costs onto consumers.

But the golden age of the factory worker was short-lived. The failure of many corporations to modernize their older plants, the relocation of businesses to states and countries with cheaper labor, the rise of automation, and union featherbedding practices all contributed to the deindustrialization of America. Clearly, America has entered the postindustrial phase of its history. The manufacturing sector of the economy is still important but not dominant, and it is run in a more decentralized manner. Output remains high and efficient even with a declining labor force. White-collar jobs dominate, although not all are high paying. "Symbolic interactionists" control Wall Street and the high-technology industries in America.

Has America entered a period of decline like those that occurred in nineteenth-century England and third-century Rome? In the following selection, Paul Kennedy asserts that within 25 years Europe and China may equal or exceed the United States' economic power. Gregg Easterbrook, in the second selection, contends that in terms of health, wealth, and moral values, life has never been better for the vast majority of Americans.

Paul Kennedy

 **YES**

The Next American Century?

The American Century. These three words surely constitute one of the best-known expressions of modern international history. The phrase was first coined by the highly successful American publisher, Henry Luce, as the title for an article he wrote in a February 1941 edition of his own LIFE magazine. Composed months before Hitler attacked the Soviet Union and Japan bombed Pearl Harbor, it was an amazingly confident prescription for the era to come. "American experience," exulted Luce in his article, "is the key to the future.... America must be the elder brother of nations in the brotherhood of man." Given Congress's desire to avoid war, the still-minuscule American army, and the massive ambitions of other, heavily armed, Great Powers, this was a risky vision to advance.

Yet how much more unlikely must the idea have seemed to foreign observers if it had been advocated 40 years earlier, at the beginning of the century Luce claimed as the "American" century? Around 1900, it is true, several of the more traditional powers (France, Spain, the Hapsburg Empire) seemed to be fading, and the idea was being advanced that the twentieth century would be dominated by four great empires—the British, the Russian, the American, and the German—that would compete against each other. This Darwinian view of a future struggle among the "Big Four" certainly influenced Admiral von Tirpitz as he strove to create the High Seas Fleet, galvanized British imperialists like Joseph Chamberlain to push for reforms of their own empire, and motivated all sorts of Russian expansionist visions. True, turn-of-the-century Americans also spoke of their country's "manifest destiny"; but the point is that the race to dominate the global scene during the next 100 years was a wide open one to most strategic experts. Only a few prescient figures outside the United States—such as the British prime minister William Gladstone, and perhaps even Wilhelm II himself, who in 1896 had called for the nations of Europe to unite against a future American economic and political domination—sensed that Washington would one day come to be the center of world affairs.

An Amazing Country

What did they, and the more numerous U.S. nationalists themselves, see in this amazing country that caused them to assume an ever greater American world influence? The first factor, surely, was sheer economic power. One did not have to be a Marxist to recognize that America's material assets—abundant land, vast mineral resources, bounding industrial production, immense railway and road networks, bustling harbors, multimillionaires galore—translated into political and strategic significance as well. By the eve of the First World War, the national product of the United States was already equal to that of *all the other Great Powers combined,* a statistic that would have amazed (and disturbed) Bismarck or Palmerston.

But there were other, less quantifiable signs that suggested a country on the rise. There was an energy among the people, whether corporate robber barons or frontier farmers, that contrasted sharply with the staider habits of the Old World. There was a sense that no limits existed to potential future growth, a confidence imbued by the vastness of the country itself compared with crowded little states like England, Italy, the Netherlands. And this broad picture of upward mobility in turn drew millions of new immigrants eager to make their own fortunes to the United States each year, thus boosting the collective national wealth.

There were, of course, many negative aspects to this bustling, rambunctious American society that appalled more traditional foreign observers. Its political affairs, especially at election times, seemed extremely corrupt even by European standards; it was widely assumed that every vote in Congress could be purchased. Its popular culture repelled European aesthetes and intellectuals, as it does to this day. Its raw social energies suggested a lack of control, excess, instability. It was probably comforting to these observers that the United States also seemed of little import in world affairs after its brief war with Spain in 1898. It rejoiced in its isolationism from Europe, its executive branch was weak, and, although it possessed a considerable navy, its army was minor. America was eccentric (in both senses of the word) but harmless. This was a common misperception of the day.

As it turned out, those who instinctively felt that America's great energies would sooner or later have an impact on the global balances—one thinks here also of Sir Edward Grey or of the young Winston Churchill, both of whom described the United States as being "a vast industrial machine"—got it right. When the European powers went to war in August 1914, most experts looked forward to a swift and decisive outcome; but the very fact that each side consisted of an extensive coalition of states, with huge productive and personnel resources, meant that the conflict would not end quickly. As the costs of the war rapidly mounted, both alliances looked for new members, courting Turkey, Italy, Bulgaria, Romania, Greece, Japan.

Yet, as the British historian A. J. P. Taylor pointed out years ago, the *only* country that had the power to change the global balances was that puzzling transatlantic nation, the United States. Already by 1915 its financial influence was marked, and in the climactic year of 1918 its military forces were ending the stalemate on the Western Front. Moreover, leaders and publics across the world had to grapple with the immense ideological impact of the American presence; Woodrow Wilson's calls for national self-determination, a peace without victory, freedom of the seas, and a new international order resonated everywhere from Danzig to Dehli, altering the political discourse forever.

An Erratic Path to Primacy

But if the United States was destined to be the next world hegemon, its path to primacy was both erratic and half-hearted. After 1919, America was an extremely reluctant superpower. By all sorts of measures, Congress voted for isolationism and neutrality. The League of Nations, Wilson's proudest creation, was abandoned. The army, massively augmented in 1917–18, was just as massively slashed. There were proposals made to abolish the Marine Corps, and some even wondered about preserving the State Department. The secret office that deciphered foreign codes was closed down. Economically, the nation opted for policies of almost complete self-centeredness, and the share of its national product derived from foreign trade became smaller than ever. Yet, paradoxically, the impact of American commercial and financial policies abroad was more important than ever before, as was to be seen in the international ripple of calamities that followed the 1929 Wall Street crash and the virtual elimination of open international trade that was provoked by the 1930 Hawley-Smoot Tariff Act. The world desperately needed a "lender of last resort," and only America had the resources to play that role; but it chose not to do so. During the 1930s, therefore, it no longer occupied its natural place at the center of the world stage but, like its equally puzzling Soviet equivalent, stood in the wings as the weakened Western democracies were faced with the rise of fascist dictatorships.

It is difficult to know how long this curious situation would have lasted— for President Roosevelt and his advisors alone could not have brought America out of its isolationism—had it not been for the repeated and growing aggressions of Adolf Hitler and the Japanese military leadership. Much as the isolationist lobby resisted it, the United States was being forced to confront the threats in Europe and the Pacific, and to formulate a strategy to deal with those threats. With France and the smaller European states destroyed, the Soviet Union invaded, and Britain besieged, America was compelled once again to occupy the center of the world stage. This was the meaning behind Henry Luce's 1941 call to his countrymen to step forward into the American Century.

And, indeed, America's time had come. Only the United States had the reserve industrial capacities to outbuild the fascist states and supply both its own troops and those of its bankrupt allies through the unique system of lend-lease. As the war unfolded, the more that potential was realized. For every merchant ship sunk by German U-boats, America was building another three. For every Allied aircraft shot down over Europe or the South Pacific, America was building another five. In 1944 alone, it assembled the staggering total of 96,000 aircraft and launched an aircraft carrier every few weeks. When the operations of the German and Japanese air forces were suspended because of lack of fuel, the United States had the spare capacity to fly Christmas packages to its soldiers everywhere in the world. Nothing was impossible. If it would take billions of dollars to construct the new and untried atomic bomb, those monies would be forthcoming.

The Elder Brother

By 1945, then, Luce's purposes had been accomplished in many parts of the world. Like it or not, America was the "elder brother" everywhere from Brazil to Australia to the Mediterranean. Amid the national bankruptcy and exhaustion of most other countries, it alone was healthy and strong, it alone could pour out monies for postwar reconstruction. It had by now largely replaced the British Empire as the greatest maritime, trading, and financial nation, as the new hegemon. It had been the chief artificer of the new international architecture, so it was not surprising that the Bretton Woods institutions (the World Bank; the International Monetary Fund) were located in Washington, not London, and that the United Nations Organization was set up in New York, not Geneva, thus reflecting this new reality. Its armed forces were massive, and it had a monopoly on the atomic bomb.

How much of America's global reach would have been trimmed back by Congress and the public had foreign affairs been stable after 1945, it is hard to say; there were many withdrawals from overseas army and air bases, and a drastic reduction in military personnel. And there were many Americans who wanted to return to the old, prewar days. But all such calculations were upset by the sudden deterioration of relations with the Soviet Union and the onset of the Cold War. Appealing to the "lessons learned" from the years of appeasement and isolationism, American leaders swiftly reversed course and, as in the Truman Doctrine, pledged support to all democracies who asked for it. Military assurances were handed out with a liberality that would have astounded the Founding Fathers—to Greece and Turkey, to other NATO allies, to Japan, to Australia, to the rest of the Americas. U.S. bomber squadrons returned to their former British air bases; American troops returned to their barracks in the Rhineland and Bavaria. It was not long before the words "Pax Americana" were a commonplace. And, in fact, American power vis-à-vis the other nations of the globe was possibly more pronounced than at any time since that of Imperial Rome vis-à-vis its neighbors.

While the Cold War stimulated American engagement in the world, curiously enough it also disguised its unique position. The existence of the Soviet Union, with its vast conventional forces and (a little later) its nuclear arsenal, possessing its own array of allies in Eastern Europe and in the developing world, and brandishing its own competing ideology, combined to suggest that this was a bipolar system, a world of two superpowers. By the late 1960s, Khrushchev was promising to overtake the United States and bury capitalism in the process. Then there were other negatives. Many developing countries disliked both alliance blocs. There was considerable anti-Americanism in Europe, and at the United Nations. The Vietnam War caused not only convulsions at home but bitter criticism of America abroad. The ending of the Bretton Woods system in 1971 pointed to growing economic weaknesses. The Watergate scandal weakened the U.S. presidency. The American failure in Iran was a humiliation. The rise of Japan, and of East Asia in general, led to criticisms of U.S. industrial techniques and a fear of being overtaken. All this suggested not an American century but an America in relative decline.

Forecasters of Doom

There was much truth in such negatives, but the forecasters of doom missed a number of important points. The first was that America's archrival, the Soviet Union, was exhibiting even greater economic weaknesses, although many Cold War advocates refused for years to admit this. Russia, to use the author Paul Dibbs's term, was "the incomplete superpower"—and not just incomplete but steadily losing ground and unraveling. As the Soviet Union weakened, it lost its hold over Eastern Europe and then over its own non-Russian states within the union. This dealt a virtual deathblow to the international appeal of communism and, by extension, to the popularity of socialist planning and policies.

The second factor was the remarkable capacity of American industry to "re-tool" itself from the early 1980s onward, and thus regain a great deal of its earlier leadership in manufacturing and production. This renewal of the industrial spirit was usually accompanied by brutal measures—downsizing the workforce; destroying, or at least weakening, the trade unions; creating millions of uninsured, part-time jobs; relocating production to cheap-labor sites in the developing world. No European country, except Margaret Thatcher's Britain, felt it could do the same, the others being constrained by their postwar "social contracts." Even today there is strong resistance to American-style capitalism. But such critics can hardly deny that the end result of the American industrial renewal was that the U.S. economic machine became much more competitive and the envy of many a foreign businessman.

Furthermore, the bold new technologies of the 1970s and 1980s played to American strengths. Computers, communications systems, new software applications, and the coming of the Internet together constituted a "knowledge revolution" that could only have emerged from a decentralized economy and society, yet also benefited such a society much more than it could a sclerotic Soviet Union or a bureaucratically encumbered Europe and Japan. The knowledge revolution produced a feedback loop, giving an advantage to the people (like Bill Gates) who had created it in the first place. And this was not merely of commercial benefit, for the U.S. armed forces also profited greatly from adopting these new technologies to enhance their combat effectiveness, making the American military unequaled in many operational and strategic aspects of warfare.

A Culture That Knew No Limits

And while European intellectuals might sneer at the crassness and greed and uncaring nature of Ronald Reagan's America, tens of millions of people from other societies—in Eastern Europe, the Caribbean, East Asia—were all panting to get to the United States, where they hoped to achieve a better life for their families. With millions of additional immigrants being admitted in each decade, there was reinforced the sense of a special American culture that knew no limits.

Moreover, U.S. politicians, from Reagan to Clinton, deliberately pushed for further economic transformations, seeking to reduce government spending (and public expectations of what government could provide its citizens), slashing taxes, and eliminating all forms of exchange controls on currencies and capital. This liberalization of capital, which was also pursued eagerly by the British, but more slowly and reluctantly by other countries, meant that a vast amount of venture capital was now circling the globe, looking for investment opportunities, rewarding countries and regions that followed American laissez-faire practices, and punishing those who tried to resist, whether it be Mitterrand's France or Suharto's Indonesia.

Since the communications revolution of the past two decades was chiefly U.S.-based, this also led to the export, intentionally and unintentionally, of American culture. This did not simply mean the spreading of American free-market rules in the businessplace, or American dress styles, or American hotels (so that the Hilton in Singapore looks no different from the Hilton in Dallas). It also included the perhaps even more important spreading of American youth culture—MTV, casual dress, blue jeans, Hard Rock Cafes, Hollywood movies, and the rest. None of this had much intellectual content; it was crass and noisy, offering immediate gratification—but to the young people of the world it was immensely attractive because of its liberating messages. It was also insidious, and evaded the attempts of Muslim ayatollahs, Soviet commissars, and French education ministries to prevent penetration of these "dangerous" American habits.

Yet while Hollywood films and American youth culture might be intellectually low, there were other strands to the U.S. resurgence of the past two decades that pointed to the increasing concentration of the world's scholarly, scientific, and technological skills within the boundaries of this single nation. It is home to the great science laboratories, developed by Bell Labs and IBM or by the rising biotechnology and pharmaceutical industries. It has come to dominate the world's computer software industry. It possesses incredible intellectual assets in its great research universities, with which the higher education systems of other countries nowadays simply cannot compete. The annual roll call of Nobel science prizewinners provides a regular witness to this dominance. Young scholars from Scotland and Cambodia, India and Brazil, flock to study in America. German pharmaceutical companies have moved their research laboratories across the Atlantic, while their boards of directors conduct company business in the English language.

Thus, in virtually all dimensions of power, whether it be the "soft power" of youth culture or the "hard power" of military hardware, in all areas from finance to scholarship, the United States seems at present in a relatively more favorable position in the world than at any time since the 1940s. Partly this is due to the exploitation and recovery of its own inherent strengths, but this is also surely caused by the serious weaknesses of its competitors. The Soviet

Union has broken up, and Russia can hardly feed or govern itself. The Japanese banking system is dangerously close to a meltdown. China is grappling with the problems that affect all of Asia. And Europe, while inching toward monetary unity, is a long way from unitary political coherence and effectiveness. With the other major units of power in disarray, the United States at the end of this decade may be closer than ever to Henry Luce's dream of the coming of the American Century.

America's Prospects

What, then, could be said of America's prospects for the century to come? Will its relative position improve still further? There are certain indications that it could do so: the globalization of U.S. commercial standards continues apace, American culture continues to extend its reach, and democratization is spreading into newer regions of the planet. While domestic patriots look forward to the "Americanization" of everything, foreign nationalists from Canada to Malaysia are appalled. Nonetheless, a large number of people clearly do anticipate an increase of the American position in the world.

Other trends, however, point in the opposite direction. The more Americanization and globalization that occurs, the greater the likelihood of a backlash, as we are now witnessing in Russia and Indonesia, and in many other places where the inhabitants feel that they have been left vulnerable to the creative gales of international capitalism.

Second, while it is difficult to forecast the condition of, say, Europe or China in 25 years' time, both of them have the potential to equal or exceed the United States, at least in economic power. Moreover, while it was relatively easy for the U.S. government to unite its people, and its allies, against the common Cold War foe, it is much harder to unite them now when threats to American interests seem much more diffuse and much more complicated. Finally, America's own troubled domestic scene, and the inwardness of its own special cultural wars, suggests that it may have more difficulty in producing leaders who can focus on international issues than it had during the Cold War. All or any of the above could diminish America's global lead.

The question arises whether it is wise to measure "power" and "influence" in the future simply from the perspective of nation-states like America and Russia, or conglomerate-states like the European Union. The decentralization of knowledge is working to the advantage of individuals and companies, but not to that of nations themselves. World finance is "unhinged," in free float, and it is difficult to think of how it can be controlled. Many observers think that the large multinational corporations, with their ability to shift resources from one part of our planet to another, are really the sovereign players on the world stage. Global drug traffickers and international terrorists also pose new and difficult threats to traditional state powers. So how much "influence" can really be defined as American, or non-American?

More than that, as the end of the century approaches, it is difficult not to hear many parts of the structure of international affairs creaking and groaning under the newer pressures for change. Many experts think we are approaching real thresholds—in the environmental damage we have inflicted on our planet, in the continuing enormous increases in human population, in the uncontrollable volatility of our financial system—and that major societies will simply collapse under these strains.

Will the United States, with or without allies, be able to handle these newer challenges, especially in an age of divided government in Washington? It is not clear that it can, which may mean that we have to think differently about the twenty-first century than we have thought about our present century.

Undoubtedly, the United States of America has had more influence upon our world over the past 100 years than any other country, and to that extent this century may be termed, in shorthand, "America's," even more than the sixteenth century seemed to be Spain's, the eighteenth France's, and the nineteenth Britain's. There is equally little doubt that the United States will enter the twenty-first century as the world's number-one power. But whether it will continue to be so into and through the next century is open to question. For the pace of the technological, financial, demographic, and environmental changes that affect our planet in the present age are so profound that it would be rash to claim that the next century, too, must be America's. By choosing intelligent policies, it is possible that the United States could stay at the top for many years to come. Yet it is wise to recall Voltaire's question: "If Rome and Carthage fell, which Power is then immortal?" His answer was "None."

Gregg Easterbrook  **NO**

America the O.K.

I don't wish to alarm you, but American life is getting better. Crime has fallen sharply. The economy is booming. Teen pregnancy is declining. The federal budget is in surplus. The air and water are getting cleaner. Health is improving by almost every measure, including the first-ever decline in cancer incidence. Deaths in accidents are decreasing. Standards of living continue to improve. The use of drugs and cigarettes is waning. Levels of education keep rising. Women and minorities are acquiring an ever-larger slice of the national pie. Personal liberty has never been greater, while American culture becomes more and more diverse. Even home runs are at an all-time high!

Yet the steady betterment of American life is practically a taboo subject for intellectual debate. Left-wing thinkers shy from it because it smacks of triumphalism or simply spoils the doomsday script. Right-wing thinkers are terrified of having to admit that recent decades of progress have occurred under a regime of strong central government. Pundits and politicians see only calamity –in 1995, Newt Gingrich called the United States "a civilization in danger of simply falling apart"–while the country around them indecorously gets better. Right now, Washington is busily sinking to an all-time low in the disconnect between governors and governed, obsessively generating an institutional crisis, in part, just to make sure there's some really bad news.

To the extent favorable trends are remarked upon, they are often treated as ephemera of a strong economy—though impressive social transitions, such as pollution reduction, exist outside the business cycle. Notes Orlando Patterson, a Harvard sociologist: "It's astonishing how the Washington and New York elites, the people who benefit most from the improvement of the United States, are so out of sync with it, endlessly talking about how things are getting worse when the country is clearly improving."

As David Whitman points out in his cogent new book, *The Optimism Gap*, polls show that personal optimism is at or near record levels—most people rating their own prospects around eight on a scale of ten—but national optimism has never been lower, most people thinking that the country is in decline. Whitman calls this the "I'm O.K., they're not" syndrome. Failure to heed the improvement of the United States feeds cynicism and robs us of valid congratulation: after race riots, Vietnam, and stagflation, isn't it good for everyone if

America can like what it sees in the mirror again? And inattention to the optimistic deprives public thought of the chance to benefit from the lessons of successful reform.

Of course, there are gloomy trends, worst among them the persistence of poverty. Today, about 13 percent of U.S. households live below the poverty level, which seems ever less tolerable as the nation grows richer. As Michael Novak has noted, when the Bible declared, "You always have the poor with you," the context was a feudal agrarian economy in which some poverty was unavoidable. Today's high-tech, knows-no-obstacle economy could transfer enough goods to everyone, and, until it does, a sword will hang over American abundance.

And, of course, the international scene presents anxieties. Beyond the specters of war and ethnic hostility, the developing world's ecosystems continue to deteriorate. Global population will rise to around nine billion before stabilizing in the twenty-first century. This means the world must eventually feed, educate, employ, and care for the health of a human race half again its present size. There's no way the United States will be able to sit out that great challenge and no sign we are preparing for it. But, overall, the American scene is progressively more encouraging. Let's review the facts:

Accidents Despite the sirens-and-carnage images projected by local TV news, accidents have been declining pretty much across the board for more than a decade. In 1985, 40 Americans out of every 100,000 died accidental deaths; by 1996, the rate was down to 35 of 100,000, a twelve percent decline. Workplace fatalities dropped spectacularly during this period, from about 11,600 in 1985 to 6,218 in 1997. Traffic fatalities have been declining, too, and in 1997 reached a record low of just 1.6 deaths per 100 million miles driven, the smallest such figure since federal agencies began keeping traffic-death statistics in the 1960s. Highway fatalities are going down in absolute numbers—in 1984, there were 46,200 traffic deaths, for example, versus 41,967 in 1997—even as there are more people driving more cars at faster speeds for more total miles.

On a related front, building fires are steadily declining. The National Fire Protection Association reports that the total number of "structure" fires in the United States went from three million in 1980 to slightly less than two million in 1996. Jill Leovy recently reported in the *Los Angeles Times* that, in her city, building fires fell from 8,557 in 1979 to 3,406 in 1997. Firefighters now have so much free time that they are teaching boating and bicycle safety. More than 6,000 Americans died in home fires in 1960; in 1996, just 2,900 did, though the population had risen almost 50 percent through the period. Trends like this have nothing to do with the economy.

What's behind such developments? Liability pressure, consumer activism, and improving technology have made cars notably safer. Automakers spent years resisting air bags and crash-impact engineering, claiming cars would become exorbitantly expensive while losing functionality. Instead, auto offerings are getting zippier and roomier—today's Ford Taurus, loaded with new safety features plus air-conditioning and a CD player, costs 70 percent less in real-dollar terms than a Model T did. Never underestimate the ability of industry to make products less dangerous—or excuse corporations from doing so.

While auto manufacturers have improved the safety engineering of products, crusades against drunken driving, plus lower legal tolerance for the same, have had the desired effect. Once, to get behind the wheel after knocking back a few was viewed as boys-will-be-boys behavior; now, it's viewed as idiocy and dishonor. The lesson: Public awareness campaigns really can work.

The drop in fires stems from a similar mix of awareness, regulation, and better management. In the past 20 years, smoke detectors have become ubiquities, a reform driven both by government rules and awareness campaigns. Federal regulators have required increasingly strict standards for fire-resistance in products and building materials. Local fire codes have become ever-tighter: Scottsdale, Arizona, now requires built-in sprinklers in every newly constructed room, even confessional booths. Fire departments and building-code writers have switched from a philosophy of fire fighting to one of prevention, with an emphasis on careful inspections of buildings or blueprints. Many big-city fire departments are becoming ambulance departments that fight fires as a sidelight. It's a wonderful transition.

Crime   Homicide is down about 20 percent from the level of the early '90s; in 1997, it reached the lowest rate in 30 years. During the '80s, Brooklyn averaged two murders per day; last March, Brooklyn went a full week without a homicide for the first time in a generation. Crime is down in nearly every category, including burglary and robbery. Since 1993, not only has the felony rate dropped, but the total number of violent felonies has fallen 14 percent, even while the population continues to grow. As Gordon Witkin has written, "It's hard to think of a social trend with greater significance."

Many factors are at play here, among them the sheer reduction in perpetrators. Tougher laws and sentences have led to a furious rate of incarceration, with 1.8 million Americans now jailed, more than double the figure of a decade ago. The shift toward "community policing" has helped, though felonies are also falling in cities that have not adopted this system. It's important to note that, while most policing has improved in the past decade, there has been no national initiative on this score, just lots of local experiments.

The adoption of James Q. Wilson's "broken windows" theory of civic propriety has helped, too. Annoying as New York City Mayor Rudy Giuliani's anti-jaywalking campaign might be, there is no doubt that an environment in which people take petty laws seriously creates sociological pressure to respect the sort of laws we really care about. Putting more officers on the street has helped, as has the upgunning of law enforcement. During the '80s, when most police carried revolvers, drug-runners had superior weapons. Now that half of all cops bear the high-rate-of-fire Glock semiautomatic, only a fool would try to shoot his way out of an arrest.

Conspicuous in recent crime trends is the decline of crack. The nature of this drug product—packaged for volume sales of inexpensive rocks that produce only a brief high, requiring the user to make multiple purchases—made it a street-corner enterprise. Lots of salesmen were needed, so the young and intemperate were recruited. As Alfred Blumstein, a criminologist at Carnegie Mellon University, describes it, crack crews carrying wads of cash themselves became the targets of crime, and, since drug dealers who were robbed couldn't exactly dial 911, they armed themselves. The result was thousands of teenagers toting guns in tense situations.

Thus, not the intoxicating effects of crack but its distribution by armed, fidgety teenagers caused the '80s homicide wave. Nearly all the murder surge occurred among under-30 males; the homicide rate in other groups actually declined during the very period of the murder epidemic. Leading the current homicide decline is a rapid drop in killings among those under 30—though the rate among those under 18 remains historically high.

Then there's the "younger brother effect." The '90s generation of inner-city kids, having seen the medically destructive effects of crack and the self-genocide it produced in minority communities, wants little to do with the opiate of the '80s. Crack use continues, but mostly among older addicts who do their buying from a new breed of dealers, who work from client lists and beepers, avoiding street confrontations.

For police, an essential policy shift was a campaign against weapons possession. Traditionally, police departments have looked the other way regarding guns alone: If someone had an illegal weapon but hadn't used it, he'd get off lightly. Beginning around 1990, patrol officers and prosecutors began going after the guns themselves. It proved easier to make cases involving traceable firearms than cases based on plastic bags of crack the suspect could claim he never saw before. Arrests of minors for weapons possession peaked in 1993; by 1994, the incidence of minors carrying firearms began to decline. Perhaps not coincidentally, it was also in 1994 that the homicide rate began its fall.

Both a growth economy and social circumstances now work against violent crime. As Jeffrey Fagan, a professor of public health at Columbia University, notes, the kids who became crack-runners in the '80s had been born into a period of upheaval: inner cities were in decline, parents were losing jobs as industry fled urban areas, welfare was pushing fathers out of homes, and, to many whose parents traversed the '60s, rioting—violent contempt for law—had briefly been seen as somehow useful to minority aspirations. Now, Fagan says, "the phase of social reorganization is basically over for the inner city." Downtown areas have stopped declining, and some are improving. People have made their peace with the new service industries, rendering legitimate employment possible again. Stability is returning, and, with it, community contempt for crime.

Within the positive trends an obvious worry is that some new street drug or an economic downturn could cause a new spate of crime. But what's most striking about falling homicide rates is that they represent rapid progress in an area where bad news was widely believed inevitable. "It's possible you won't be able to solve this problem," New York Governor Mario Cuomo said of the murder rate in 1989. Nine years later, the arrows point up.

Drink, drugs, and fooling around   Crack is hardly the only bane in decline. On the key barometer of ingestion by high school seniors, cocaine has declined from something tried by 17 percent of students in 1985 to seven percent in 1996. Twenty-two percent of high school seniors in 1975 had tried stimulant drugs; by 1996, the figure was down to 15 percent. Use of some, though not all, other illegal drugs is also down.

Even legal, socially acceptable forms of indulgence are in remission. In 1965, 42 percent of American adults smoked; today, 25 percent do. Per capita U.S. consumption of spirits has been going down for years. In 1980, 72 percent of high school seniors reported having consumed alcohol recently. This figure has gone down steadily since, falling to 51 percent in 1996. Can it be that half of America's young aren't even sneaking beers anymore?

Another entirely legal (except in Washington) form of earthly pleasure, sex, also seems in decline, at least among the supposedly incorrigible young. The portion of teenage girls reporting to have had intercourse had been climbing steadily since the '60s, a statistic commonly cited—often by middle-age commentators who themselves once devoted countless hours to the pursuit of teenage sex—as a sign of American moral erosion. Now, according to the National Center for Health Statistics, the percentage of sexually active girls ages 15 to 19 has dropped from a peak of 53 percent in 1988 to 50 percent in 1995. Teen pregnancy rates have begun to decline; in 1995, teen pregnancy fell to the same rate as that of 1975, and the downward statistical slope continues. Births to teens have dropped twelve percent since 1991. The number of teen abortions has fallen for seven consecutive years.

Smoking's decline clearly reflects improved awareness of lung cancer. Drug declines probably result from a combination of law-enforcement intensification and rising understanding of the fact that, with the possible exception of marijuana, drugs simply aren't innocuous private choices. Less drinking seems to stem from anti-drunken-driving campaigns and a changing anthropology of the social event, today less viewed as a sanctioned time during which to get schnockered (think *Virginia Woolf*) than as a time at which to sip wine and listen to music.

Less sexual activity among young people may be influenced by concern about sexually transmitted diseases and by religious feeling. A reaction against cultural pressure in favor of sex, especially the repulsively phony Hollywood and rock-video conceptions of sex, might be just as important. Teenage pregnancy decline results directly from higher birth control use—contraceptive use at first intercourse is up from 48 percent among females in the early '80s to 78 percent in 1995. Contraceptives are getting safer (the low-dose Pill) and more convenient (the inject-and-forget Depo-Provera). As important, probably, is a shifting sociology of birth control—which is increasingly seen as smart and responsible.

Less drug use, less drinking, less smoking, and less fooling around hardly synchronize with conventional hand-wringing about the United States as a self-indulgent, libertine realm where anything goes. Rather, these trends suggest that public habits can be moderated through awareness campaigns, rational arguments, and common sense.

The economy Financial situations can change rapidly, so the milk might curdle; that admonition aside, the American economic outlook is the best it's ever been. Unemployment and inflation are at their lowest points in a quarter-century. Growth is strong, though below record levels. Economic troubles elsewhere in the world seem barely to have dented the system here. Gasoline prices are at a postwar low in real-dollar terms, while mortgage rates are at 30-year lows. Industry isn't disappearing, as is commonly assumed—current U.S. industrial production is 90 percent greater than in 1970, though that figure is achieved with fewer workers. It's common to hear analysts bemoaning the fact that median household income has risen only slightly in the past quarter-century. But the standard concept doesn't take into account that fewer and fewer people live in the median household: factor that in, and household income is up about 15 percent since 1970. The only major negative indicators are the savings rate and the balance-of-trade deficit. As problems go, that's not bad.

The transition from federal deficit to surplus should remind us how often "impossible" problems are solved. Think back to the hollow legislative rituals of the Gramm-Rudman-Hollings law, written to be vacuous on the assumption that real deficit reduction simply could not happen. Now the federal balance sheet has improved so much that lower government borrowing helps drive down interest rates, benefiting everyone. And this has been accomplished without punitive taxation. As Derek Bok pointed out in his 1996 *The State of the Nation,* the American tax burden is 27 percent of GDP, versus 44 percent in France or 50 percent in Sweden.

Having lived the past few years in Europe, I often heard Euros express astonishment at the American economic engine. How could it be, they would ask, that your system has so much litigation, adversarial confrontation, hype, spin, glibness, and overwrought scandal, and yet functions so marvelously? I liked to reply that lawsuits, hype, spin, and scandal must in some way aid American success, forcing our society to accept perpetual change. The sincere answer might be that positive trends in U.S. national wealth have been sparked by ever-greater acceptance of true market economics, with its tumult and endless unanticipated results.

"It's only in the last generation that most people have been converted to the belief that market economics is good for everybody, not just a tool of the wealthy," says John Mueller, a political scientist at the University of Rochester and a rising star in the study of what makes societies run well. Stagflation stopped after Jimmy Carter began deregulation, freeing air travel, energy, and telecommunications. National economic performance shot upward not long thereafter, and, though not all results of deregulation have been favorable, each year brings more evidence that the country is better off with market forces driving most decisions.

Environment Twenty-five years ago, only one-third of America's lakes and rivers were safe for fishing and swimming; today two-thirds are, and the proportion continues to rise. Annual wetlands loss has fallen by 80 percent in the same period, while soil losses to agricultural runoff have been almost cut in half. Total American water consumption has declined nine percent in the past

15 years, even as the population expands, especially in the arid Southwest. Since 1970, smog has declined by about a third, even as the number of cars has increased by half; acid rain has fallen by 40 percent; airborne soot particles are down 69 percent, which is why big cities have blue skies again; carbon monoxide or "winter smog" is down 31 percent; airborne lead, a poison, is down 98 percent. Emissions of CFCs, which deplete stratospheric ozone, have all but ended.

Other environmental measures are almost uniformly positive. Toxic emissions by industry declined 46 percent from 1988 to 1996, even as petrochemical manufacturers enjoyed record U.S. production and copious profits. About one-third of Superfund toxic waste sites are now cleaned up, with the pace of cleanup accelerating. The forested acreage of the United States is expanding, with wildlife numbers up in most areas, led by the comeback of eastern deer, now thought to be at precolonial numbers. Since the Endangered Species Act was passed, only a few U.S. species have fallen extinct, not the thousands predicted, while species such as the bald eagle, gray whale, and peregrine falcon have recovered enough to no longer require full legal protection. Only two major U.S. environmental gauges are now negative: continuing inaction against greenhouse gases and continuing loss of wildlife habitats to urban expansion.

An important conceptual lesson is being learned: When pollution stops, natural recovery does not require ponderous geological time. Consider Boston Harbor, whose filth was an issue in George Bush's 1988 campaign against Massachusetts Governor Michael Dukakis. Even as Bush filmed his memorable commercial standing on the sludge-caked Boston shore, a $4 billion water treatment plant was rising in the background. At the time, most experts predicted that it would take 50 years or more to rinse the harbor. Instead, cleanup has been so rapid that Boston Harbor is already safe again for swimming and fishing. Activists, who once had to rail against sludge by the ton, are down to complaining about detection in the harbor of trace parts-per-billion or even parts-per-trillion of compounds. As Paul Levy, who ran the first phase of the cleanup project, has said, the fact that activists now remonstrate about smaller and smaller issues shows that the big issues are under control.

The left side of the environmental debate can't seem to deal with the fact that technology has (for the moment, at least) entered a relatively benign phase in which products and industrial processes consume steadily fewer resources and produce steadily less waste. Says Jesse Ausubel, director of the environment program at Rockefeller University and a leading thinker in the new field of industrial ecology: "The larger lesson here is about the sparing of resources," driven by new technological ideas. The right can't seem to deal with the fact that, if it weren't for ecological regulations, most positive trends in the environment would not have happened. Tailpipe controls on automobiles, for example, not only cleared the air but also saved the car industry. If cars still spewed smog as they once did, Los Angeles's air would be poison gas; mandatory driving bans would be unavoidable.

Because the character of environmental progress is nonideological—reflecting well both on federal initiatives and on business—neither political camp knows how to extol what's happened. That no interest group sees itself as

benefiting from public awareness of environmental success might be just a political foible, but it has the effect of preventing commentators and voters from
focusing on the locus of the real environmental emergencies—the developing
world.

Health   Both incidence and death rates for cancer began to ebb in the early
'90s, reversing a 20-year trend of increase. Cancer incidence, or the occurrence
of new cases, had risen about 1.2 percent per year from 1973 to 1990; since then,
incidence has fallen by almost one percent per year, with the decline manifest-
ing in the big-four cancer forms (lung, prostate, breast, and colon-rectum) for
both genders and across all major age and ethnic groups other than black males.
Mortality for most cancers is now either level (as it is for breast cancer) or in
slight decline. Only melanoma and non-Hodgkin's lymphoma are now rising.

By nearly all other measures, U.S. public health is getting steadily better. Heart disease and stroke are both in decline relative to population growth,
with heart disease deaths, the number-one medical killer, falling 3.4 percent
from 1996 to 1997. Infant mortality is now down to 0.7 percent of live births,
the lowest such figure ever for the United States. (Some European countries do
slightly better.) AIDS deaths are declining markedly in the United States. The
rate of suicides is declining, falling 4.6 percent in 1997. There are a few worrisome public-health trends, such as the reappearance of TB and the emergence
of microbes that resist currently available antibiotics. But, in the main, public
health is getting better by leaps and bounds.

Most remarkable is the continued rise in life expectancy, now 76 years
at birth for the typical American, up from 54 years when the World War II
generation was being born. The rise in life expectancy is global, expressing
itself in nearly every country in the world, outside Central Africa. Indeed, the
reason there is global population growth is not that the world's women are having more babies—per capita they are having steadily fewer, even in developing
nations—but that people the world over are living so much longer.

Most of what's going on in public health appears to be a mix of advancing
medical knowledge and public awareness. The biggest factor in the cancer decline, for example, is the drop in smoking. Heart disease decline has been aided
by better drugs, better therapy (the coronary-artery bypass operation, touch-
and-go 20 years ago, has gotten so much more efficacious that it's now working
even for the elderly), and advancing understanding of lifestyle issues such as
fat intake. The improving sophistication of medical education and other factors
are also at play.

Better public health hasn't come cheaply: medical spending was seven percent of GDP in 1970 and is almost 14 percent now. Yet, much as you may detest
your HMO, keep in mind that most trends in health care costs are favorable,
too. During the late '80s, costs were rising so rapidly that it was common to
predict that 15 to 20 percent of GDP would be spent on health care by the end
of the century. If that had happened, American prosperity would have been
damaged. Instead, in the past five years, there has been little medical inflation.
Managed care creates annoying preapproval hassles and longer waits for some

appointments. But on the key points—protecting health at an affordable cost—the system is doing well.

Public debate   Despite so many auspicious indicators, the America depicted in political and intellectual debate is invariably a place we should be building starships to flee. To the left, the United States remains a land of racial and sexual repression, corporate oligarchy, and environmental decay; to the right, a country where all things pure are collapsing. Such views hold considerable sway. Whitman's *The Optimism Gap* reports that 1996 polls showed that only 15 percent of Americans believe the country is getting better. In similar polls, about half said the nation is worse off compared to how it was when their parents were growing up, and 60 percent believed the United States in which their children dwell will be worse still. Though most Americans are today healthier, better housed, better fed, better paid, better educated, better defended, more free, and diverted by a cornucopia of new entertainment products and services, somehow they've managed to convince themselves their parents had it better during the Dust Bowl.

As Robert J. Samuelson noted in his skillful *The Good Life and Its Discontents,* the revolution of rising expectations has taken on a life of its own: "[T]here can never be enough prosperity." (Polls now suggest that, regardless of how much money an American has, he or she believes that twice as much is required.) Samuelson further contends that one reason for all the unfocused anxiety is that the media have gotten so much better at emphasizing things to worry about. Tropical storms that *might* hit the United States get more network coverage than any favorable turn of events.

Television crime coverage, especially, now seems pitched to cause civic fright, while movies and network entertainment programming depict violence as far more pervasive than it actually is. As Christopher Jencks, a professor of government at Harvard University, notes: "When I was growing up there was violence on TV, but it was cowboys having shootouts. I never worried that rustlers would come over the hill into my neighborhood. Now the violence on television is presented as if it's about to get you personally. Every screen you look at, at home or in theaters, has something disastrous on it. No wonder people think the country is out of control."

Conservative thinkers and politicians seem distressed by the contemporary milieu in part because Americans are more or less willingly adopting gender equality and cultural openness, including a culture in which minority writing and art are being admitted to the canon. (Recent polls have found that three of the most admired people in the United States are Colin Powell, Oprah Winfrey, and Michael Jordan.) The political and academic left can't stand the contemporary milieu in part because class war, economic breakdown, and environmental calamity seem less and less likely. "The left elites talk with obsessive negativism about the religious right because it's one of the few things they can find to still get upset about," notes Orlando Patterson of Harvard. "The right elite is similarly obsessive about the supposed culture war, when all the evidence is that the United States is becoming ever more tolerant and ever more at peace with diversity."

Of course, generations at least as far back as Plato have felt that nations were sweetly ordered in their youths but now decline. "When we think about the past, we focus on our childhoods, to a time when our parents protected us from the world," Jencks notes. "Now as adults, even if society's gotten better, the sense of being sheltered is gone. Nobody's taking care of you anymore, so it feels like everything is getting more worrisome, even if objectively it's getting better." Mueller of the University of Rochester has memorably phrased it this way: "Golden ages do happen, but we are never actually *in* them."

Race   As William Julius Wilson has extensively documented, attention to the problems of inner-city dysfunction causes us to overlook what history will judge as the big racial story of late-twentieth-century America: the emergence of a black middle class.

Through the last generation, the portion of African Americans living in middle-class circumstances has more than doubled. Some kind of watershed was crossed in 1994, when the average income of black families in Queens, long a community treated as symbolic of working-class to middle-class transition, surpassed the average income of white families there. Georgia, Maryland, and other states now contain large, economically independent black middle-class areas where life is suburban, family structures conventional, and values entirely middle-American.

African American income still lags significantly behind that of whites, but, as Steven Holmes has written, in the past few years poverty rates "have dipped below 30 percent of black households for the first time in the country's history." Black male college graduates now make, on average, twelve percent less than their white counterparts, a much smaller gap than a generation ago, while black female college grads now earn slightly more than white female grads. Jencks's 1972 book, *Inequality,* argued that, even if minority education rose, minority income levels would not, owing to barriers of prejudice. Jencks now feels the situation has changed, with minority education "look[ing] far more important than it did in the 1960s," because African American accomplishment in school can now translate into economic success.

Minority educational accomplishment continues to improve. In 1996, black high school graduation rates became about the same as white rates— needless to say, a historical first. The black-white math SAT score gap, which was 140 points in 1976, is 110 points now, owing to black improvement, not white erosion. Bok and William Bowen write in *The Shape of the River* that, although African Americans entering most colleges have lower overall grades and SAT scores than white schoolmates, on the real-world test of what they do when they leave the university, top black students now have about the same career achievement as top whites.

At the turn of this century, many African Americans weren't even literate; today, the college-completion rates of black Americans exceed the comparable figures for much of Europe. If one views African Americans as an immigrant co-hort that "arrived" in the United States with the passage of the civil rights laws, black rates of social progress are similar to those previously displayed by white ethnic immigrant groups, which typically required two to three generations to join the establishment.

Standards of living Living standards are improving so fast and so consistently that to mention them today seems almost banal. Most fundamental is housing. The typical contemporary home is 40 percent larger than a 1970 house, while only three percent of Americans, the lowest percentage ever, live in overcrowded conditions, defined as more than one person per room. That every person should have at least one room to call his or her own is a social innovation of the American present. The majority of today's dwellings have air-conditioning and other improvements. More than half of Americans now live in suburbs, which may be superficial and intellectually insufferable but are physically pleasant: the reason they are popular.

The metric of living standards is rising so rapidly that merely how to track its ascent has become a controversy, centering on whether the Consumer Price Index adequately recognizes such once-rare, now-quotidian indicators as computer ownership or eating out. Another way to meter the evolution of living standards, championed by Richard Alm and W. Michael Cox in the forthcoming book *Myths of Rich and Poor,* is how long the typical person must work to acquire consumer items. Between rising wages and larger dwellings, for example, in 1956 the typical worker had to invest 16 weeks at labor to buy 100 square feet of home; now the figure has fallen to less than 14 weeks. The McDonald's brothers' first burgers cost half an hour of work at the time; now 180 seconds buys one. Only health care and university-level education are growing more expensive when measured by work hours required for purchase.

"A seven-day Caribbean cruise," Alm and Cox write, "slipped from 51 hours in 1972 to 45 hours in 1997." Not only are they getting cheaper, excursions on 42-deck luxury liners with names like *Insatiable Princess* are another indication of the rising standard of living: such experiences may be stupefying, but what matters is that they are becoming standard middle-class events. Leisure and tourism barely existed as economic sectors a generation ago; today they are a hefty slice of the GDP [gross domestic product].

As Robert J. Samuelson has written, overall the U.S. standard of living has continued to rise in the '80s and '90s roughly as rapidly as it did in the '50s and '60s; it's just that we now take out a considerable share of national wealth in forms that don't show up well in price indexes, such as better health, cleaner air, and the ability to fly anywhere, anytime, at an affordable price.

Wedlock The family-breakup wave may have crested. The divorce rate, which was 2.5 per 1,000 people in 1966, peaked at 5.3 per 1,000 in 1981. The rate leveled off in the early '90s at about 4.7 and now appears to be in a shallow decline. A few years ago, half of all new marriages were expected to fail; now only 40 percent are, with the average length of a marriage starting to creep back up again. And Census Bureau figures suggest that the reduction in conventional two-parent families—which dominated American demographics from 1970 to 1990—is "flattening" and might be about to end.

Whether the decline of divorce is just a blip or suggests some larger social trend can't be determined by only a few years of data. But it's worth noting that sociologists and writers have spent the past decade elaborately documenting the fact that, whatever it means in terms of adult personal freedom, family breakup harms children. That message may be sinking in.

                                                                    ◦◦◦

At first glance, there seems no single thread that runs through the subjects where life is improving. Some seem a case for more Washington: environmental protection is arguably the most impressive achievement of progressive government since the establishment of the Social Security system. But "outside of pollution control, it's hard to see where federal regulations have been the driving factor in recent social improvements," says Gary Becker, a Nobel Prize-winning economist at the University of Chicago. Economic vigor has been aided by deregulation. Crime reduction, welfare reform, and other positive trends have arisen mainly through state and local initiatives. Public health has certainly benefited from federal investments, but advancing knowledge is the primary factor. Betterment of personal behavior, such as the reduction in drunken driving, has been inspired mainly through private efforts.

It's possible that what the surge of national good news tells us is that, as pragmatism supplants ideology, society will get better at fixing things. "We're living in an age with very few romantics and revolutionaries," says Mueller of the University of Rochester. "People with vast, sweeping visions caused most of this century's problems. Most of the time you don't want leaders with visions, you want society run by cautious pragmatists. At the moment, the pragmatists are in control of most nations, and it's making things better."

It's possible that the upswing in good news tells us that reform initiatives of the '60s and '70s have finally begun to work. Pollution-control regulations, affirmative action programs, crime crackdowns—all started off clunky and problem-plagued, but, as the snafus were ironed out, results began to flow. And it's possible that what the late-century tidings convey is simply what the United States would have looked like all along if so much of its brainpower and resources had not been diverted to the cold war.

But what the good news unequivocally tells us is that it's never too late to change the world. In that sense, there is a bright thread running through all these examples: intractable or "impossible" dilemmas can be solved. Our efforts matter; when we attempt reform, we can be crowned with success. It is no coincidence that the aspects of life that have gotten better are those that people have dedicated themselves to improving. America can still become whatever it wants to be. We do not have to accept what we see out the window; rather, we can make the view the one of our choosing.

Knowing that reform still works should grant us courage to strive for change in areas where progress now seems "impossible." For instance, the greenhouse effect may seem unstoppable today, but that's only because we have not yet tried to stop it. There is no reason we need accept poverty: it can be bested. Polls show that, far from thinking society spends too much to lift up the poor, 60 percent of Americans think the country should take more action against poverty. So let's—because it will work!

Consider an astonishing figure: The United Nations estimates that it would cost $40 billion per year to provide the basics of life—adequate food, clean water, health care, shelter, and literacy—to every person on the planet. That works out to $151 per American. Every one of us would gladly write that check, if only there were a way to be sure the money were properly used. All that's stopping us from attempting reform of this noble magnitude is the false belief that life is rolling irrevocably downhill.

It's not, and the proof gets stronger each day.

POSTSCRIPT

Is America Entering the Twenty-First Century in a Period of Decline?

In the late 1980s Kennedy's books and articles—especially the final chapter in *The Rise and Fall of the Great Powers: Economic Change and Military Conflict From 1500 to 2000* (Random House, 1987)—created a major debate about the moral health and economic well-being of the United States. As a historian, Kennedy was careful not to make facile comparisons of the contemporary United States with the declines of the Roman Empire in the early middle ages, Spain in the nineteenth century, and England in the twentieth century. In his book Kennedy uses the phrase "relative decline" because of the United States' size, abundance of resources, and (in his view) a homogeneous population.

Easterbrook is extremely optimistic about the health and economic well-being of the United States at the end of the twentieth century. The author creates a long list of everything that is right in America: Crime is down, as are accidents from drunk driving. Individuals are more concerned with their own health, which has resulted in a decline in the use of alcohol, tobacco, and illegal drugs. If there is a problem with Social Security, it is because people are living longer. The quality of people's daily living spaces has also improved. Houses are larger and cleaner, and so is the air. Even race relations—a constant blight on American history—have vastly improved with the creation of a large and at least economically integrated middle class.

If Easterbrook is correct that life in the United States has never been better, then why is there so much pessimism? The author points out two paradoxes. First the politicians in Washington, especially the conservative right wing, cannot admit that so much progress has been made in the past 55 years under a strong central government. Secondly, the American people themselves are victims of the phenomenon that David Whitman describes in his book *The Optimism Gap* (Walker, 1998). Most people, says Whitman, are very optimistic about their current and future lifestyles; yet national optimism is at an all-time low because the majority of people think that the country is in decline.

There are a number of other books worth mentioning. On the negative economic side is Robert J. Shiller, *Irrational Exuberance* (Princeton University Press, 2000), in which the author argues that the soaring stock market will crash once again. This viewpoint is supported by Paul Krugman in *The Return of Depression Economics* (W. W. Norton, 1999). Also see James D. Hunter, *Culture Wars: The Struggle to Divine America* (Basic Books, 1991); Francis Fukuyama and Paul Berman, "Reconstructing America's Moral Order," *The Wilson Quarterly* (Summer 1999); and David Hackett Fischer, *The Great Wave: Price Revolutions and the Rhythm of History* (Oxford University Press, 1997).

Contributors to This Volume

EDITORS

LARRY MADARAS is a professor of history and political science at Howard Community College in Columbia, Maryland. He received a B.A. from the College of the Holy Cross in 1959 and an M.A. and a Ph.D. from New York University in 1961 and 1964, respectively. He has also taught at Spring Hill College, the University of South Alabama, and the University of Maryland at College Park. He has been a Fulbright Fellow and has held two fellowships from the National Endowment for the Humanities. He is the author of dozens of journal articles and book reviews.

JAMES M. SoRELLE is a professor of history in and chair of the Department of History at Baylor University in Waco, Texas. He received a B.A. and an M.A. from the University of Houston in 1972 and 1974, respectively, and a Ph.D. from Kent State University in 1980. In addition to introductory courses in American history, he teaches upper-level sections in African American, urban, and late-nineteenth- and twentieth-century U.S. history. His scholarly articles have appeared in the *Houston Review, Southwestern Historical Quarterly,* and *Black Dixie: Essays in Afro-Texan History and Culture in Houston* edited by Howard Beeth and Cary D. Wintz (Texas A&M University Press, 1992). He has also contributed entries to *The Handbook of Texas, The Oxford Companion to Politics of the World,* and *Encyclopedia of the Confederacy.*

STAFF

Theodore Knight   List Manager
David Brackley   Senior Developmental Editor
Juliana Gribbins   Developmental Editor
Rose Gleich   Administrative Assistant
Brenda S. Filley   Director of Production/Design
Juliana Arbo   Typesetting Supervisor
Diane Barker   Proofreader
Richard Tietjen   Publishing Systems Manager
Larry Killian   Copier Coordinator

AUTHORS

STEPHEN E. AMBROSE (1936–2002) was the Boyd Professor of History at the University of New Orleans in New Orleans, Louisiana, until his retirement in 1995. He also taught at the Johns Hopkins University, the University of California, Berkeley, the Army War College, the Navy War College, and Louisiana State University, among others. The founder of the Eisenhower Center and president of the National D-Day Museum in New Orleans, he is the author of over 20 books, including biographies of Dwight D. Eisenhower and Richard M. Nixon. His publications include *Eisenhower and Berlin, 1945: The Decision to Halt at the Elbe* (W. W. Norton, 2000) and *Comrades: Brothers, Fathers, Heroes, Sons, Pals* (Simon & Schuster, 2000).

DAVID H. BENNETT is a professor of history at Syracuse University, where he specializes in modern American history and modern military history. He is the author or coauthor of numerous publications, including *The Party of Fear: The American Far Right From Nativism to the Militia Movement* (Vintage Books, 1995) and *Demagogues in the Depression: American Radicals and the Union Party, 1932–36* (Rutgers University Press, 1969). He earned his Ph.D. from the University of Chicago in 1963.

IRVING BRANT was an editorial writer for several major newspapers, including the *St. Louis Star-Times* and the *Chicago Sun*. He is the author of over a dozen books, including the six-volume biography *James Madison* (Bobbs-Merrill, 1941–1961) and *The Bill of Rights: Its Origin and Meaning* (Bobbs-Merrill, 1965).

JAMES MACGREGOR BURNS is the author of noted studies of presidents and other political leaders. As senior scholar, he teaches and researches leadership at the James MacGregor Burns Academy of Leadership at the University of Maryland in College Park, and he is an emeritus professor of political science at Williams College. He is the author of *State and Local Politics: Government by the People* (Prentice Hall, 2000) and editor of *Government by the People: National, State, and Local* (Simon & Schuster, 2000).

STANLEY COBEN (d. 2000) was a professor of history at the University of California, Los Angeles, for 30 years. He earned his Ph.D. in history from Columbia University in 1961, and he also taught at Princeton University. Coben is best known for his research on the American Red Scare of the early 1900s, and he is the author of *Reform, War, and Reaction: 1912–1932* (University of South Carolina Press, 1973).

DANIEL DEUDNEY is an assistant professor in the Department of Political Science at the Johns Hopkins University in Baltimore, Maryland. He is the author of *Pax Atomica: Planetary Geopolitics and Republicanism* (Princeton University Press, 1993).

GREGG EASTERBROOK is a senior editor at *The New Republic* and the author of several books, including *A Moment in Earth: The Coming Age of Environmental Optimism* (Viking, 1995).

RICHARD M. FRIED is a professor of history at the University of Illinois at Chicago and the author of *The Russians Are Coming! The Russians Are Coming! Pageantry and Patriotism in Cold-War America* (Oxford University Press, 1998).

JOHN LEWIS GADDIS is the Robert A. Lovett Professor of History at Yale University in New Haven, Connecticut. He has also been the Distinguished Professor of History at Ohio University, where he founded the Contemporary History Institute, and he has held visiting appointments at the United States Naval War College, the University of Helsinki, Princeton University, and Oxford University. He is the author of many books, including *The Long Peace: Inquiries Into the History of the Cold War* (Oxford University Press, 1987).

ERNEST S. GRIFFITH (1896–1981), an editor and writer, was a professor of political science and political economy in the School of International Service at the American University in Washington, D.C. He also held academic appointments at Harvard University and Syracuse University, and he served as director of the legislative reference service at the Library of Congress. He is the author of *The American System of Government,* 6th edition (Routledge, 1984).

JACQUELYN DOWD HALL is the Julia Cherry Spruill Professor and director of the Southern Oral History Program at the University of North Carolina, Chapel Hill. Her research interests include U.S. women's history, southern history, working-class history, and biography. She has won a number of awards, including a Distinguished Teaching Award for graduate teaching. She is coauthor of *Like a Family: The Making of a Southern Cotton Mill World* (University of North Carolina Press, 1987).

JOHN EARL HAYNES is a twentieth-century political historian with the Library of Congress. He is coauthor, with Harvey Klehr and K. M. Anderson, of *The Soviet World of American Communism* (Yale University Press, 1998) and, with Harvey Klehr and Fridrikh I. Firsov, of *The Secret World of American Communism* (Yale University Press, 1996).

MURIEL E. HIDY taught at the Harvard Business School for many years and was a pioneer in the field of business history. She is the author of *George Peabody, Merchant and Financier: 1829–1854* (Ayer, 1979) and coauthor, with Ralph W. Hidy and Roy V. Scott, of *The Great Northern Railway* (Harvard Business School Press, 1988).

RALPH W. HIDY taught at the Harvard Business School for many years and was a pioneer in the field of business history. He is the author of *House of Baring in American Trade and Finance: English Merchant Bankers at Work, 1763–1861* (Harvard University Press, 1949) and coauthor, with Muriel E. Hidy and Roy V. Scott, of *The Great Northern Railway* (Harvard Business School Press, 1988).

HAROLD M. HYMAN was the William P. Hobby Professor of History at Rice University from 1968 to 1996. He has also taught at Arizona State University, the University of California, and the University of Illinois. He is the author of many books, including *To Try Men's Souls: Loyalty Tests in American History* (University of California Press, 1959), which won the Sidney Hillman Award in 1960, and *A History of the Vinson and Elkins Law Firm of Houston, 1917–1997* (University of Georgia Press, 1998).

G. JOHN IKENBERRY, currently a Wilson Center Fellow, is a professor of political science at the University of Pennsylvania and a nonresident senior fellow at the Brookings Institution. He is the author of *After Victory: Institutions, Strategic Restraint and the Rebuilding of Order After Major Wars* (Princeton University Press, 2000) and *American Foreign Policy: Theoretical Essays,* 3rd ed. (Addison-Wesley Longman, 1998).

D. CLAYTON JAMES holds the John Biggs Chair of Military History at Virginia Military Institute in Lexington, Virginia. He is the author of the best-selling and prize-winning three-volume work *The Years of MacArthur* (Houghton Mifflin, 1970–1985), as well as numerous other works of military history.

MATTHEW JOSEPHSON, who figured among the literary expatriots in France in the 1920s, is the author of numerous critical biographies and histories of the Gilded Age, including *Edison: A Biography* (McGraw-Hill, 1963) and *The President Makers: The Culture of Politics in an Age of Enlightenment* (Putnam, 1979).

PAUL KENNEDY is the J. Richardson Dillworth Professor of History at Yale University and the author of several books on contemporary international relations, including *The Rise and Fall of the Great Powers: Economic Change and Military Conflict From 1500 to 2000* (Random House, 1987).

HARVEY KLEHR is the Andrew W. Mellon Professor of Politics and History at Emory University. He is coauthor, with Kyrill M. Anderson and John Earl Haynes, of *The Soviet World of American Communism* (Yale University Press, 1998) and, with John Earl Haynes and Fridrikh I. Firsov, of *The Secret World of American Communism* (Yale University Press, 1996).

ROBERT KORSTAD is an assistant professor in the Department of Public Policy Studies at Duke University, where he has been teaching since 1980. He has also taught at North Carolina Central University, and he has won a number of honors and awards. His work has appeared in such journals as *Journal of American History* and *Social Science History,* and he is coauthor of *Like a Family: The Making of a Southern Cotton Mill World* (University of North Carolina Press, 1987).

RICHARD D. LAMM is a former governor of Colorado. He has also served as executive director of the University of Denver's Center for Public Policy and Contemporary Issues, and he is the author or coauthor of several books, including *The Immigration Time Bomb: The Fragmenting of America* (Dutton/ Plume, 1985).

JAMES LELOUDIS is an associate professor, the associate dean for honors, and director of the James M. Johnston Center for Undergraduate Excellence at the University of North Carolina, Chapel Hill. His chief interest is in the history of the modern South, with emphases on women, labor, race, and reform. He is the author of *Schooling the New South: Pedagogy, Self, and Society in North Carolina, 1880–1920* (University of North Carolina Press, 1999).

LEON F. LITWACK is the Alexander F. and May T. Morrison Professor of American History at the University of California, Berkeley. He is the author of *Been in the Storm So Long: The Aftermath of Slavery* (Alfred A. Knopf, 1980).

ELAINE TYLER MAY is a professor of American studies and history at the University of Minnesota in Minneapolis, Minnesota. She has also taught at Princeton University, and her research interests include family history and gender issues. She is the author of *Barren in the Promised Land: Childless Americans and the Pursuit of Happiness* (Basic Books, 1995).

DAVID NASAW is a professor of U.S. social history in the Graduate School and University Center of the City University of New York. He is the author of *Going Out: The Rise and Fall of Public Amusements* (Harvard University Press, 1999) and editor of *Course of U.S. History* (Wadsworth, 1987).

LARS-ERIK NELSON (1941–2000) was a Washington columnist for the *New York Daily News* and a frequent contributor to *The New York Review of Books*.

WILLIAM L. O'NEILL is a professor in the Department of History at Rutgers University in New Brunswick, New Jersey, who specializes in twentieth-century American history. He is the author of many books, including *A Democracy at War: America's Fight at Home and Abroad in World War II* (Harvard University Press, 1995).

HOWARD N. RABINOWITZ (d. 1998) was a professor of history at the University of New Mexico and a historian of the urban South. Among his authored works are *Race Relations in the Urban South, 1865–1890* (University of Georgia Press, 1996) and *Race, Ethnicity, and Urbanization: Selected Essays* (University of Missouri Press, 1993).

ARTHUR M. SCHLESINGER, JR., was the Albert Schweitzer Professor of the Humanities at the Graduate School of the City University of New York until his retirement in 1993. His publications include *The New Deal in Action* (Folcroft Library Editions, 1977) and prize-winning books on Presidents Andrew Jackson, Franklin D. Roosevelt, and John F. Kennedy.

ANNE FIROR SCOTT is the William K. Boyd Professor of History Emeritus at Duke University in Durham, North Carolina. She has received numerous honors and professional citations, and she has served a term as president of the Organization of American Historians. She has contributed to many books on women's history, and she is the editor of *Unheard Voices: The First Historians of Southern Women* (University Press of Virginia, 1993).

THEODORE C. SORENSEN, special counsel to the president from January 1960 to February 1964, is the author of *Kennedy* (Harper & Row, 1965), one of the standard accounts of the Kennedy presidency, and *A Different Kind of Presidency* (HarperTrade, 1984).

GEORGIA J. SORENSON is a senior scholar and founding director of the James MacGregor Burns Academy of Leadership at the University of Maryland.

Formerly a senior policy analyst with the Carter administration, she has served as a consultant to four presidential campaigns.

JOHN S. SPANIER is a professor of political science at the University of Florida. In addition, he has lectured extensively at other universities, including the United States Military Academy at West Point and the Naval War College, where he was a visiting professor of strategy in 1983–1984. He is the author or coauthor of a number of publications, including *Games Nations Play*, 4th ed. (CQ Press, 1993) and *American Foreign Policy Since WWII*, coauthored with Steven W. Hook (CQ Press, 2000).

W. A. SWANBERG was a freelance journalist and story writer who also had experience working on a railway. He studied English literature at the University of Minnesota, and during World War II he worked for a year and a half in the Office of War Information. He has written a number of biographies, including *Pulitzer* (Scribner, 1967).

JON C. TEAFORD is a professor of history at Purdue University in West Lafayette, Indiana. His publications include *Post-Suburbia: Government and Politics in the Edge Cities* (Johns Hopkins University Press, 1996) and *Cities of the Heartland: The Rise and Fall of the Industrial Midwest* (Indiana University Press, 1994).

ROBERT A. THEOBALD was a retired rear admiral before his death. He was the commanding officer of Flotilla One, Destroyers, Pacific Fleet, and was present at the Pearl Harbor attack. He testified on behalf of Admiral Husband E. Kimmel before the Roberts Commission, which had accused Kimmel of "dereliction of duty."

REED UEDA teaches history at Tufts University and has been a visiting professor at Harvard and Brandeis Universities. He is the author of *Postwar Immigrant America: A Social History* (St. Martin's Press, 1994).

ANNE SHARP WELLS is an assistant editor with *The Journal of Military History*. She is the author of *Historical Dictionary of World War II: The War Against Japan* (Scarecrow Press, 1999) and coauthor, with D. Clayton James, of *America and the Great War, 1914–1920* (Harlan Davidson, 1998).

MARK J. WHITE is an assistant professor of history at Eastern Illinois University, and he has also taught at the University of St. Andrews, Scotland. He received his doctoral degree from Rutgers University, and his articles have appeared in such journals as *Mid-America, Journal of Strategic Studies* and *Illinois Historical Journal*. He is the editor of *Kennedy: The New Frontier Revisited* (New York University Press, 1998) and the author of *Missiles in Cuba: Kennedy, Khrushchev, Castro, and the 1962 Crisis* (Ivan R. Dee, 1997).

ROBERTA WOHLSTETTER is a historian and a member of the Steering Committee of the Balkan Institute, which was formed to educate the public on the nature of the crisis in the Balkans and its humanitarian, political, and military consequences. She has earned the Presidential Medal of Freedom, and she is coauthor of *Nuclear Policies: Fuel Without the Bomb* (Harper Business, 1978).

Index

accidents, decline in, 385–386
Acheson, Dean: the Cuban Missile Crisis and, 294, 298; and controversy over Harry Truman's firing of Douglas MacArthur during the Korean War, 260, 261, 262, 263, 264
Adams, Sherman, 286–287, 288
African Americans: controversy over racial segregation and the status of, 120–139; the Ku Klux Klan of the 1920s and, 155, 163–165. *See also* racial issues
agriculture, Dwight Eisenhower and, 271–272
alcohol use, decline in, 388
Ambrose, Stephen E., 282, 284, 286; on the performance of Dwight Eisenhower as president, 270–277,
American Business Consultants (ABC), 238
American Communist party (CPUSA), espionage and, 221, 224, 230
American Legion, 238, 239, 240
Andrews, Samuel, 26, 31
Anthony, Susan B., 176
Archbold, John B., 41, 42
architecture, urban, 81
Army Appropriations Act, 15
Atoms for Peace, 287
Aware, Inc., 238

Bay of Pigs, 273–274, 299
Benedict, M. L., 19, 20, 21
Bennett, David H., on the Ku Klux Klan of the 1920s, 144–153
Bentley, Elizabeth, 222–223, 224, 225, 227
Berkeley, Martin, 236
Berlin crisis, 292
bills of attainder, and controversy over the impeachment of Andrew Johnson, 4, 8–9, 10, 11, 12
bills of pains and penalties, and controversy over the impeachment of Andrew Johnson, 4, 12
Bingham, Hiram, 233
Bingham, John A., 6–7, 9, 11, 13
Black Codes, 132
Black, Jeremiah, 17
blacklisting, 238–239
blackmail, city government in late-nineteenth-century America and, 75, 76–77
blacks. *See* African Americans
Blanco y Erenas, Ramón, 96, 99

blue-collar workers, and controversy over the influence of the Industrial Revolution on the family, 53–56
Boehm, Keith, 162
Bogart, Humphrey, 239
Boston Harbor, 390
Boutwell, George S., 6–7
Bowles, Samuel, 22
Bradley, Omar N., 225, 252–253, 261
Brady Bill, 353
Brant, Irving, on the impeachment of Andrew Johnson, 4–14
Brewer, Roy, 239
bribes, city government in late-nineteenth-century America and, 72, 74, 75
Bridges, Harry, 235
"broken windows" theory, 386
Bruce, David, 283
Bryce, James, 79, 81
Budenz, Louis, 232
Bulgin, E. E., 162–163
Burgess, Guy, 222
Burke, Edmund, 11, 12–13
Burns, James MacGregor, on the historical view of the Clinton presidency, 359–371
Butler, Benjamin J., 6–7, 8, 9–10
Butler, John Marshall, 234

Carey, James, 234–235
Carnegie, Andrew, 27
Carpenter, Matthew, 17
Carter, Jimmy, 366
Castro, Fidel, the Cuban Missile Crisis and, 297–298, 299–300, 301
Catholics, the Ku Klux Klan of the 1920s and, 144–145, 147, 163–165
cemeteries, racial segregation in, 121, 124, 137
censorship, anticommunism and, 240
Central Intelligence Agency (CIA), and controversy over the performance of Dwight Eisenhower as president, 282–284
centrism, in the Clinton presidency, 349, 360–361, 362, 363–364
Chamber, Whitaker, 225, 227
charities, anticommunism and, 239
Chase, Salmon P., 16, 18
China Hands, and controversy over communism in America after World War II, 232–233
China, and controversy over Harry Truman's firing of Douglas MacArthur during the Korean War, 246–265
CIO, 234, 235

city government, controversy over, in late-nineteenth-century America, 70–87
Civil Rights Act of 1875, 123, 128
civil rights, Dwight Eisenhower and, 271, 274, 275, 280
Clarke, Carter, 220
Cleveland, Grover, 101
Clinton, Bill, controversy over the historical view of the presidency of, 348–371
Clinton, Hillary Rodham, 366, 369, 370
Coben, Stanley, on the Ku Klux Klan of the 1920s, 154–165
Cocoltchos, Christopher, 157, 158–159
code, Japanese, 203
cold war: and controversy over communism in America after World War II, 220–242; controversy over Ronald Reagan and the end of the, 324–343; Dwight Eisenhower and, 272–273, 281–282, 286–288
Collins, Joseph L., 249, 252, 257, 264, 285
Colorado, the Ku Klux Klan in, 157, 159, 162
Colville, John, 288
Comer, James, 148
communism: controversy over, in America after World War II, 220–242; and controversy over Ronald Reagan and the end of the cold war, 324–343
"community policing," 386
Congress, the Spanish-American War and, 114–115
containment doctrine, 327, 338–339
Coplon, Judith, 222, 223
corruption, and controversy over city government in late-nineteenth-century America, 70–87
Corwin, Edward S., 20
Cosio y Cisneros, Evangelina, 110–112
cotton mills: and controversy over the influence of the Industrial Revolution on the family, 57–65; women's suffrage and, 180
Counterattack, 238
courts, city government in late-nineteenth-century America and, 77–78
Cox, Eugene, 239
crack, 386–387
crime, decrease in, 386–387
crop lien, 57, 59–60
Crucible, The (Miller), 237
Cuban Missile Crisis, controversy over the performance of John Kennedy during, 292–303
culture, adaptation to, by immigrants, 318
Cummings v. Missouri, 4
Currie, Lauchlin, 221
Curtis, Benjamin, 10, 11
customs, versus laws, and racial segregation in the South, 120, 129–130, 131–132

Davis, Richard Harding, 109–110
de Lome, Dupuy, 97, 98, 105, 106, 112
Decker, Karl, 96, 97, 111

Deudney, Daniel, on Ronald Reagan and the end of the cold war, 334–343
diversity, ethnic, 82; and controversy over immigration, 308–320
Divine, Robert A., 280–281, 282, 284, 285
divorce: and controversy over the influence of the Industrial Revolution on the family, 48–49, 50–52, 53–56, 65; decrease in rate of, 394–395
Dodd, Bell, 235
Dodd, C. T., 38, 42
domestics, racial segregation and, 137–138
Donnelly, Ignatius, 22
Douglass, Frederick, 125
drugs: crime and, 386–387; decline in use of, 388
Duffus, Robert L., 148–149, 150
Duggan, Laurence, 227

Easterbrook, Gregg, on the current state of America, 384–396
education, the Clinton presidency and, 349–350, 363–364, 370
Eisenhower and the Cold War (Divine), 280–281, 282
Eisenhower Diaries, The, 279
Eisenhower, Dwight D., 255, 258; controversy over the performance of, as president, 270–288
Eisenhower the President (Ewald), 277
employment, municipal, 71, 84
entertainment industry, and controversy over communism in America after World War II, 236–238
environment, improvement of, 389–391
espionage, and controversy over communism in America after World War II, 220–230
Evans, Hiram Wesley, 144, 146, 148, 149, 150, 151, 152, 164
Evarts, William M., 7, 12–13
Ewald, William, 270
extortion, city government in late-nineteenth-century America and, 75, 76–77

factories: protests in, 64; racial segregation in, 135; supervision in, 62–63
families, controversy over the influence of the Industrial Revolution on, 48–65
Field, David Dudley, 17
Field, Stephen J., 6
Fifth Amendment, anticommunist movement and, 236–237
film industry. *See* entertainment industry
First Amendment, and controversy over the impeachment of Andrew Johnson, 10–11, 13–14
5412 Committee, NSC control of the CIA and, 283–284
Flagler, Henry M., 30, 31, 33, 38, 41

Flynn, John T., 26, 27, 30
Formosa, and controversy over Harry Truman's firing of Douglas MacArthur during the Korean War, 248, 257, 260, 261
Forrestal, Jim, 281
Freedom of Information Act (FOIA), 228
freedom of speech, and controversy over the impeachment of Andrew Johnson, 10–11, 13–14
Frick, Henry, 27
Fried, Richard M., on communism in America after World War II, 231–242
Fuchs, Klaus, 221–222, 223, 226
Fur and Leather Workers, 235

Gaddis, John Lewis, on Ronald Reagan and the end of the cold war, 324–333
gambling, city government in late-nineteenth-century America and, 72, 73
Garfield, James, 239
Garvey, Marcus, 155
Geer, Will, 236
Gelpcke v. Dubuque, 17
Gingrich, Newt, 353
Goldberg, Robert, 157, 159
Good Life and Its Discontents, The (Samuelson), 392, 393
Gorbachev, Mikhail, the cold war and, 324, 328–333, 336, 337, 339, 341
Gore, Al, 364, 369, 371
Gouzenko, Igor, 224
graft, city government in late-nineteenth-century America and, 72–75
Grant, Ulysses S., 9, 16
Gray, Gordon, 283
Greenglass, David, 221–222, 223, 226
Greenstein, Fred I., 279–280
Griffith, Ernest S., on city government in late-nineteenth-century America, 70–78
Groesbeck, W. S., 7, 11

Hall, Jacquelyn Dowd, on the influence of the Industrial Revolution on the family, 57–65
Hall, Theodore, 221–222, 226
Halperin, Maurice, 221
Hannah, Mark, 102, 104
Harkness, S. V., 30, 32
Hastings, Warren, the trial of, and controversy over the impeachment of Andrew Johnson, 7–8, 11, 12–13
Haw River strike, 63–64
Haynes, John Earl, on communism in America after World War II, 220–230
health care, improvements in, 391–392
health care plan, the Clinton presidency and, 352, 360–361, 370
Hearst, William Randolph, the influence of yellow journalism on the Spanish-American War and, 94–115

Hellman, Lillian, 237
"hidden-hand" leadership, Dwight Eisenhower and, 279–280
Hidy, Muriel E., on John D. Rockefeller, 36–44
Hidy, Ralph W., on John D. Rockefeller, 36–44
high crimes and misdemeanors, and controversy over the impeachment of Andrew Johnson, 6, 7, 9–10
Hiss, Alger, 224, 227
Hollywood Ten, 237
"honest graft," city government in late-nineteenth-century America and, 73–74
Hoover, Herbert, 278
House Un-American Activities Committee (HUAC), and controversy over communism in America after World War II, 231, 233–234, 236–239
housing: lack of, and divorce, 54–55; racial segregation and, 136
Hughes, Emmet, 288
Hyman, Harold M. on the impeachment of Andrew Johnson, 15–22

Ikenberry, G. John, on Ronald Reagan and the end of the cold war, 334–343
immigration, 82; controversy over, 308–320
impeachment, controversy over the, of Andrew Johnson, 4–22
Imperial Presidency, The (Schlesinger), 271
income inequality, 350, 371
Indiana, the Ku Klux Klan in, 150–152, 157–158, 159–162
Industrial Revolution, controversy over the influence of the, on the family, 48–65
Institute of Pacific Relations (IPR), 232–233
integration, 130
intermarriage, immigrant assimilation and, 311
International United Electrical Workers Union (IUE), 234–235
Interstate Commerce Commission, racial segregation and, 126

Jackson, Ed, 152
James, D. Clayton, on Harry Truman's firing of Douglas MacArthur during the Korean War, 256–265
Jefferson, Thomas, 365
Jencks, Christopher, 392, 393
Jews, the Ku Klux Klan and, 145–146
jobs, immigrants and, 316–317
Johnson, Andrew, controversy over the impeachment of, 4–22
Joint Chiefs of Staff (JCS), and controversy over Harry Truman's firing of Douglas MacArthur during the Korean War, 248, 249–250, 252, 257, 260–262, 264–265
Josephson, Matthew, on John D. Rockefeller, 26–35
Judiciary Act of 1789, 16

Kazan, Elia, 237
Keating, Kenneth, the Cuban Missile Crisis and, 297, 298
Kempton, Murray, 270
Kennan, George F., 320, 328, 333, 340
Kennedy, John F., controversy over the performance of, during the Cuban Missile Crisis, 292–303
Kennedy, Joseph P., 283
Kennedy, Paul, on the current state of America, 376–383
Kennedy, Robert, the Cuban Missile Crisis and, 294–295, 296, 298, 301
Khrushchev, Nikita, and controversy over the performance of John Kennedy during the Cuban Missile Crisis, 292, 293, 295, 296, 297–298, 299–300, 301, 302–303
Kimmel, Husband E., 192, 193, 194, 198, 199–200, 201, 207, 209, 210, 212
Kissinger, Henry A., 340
Klehr, Harvey, on communism in America after World War II, 220–230
Knights of Labor, 63
Korean War: controversy over Harry Truman's firing of Douglas MacArthur during, 246–265; Dwight Eisenhower and, 284–285
Korstad, Robert, on the influence of the Industrial Revolution on the family, 57–65
Ku Klux Klan (KKK), controversy over, of the 1920s, 144–165

labor unions. See unions
Lait, Jack, 240
Lamm, Richard D., on immigration, 314–320
Larson, Arthur, 280, 288
Latham, Earl, 233
Lattimore, Owen, 232, 233
Lawrence, William, 7, 8, 9–10
laws, versus customs, and racial segregation in the South, 120, 129–130, 131–132
League of Woman Voters (LWV), 171, 172, 174–175, 180, 182, 184
Leloudis, James, on the influence of the Industrial Revolution on the family, 57–65
Lend-Lease arrangement, Soviet espionage and, 229–230
Lewinsky, Monica S., 365–366, 369
libraries, anticommunism and, 240
Lippmann, Walter, 288, 340
liquor, corruption in city government and, 72, 76
Litwack, Leon F., on racial segregation and the status of African Americans, 131–139
Locke, John Galen, 162
Logan, John A., 11
Long, John D., 99, 102, 103
Longshoremen's Union, 235
Lovett, Robert A., 283
loyalty oaths, bills of attainder and, 4
Luce, Henry, 376

MacArthur, Douglas, controversy over Harry Truman's firing of, during the Korean War, 246–265
Maclean, Donald, 222
Madison, James, 9
MAGIC, 194, 198, 202, 204–205, 208, 209, 210, 211–212
Maine, sinking of, and the Spanish-American War, 94–115
marriage, 394–395; and controversy over the influence of the Industrial Revolution on the family, 48–49. See also divorce
Marshall, George, 249, 259, 261, 262, 263–264
Martin, Joseph W., 254, 261
Mason, Lucy Randolph, 181, 183, 186
May, Elaine Tyler, on the influence of the Industrial Revolution on the family, 48–56
McCardle, William, 17–18
McCarran, Pat, 231–233
McCarthy, Joseph, 226–227, 249, 271, 280
McKinley, William, 96, 97, 98, 102, 103, 104, 112, 113, 114–115
media: American, and the presidency, 368–369; and controversy over the influence of yellow journalism on the Spanish-American War, 94–115; Japanese, and Pearl Harbor, 204
melting pot, 82, 85; and controversy over immigration, 310–311, 318
mill villages, and controversy over the influence of the Industrial Revolution on the family, 57–65
Miller, Arthur, 237
Mine, Mill and Smelter Workers Union, 235
Moore, Leonard, 157–158, 159–161
Morgenthau, Hans, 340
Mortimer, Lee, 240
Mostel, Zero, 238–239
movie industry. See entertainment industry
multicultural pluralism, and controversy over immigration, 310–311, 312
municipal government. See city government
Musmano, Michael, 234

Nasaw, David, on the influence of yellow journalism on the Spanish-American War, 108–115
National Security Council (NSC), CIA and, under Dwight Eisenhower, 283–284
National Union of Textile Workers (NUTW), 63–64
Nelson, Lars-Erik, on the historical view of the Clinton presidency, 348–358
Nelson, Thomas A. R., 7
New York Teachers Union, 235
newspapers, and controversy over the influence of yellow journalism on the Spanish-American War, 94–115

Nineteenth Amendment, of the U.S. Constitution, 186
North American Free Trade Agreement (NAFTA), 352–356
North Korea. *See* Korean War
nuclear power, Dwight Eisenhower and, 272
Nuclear Test Ban Treaty, 295, 296
nuclear weapons: and controversy over the performance of Dwight Eisenhower as president, 281–282, 284–286, 287–288; and controversy over the performance of John Kennedy during the Cuban Missile Crisis, 292–303; and controversy over Ronald Reagan and the end of the cold war, 324–343; and controversy over Harry Truman's firing of Douglas MacArthur during the Korean War, 251, 258; Soviet spying and, 221–222, 224–225

Oberholtzer, Madge, 151–152, 161–162
oil industry, and controversy over John D. Rockefeller, 26–44
On the Waterfront, 237
O'Neill, William L., on the women's movement in the 1920s, 170–177
Open Skies plan, 287
Optimism Gap, The (Whitman), 384–385, 392
Orange County, California, the Ku Klux Klan in, 157, 158–159, 162–163
Ordeal of Power, The (Hughes), 288
Order of American Women, 148

Pacific Affairs, 232, 233
Pacific Fleet, and controversy over the attack on Pearl Harbor, 194, 195–196, 198, 201
Panay incident, 195
parks: city, 81; racial segregation and, 123–124, 135
Parks, Larry, 236
Patterson, Orlando, 384, 392
Payne, Oliver H., 51, 57
Pearl Harbor, controversy over the attack on, 192–213
Perl, William, 221
Philippines. *See* Spanish-American War
police: city government in late-nineteenth-century America and, 77–78; racial segregation and, 139
political parties: city government and, 84–85; the Clinton presidency and, 366–367
Pomeroy, John Norton, 19–20
poorhouses, racial segregation and, 121
poverty: the Clinton presidency and, 371; immigrants and, 316–317
pragmatism, the Clinton presidency and, 367–368
President's Board of Consultants on Foreign Intelligence Activities, 283
press. *See* media

privacy, the Clinton presidency and, 365–366
prostitution, 73; racial segregation and, 123
Pulitzer, Joseph, and controversy over the influence of yellow journalism on the Spanish-American War, 94–115

Quemoy-Matsu Crisis, Dwight Eisenhower and, 285–286

Rabinowitz, Howard N., on racial segregation and the status of African Americans, 120–130
racial issues: controversy over racial segregation and the status of African Americans, 120–139; the Clinton presidency and, 350; improvements in, 393–394
railroads, corruption and, 74, 83
Randolph, John, 279
Reagan, Ronald, controversy over, and the end of the cold war, 324–343
Reconstruction, and controversy over the impeachment of Andrew Johnson, 4–22
Red Channels, 238
Redeemers, 121, 122, 127
Remington, Frederic, 109–110
Ridgway, Matthew, 248, 250, 251, 254–255, 257
Rise of the City, The (Schlesinger), 80
robber barons, and controversy over John D. Rockefeller, 26–44
Roberts Commission, 192, 193
Rockefeller, Frank, 34, 41
Rockefeller, John D., controversy over, 26–44
Rogers v. U.S., 237
Roosevelt, Franklin D., 363; and controversy over the attack on Pearl Harbor, 192–213
Roosevelt, Kermit, 282
Roosevelt, Theodore, 79
Rosenberg, Ethel, 224–226, 227
Rosenberg, Julius, 222, 223, 224–226, 227

safety, increase in, 385–386
Samuelson, Robert J., 392
Schlesinger, Arthur M., Jr., 271, 364; on the performance of Dwight Eisenhower as president, 278–288
Schlesinger, Arthur, Sr., 80, 81–82
school libraries, anticommunism and, 240
schools, racial segregation and, 121
Schulberg, Budd, 236
Scott, Anne Firor, on the women's movement in the 1920s, 178–187
Screen Actors Guild, 236
Screen Directors Guild, 236
Searchlight, 155

Sedition Act of 1798, and controversy over the impeachment of Andrew Johnson, 13–14
segregation: controversy over racial, and the status of African Americans, 120–139; economic change and, 57
Senate Internal Security Subcommittee (SISS), and controversy over communism in America after World War II, 231–233, 235
separate but equal doctrine, 122
servants, racial segregation and, 137–138
services, increased demand for municipal, 82–83
sexual activity, decline in teen, 388
Shame of the Cities, The (Steffens), 80
Sherman, William T., 9, 13
Shivers, Allen, 235
Short, Walter, 193, 194, 199–200, 201, 207, 212, 213
Sickles, Daniel, 16
Sigsbee, Charles E., 97, 99, 100
Silvermaster, Gregory, 221
Soble, Jack, 222, 223
Soblen, Robert, 222, 223
Sondergaard, Gale, 236
Sorensen, Theodore C., on the performance of John Kennedy during the Cuban Missile Crisis, 292–296
Sorenson, Georgia J., on the historical view of the Clinton presidency, 359–371
South Korea. See Korean War
Soviet Union: and controversy over communism in America after World War II, 220–230; and controversy over Ronald Reagan and the end of the cold war, 324–343. See also cold war
Spanier, John S., on Harry Truman's firing of Douglas MacArthur during the Korean War, 246–255
Spanish-American War, controversy over the influence of yellow journalism on the, 94–115
spying, and controversy over communism in America after World War II, 220–230
Stalin, Joseph, 222, 228–230, 314
Stanbery, Henry, 15
standard of living, improvements in, 394
Standard Oil Company, and controversy over John D. Rockefeller, 26–35
Stanton, Edwin, 5, 15, 16
Steffens, Lincoln, 80
Stephenson, David D., 150–152, 161–162
Stevens, Thadeus, 5, 7, 11–12
Stevenson, Adlai, the Cuban Missile Crisis and, 297–299, 301–302
Strategic Arms Reduction Talks (START), 328, 330, 331, 332
Strategic Defense Initiative (SDI), 324, 327, 329, 331, 332, 335
Stratemeyer, George E., 249–250
subsistence strategies, and controversy over the influence of the Industrial Revolution on the family, 53–56, 60–61

suffrage, women's, and controversy over the women's movement in the 1920s, 170–187
Sumner, Charles, 5
Supreme Court, U.S., and controversy over the impeachment of Andrew Johnson, 4, 15–16, 17–18
Swanberg, W. A., on the influence of yellow journalism on the Spanish-American War, 94–107

Taiwan. See Formosa
Tarbell, Ida, 28, 29
Task Force Investigating Communist Domination of Certain Labor Unions, 234
teachers unions, communism and, 235–236
Teaford, Jon C., on city government in late-nineteenth-century America, 79–87
Tenure of Office Act, and controversy over the impeachment of Andrew Johnson, 5, 10, 13, 15, 18
textile mills: and controversy over the influence of the Industrial Revolution on the family, 57–65; women's suffrage and, 180
Theobald, Robert A., on the attack on Pearl Harbor, 192–202
Thomas, Lorenzo, 9
Thurston, John W., 102, 103
"transactional opportunists," 367
transportation, racial segregation and, 121, 122–123, 124–128, 132–134
Tripartite Treaty, 194, 197
Truman, Harry S.: controversy over the firing of Douglas MacArthur by, during the Korean War, 246–265; Soviet espionage and, 223–224
Trumbull, Lyman, 14, 17

U.S.A. Confidential, 240
Ueda, Reed, on immigration, 308–313
unions, 63–64; and controversy over communism in America after World War II, 234–236
United Electrical Workers (UE), 234–235
United Public Workers, 235
Unwanted War, An (Offner), 114
urban governance. See city government
urban rule, city government in late-nineteenth-century America and, 79–87
utilities, 81, 82, 83; corruption and, 74

Van Buren, Martin, 279
Vandenberg, Hoyt S., 252, 257, 261, 264
Vanderbilt, Cornelius, 30
Venona Project, and controversy over communism in America after World War II, 220–230
Vietnam, Dwight Eisenhower and, 285

Vincent, John Carter, 232

Wade, Ben, 20–21
Walter, Francis, 236
Washington conference, and controversy over the attack on Pearl Harbor, 194, 197, 198–199, 200
welfare, immigration and, 316–317
Welker, Herman, 234
Wells, Anne Sharp, on Harry Truman's firing of Douglas MacArthur during the Korean War, 256–265
What Makes Sammy Run (Schulberg), 236
White, Harry, 221, 227
White, Mark J., on the performance of John Kennedy during the Cuban Missile Crisis, 297–303
white-collar workers, economic status and, 50–52
Whitman, David, 384–385, 392
Wills, Garry, 270

Wilson, James Q., 386
winds code, 207, 208
Wohlstetter, Roberta, on the attack on Pearl Harbor, 203–213
Woman's Party, 171, 174, 175–176, 177
women: and controversy over segregation and the status of African Americans, 122–123, 132; and controversy over the influence of the Industrial Revolution on the family, 49–50, 59, 62–63, 64, 65; the Ku Klux Klan of the 1920s and, 146–149
women's movement, controversy over, in the 1920s, 170–187
Woodford, Steward, 105
World War II, and controversy over the attack on Pearl Harbor, 192–213

yellow journalism, controversy over the influence of, on the Spanish-American War, 94–115
"younger brother effect," 387